Digital Technologies in Modeling and Management:

Insights in Education and Industry

G. S. Prakasha
Christ University, India

Maria Lapina
North–Caucasus Federal University, Russia

Deepanraj Balakrishnan
Prince Mohammad Bin Fahd University, Saudi Arabia

Mohammad Sajid
Aligarh Muslim University, India

A volume in the Advances in Systems Analysis,
Software Engineering, and High Performance
Computing (ASASEHPC) Book Series

Published in the United States of America by
  IGI Global
  Information Science Reference (an imprint of IGI Global)
  701 E. Chocolate Avenue
  Hershey PA, USA 17033
  Tel: 717-533-8845
  Fax: 717-533-8661
  E-mail: cust@igi-global.com
  Web site: http://www.igi-global.com

Library of Congress Cataloging-in-Publication Data

Names: Prakasha, G. S., editor.
Title: Digital technologies in modeling and management : insights in
  education and industry / edited by GS Prakasha, Maria Lepina, Deepanraj
  Balakrishnan, and Mohammad Sajid.
Description: Hershey, PA : Engineering Science Reference, 2024. | Includes
  bibliographical references and index. | Summary: "Digital Technologies
  in Modeling and Management: Insights in Education and Industry explores
  the use of digital technologies in the modeling and control of complex
  systems in various fields, such as social networks, education, technical
  systems, and their protection and security. The book consists of two
  chapters, with the first chapter focusing on modeling complex systems
  using digital technologies, while the second chapter deals with the
  digitalization of economic processes and their management"-- Provided by
  publisher.
Identifiers: LCCN 2023021229 (print) | LCCN 2023021230 (ebook) | ISBN
  9781668495766 (h/c) | ISBN 9781668495773 (s/c) | ISBN 9781668495780
  (ebook)
Subjects: LCSH: Artificial intelligence--Educational applications. |
  Chatbots. | Teleshopping.
Classification: LCC LB1028.73 .D54 2023 (print) | LCC LB1028.73 (ebook) |
  DDC 006.3--dc23/eng/20230517
LC record available at https://lccn.loc.gov/2023021229
LC ebook record available at https://lccn.loc.gov/2023021230

This book is published in the IGI Global book series Advances in Systems Analysis, Software Engineering, and High Performance Computing (ASASEHPC) (ISSN: 2327-3453; eISSN: 2327-3461)

British Cataloguing in Publication Data
A Cataloguing in Publication record for this book is available from the British Library.

For electronic access to this publication, please contact: eresources@igi-global.com.

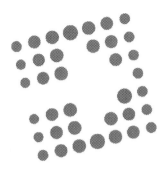

Advances in Systems Analysis, Software Engineering, and High Performance Computing (ASASEHPC) Book Series

Vijayan Sugumaran
Oakland University, Rochester, USA

ISSN:2327-3453
EISSN:2327-3461

MISSION

The theory and practice of computing applications and distributed systems has emerged as one of the key areas of research driving innovations in business, engineering, and science. The fields of software engineering, systems analysis, and high performance computing offer a wide range of applications and solutions in solving computational problems for any modern organization.

The **Advances in Systems Analysis, Software Engineering, and High Performance Computing (ASASEHPC) Book Series** brings together research in the areas of distributed computing, systems and software engineering, high performance computing, and service science. This collection of publications is useful for academics, researchers, and practitioners seeking the latest practices and knowledge in this field.

COVERAGE

- Performance Modelling
- Virtual Data Systems
- Enterprise Information Systems
- Parallel Architectures
- Engineering Environments
- Computer System Analysis
- Metadata and Semantic Web
- Distributed Cloud Computing
- Storage Systems
- Computer Graphics

IGI Global is currently accepting manuscripts for publication within this series. To submit a proposal for a volume in this series, please contact our Acquisition Editors at Acquisitions@igi-global.com or visit: http://www.igi-global.com/publish/.

Titles in this Series

For a list of additional titles in this series, please visit: http://www.igi-global.com/book-series/advances-systems-analysis-software-engineering/73689

Technological Advancements in Data Processing for Next Generation Intelligent Systems
Shanu Sharma (ABES Engineering College, Ghaziabad, India) Ayushi Prakash (Ajay Kumar Garg Engineering College, Ghaziabad, India) and Vijayan Sugumaran (Oakland University, Rochester, USA)
Engineering Science Reference • copyright 2024 • 357pp • H/C (ISBN: 9798369309681) • US $300.00 (our price)

Advanced Applications in Osmotic Computing
G. Revathy (SASTRA University, India)
Engineering Science Reference • copyright 2024 • 370pp • H/C (ISBN: 9798369316948) • US $300.00 (our price)

Omnichannel Approach to Co-Creating Customer Experiences Through Metaverse Platforms
Babita Singla (Chitkara Business School, Chitkara University, Punjab, India) Kumar Shalender (Chitkara Business School, Chitkara University, India) and Nripendra Singh (Pennsylvania Western University, USA)
Engineering Science Reference • copyright 2024 • 223pp • H/C (ISBN: 9798369318669) • US $270.00 (our price)

Uncertain Spatiotemporal Data Management for the Semantic Web
Luyi Bai (Northeastern University, China) and Lin Zhu (Northeastern University, China)
Engineering Science Reference • copyright 2024 • 518pp • H/C (ISBN: 9781668491089) • US $325.00 (our price)

Bio-Inspired Optimization Techniques in Blockchain Systems
U. Vignesh (Vellore Institute of Technology, Chennai, India) Manikandan M. (Manipal Institute of Technology, India) and Ruchi Doshi (Universidad Azteca, Mexico)
Engineering Science Reference • copyright 2024 • 288pp • H/C (ISBN: 9798369311318) • US $300.00 (our price)

Enhancing Performance, Efficiency, and Security Through Complex Systems Control
Idriss Chana (ESTM, Moulay Ismail University of Meknès, Morocco) Aziz Bouazi (ESTM, Moulay Ismail University of Meknès, Morocco) and Hussain Ben-azza (ENSAM, Moulay Ismail University of Meknes, Morocco)
Engineering Science Reference • copyright 2024 • 371pp • H/C (ISBN: 9798369304976) • US $300.00 (our price)

Frameworks for Blockchain Standards, Tools, Testbeds, and Platforms
Yanamandra Ramakrishna (School of Business, Skyline University College, Sharjah, UAE) and Priyameet Kaur Keer (Department of Management Studies, New Horizon College of Engineering, India)
Engineering Science Reference • copyright 2024 • 244pp • H/C (ISBN: 9798369304051) • US $285.00 (our price)

Machine Learning Algorithms Using Scikit and TensorFlow Environments

701 East Chocolate Avenue, Hershey, PA 17033, USA
Tel: 717-533-8845 x100 • Fax: 717-533-8661
E-Mail: cust@igi-global.com • www.igi-global.com

Table of Contents

Detailed Table of Contents

Chapter 1

Mohammad Izzuddin Mohammed Jamil, Universiti Brunei Darussalam, Brunei

Digital transformation is a field of study that has been extensively studied in academic literature. Major topics that have been explored include its definitions, concepts, strategies, enablers, managerial and organisational capabilities, orientations, and digital literacy. Because digital transformation entails the transformation across all levels of an organisation, new business models and practices must be conjured. This chapter is composed with the aim of assessing and discoursing the relevance of digital transformation for the application of MSMEs. The scope of digital transformation encompasses various aspects and concepts for organisations that are useful to support MSMEs survive in developed and emerging economies. This chapter would also state the conditions necessary for digital transformation to occur, such as a degree of digital literacy is needed for proper understanding of digitised activities by both managers and employees, and efforts must be made to ensure equal access to technology as the phenomenon of digital divide is a hindrance towards digital transformation.

Chapter 2

Mehul Anil Waghambare, Symbiosis Institute of Digital and Telecom Management,
*   Symbiosis International University, India*
Sandeep Prabhu, Symbiosis Institute of Digital and Telecom Management, Symbiosis
*   International University, India*
P. Ashok, Symbiosis Institute of Digital and Telecom Management, Symbiosis International
*   University, India*
N. A., Symbiosis Institute of Digital and Telecom Management, Symbiosis International
*   University, India*

The COVID-19 pandemic is changing the way we connect, communicate, and collaborate. the crisis rapidly re-shape both the "what" and the "how" of companies. Businesses now move to doing business online, that involves selling of products, generating leads and connecting with customers. The chatbot, a software application designed for human-like conversations, emerged as a trend that is helping to close the social distance gap between customers and businesses. Many business have incorporated the tool in their communication strategy, this paper aims to understand to what extent, tries to put-forward an understanding of chatbots marketing and the use of chatbots in online shopping process. Furthermore, the paper tries to speaks extensively about the design in such a way that it will peak its performance for user acquisition.

Chapter 3

Mohan Kumar Dehury, Amity University, India
Ronit Kumar Gupta, Amity University, India
Tannisha Kundu, Amity University, India

The field of artificial intelligence (AI) is very promising with the emergence of machine learning and deep learning algorithms. The rise of convolutional neural networks (CNN) is very propitious in deep learning as it is more accurate and powerful than previously known soft computational models like artificial neural networks (ANN) and recurrent neural networks (RNN). CNN is ANN with steroids. These soft computational models are inspired by biological models that give an approximate solution to image-driven pattern recognition problems. The near perfect precision of CNN models offers a better way to recognize patterns and solve real-world problems and provide approximate solutions which are near precision. These technologies have enhanced the trust with humans. Its results have been accepted widely. This chapter aims to provide brief information about CNNs by introducing and discussing recent papers published on this topic and the methods employed by them to recognize patterns. This chapter also aims to provide information regarding dos and don'ts while using different CNN models.

Chapter 4

Thivashini B. Jaya Kumar, Taylor's University, Malaysia
Thanuja Rathakrishnan, Taylor's University, Malaysia

Escape rooms are a cutting-edge method of evaluating student learning because they give them a scenario in which they must solve issues and solve puzzles using numerous clues and contextual suggestions. The chapter intends to explore a discussion and reflection on the potential of immersive learning environments for formative assessments (escape room as a quiz) in enhancing students' learning experiences. The theoretical framework, the idea of an escape room, and how it might improve the learning process will be covered at the beginning of the chapter. This study employed a quasi-experimental design to investigate the effects of quiz format (digital quiz vs. digital escape room) on academic performance. Finally, the chapter discusses the potential challenges and limitations of escape room games in education. The chapter concludes by highlighting the insights, practical guidance, and future directions for educators interested in implementing escape room games in their teaching.

Chapter 5

Sameer Saharan, Mody University of Science and Technology, India
Shailja Singh, Mangalayatan University, Jabalpur, India
Debasis Bora, Mandsaur University, India
Geetika Saxena, Mody University of Science and Technology, India

Cyber forensics is a vital ally in safeguarding our digital world. This abstract explores its symbiotic relationship with cybersecurity. Cyber forensics not only investigates cybercrimes, but also aids in threat detection, incident response, and risk mitigation. Technology, including AI, empowers professionals in navigating digital crime scenes. Ethical and legal considerations remain pivotal. Cyber forensics, as an indispensable part of cybersecurity, fortifies our digital landscape against evolving threats, ensuring a safer digital future.

Success and efficiency of today's business depends on many factors across various industries. Among the many factors, supply chain plays a crucial role. The well-functioning of distribution system may lead to customer satisfaction, cost reduction, risk management, competitive advantage, collaboration and integration, innovation and adoptability and sustainability. Adopting technology in supply chain systems is another way of increasing business growth in the present era. The technologies used in today's business organizations are blockchain, internet of things (IoT), cloud technology, etc. To what extent technology is used to improve supply chain visibility in business is a matter of concern. With this background, the study aims to explore the relationship and impact of different technology on supply chain visibility in fast moving consumer goods sector. To meet the objective of the study, the study chose the top 20 FMCG companies based on highest market share and collected the data from 20 supply chain managers. The variables considered for the study were internet of things (IoT), blockchain, artificial intelligence (AI), radio frequency identification (RFID), cloud technology and information technology. relevant statistical analysis was used to prove the results and it is evident that technology positively correlates with the supply chain visibility. Artificial Intelligence has the most significant impact on the supply chain visibility of a firm. Hence, there is a significant impact of technology on supply chain visibility and the extent impact is high.

Chapter 7

This literature review aims to understand the recent developments in the field of upscaling and upskilling in the digital transformation of business, from an Industry 5.0 prospective. It used a comprehensive search of relevant peer-reviewed journal articles, industry reports, and online sources to gather the relevant data. The findings indicate that upscaling is essential for industry 5.0, and that businesses should invest in upskilling and upscaling programs to meet the changing demands of the digital economy. This literature review provides a comprehensive analysis of the current state of upscaling and upskilling in the digital transformation of business and provides insights into the future direction of this field. It also highlights the importance of collaboration between businesses, governments, and educational institutions to ensure that the workforce is prepared for the future of work.

Knowledge is recognized as a central component for an organisation to remain competitive. In this current phase, the blend of artificial intelligence (AI) and knowledge management (KM) frameworks can upgrade and improve organizational success. The role of knowledge management (KM) frameworks has evolved because of fast changing environment technology and continuously upgrading technology. AI combining KM can become that thriving component for organizations to be more progressive. Application of AI can be used in different forms of KM, like creation, storage, share and usage of knowledge. Different forms of AI technologies such as expert systems, intelligent search, chatbots, Robotics process automation, machine learning (ML) and natural language processing (NLP), can help to process large data and extract valuable information. AI-enabled KM systems in organisations can bring transformation through improved organisation learning, better decision-making based on data analysis, upgraded technology and innovation, and can provide aid to be more informed, intelligent, and adaptable to respond quickly with unpredictable corporate settings. If a business were to leverage the power of AI in organisation systems in India, they can gain competitive advantage, improve their innovation and agility in today's fast changing scenario. However, there are challenges in integrating AI and KM frameworks, such as data privacy and ethical concerns. This study explores the integration of KM frameworks and AI to increase organisation effectiveness also it examines how technologies of AI can help with creation of knowledge, its storage, knowledge sharing and application of knowledge. Though, it is also significant to consider challenges of using AI in KM frameworks, like data privacy and ethical concerns are particularly important, so that organization's sensitive information should not be compromised and can use AI technologies in transparent, accountable, and ethical manner.

Chapter 9

Alejandro Sánchez-Villarin, University of Seville, Spain
Alejandro E. Santos, University of Seville, Spain
José E. Gonzalez-Enriquez, University of Seville, Spain
Javier J. Gutierrez, University of Seville, Spain
Nicolas E. Sanchez-Gomez, University of Seville, Spain
Nora E. Koch, University of Seville, Spain
Maria Jose Escalona, University of Seville, Spain

Prototyping is a requirement technique frequently used for communication between customers and developers. Software prototypes help to understand users' expectations, but they are often seen as disposable artifacts because it is not easy to manage the transfer of knowledge from prototypes to software models or code. This chapter studies whether suitable solutions already exist for exploiting the knowledge acquired during the building of prototypes in the early phases of the lifecycle. The objective is addressed by means of a systematic literature review of approaches offering solutions for transforming software prototypes into analysis models. We propose a characterization schema for comparing them and describing the current state-of-the-art. The results reveal a need for more automated solutions that are more economical in terms of time and effort for transforming prototypes into models and thereby ensuring traceability between requirements and design artifacts.

Chapter 10

Wasswa Shafik, School of Digital Science, Universiti Brunei Darussalam, Uganda
Kassim Kalinaki, Islamic University in Uganda, Uganda

Smart cities are imperative in terms of smart buildings, transportation, parking, healthcare, agriculture, traffic systems, and public safety aided by the fifth generation (5G) computation standards. They are entirely capable of controlling real-time devices and delivering relevant smart information to the citizens. However, different architectural stages experience privacy and security concerns. Therefore, in this survey, an internet of things (IoT) based architecture is proposed, showing the critical layers that are key to ensure secure smart IoT implementation. The study further covers the recent approaches to security applications for information centric SCs. 5G security solutions have been highlighted in SCs' settings and proposed. Comparably, a comprehensive SC current 5G security and numerous open security concerns are demonstrated. Lastly, offer potential research directions and motivations mainly in academia and industry, outlining these concerns that need to be considered to enhance smart daily operations.

Chapter 11

    Sumit Kumar, Rajan Mamta Degree College, India
    Samta Jain Goyal, Amity University, India
    Ipseeta Nanda, Gopal Narayan Singh University, Sasaram, India
    Rajeev Goyal, Amity University, India
    Chandra Shekhar Azad, National Institute of Technology, Jamshedpur, India

With the prompt evolution of the internet, the growth of the data rate is increasing day by day. Most of the current technologies, including 5G, provide high data rate services to handle and process those data. For this reason, machine learning came into its role. Machine learning is quite different from the traditional programming paradigm. Machine learning takes a massive, huge amount of data and results to produce such programs or models used for prediction purposes. The key enabling technologies with 5G are IoT and ML, which are used to change the picture of the real world, change their trends, and explore their applications worldwide. This review chapter starts with relating 5G with the opportunities of machine learning, and its techniques to manage these challenges.

Chapter 12

    Dipti Chauhan, Department of Artificial Intelligence & Data Science, Prestige Institute of
        Engineering Management and Research, Indore, India
    Jay Kumar Jain, Department of Mathematics, Bioinformatics and Computer Applications,
        Bhopal, India

Smart cities are gradually becoming a reality rather than a distant vision. Governments, companies, and everyday people are using technology more and more these days to boost productivity at work and at home. On the one hand, smart cities have enacted a number of modifications in an effort with the goal of revolutionizing people's lives. On the other side, while smart cities offer improved quality of life and more convenience, there are also increased hazards to cyber security, including data leaks and malicious cyberattacks. As smart cities are evolving with more connected, as well as enhanced digital infrastructures becoming more sophisticated, these services will become increasingly exposed to cyber intrusions. Cities can only be as strong as their weakest link, and even the tiniest flaws can be used to deadly advantage. Governments must invest more money in cyber security and threat reduction as a result. In this proposed chapter we will be discussing about the measures need to be taken for the development of Smart city and what are the preventions of cyber policies in smart cities.

Munir Ahmad, Survey of Pakistan, Pakistan
Asmat Ali, Survey of Pakistan, Pakistan
Hassan Nawaz, Huawei MiddleEast Cloud, Pakistan
Muhammad Arslan, Chenab College of Advance Studies, Faisalabad, Pakistan
Nirmalendu Kumar, Survey of India, India

Fog computing offers key features such as real-time communication, physical distribution, position awareness, compatibility, scalability, and energy efficiency, which collectively enhance the management of integrated spatial data. It provides benefits such as real-time data processing, seamless data sharing, improved efficiency, enhanced data security and privacy, and effective resource utilization. The distributed architecture and edge processing capabilities of fog computing enable real-time spatial data processing, faster insights, and localized decision-making. It presents opportunities for web-based analytics, real-time analysis, fault tolerance, event-triggered actions, and context-aware applications. However, challenges exist in terms of user needs and requirements, collaboration and partnership, data quality and interoperability, technical infrastructure, and policy and governance. Future work should focus on addressing these challenges and exploring new opportunities.

Nayanika Nandy, Illinois Institute of Technology, USA

In the era of technological advancements and widespread internet access, numerous issues have emerged, including cyber bullying, cyber extortion, and the disturbing trend of revenge pornography. Revenge pornography, also known as non-consensual pornography, involves the malicious act of sharing explicit photos or videos of individuals without their consent, aimed at compromising their sexual integrity. While the term "revenge porn" may suggest that the content is leaked by vengeful ex-intimate partners, it is important to note that many cases involve the illegal acquisition of explicit material through means such as hacking, with perpetrators seeking personal gain, amusement, or notoriety.

Vivek Topno, Amity University, India
Tannisha Kundu, Amity University, India
Mohan Kumar Dehury, Amity University, India

Quantum computing is a revolutionary technology that has the potential to transform various industries, including government operations, defence strategies, and national security. The chapter discusses its fundamental principles, advantages, limitations, and applications in cryptography, optimization, resource allocation, quantum sensing, and metrology. It highlights the need for quantum-resistant cryptography and post-quantum cryptographic algorithms to safeguard sensitive information. Quantum algorithms can improve decision-making processes, enhance efficiency, and address logistical challenges in defense strategy planning and disaster management. Quantum communication and secure networks are crucial for secure communication among government agencies, military units, and allied nations. Challenges include high costs, skilled personnel, and ethical and legal implications. The chapter concludes with a discussion on the future outlook of quantum computing in these sectors, emphasizing the need for continued research and investment.

Chapter 16

Cagla Ozen, Yeditepe University, Turkey
Zehra Mine Tas, Yeditepe University, Turkey

When examining domestic and foreign literature, surprisingly, very few studies examining the effects of AI on product efficiency have been observed in the domestic literature. Therefore, this study aims to contribute to domestic literature by focusing on the effects AI on product development efficiency. When the studies in foreign literature are examined, it is seen that AI increases the efficiency in product development, data analysis, management, control, and supply process. The overall result of this study shows that AI, which plays an important role in the design of high scalable algorithms that analyze complex and large-scale data, increases the efficiency of product development from the production process to supply chains.

Chapter 17

Cagla Ozen, Yeditepe University, Turkey
İremnaz Yolcu, Yeditepe University, Turkey

The purpose of this book chapter is to delve into the role of the internet of things (IoT) in disaster management. Specifically, this chapter will address the following research questions and subjects: How can IoT be utilized in early warning systems for natural disasters? How does big data analytics contribute to disaster management when combined with IoT? Furthermore, a review of literature on the analysis of case studies involving IoT-based disaster management approaches will also be discussed.

Preface

In the ever-evolving landscape of the information and knowledge society, the intricate dance between trust and technology has emerged as a pivotal force shaping the realms of education and industry. As editors of *Digital Technologies in Modeling and Management: Insights in Education and Industry*, we are delighted to present this comprehensive reference book, meticulously curated to illuminate the multifaceted facets of trust in the digital era.

This collaborative effort, spearheaded by GS Prakasha, Maria Lapina, Deepanraj Balakrishnan, and Mohammad Sajid, is a testament to the imperative role trust plays at different levels within organizations. The recognition of trust as a linchpin in the network economy underscores the need for a deeper understanding of its manifestations and the avenues through which it can be fortified. Crucially, the nexus of trust in both human and technological interactions stands as the cornerstone for refining information and knowledge-related processes, thereby fostering the creation of new knowledge and enhancing strategic capabilities.

This edited collection is designed to address a conspicuous gap in the existing literature within the fields of information studies, information systems, and knowledge management. The need for a compendium of original research on trust, spanning global economies, networks, organizations, teams, information systems, and individual actors, has motivated the assembly of this book.

Our target audience comprises professionals and researchers immersed in the dynamic field of information and knowledge management across diverse disciplines. From library and information sciences to administrative sciences and management, education, adult education, sociology, computer science, and information technology, this book endeavors to provide valuable insights to a broad spectrum of readers. Furthermore, executives grappling with the complexities of expertise, knowledge, information, and organizational development in varied work communities and environments will find pragmatic guidance within these pages.

The book encompasses an array of topics at the intersection of trust and technology, including Artificial Intelligence, AI Model Training, Machine Learning, AI for Robotics and Control Management UAVs, Data Privacy, Privacy-Enhancing Technologies, Cybersecurity Management, Virtual Learning Environments, Augmented Reality Educational Technologies, and Digital Tools for Collaborative Learning.

Each chapter unfolds a unique facet of the intricate tapestry that binds trust and digital technologies. They open up a comprehensive exploration of the intricate relationship between trust and technology in the dynamic landscapes of education and industry. Written by esteemed professionals all across the globe, each chapter delves into a unique facet of the digital realm, offering profound insights and cutting-edge perspectives. From the transformative impact of Digital Transformation on Micro, Small, and Medium Enterprises (MSMEs) to the role of chatbots in reshaping communication strategies amidst the COVID-19 pandemic, and the promising advances in fields such as Artificial Intelligence, cyber forensics, and smart cities, the chapters collectively form a rich tapestry of knowledge. As the digital era continues to evolve, this compilation serves as a valuable resource for professionals and researchers navigating the complex intersections of trust, technology, and knowledge management across diverse disciplines.

Chapter 1: In this opening chapter, the focus is on Digital Transformation, a widely explored field in academic literature. The paper delves into key topics such as definitions, concepts, strategies, enablers, and organizational capabilities associated with Digital Transformation. However, the unique contribution lies in assessing its relevance for Micro, Small, and Medium Enterprises (MSMEs). The chapter addresses the need for new business models and practices and outlines conditions necessary for digital transformation, emphasizing the importance of digital literacy and equal access to technology.

Chapter 2: As the COVID-19 pandemic reshapes business dynamics, Chapter 2 explores the profound changes in how companies connect, communicate, and collaborate. The spotlight is on the adoption of online business practices, particularly the emergence and impact of chatbots in narrowing the social distance gap between customers and businesses. The chapter investigates the extent to which businesses have incorporated chatbots into their communication strategies and delves into the design principles that enhance their performance, especially in online shopping processes.

Chapter 3: Focused on the promising field of Artificial Intelligence (AI), this chapter delves into the rise of Convolutional Neural Networks (CNN) and their superiority in image-driven pattern recognition over previous soft computational models. The discussion revolves around the precision and acceptance of CNN models, offering insights into recent papers and methods used for pattern recognition. Additionally, the chapter provides practical guidance by highlighting do's and don'ts when employing various CNN models.

Chapter 4: Addressing innovative approaches to student assessment, Chapter 4 explores the use of escape rooms as a formative assessment tool. The theoretical framework is presented, along with a discussion on how escape rooms can enhance the learning process. The chapter employs a quasi-experimental design to compare the effects of digital quizzes versus digital escape rooms on academic performance. It concludes with insights, practical guidance, and considerations for educators interested in incorporating escape room games in their teaching.

Chapter 5: Cyber forensics takes center stage in Chapter 5, exploring its role as a vital ally in safeguarding the digital world. The chapter highlights the symbiotic relationship between cyber forensics and cybersecurity, emphasizing their collective impact on threat detection, incident response, and risk mitigation. The integration of technology, including AI, is discussed as a powerful tool for navigating digital crime scenes while considering ethical and legal considerations in fortifying the digital landscape.

Chapter 6: Chapter 6 delves into the impact of various technologies on supply chain visibility in the fast-moving consumer goods sector. The study, based on data from top FMCG companies, explores the positive correlation between technology (IoT, Blockchain, AI, RFID, Cloud Technology, and Information Technology) and supply chain visibility. Artificial Intelligence emerges as the most influential factor, emphasizing the significant impact of technology on enhancing supply chain visibility.

Chapter 7: A comprehensive literature review in Chapter 7 focuses on upscaling and upskilling in the digital transformation of business, from an Industry 5.0 perspective. Drawing on peer-reviewed articles and industry reports, the review emphasizes the essential role of upscaling and upskilling programs in meeting the changing demands of the digital economy. Collaboration between businesses, governments, and educational institutions is highlighted as crucial for workforce preparation in the future of work.

Chapter 8: Chapter 8 explores the synergy between Artificial Intelligence (AI) and knowledge management (KM) frameworks. Recognizing knowledge as a central component for organizational success, the discussion revolves around how the combination of AI and KM can enhance organizational progress in the rapidly changing technological environment. The evolving role of KM frameworks and the thriving potential of AI in organizational development are key focal points.

Chapter 9: Focusing on prototyping as a requirement technique, Chapter 9 investigates the challenges of transferring knowledge from prototypes to software models or code. The chapter conducts a Systematic Literature Review to identify existing solutions for transforming software prototypes into analysis models. It proposes a characterization schema for comparison and highlights the need for more automated solutions to ensure traceability between requirements and design artifacts.

Chapter 10: Addressing the imperative of smart cities, Chapter 10 proposes an IoT-based architecture for ensuring secure smart IoT implementation. The study covers various architectural stages, emphasizing privacy and security concerns. It highlights recent approaches to security applications, with a comprehensive analysis of current 5G security in smart cities. The chapter concludes by offering potential research directions to enhance smart daily operations.

Chapter 11: Chapter 11 explores the synergy between 5G and machine learning in the context of technological advancements and increasing data rates. The review begins by establishing the connection between 5G and opportunities in machine learning, addressing challenges and techniques to manage them. It underscores the key enabling technologies with 5G, namely IoT and ML, in changing real-world trends and applications worldwide.

Chapter 12: As smart cities evolve, Chapter 12 discusses the measures needed for their development and the preventive measures for cybersecurity. The chapter explores the modifications enacted in smart cities to revolutionize people's lives while acknowledging the increased cybersecurity risks. It emphasizes the need for governments to invest more in cybersecurity and threat reduction to safeguard against cyber intrusions.

Chapter 13: Focusing on fog computing, Chapter 13 explores its key features and benefits for managing integrated spatial data. The discussion includes real-time data processing, seamless data sharing, improved efficiency, enhanced data security and privacy, and effective resource utilization. The chapter identifies challenges in user needs, collaboration, data quality, technical infrastructure, and policy, emphasizing the need for future work to address these issues.

Chapter 14: Chapter 14 addresses the disturbing trend of revenge pornography in the era of technological advancements. It defines revenge pornography and explores its malicious implications, emphasizing that it extends beyond acts of vengeance by ex-partners. The chapter underscores the need for legal measures to combat revenge pornography and protect individuals from non-consensual sharing of explicit material.

Chapter 15: Quantum computing takes center stage in Chapter 15, discussing its revolutionary potential to transform various industries, including government operations, defense strategies, and national security. The chapter explores fundamental principles, advantages, limitations, and applications in cryptography, optimization, resource allocation, quantum sensing, and metrology. It emphasizes the need for quantum-resistant cryptography and post-quantum cryptographic algorithms to safeguard sensitive information.

Chapter 16: Chapter 16 contributes to the domestic literature by examining the effects of AI on product development efficiency. Drawing on foreign studies, the chapter highlights the positive impact of AI on product development, data analysis, management, control, and supply processes. It concludes that AI, particularly in designing high-scalable algorithms, significantly increases efficiency throughout the production and supply chains.

Chapter 17: The final chapter delves into the role of the Internet of Things (IoT) in disaster management. Addressing research questions on early warning systems and the contribution of big data analytics when combined with IoT, Chapter 17 reviews case studies involving IoT-based disaster management approaches. The chapter contributes to the understanding of how IoT can enhance disaster management efforts in various contexts.

As editors, we extend our gratitude to the contributors for their invaluable insights and rigorous research that enriches the content of this book. It is our fervent hope that this collection not only deepens the scholarly discourse on trust but also serves as a practical resource for professionals navigating the complex terrain of the information and knowledge society.

Editors,

GS Prakasha
Christ University, India

Maria Lapina
North-Caucasus Federal University, Russia

Deepanraj Balakrishnan
Prince Mohammad Bin Fahd University, Saudi Arabia

Mohammad Sajid
Aligarh Muslim University, India

Chapter 1
A Discourse of the Underlying Concepts of Digital Transformation for MSMEs

Mohammad Izzuddin Mohammed Jamil
ⓘ https://orcid.org/0000-0002-2967-7870
Universiti Brunei Darussalam, Brunei

ABSTRACT

Digital transformation is a field of study that has been extensively studied in academic literature. Major topics that have been explored include its definitions, concepts, strategies, enablers, managerial and organisational capabilities, orientations, and digital literacy. Because digital transformation entails the transformation across all levels of an organisation, new business models and practices must be conjured. This chapter is composed with the aim of assessing and discoursing the relevance of digital transformation for the application of MSMEs. The scope of digital transformation encompasses various aspects and concepts for organisations that are useful to support MSMEs survive in developed and emerging economies. This chapter would also state the conditions necessary for digital transformation to occur, such as a degree of digital literacy is needed for proper understanding of digitised activities by both managers and employees, and efforts must be made to ensure equal access to technology as the phenomenon of digital divide is a hindrance towards digital transformation.

INTRODUCTION

Possessing the willingness and capability to embrace and adopt digital technology in order to revolutionise business processes or modify existing ones is widely known as digital transformation (Lankshear & Knobel, 2008). Digital technology, with acceptance or otherwise, has reshaped global daily lives in past decades, and millions of people work, shop, book holidays, play games, and listen to music via online means. At present day, communications are made via mobile rather than traditional landline phones, and close to half of the world's population utilizes social media. Digital technology is an essential aspect for most organisations, and must be managed effectively in order to fully reap its benefits. For

DOI: 10.4018/978-1-6684-9576-6.ch001

instance, in some organisations, digital technology forms the basis of the foundation of their Information Technology (IT), while others link it to their marketing section via the management of social media channels. Managers working in the field of digital technology need to understand the potential of digital technology for it to be successfully utilised across all departments of an organisation. This may include understanding the use of social media to market goods and allure customers, as well as collecting data and analyzing information to find ways of increasing profitability. A manager involved in formulating an organisation's digital strategy, and who recognizes its role in the overall business plan, is in the best position to initiate new technologies and explain the importance of digital technology to employees. Managers must embrace the opportunities digital technology presents for their market scope to reach to an ever-increasing global audience via digital means.

For some organisations, they are still under the obligation to do yearly repayments on their loans, mortgages and debentures to trade payables and suppliers. In addition, they have had to cover their operating expenses which include salaries and wages, water and electricity, heating and lighting, while having to make do with limited sales. COVID-19 has brought a dramatic fall in economic activities (Cavallo, & Forman, 2020); products and services are not consumed, supply lines are prevented from reaching, customers are unwilling to spend their money, banks are unwilling to lend especially to smaller organisations due lack of collaterals. COVID-19 has brought about the largest collapse in the number of outputs, since the Great Depression in 1930 (Fairlie, Couch, & Xu, 2020).

Above all, Micro, Small and Medium-sized Enterprises (MSMEs) are affected due their inexperiences, lack of brand recognition and relatively small size which limits their assets and resources. The outbreak of the pandemic of COVID-19 only serves to increase the hostility of business environments, and decreasing survival chances of start-ups and MSMEs around the globe that is devastated by COVID-19. In other words, the failure rate of MSMEs are even higher than they already are.

The sudden outbreak of COVID-19 and its spread at an alarming rate have ravaged the world (Chen, Wang, Huang, Kinney & Anastas, 2020), infecting millions and has had profound negative social and economic consequences due to countries imposing tight restrictions on movement of people and goods in order to halt the spread of the virus. The pandemic has affected educational systems around the world, leading to closures of universities and schools and low-income earners are the first ones to be infected due to them living in congested housings. COVID-19 has also affected people at psychological level (Groarke, Berry, Graham-Wisener, McKenna-Plumley, McGlinchey, & Armour, 2020), as there have a rapid increase in number of suicides (Sher, 2020) due to fear and unemployment, and domestic violence skyrockets due to financial insecurity and stress. Preventive measures (Wong, Hung, Alias, & Lee, 2020) such as social distancing, wearing of face masks, mandatory hand washing, self-isolation and self-quarantine for those who have travelled far and wide are implemented to slow down the spread of the virus, to the point where the world has been forced to embrace that Social Distancing has become the societal norm. However, one way of allowing organisations to operate their daily business while also adhering to the regulations of COVID-19 preventive measures is by transforming the entire process including end-products into digital forms, in a process known as digital transformation (Korachi, & Bounabat, 2020). In a world that is slowly becoming digitised, people have taken to call it the digital economy or network economy.

The amount, volume, and complexity of data being created is increasing at a rapid rate. According to Google, humanity have created an estimated five exabytes of data from the start of civilisation until 2003 (Morvan, 2016). Every day, 2.5 exabytes of data are created, and the International Data Corporation (IDC) predicts that this number will double every two years until 2020 Chandralekha & Shenbagavadivu,

2017). In 2013, the total amount of data reached 4.4 zettabytes, and this amount is anticipated to quadruple every two years, reaching a staggering 44 zettabytes by 2020 (Chandralekha & Shenbagavadivu, 2017).. It is also expected that by 2020 there will be more than 16 zettabytes (or 16 Trillion GB) of useful data (Gantz, Reinsel, Turner, & Minton, 2014). Useful data are of the utmost importance for businesses make informed business decisions.

Thus, data has fuelled the growth of digital and network economy. The Digital economy is redefining business and society at an astonishing rate and the ways in which business interactions are done is increasingly digital. According to Accenture Strategy (Morvan, 2016), an approximate 2.2 percent of the global economy are attributed to digital skills and capital. Despite this, the ability of digital interactions to improve productivity and boosts growth is far from being exploited. Digital economy is an important contribution to an economy's growth. In the United States (U.S.), the digital economy accounted for about 6.9 percent of the U.S. Gross Domestic Product (GDP), which translates to roughly $1.35 trillion (Brynjolfsson & Collis, 2019)

Thus, the emergence of digital economy and the exponential increase in data enables the possibility of digital transformation; there exists a great opportunity for Micro, Small and Medium-sized Enterprises (MSMEs) everywhere; digital transformation will enable MSMEs to provide goods and services to customers at lower costs, at greater efficiency via effective business processes that creates better value of products. Digital transformation is seen as the next step in business processes, whereby face-to-face interactions are at a minimal, saving fuel and other travelling expenses, while also seamlessly interacting with customers at high speed broadband.

In some cases, the unrealised technological application of Digital Transformation can be considered a form of emerging technologies. Lately, the question has not been whether or not the emerging technologies are useful for practical applications and real-world scenarios, rather how can MSMEs everywhere, particularly in emerging or developing economies can successfully utilise those technologies, in order to overcome the typical and usual challenges that MSMEs often face, and turn themselves into a driving force of growth. Instances of such challenges include the lack of funding due to banks unwilling to lend, the inability to grow and scale operations, data forgery or fraud, lack of technical knowhow and skills, and no brand recognition. These challenges are enough to prevent and stunt the growth of MSMEs which can lead to them failing in just their first few years of operation.

MSMEs tend to struggle to survive the most in the business environment and the failure rates are often high, despite a microeconomic framework which include policies that are friendly for MSMEs such as low taxation rates to enable MSMEs to supply the goods, low interest rates to increase consumer spending, best efforts by governments in creating an ecosystem that boosters entrepreneurship, and an education system that encourages entrepreneurial intention. According to a recent figure in the global economy by Carrigan (2020), around 21.5 percent of MSMEs fail in the first year of operation, over 30 percent in the second year, over 50 percent in the fifth year, and a staggering 70 percent in the tenth year of business. Paffenholz (1998) and Woywode (1998) found that around half of MSMEs survive for more than five years. According to some authors, only approximately half of MSMEs are still operational after only three years after their initial start-up (Watson, 2003).

LITERATURE REVIEW

Digital Transformation is a phenomenon that is gaining in popularity in both literature and practical applications, especially in today's COVID-19 era that mandates the populace to undertake preventive measures such as self-isolation and social distancing in order to mitigate the spread of the virus. Despite the many theories composed for digital transformation in organisational context, the researches that have been made for the application in MSMEs are still at its early conceptual stages. Furthermore, this paper implores that more emphasis must be placed in the context of MSMEs, as many papers by researchers have been composed for large corporations and organisations. The application of digital transformation frameworks for MSME can help improve their odds of survival, and by digitally transforming goods and services, MSMEs can compete successfully against large corporations. Dimensions of Digital Transformation included in this paper are: Strategies, Enablers or Drivers, Capabilities, the need for Digital Managers, Digital Literacy, Digital Divide, as well as covering the aspects of digital transformation that are often misunderstood. Ironically the increased amount of articles on digital transformation serves to increase ambiguity and confusion rather than reduce them. Thus, this paper is aimed at providing a brief overview as well as covering the main range of digital transformation aspect that can potentially be applied at MSME level.

The justification for this research is glaring; most researches and discussions regarding digital transformation are only mostly suited for large corporations due to their propensity to possess larger than average asset value and the capability earn above average sales revenue due to larger consumer base, in comparison to smaller organisations. In particular, digital transformation is seen as not feasible in the context of MSMEs. With the dawn of industry 4.0, and the rapid technological advancement at global level, the readily available of technology means tha t costs of production are reduced, and that organisations including MSMEs can exploit digital transformation to prevent from getting left behind in competitiveness.

This section showcases the theories and concepts that have been covered by scholars regarding digital transformation. For each theory, the paper evaluates the manner in which MSMEs can properly utilise them to increase their chances of surviving in a business environment, and this is also useful for MSMEs located in economies that are severely affected by COVID-19. The potential issues are also covered in an attempt for fair evaluation, and the paper answers whether they are relevant in the context of MSMEs.

BACKGROUND OF DIGITAL TRANSFORMATION

The inspiration on digital transformation began with the advent of a set of connected computer system called the Internet in the late 20th century (Chen, 2016), resulting in the establishment of World Wide Web (Ghantz, 2014) which allowed for the immediate sharing of information, without the need for physical intermediaries. It is this World Wide Web phenomenon that began a series of digitisation trends and changes that enables for the first time in history the reading, sharing of information without requiring a physical of tangible asset, effectively igniting the call for digital transformation across all levels and industries such as healthcare, financial, manufacturing and education (Chen, 2016; Ghantz, 2014).

With the ensuing confusion is due to various terms and definitions associated with digital transformation, coupled with the fact that digital transformation as a topic is still at its infancy, whereby people are generally unaware of the term, it important to note the slight differences in common terms. Digitalisation also entails the transformation of business processes into digital technologies, while digitisation is simply the conversion of simple media such information into digital format. However, there is gap between the two former terms and digital transformation.

Digital transformation embodies more than both digitalisation and digitisation; it requires the use of various strategies, aligned, the composing of a long-term plan to lay out a set of actions, as well as the identification of the correct tools. The process of transforming information from a physical to a digital representation is called digitization. In this format, data is arranged into discrete data units called bits that may be independently addressed, often in groupings of several bits called bytes. Digitalisation is the use of digital technology to enhance corporate operations. Digitalization is the use of digital technology to transform a company model and create new revenue and value-generating possibilities; it is the transition to a digital business. Thus, digital transformation provide a more broader, more accurate depiction of digitalisation. In the below table, this paper presents a process for easier grasping the differences.

Definition of Digital Transformation

Before diving into the theories, it is important to grasp the concept of digital transformation.

The term 'digital transformation' is simply defined as the adoption of digital technology in organisations (Schallmo, & Williams, 2018). The purpose of this adoption is to convert, transform, and change completely an organisation's entire infrastructure which include automating all manual processes, replacing obsolete digital technology with the latest state-of-the-art digital technology, the removal of non-digital aspects of the organisation in line with a concept known as 'paperless society' (Dhumne, 2017).

Digital Transformation is a field of study that has been extensively studied in academic literature Ebert & Duarte, 2018). Major topics that have been explored include its definitions concepts, and strategies (Ebert & Duarte, 2018; Matt, Hess & Benlian, 2015). It is found because digital transformation entails the transformation across all levels of an organisation, new business models and practices must be conjured (Matt, Hess & Benlian, 2015). However, studies on digital transformation in the context of MSMEs have only begun to surface over the last demi-decade (Ulas, 2019). The nature of large corporations mean that they have superior assets and equity, enabling them to invest in digital transformation. This is especially the case of MSMEs whose structure are more malleable and maintain assets below a certain threshold, and are thus faces limitation in digital transformation. For example, some theories may only be applicable for large corporations and thus are not suited for MSME applications. MSMEs include new ventures and start-ups and thus, are different in that they possess relatively few number of employees, and sales revenue and operating expenses that are typically meagre.

With the ensuing confusion is due to various terms and definitions associated with digital transformation, coupled with the fact that digital transformation as a topic is still at its infancy, whereby people are generally unaware of the term, it important to note the slight differences in common terms. Digitalisation also entails the transformation of business processes into digital technologies (Rijswijk,

Figure 1. Digitisation and digitalisation forming the foundation of digital transformation

Bulten, Klerkx, den Dulk, Dessein, Debruyne & en Nematoden, 2020), while digitisation is simply the conversion of simple media such information into digital format (Gobble, 2018). However, there is gap between the two former terms and digital transformation. Digital transformation embodies more than both digitalisation and digitisation; it requires the use of various strategies, aligned, the composing of a long-term plan to lay out a set of actions, as well as the identification of the correct tools. Thus, digital transformation provide a more broader, more accurate depiction of digitalisation.

Out of the various type of organisations, none are more important than MSMEs. MSMEs are the backbone of every economy; they are the source of employment, provide revenues in the form taxes for the government, the main source of product innovation and the creation of new differentiated products, and the encouragement of competitions. When combined with digital economy, the GDP of economies are further boosted, and MSMEs are able to keep up and compete with large corporations in an economy that is going digital.

One prime example of digital transformation in organisations is cloud computing (Arora, Parashar, & Transforming, 2013), an emerging technology that has also gained great popularity due to its practical applications that goes beyond the development and prototype stages. While emerging technology is usually only available for large corporations, the implementation of cloud computing in developed and emerging economies means the services have been made affordable for utilisation by MSMEs, whereby subscription at low costs are available. Cloud computing enables MSMEs to rely on cloud services, which allows them to save the costs of spending lump sum on hardware devices which large capacity.

Strategies for MSMEs

In order to better understand the strategies behind digital transformation, it is important to define the underlying concept of digital transformation to prevent confusion and ambiguity. While different authors have variable ways of defining and explaining digital transformation with the use of their own complex and contemporary words, the underlying concept remains the same. Vial (2019) had developed a grounded conceptual definition of Digital Transformation from various articles as the process with aims of improving a business aspect with dramatic changes to its processes. This is done via a combination of many elements such as information, computing, communication, and connectivity technologies. Bloomberg (2018) refers digital transformation in a broader that stems the long-term strategic customer-oriented business transformation that requires cross-cutting organisational change as well as the implementation of digital technologies. Another definition explains that digital transformation is the integration of any digital technologies into business processes in line with the rise of digital economy and industry 4.0 (Ziyadin, S., Suieubayeva, S., & Utegenova, A. (2019, April). Schallmo, D., Williams, C. A., & Boardman, L. (2020) have composed a framework for digital transformation which explains the role of various actors such as organisations and consumers in the creation of value chains, and these actors are dubbed the 'elements'.

Much definitions have been proposed in literature but that only serves to increase uncertainty. On a more broader perspective, digital transformation can be looked upon from a social phenomenon (Vial, 2019), explaining that the movement towards digital transformation is being normalized in every aspect of society. Authors have also defined digital transformation from a cultural evolution standpoint (Ziyadin, 2019), where it is referred to as a change of culture over time (Schallmo, 2020). The information brought about by digital transformation are capable of influencing organisational and consumer behaviour, and businesses have to follow suit. It is noteworthy to point out while the context of digital transformation is often explained from a business standpoint, it is also discussed in other industries particularly healthcare, financial, manufacturing and education.

Arguably an important part for business managers is that digital transformation is about the creation of new business models, as the new business activities entails the scrapping of traditional business models. It is important to note that unlike traditional business models, the new model demands it to be multi-sided in nature due to alignment of strategies such as IT platforms, marketing platform, human resource platform and others.

From the aforementioned definitions, one can notice a set of patterns. The patterns that these definitions had in similarity regarding the digital transformation is the emphasis on 'strategies', 'elements' or 'enablers', and 'business model'. For 'strategies', the cross cutting and alignment of various strategies are needed for digital transformation to happen by linking traditionally separate or independent strategies such Information Technology (IT) strategies, Operational Strategies, and Functional Strategies. For easier navigation on the various terms associated with digital transformation, this paper has devised a process model of digital transformation (Figure 2).

Overall, there are two conditions that must be satisfied for a process to be coined the term 'digital transformation', firstly objectives have to be set to point out where specific objectives and instructions are named to ensure employees comprehend the process. The process of digital transformation is a complex process that requires round-the-clock efforts from managers and employees from top, middle and low level management. In addition, stakeholders that are not part of the organisation play a role in shaping the strings of complicated process. Thus, it is vital to formulate and devise a digital transformation strategies. This is to ensure coordination and cohesion amongst the various departments.

While the explanation on what is digital transformation strategies are simple and concise in order for the masses to understood, further analysis reveals more dimensions in digital transformation strategies. In order to make possible digital transformation, it is essential to incorporate digital transformation strategies. Digital Transformation strategies encompasses more than just a single pathway for guidance; it involves the cutting across and the involvement of other strategies, and thus must be aligned together (Vial, 2019; Ziyadin, 2019) An organisation is bound to have more than one strategies at a time, and thus faces difficulty in prioritising relevant strategies that suit the needs of the organisation.

Despite the fact that digital transformation emphasizes a mix of aligned strategies, including IT strategies, there is a growing focus in the literature on the strategy itself rather than technology. This is owing to the discovery that, of the $1.3 trillion invested on digital transformation in the United States, nearly $900 billion were lost due to implementation errors (Dhumne, 2017; Schallmo, & Williams,

Figure 2. Process model of digital transformation

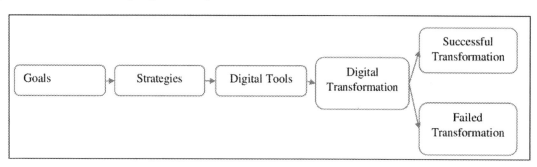

2018). In addition, if digital transformation is effectively executed, there is a possibility that rather than resolving difficulties and improving operational efficiency, digital transformation will exacerbate the organization's present weaknesses in business operations. Without the necessary skills, expertise, and mentality, digital transformation programs will fail to achieve their desired results. Despite the allure of technology and how it is sometimes idealized as the personification of problem-solvers and forward-thinking, caution must be used while investing in and using it. In order to select the appropriate digital technologies, the emphasis must be on which particular areas of an organization need development. By defining the precise regions, specific objectives and long-term plans may be formulated.

Business strategies are the means by which an organization sets out which include the outline of the actions and decisions it takes to achieve its desired objectives. Examples of concrete goals include to improve profitability by increasing sales revenue. The digital tool that is relevant in this case is Machine Learning (ML), as it help study transaction patterns and customer behaviour to do a social sentiment analysis. This can help determine which customers are at the highest risk of leaving, thereby helping to map retention strategies. Thus It can also help improve profitability based on buying patterns.

Another concrete goal is to improve design processes, the right digital tools to implement are Augmented Reality (AR) and Virtual Reality (VR). AR helps improve design speeds by reducing the amount of time consumed for a product to reach the market by removing the need for a physical prototype. VR helps designers, managers, and office workers to easily visualise and design innovative products, which will improve workflow, and provide feedback for management come up with new ideas, as well as provide product demonstration for consumers.

From these examples, it is clear that the only way to identify the correct digital tool is by identifying the broader business strategy and goals. Thus, arguably the most important question that needs to be addressed in digital transformation revolves on how can it be implemented properly, and what are the proper accompanying digital tools to reach organisational objectives.

Four Dimensions of Digital Transformation Strategies

Digital Transformation is seen as a long-term strategy for enterprises, which consists of a plan of actions to be taken in order to achieve objectives under business uncertainty (Correani, De Massis, Frattini, Petruzzelli, & Natalicchio, 2020). Under the perspective of 'strategy', scholars have composed the Four Dimensions of Digital Transformation Strategies (Matt, Hess, & Benlian, 2015), which consists of the dimension of the use of technologies, changes in value creation, structural changes, and financial aspects.

The first dimension, 'use of technologies' indicate that organisations have to decide whether to become a market leader in technology usage or rely on technological standards that have been determined by industry average (Matt, Hess, & Benlian, 2015). The dimension assesses an organisation's apparent attitude towards new technologies, while being a market leader may lead to competitive advantage, the risks associated with technological competences may warrant relying on existing technological standards.

When applying in the context of MSME, this dimension is of the utmost importance. MSMEs especially start-ups who have recently created a new venture would have to decide to become either the first mover that leads the industry, or fast follower of the first mover (Wunker, 2012). The former refers to being the first with a product that is often characterised by strong brand recognition, high switching costs, and technical economies of scale. First movers in an industry are always followed by competitors in an attempt to capitalize and imitate on the first mover's success, known as fast follower, who aims for a portion of the new market share. The last strategy, late-mover is based on the idea that an organisation learns from mistakes of first movers and fast followers and is the safest of the strategies. MSMEs can utilise any of the three methods above, but which one is suitable for growth of business, especially in the era ridden with COVID-19?

The restriction on the movement of goods due to consequences from COVID-19 means that supply lines and technology transfer is potentially affected (Guerrieri, Lorenzoni, Straub, & Werning, 2020). Thus, this paper advocates that MSMEs stick with becoming fast follower, as this is a safer option. The uncertainty of technology transfer and imports into an economy means that technology may not advance as fast as expected, and the nature of fast follower means that MSMEs are not far behind in terms of product differentiation. Undertaking a late-mover strategy however may prevent any potential advantage to be gained in a market that is already saturated with similar products. However, one can argue that this is the most opportune time become first-mover and enter the market, provided that the MSMEs are capable of bearing the high initial cost. COVID-19 has resulted in increase in the costs of borrowing, potentially decreasing investments, allowing the MSME to be far ahead of its competition and establish high barriers to entry.

The financial aspect dimension is the most important of the theory (Matt, Hess, & Benlian, 2015), as without it the other dimensions cease to exist. For both large corporations and MSMEs, should a form of urgency to act exist, be it due to under constant financial pressure or other reasons that diminishes the business core, the rate of digital transformation is based on this urgency. Any financial aspect is driver of digital transformation, and organisations with lower financial pressure may have reduced perception to act. However, it should be noted that organisations under greater financial pressure may lack the necessary external finance to initiate digital transformation. The recessions brought about by COVID-19 however, may have further increased the difficulty of finding external sources of finance, forcing MSMEs to rely on its internal funding such as retained profits from previous years or self-funding to survive.

The 'changes in value creation' dimension entails the extent to which an organisation deviates away from its original values upon implementation of a digital transformation strategy (Matt, Hess, & Benlian, 2015). Specifically, it assesses how the new digital activities are different from the organisation's classical core competences. It is the notion that in an MSME, the further the gap between the digital activities and the former values, the more opportunities there are to improve and add new features to current products and services.

The last of the 'Four dimension of digital strategies', structural changes is the least relevant for MSMEs (Matt, Hess, & Benlian, 2015). Unlike large corporations, MSMEs by its very nature are malleable and dynamic in nature due to the need to adapt to markets in its first few years of operation. The dimension of structural changes believe that the effects of digital changes in an organisation's structure and setup have to be assessed to prevent negative consequences. Managers and employees in MSMEs however are inclined to make any changes in organisations, as they understood that implementation of digital activities are necessary in today's digital age. Consequences must be assessed in terms of products, business processes or skills of employees. This assessment is vital during the ongoing COVID-19 pandemic as digitalisation is essential for the adherence of preventive measures such as social distancing.

Procedural Aspects of Digital Transformation Strategies

Another perspective of strategic management that has been proposed is the 'Procedural Aspects of Digital Transformation Strategies' (Li, Su, Zhang, & Mao, 2018). This theory is based on the idea that responsibilities must be delegated with clarity to ensure proper implementation of digital transformation.

This means equipping operational employees with the right mindset and technical know-how, while also aligning them with the organisation's objectives.

Procedures (Li, Su, Zhang, & Mao, 2018) must be drafted for digital transformation which is vital for formulating, implementing, evaluating and adopting digital transformation strategies. While this often entails a complicated process, it has been necessitated because employees with the expertise and outsourced services may need additional support. The high risk and uncertainty of new digital technologies that is often malleable to changes warrants procedures for every digital activity in the process. This includes contingency planning for various unusual scenarios that may happen in order to reduce the impact of negative consequences. The benefits conferred by this strategy is sustained management credibility, avoidance of biased decision-making, whereby decisions are made on the basis of emotions rather than facts.

With every completion of the activities and stages of the digital transformational process, continuous reassessment is mandatory to ensure performance for digital transformation are up to par, and should expectations are not met, the procedures would provide clarity as to what is the next step. Not only will procedures and reassessment provide confidence and assurance for both managers and employees, it will serve to remind them on how far they have achieved towards the implementation of digital transformation strategies. However, questions are still being asked as who should be overseeing the strategy of digital transformation. There are arguments that instead of the traditional hierarchy of Chief Executive Officer (CEO) being given the task of overseeing (Singh, & Hess, 2017), the creation of a new role known as Chief Digital Officer (CDO) is better suited to focus solely on managing all activities associated with Digital Transformation. This applies to MSMEs, and it is worth noting that any form of digital transformation is a tedious and long process that often entails one person being consistent and able to continue in the foreseeable future.

As with any changes in an organisation, resistance to organisational change is bound to happen (Bolognese, 2002). This is especially true for large corporations that is often characterised by a large and rigid structure that is not subjected to rapid changes. One way to circumvent this issue is the application of transformational leadership skills (Diaz-Saenz, 2011). Under this concept, each stakeholder is implored to be involved in the digital changes, whereby they can offer feedback which will help further smoothen the transition to a digital structure.

The nature of MSMEs means that they often hire employees at minimum wage in an attempt to minimise costs. This came at the cost of hiring employees who are unskilled and unqualified which is detrimental for digital transformation process. Thus, the 'Procedural Aspects of Digital Transformation Strategies' provides the necessary procedures to act as a guidance for these employees. It should be noted however that the procedures can only do so much, for employees that is without a degree of digital literacy may still find it baffling to comprehend the procedures (Jamil, M. I. M., & Almunawar, M. N).

Digital Transformation Enablers

For digital transformation to be made possible, there are enablers that allows the seamless transition for any organisation (Schallmo, & Williams, 2018; Chatterjee, Grewal, & Sambamurthy, 2002). These serve as change drivers, which include digital data, automation, digital customer access, and networking.

Data must be digitised and not written on paper, which entails organisations to have the necessary hardware or outsource from a subscription-based cloud-service. The digitised data is then collected in order to be processed to make informed decision-makings, and analysed to make predictions of potential future outcomes, especially when taking into account the COVID-19 pandemic.

Manual labour is ultimately replaced with automation process (Moffitt, Rozario, & Vasarhelyi, 2018). The advantages of automation include increased in efficiency of producing output, reduction of costs from economies of scale, and reduction of errors. The sophisticated technologies employed include artificial intelligence system that is capable of enabling autonomous work, and able to self-organise in a process known as machine learning, which refers to the ability to automatically learn and improve from experience without being explicitly programmed. However, this comes at the cost of redundancy of employees. This paper advocates that automation will not remove jobs, rather they create new ones, as automation is driving job creation. Human labour can remain competitive as human-system relationships can exists provided adequate digital literacy exists. Most experts in the three industries of manufacturing, logistics, and healthcare predict a future in which humans and machines work together. Automation can create rewarding job profiles for long-term employees. While MSMEs can retain the same employees to avoid issue of redundancy, resources have to be spent on retraining on equipping employees with skills on operating automated hardware and software.

Digital Customer Access is an enabler that allows any organisation to contact new and existing customers (Chatterjee, Grewal, & Sambamurthy, 2002). The benefits conferred include high level of transparency, and the provision of new services that allows customers to consistently buy from the same organisation and establish customer relationship. This is crucial for MSMEs, as it will enable profits to be made from Lifetime Value of a Customer (CLV), which is defined as the total amount of money to be made from one customer spending on goods and services during their lifetime (Sunder, Kumar, & Zhao, 2016). This necessitates excellent customer relationship management (CRM), whereby an organisation must manage and analyse customer interactions and data throughout a customer lifecycle (Raab, Ajami, & Goddard, 2016), to ensure repeat purchase from the same customer over a prolonged duration and increase CLV.

Networking is essential for the alignment of supply chain customers (Chatterjee, Grewal, & Sambamurthy, 2002); high-speed internet infrastructure allows for a more aligned supply chain which reduces production time and innovation cycles. This is all the more important for MSMEs in emerging economies that aims to reduce intermediaries as much as possible in a supply chain, and will have to rely on good infrastructure to constantly innovate and allow goods to reach the MSME from suppliers and producers with minimal costs. This is vital as supply lines are even more unreliable due to restriction imposed to counteract the effects of COVID-19.

However, this paper argues that not all MSMEs have the assets to implement such enablers. For instance, some economies lack the proper technological infrastructure that is characterised by slow download speed. In fact, traditional papers are still used to store data and information in favour digital data. In addition, technology transfer and import is slow in certain regions across the world, in a process known as digital divide (Jamil, M. I. M., & Almunawar, M. N). Policy makers and private sector firms are implored to create an create an entrepreneurial ecosystem and infrastructure that is supportive towards the growth of MSMEs. This includes a microeconomic framework that has low taxation rate, strong technological infrastructure that is based on digitised processes, low interest rates, and increase in the circulation of money supply to encourage consumer spending on MSME products.

Dynamic Managerial Capabilities

Aside from strategy, authors throughout the decades have informed that the two aspects that must exist in any organisation to initiate value creation is resources and capabilities (Leiblein, 2011). A dimension of digital transformation that is often talked about by researchers is the capabilities (Li, Su, Zhang & Mao, 2018), which is further subdivided into dynamic managerial capabilities and organisational capabilities.

Under the theory of dynamic managerial capabilities (DMC), "the capabilities with which managers build, integrate, and reconfigure organizational resources and competences" (Helfat, & Winter, 2011; Adner, & Helfat, 2003; Helfat, & Martin, 2015). These capabilities indicate the extent to which an organisation able to undertake digital transformation.

Previous research has suggested that DMC is built on three core underpinnings: managerial cognition, managerial social capital, and managerial human capital (Helfat, & Winter, 2011). Managerial cognition is the personal beliefs of managers which includes managers' knowledge and understanding of current events and predictions of future developments, which greatly influences their decision-making. While decision-making in MSMEs is not often complex, informed decisions still need to be made, and cognitive managers is able to detect changes in market structure, and how they are adapting to his change.

Managerial social capital outlines the relationship managers have with the people around him, both formally and informally (Helfat, & Winter, 2011). This is crucial as it can help managers obtain information by conversing with others, and establish networks for resource acquisition. This is of utmost importance for MSMEs as information about market opportunities are often one-off and may require quick action in order to acquire competitive advantage in the early stages.

Managerial Human Capital includes the knowledge, experience, skills, and education (Helfat, & Winter, 2011) of both individual managers and teams of managers. In this instance, it is vital that MSME possesses employees with wide variety of diverse skills to ensure different knowledge can complement each other. This is useful for MSME adaption to a dynamic business environment.

Theory of Organisational Capabilities

The theory of Organisational Capabilities is defined as the capacity by which an organization "performs a particular activity in a reliable and at least minimally satisfactory manner" (Helfat & Winter, 2011). In other words, specific organisational capabilities are needed in different organisations in different industry. An example is an MSME competing in a monopolistic competition industry which is filled with competitors must be capable of differentiating their products, while MSMEs in a technology-based industry that is subjected to rapid changes in technological advancement must be ready to embrace new technology and must devote their resources to research and development.

Digital Transformation has also been applied at the context of organisational performance with the use of a qualitative and quantitative approach (Chen, Jaw, & Wu, 2016). To an extent, digital transformation has been proven empirically to have an impact on organisational performance. In particular, the service-oriented portal function dimension, such as portal maintenance service, B2B function, and cloud computing, has been found to have a positive correlation on organisational performance. However, extrinsic factors such as information on industry benchmark is stated to have a negative relationship with organisational performance. What is important to note here is that, the dimensions that have positive correlation are intrinsic or occurs within the organisation, and are focused on improving the strategy of the organisation such as its services. The emphasis is not on technology.

Strategy Orientation and Technology Orientation

In addition, many authors have argued with great emphasis that for digital transformation to be made possible, the infrastructure and mindset of the enterprise has to be based on strategy rather than technology (Kane, Palmer, Phillips, Kiron, & Buckley, 2015; Hess, Matt, Benlian & Wiesböck, 2016; GERALD, 2015; Matt, Hess, & Benlian, 2015; Chen, Jaw, & Wu, 2016). This means that investments should be focused on the transformation of products, processes and organisational aspects, whereby activities are digitised such as the process of converting input to output, the end-user products itself, as well as post-products the customer interfaces or relationship. The digitised activities at every processes will create a culture and core competences (Prahalad, 1993) that is heavily reliant on a plan of action, and when synchronised at every levels and departments, will ultimately lead to achievement of a the long-term goal. The concept is similar to the theory popularised by Drucker (McLaren, Mills, & Durepos, 2009) known as management by objectives (MBO). Under the MBO model, the performance of an organization is improved by clearly defining and synchronising objectives that are must be agreed upon by both management and employees. Without proper coordination from each employee, the long-term goal set may not be achieved on time.

This scenario can be applied to the case of an MSME. Due to the limited sources of finance and the constraint amount of funding for MSME, it would be unwise to invest the relatively small amount of resources they have on new technology that is often characterised by high initial cost. The main objective of an MSME should be cost-reduction, thus an organisation-wide emphasis on strategy would not only provide directions for employees, but also motivate them, especially with the use of Key Performance Indicators (KPI).

Digital Literacy and Digital Divide

Above all, digital transformation is not possible without an organisation possessing a degree of digital literacy. Digital literacy has been defined as an individual's skills and competences in using Information and Communication technology (ICT) (Jamil, M. I. M., & Almunawar, M. N.). It is more than just the ability to use technology; the individual must be able to discover, compose and assess information that is available in digital format such as text, audio and images. The individual is then able to distribute these digital data and information via various digital platforms such as Google, Facebook and Amazon. Unfortunately, there is an uneven distribution of access to ICT, which includes hardware and software, and the Internet in different regions across the world. Certain regions lack the necessary ICT infrastructure, which limits the potential of digital literacy, while developed regions is able to boost digital skills of the populace, causing a phenomenon known as digital divide. For instance, in the United States, it is reported that youths are connected to the Internet at a rate of 94 to 98 percent, while in regions such as Africa, only 7% of the continent's inhabitants that are online (Cohen, & Kahne, 2011). Digital divide may render the certain digital transformation theories null due to the existing conditions being that data must in digital format and digital network must exist for interactions to occur.

As the severity of COVID-19 spreads throughout the world, and its effect is felt by businesses in both developed and emerging economies, it comes as no surprise that the study of COVID-19 has started to appear in literature, especially in the application of business organisations. In addition, literature has burst on COVID and its impacts. New research interests have emerged in regards to how MSMEs can survive COVID-19. Gourinchas, Kalemli-Özcan, Penciakova, & Sander (2020) have empirically proven that failure rates are even higher in many industries than in the pre-COVID era. However, while some industries are badly affected, there are others that are only moderately affected such as the financial sector due to their huge amount of reserves that they able to use in the event of a bankruptcy, and potential financial crisis. The financial crisis in 2008 has increased the risk perception of the financial sector (Purfield, & Rosenberg, 2010). Smaller organisations are not so lucky as they had to make do with limited resource, which means lack of capital and revenue reserves to be used for emergency purposes.

It has been argued in adapting to COVID-19 era, for MSMEs to succeed in undergoing digital transformation, they have to possess a quality known as digital resilience in order to be able to make informed decisions on which is the best digital transformation strategy (Fitriasari, 2020). Digital resilience is defined as the perfect balance between undertaking risks associated with taking advantage of available opportunities by weighing out the financial and personal risks, as well the striking a balance between the consumption of human resources and capital machinery, undertaking either labour-intensive or capital-intensive approach.

COVID-19 has undoubtedly caused an adverse effect on the perception of risks (Cepel, Gavurova, Dvorský, & Belas, 2020). Prior to outbreak of COVID-19, over 30% of MSMEs in Czech Republic and Slovakia considers financial risk as one of the most significant risks. In the era of COVID-19, these percentages have increased to more than 50%. Aside from financial risks, there is also increase in perception risk from over 20% in the pre-COVID era, to more than 60% at present day. In other words, COVID-19 have made organisations everywhere more risk-averse, meaning less investments on capital and foreign direct investment, and less spending on goods and service for in favour of savings money for future survival.

Implementation Issues of Digital Transformation

Once solidarity and clarity has been confirmed with the publications of empirical researches, researchers have begun to ask how MSMEs can utilise digital transformation. However, it should be said that researches of digital transformation in the context of MSMEs are lacklustre. This is largely due to the stereotypical belief that MSMEs are entities that lack the necessary resources to and would not have capabilities to endeavour on the insurmountable task of digital transformation. Researches are more inclined towards large corporations that are usually given leniency in terms of finance due to their vast amount of assets as collaterals. Their reputation also gives them an advantage as consumers often flock towards buying branded and recognised goods.

However, this paper argues that digital transformation is possible to be applied at MSME level. MSMEs confer the advantage of having a structure that is flexible and open to changes. This means that they are adaptable to the rapidly changing and dynamic environment. Investments in technology are often risky due to its rapid advancement and MSMEs are in the advantageous position of being able adapt quickly to digital transformation. MSMEs are able to spare the time and effort to establish close relationships with customers, boosting sales and employees are often easily managed due to their small structure. Above all costs are low and manageable, simplifying the task of going beyond the breakeven line. These factors are important as it proves that not only large corporations are able to initiate digital transformation but MSMEs as well.

More importantly, studies have emerged on how the issues that MSMEs face related to the implementation of Digital Transformation at various aspects of an organisation (Khitskov, Veretekhina, Medvedeva,

Mnatsakanyan, Shmakova, & Kotenev, 2017). Specifically, these issues pertain to the lack of digital literacy, misunderstandings related to need for digital transformation.

One of the first problem that has been identified is the lack of digital literacy in terms of understanding the digital processes which include human-system relationship. Digital transformation consists of a synthesis between labour and capital, such as human resources and machinery. For human-system relationship to occur, digital literacy must be enhanced.

The second most important issue relates to the various perceptions as to the increase in the number of IT-specialists in an organisation, in order to put into effect digital transformation. In comparison to previous years, questions have been asked as to how much percentage should there be in the increase in number of IT-specialists. The variety of answers provided by respondents is a clear indication on the lack of comprehension on importance of retraining and reorientation in technology and technical skills. Organisations with traditional jobs may need to be revamped in favour of jobs that require core competence in digital skills and literacy. However, the advantage provided is the increase in the number of job opportunities.

The next problem is an advanced issue whereby there is a lack of synchronisation between devices. This indicates a lack of cloud computing system. Lack of content creation is symbolic to the lack of efforts to produce educational contents, and payments for transactions are still conducted in traditional currency such as cash. The ideal currency for digital transformation is the use of virtual currencies such as bitcoin, that utilises advanced form of technology called blockchain that enables the storing of unchangeable data.

Lastly, the problem is related to partial understanding to the importance of embracing a digital culture, digital ethics and digital reputation. These concepts are needed for quick adaptation of employees in a digitally transformed organisation. Digital Culture refers to values, core competences, skills, attitudes and behaviours associated with a digital environment. Digital culture encompasses digital society in that digital culture aims to create and maintain a culture that adheres to a set of ethnic principles, with the aim of becoming a symbol of role model, freedom and creativity in an era of digital society. Out of the three, digital reputation is arguably the most important, as it speaks of consequences of placing information in a medium such as the Internet and social media. In the aftermath, the consequences and feedback of said information may either be positive or negative.

Other researchers are focused on the problems related to the availability of data and the emerging technologies that enables the use of data (Ianenko, Ianenko, Huhlaev, & Martynenko, 2019, March). While digital economy is all the rage, certain poor and emerging economies are still based on traditional economy, which results in lack of data in digital forms. Information are still noted in papers, applications are still submitted by travelling all the way to the counter, processes take time due to the passing of paper applications from bottom to top of the hierarchy.

The unavailability of emerging technologies or utilisers of digital economy such as big data, Internet of Things (IoT), Artificial Intelligence (AI), Robotics, Augmented Reality (AR), Virtual Reality (VR), Mixed Reality (MR), Machine Learning (ML), Blockchain, etc is a potential hindrance. The absence of these utilisers would make it nigh difficult for data to flow, be collected and analysed for benefits and organisations, and growth of digital economy would be stunted.

PROPOSED THEORETICAL FRAMEWORK

Figure 3. Framework showcasing underlying concepts of digital transformation

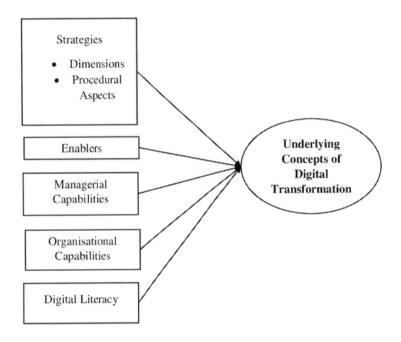

CONCLUSION

Digital Transformation is a phenomenon that is gaining in popularity in both literature and practical applications, especially in today's COVID-19 era that mandates the populace to undertake preventive measures such as self-isolation and social distancing in order to mitigate the spread of the virus. Despite the many theories composed for digital transformation in organisational context, few researches have been made for application in MSMEs. This paper implores that more emphasis must be placed in the context of MSMEs, as many papers by researchers have been composed for large corporations and organisations. For easier comprehension, a figure 3 is composed to summarise the various theories.

It is the opinion of this paper that the application of digital transformation frameworks for SME can help improve their odds of survival, especially in an economy ridden with COVID-19. The reasons are twofold: Digital Transformation helps MSMEs conduct business as usual while also adhering to the regulations of COVID-19 preventive measures; the impact of globalisation has brought about the growth of digital economy, and by digitally transforming goods and services, MSMEs can compete successfully against large corporations.

The world is approaching an era where everything is digitised for the sake improved efficiency, thus Digital Transformation is of the utmost importance for MSMEs. Its strategies and infrastructure can provide MSMEs an unprecedented competitive advantage in the field of business that not only will put them ahead of its competitors which include large corporations, but also an advantage in the field of technology. As time moves on however, these technologies can be made for MSMEs at affordable rates, such as the case of cloud computing that used to only be available for large corporations. Overall, Digital Transformation can reduce the failure rates of MSMEs, and assist MSMEs survive, especially to survive the economies impacts of COVID-19, and venture into the growth phase indicated by the increase in sales turnover and rise in the number of employment.

This paper has pointed the future research directions to more specific details such as how digital transformation changes framework of supply chains, processes in healthcare, the equity of financial sector and its similarity to e-Commerce models. Elements of digital transformation may have skirted around digital literacy and digital divide, but researches in both aspects are saturated, unless redirected to the context of MSMEs. More questions must be asked, and in more specific details, on how MSMEs can successfully apply the concept of digital transformation, assessment must be made as how much improvement and impacts have been reaped by MSMEs, for instance, changes in indicators or metrics such as productivity, efficiency, sales, equity, brand recognition, motivation, etc.

REFERENCES

Adner, R., & Helfat, C. E. (2003). Corporate effects and dynamic managerial capabilities. *Strategic Management Journal*, *24*(10), 1011–1025. doi:10.1002/smj.331

Arora, R., Parashar, A., & Transforming, C. C. I. (2013). Secure user data in cloud computing using encryption algorithms. *International Journal of Engineering Research and Applications*, *3*(4), 1922–1926.

Bloomberg, J. (2018). Digitization, digitalization, and digital transformation: confuse them at your peril. *Forbes*.

Bolognese, A. F. (2002). *Employee resistance to organizational change*. Research Gate.

Brynjolfsson, E., & Collis, A. (2019). How should we measure the digital economy. *Harvard Business Review*, *97*, 140–148.

Carrigan, M. (2020). *2019 Small Business Failure Rate: Startup Statistics by Industry*. National Biz. https://www.national.biz/2019-small-business-failure-rate-startup-statistics-industry/

Cavallo, J. J., & Forman, H. P. (2020). The economic impact of the COVID-19 pandemic on radiology practices. *Radiology*, *296*(3), 201495. doi:10.1148/radiol.2020201495 PMID:32293225

Cepel, M., Gavurova, B., Dvorský, J., & Belas, J. (2020). The impact of the COVID-19 crisis on the perception of business risk in the SME segment. *Journal of International Students*, *13*(3), 248–263. doi:10.14254/2071-8330.2020/13-3/16

Chandralekha, M., & Shenbagavadivu, N. (2017). AN INSIGHT INTO THE USAGE OF BIG DATA ANALYTICS. *International Journal of Advanced Research in Computer Science*, *8*(9).

Chatterjee, D., Grewal, R., & Sambamurthy, V. (2002). Shaping up for e-commerce: Institutional enablers of the organizational assimilation of web technologies. *Management Information Systems Quarterly*, *26*(2), 65–89. doi:10.2307/4132321

Chen, K., Wang, M., Huang, C., Kinney, P. L., & Anastas, P. T. (2020). Air pollution reduction and mortality benefit during the COVID-19 outbreak in China. *The Lancet. Planetary Health, 4*(6), e210–e212. doi:10.1016/S2542-5196(20)30107-8 PMID:32411944

Chen, Y. Y. K., Jaw, Y. L., & Wu, B. L. (2016). Effect of digital transformation on organisational performance of SMEs. *Internet Research, 26*(1), 186–212. doi:10.1108/IntR-12-2013-0265

Cohen, C. J., & Kahne, J. (2011). *Participatory politics. New media and youth political action.*

Correani, A., De Massis, A., Frattini, F., Petruzzelli, A. M., & Natalicchio, A. (2020). Implementing a digital strategy: Learning from the experience of three digital transformation projects. *California Management Review, 62*(4), 37–56. doi:10.1177/0008125620934864

Dhumne, K. M. (2017). Paperless Society in Digital Era. *International Journal of Library and Information Studies, 7*(4), 317–319.

Diaz-Saenz, H. R. (2011). Transformational leadership. The SAGE handbook of leadership, 5(1), 299-310.

Ebert, C., & Duarte, C. H. C. (2018). Digital Transformation. *IEEE Software, 35*(4), 16–21. doi:10.1109/MS.2018.2801537

Fairlie, R. W., Couch, K., & Xu, H. (2020). The impacts of covid-19 on minority unemployment: First evidence from april 2020 cps microdata (No. w27246). National Bureau of Economic Research.

Fitriasari, F. (2020). How do Small and Medium Enterprise (SME) survive the COVID-19 outbreak?. *Jurnal Inovasi Ekonomi, 5*(02).

Gantz, J. F., Reinsel, D., Turner, V., & Minton, S. (2014). The Digital Universe of Opportunities: Rich Data and the Increasing Value of the Internet of Things. *IDC iView: IDC Analyze the Future.*

Gerald, C. (2015). *Research Report Strategy, Not Technology, Drives Digital Transformation.* Research Gate.

Gobble, M. M. (2018). Digitalization, digitization, and innovation. *Research Technology Management, 61*(4), 56–59. doi:10.1080/08956308.2018.1471280

Gourinchas, P. O., Kalemli-Özcan, Ş., Penciakova, V., & Sander, N. (2020). COVID-19 and SME Failures (No. w27877). National Bureau of Economic Research.

Groarke, J. M., Berry, E., Graham-Wisener, L., McKenna-Plumley, P. E., McGlinchey, E., & Armour, C. (2020). Loneliness in the UK during the COVID-19 pandemic: Cross-sectional results from the COVID-19 Psychological Wellbeing Study. *PLoS One, 15*(9), e0239698. doi:10.1371/journal.pone.0239698 PMID:32970764

Guerrieri, V., Lorenzoni, G., Straub, L., & Werning, I. (2020). *Macroeconomic Implications of COVID-19: Can Negative Supply Shocks Cause Demand Shortages?* (No. w26918). National Bureau of Economic Research.

Helfat, C. E., & Martin, J. A. (2015). Dynamic managerial capabilities: Review and assessment of managerial impact on strategic change. *Journal of Management, 41*(5), 1281–1312. doi:10.1177/0149206314561301

Helfat, C. E., & Winter, S. G. (2011). Untangling dynamic and operational capabilities: Strategy for the (n)ever-changing world. *Strategic Management Journal, 32*(11), 1243–1250. doi:10.1002/smj.955

Hess, T., Matt, C., Benlian, A., & Wiesböck, F. (2016). Options for formulating a digital transformation strategy. *MIS Quarterly Executive, 15*(2).

Ianenko, M., Ianenko, M., Huhlaev, D., & Martynenko, O. (2019, March). Digital transformation of trade: Problems and prospects of marketing activities. [). IOP Publishing.]. *IOP Conference Series. Materials Science and Engineering, 497*(1), 012118. doi:10.1088/1757-899X/497/1/012118

Jamil, M. I. M., & Almunawar, M. N. Importance of Digital Literacy and Hindrance Brought About by Digital Divide. In *Encyclopedia of Information Science and Technology* (5th ed., pp. 1683–1698). IGI Global.

Kane, G. C., Palmer, D., Phillips, A. N., Kiron, D., & Buckley, N. (2015). Strategy, not technology, drives digital transformation. *MIT Sloan Management Review and Deloitte University Press, 14*, 1–25.

Khitskov, E. A., Veretekhina, S. V., Medvedeva, A. V., Mnatsakanyan, O. L., Shmakova, E. G., & Kotenev, A. (2017). Digital transformation of society: Problems entering in the digital economy. *Eurasian Journal of Analytical Chemistry, 12*(5), 855–873. doi:10.12973/ejac.2017.00216a

Korachi, Z., & Bounabat, B. (2020). General Approach for Formulating a Digital Transformation Strategy. *Journal of Computational Science, 16*(4), 493–507. doi:10.3844/jcssp.2020.493.507

Leiblein, M. J. (2011). *What do resource-and capability-based theories propose?* Research Gate.

Li, L., Su, F., Zhang, W., & Mao, J. Y. (2018). Digital transformation by SME entrepreneurs: A capability perspective. *Information Systems Journal, 28*(6), 1129–1157. doi:10.1111/isj.12153

Matt, C., Hess, T., & Benlian, A. (2015). Digital transformation strategies. *Business & Information Systems Engineering, 57*(5), 339–343. doi:10.1007/s12599-015-0401-5

McLaren, P. G., Mills, A. J., & Durepos, G. (2009). Disseminating Drucker. *Journal of Management History, 15*(4), 388–403. doi:10.1108/17511340910987310

Moffitt, K. C., Rozario, A. M., & Vasarhelyi, M. A. (2018). Robotic process automation for auditing. *Journal of Emerging Technologies in Accounting, 15*(1), 1–10. doi:10.2308/jeta-10589

Morvan, L. (2016). Data: The Fuel of the Digital Economy and SME Growth. *Accenture Report.*

Paffenholz, G. (1998). Krisenhafte Entwicklungen in mittelständischen *Unternehmen: Ursachenanalyse und Implikationen für die Beratung.* Ifm.

Prahalad, C. K. (1993). The role of core competencies in the corporation. *Research Technology Management, 36*(6), 40–47. doi:10.1080/08956308.1993.11670940

Purfield, C., & Rosenberg, C. B. (2010). Adjustment under a currency peg: Estonia, Latvia and Lithuania during the global financial crisis 2008-09. *IMF Working Papers*, 1-34.

Raab, G., Ajami, R. A., & Goddard, G. J. (2016). *Customer relationship management: A global perspective.* CRC Press. doi:10.4324/9781315575636

Rijswijk, K., Bulten, W., Klerkx, L. W. A., den Dulk, L. S., Dessein, J., Debruyne, L., & en Nematoden, O. T. E. (2020). *Digital Transformation: Ongoing digitisation and digitalisation processes.*

Schallmo, D., Williams, C. A., & Boardman, L. (2020). Digital transformation of business models—best practice, enablers, and roadmap. *Digital Disruptive Innovation*, 119-138.

Schallmo, D. R., & Williams, C. A. (2018). History of digital transformation. In *Digital Transformation Now!* (pp. 3–8). Springer. doi:10.1007/978-3-319-72844-5_2

Sher, L. (2020). The impact of the COVID-19 pandemic on suicide rates. *QJM, 113*(10), 707–712. doi:10.1093/qjmed/hcaa202 PMID:32539153

Singh, A., & Hess, T. (2017). How Chief Digital Officers promote the digital transformation of their companies. *MIS Quarterly Executive, 16*(1).

Sunder, S., Kumar, V., & Zhao, Y. (2016). Measuring the lifetime value of a customer in the consumer packaged goods industry. *JMR, Journal of Marketing Research, 53*(6), 901–921. doi:10.1509/jmr.14.0641

Ulas, D. (2019). Digital transformation process and SMEs. *Procedia Computer Science, 158*, 662–671. doi:10.1016/j.procs.2019.09.101

Vial, G. (2019). Understanding digital transformation: A review and a research agenda. *The Journal of Strategic Information Systems, 28*(2), 118–144. doi:10.1016/j.jsis.2019.01.003

Watson, J. (2003). The potential impact of accessing advice on SME failure rates. In The potential impact of accessing advice on SME failure rates (pp. CD-Rom). University of Ballarat.

Wong, L. P., Hung, C. C., Alias, H., & Lee, T. S. H. (2020). Anxiety symptoms and preventive measures during the COVID-19 outbreak in Taiwan. *BMC Psychiatry, 20*(1), 1–9. doi:10.1186/s12888-020-02786-8 PMID:32677926

Woywode, M. (1998). *Determinanten der Überlebenswahrscheinlichkeit von Unternehmen: Eine empirische Überprüfung organisationstheoretischer und industrieökonomischer Erklärungsansätze.* Nomos.

Wunker, S. (2012). Better growth decisions: Early mover, fast follower or late follower? *Strategy and Leadership, 40*(2), 43–48. doi:10.1108/10878571211209341

Ziyadin, S., Suieubayeva, S., & Utegenova, A. (2019, April). Digital transformation in business. In *Digital Transformation of the Economy: Challenges, Trends, New Opportunities* (pp. 408-415). Springer, Cham.

Chapter 2
Artificial Intelligence (AI)–Powered Chatbots for Marketing and Online Shopping

Mehul Anil Waghambare

Symbiosis Institute of Digital and Telecom Management, Symbiosis International University, India

Sandeep Prabhu

(iD) https://orcid.org/0000-0002-2146-1960

Symbiosis Institute of Digital and Telecom Management, Symbiosis International University, India

P. Ashok

(iD) https://orcid.org/0000-0002-5859-6041

Symbiosis Institute of Digital and Telecom Management, Symbiosis International University, India

N. A.

(iD) https://orcid.org/0000-0002-8726-5284

Symbiosis Institute of Digital and Telecom Management, Symbiosis International University, India

ABSTRACT

The COVID-19 pandemic is changing the way we connect, communicate, and collaborate. the crisis rapidly re-shape both the "what" and the "how" of companies. Businesses now move to doing business online, that involves selling of products, generating leads and connecting with customers. The chatbot, a software application designed for human-like conversations, emerged as a trend that is helping to close the social distance gap between customers and businesses. Many business have incorporated the tool in their communication strategy, this paper aims to understand to what extent, tries to put-forward an understanding of chatbots marketing and the use of chatbots in online shopping process. Furthermore, the paper tries to speaks extensively about the design in such a way that it will peak its performance for user acquisition.

DOI: 10.4018/978-1-6684-9576-6.ch002

ARTIFICIAL INTELLIGENCE (AI) POWERED CHATBOTS FOR MARKETING AND ONLINE SHOPPING

Introduction

The COVID-19 pandemic is changing the way we connect, communicate, and collaborate. the crisis rapidly re-shape both the "what" and the "how" of companies. Businesses now move to doing business online, that involves selling of products, generating leads and connecting with customers. The chatbot, a software application designed for human-like conversations, emerged as a trend that is helping to close the social distance gap between customers and businesses. Many business have incorporated the tool in their communication strategy, this chapter aims to understand to what extent, tries to put-forward an understanding of chatbots marketing and the use of chatbots in online shopping process. Furthermore, the chapter tries to speaks extensively about the design in such a way that it will peak its performance for user acquisition.

The largest influence on the rate of economic progress in many countries will come from IoT and AI. (*Panetta, 2016*). One factor that enables the acceptance of these technologies in the corporate, consumer, and social dimensions is undoubtedly the rising functionality of their devices, systems, applications, and equipment. On the one hand, their presence acts as a spur for the development of new solutions, and on the other hand, they serve as the digital economy's unique DNA code, subjected to ongoing processes that increase their potential (*Kaczorowska-Spychalska et al, 2019*). Digital change is unavoidable, and it contributes to the current culture and technology system, which fosters new social behaviours while also accelerating the creation of new, impossible things. Computers and other digital innovations rely on our brains' ability to comprehend and modify our surroundings. Digital technologies are currently thought to expand the functionality of implemented solutions, increase operational effectiveness, and improve and optimise existing processes and tools in an individual organisation.

Over the past 20 years, the "digital revolution" has fundamentally altered the customer experience. Consumer preferences have evolved, technology has advanced, and communication is no longer constrained by distance or time and is diversified in different areas as in Figure 1.

The convenience and speed of this transaction also contribute to the growth of online businesses all over the globe. Even across borders, the cost of joining various markets has decreased thanks to digital technologies. Digitalization has also made it easier for newcomers to scale up production, advertising, and distribution (*OECD et al, 2018*). The ease of starting a business online has resulted in the growth of thousands of businesses in every industry online (*Avis et al, 2015*). This possibly could create a market full of perfect competition. Businesses hence are looking into different marketplaces, exploring ways to market their services differently in order achieve competitive differentiation. In a fast-paced market that is full of competition, it becomes almost essential for businesses to cater to their consumers efficiently and well in time. Customers are demanding 24-hour service for everything from banking and finance to healthcare. In this century, quick and efficient technology has become the norm and consumers have high expectations. If a business does not address a consumer's needs, the individual has enough options to let go and turn to a competitor business. Hence, it has become imperative for companies to put into place an enhanced digital system to cater to their consumers.

Figure 1. Digital Customer Experience Areas

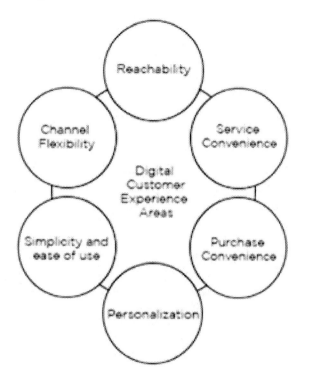

Effect of COVID-19 on Customer Behaviour and Shopping

COVID-19 has had a huge and immediate impact on customer behaviour. Spending is down across most industries, purchases are changing from physical to the online platform, and consumer well-being has become a primary consideration for businesses. Companies have acknowledged that customer experience would be shaped by current behaviours in the upcoming years. They should next make sure these opportunities are compatible with their firm's objectives and capabilities. Dynamic customer data, Safe and contactless engagements and Digital excellence will define the post-pandemic customer experience. Each organisation will pursue these priorities in their own way, depending on its industry competitive landscape as well as the starting point. Some organisations have begun to demonstrated their awareness of what customers value as well as have innovated strategies to fulfil both their previous and new expectations. These early adopters provide a useful guide for how to proceed.

While financial flexibility is becoming more limited, many customers now have more time on their hands. Physical and in-person activities are increasingly being replaced or supplemented by digital alternatives as a result of shelter-in-place requirements, as a result, internet and digital channels have seen unprecedented levels of participation. Globally, businesses have quickly responded to the tremendous transition to digital platforms. From education to fitness, from meals and groceries to money, every potential activity now has a digital or online equivalent, and many of them have seen a surge in usership.

COVID-19's impact on customer behaviour has resulted in boosting of projected trends, formation of new preference, and the full reversal of some pre-existing behaviours. As a whole, this combination will keep developing, laying the groundwork for the future normal. Businesses can use nudging to not only influence future customer behaviour that will likely persist after the pandemic, but also in the post-pandemic age, they are establishing themselves at the forefront of influencing client experience.

The Commerce industry has been hit the hardest by the economic downturn. Consumers who have never purchased products from an e-commerce website are now more inclined to do so. They have been forced to start browsing e-commerce sites, and some of them may become accustomed to it even after the crises have passed. With the increase in the number of consumers, many businesses have begun to place a greater emphasis on their online portals in order to generate more leads and sales. However, as more businesses began to focus on e-commerce markets, competition has increased, as everyone is attempting to capture as many potential leads as possible. Because fierce competition necessitates new strategies and planning, the question is: what is the best strategy for businesses to employ in this situation?

Chatbots as a latest trend

Chatbots, as an emerging technology, will eventually become an essential part of an organization's process more so in pandemic and post-pandemic era. On-demand messaging has grown significantly over the past several years, changing how consumers interact with brands. To deliver superior client service, over the last decade, chat services have surpassed telephone help as the primary method of accessing customer service (*Charlton et al, 2013*). Chatbots are a type of conversational, intelligent software that may respond to text, voice, or both forms of natural language input. (*Nicole Radziwill et al, 2017*) Personalization has become a key trend in the market's shifting paradigm and companies have identified chatbots as an excellent opportunity to exploit social network and set up streams of human-to-computer communication that will provide a personalized experience and boost relationship marketing in the digital environment (*Zumstein et al, 2018*). One of the modern technology advancements for client communication is chatbots. (*Letheren and Glavas, 2017*). Moreover, chatbots also assist businesses in reducing customer service costs by reducing response time and answering common routine questions. The existence of chatbots first came into being in 1966 and the first chatbot was called ELIZA (*Pereira et al, 2019*). Joseph Weizenbaum's creation, ELIZA could communicate with people and act like one. Because humans couldn't tell whether they were speaking with a robot or another human, the first conversational agent was successful (*Pereira et al, 2019*). ELIZA was quickly followed by a variety of other chatbot models developed to delve deeper into the interesting field of artificial intelligence and take advantage of this cutting-edge technology. Chatbots have drastically evolved since then, becoming much easier to train and implement.

In today's world, chatbots are becoming increasingly popular among businesses and consumers. In fact, Microsoft CEO Satya Nadella predicted that chatbots would overtake the graphical user interface, web browser, and touch screen as the most popular technologies in March 2016 (*Dale et al, 2016*) From 2015 to 2017, nearly half of all online conversations have been aided by chatbots (*Tsvetkova et al, 2016*). The magnitude of this can be gauged by looking at the massive increase in Facebook Messenger chatbots which increased from 30,000 in 2016 to over 100,000 in 2017 (*Zumstein et al, 2018*). Along with the number, the variety of chatbots have also skyrocketed and there is a new type of chatbot for every business - right from ordering food to shopping, from finding like-minded people to booking flights, and from reading the news to chit-chatting. Chatbot transactions are projected to produce up to 32 billion US dollars in yearly revenue globally (*Zumstein et al, 2018*).

Despite being widely used, chatbots frequently fall short of consumer expectations because they don't comprehend user input. According to reports, Facebook's Project M, a text-based virtual assistant, failed in more than 70% of engagements (*Weinberg, 2017*). Even the most advanced chatbots make mistakes. In this paper Web-based conversational agents will be discussed, chatbots in particular, with a focus on their significance in online purchasing and user acquisition.

Traditional application of chatbots

Many people favour shopping in actual stores. Many people go supermarkets each week, where they are exposed to a wide variety of product choices. To add to the experience, customer service representatives (CSRs) are employed in many shopping centres to answer questions from customers about products. The CSRs also play a huge role in influencing and consulting their potential customers and leading them to make their purchasing decisions. According to one study (*Froehle et al, 2006*), CSRs can influence customer satisfaction by their thoroughness, knowledge, and preparedness, hence they are also trained accordingly. However, if all CSRs are busy interacting with other customers, a customer may have to wait a long time for assistance. This could be a downside to retail industry as they would have a stream of customers coming in but less employees to deal with them, further straining on expenses of hiring and training. For services providing businesses, it is very important to strike a balance between service efficiency and quality. The businesses that are able to maintain this in a long run are likely to find success in their respective ventures (*Meuter et al, 2005*). In Addition, customers today expect quick, convenient, and personalised service, thus, businesses are under increasing pressure to innovate (*Panetta, 2016*). The large proportion of customer service expenses spent to training and labour can be dramatically be lowered by employing automated solutions. Retailers are leveraging data and new technologies more frequently to enhance the shopping experience for customers both online and offline. This technology-driven retail revolution is built on the four pillars of speed, immersion, automation, and convenience.

The only approach that retailers utilise that is consumer-friendly to fulfil these tenets is conversational AI (*Analytics et al, 2020*). With the help of these automated humanised interfaces, businesses may offer support seven days a week, twenty-four hours a day. Thousands of brands are using chatbots effectively leveraging artificial intelligence technology. What is the relation of personalization and chatbots? AI-powered or Machine Learning Chatbots can provide answers to ambiguous questions. In other words, you don't have to be specific when asking these chatbots questions. Natural language processing is used by the chatbots to generate responses from scratch. Artificial intelligence will serve as the cornerstone for a level of customer personalization that will be sought by fickle consumers around the world (*Pearson et al, 2019*). In the course of resolving any of the customer's issues, a human personnel spends 33% of their time understanding the nature of the inquiry and 25% of their time finding the correct information for the customer (*Reddy et al, 2017*), chatbots become smarter over time as they learn from previous questions and answers. That means, Chatbots have the potentiality to create a personalized experience while carrying out the programmed task. According to (*Schumaker et al, 2007*) a chatbot is a system that "seeks to mimic conversation rather than understand it". Whereas (*Schumaker et al, 2007*) place a greater emphasis on mimicry and simulation than on comprehension, Mauldin (*Pereira et al, 2019*) described chatbots as systems with the goal of "thinking". According to (*Michiels et al, 2017*), Chatbots can be used everywhere and at any time to provide customer care.

Chatbots have mostly been employed in messenger apps, rather than computer programs, since the emergence of smartphones and mobile applications (*Letheren and Glavas, 2017*). We shall take a closer look at how chatbots are used on social media. Chatbots are increasingly widely used in electronic marketplaces and customer service across a wide range of websites, social media platforms, and messaging apps. Instead of calling a call centre or sending an email, customers can, for example, address issues with CAs that are accessible 24/7. Think about how many Facebook chatbots there are. Facebook Messenger, for instance, had over 1.2 billion active users monthly in 2017. Around 300,000 developers used the platform in 2019, and users and businesses sent over 20 billion messages each month (*Business et al, 2019*).

The biggest advantages a CA can bring to any business is the enhanced customer experience (*Gnewuch et al, 2017 and LUCIA et al, 2003*). CSRs can be burdened with the overwhelming amount of customers' requests coming in at each hour, bot can easily handle all of them at once without becoming overworked. According to studies, each year, 265 billion customer support calls cost $1.3 trillion to businesses. Chatbots can save organisations money on customer service by reducing response times, allowing contact center employees to take their time and deliver better service by freeing up human agents to answer more difficult enquiries, while catering to up to 80% of common questions (*Reddy et al, 2017*). Annual salary savings of $23 billion might be achieved by businesses using chatbots (*Business Insider Intelligence et al, 2016*).

Types of Chatbots

The convergence of two enabling technologies has fueled recent growth in conversational agents. First, the Internet became a universal communication medium. Web-based conversational agents are scalable business solutions that make advantage of the internet to offer chat-based services to large groups of people at once. Secondly, substantial progress has been made in computational linguistics, an area of artificial intelligence concerned with natural language software. For example, the ability to comprehend natural language has substantially improved because for parsing technology advancements. Chatbots are of two types: Rule-Based Chatbots (Linguistic Based) and Natural Language Processing (Artificial Intelligence-Based) Chatbots.

Rule based Chatbots

Rule-based chatbots rely on pre-established rules to communicate. User input must adhere to these established guidelines in order to receive a response. Frequently, these bots merely use buttons. As they merely adhere to a set of predetermined rules based on identifying the lexical form of the input text without producing any new text answers, they are also known as decision-tree bots (*Adamopoulou et al, 2020*). The chatbot's knowledge is organised and presented using conversational patterns, and it is hand-coded by humans (*Adamopoulou et al, 2020*). These sorts are most suited for frequent inquiries like business inquiries, delivery status, or tracking information, and a larger rule-database will enable the bot to reply to a wider range of user input. They are particularly appropriate to customer service roles. Customers think of chatbots as a quicker way to connect people. 34% of all consumers believe chatbots can assist in locating human services (*Salesforce UK et al, 2018*). This type of model, on the other hand, is not resistant to grammatical and spelling errors in user input (*Adamopoulou et al, 2020*).

AI based Chatbots

Contrary to rule-based bots, AI-based chatbots employ algorithms to interpret natural language (neural networks). This is done using Machine Learning, a feature of AI that makes bots smarter over time and with use. NLP and Machine Learning are two major elements of AI chatbots and they go hand in hand.

The chatbot employs machine learning to learn from user requests and data as it is being trained. When a query is received, machine learning helps the bot monitor the prior discussion it had with the user before responding appropriately. A type of artificial intelligence called natural language processing, or NLP, enables a bot to comprehend and interpret data. Natural language processing (NLP) enables you to teach your chatbot a variety of user intentions that they might express during a conversation. These intents will simplify the response to the query. AI Based chatbots come with major benefits and scope that is yet to be completely explored.

Recent developments in natural language processing and a move toward messaging as the primary form of communication have helped chatbots become more popular in the retail sector (*Gnewuch et al, 2017*). One important scope this paper tries to explore is the use of these chatbots in customer acquisition and purchasing initiation. This can be powered by personalized marketing, a process of using data to deliver targeted and individual brand messages, also known as one-to-one marketing. Customers can receive personalised offers from AI-based chatbots based on their life events or profile data. Chatbots can qualify leads by asking pertinent questions before directing them to a sales representative or an appointment scheduler. This reduces the amount of time the sales team spends searching for qualified leads. It speeds up the lead generation process and makes it more profitable. As a result, companies across a wide range of industries are eager to use intelligent bots to optimise operations, automate procedures, boost productivity, improve customer acquisition and retention, and raise employee and client engagement (*Toader et al, 2020*). These bots can also completely be transformed into selling agents to add another touchpoint for new users and to explore and provide a peculiar yet potentially very personal shopping experience to customers. They have a lot of potential for lead generation and can be integrated in sales funnel to streamline sales cycle.

Design of Chatbots

(*Medhi Thies et al, 2017*) to determine which chatbot personalities are the most appealing to India's youthful, urban users. They experimented with three different chatbots, each with a different personality. Participants wished for a chatbot that would enrich their lives by offering useful recommendations and being comforting, sympathetic, and non-judgmental. As a result, the paper demonstrates that people who use the chatbots have a higher expectation with its output, It does not, however, include insights on how well current chatbots meet these expectations. (*Liao et al, 2016*) observed incorporation of a chatbot into a Human Resource Management System (HRMS) in the workplace. They discovered that, in addition to being functional, participants were interacting with the chatbot in a playful manner, which can be interpreted as a positive experience and promising signs for future research. Another study (*Jain et al, 2018*) carried about by IBM researchers in which they made 16 participants of different demographics interact with 8 chatbots (chatShopper, CNN, Call of Duty, Pandorabots, Alterra, Hi Poncho, Trivia Blast, Swelly) to counteract order effects, in a randomised order. Participants expressed disappointment and even annoyance with the chatbots' "mediocre natural language capabilities" after the experiment. They held the opinion that chatbots occasionally failed to perceive or understand their text inputs and were unable to interact with or effectively respond to them.

The research came to the conclusion that chatbots will need to fast develop their key capabilities in order to effectively engage and retain users as a result of the feedback. Moreover, during the study A few chatbots received positive feedback. Pandorabots' witty human-like conversational skills were particularly popular with participants. It appeared to be able to comprehend the user's input and respond in a timely and intelligent manner. Hi Poncho bot was thought to have a pleasant and enjoying personality. Participants also liked Trivia Blast, which despite having a non-chatty and click-based interface, within a messaging interface, delivered an entertaining quiz experience.

The following key lessons for next generation chatbots are highlighted by these three top-rated bots: Either natural language functionality with sufficient conversational delight, or an interesting app-like experience designed expressly for the well-known turn-based messaging interface, must be provided by chatbots. The higher the users' positive appraisals of the agents and the better the emotional and social relationships they build with them, the more emotions they communicate and the more empathy and sympathy they show.

Personality

A chatbot's personality can help establish a predictable pattern for how it will be viewed, resulting in a more consistent user experience. The bot personality chosen; determines the type of interactions the audience will have with it. The chatbot's personality must reflect the brand in a consistent manner. In a study (*Ruane et al, 2021*) noted, qualities of personality can be reliably reproduced via text and without the usage of extra audio or visual cues can still be viewed as the users intend, also that the user experience is influenced by the personality of a chatbot and is thus a significant design concern. A chatbot can appear empty and cold without a persona. Creating an identity based on the brand fosters user empathy and reflects the personalized service they receive from the team.

Design bot to be cheeky if the company is a cheeky retailer. A brand with target audience as young urban teenagers can design a chatbot's personality to be trendy and witty. Because humour is still too difficult to produce automatically, (*Medhi Thies et al, 2017*) suggest including a variety of jokes in response to frequent inquiries. A chatbot is a virtual representation of a person, and represents the company ideas and image, so it should have a personality that reflects that. Bots with strong personalities and well-named names are more likely to be remembered, whereas bots with weak names are more likely to be forgotten. A bot that performs poorly and bears a company's brand name will be forever linked to the company. In a study done by (*Medhi Thies et al, 2017*) users of experimental chatbots have stated that they want the bot to be comforting, empathic, and nonjudgmental, while also not being overly caring. Other research has looked into whether a personality match between the agent and the user improves the user experience. (*Land et al, 2013*) studied. In a low-stakes discussion activity, how an agent's perceived extraversion/introversion affects user experience. Users value consistency in both verbal and nonverbal personality cues, as well as personality cues that are complementary rather than identical to their own. Lexical characteristics, such the amount of characters or words used per turn, can be used to gauge user engagement, but they may also represent the chatbot's personality and be connected to the agent's efficiency and knowledge-sharing abilities from the user's point of view. Emoticons and expressive punctuation are examples of syntactic features that can be used to express feelings or emotions. Finally, reaction time and duration of each turn will vary substantially based on the chatbot and user interaction.

(*Horzyk et al, 2009*) proposed the Human Personality Traits (HPT) model. It identifies various demands connected to a particular personality and describes particular human behaviors and activities in relation to their personality. Each HPT has its own unique vocabulary. Furthermore, HPT can assist businesses in deciding how to manage each customer individually and make sure that they are satisfied when interacting with a sophisticated chatbot system. This psycholinguistic paradigm identifies 11 different human personality types: the dominant, maximalist, inspiring, discovering, verifying, methodical, Assurant, harmonious, emphatic, task-oriented, and balancing personality types. Chatbots that can recognize HPTs and their demands can utilize the right algorithms to negotiate with clients, persuade them, and reinforce their activities. Words and phrases are used to help identify HPTs, and consumers are handled properly to evoke favorable reactions. The incorporation of a chatbot engine into an e-commerce system enables a business to understand the thought processes of its clients, which may result in novel e-commerce prospects as in Figure 2.

Personalization

Nowadays, information is constantly being thrown at people, whether it's through billboard advertisements, TV commercials, emails, social media, or hundreds of brands fighting for their attention. Customers will therefore naturally shut out the majority of the information, especially if it doesn't pertain to them personally. That means, the businesses that reach out to their customers with content that is generic and impersonal, are missing out on a huge opportunity of engaging them into their brand. It's not just initial communication that matters in this case, but also the approach taken by businesses. Personalization of chatbots, in particular, is gaining traction. Users like chatbots that have human-like personality qualities, according to studies by (*Pearson et al, 2019*).

Personalization can range from simply naming a chatbot or inserting an image into the conversation to reacting to user emotions. In a word, marketing personalization refers to engaging your audience and clients in a way that seems genuine and personal while taking into account their likes, preferences, and interests. Advertisers use personalization to personalize advertisements to a person's preferences and attributes (*Sundar et al, 2010*). The term "digital assistants" that are conscious of human skills is another name for chatbots. Bots interpret user requests, ascertain their intentions, and provide speedy, accurate responses. A new kind of customer support experience made possible by developments in artificial intelligence and natural language processing is chatbots (*Um et al, 2020*).

Figure 2. Chatbot engine recognizing a customer personality (Horzyk et al, 2009)

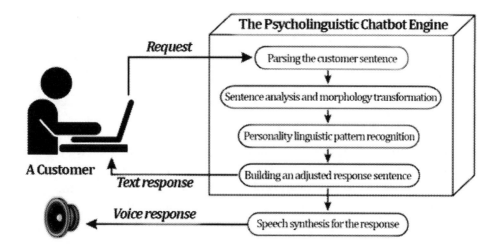

Bots' strength lies in their ability to have personalized conversations, provide personalized offers, and make quick purchases. They can use data and serious computing to analyse trends in our speech in order to plan when and what to advertise. They can also raise engagement and bring your brand personality to life (*Letheren and Glavas, 2017*). Facebook has even added the ability to send audio, video, GIFs, and other types of responses in addition to text. This has only added more personalization capabilities to the chatbots technology. In this era, where Internet is not only a place to seek for information but also a place for humor, chatbots interface can be personalized with respect to the type of audience the business hopes to cater to. For example, a hyper casual Business that caters to a young audience can add a fun quotient to their chatbot's chatting style. Because advertising and assistance are so closely intertwined, chatbots are well-suited to perform both because they are the next step in tailored advertising (*Letheren and Glavas, 2017*). Facebook, on its Messenger platform has begun to offer advertising via chatbots, which they define as "sponsored messages" to the customers that have already been reached out to be the advertisers, either through a Messenger bot or live chat assistance (*Weinbergl, 2017*).

14.4 Chatbot Shopping Experience

Because of its ability to have automated conversations with consumers using human language, prompting them to create content (via questions) and apply brand and customer-specific content, chatbot messaging lays the groundwork for greater customer engagement (through tailored automated responses based on data previously obtained from users). Customer Experiences with Chatbots, according to the Customer Acceptance of Technology Model, a unified theory of technology acceptance, cognitive elements including perceived usefulness, perceived ease-of-use, and perceived helpfulness are linked to customers' attitudes toward technology adoption. It also claims that consumer attitudes have an effect on adoption intentions (*Ting Yan Chan et al, 2021*). Same way, (*Brandtzaeg et al, 2017*) underlined the utility in the adoption of chatbots and people's attitude toward them. They were also discovered to be two important predictors of chatbot experience, which is typically the goal of commercial chatbots. When chatbots help people save time or find information more quickly, they are perceived as very helpful (*Brandtzaeg et al, 2017*). (*Gefen et al, 2003*) study explicates, a stronger priority should be placed on detecting conversational cues that increase users' impressions of social presence. Perceived in social media advertising, it was discovered that intrusiveness was a bad thing that might irritate people and have a negative effect on how well messages were received (*Van den Broeck et al, 2019*) and chatbot interactions. Changing the linguistic style of an e-commerce chatbot can affect overall customer satisfaction, service engagement, product interest and the perceived value of the product. Chatbots could be used to develop prediction models that improve client commitment and loyalty by combining transaction information and customer profiles., resulting in a long-term relationship.

Customer Engagement Cycle

The process of constructing customer engagement for a corporation is described by the proposed customer engagement cycle by (*Sashi et al, 2012*) as in Figure 3. The client passes through seven phases in this model: engagement, connection, interaction, satisfaction, retention, commitment, and advocacy. Chatbots have a part to play in each of these stages thanks to its functionality, personality, conversational intelligence, and UI components. Client engagement, in the opinion of (*Sashi et al, 2012*), should be concentrated on gaining long-term customer loyalty by offering value that is superior to that of competitors.

Figure 3. The Customer Engagement Cycle (Sashi et al, 2012)

- Connection

To create customer engagement, you must first establish contact with potential customers. Traditional offline methods as well as digital technologies such as chatbots can be used to make these connections (*Sashi et al, 2012*). A Chatbot can be designed as a sales assistant and be used in marketing programs to establish interactive engagement session with potential leads and customers.

- Interaction

The tools that enable more frequent, richer, and quicker interactions with leads and potential consumers include texting, instant messaging, blogging, social networking, and, in especially, chatbots. By communicating with customers more regularly, businesses may get more information about their wants. Chatbots can be a key component of engagement if user experience is elevated because the design and responses will reflect the brand's personality.

- Satisfaction

A satisfied consumer is more likely to be loyal to the business and will express their satisfaction with the interaction. As in this context, chatbots are the starting point of contact with the customers, they must be designed in such a way that it able to assist all requests in a way that pleases the outcome. Customer satisfaction is important for creating customer engagement, but it isn't enough because it doesn't guarantee customer repurchase. Because of its ability, it can handle the emotions of a disgruntled customer, that will directly improve the user experience. Customers are always pleased when their issues are resolved quickly, which improves the overall experience.

- Retention

Customer retention, which can result in a long-term consumer-seller connection, is a result of customer happiness and general positive attitudes toward a brand. A chatbot designed to increase engagements might astound clients with its incredibly engaging response and increase the possibilities for retargeting.

- Commitment

Chatbots have the potential to develop Affective commitment. Customers who are emotionally in-vested in a brand are more likely to be loyal to the business that produces the goods they value. They feel a personal connection to the brand and, at times, see it as an extension of themselves or a close friend. This can be triggered when customers are able to relate with the brand's personality.

- Advocacy

When a consumer is content with a service, business, or product, they can tell others about it to spread the word about their experiences (*Sashi et al, 2012*). In the linked world of today, people talk about brands and share their experiences on social media. If the service offered is satisfactory, customers can easily be directed to utilize a chatbot by way of a link or a few clicks.

- Engagement

A customer is more engaged with a brand if they are both satisfied with it and feel some loyalty to it (*Sashi et al, 2012*). Consumer engagement demands both an effective and calculative commitment, as it calls for a solid link and better value for the customer. Through word-of-mouth and technical channels like social media, engaged customers can become brand ambassadors and attract new interested potential customers (*Sashi et al, 2012*).

Purchasing Behavior

It is essential for businesses to comprehend what their customers' demands are and how to address them because marketing comprises everything a company does to sell things to customers and influence their purchasing behaviour (*Todor et al, 2016*). As a result of the increased access to information, consumers have become less reliant on sales and marketing. Instead, today's consumers are more inclined to rely on online evaluations and word-of-mouth recommendations that come from other customers.

Environmental cues have also been proven to influence impulse buying, with people feeling compelled to buy impulsively when aroused by particular situational elements during a shopping interaction (e.g., ambient elements such as music, lighting, etc.) (*Youn et al, 2000*). A more complete description of emo-tional and behavioural responses is offered by the environmental psychology model. Several researchers have looked into the aspects of the internet environment that lead to impulse buying in an online context (*Adelaar et al, 2003*). In chatbots' context, we can associate the environment with the chatting style of the bot and the interface. Behavioral cues and social signals are part of conversational language, and they transmit additional information and have a significant impact on conversational engagement (*McTear et al, 2016*). Functionality, personality, conversational intelligence and interface are the 4 main aspects of a chatbot's design. Functionality focuses on how well the chatbot carries out the requested tasks. An interaction without error could incline the customers to make a purchase (*Toader et al, 2020*). For a chatbot to be successful, its functionality must be up to par. Numerous media content representations can represent a variety of human sensory modalities, including taste, touch, smell, kinesthesia, vision, and hearing. People's perception of external cues, as well as their emotional and behavioural responses, can all be influenced by how linguistic or visual information is processed individually. Businesses may provide consumers particular media experiences that are used to establish the scene or create the environment for the promotion or sale of associated goods and/or services (*Rifkin et al, 2001*). (*Gefen et al, 2003*) study explicates, Similar to how personal photographs and pictures do, texts also provide a sense of the individual. The behavioural intent to purchase is distinguished from the actual purchasing behaviour by the intention to purchase a particular good or service. In other words, a consumer's actual purchase behaviour is predicated on the idea that they might decide to buy a good or service on a whim. Shopping assistant oriented chatbots have the power to evoke a spontaneous purchasing behavior triggering impulse buying behavior.

Conversational intelligence, personality and interface can be tweaked in a way to maximize personalization potential. The personality of a chatbot has a significant impact on the user experience and shapes how the user perceives the discussion, as discussed above in this literature (*Ruane et al, 2021*). Several elements, such as the company's brand identity, the activities, the tasks of the chatbots, and target audience preferences, all play a part in building a chatbot personality that matches the business. During the study done by (*Jain et al, 2018*) chatbots with distinct personalities were popular among the participants. They anticipated that the chatbot's temperament would correspond to its area of expertise; for instance, a news chatbot should be serious, but a shopping chatbot can be lighthearted and informal. Consistent personality makes a chatbot easier for users to interact with (*Jain et al, 2018*). Researchers across different disciplines have proposed that CAs should imitate human communication qualities to be more organic and interesting. (*Gnewuch et al, 2017*). (*Schumaker et al, 2007*) suggested that conversational knowledge aids users in making decisions. Furthermore, the experiment conducted by (*Toader et al, 2020*) indicated that Gender signals are crucial in eliciting favorable responses from customers. Study participants who interacted with a virtual assistant posing as a female displayed higher readiness to share personal information, showed increasingly higher level of patronage intentions, were more forgiving to the chatting errors, and were just happy and intrigued to interact.

Chatbots as Marketing Agents

Chatbots allow companies to contact their target audience using messaging applications such as WeChat Messenger, WhatsApp Messenger, Facebook Messenger as they are looked at as a new information, communication, and transaction channel. The essential beauty of an artificially intelligent bot is that it can work on an endless number of channels. Bot frameworks allow developers to create a single A bot that reacts to users in the same way across many platforms, including web chat, Facebook Messenger, Skype, and others. Artificial Intelligence (AI) has the potential to significantly advance the methods used by businesses to address a variety of marketing issues. The latest advancements in chatbots in customer service and sales are impressive and one of the most recent technology developments in consumer communication is AI chatbots. (*Letheren and Glavas, 2017*; *Van den Broeck et al, 2019*). Customers' demands for personalized services are becoming increasingly sophisticated. In order to satisfy customers, businesses must implement new technologies that enable human-like contact in real time. However, the use of intelligent conversational agents, or Chatbots-AI, for personalized marketing is still in its early stages around the world.

Chatbots can be used to promote more intimate consumer-brand relationships, greater trust, and can be incorporated into customers' shopping process. With the power of personalization, businesses can witness chatbots' upselling potential. The majority of customers in the instant gratification era seek service speed. Chatbots can assist in cross-selling a company's services or products while keeping customers engaged by providing solutions to their problems. The more a customer is engaged, the more profitable an organization becomes as a result of increased customer satisfaction. To keep customers interested, many chatbots use visual content such as images and videos. A character-driven experience has also aided in better customer engagement on occasion. On a single platform, chatbots educate, inform, and entertain users. As a result, any company with a social media account should make sure that its potential customers can have a useful conversation with them. According to recent reports, chatbots' strength lies on their capacity to obfuscate the distinction between aid and advertising (*Letheren and Glavas, 2017*; *Van den Broeck et al, 2019*). Users feel more like they are being serviced by the company than being sold to when a chatbot presents relevant apparel options that are catered to their preferences and prior purchasing history. This is an example that could illustrate the aforementioned assertion (*Van den Broeck et al, 2019*). (*Toader et al, 2020*) believes, companies may be able to make up for the loss of human connection in online environments while simultaneously increasing their willingness to trust technology and taking part in productive consumer engagement, despite the complexity of consumers' psychological and behavioural responses to virtual assistants, which further blurs this barrier. As it was mentioned in this literature, tweaking three (personality, interface and conversational intelligence) of the four functionalities of a chatbot, organizations can explore chatbot's customer acquisition potential. Either natural language skills with engaging conversational experiences, or a fun app-like experience designed for the well-known turn-based messaging interface, must be provided by chatbots (*Jain et al, 2018*). At its best potential with respect to its functionality, A chatbot can possibly facilitate the following: Making it simple for customers to find information and make purchases wherever they are, providing personalised products, recommendations, and content that is more likely to meet their needs, offering agents decision-support with suggestions for the next best offer, and quickly scaling up and down to always provide new clients with cost-effective services. These services' use of natural language in online interactions makes automated marketing and communication services viable candidates for new business growth (*Brandtzaeg et al, 2017*). In order to be more natural and engaging, CAs should take on the qualities of human communication. Moreover, When CAs become orchestrators of consumer interactions and engagements, they might provide a point of difference and a competitive advantage, not just within the company, but across other companies as well (*Thomaz et al, 2020*).

Chatbots as Shopping Assistants

Consumer buying behavior is expected to change as a result of the increased use of chat applications. Chatbots are becoming more recognised by businesses as a fantastic chance to better utilise social networks and establish competitive differentiator. Chatbots suggest a potential change in how people interact with internet businesses (*Brandtzaeg et al, 2017*). The survey's findings indicate that users favor chatbots because they are convenient, easy to use, and may help with online purchases. Nevertheless, respondents expected the chatbot's performance to improve with time. Marketing is anticipated to strengthen the perception of human-like communication and improve the amusement characteristics of chatbots in addition to making them simple to utilise. (*Ting Yan Chan et al, 2021*). The results of the survey also suggested that respondents favored natural language chatbot communication (*Ting Yan Chan et al, 2021*). While some Conversational Agents may offer an impersonal or cold experience, the most effective agents will be built to personalize and engage the users (*Thomaz et al, 2020*). Consumers expect a Chatbot's demeanor to fit its domain; for example, a news chatbot should be serious, but a retail chatbot might be lighthearted (*Jain et al, 2018*). CAs must develop social signals (e.g., appearance or language) which are both also consistent with these service agent characteristics and appropriate for the context in which they are used (*Gnewuch et al, 2017*). In terms of the user experience, chatbots can mimic an interpersonal conversation, both in terms of communication and prospective offers to consumers, with a high level of personalization (*Letheren and Glavas, 2017*). Maintaining context improves user input efficiency by reducing required amount of user inputs. This capability can range from keeping context within a single chat to keeping context across numerous conversations. Users perceive context resolution as a quality of a customised, sympathetic, and intelligent chatbot (*Jain et al, 2018*). The secret to designing a successful shopping assistant bot is personalization. Chatbots can provide specialized customer service conversations, individualized information, and ideas (*Zumstein et al, 2018*). Additionally, chatbots can save user preferences based on past purchases, requests, and other behaviors (*Zumstein et al, 2018*) and offer suggestions for future purchases and keep delivery information current (*Brandtzaeg et al, 2017*). The value of chatbots is amply demonstrated when they offer customers relevant apparel selections that are catered to their interests and previous shopping behaviour. Users are more likely to feel supported by the business than like they are being sold to (*Van den Broeck et al, 2019*). A virtual assistant can help your customers wherever they need information, guidance, or buying ideas. When speaking with a bot via a messenger app or a physical installation in a store, airports, or customer service desk, the functionality of the bot is easily provided.

By putting a chatbot in charge of capturing customers, the company can spend less money per customer to persuade them to complete their purchase than if it used traditional conversion methods. CAs can use the collected personal data in future contacts to further personalize dialogues with people on a large scale (*Thomaz et al, 2020*). CAs have the potential to voluntarily encourage the users to share personal information by providing a sense of companionship an entertaining chatting experience (*Brandtzaeg et al, 2017*). The perceived benefits of CAs will be amplified to the degree that they are regarded as more engaging, pleasurable, and useful, while the perceived privacy dangers will be reduced to the extent that they are perceived as more trustworthy (*Thomaz et al, 2020*). Designers should use humor and a wide variety of chatbot responses to diversify the conversation. Positive characteristics include wit, sarcasm, and playfulness. Excessive politeness, on the other hand, is regarded as a negative trait (*Jain et al, 2018*). Chat applications will be able to accept payments in the future, allowing for a seamless shopping experience without having to leave the interface (*Braveen Kumar et al, 2016*). The messaging app can handle the order, billing, and delivery while the bot evolves into a personal assistant capable of performing a variety of consumer-focused tasks. WeChat, a popular Asian messaging app, already offers a number of services within the app. Some of the integrated functionalities include money transfers, food ordering, movie ticket purchases, and flight booking. Additionally, search engines might be integrated with chatbots to identify, pick, and offer the user the best options based on past decisions, preferences, and online interactions.

Discussion

The coronavirus pandemic has caused companies to reconsider how they approach their customers, how they continue to provide relevant customer experiences, and how they may use digital channels to remain in operation both during and after the crisis. Businesses need to evolve the way they provide their services and can leverage on the AI technology to test the chatbot trends. When leveraged properly, features of chatbots not only can not only help the e-commerce industry to overcome the challenges, but can also help provide a superior online shopping experience. Companies must provide an omnichannel approach to customer engagement. However, from a data retention and engagement standpoint, it's also critical to ensure that these various channels intersect. Companies that are already operating on the digital landscape can capitalize by experimenting on chatbots and integrate it in their online sales funnel. Businesses are starting to use chatbots more frequently as a strategy to better utilise social media and outperform rivals online who do not use them. Personalization has been identified as one of the most effective ways for businesses to build relationships. Chatbots are a new technology that is expected to take over mobile commerce and shopping apps in the near future. Companies who identify its application with the help of this study, could build bots best suited for shopping. Integration of chatbots in sales funnel could help business online explore an unchartered opportunity, provided that the development of the bot is aligned and built to the best of its ability with respect to its scope of customizable functions like, personality, interface and conversational intelligence as elaborated.

REFERENCES

Adamopoulou, E., & Moussiades, L. (2020). An Overview of Chatbot Technology. In IFIP Advances in Information and Communication Technology (Vol. 584 IFIP). Springer International Publishing. doi:10.1007/978-3-030-49186-4_31

Adelaar, T., Chang, S., Lancendorfer, K. M., Lee, B., & Morimoto, M. (2003). Effects of media formats on emotions and impulse buying intent. *Journal of Information Technology*, *18*(4), 247–266. doi:10.1080/0268396032000150799

Ai, C. (n.d.). *The New wave of customer and employee experiences*. Deloitte Digital.

Analytics, C. (2020). *Key Factors Driving the Growth of Conversational AI in Retail*. Uniphore. https://www.uniphore.com/key-factors-driving-the-growth-of-conversational-ai-in-retail/

Avis, E. (2015). The Rise of Digital Challengers. *Independent Banker, 65*(11), 28–30. http://search.ebscohost.com/login.aspx?direct=true%7B&%7Ddb=bth%7B&%7DAN=111109565%7B&%7Dsite=ehost-live

Brandtzaeg, P. B., & Følstad, A. (2017). Why people use chatbots. Lecture Notes in Computer Science (Including Subseries Lecture Notes in Artificial Intelligence and Lecture Notes in Bioinformatics). Springer. doi:10.1007/978-3-319-70284-1_30

Charlton, G. (2013). *Consumers Prefer Live Chat For Customer Service: Stats*. Econsultancy. https://econsultancy.com/blog/63867-consumers-prefer-live-chat-for-customer-service-stats#i.1nockyz1cffd8a

Dale, R. (2016). The return of the chatbots. *Natural Language Engineering, 22*(5), 811–817. doi:10.1017/S1351324916000243

Elevating customer experience excellence in the next normal. (n.d.). McKinsey. https://www.mckinsey.com/business-functions/operations/our-insights/elevating-customer-experience-excellence-in-the-next-normal#

Froehle, C. M. (2006). Service personnel, technology, and their interaction in influencing customer satisfaction. *Decision Sciences, 37*(1), 5–38. doi:10.1111/j.1540-5414.2006.00108.x

Gefen & Straub. (2003). Managing User Trust in B2C e-Services. E-Service Journal, 2(2), 7. https://doi.org/ doi:10.2979/esj.2003.2.2.7

Gnewuch, U., Morana, S., Adam, M., & Maedche, A. (2017). This is the author ' s version of a work that was published in the following source Please note : Copyright is owned by the author and / or the publisher. Commercial use is not allowed. Institute of Information Systems and Marketing (IISM) The psychop. *Thirty Eighth International Conference on Information Systems*, South Korea.

Horzyk, A., Magierski, S., & Miklaszewski, G. (2009). An Intelligent Internet Shop-Assistant Recognizing a Customer Personality for Improving Man-Machine Interactions. *Recent Advances in Intelligent Information Systems*, 13–26.

Jain, M., Kumar, P., Kota, R., & Patel, S. N. (2018). Evaluating and informing the design of chatbots. *DIS 2018 - Proceedings of the 2018 Designing Interactive Systems Conference,* 895–906. ACM. 10.1145/3196709.3196735

Kaczorowska-Spychalska, D. (2019). How chatbots influence marketing. *Management, 23*(1), 251–270. doi:10.2478/manment-2019-0015

Land, R., Beetham, H., Sharpe, R., DeNoyelles, A., Zydney, J., Chen, B., Sendall, P., Shaw, R., Round, K., Larkin, J., Barczyk, C. C., Duncan, D. G., Abes, E. S., Jones, S. R., McEwen, M. K., Boon, S., Sinclair, C., Borup, J., West, R. E., & Tu, C.-H. (2013). Social Presence and Cognitive Engagement in Online Learning Environments. *Language Learning & Technology, 10*(1), 1–22. doi:10.1111/j.1467-8527.2008.00397_1.x

Letheren, K., & Glavas, C. (2017). Embracing the bots: How direct to consumer advertising is about to change forever. QUT Business School, 11–13. https://eprints.qut.edu.au/107945/

Liao, Q. V., Davis, M., Geyer, W., Muller, M., & Shami, N. S. (2016). What can you do? Studying social-agent orientation and agent proactive interactions with an agent for employees. *DIS 2016 - Proceedings of the 2016 ACM Conference on Designing Interactive Systems: Fuse,* (pp. 264–275). ACM. 10.1145/2901790.2901842

Lucia, P., Schmid, B. F., Wolfgang, M., & Müller, J. P.LUCIA. (2003). Editorial: Software Agents. *Electronic Markets, 13*(1), 1–2. doi:10.1080/1019678032000062195

McTear, M., Callejas, Z., & Griol, D. (2016). The conversational interface: Past and. *The Conversational Interface: Talking to Smart Devices*, 1–422.

Medhi Thies, I., Menon, N., Magapu, S., Subramony, M., & O'Neill, J. (2017). How do you want your chatbot? An exploratory Wizard-of-Oz study with young, Urban Indians. Lecture Notes in Computer Science (Including Subseries Lecture Notes in Artificial Intelligence and Lecture Notes in Bioinformatics). Springer. doi:10.1007/978-3-319-67744-6_28

Meuter, M. L., Bitner, M. J., Ostrom, A. L., & Brown, S. W. (2005). Choosing among alternative service delivery modes: An investigation of customer trial of self-service technologies. *Journal of Marketing*, *69*(2), 61–83. doi:10.1509/jmkg.69.2.61.60759

Michiels, E. (2017). Modelling Chatbots with a cognitive system allows for a differentiating user experience. *CEUR Workshop Proceedings*, *2027*, 70–78.

Nicole Radziwill and Morgan Benton. (2017). *Evaluating Quality of Chatbots and Intelligent Conversational Agents*. Arxiv.Org.

OECD. (2018). *Maintaining competitive conditions in the era of digitalisation*. OECD. https://www.oecd.org/g20/Maintaining-competitive-conditions-in-era-of-digitalisation-OECD.pdf

Panetta, K. (2016). *Artificial intelligence, machine learning, and smart things promise an intelligent future*. Gartner. https://www.gartner.com/smarterwithgartner/gartners-top-10-technology-trends-2017/

Pearson, A. (2019). Personalisation the artificial intelligence way. *Journal of Digital and Social Media Marketing*, *7*(3), 245–269.

Pereira, M. J., Coheur, L., Fialho, P., & Ribeiro, R. (2019). Chatbots' greetings to human-computer communication. *CEUR Workshop Proceedings, 2390*(1994), 61–66.

Reddy, T. (2017). *How chatbots can help reduce customer service costs by 30% - Watson Blog*. Ibm.Com. https://www.ibm.com/blogs/watson/2017/10/how-chatbots-reduce-customer-service-costs-by-30-percent/

Rifkin, J. (2001). *The Age of Access: The New Culture of Hypercapitalism, Where all of Life is a Paid-For Experience*. Amazon. https://www.amazon.com/The-Age-Access-Hypercapitalism-Experience/dp/1585420824

Ruane, E., Farrell, S., & Ventresque, A. (2021). User Perception of Text-Based Chatbot Personality. Lecture Notes in Computer Science (Including Subseries Lecture Notes in Artificial Intelligence and Lecture Notes in Bioinformatics), 12604 LNCS(February), 32–47. Springer. doi:10.1007/978-3-030-68288-0_3

Sashi, C. M. (2012). Customer engagement, buyer-seller relationships, and social media. *Management Decision*, *50*(2), 253–272. doi:10.1108/00251741211203551

Schumaker, R. P., Ginsburg, M., Chen, H., & Liu, Y. (2007). An evaluation of the chat and knowledge delivery components of a low-level dialog system: The AZ-ALICE experiment. *Decision Support Systems*, *42*(4), 2236–2246. doi:10.1016/j.dss.2006.07.001

Sundar, S. S., & Marathe, S. S. (2010). Personalization versus customization: The importance of agency, privacy, and power usage. *Human Communication Research*, *36*(3), 298–322. doi:10.1111/j.1468-2958.2010.01377.x

Talking the Talk: The Beginner's Guide to Designing a Chatbot Conversation. (2017). Hubspot. https://blog.hubspot.com/marketing/beginners-guide-to-designing-a-chatbot-conversation

Thomaz, F., Salge, C., Karahanna, E., & Hulland, J. (2020). Learning from the Dark Web: Leveraging conversational agents in the era of hyper-privacy to enhance marketing. *Journal of the Academy of Marketing Science, 48*(1), 43–63. doi:10.1007/s11747-019-00704-3

Ting Yan Chan, W., & Hong Leung, C. (2021). Mind the Gap: Discrepancy Between Customer Expectation and Perception on Commercial Chatbots Usage. *Asian Journal of Empirical Research, 11*(1), 1–10. doi:10.18488/journal.1007.2021.111.1.10

Toader, D. C., Boca, G., Toader, R., Măcelaru, M., Toader, C., Ighian, D., & Rădulescu, A. T. (2020). The effect of social presence and chatbot errors on trust. *Sustainability (Basel), 12*(1), 1–24. doi:10.3390/su12010256

Todor, R. D. (2016). Blending traditional and digital marketing. *Bulletin of the Transilvania University of Brasov, Series I: Engineering Sciences, 9*(1), 51–56. http://ezproxy.leedsbeckett.ac.uk/login?url=http://search.ebscohost.com/login.aspx?direct=true&db=a9h&AN=116699220&site=eds-live&scope=site

TsvetkovaM.García-GavilanesR.FloridiL.YasseriT. (2016). Even Good Bots Fight. December. http://arxiv.org/abs/1609.04285

UK. S. (2018). *How Chatbots Can Redefine Your Sales Process.* UK. https://www.salesforce.com/uk/blog/2018/09/how-chatbots-can-redefine-your-sales-process.html

Um, T., Kim, T., & Chung, N. (2020). How does an intelligence chatbot affect customers compared with self-service technology for sustainable services? *Sustainability (Basel), 12*(12), 5119. doi:10.3390/su12125119

Van den Broeck, E., Zarouali, B., & Poels, K. (2019). Chatbot advertising effectiveness: When does the message get through? *Computers in Human Behavior, 98*, 150–157. doi:10.1016/j.chb.2019.04.009

Weinberg, C. (2017). How Messenger and "M" Are Shifting Gears. *The Information.* https://www.theinformation.com/articles/how-messenger-and-m-are-shifting-gears

Zumstein, D., & Hundertmark, S. (2018). Chatbots : an interactive technology for personalized communication and transaction. *IADIS International Journal on Www/Internet, 15*(1), 96–109.

Chapter 3

CNN:
A Fundamental Unit of New Age AI

Mohan Kumar Dehury
Amity University, India

Ronit Kumar Gupta
Amity University, India

Tannisha Kundu
Amity University, India

ABSTRACT

The field of artificial intelligence (AI) is very promising with the emergence of machine learning and deep learning algorithms. The rise of convolutional neural networks (CNN) is very propitious in deep learning as it is more accurate and powerful than previously known soft computational models like artificial neural networks (ANN) and recurrent neural networks (RNN). CNN is ANN with steroids. These soft computational models are inspired by biological models that give an approximate solution to image-driven pattern recognition problems. The near perfect precision of CNN models offers a better way to recognize patterns and solve real-world problems and provide approximate solutions which are near precision. These technologies have enhanced the trust with humans. Its results have been accepted widely. This chapter aims to provide brief information about CNNs by introducing and discussing recent papers published on this topic and the methods employed by them to recognize patterns. This chapter also aims to provide information regarding dos and don'ts while using different CNN models.

INTRODUCTION

The human brain consists of more than 100 billion neurons which are interconnected to each other. These neurons are made up of tissues and chemicals which facilitate the functioning of the human brain and control many processes of the human body. Some of these processes occur involuntarily like breathing, blinking, and thinking. This collection of interconnected neurons (a single neuron is connected to up to

DOI: 10.4018/978-1-6684-9576-6.ch003

200,000 other neurons) works like a microprocessor, albeit 100 times faster. We are born with neural structures and many other neural structures are formed using experiences. Each neuron structure is perceived differently when a signal is passed to them. Images are one of the key components through which humans define an object. Although images are captured using the eyes it is the brain that analyzes them using neurons and provides features through which we determine the object(s) present in the image. Although scientists haven't completely understood how biological neurons work, researchers have been successful in creating "artificial neurons". Artificial neurons are abstractions of biological neurons. Structures of these artificial neurons are trained to perform useful functions. Using these artificial neurons, we can create neural networks with layers of neurons. Each neuron in the neural network has weights associated with it. These dynamic weights are frequently changed so that the algorithm can arrive at an equation upon which the solution is predicted, and an approximate solution is given as output. These neural networks can be trained to identify handwriting, tag objects in an image, improve survival rates of heart transplant recipients etc. The fields of applications are expanding as neural networks are used in various fields outside the realm of STEM fields. Neural networks are employed in the fields such as finance, medicine, business, literature and arts where it is extensively used to identify plagiarism in the field of arts (Chitra & Rajkumar, 2016).

There are many types of neural networks such as perceptron, feed-forward networks, and convolutional neural networks. Many other such types of neural networks exist and are being developed as we read this article. To keep this article brief and short we will be only discussing the neural networks. Perceptron Networks as shown in Figure 1 are the most basic neural networks. It consists of only one neuron and based on the input weights the activation function is applied to produce a binary output. It is the oldest neural network known and is not known to produce correct output. It is based on a supervised learning algorithm where tagged data is used and classified into binary classification.

Feed-Forward Networks are types of neural networks which are used mainly in applications of speech and face recognition. ANN is one example of a feed-forward network. It consists of many layers

Figure 1. Perceptron network

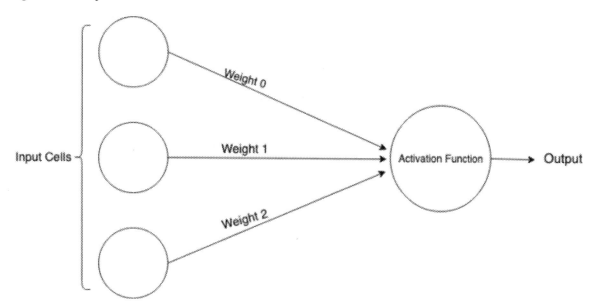

of neurons and data flow is only forward, hence its name. There is an input layer, hidden layers, and an output layer as shown in Figure 2. In some models, hidden layers may not be present. The weight of the neurons is also static as data is unidirectional.

Convolutional neural networks are mainly used for image classification. ANNs can also classify images but due to high computational cost CNNs are preferred. It contains many convolutional layers which extract important features from the image. The first convolutional layers are responsible for extracting low-level features and later convolutional layers are responsible for extracting high-level features. The level of feature extraction increases as the algorithm moves to the next convolutional layer. To extract features, filters are used where convolutional operations are employed to. Feature maps are produced once the convolution operation is completed to indicate the features present in the image. These features are later combined in the next convolutional layers to predict the object by inputting these features into the convolution function. Depending upon the number of features the filter may not be one-dimensional. The output feature maps from this convolutional layer may be further inputted in the next convolutional layer to further predict the object with greater precision. Once all the convolutional layers are completed the output data is flattened to produce a one-dimensional array using this the image is classified with very high precision. The CNN architecture is presented as shown in Figure 3.

This chapter analyzes the ongoing research going on in the field of convolutional neural network algorithms and provides a deep review of its strengths and weaknesses.

The chapter is organized as follows. Section 1 briefly introduces the topic and provides background information about neurons, artificial neurons, and its types. Section 2 provides a review of various ongoing research papers in the field of CNN. Section 3 provides the key findings and Section 4 presents the conclusion of the chapter where we discuss the various aspects of this topic like strengths, weaknesses, limitations, and future direction.

Figure 2. Feed forward network

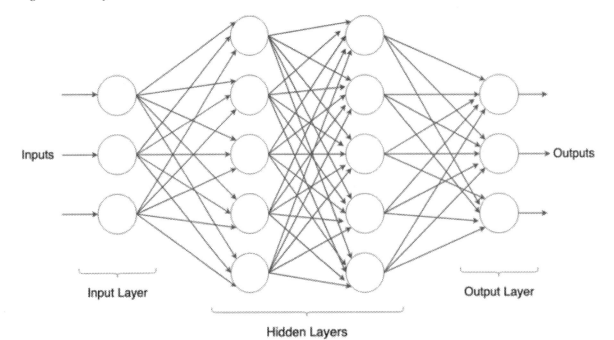

Figure 3. CNN architecture

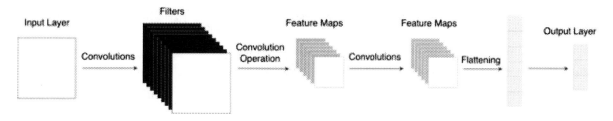

REVIEW AND ANALYSIS

In this chapter, the papers were reviewed and analyzed. The reviewed papers are categorized into following categories:

- Activation Functions
- Applications
- Popular Models

Activation Function

Activation Function decides whether a neuron should be activated or not. It is also known as the transfer function. It decides whether the output for a neural network or neuron is yes or no using the values 0 and 1 or -1 and 1. The various activation functions that are used in CNN are presented in Table 1.

Applications of CNN

The applications of CNN have been discussed and presented in Table 2 with short description in different areas.

Popular Models

Here, in Table 3 various popular models that are used in CNN are presented with a short description about them.

Sigmoid Function-Based CNN Architectures

Kim et al (2020) proposed a CNN-based intrusion detection system (IDS) that can prevent cyberattacks based on user's usage patterns. The various steps of IDS model are presented in Figure 4. Anomaly detection is the type of IDS that deals with the identification of attacks based on the user's usage pattern. There is a high number of false alarms of anomaly detection without the use of deep learning methods. The CNN model learns the normal usage pattern to identify patterns that are not normal i.e., attacker's pattern. This reduces false alarms. The dataset used to train and test the model is KDD (corrected version) which consists of denial of service (DOS), user to root (U2R), remote to load (R2L) and probing types

Table 1. Activation Function and its description

S. No	Activation Function	Short Description	Papers using the activation function
1	Sigmoid Function	Sigmoid function is also known as a logistic function that takes any real value as input and outputs a value between 0 and 1. Sigmoid Function Formula: $s(x) = \dfrac{1}{1+e^{-x}}$	(Deng et al., 2021; Gill et al., 2022; Kim et al., 2020; Sarnovský et al., 2022)
2	ReLU Function	It is also called Rectified Linear Unit function. Its output range is between 0 to ∞. It is the most used activation function in CNN. $f(x) = max(0, x)$	(Adi et al., 2022; Ahlawat et al., 2020; Belay et al., 2022; Chattopadhyay & Maitra, 2022; Dua et al., 2021; Goyal et al., 2022; Katoch et al., 2022; Lee, 2022; Liu et al., 2021; Muhammad et al., 2021; Ouichka et al., 2022; Paymode & Malode, 2022; Shoeibi et al., 2021; Tiwari et al., 2022; Vieira et al., 2022; Zheng et al., 2022)
3	Softmax Function	It is most used in multiclass neural networks, and it is also found in most output layers. It takes a vector of real numbers as input to provide an output range between 0 and 1. $\sigma(\vec{z}) = \dfrac{e^{z_i}}{\sum_{j=1}^{k} e^{z_j}}$	(Altun et al., 2023; Li et al., 2021; Mao et al., 2021; Qiao et al., 2021)
4	Tanh Function	It is nearly same as the sigmoid function. It provides an output range between -1 and 1. It is mainly used for classification between two classes. $tanh(x) = \dfrac{e^{x} - e^{-x}}{e^{x} + e^{-x}}$	(Kamalraj et al., 2021; Kaur et al., 2022; Monshi et al., 2021; Xie et al., 2021)

of attacks. The model is built to detect only denial of service attacks therefore only dos data points are selected which comprise about 230,000 data points of the dataset. Along with KDD, CSE-CIC-IDS 2018 is also used as it is one of the most updated datasets available and includes data points for sophisticated dos attacks like slowloris and slowhttptest.

The CNN model is built for both binary and multiclass classification using different kernel sizes and the number of hidden layers. The results show that for all different architectures of the model, accuracy is over 99%. Increasing and decreasing the size of the kernel and layers also do not yield uniform results. When compared to the RNN model built using Keras with 5 embedded vectors and a sigmoid activation function. RNN has similar results to that of CNN with 100% accuracy for some attacks like smurf detection but the accuracy dips for attacks such as Benign and Neptune to 85% and 80% respectively. It can be said that the CNN model is able to identify attacks with similar accuracy as RNN. Gill et al (2022) created an LSTM CNN-RNN-based multi-model fruit recognition model. Fruit identification and categorization are important to both consumers and marketers. Identifying some fruit correctly depends on the number of extracted features, the kinds of features, and the quality of images. Images that have poor visibility of features of the fruit reduce the accuracy of the model. Image enhancements help to identify features of low-quality images. The paper analyses various related works and their shortcomings. Among the shortcomings, it is found that classification approaches may not perform well due to spectral reflectance values. In the proposed model, features are extracted using convolution layers of the CNN model. Optimal features are labeled using RNN with a fine and coarse strategy of the recurrent model.

Table 2. Applications of CNN with description

S. No.	Application	Short Description
1	Cyber Attacks Prevention (Kim et al., 2020)	CNN Architectures can be used to detect pattern of suspicious user behavior and prevent cyber attacks.
2	Fruit Recognition (Gill et al., 2022)	CNN can be combined with other deep learning methods to identify fruits and classify them.
3	3D Object Detector (Deng et al., 2021; Li et al., 2021; Mao et al., 2021)	CNN can be combined with machine learning and deep learning techniques to detect objects and classify them. The architecture can be made accurate and efficient by optimizing various hyperparameters.
4	Fake News Detector (Sarnovský et al., 2022; Vunnava et al., 2022)	CNN can be used to train a model which can identify fake news circulated online.
5	Handwriting recognition (Ahlawat et al., 2020)	Characters of different languages can be identified using CNN. The algorithm can be made more efficient by optimizing various hyperparameters.
6	Ship Detector for marine time surveillance (Liu et al., 2021; Xie et al., 2021)	Ships can be detected using deep learning models to improve marine time surveillance and reduce accidental risks.
7	Schizophrenia prediction (Shoeibi et al., 2021)	Schizophrenia can be predicted using CNN and other methods of deep learning and machine learning. EEG signals is used as input in the model.
8	Human activity recognition (Dua et al., 2021; Muhammad et al., 2021; Vieira et al., 2022)	Human actions like walking, running, eating, sleeping, etc. can be detected and classified using CNN based models.
9	Brain tumor detection (Chattopadhyay & Maitra, 2022; Tiwari et al., 2022)	Brain tumor can be detected in MRI scans to reduce human error when brain tumor is detected manually in MRI scans. The detection can be made using CNN based architectures which have optimized hyperparameters.
10	Image denoising (Zheng et al., 2022)	Noise from images can be removed using deep learning models such as CNN to enhance image quality. Data argumentation techniques are employed to get better results.
11	Violence prediction and detection (Vieira et al., 2022)	Violence detection is important to law enforcement personals to catch the correct person involved in criminal activity and violence prediction can help prevent riots and street fight. Based on inputs from CCTV cameras models based on CNN can detect and predict violence.
12	Moths' detection in Rice (Lee, 2022)	Moths can decrease crop yield significantly and contribute to food insecurity. These tiny insects are difficult to identify from naked eye. Deep learning based models can detect these insects with high accuracy.
13	Epileptic Seizure prediction (Ouichka et al., 2022)	CNN model can predict if a person is going to have epileptic seizure based on EEG signal readings. Large amount of training data can reduce false positive and false negative in the model.
14	Chickpea diseases detection (Belay et al., 2022)	Yield of chickpeas can be increase by detecting diseases affecting chickpeas plant during growth phase using CNN based models.
15	Foreign object detection (Adi et al., 2022)	Aviation can be made safer by accurately detecting foreign objects which can harm aviation infrastructure in the vicinity of airports by employing methods of deep learning with optimized hyperparameters and transfer learning.
16	Plant disease detection (Belay et al., 2022; Paymode & Malode, 2022)	Diseases can affect different plants and each plant can have a different symptom. Timely diagnosis of these disease is important else yield can decrease. CNN combined by transfer learning can help to detect and classify plant diseases.
17	Face mask detection (Goyal et al., 2022; Kaur et al., 2022)	Face mask detection is important to enforce masks during epidemic or pandemic. CNN models have shown high accuracy in detecting face masks in people using existing infrastructure like CCTV cameras.
18	Few-shot object detection: Detection of objects in images when training data is sparse (Qiao et al., 2021)	Classification of objects in images is essential to solve various kinds of real-world problems. Deep learning models are known for high accuracy and efficient performance but when only sparse amount of training data is available then CNN based architectures can detect objects in few-shot scenarios.
19	Monkeypox detection (Altun et al., 2023)	Monkeypox is a highly infectious disease which can be identified by analysis skin lesions. Many other diseases have similar skin lesions which can cause diagnosis difficult. Pre-trained models based on CNN can be used to effectively detect and diagnose monkeypox in patients.
20	Diabetes prediction (Kamalraj et al., 2021)	Diabetes prediction in early stages can improve health of a person. Data driven CNN architectures can predict diabetes in people in early stages so doctors can take appropriate action to prevent it.
21	Covid-19 detection using chest x-ray (Monshi et al., 2021)	Various methods to detect covid-19 in people is both expensive and time consuming. Chest x-ray machines are widespread and easy to operate. CNN models can use chest X-Ray to detect covid-19 in people with high accuracy.

Table 3. Popular CNN models

S. No	Model	Short Description	Papers using the Model
1	YOLOv3	YOLOv3 is an object detection algorithm based on CNN. It is fast and efficient that can detect objects in real time. It stands for You Only Look Once version 3. It uses Darknet-53 to classify objects and is significantly faster and more accurate than the previous version YOLO v2.	(Liu et al., 2021)
2	R-CNN	R-CNN is an object detection algorithm that is based on CNN, SVM, and Bounding box regression methods. It is a Region-based Convolutional Neural Network. It used region proposals to detect objects in images where certain locations in the image is checked first for desired objects.	(Deng et al., 2021; Li et al., 2021; Mao et al., 2021; Qiao et al., 2021; Xie et al., 2021)
3	SqueezeNet	SqueezeNet is based on a small architecture CNN. Smaller CNN architecture provides the benefit of less computational cost to models. It provides a decent accuracy with few parameters which significantly increases efficiency.	(Vieira et al., 2022)
4	MobileNet Versions	MobileNet is a CNN based model. It is a lightweight neural network. It has a very less number of parameters and performs reduced athematic operations such as addition and multiplications. It follows depthwise convolution which is then followed by point wise convolution. It is significantly lightweight and is designed to be used on mobile devices where efficiency is a huge factor.	(Altun et al., 2023; Goyal et al., 2022; Monshi et al., 2021; Vieira et al., 2022)
5	NASNet	It is a deep neural architecture that creates different architectures of CNN models for a dataset. The architecture which provides the best accuracy is selected as the architecture of the model. While developing the model human interaction is minimum as it is the hyperparameters of the model are selected automatically. The best architecture is selected using the reinforcement technique and it is computationally expensive. However, once the model is selected it is generally efficient.	(Vieira et al., 2022)
6	SURF	Speeded up robust features is a feature detection algorithm for images. It is a robust and highly efficient algorithm used in computer vision models. It is inspired by SIFT which is also used for object detection.	(Katoch et al., 2022)
7	ResNet50	It is a CNN architecture consisting of 50 layers of neurons. It uses concepts such as residual blocks to train the model efficiently and provide outstanding results in image classification, object detection, and image restoration. Similar CNN architectures with 50 layers of neurons face problems like vanishing gradient which ResNet50 control using residual blocks and residual mapping. Pre-trained versions of this model which are trained on millions of image datasets are used to solve real-world problems.	(Monshi et al., 2021; Ouichka et al., 2022)
8	VGG-16	It is a CNN-based model which is used in image classification problems. It consists of 16 layers of neurons and uses the rectified linear unit as an activation function in hidden layers and softmax during classification in the output layer. It is known as a simple architecture that can classify images in over 100 classes as it is pre-trained on a vast number of images. Its precision is also competitive. The input size of images is fixed therefore pre-processing must be done to correctly feed images in the model.	(Paymode & Malode, 2022)
9	EfficientNet-B0	It is one of the most popular image classification models which is based on CNN architecture. It has many versions of which B0 is the base version. It has high efficiency and impressive performance. Its accuracy is matched by models which consume much more resources. It can classify objects in over 1000 classes as it is trained on a large dataset of images.	(Monshi et al., 2021)
10	DarkCovidNet	DarkCovidNet is an effective deep neural network-based algorithm that uses chest X-rays for the diagnosis of covid-19 in people. It uses multiple convolutional layers to achieve the goal to detect coronavirus in people. It works well with X-ray images that were captured in low light and have dark shades where feature detection and extraction are difficult.	(Monshi et al., 2021)
11	COVID-NET	It is a deep neural network based on CNN architecture that uses chest X-ray images to determine coronavirus in patients. It uses transfer learning from the ImageNet model to predict covid-19. It is built on multiple layers of convolution.	(Monshi et al., 2021)

Classification of fruits is done using the LSTM model. The different phases of the proposed model includes acquisition of image, preprocessing of image, extraction of features, and then classification. In the image acquisition phase, image enhancements are also performed. In the image preprocessing phase, intensity levels are improved to overcome distortions in images.

During the feature extraction phase, the best features are selected and extracted. During the classification phase, based on the feature vector fruits are classified. The accuracy of the model is very high with over 98% accuracy for over 10 fruits. When compared to existing techniques like CNN, CNN, ANFIS and RNN-CNN the proposed multi-modal CNN-RNN-LSTM outperforms them. The flow chart of LSTM-CNN-RNN model is presented in Figure 5. The paper focuses on more functionality of the model to detect the growth of fruits, ripeness detection, etc. in the future. Deng et al (2021) proposed a substitute for point-based 3D object detection which is a voxel-based 3D detector called Voxel R-CNN. Point-based 3D object detection is precise but computationally expensive due to unordered storage. It is because the efficiency voxel-based is better suited for models where optimal efficiency is a requirement. Voxel-based 3D detectors have low accuracy because the antecedent is divided into grids. The paper proposes a voxel-based 3D detector with high accuracy and efficiency. The paper analyses the SECOND

Figure 4. Flow chart of IDS model (Kim et al., 2020)

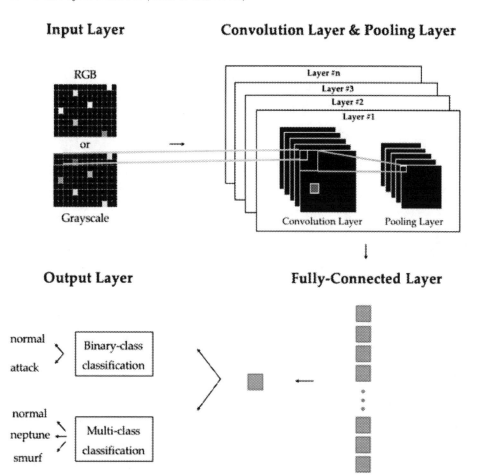

(Yan et al., 2018) and PV-RCNN (Shi et al., 2020) models on Waymo Open Dataset and KITTI dataset. It is observed that there is a significant gap between the two models' performance. A detect head is added on the 2D backbone of the SECOND model which shows an improvement of 0.6% average precision (AP) which demonstrates the notion that BEV has limited capacity to improve the performance of a model. PV-RCNN which is point-voxel-based is slower than SECOND. By the analysis, it is concluded that 3D structure is very important for 3D object detection and the point-voxel-based techniques are inefficient. The analysis motivated Deng et al (2021) to directly use the 3D voxel tensors and develop the voxel R-CNN model based only on voxels.

The developed model is tested on KITTI and Waymo Open Dataset. It is found that the performance of the model is very high on the KITTI dataset when compared to many top benchmark-achieving models which include PointCNN, 3DSSD, etc. For the Waymo Open dataset, the Voxel R-CNN model surpasses every top-performing model. It is tested in two levels, each level with 3D or BEV. Each level is differentiated by the number of points contained in it. The results of both datasets show that Voxel R-CNN can be a simple yet effective model to detect 3D objects and other downstream tasks. The flowchart of Voxel based 3D detector is presented in Figure 6.

Sarnovský et al (2022) proposed building a deep learning-based model which can detect fake news. During the period of coronavirus, much of the published content contained fake news, news that is not authentic and has sources to back the content. Many models including deep learning-based models have been developed for this kind of classification, but most are tailor-made for global languages such as English (Vunnava et al., 2022). The paper proposed to build a model which can detect fake news in local languages such as Slovak. The model comprises CNN, LSTM, and a combination of CNN + BiLSTM to classify authentic and fake news.

The dataset has been manually collected from online news publishing websites, conspiracy theory websites, and websites which have unreliable sources. The dataset is then labeled using a database where

Figure 5. Flow chart of LSTM-CNN-RNN model (Deng et al., 2021)

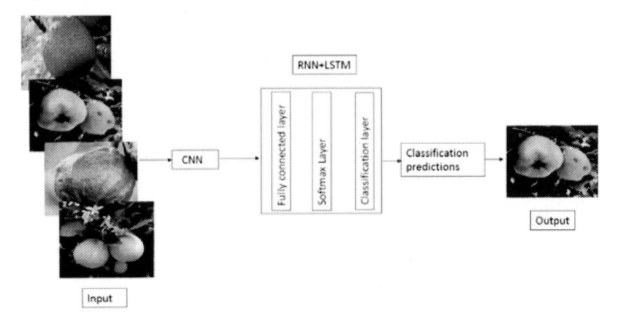

Figure 6. Flow chart voxel based 3D detector (Deng et al., 2021)

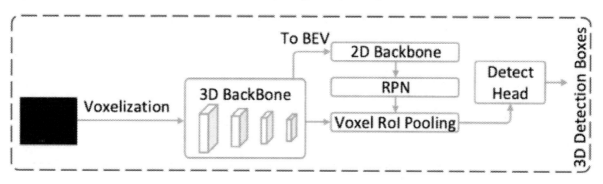

local media experts rate articles' authenticity by assigning the score. Using the score, the data is labeled as authenticated or fake. Articles that were not found in the database for scores were manually reviewed for authenticity and were labeled accordingly. The paper has limited the examination of articles to the domain of coronavirus. Therefore, articles that contained keywords such as coronavirus, covid-19, etc. were only kept in the dataset. Data preprocessing is performed on the dataset to remove attributes that do not help in making classification and reduce the performance of the model. Only the textual part of the news is kept and sources attributing to the textual content are removed. Grammatical words from the articles are removed and before being fed to the model it is converted into a vector representation format where words with similar meaning are grouped and counted as one. The data flow into the CNN model and then to an LSTM model after which data flows into a combination of CNN and BiLSTM model for classification. The flowchart of fake news detector is presented in Figure 7.

Performance of sigmoid based models

The performance of sigmoid based models in terms of accuracy is presented as shown in Figure 8.

Sigmoid Activation Function

Sigmoid function is also known as a logistic function that takes any real value as input and outputs a value between 0 and 1as presented in Figure9. Sigmoid Function formula is as follows:

$$s(x) = \frac{1}{1 + e^{-x}}$$

where, e is Euler's number (i.e., 2.71828), $s(x)$ is sigmoid function, x is the input to sigmoid function. The curve of sigmoid function is shown in Figure 9.

ReLU Function Based CNN Architectures

Ahlawat et al (2020) delineate how contemporary CNN models of ensemble architecture have improved accuracy but are computationally expensive. They describe various models that have very high predica-

Figure 7. Flow chart fake news detector (Sarnovský et al., 2022)

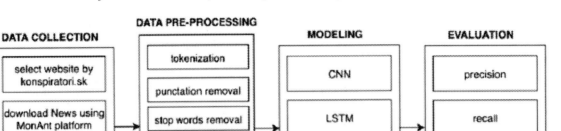

Figure 8. Performance of Sigmoid-based models

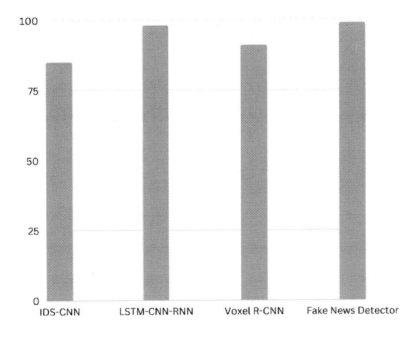

tion values on the MNIST dataset for handwriting but all of them are of ensemble architecture. Ensemble architectures increase time complexity and high testing complexity. It is built up of multiple CNN models. They propose a pure CNN architecture that can predict with comparable accuracy without increasing the time complexity. A comprehensive evaluation of various parameters such as the number of layers, padding, and dilution is also done in the paper. The proposed pure CNN architecture is then built into two variants one with three layers and the other with four layers. For the three-layer model, six cases have been considered and five cases for four-layer architecture are considered. Each case differs in the number of feature maps, padding, dilation, etc. The results show a very high accuracy for both layers of

Figure 9. Sigmoid activation function range

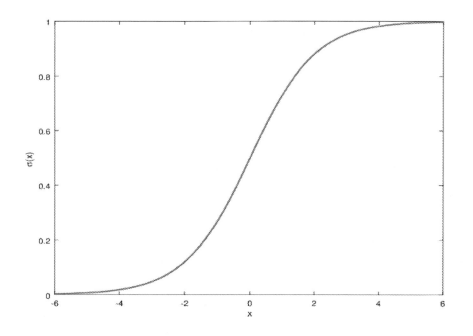

architecture each having 99.76% accuracy. Using the Adam optimizer, the accuracy is increased up to 99.89% which outperforms many other approaches of ensemble architectures.

Liu et al (2021) proposed an enhanced CNN-based model to detect ships for maritime surveillance with high precision. The model will be able to detect ships under different adverse weather conditions. The model has major changes to boost its performance. Anchor boxes are redesigned, soft non-maximum suppression (SNMS) is included and the mixed loss function is rebuilt to enhance the prediction by handling inter-class imbalance problems during training. A single Gaussian function is also introduced to localize uncertainties of predicted bounding boxes. The antecedent dataset is also augmented by enlarging its volume and diversity of it. This argumentation is beneficial for prediction when images are captured under varying conditions like rain, haze, and low illumination. An enhanced YOLOv3 network is used to extract features for the model. There are two convolutional layers with different kernels of size 3 x 3 and 1 x 1. The two kernels provide the required balance between the robustness and cost of the model. The model is tested on the TensorFlow software library using the SeaShips dataset. The result provided during the testing phase is 85.62% when data argumentation, redesigning the size of anchor boxes, SNMS, PLUBB, and loss function modifications are done. For container ships the accuracy is over 91% compared to faster R-CNN whose performance is 82.75% accuracy. The model also surpassed the performance of other methods such as SSD, YOLOv2, and YOLOv3. The paper suggests using powerful transfer learning and generative adversarial networks for data argumentation so synthetic images with a more natural-looking appearance can be produced. For small ships and boats, super-resolution methods can be introduced to improve accuracy. The flow chart of Ship Detector is presented in Figure 10.

Shoeibi et al (2021) compared various models to predict Schizophrenia using deep learning (DL) and machine learning (ML) methods using electroencephalography (EEG) signals. The deep learning

Figure 10. Flow chart of ship detector (Liu et al., 2021)

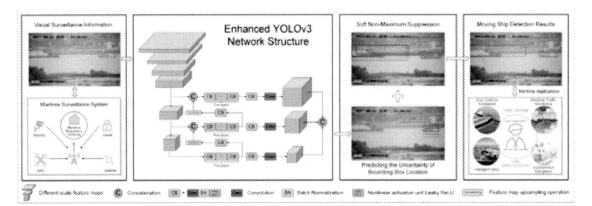

models used were long short-term memories (LSTM), one-dimensional convolutional networks (1D-CNN), and 1D-CNN-LSTM. These models were implemented with various activation functions. To test Schizophrenia diagnosis, conventional machine learning methods like SVM, KNN, Decision tree, naive Bayes, random forest, etc. were also used for classification. The K-fold cross-validation method with k=5 was used to perform all the tests. EEG is selected as a medium to detect Schizophrenia because it is one of the most practical and inexpensive neuroimaging-based methods. In EEG, the electrical activities of the brain are recorded in an appropriate spatial resolution. This recorded data can be used to detect Schizophrenia. The EEG signals were divided into 25s frames without overlapping and were normalized by z-score or norm L2. The flow chart of Schizophrenia Prediction Model is presented in Figure 11.

The 1D-CNN models had three versions: nine layers with a kernel size of 3, three layers with different kernel sizes, and two convolutional layers. The LSTM model had two versions: six layers with a kernel size of 100, with two dense layers and two dropout layers, and ReLU and Sigmoid activation functions. The second version added an extra 50-kernel layer to examine the effect of adding extra layers. The CNN-LSTM model has two versions: the first uses convolutional layers to extract features and local patterns, and the second uses 13 layers with ReLU and sigmoid activation functions. The filter size is 64, and the kernel size is 3 and 100.

The results have found that ML-based models have comparatively less accuracy than DL-based models. The bagging model gives the highest accuracy with the z-score normalization of the dataset. The accuracy is 81.22%. The DL-based models have given a better accuracy than the CNN-LSTM model with 13 layers giving an impressive 99.25% with ReLU activation function and combined normalization technique of z-score and L2. The study is conducted with limited cases of EEG dataset. The model also doesn't determine the severity of the disorder but rather diagnoses the disorder.

Dua et al (2021) proposed an end-to-end model which can recognize the human activity. Human Activity Recognition (HAR) is a methodology through which we can identify and name the activities performed by humans. The flow chart of Human Activity Recognition model is presented in Figure 12. The paper proposes a CNN-GRU model for automatically extracting features and predicting activities from wearable sensor data, eliminating feature engineering and time-consuming feature engineering. The model uses three convolutional filter sizes and uses both CNN and RNN for feature extraction. The model achieved 96.2% accuracy in UCI-HAR, 96.19% F1 score in WISDM, and 97.21% F1 score in PAMAP2 datasets. It outperformed other neural networks in accuracy and F1 scores.

Figure 11. Flow chart of schizophrenia prediction model (Shoeibi et al., 2021)

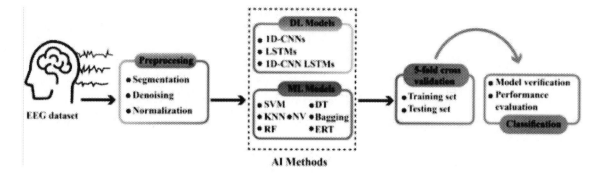

Muhammad et al (2021) proposed a bi-directional long short-term memory (BiLSTM) with a DCNN (dilated convolutional neural network) for human action recognition (HAR) in videos. It is stated that contemporary systems to recognize human behavior and action use pre-trained weights in their architecture for the visual representation of video frames during the training phase. This affects the feature discrepancy determination negatively. The proposed model selectively focuses on effective features in video frames using DCNN, overcoming handcrafted-based feature selection and handcrafted-based performance issues. It uses more inclusive receptive fields and upgrades learned features using residual blocks. The model classifies HAR using BiLSTM and Softmax loss function. Video conversion from 2D to 3D ensures precise information capture. The flow chart of BiLSTM + DCNN HAR Recognition Model is presented in Figure 13.

The model was tested on three datasets: UCF11, UCF Sports, and J-HMDB. UCF11 had 1600 videos with 30FPS quality, UCF Sports had 150 videos, and J-HMDB had 923 videos. Different versions were tested, with the third version achieving the highest accuracy. The model outperformed other state-of-the-art models, with 98.3% accuracy in UCF11, 99.1% in UCF Sports, and 80.2% in J-HMDB. The paper analyzed swing class activities' accuracy in the UCF Sports dataset, highlighting the importance of spatial and spatiotemporal features for accurate video stream classification.

A convolutional neural network-based brain tumor detection is proposed by Chattopadhyay and Maitra (2022). The flow chart of brain tumor detection model is presented in Figure 14. Brain tumor detection is time-consuming, and MRI images are similar. A CNN-based model is proposed for 2D MRI tumor identification, with 9 layers and a 2 kernel size using ReLU activation function. Batch normalization proposed by Ioffe and Szegedy (2015) is also applied to form the algorithm quicker. The BraTS 2020 dataset is used for training and testing models, with various activation functions and optimizers evaluated. The model's accuracy is influenced by training data, with Softmax activation function and RMSProp optimizer being the best. The model provides an accuracy of 99.74% which is higher than other state-of-the-art models presented by Seetha and Raja (2018) and Hossain et al (2019). It is stated that some images from the dataset were removed to overcome overfitting.

Zheng et al (2022) proposed a hybrid CNN model for image denoising. Contemporary image denoising does not provide good performance for complex images. The proposed model uses a hybrid CNN technology to overcome this issue. It is called hybrid denoising CNN (HDCNN). The flow chart of HDCNN Model is presented in Figure 15. This paper proposes a high-performance denoising CNN model by embedding BN and ReLU components. The model consists of 34 layers, including a dilated block, RepVGG block, single convolution, and feature refinement block. The DB extracts knowledge

Figure 12. Flow chart of human activity recognition model (Dua et al., 2021)

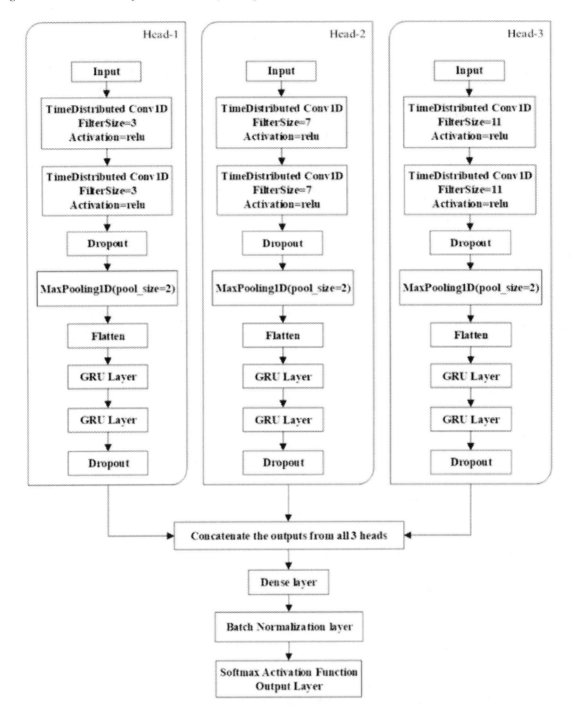

from the antecedent image, while the RVB refines object features. The FB extracts knowledge from the antecedent image, and the single convolution combines the knowledge to create a clear image. The kernel size is 3x3.

Figure 13. Flow chart of BiLSTM + DCNN HAR recognition model (Muhammad et al., 2021)

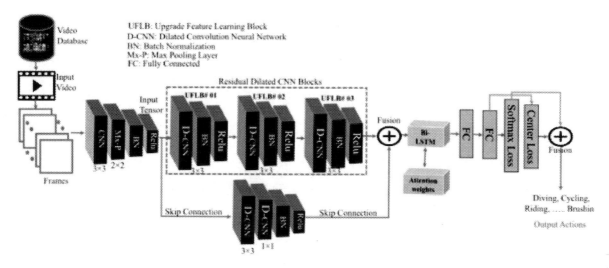

Figure 14. Flow chart of brain tumor detection model (Chattopadhyay & Maitra, 2022)

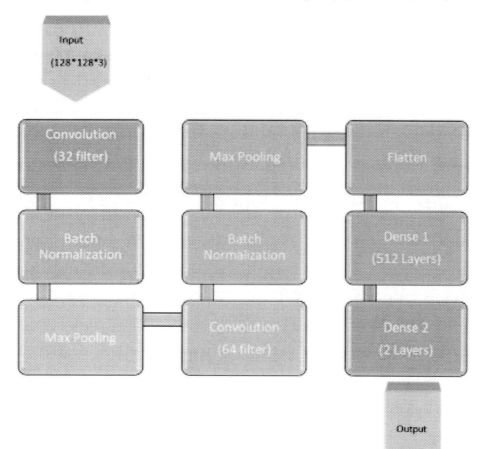

The model is trained on the Berkeley Segmentation dataset which contains 432 images. To test the model, BSD68 and Set12 are used. The model is tested with all the components given above and gives a 31.74 PSNR (peak signal to noise ratio) value on BSD68 with a Gaussian noise of standard deviation(σ) of 15. Different versions of HDCNN are also trained and tested where in each version one component is removed. Components include FB, RVB, dilated convolution, BN, and DB. HDCNN without dilated convolution and HDCNN without DB gave nearly the same performance. When compared to other models its performance is highest for $\sigma = 15$ and $\sigma = 25$. It is the second best performing model when $\sigma = 50$. The proposed model has also outperformed other models for the Set12 dataset. When $\sigma = 15$ then it has the second highest PSNR.

Vieira et al (2022) proposed a CNN-based automatic violence recognition embedded system. The CNN model is to monitor people in crowded and uncrowded environments for suspicious events. For the model to work it must be able to classify different human actions such as punching, jumping, shooting, hugging, etc in violent and nonviolent classes. Data augmentation is performed to avoid overfitting. The model is created in four versions. Each version had different architectures namely SqueezeNet, MobileNet v1, MobileNet v2, and NASNet. Adam optimizer is used in each of these versions. SqueezeNet offers a low-parameter architecture. This helps to reduce computational costs. The MobileNet v2 architecture was trained and tested on four datasets: Violent-Flow, UCF-101, HMDB, and Moments in Time. The model was compared for accuracy against epoch and error against epoch. A prototype was created using an embedded Raspberry Pi platform for mobile application, achieving an accuracy of 92.05%. The system can execute up to 4 frames per second and recognize pre-fight behavior and anticipate violent acts.

Lee (2022) used a convolutional neural network to recognize and classify small insects like moths. The neural network can be used to identify rice pests and use the identification to prevent the early spread of rice pests. The flow chart of Moth Detector Model is presented in Figure 16. The moths which are targeted are less than 1mm in size therefore and due to poor-quality images, they could be difficult to identify. Therefore, a data booster is used in the classification object. The rectified linear unit (ReLU) activation function is used as the activation function. The sigmoid function is not used because it can create errors because of the slope at both ends. Two convolutional layers are used with a kernel size of 3. The dataset used for training and testing consists of 9700 images. The accuracy is over 90%.

Katoch et al (2022) proposed an Indian Sign Language (ISL) recognition model. A sign is used to communicate with deaf persons. The flow chart of ISL Recognition Model is presented in Figure 17.

Figure 15. Flow chart of HDCNN model (Zheng et al., 2022)

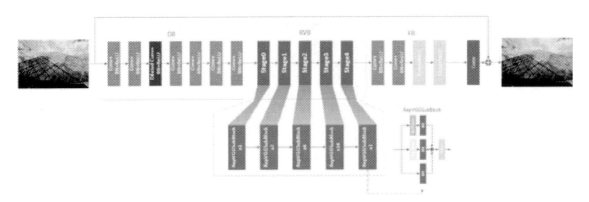

Figure 16. Flow chart of moth detector model (Lee, 2022)

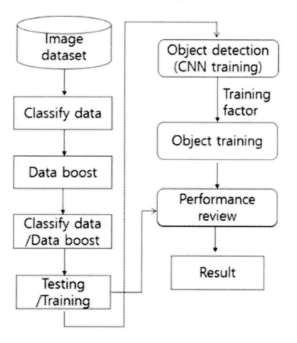

ISL is a complex sign language in India, using Bag Of Visual Words (BOVW) to recognize alphabets and digits, Speeded Up Robust Features (SURF) for video streams, and SVM and CNN for classification. The dataset is custom-built with 36,000 images and a 250x250 resolution, with a 4:1 training and testing ratio. Segmentation and background subtraction are performed to detect hands. The CNN architecture consists of 6 convolutional layers divided into three groups: 3 with 32 filters, 64 with 64 filters, and 3 with ReLU activation and softmax activation functions. It outperforms SVM in accuracy, providing 99.64%. A GUI and Tkinter library are developed for speech conversion and simple word formation.

Tiwari et al (2022) proposed a CNN-based model to detect brain tumors consisting of many layers six of the layers have weight and another six are batch normalization layers. The model uses input, output, and max-pooling layers to automatically classify and detect brain tumors from MRI images. It uses Rectified Linear Unit activation for hidden layers and softmax activation in the output layer. The main goal is to minimize parameters and training phases. The model achieves over 99% accuracy using a dataset of MRI images with both tumors and no tumors, with a 22:3 training/testing ratio. Ouichka et al (2022) proposed various models to predict epileptic seizures using EEG signals. EEG signals are

Figure 17. Flow chart of ISL recognition model (Katoch et al., 2022)

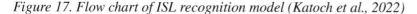
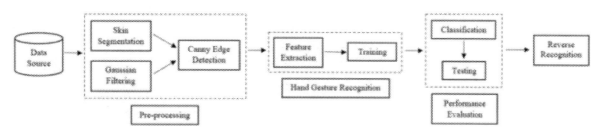

recorded by placing electrodes on the skull to detect electric signals both during and after a seizure. A total of 5 models are developed to compare the accuracy of epileptic prediction. Each of the models has different architecture: the first model consists of one CNN network, the second model consists of two CNN networks, the third model consists of three CNN models and the fourth consists of four CNN models to predict epileptic seizures. The fifth is ResNet50, a model consisting of 50 layers of a CNN network. The models use the Adam optimizer during training and use the softmax activation function. The third model, consisting of three CNN networks, combines the first two CNN networks and the result is then combined with the next CNN network. The flow chart of 3-CNN Model is presented in Figure 18. The fourth mode uses four CNN networks to predict epilepsy seizures, trained and tested against a dataset of intracranial EEG signals from humans and dogs, recorded under general anesthesia. The accuracy for the third and fourth models is highest, giving over 95% accuracy while the accuracy of the first model is 91%. The accuracy of the second model is 76%. The accuracy of ResNet50 which has 50 convolutional layers is the lowest at 66.5%. The training and testing dataset is in a ratio of 97: 3. It is discussed that accuracy can be improved by combining the EEG data with electrocardiogram data.

An accuracy of 92.55% is achieved to classify chickpea diseases like fusarium wilt and ascochyta blight by Belay et al (2022) using deep learning methods. These diseases impact the yield of chickpea production negatively and impact the economies and livelihoods of countries and people respectively. The flow chart of Chickpeas Disease Detector is presented in Figure 19. The proposed method uses CNN and LSTM to develop a Python-based classification model for diseases. Data pre-processing and image resizing are used to prevent noise and overfitting. The CNN architecture consists of six layers, with a ReLU activation function applied. Features are extracted using Softmax and SVM. A dataset of chickpeas-producing farms is used, and disease characteristics are labeled using plant leaves. Data aug-

Figure 18. Flow chart of 3-CNN model (Ouichka et al., 2022)

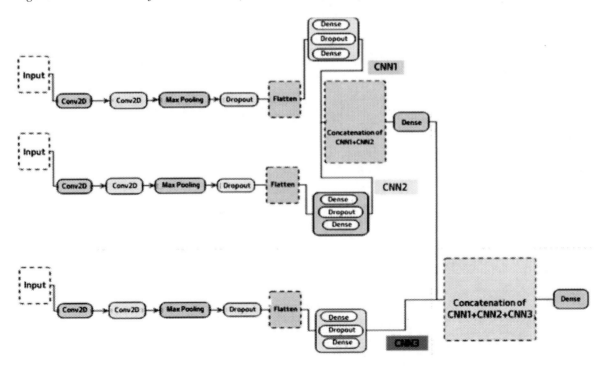

mentation is done using computer graphics techniques. A 4:1 training and testing dataset is used, with softmax being the best performer. The model provides three classes of classification: healthy plants, fusarium wilt, and ascochyta blight plants.

Airport infrastructure contains foreign objects that can cause significant damage to airplanes, monetary loss to owners, and loss of lives. These objects can be part of airplanes, engine maintenance, rubber parts, or waste thrown by passengers. Adi et al (2022) proposed a model which can detect these objects without requiring too much human interaction which increases the accuracy of detection. The proposed model is the deep learning method convolutional neural network to identify the features and classify the objects using the selected features. It takes images of airport infrastructure where airplanes operate like runways, hangers, etc. The CNN architecture was tested against various factors, including learning rates, image size, kernel size, and object detection. The model achieved 90% accuracy with 4 classes, with a single convolutional layer and higher image size. The model performed better with softmax activation function and ReLU after each convolutional layer.

Figure 19. Flow chart of chickpeas disease detector (Belay et al., 2022)

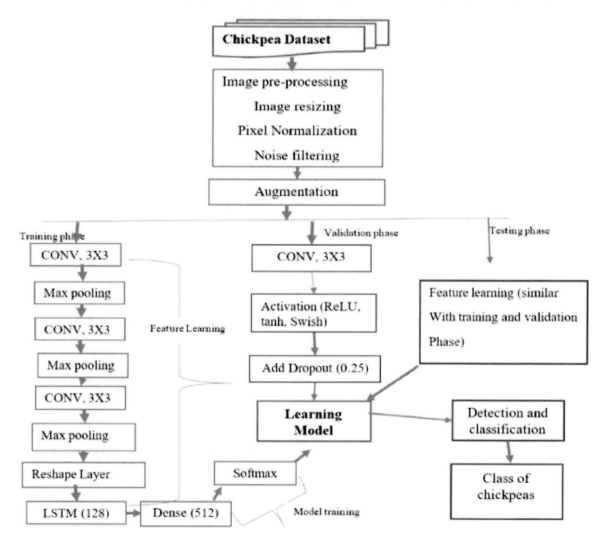

Controlling disease in plants is important during the growth phase to increase the yield of crops. Paymode and Malode (2022) propose a model which can detect different kinds of illnesses plants have. The paper focuses on two kinds of plants namely grapes and tomatoes and proposes a transfer learning-based model which can detect the illness on these plants. The detection is based on images of plant leaves. The training dataset has been collected from a university while data is tested on real-world images collected from different kinds of imaging gadgets with different configurations. The model comprises a Visual Geometry Group (VGG) based CNN neural network and archives an accuracy of 98.4% for grapes and 95.71% for tomatoes. Before the images are input, they are pre-processed using various techniques. In the training phase data is augmented to improve the model using methods such as scaling, rotation, and shearing. CNN-VGG16 model is used for transfer learning and classification of crop images. The flow chart of VGG16 Based Plant Disease Detector is presented in Figure 20. The model is trained and tested on various hyperparameters and using the best set of hyperparameters.

Figure 20. Flow chart of VGG16 based plant disease detector (Paymode & Malode, 2022)

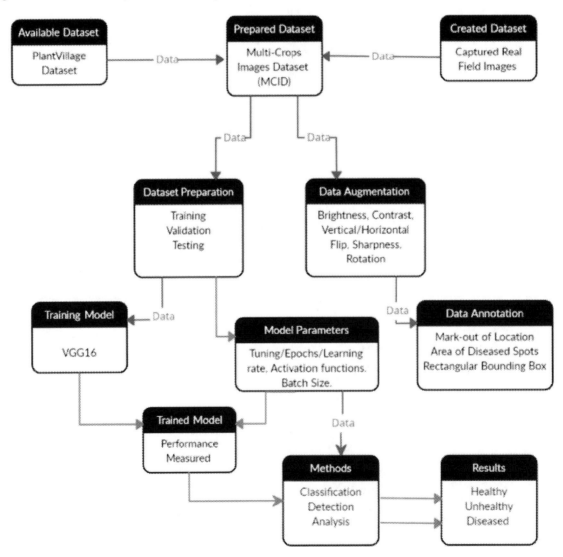

Goyal et al (2022) proposed a face mask detection model which is highly precise and efficient. The proposed method for detecting face masks uses deep learning techniques and a CNN architecture with 10 layers, including convolutional and max pooling layers. The model uses ReLU activation functions and data pre-processing from a 52-layer MobileNet V2 CNN model. The dataset includes 4000 images, with a 4:1 training/testing ratio. The model uses the Adam optimizer for training and the softmax function for output. It achieves 98% accuracy against the testing dataset and excels on low-configuration GPUs. It first detects the face and then the face masks. The flow chart of Face Mask Detection Model is presented in Figure 21. It is proposed that in the future physical distance will be used as a feature to make the model more accurate and dynamic.

Figure 21. Flow chart of face mask detection model (Goyal et al., 2022)

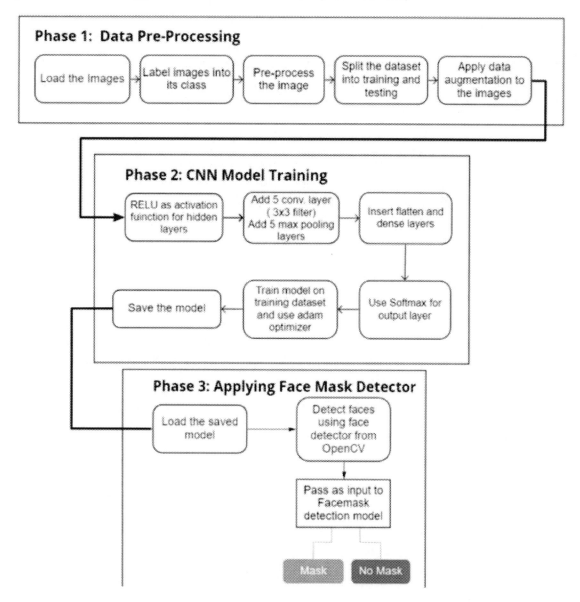

Performance of ReLU Based Models

The performance of ReLU based models which provides accuracy have been presented in Figure 22.

ReLU Activation Function

It is also called Rectified Linear Unit function. Its output range is between 0 to ∞. It is the most used activation function in CNN.

$$f(x) = max(0, x)$$

where, $f(x)$ is the ReLU activation function, x is the input to ReLU activation function, $max()$ returns the maximum value present inside the bracket. The curve for ReLU activation function is shown in Figure 23.

Figure 22. Performance of ReLU based models

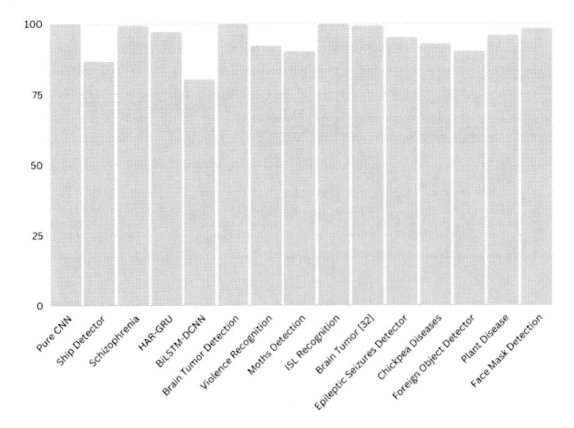

Figure 23. ReLU activation function range

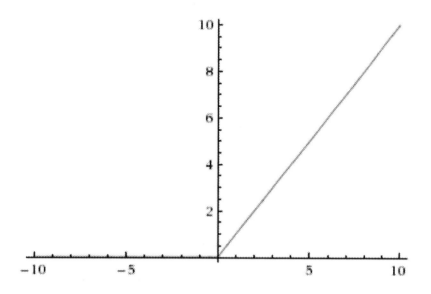

Softmax Function Based CNN Architectures

Qiao et al (2021) used Gradient Decoupled Layer (GDL) and Prototypical Calibration Block (PCB) to create a simple but effective architecture named Decoupled Faster R-CNN (DeFRNC) for the detection of objects in few-shot scenarios. The architecture extends Faster R-CNN by introducing GDL for multi-stage decoupling and PCB for multi-task decoupling. DeFRNC is effective when limited data is available, as it modifies feature-forward operations. GDL modifies feature-forward operations, while PCB boosts original classification scores for calibration. DeFRNC helps train models with limited data without compromising detection accuracy. GDL significantly improves conventional detection, with faster R-CNN achieving 7.9%/12.2% for 10/30 shots, while DeFRCN achieves 10.6%/10.4% for the same dataset.

Mao et al (2021) presented a framework named pyramid R-CNN which is for a two-stage 3D object detection model. Pyramid R-CNN improves 3D object detection performance by adaptively learning features from sparse points of interest. It outperforms traditional voxels-based approaches, outperforming Pyramid-PV and Pyramid-P in Waymo Open datasets. Li et al (2021) explain how voxel-based 3D object detection suffers from point sparsity and a very large search space in 3D space. The accuracy of voxel-based 3D object detection has decreased significantly along with the efficiency. The paper proposes a point-based CNN model named LiDAR R-CNN which can detect 3D objects with greater accuracy and efficiency. Earlier other models have also been made using point-based techniques, but it is observed that most of them used native point-based methods like PointNet. Native point-based methods can overlook proposal size, so techniques like normalization, anchoring, voxelization, boundary offset, and spacing with virtual points were employed. The LiDAR R-CNN 3D detector outperformed baseline models in the Waymo Open Dataset (WOD) and KITTI datasets, with high average precision for vehicles, pedestrians, and cyclists. The model's performance surpasses most baseline models.

Altun et al (2023) optimized existing models to detect monkeypox through skin lesions images. The various models were customized using transfer learning tools and providing an optimal hyperparameter value. The flow chart of Monkeypox Detection Model is presented in Figure 24. The model works when images of skin are fed to the model. The images can be taken from any type of gadget. The CNN architecture uses both the Softmax and Rectified linear unit of activation functions in consecutive turns. Various optimizers were used to check the performance of the models of those the Adam Optimizer is found to be best performing and selected. Adaptive Algorithms are also used to substitute SGD. The dataset used to train and test the model is scraped from the Internet. The positive labeled images have skin lesions belonging to monkeypox while negative labeled images have skin lesions belonging to other types of diseases. Data argumentation is also performed. The training and testing ratio of the dataset is 17: 3. The MobileNetV3-s provided the best AUC result at a score of 99.7% and an accuracy of 99.1% among the different models considered. Most of the models gave an accuracy of over 90%. The best-performing model is compared to the other relevant studies, and it surpasses them in all measures of performance.

Performance of Softmax based models

The performance of Softmax based models which provides accuracy have been presented in Figure 25.

SoftMax Activation Function

It is mostly used in multiclass neural networks, and it is also found in most output layers. It takes a vector of real numbers as input to provide an output range between 0 and 1.

$$\sigma\left(\vec{z}\right) = \frac{e^{z_i}}{\sum_{j=1}^{K} e^{z_j}}$$

Figure 24. Flow chart of monkeypox detection model (Altun et al., 2023)

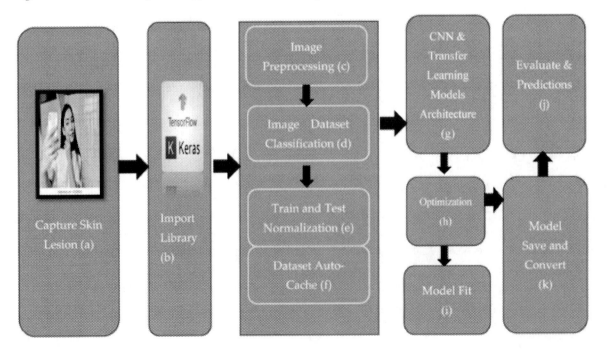

Figure 25. Performance of Softmax-based models

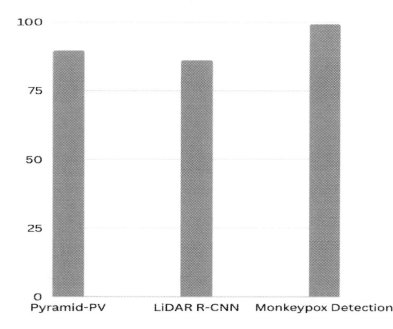

where, σ is softmax, $\vec{z}$ is input vector, e^{z_i} is standard exponential function for input vector, K is the number of classes in the multi-class classifier, e^{z_j} is the standard exponential function for output vector. The curve for SoftMax activation function is shown in Figure 26.

2.7 CNN Architectures Based on Other Functions

Xie et al (2021) proposed an effective yet simple oriented object detection framework called Oriented R-CNN, a two-stage detection algorithm with high accuracy and efficiency. The proposed algorithm uses an Oriented Region Proposal Network (RPN) to generate high-quality oriented proposals without requiring significant computing resources. It uses an oriented R-CNN head to purify oriented regions of interest and detect objects using classification and regression. The algorithm is lightweight, takes fewer parameters, and achieves an accuracy of 75.87% mAP on a DOTA dataset and 96.50% mAP on an HRSC2016 dataset. The algorithm uses a single RTX 2080Ti graphics card and aims to balance inference speed and detection accuracy. The flow chart of Oriented R-CNN Model is presented in Figure 27. The computational cost of the proposed algorithm-oriented R-CNN is close to one-stage detectors but with much higher accuracy than one-stage detectors.

Kamalraj et al (2021) proposed an Interpretable Filter based CNN (IF-CNN) based model to predict the severity and risk factor of diabetes. The paper aims to create a ML-based model to predict diabetes using the Pet Dog-Smell Sensing (PD-SS) algorithm. The optimized CNN-LSTM model achieved 95.1% accuracy, using ML-based algorithms. The model uses seven neurons and attributes like glucose, skin size, blood pressure, age, diabetes function, BMI, and insulin. Interpretable filters extract features and reduce time differences between glucose and glucose levels. The results of the models are quite good. The SVM gives a 90% accuracy while CNN-LSTM provides a 92% and the IF-CNN provides the highest 96.26% accuracy. The flow chart of IF-CNN algorithm is presented in Figure 28. The efficiency of

Figure 26. Softmax activation function range

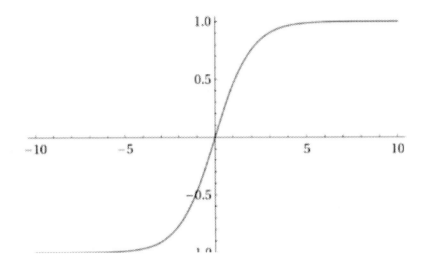

Figure 27. Flow chart of oriented R-CNN model (Xie et al., 2021)

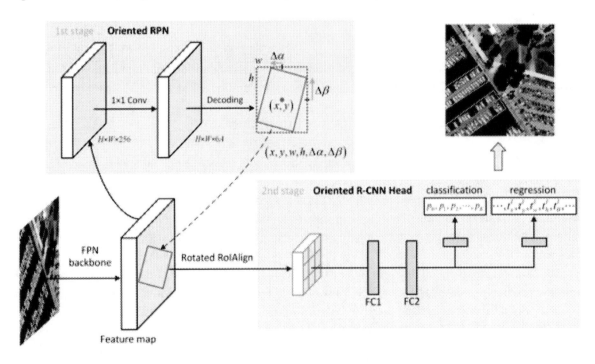

IF-CNN is also highest among the others with SVM performing the least. The paper specifies that the accuracy can be increased when the dataset size is increased without any missing values. The PIMA dataset had some cases which had missing values. These cases were removed from the dataset.

Kaur et al (2022) proposed a face mask recognition model to detect whether a person is wearing a mask or not. It uses a conventional CNN technique to recognize if a person is wearing a mask or not. It

Figure 28. Flow chart of IF-CNN algorithm (Kamalraj et al., 2021)

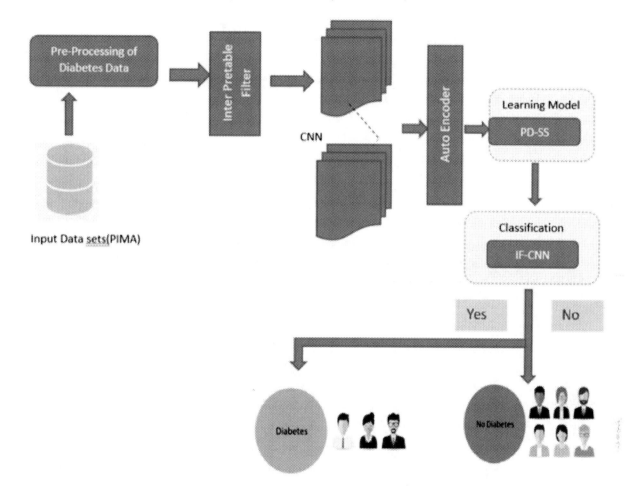

uses tensor flow to implement the model. The flow chart of CNN Based Face Mask Detection Model is presented in Figure 29. The model extracts features from images without or with masks, transforming them into smaller images. It uses a dataset from Kaggle and a webcam to train and test. The model can detect multiple faces in a single frame and requires no cost to set up infrastructure for identifying people without masks in streets.

Monshi et al (2021) optimized the CNN hyperparameters and data argumentation to increase the accuracy of popular CNN architectures for the diagnosis of COVID-19 using Chest X-Ray (CXR). Data augmentation also prevented overfitting in the model. Resizing, rotating, zooming, warping, normalizing, and other methods were examined during data argumentation. The proposed data argumentation and optimization of hyperparameters of CNN increased the accuracy of the Visual Geometry Group Network (Simonyan & Zisserman, 2014) (VGC-19) by 11.93% and 4.93% for the Residual Neural Network (He et al., 2016) (ResNet-50). The paper proposes a model using EfficientNet-B0 and optimization results, including data argumentation, Adam optimizer, and Label Smoothing Cross Entropy Loss function, resizing CXR images. The model is called CovidXrayNet and is performed on two datasets COVIDcxr and COVIDx (Wang & Cheng, 2020). The flow chart of CovidXrayNet is presented in Figure 30. The datasets contained three classes of CXR. The three classes are covid-19 (coronavirus infection), pneu-

Figure 29. Flow chart of CNN based face mask detection model (Kaur et al., 2022)

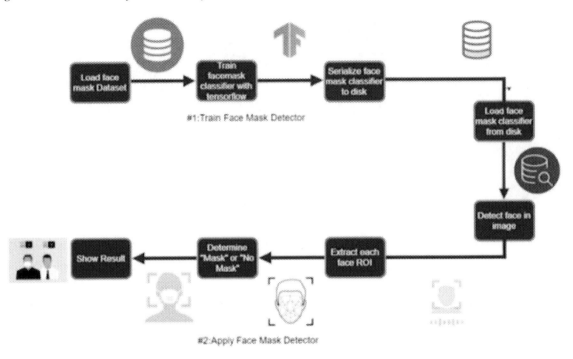

monia (other chest infection), and normal (no infection). The COVIDcxr has been generated using two other datasets, ChestX-Ray14 (Wang et al., 2017), and Covid-19 image data collection (Cohen et al., 2020). The COVIDx dataset, with 15,496 CXR images, is a balanced, complete, and unbiased dataset. Training with 32 batch sizes and 30 epochs, the model achieves 95.82% accuracy, surpassing popular methods like DarkCovidNet, COVID-Net, and MobileNet v2. However, CovidXrayNet has errors, making it a second option for COVID-19 diagnosis.

Figure 30. Flow chart of CovidXrayNet (Monshi et al., 2021)

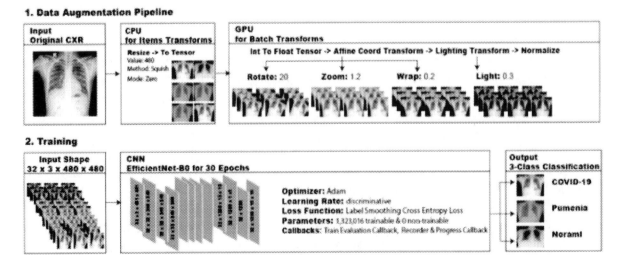

Performance of Models

Model which provides accuracy have been presented in Figure 31.

Tanh Activation Function

It is nearly same as the sigmoid function. It provides an output range between -1 and 1. It is mainly used for classification between two classes.

$$\tanh(x) = \frac{e^x - e^{-x}}{e^x + e^{-x}}$$

where, e is Euler's number, $\tanh(x)$ is tanh activation function, x is input to tanh function. The curve for Tanh activation function is shown in Figure 32.

FINDINGS

The papers analyzed have shown that CNN can be used to solve a variety of problems. Some papers (Monshi et al., 2021; Ouichka et al., 2022; Vieira et al., 2022) have thoroughly analyzed different architectures to achieve near-perfect precision. Different kernel sizes and the number of convolutional layers

Figure 31. Performance of models

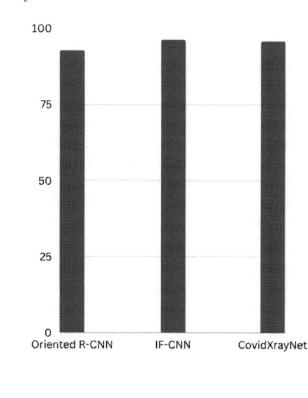

Figure 32. Tanh activation function range

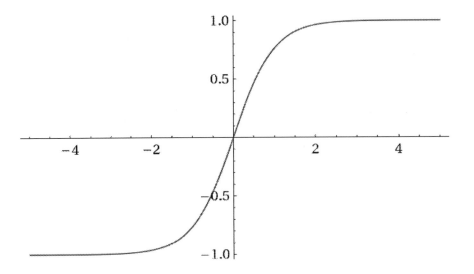

involved can have a major impact on the model. For each of the models presented it is found that the performance increases as the training data increases. The cross-validation of the dataset is also important and each of the cross-validation techniques should be tested against the model to find the best way to divide the dataset into training and testing subsets. Some papers (Kaur et al., 2022) have not provided any performance metrics which could have been provided for performance evaluation. Some papers have been analyzed where the dataset is thin, and a dense dataset would have given a more accurate performance measure.

CONCLUSION

It can be said that convolutional neural networks can be used to solve various kinds of real-world problems which either couldn't be solved earlier or solved with much less efficiency and speed. Problems that were solved earlier can now be refined using CNN to provide better performance and efficiency. Its ability to interact with other technologies and methods of DL and ML makes it quite dynamic and robust. It requires enough training data else the performance may dip though there are methods that can be used when a sparse amount of data is available. Many papers have shown that it provides better performance across all metrics when compared to other classification methods such as SVM, Random Forest, RNN, etc. It can be concluded that more research is needed in this field to completely exploit the potential of this technology. The critical review provided above points to the wide range of applications where CNN is used. From the field of medical science to violence detection in social places and from image denoising to network security CNN has shown its applications and precision. Models like CovidXrayNet have shown that it is better than other classification technologies like SVM, ANN, KNN, etc. In the future, this neural network can be used to improve existing models by testing different architectures and hyperparameters. CNN should be considered along with existing technologies to check if a more suitable solution can be provided. Different versions of the architecture should be built and tested to check if better solutions can be provided.

REFERENCES

Adi, K., Widodo, C. E., Widodo, A. P., & Margiati, U. (2022). Detection of foreign object debris (Fod) using convolutional neural network (CNN). *Journal of Theoretical and Applied Information Technology*, *100*(1), 184–191.

Ahlawat, S., Choudhary, A., Nayyar, A., Singh, S., & Yoon, B. (2020). Improved handwritten digit recognition using convolutional neural networks (CNN). *Sensors (Basel)*, *20*(12), 3344. doi:10.3390/s20123344 PMID:32545702

Altun, M., Gürüler, H., Özkaraca, O., Khan, F., Khan, J., & Lee, Y. (2023). Monkeypox detection using CNN with transfer learning. *Sensors (Basel)*, *23*(4), 1783. doi:10.3390/s23041783 PMID:36850381

Belay, A. J., Salau, A. O., Ashagrie, M., & Haile, M. B. (2022). Development of a chickpea disease detection and classification model using deep learning. *Informatics in Medicine Unlocked*, *31*, 100970. doi:10.1016/j.imu.2022.100970

Chattopadhyay, A., & Maitra, M. (2022). *MRI-based brain tumor image detection using CNN based deep learning method*. Neuroscience Informatics.

Chitra, A., & Rajkumar, A. (2016). Plagiarism detection using machine learning-based paraphrase recognizer. *Journal of Intelligent Systems*, *25*(3), 351–359. doi:10.1515/jisys-2014-0146

Cohen, J. P., Morrison, P., & Dao, L. 2020. COVID-19 image data collection. *arXiv preprint arXiv:2003.11597*.

Deng, J., Shi, S., Li, P., Zhou, W., Zhang, Y., & Li, H. (2021, May). Voxel r-cnn: Towards high performance voxel-based 3d object detection. *Proceedings of the AAAI Conference on Artificial Intelligence*, *35*(2), 1201–1209. doi:10.1609/aaai.v35i2.16207

Dua, N., Singh, S. N., & Semwal, V. B. (2021). Multi-input CNN-GRU based human activity recognition using wearable sensors. *Computing*, *103*(7), 1461–1478. doi:10.1007/s00607-021-00928-8

Gill, H. S., Khalaf, O. I., Alotaibi, Y., Alghamdi, S., & Alassery, F. (2022). Multi-Model CNN-RNN-LSTM Based Fruit Recognition and Classification. *Intelligent Automation & Soft Computing*, *33*(1).

Goyal, H., Sidana, K., Singh, C., Jain, A., & Jindal, S. (2022). A real time face mask detection system using convolutional neural network. *Multimedia Tools and Applications*, *81*(11), 14999–15015. doi:10.1007/s11042-022-12166-x PMID:35233179

He, K., Zhang, X., Ren, S., & Sun, J. (2016). Deep residual learning for image recognition. In *Proceedings of the IEEE conference on computer vision and pattern recognition* (pp. 770-778). IEEE.

Hossain, T., Shishir, F. S., Ashraf, M., Al Nasim, M. A., & Shah, F. M. (2019, May). Brain tumor detection using convolutional neural network. In *2019 1st international conference on advances in science, engineering and robotics technology (ICASERT)* (pp. 1-6). IEEE. 10.1109/ICASERT.2019.8934561

Ioffe, S., & Szegedy, C. (2015, June). Batch normalization: Accelerating deep network training by reducing internal covariate shift. In *International conference on machine learning* (pp. 448-456). PMLR.

Kamalraj, R., Neelakandan, S., Kumar, M. R., Rao, V. C. S., Anand, R., & Singh, H. (2021). Interpretable filter based convolutional neural network (IF-CNN) for glucose prediction and classification using PD-SS algorithm. *Measurement*, *183*, 109804. doi:10.1016/j.measurement.2021.109804

Katoch, S., Singh, V., & Tiwary, U. S. (2022). Indian Sign Language recognition system using SURF with SVM and CNN. *Array (New York, N.Y.)*, *14*, 100141. doi:10.1016/j.array.2022.100141

Kaur, G., Sinha, R., Tiwari, P. K., Yadav, S. K., Pandey, P., Raj, R., Vashisth, A., & Rakhra, M. (2022). Face mask recognition system using CNN model. *Neuroscience Informatics (Online)*, *2*(3), 100035. doi:10.1016/j.neuri.2021.100035 PMID:36819833

Kim, J., Kim, J., Kim, H., Shim, M., & Choi, E. (2020). CNN-based network intrusion detection against denial-of-service attacks. *Electronics (Basel)*, *9*(6), 916. doi:10.3390/electronics9060916

Lee, S. (2022). A study on classification and detection of small moths using CNN model. *Computers, Materials & Continua*, *71*(1), 1987–1998. doi:10.32604/cmc.2022.022554

Li, Z., Wang, F., & Wang, N. (2021). Lidar r-cnn: An efficient and universal 3d object detector. In *Proceedings of the IEEE/CVF Conference on Computer Vision and Pattern Recognition* (pp. 7546-7555). IEEE. 10.1109/CVPR46437.2021.00746

Liu, R. W., Yuan, W., Chen, X., & Lu, Y. (2021). An enhanced CNN-enabled learning method for promoting ship detection in maritime surveillance system. *Ocean Engineering*, *235*, 109435. doi:10.1016/j.oceaneng.2021.109435

Mao, J., Niu, M., Bai, H., Liang, X., Xu, H., & Xu, C. (2021). Pyramid r-cnn: Towards better performance and adaptability for 3d object detection. In *Proceedings of the IEEE/CVF International Conference on Computer Vision* (pp. 2723-2732). IEEE. 10.1109/ICCV48922.2021.00272

Monshi, M. M. A., Poon, J., Chung, V., & Monshi, F. M. (2021). CovidXrayNet: Optimizing data augmentation and CNN hyperparameters for improved COVID-19 detection from CXR. *Computers in Biology and Medicine*, *133*, 104375. doi:10.1016/j.compbiomed.2021.104375 PMID:33866253

Muhammad, K., Ullah, A., Imran, A. S., Sajjad, M., Kiran, M. S., Sannino, G., & de Albuquerque, V. H. C. (2021). Human action recognition using attention based LSTM network with dilated CNN features. *Future Generation Computer Systems*, *125*, 820–830. doi:10.1016/j.future.2021.06.045

Ouichka, O., Echtioui, A., & Hamam, H. (2022). Deep Learning Models for Predicting Epileptic Seizures Using iEEG Signals. *Electronics (Basel)*, *11*(4), 605. doi:10.3390/electronics11040605

Paymode, A. S., & Malode, V. B. (2022). Transfer learning for multi-crop leaf disease image classification using convolutional neural network VGG. *Artificial Intelligence in Agriculture*, *6*, 23–33. doi:10.1016/j.aiia.2021.12.002

Qiao, L., Zhao, Y., Li, Z., Qiu, X., Wu, J., & Zhang, C. (2021). Defrcn: Decoupled faster r-cnn for few-shot object detection. In *Proceedings of the IEEE/CVF International Conference on Computer Vision* (pp. 8681-8690). IEEE. 10.1109/ICCV48922.2021.00856

Sarnovský, M., Maslej-Krešňáková, V., & Ivancová, K. (2022). Fake news detection related to the co-vid-19 in slovak language using deep learning methods. *Acta Polytechnica Hungarica, 19*(2), 43–57. doi:10.12700/APH.19.2.2022.2.3

Seetha, J., & Raja, S. S. (2018). Brain tumor classification using convolutional neural networks. *Biomedical & Pharmacology Journal, 11*(3), 1457–1461. doi:10.13005/bpj/1511

Shi, S., Guo, C., Jiang, L., Wang, Z., Shi, J., Wang, X., & Li, H. (2020). Pv-rcnn: Point-voxel feature set abstraction for 3d object detection. In *Proceedings of the IEEE/CVF Conference on Computer Vision and Pattern Recognition* (pp. 10529-10538). 10.1109/CVPR42600.2020.01054

Shoeibi, A., Sadeghi, D., Moridian, P., Ghassemi, N., Heras, J., Alizadehsani, R., Khadem, A., Kong, Y., Nahavandi, S., Zhang, Y. D., & Gorriz, J. M. (2021). Automatic diagnosis of schizophrenia in EEG signals using CNN-LSTM models. *Frontiers in Neuroinformatics, 15*, 58. doi:10.3389/fninf.2021.777977 PMID:34899226

Simonyan, K., & Zisserman, A. (2014). Very deep convolutional networks for large-scale image recognition. *arXiv preprint arXiv:1409.1556.*

Tiwari, P., Pant, B., Elarabawy, M. M., Abd-Elnaby, M., Mohd, N., Dhiman, G., & Sharma, S. (2022). Cnn based multiclass brain tumor detection using medical imaging. *Computational Intelligence and Neuroscience, 2022*, 2022. doi:10.1155/2022/1830010 PMID:35774437

Vieira, J. C., Sartori, A., Stefenon, S. F., Perez, F. L., De Jesus, G. S., & Leithardt, V. R. Q. (2022). Low-cost CNN for automatic violence recognition on embedded system. *IEEE Access : Practical Innovations, Open Solutions, 10*, 25190–25202. doi:10.1109/ACCESS.2022.3155123

Vunnava, R., Bodla, L., Dehury, M. K., & Mohanta, B. K. (2022). Performance Analysis of ML Techniques in Identification of Fake News. *2022 International Conference on Sustainable Computing and Data Communication Systems (ICSCDS)*, Erode, India. 10.1109/ICSCDS53736.2022.9760905

Wang, L., & Cheng, J. (2020). Robust disturbance rejection methodology for unstable non-minimum phase systems via disturbance observer. *ISA Transactions, 100*, 1–12. doi:10.1016/j.isatra.2019.11.034 PMID:31818485

Wang, X., Peng, Y., Lu, L., Lu, Z., Bagheri, M., & Summers, R. M. (2017). Chestx-ray8: Hospital-scale chest x-ray database and benchmarks on weakly-supervised classification and localization of common thorax diseases. In *Proceedings of the IEEE conference on computer vision and pattern recognition* (pp. 2097-2106). IEEE. 10.1109/CVPR.2017.369

Xie, X., Cheng, G., Wang, J., Yao, X., & Han, J. (2021). Oriented R-CNN for object detection. In *Proceedings of the IEEE/CVF International Conference on Computer Vision* (pp. 3520-3529). IEEE.

Yan, Y., Mao, Y., & Li, B. (2018). Second: Sparsely embedded convolutional detection. *Sensors (Basel), 18*(10), 3337. doi:10.3390/s18103337 PMID:30301196

Zheng, M., Zhi, K., Zeng, J., Tian, C., & You, L. (2022). A hybrid CNN for image denoising. *Journal of Artificial Intelligence and Technology, 2*(3), 93–99.

Chapter 4
Cracking the Code:
Creating an Immersive Learning Environment Through a Digital Escape Room Adventure

Thivashini B. Jaya Kumar
https://orcid.org/0000-0002-3265-3191
Taylor's University, Malaysia

Thanuja Rathakrishnan
https://orcid.org/0000-0002-5470-8931
Taylor's University, Malaysia

ABSTRACT

Escape rooms are a cutting-edge method of evaluating student learning because they give them a scenario in which they must solve issues and solve puzzles using numerous clues and contextual suggestions. The chapter intends to explore a discussion and reflection on the potential of immersive learning environments for formative assessments (escape room as a quiz) in enhancing students' learning experiences. The theoretical framework, the idea of an escape room, and how it might improve the learning process will be covered at the beginning of the chapter. This study employed a quasi-experimental design to investigate the effects of quiz format (digital quiz vs. digital escape room) on academic performance. Finally, the chapter discusses the potential challenges and limitations of escape room games in education. The chapter concludes by highlighting the insights, practical guidance, and future directions for educators interested in implementing escape room games in their teaching.

INTRODUCTION

Gamification in all its manifestations, including game-based learning, is rising in popularity within the educational system. One of the reasons is that playing educational games allows students to feel playfulness, which inspires them. The social aspect of games, which encourages student cooperation, is

DOI: 10.4018/978-1-6684-9576-6.ch004

another factor. One such game in game-based learning is the escape room. Over the past few years, the phenomenon of escape rooms has skyrocketed in popularity.

Escape rooms were first created as a type of physical adventure game, but they have since expanded into many other areas. In educational settings, these games have the potential to have an enormous influence (Vidergor, 2021). When employed in an educational setting, they can be used right there in the classroom, transforming it into an escape room where students are exposed to a timely narrative that must be resolved in groups within a set amount of time. The students are faced with a hurdle because they must find codes and unlock boxes in order to crack the case. Another difficult scenario is when the escape room game is made available to students digitally online and asks them to work together from home to solve a case involving a subject they have covered in class, depending on an internet connection, and restricting face-to-face interaction. Escape rooms are a cutting-edge method of evaluating student learning because they give them a scenario in which they must solve issues and solve puzzles using numerous clues and contextual suggestions (LaPaglia, 2020). Escape games are a fantastic way to encourage student engagement and learning since they place a strong emphasis on problem-solving, critical thinking, and teamwork.

This chapter will examine the benefits and challenges of using escape games in education, as well as practical considerations for implementation. In higher education, management and marketing modules are significant because they give students a thorough understanding of key business concepts, such as management theories, decision-making, and marketing tactics. Innovation and originality are now essential to the success of any business organization due to the increased competition and the necessity to keep ahead of the competitors in the market. As a result, combining cutting-edge teaching methods can help students achieve a competitive edge. This chapter investigates the use of escape rooms as a test in higher education management module.

Due to the novelty of the escape room concept, there is a dearth of research studying the usage of escape rooms in educational settings. Recently published research on escape rooms frequently discusses design or logistics (Clarke et al., 2017; Duggins, 2019; Karageorgiou, Mavrommati, & Fotaris, 2019; Merx, Veldkamp, & van Winden, 2020); and focus on higher education in general (Fotaris & Mstoras, 2019). In the higher education sector, educational escape rooms have been used with success in the subjects of nursing (Adams et al., 2018; Gómez-Urquiza et al,2019), pharmacy (Cain, 2019), chemistry (Dietrich, 2018), computer networks (Borrego, Fernández, Blanes, & Robles, 2017), and computer programming (Lopez-Pernas et al., 2019), computer education (Borrego et al., 2017), engineering (Queiruga-Dios et al., 2020), and medicine (Jambhekar, Pahls, & Deloney, 2020).

With the sole purpose of exercising soft skills like teamwork, leadership, and communication, some instructors have also run escape rooms that are strictly for fun (their puzzles don't have any educational content). However, earlier study has not adequately addressed students' perspectives of the use of educational escape rooms for teaching management module. The objective of the current study was to fill in knowledge gaps regarding educational escape rooms and their effects on management students. It concentrated on the impact of using a digital escape room for learning in higher education and tried to comprehend the effects on the gaming experience, student collaboration, and student motivation, as well as their influence by grade. Researchers and educators interested in the effects of virtual escape rooms and how they may be used as teaching aids in online learning environments may find this study to be insightful.

BACKGROUND

Formative Assessments

Formative assessments, which are part of the regular teaching and learning cycle, offer prompt feedback as well as chances for improvement. Furthermore, formative evaluations combined with immersive learning environments can change the way students learn and promote an experience pedagogy (Schildkamp et al., 2020). Through the creation of a gamified environment that motivates them to think creatively, pose questions, and participate in an exciting learning experience, immersive learning environments awaken students' curiosity and motivation.

Quizzes are typically viewed as a tiresome task that students must do to obtain a mark. However, escape rooms provide conventional quizzes with a novel twist by giving students a difficult but enjoyable experience. With the advancement of technology, teachers are continuously looking for fresh approaches to enthuse students about learning and give assessments more significance. Digital escape rooms used as classroom quizzes is one creative strategy. By posing real-world scenarios and asking them to use the principles they have learnt throughout the programme, they assess students' understanding of the subject.

For students, educators can create an interactive and interesting learning environment by using digital escape rooms as quizzes. Students are motivated to actively participate in the learning process and are more likely to remember material when game-based learning is incorporated into the curriculum. Digital escape rooms can also be customized for topic areas and academic objectives. Overall, the use of digital escape rooms as quizzes in the classroom has the potential to improve student engagement, promote critical thinking skills, and provide meaningful assessment opportunities for educators.

Game-Based Learning

Design components that produce a playful experience help game-based learning by facilitating affective, behavioral, cognitive, and social/cultural engagement factors (Plass, Homer, & Kinzer, 2015). There are two categories of learning games: those made for educational reasons and those made for commercial usage, according to Stewart et al. (2013). Games that are primarily designed to educate or teach people typically combine demanding activities that need focus with the enjoyment that comes from using one's talents to the fullest (Makri et al., 2021). A game-based learning strategy may be useful in helping students build 21st-century skills, according to Qian and Clark (2016).

Game-based learning offers numerous benefits that contribute to its effectiveness. First, games offer a secure and encouraging learning environment that lets students try new things, make mistakes, and learn from them without worrying about the repercussions. As a result, there is an uptick in motivation and involvement among students. Second, games encourage active learning by requiring students to engage with the material. This practical method encourages greater comprehension and memory of the material. Thirdly, games frequently include customized feedback mechanisms that let students pinpoint their areas of progress and modify their learning techniques as necessary.

A number of variables have been found to have an impact on game-based learning results. According to Hainey et al. (2011), learner attributes including motivation and prior gaming experience can have a big impact on engagement and performance. The design of the game itself also affects student engagement and cognitive load, including the storyline, game mechanics, and difficulty levels (Koivisto & Hamari, 2019). Additionally, the facilitator's involvement in providing game-based learning experiences is vital. Support and direction provided by the instructor have an impact on students' motivation and comprehension (Becker et al., 2020).

Escape Room

Escape rooms are utilized as a game-based activity or as a game-like experience to encourage learning. While gamification employs game aspects and thinking to boost motivation and enhance problem solving, game-based learning is described as learning while playing or gaming (Ceker & Ozdamh, 2017; Chapman & Rich, 2018). According to Nicholson (2015), a combination of several activities with recurring themes, such as treasure hunts, adventure games, television shows, live action role-playing, interactive theatre, haunted houses, and video games, gave rise to the escape room concept.

In Japan, recreational escape rooms were first utilized in 2007 (Corkill, 2009), and their popularity skyrocketed in 2012–2013. It has been said that escape rooms are "live-action collaborative games where players discover clues, resolve puzzles, and achieve a specific goal (usually escaping from a room) in a brief duration of time" (Nicholson, 2015). 'Escapes' from a room were the main objectives of first-generation escape room games. The objectives are now more varied; players can open a safe, investigate a murder, or neutralize an explosive device. Escape rooms are being adopted by enthusiastic teachers as teaching and learning settings in education (Veldkamp et al., 2020).

The nature of escape rooms as team-based games tends to ensure that each player is engaged and able to contribute (Wiemker et al., 2015). All tasks in an escape room are referred to as puzzles, and they follow a straightforward formula: a problem to solve, a reward (such as the key to a lock or information needed for the next puzzle), and an obstacle to overcome. Players need abilities like seeking, observation, correlation, memorization, math, reading, pattern identification, and compartmentalization to solve cognitive problems in escape rooms, according to Nicholson (2015). When it comes to solving the riddles, a gamemaster may give players tips and briefings on the procedure and their progress.

Educational Escape Rooms

Escape rooms have recently started to appear in classrooms all across the world, from primary education to professional development (Fotaris and Mastoras, 2019; Veldkamp et al., 2020). Similar to recreational escape rooms, a team must complete a mix of physical and mental activities in a short amount of time. These puzzles are content-based activities found in educational escape rooms. For example, when it is unclear how to solve the task, clues are hidden, or essential information needs to be found. According to Glava and Stacik (2017), López-Pernas et al. (2019), and Peleg et al. (2019), completing one task frequently results in the availability of a new task, piece of information, or tool. Locks only unlock if a task is successfully completed. With this framework, students receive rapid feedback on whether their response is valid. This is seen by Monaghan and Nicholson (2017) as one of the escape room's potent features.

Typically regarded as thematic games, escape room games are described as games in which players, working as a group, are trapped in a room and must solve a series of puzzles, to achieve a goal which leads to escaping the room within allocated time limit (Beguin et al., 2019). It is thought of as a metaphorically "locked" classroom that is used for peer collaboration in particular educational environments. Educational escape rooms are described as rooms that incorporate a portion of the module materials or chapters within the puzzles which require students to master these materials in order to solve the puzzles and succeed in the escaping the room (Lopez-Pernas et al., 2019b). Escape room can also be used to describe replicas of reality as simulated situations where students must work together as a group to "escape" the scenario in a given amount of time. They may be used to assess a team's capacity for collaboration and offer a chance for both individual and group-focused learning reflection (Baker et al., 2020).

Botturi and Babazadeh (2020) developed a star model indicating that the educational escape rooms have five elements including the narrative, which is the story of the game scenario, the game flow refer as the structure of the game, the puzzles refer as the type of problems or questions implemented, equipment items such as locks, keys, hints and lastly the learning process, objective of the game. Another two important aspects comprising pre-learning goals and their post evaluation of the experience were introduced by Clarke et al. (2017) in their model. Figure 1 shows the seven elements of developing an escape room.

Goals for educational escape rooms should be divided into game goals and instructional goals, according to Veldkamp and van de Grint (2020). They advocate integrating escape rooms into the curriculum and conducting a thorough assessment of student progress is vital. Eukel and Morrell (2020) propose a cycle design approach to support learning and evaluation that entails planning and designing, piloting, evaluating, redesigning, re-evaluating, and repetition in order to foster deep learning and favorable student impressions. Figure 2 shows the cycle design approach of the escape room.

There are obstacles to overcome in the creation of an educational escape room (Botturi & Babazadeh, 2020), such as a lack of funding, time commitment, and classroom space. They added that teachers should take into account the preparation stage, testing of the game and riddles, and post-game debriefing stage. The limited number of participants that can participate in an on-site activity during a single session, the need to multiply materials to accommodate the number of participants, the supervision of the game by at least one guide who is familiar with it, and the careful integration of the learning context into the various riddles are additional difficulties or limitations mentioned by Guigon, Humeau, and Vermeulen (2018). Digital educational escape rooms were created in response to the challenges with physical escape rooms.

Figure 1. The seven elements of developing an escape room

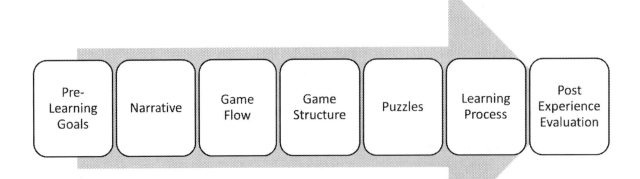

Figure 2. The cycle design approach for an escape room

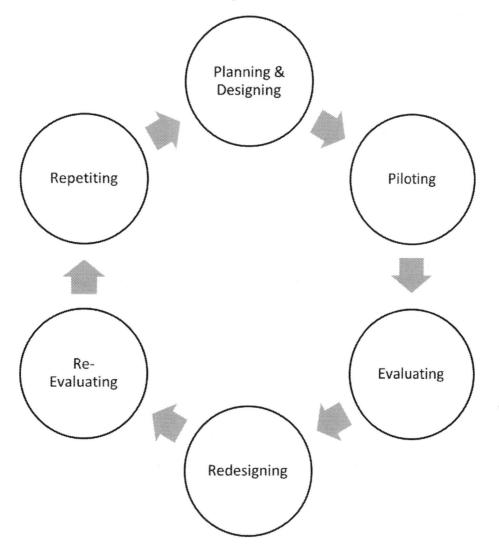

Digital Escape Room

Digital technology's rise has transformed many elements of education, including the introduction of cutting-edge instructional techniques like educational escape rooms. To get students involved in active learning, a digital educational escape room combines elements of game-based learning and problem-solving. Virtual, immersive learning experiences called "digital educational escape rooms" are intended to foster participation and critical thinking abilities. Students must solve challenges, puzzles, and riddles in order to advance in these gamified learning environments.

Students can work together, interact, and improve their problem-solving skills in a digital context by participating in these escape rooms using online platforms, smartphone applications, or virtual reality environments. It is possible to use digital escape rooms, which can result in flexible learning experiences, cost-effectiveness, accessibility, and ease of use in virtual learning settings. In an online learning environment, digital escape rooms are immersive, captivating, dynamic, and activity focused. They imitate a succession of locks that must be opened, riddles that must be solved, and adventures that must be carried out using a variety of free web-based applications. (Kroski, 2020). Digital escape rooms are a novel method to incorporate technology and critical thinking into online learning, and they have numerous advantages. Dedication to a learning environment is accomplished, and interaction through collaboration aids in the development of social skills in students.

The effects of digital educational escape rooms on student learning outcomes have been evaluated in several research. Positive outcomes have been found in the research, with better academic achievement, more knowledge retention, and improved problem-solving skills. Firstly, digital educational escape rooms have gained recognition as cutting-edge learning resources that encourage motivation and involvement in students. According to a study by Vega-Canaveras et al. (2019), students were more inspired to actively engage in the learning process and had a good perception of gamified digital escape rooms. According to meta-analytic data, gamification enhances learning and motivation (Sailer & Homner, 2020). According to authors, games and gamification are employed in education because students' enthusiasm for learning can be increased and they can reach a state of flow while playing, which sharpens their focus. This is because traditional classroom instruction can be dull. Intrinsic and extrinsic motivation are the two fundamental constructs that make up motivation. The desire to carry out an action for oneself is referred to as intrinsic motivation. Players that are intrinsically motivated do so either out of a desire to learn more about the game and develop their skills, or because they love the excitement and intense feelings it evokes (Lafreniere, Verner-Filion, & Vallera, 2012). Extrinsic motivation refers to doing something for a purpose other than enjoyment. As a result, extrinsically motivated people engage in an activity in order to gain something favourable or avoid a disadvantage (Lafreniere, Verner-Filion, & Vallera, 2012).

Secondly, gamified components are frequently used in digital educational escape rooms to increase student engagement. An ensemble made up of the player's sensations, thoughts, feelings, actions, and meaning making in a gameplay setting is how the term "game experience" is used. Although enjoyment could be viewed as both a result and a component of the gaming experience, it must be distinguished from both (Hogberg, Hamari, & Wastlund, 2019). Gamified services are designed to have effects that continue after the game is over. They incorporated elements like achievement, challenge, competitiveness, guided use, and immersion. Games for learning purposes could also fit inside the concept and elements listed above. Challenge, according to Vorderer, Klimmt, and Ritterfeld (2004), is related to the degree of difficulty of the game, which tests players' skills and motivates them to succeed. Hamari and colleagues (2016) discovered that the game's difficulty had a beneficial impact on learning both directly and through elevated engagement. They came to the conclusion that the design of educational games needs to take the game's level of difficulty into account in order to foster ongoing learning in game-based learning environments.

Thirdly, digital educational escape rooms are now acknowledged as revolutionary learning tools that promote student collaboration. According to a research by Thompson (2018), digital escape rooms encourage group problem-solving among students, which in turn fosters collaborative learning. The author also emphasized how virtual escape rooms may improve classroom instruction and better prepare students for the demands of the job market in the future. Collaboration promotes teamwork, which gives students a sense of importance (Sailer & Homner, 2020), as well as allowing students to master obstacles they otherwise might not be able to handle on their own. This can foster feelings of competence. This implies that game experience and teamwork are closely related.

Last but not least, online educational escape rooms give chances for formative assessment and quick feedback in addition to opportunities for active learning. Digital escape rooms were studied as a potential assessment tool in a higher education setting by Corcoran and White (2020). The researchers discovered that digital escape rooms might efficiently gauge students' comprehension of the material covered in class and offer pertinent feedback to aid in their learning. The use of digital educational escape rooms has been linked to a number of advantages, including greater student motivation and engagement, higher critical thinking abilities, and increased student collaboration. The gamification of these escape rooms has been continuously demonstrated in research to help pupils pay better attention, concentrate better, and retain information. Additionally, it has been demonstrated that using digital educational escape rooms can help students acquire important 21st-century abilities including creativity, communication, cooperation, and critical thinking.

METHODOLOGY AND RESULT

Research Design

This study employed a quasi-experimental design to investigate the effects of quiz format (digital quiz vs. digital escape room) on academic performance. The type of quiz (digital quiz vs. digital escape room) will be the independent variable, and the quiz results will be the dependent variable. Traditional quizzes will be given to the control group, whereas digital quizzes based on an escape room will be given to the experimental group.

Quantitative techniques of data collecting will be used to give researchers a more complete picture of the success of employing online quizzes as digital escape rooms in the classroom. Pre-test and post-test quiz results from both the control and experimental groups will be used to gather quantitative data. The purpose of the tests is to gauge the students' knowledge and comprehension of the subject matter given in class. A spreadsheet will contain the quiz results for later analysis.

Participants

The study involved 100 undergraduate students from a university enrolled in a management module. This study aims to investigate the effectiveness of using digital escape rooms as a quiz in the classroom. To achieve this, the participants in this study will be split into two groups—a control group and an experimental group.

The distribution of participants among the groups was done at random to ensure fairness while eliminating bias. Students are assigned to groups at random, following no discernible or systematic pattern. By distributing the groups randomly, the potential impact of confounding variables is reduced, and the groups are as similar as feasible prior to the intervention.

By lowering the possibility of bias and supplying a more trustworthy foundation for making results, this randomization approach contributes to improving the internal validity of the study. Participants were randomly assigned to either the control group (n=50) or the experimental group (n=50). An equal number of people will be in both groups, and they will both take identical quizzes on the same subjects.

Procedure

The study was conducted following steps shown below in Figure 3.

All participants took a pre-test to gauge their academic background at the start of the study (pre-test). To make sure that participants' initial levels of knowledge of the study's subject were comparable, this pre-test was given to both the control and experimental groups. After the pre-test followed the intervention, in which the experimental group received a digital escape room quiz while the control group received a traditional digital quiz. The topic, degree of difficulty, and time restriction were the same for both types of quizzes, which each featured 12 questions. Both the control group and experimental group then completed the quiz using personal devices (such as computers, cellphones, and tablets) on a web-based platform. To maintain consistency and get rid of any potential day-of-the-week effects, the tests were given at the same time. Participants were given instructions on how to access and complete the quiz. Finally, a post-test was given to both the control and experimental groups after the quizzes had been finished in order to evaluate the academic results. This post-test, which was the same as the pre-test, was used to assess how well academic performance had improved following the quiz intervention.

Data Analysis

Descriptive statistics, such as mean and standard deviation, were computed independently for the control and experimental groups in order to evaluate the effectiveness of online quizzes. To determine whether there were any notable changes between the groups, the pre- and post-test mean scores were compared using independent t-tests. The practical significance of the observed results was also evaluated using effect size measures like Cohen's d.

The research design, participant selection, steps, and data analysis strategy for a study using a quasi-experimental design, with a control group using a traditional digital quiz and an experimental group using a digital escape room, were all discussed in this section. The investigation that follows will shed light on how quiz structure affects academic performance.

Overall Performance

The mean scores and corresponding standard deviation (SD) must be considered when contrasting the performance of the experimental and control groups. We can identify any performance disparities and reach judgements about the usefulness of the digital escape room in comparison to the digital quiz by examining these indicators. The analysis showed a statistically significant difference in the mean post-test scores between the experimental group and control group (M = 78.2, SD = 6.2 vs. M = 72.4, SD = 5.8), with a p-value < 0.001. Digital escape room quizzes have a sizable practical impact on student learning outcomes, according to the effect size calculation (Cohen's d = 0.93). These results imply that

Figure 3. The steps conducted for the study

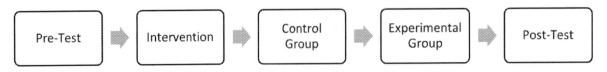

the addition of digital escape rooms enhanced academic performance in the experimental group relative to the control group.

Results Summary

Several important conclusions were drawn after data analysis. First, it was discovered that both the escape room quiz and the digital quiz were capable of assessing the learning outcomes of students. In terms of motivation, engagement, and performance, however, subtle differences were found. Below are more details about these distinctions.

Engagement and Motivation

Compared to a digital quiz, the escape room quiz seems to increase student engagement and motivation because it is an interactive and immersive tool. Due to the fact that the escape room quiz involved teamwork, problem-solving, and critical thinking skills, students engaged more enthusiastically and actively. The digital quiz, in comparison, lacked the same level of engagement, which could have lowered motivation and resulted in fewer successful learning results.

Immediate Feedback and Learning

The experimental group received fast feedback from the escape room quiz, enabling the students to quickly recognize and correct their errors. This feature of the escape room most likely helped the students learn and understand the material better. Although a digital quiz also provides immediate feedback, doing so after the complete test may impair the learning process for the students in the control group.

Time Efficiency

We observed the potential time benefits obtained from the escape room by comparing how long it took the control and experimental groups to finish their quizzes. According to the analysis, the experimental group finished the test about 20% quicker than the control group did. This result is partially attributable to the escape room's expedited assessment process, which included automated grading and fast feedback. Additionally, it was noted that despite having the chance to retake the questions on the digital quiz, students did not do so. In contrast, students in the escape room continuously tried the questions to get the correct answers and eventually succeeded in escaping the room.

Performance Comparisons

Interesting findings were obtained from the analysis of student performance. The knowledge retention was successfully examined by both the digital quiz and the escape room quiz, but the experimental group (escape room quiz) performed marginally better. This shows that the escape room quiz can promote a deeper comprehension and application of acquired concepts due to its gamified and immersive nature.

Retention and Transfer of Knowledge

Notably, compared to the digital quiz, the escape room quiz seems to encourage higher information retention and transfer. Students probably had a more memorable learning experience thanks to the immersive and engaging aspect of the escape room atmosphere, which allowed them to relate concepts to practical applications. The digital quiz, on the other hand, might have limited students to a recall-based assessment.

DISCUSSION

The purpose of this section is to encourage discussion and thought on how immersive learning settings, such as an escape room used as a quiz, might improve students' learning experiences.

First off, the capacity to improve student engagement is one advantage of employing escape rooms as quizzes. Digital quizzes frequently lack enthusiasm, which causes students to lose interest or put less effort into studying. On the other hand, escape rooms offer a lively and engaging learning environment that has proven to be quite successful in attracting students' attention. Students are motivated to engage because the escape room puzzles are difficult, which increases retention and motivation. The findings of this study are consistent with those of Vega-Canaveras et al.'s research (2019), which found that gamified digital escape rooms increased students' motivation to actively participate in their studies. Second, escape rooms are made to be psychologically challenging by asking players to solve puzzles, crack codes, and exercise critical thinking. Instructors can evaluate their students' problem-solving abilities and their capacity for creative thought under duress by employing escape rooms as quiz questions. These activities encourage imaginative problem-solving strategies, critical thinking, and logical reasoning—skills that are important for both academic achievement and future professions. The findings of this study are consistent with a study by Thompson (2018), which found that students use problem-solving and critical thinking to solve problems in digital escape rooms.

Thirdly, escape rooms naturally foster teamwork and collaboration, which are vital abilities in today's interconnected society. Digital tests sometimes involve solo work, which limits pupils' exposure to group problem-solving situations. Quizzes using escape rooms, on the other hand, call for teamwork, excellent communication, and the use of the individual strengths of each team member. This collaborative aspect improves social skills, fosters trust, and enriches the learning process as a whole. The study's findings are in line with those of Sailer and Homner (2020), who found that collaboration fosters teamwork, which provides students a sense of importance and helps them overcome challenges they otherwise might not be able to overcome on their own. Fourthly, quizzes have historically been seen by many students as stress-inducing and anxiety-provoking experiences. But using escape rooms as tests instead of scheduled, graded exams turns the exercise into a team-building exercise. The usefulness of escape rooms as tests encourages intrinsic motivation and frees students from undue stress to enjoy the process of learning and problem-solving. Following the escape room experience, there is an opportunity for constructive criticism and positive reinforcement, highlighting the students' successes and areas for development.

Finally, the escape room quiz examines students' subject-specific knowledge as well as their ability to apply that information in a practical setting. Escape room riddles can be customized to match the information being assessed, ensuring that the assessment is in line with the objectives of the curriculum. By doing this, teachers can urge students to show their understanding through real-world problem-solving situations rather than the more common multiple-choice questions. The study analysis is consistent with Corcoran and White (2020), who also investigated the use of digital escape rooms as a potential evaluation tool in a higher education setting. Digital escape rooms may effectively assess students' understanding of the content given in class and provide useful feedback to support their learning, according to the researchers.

Digital Escape Room. vs Digital Quiz

Teachers are continuously looking for novel approaches to include their students in interactive and enjoyable learning experiences in the age of rapid technological advancement and remote learning. Digital quizzes and digital escape room quizzes are two well-liked possibilities. Both aim to improve learning results, but they are different in terms of format, gameplay, chance for collaboration, and customizability.

Firstly, the formats of digital quizzes and digital escape room quizzes are different. A multiple-choice quiz with a time limit can be created by educators online using the digital quiz platform, and students can take the quiz in real-time using their devices. Digital escape room quizzes, on the other hand, mimic the feeling of solving puzzles and completing tasks in a virtual escape room environment. To move forward, students must complete each of the activities that are given to them in order. Digital escape room quizzes have a format that naturally lends itself to a more immersive and engaging experience, enabling a deeper connection with the subject matter. The second feature that is different between digital quiz and escape room quiz is the gameplay. Digital quiz gameplay moves quickly, is competitive, and is based on player performance. In order to earn points and surpass their peers, students are motivated to respond to questions accurately and promptly. The leaderboard function ups the excitement level and promotes friendly competition. Digital escape room quizzes, on the other hand, depend on cooperation and teamwork. To accomplish a common objective, students collaborate to solve puzzles and uncover hints. This cooperative character encourages the development of communication, analytical thinking, and problem-solving skills.

Thirdly, collaborative potential is the next difference between digital quiz and escape room quiz. While digital quizzes are primarily intended for individual participation, team mode allows them to be changed into a collaborative activity. Students can form teams and compete together while combining their knowledge and abilities. But the competitive aspect of digital quizzes frequently inhibits teamwork and emphasizes individual success. Digital escape room games, on the other hand, are designed to encourage cooperation and teamwork. Due to the difficulty of the obstacles, students must work together, foster communication, delegate tasks, and support one another. The next key difference between digital quizzes and escape room quiz is customization. Digital escape room quizzes and digital quizzes both provide personalization choices, but in different ways. With digital quizzes, educators may design custom assessments for a range of subjects and grade levels. To improve the learning process, educators can add images, videos, and other multimedia components. Digital escape room quizzes, on the other hand, allow for customisation through original storytelling and theme choice. Themes and difficulties can be altered by teachers to better fit the learning objectives, resulting in a more immersive and interesting experience.

Last but not least, one further difference between a digital quiz and a digital escape room is the atmosphere. Digital quizzes are renowned for their colourful graphics, upbeat music, and rapid-fire format, which grabs students' attention and fosters a stimulating environment. Students are driven and laser-focused because of the competitive aspect, as well as the immediate feedback and prizes. But for some students, the rapid-fire pace of digital quizzes might be overwhelming, resulting in anxiety or disengagement. Digital escape room quizzes, in comparison, offer a more leisurely, suspenseful experience that immerses pupils in an engrossing narrative. The sense of accomplishment that comes from advancing through the virtual escape room and conquering obstacles is a strong motivation. The below figure shows the key difference in the setting of digital quiz and escape room quiz.

In short, there are important distinctions between digital quizzes and digital escape room quizzes. Digital quizzes thrive in terms of competitiveness that moves quickly, personal accomplishment, and customization. Digital escape room games, on the other hand, provide a more immersive and group experience, encouraging cooperation and problem-solving abilities. The digital escape room quizzes can, in the end, be used in any type of educational environment and pedagogical method. When choosing a digital escape room, educators should take into account the objectives of the class, the expected learning results, and the unique needs of their students.

CHALLENGES

Despite the numerous advantages of using digital escape rooms for formative assessment, it is important to be aware of potential challenges. To guarantee that the escape room serves as a relevant assessment of learning outcomes, educators must first make sure that the aims and content of the game are in line with the curriculum. Furthermore, it can be difficult to make sure that the escape room is accessible to all students, especially those who have disabilities or learning problems. Different learning styles must be taken into account, and students who might find the escape room challenging should be given accommodation or other options. Secondly, using a virtual escape room as a formative test might not fully represent a student's comprehension of the subject. Instead of evaluating a student's breadth of knowledge on a particular subject, digital escape rooms frequently place a premium on problem-solving and critical thinking abilities. This means that even if students have a strong comprehension of the material being

Figure 4. The key difference in the setting of digital quiz and escape room quiz

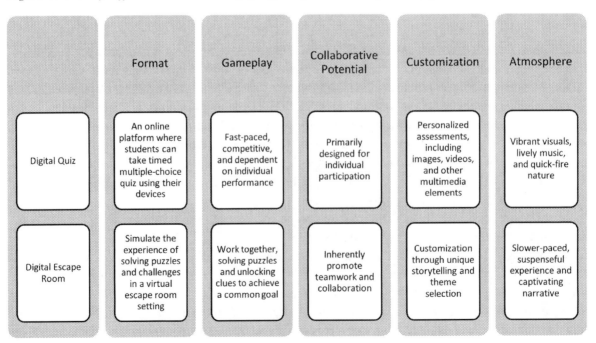

assessed, they may not score well if they have trouble with the escape room's puzzle-solving component. Additionally, the time constraints present in escape rooms could make some students feel hurried and uneasy, which might make it harder for them to show off their genuine skills.

Thirdly, producing excellent, captivating puzzles and challenges that accurately evaluate the desired learning outcomes can take time and demand a high level of instructional design knowledge. One of the biggest barriers to any innovation, whether at the individual, classroom, or school level, is time, which is a finite resource for instructors. It is therefore remarkable that so many educators find the time to modify the escape room concept for their classes. Alignment to the curriculum, testing prototypes, and organizing the gameplay are specific time-consuming parts. Although the development process takes a while, especially when compared to the amount of time spent actually working with the students, it is rewarding to observe engaged students. Finally, there may be technical issues or access issues with the escape room platform. These issues can prevent students from completing the activities and interrupt the evaluation process.

LIMITATIONS AND FUTURE DIRECTION

Several limitations of this study should be acknowledged. First, the sample consisted of undergraduate students from a single university, which may limit the generalizability of the findings. Future research with larger sample sizes and diverse populations is necessary to validate and expand upon these findings. Additionally, factors such as technological familiarity and access to digital devices may have influenced the outcomes. Future research should consider a broader and more diverse sample to strengthen the generalizability of the findings. Lastly, the study only assessed short-term effects and did not investigate long-term retention of the learned material.

CONCLUSION

Digital escape rooms have become a cutting-edge and useful formative evaluation tool in the field of education. Traditional evaluation techniques, especially when used in conjunction with remote or hybrid learning, are becoming less and less effective as technology develops. By involving students in interactive, problem-solving tasks, digital escape rooms are a useful alternative to conventional exams. These escape rooms stimulate students' interest and promote active engagement in the learning process by establishing an engaging and immersive learning environment. Additionally, digital escape rooms give educators timely insights into students' progress, allowing for personalized feedback and targeted interventions.

Additionally, digital escape rooms offer a unique advantage in assessing students' knowledge retention and application. Instead of relying solely on traditional exams or quizzes, these activities provide students with an opportunity to apply their knowledge to real-world scenarios. By incorporating authentic and relevant content, escape rooms challenge students to transfer their learning to practical contexts, thus gauging their depth of understanding and ability to apply knowledge creatively. Importantly, digital escape rooms also present a flexible and adaptable assessment tool. Educators can tailor the content, style, and difficulty level of the escape room to meet the specific needs and learning goals of their students. This adaptability allows for differentiation, ensuring that students are challenged appropriately and supported in their individual learning journeys. The cooperative atmosphere of escape rooms encourages teamwork and gets students ready for the workplace.

Additionally, using digital escape rooms to test students' recall and application of knowledge has a distinct advantage. These exercises give students the chance to apply their knowledge to real-world settings as opposed to only standard tests or quizzes. Escape rooms test students' comprehension and creative application of knowledge by presenting them with authentic and pertinent content that forces them to apply what they have learned to real-world situations. Importantly, online escape games offer an adjustable and versatile testing technique. In order to match the unique requirements and learning objectives of their students, educators can modify the escape room's content, style, and level of difficulty. By allowing for differentiation, this adaptability makes sure that students are suitably challenged and supported in their unique learning journeys. Important ramifications for educational practices flow from this study. Quizzes based on escape rooms could improve student motivation, engagement, and long-term memory. However, the availability of resources and time restrictions must be taken into account when evaluating the viability and scalability of applying such approaches.

In a nutshell up, digital escape rooms have transformed formative assessment in the classroom. These exercises engage students, develop critical thinking and problem-solving abilities, encourage cooperation, and test knowledge retention and application in real-world situations thanks to their interactive and immersive character. Digital escape rooms present a viable method for efficiently involving and evaluating students as educators continue to navigate the rapidly changing educational landscape. By utilizing this cutting-edge tool, educators can design a comprehensive learning experience that equips students with the skills they need to succeed in the digital age.

REFERENCES

Adams, V., Burger, S., Crawford, K., & Setter, R. (2018). Can you escape? Creating an escape room to facilitate active learning. *Journal for Nurses in Professional Development*, *34*(2), E1–E5. doi:10.1097/NND.0000000000000433 PMID:29481471

Baker, C. M., Crabtree, G., & Anderson, K. (2020). Student pharmacist perceptions of learning after strengths-based leadership skills lab and escape room in pharmacy practice skills laboratory. *Currents in Pharmacy Teaching & Learning*, *12*(6), 724–727. doi:10.1016/j.cptl.2020.01.021 PMID:32482276

Beguin, E., Besnard, S., Cros, A., Joannes, B., Leclerc-Istria, O., Noel, A., Roels, N., Taleb, F., Thongphan, J., Alata, E., & Nicomette, V. (2019). Computer-security-oriented escape room. *IEEE Security and Privacy*, *17*(4), 78–83. doi:10.1109/MSEC.2019.2912700

Borrego, C., Fernández, C., Blanes, I., & Robles, S. (2017). Room escape at class: Escape games activities to facilitate the motivation and learning in computer science. *JOTSE*, *7*(2), 162–171. doi:10.3926/jotse.247

Botturi, L., & Babazadeh, M. (2020). Designing educational escape rooms: Validating the star model. *International Journal of Serious Games*, *7*(3), 41–57. doi:10.17083/ijsg.v7i3.367

Cain, J. (2019). Exploratory implementation of a blended format escape room in a large enrollment pharmacy management class. *Currents in Pharmacy Teaching & Learning*, *11*(1), 44–50. doi:10.1016/j.cptl.2018.09.010 PMID:30527875

Ceker, E., & Ozdamh, F. (2017). What "gamification" is and what it's not. *European Journal of Contemporary Education*, *6*(2), 221–228.

Chapman, J., & Rich, P. (2018). Does educational gamification improve students' motivation? If so, which game elements work best? *Journal of Education for Business*, *93*(7), 314–321. doi:10.1080/08832323.2018.1490687

Clarke, S., Peel, D. J., Arnab, S., Morini, L., Keegan, H., & Wood, O. (2017). escapED: A framework for creating educational escape rooms and Interactive Games For Higher/Further Education. *International Journal of Serious Games*, *4*(3), 73–86. doi:10.17083/ijsg.v4i3.180

Dietrich, N. (2018). Escape classroom: The leblanc process—an educational "Escape Game". *Journal of Chemical Education*, *95*(6), 996–999. doi:10.1021/acs.jchemed.7b00690

Duggins, R. (2019). Innovation and problem-solving teaching case: The breakout box–a desktop escape room. *Journal of Organizational Psychology*, *19*(4).

Eukel, H., & Morrell, B. (2021). Ensuring educational escape-room success: The process of designing, piloting, evaluating, redesigning, and re-evaluating educational escape rooms. *Simulation & Gaming*, *52*(1), 18–23. doi:10.1177/1046878120953453

Fotaris, P., & Mastoras, T. (2019, October). Escape rooms for learning: A systematic review. In *Proceedings of the European Conference on Games Based Learning* (pp. 235-243). IEEE.

Glavaš, A., & Staščik, A. (2017). Enhancing positive attitude towards mathematics through introducing Escape Room games. *Mathematics Education as a Science and a Profession*, *281*, 293.

Gómez-Urquiza, J. L., Gómez-Salgado, J., Albendín-García, L., Correa-Rodríguez, M., González-Jiménez, E., & Cañadas-De la Fuente, G. A. (2019). The impact on nursing students' opinions and motivation of using a "Nursing Escape Room" as a teaching game: A descriptive study. *Nurse Education Today*, *72*, 73–76. doi:10.1016/j.nedt.2018.10.018 PMID:30453202

Guigon, G., Humeau, J., & Vermeulen, M. (2018, March). A model to design learning escape games: SEGAM. In *10th International Conference on Computer Supported Education* (pp. 191-197). SCITE-PRESS-Science and Technology Publications. 10.5220/0006665501910197

Hainey, T., Connolly, T., Boyle, E., Azadegan, A., Wilson, A., Razak, A., & Gray, G. (2014, October). A systematic literature review to identify empirical evidence on the use of games-based learning in primary education for knowledge acquisition and content understanding. In *8th European Conference on Games Based Learning: ECGBL* (p. 167). IEEE.

Hamari, J., Shernoff, D. J., Rowe, E., Coller, B., Asbell-Clarke, J., & Edwards, T. (2016). Challenging games help students learn: An empirical study on engagement, flow and immersion in game-based learning. *Computers in Human Behavior*, *54*, 170–179. doi:10.1016/j.chb.2015.07.045

Högberg, J., Hamari, J., & Wästlund, E. (2019). Gameful Experience Questionnaire (GAMEFUL-QUEST): An instrument for measuring the perceived gamefulness of system use. *User Modeling and User-Adapted Interaction*, *29*(3), 619–660. doi:10.1007/s11257-019-09223-w

Jambhekar, K., Pahls, R. P., & Deloney, L. A. (2020). Benefits of an escape room as a novel educational activity for radiology residents. *Academic Radiology*, *27*(2), 276–283. doi:10.1016/j.acra.2019.04.021 PMID:31160173

Karageorgiou, Z., Mavrommati, E., & Fotaris, P. (2019, October). Escape room design as a game-based learning process for STEAM education. In *ECGBL 2019 13th European Conference on Game-Based Learning* (p. 378). Academic Conferences and publishing limited.

Kroski, E. (2020). What is a digital breakout game? *Library Technology Reports*, *56*(3), 5–7.

Lafreni'ere, M. A. K., Verner-Filion, J., & Vallerand, R. J. (2012). Development and validation of the gaming motivation scale (GAMS). *Personality and Individual Differences*, *53*(7), 827–831. doi:10.1016/j.paid.2012.06.013

LaPaglia, J. A. (2020). Escape the evil professor! Escape room review activity. *Teaching of Psychology*, *47*(2), 141–146. doi:10.1177/0098628320901383

López-Pernas, S., Gordillo, A., Barra, E., & Quemada, J. (2019). Analyzing learning effectiveness and students' perceptions of an educational escape room in a programming course in higher education. *IEEE Access : Practical Innovations, Open Solutions*, *7*, 184221–184234. doi:10.1109/ACCESS.2019.2960312

López-Pernas, S., Gordillo, A., Barra, E., & Quemada, J. (2019b). Examining the use of an educational escape room for teaching programming in a higher education setting. *IEEE Access : Practical Innovations, Open Solutions*, *7*, 31723–31737. doi:10.1109/ACCESS.2019.2902976

Makri, A., Vlachopoulos, D., & Martina, R. A. (2021). Digital escape rooms as innovative pedagogical tools in education: A systematic literature review. *Sustainability (Basel)*, *13*(8), 4587. doi:10.3390/su13084587

Merx, S., Veldkamp, A., & van Winden, J. (2020). *Educational escape rooms: Challenges in aligning game and education.*

Monaghan, S. R., & Nicholson, S. (2017). Bringing escape room concepts to pathophysiology case studies. *HAPS Educator*, *21*(2), 49–65. doi:10.21692/haps.2017.015

Nicholson, S. (2015). *Peeking behind the locked door: A survey of escape room facilities.*

Peleg, R., Yayon, M., Katchevich, D., Moria-Shipony, M., & Blonder, R. (2019). A lab-based chemical escape room: Educational, mobile, and fun! *Journal of Chemical Education*, *96*(5), 955–960. doi:10.1021/acs.jchemed.8b00406

Plass, J. L., Homer, B. D., & Kinzer, C. K. (2015). Foundations of game-based learning. *Educational Psychologist*, *50*(4), 258–283. doi:10.1080/00461520.2015.1122533

Qian, M., & Clark, K. R. (2016). Game-based learning and 21st-century skills: A review of recent research. *Computers in Human Behavior*, *63*, 50–58. doi:10.1016/j.chb.2016.05.023

Queiruga-Dios, A., Santos Sánchez, M. J., Queiruga Dios, M., Gayoso Martínez, V., & Hernández Encinas, A. (2020). A virus infected your laptop. let's play an escape game. *Mathematics, 8*(2), 166. doi:10.3390/math8020166

Sailer, M., & Homner, L. (2020). The gamification of learning: A meta-analysis. *Educational Psychology Review, 32*(1), 77–112. doi:10.1007/s10648-019-09498-w

Schildkamp, K., van der Kleij, F. M., Heitink, M. C., Kippers, W. B., & Veldkamp, B. P. (2020). Formative assessment: A systematic review of critical teacher prerequisites for classroom practice. *International Journal of Educational Research, 103*, 101602. doi:10.1016/j.ijer.2020.101602

Smith, M. M., & Davis, R. G. (2021). Can you escape? The pharmacology review virtual escape room. *Simulation & Gaming, 52*(1), 79–87. doi:10.1177/1046878120966363

Stewart, J., Bleumers, L., Van Looy, J., Mariën, I., All, A., Schurmans, D., & Misuraca, G. (2013). *The potential of digital games for empowerment and social inclusion of groups at risk of social and economic exclusion: evidence and opportunity for policy*. Joint Research Centre, European Commission.

Veldkamp, A., Daemen, J., Teekens, S., Koelewijn, S., Knippels, M. C. P., & van Joolingen, W. R. (2020). Escape boxes: Bringing escape room experience into the classroom. *British Journal of Educational Technology, 51*(4), 1220–1239. doi:10.1111/bjet.12935

Veldkamp, A., van de Grint, L., Knippels, M. C. P., & van Joolingen, W. R. (2020). Escape education: A systematic review on escape rooms in education. *Educational Research Review, 31*, 100364. doi:10.1016/j.edurev.2020.100364

Vidergor, H. E. (2021). Effects of digital escape room on gameful experience, collaboration, and motivation of elementary school students. *Computers & Education, 166*, 104156. doi:10.1016/j.compedu.2021.104156

Vorderer, P., Klimmt, C., & Ritterfeld, U. (2004). Enjoyment: At the heart of media entertainment. *Communication Theory, 14*(4), 388–408. doi:10.1111/j.1468-2885.2004.tb00321.x

Wiemker, M., Elumir, E., & Clare, A. (2015). Escape room games. *Game based learning, 55*, 55-75.

KEY TERMS AND DEFINITIONS

Digital Escape Room: Using technology (phones, tablets, or computers), the escape room concept is used to run through the scenarios and solve the challenge.

Digital Quiz: Using web platforms or published on the Internet to test knowledge.

Educational Escape Rooms: Utilized escape room concept as a game-based activity or as a game-like experience to encourage learning.

Escape Room: A room where players are locked in order to participate in a game that calls for them to solve a series of riddles in order to complete a task, usually locating the key to unlock the room.

Formative Assessments: The term "formative assessment" refers to a broad range of techniques used by teachers to assess student understanding, learning requirements, and academic achievement as they occur throughout a lesson or course.

Game-Based Learning: When learning activities incorporate game mechanics and principles, this is referred to as game-based learning.

Quizzes: A knowledge test, particularly one that serves as a type of entertainment competition between individuals or teams.

Chapter 5
Cyber Forensics:
A Boon to Cybersecurity

Sameer Saharan
 https://orcid.org/0000-0002-7487-6297
Mody University of Science and Technology, India

Shailja Singh
 https://orcid.org/0000-0002-6425-1699
Mangalayatan University, Jabalpur, India

Debasis Bora
Mandsaur University, India

Geetika Saxena
Mody University of Science and Technology, India

ABSTRACT

Cyber forensics is a vital ally in safeguarding our digital world. This abstract explores its symbiotic relationship with cybersecurity. Cyber forensics not only investigates cybercrimes, but also aids in threat detection, incident response, and risk mitigation. Technology, including AI, empowers professionals in navigating digital crime scenes. Ethical and legal considerations remain pivotal. Cyber forensics, as an indispensable part of cybersecurity, fortifies our digital landscape against evolving threats, ensuring a safer digital future.

INTRODUCTION

The advent of the Digital Age has heralded a new era of extraordinary connection, information sharing, and technological innovation. The globe has grown more interconnected than ever before, thanks to the increasing integration of digital technologies into every aspect of our lives, from communication and business to governance and healthcare (Miller & West, 2009). This fundamental transformation has provided

DOI: 10.4018/978-1-6684-9576-6.ch005

tremendous benefits, but it has also exposed individuals, businesses, and society to a slew of cybersecurity dangers that necessitate strong safeguards. Data has become the vitality of modern civilisation in this Digital Age. Data is at the centre of innumerable activities and transactions, ranging from personal information and financial records to intellectual property and national security secrets (Huang et al., 2022). However, this reliance on data-driven procedures has created a vulnerability that malevolent actors can exploit. Cyber-attacks have evolved into a sophisticated and ubiquitous threat capable of destroying key infrastructure, stealing sensitive information, and incurring worldwide financial damages. The rising frequency, complexity, and severity of cyber threats necessitates the need for cybersecurity. Malware, phishing assaults, ransomware, and Distributed Denial of Service (DDoS) attacks are just a handful of the methods used by cybercriminals to circumvent security measures and corrupt digital systems (Li & Liu, 2021). These attacks have the potential to have far-reaching implications, affecting not only individuals but potentially organisations, governments, and even entire countries. In the Digital Age, the interconnection of devices and systems magnifies the potential impact of cyber threats. The Internet of Things (IoT) has introduced a slew of networked gadgets, ranging from smart home appliances to industrial control systems, resulting in a vast attack surface (Huang et al., 2022). Furthermore, the increasing reliance on cloud computing and internet platforms has broadened the channels via which hostile actors might infiltrate networks and access sensitive data. The consequences of a successful cyberattack go beyond monetary damages. Cyber incidents have the potential to undermine trust in organisations, interrupt key services, and jeoparadize personal privacy (Sukri et al., 2023). High-profile data breaches have exposed millions of people to identity theft and financial crime, emphasising the importance of protecting digital assets. Furthermore, state-sponsored cyber-attacks and cyber espionage endanger national security by targeting sensitive information and essential infrastructure. Strong cybersecurity measures are required to solve these concerns (Sukri et al., 2023). To secure their networks and data, organisations must invest in advanced threat detection, intrusion prevention systems, and encryption techniques. Furthermore, cybersecurity awareness and training programmes are critical for educating people about the dangers of digital interactions and promoting safe online behaviour.

Cyber forensics develops as a critical and dynamic component in the arena of modern cybersecurity, where the digital terrain is riddled with ever-evolving threats. Cyber forensics, also known as digital forensics, is critical in detecting, investigating, and mitigating cybercrime, ensuring that the digital environment is secure and resilient. Incident response is one of the key functions of cyber forensics (Saharan & Yadav, 2022). When a cyber incident occurs, whether it is a data breach, a malware assault, or unauthorised access, cyber forensics specialists are entrusted with determining the extent and scale of the breach as soon as possible. They acquire and preserve digital evidence in a forensically sound manner by using specialised tools and techniques. This data not only helps to understand the attack, but it also acts as an important foundation for legal procedures. Furthermore, cyber forensics helps with cybercrime attribution. Investigators can identify cyber incidents to specific individuals, groups, or businesses by tracing the origin of assaults, discovering digital traces, and analysing malware signatures. This attribution capacity acts as a deterrent, warning potential attackers about the risks of being recognised and held accountable (Brinson et al., 2006; Saharan & Yadav, 2022). Cyber forensics role extends beyond identifying and attributing cybercrimes. It helps organisations detect vulnerabilities and flaws in their systems and networks by assisting in root cause analysis. As a result, they may strengthen their cybersecurity procedures, close gaps, and prevent repeat attacks. Cyber forensics responds to obstacles like as encryption and obfuscation techniques used by cybercriminals by creating creative approaches to unearth buried tracks. Furthermore, its ability to coordinate with law enforcement authorities across borders increases its effectiveness in tackling cybercrime on a global basis (Saharan & Yadav, 2022).

In this chapter, the primary objectives are to introduce the critical intersection of "Cyber Forensics: A Boon to Cybersecurity." The chapter begins by tracing the historical evolution of cyber forensics and its foundational principles, illuminating its pivotal role in addressing modern cyber threats. It delves into the cyber forensics process, encompassing evidence collection, preservation, analysis, and reporting, showcasing its invaluable contributions to incident response and overall cybersecurity. Moreover, the chapter sheds light on the legal and ethical framework underpinning cyber forensics, emphasizing the significance of evidence admissibility. Real-world cases illustrate its role in attributing cybercrimes and fostering accountability, while it also discusses the challenges faced by practitioners and innovative solutions. The chapter underscores the importance of public-private collaboration and concludes by exploring the future of cyber forensics, considering emerging trends and technologies that will continue to fortify digital defences. Throughout, this chapter aims to provide a comprehensive understanding of how cyber forensics serves as an indispensable boon to modern cybersecurity.

The Evolution of Cyber Threats

The evolution of cyber threats has seen a transition from basic hacking to complex, nation-state-sponsored attacks. Today's threats encompass sophisticated malware, ransomware, and social engineering. Cybercriminals continually adapt, targeting critical infrastructure, data, and individuals, making cybersecurity an ever-pressing concern in the digital age.

1. Types of cyber threats:

In present scenario there are following types of cyber threats (Figure 1):

Malware: Malware, short for "malicious software," encompasses a wide range of harmful software programs that can infiltrate computer systems and cause damage (Pachhala et al., 2021). These include:

Viruses: These programs attach themselves to legitimate software or files, and when executed, they replicate and spread. This can lead to the corruption of data or system files.

Worms: Worms are self-replicating malware that can spread across networks and systems without any user interaction. They can rapidly consume network bandwidth and resources.

Trojans: Often disguised as legitimate software, Trojans deceive users into installing them. Once installed, they can provide unauthorized access to the attacker.

Ransomware: Ransomware encrypts a victim's data and demands a ransom for the decryption key. It can lead to data loss and financial extortion.

Spyware: Spyware secretly gathers user information and transmits it to attackers. It can be used for purposes such as stealing login credentials or monitoring user activities.

Adware: Adware displays unwanted advertisements on a user's device, often bundled with legitimate software. While not as malicious as other malware types, it can be intrusive and compromise user experience.

Phishing: Phishing attacks involve cybercriminals impersonating trustworthy entities, often via email, to deceive individuals into revealing sensitive information or taking malicious actions (Chiew et al., 2018). This can include:

Figure 1. Types of cyber threats

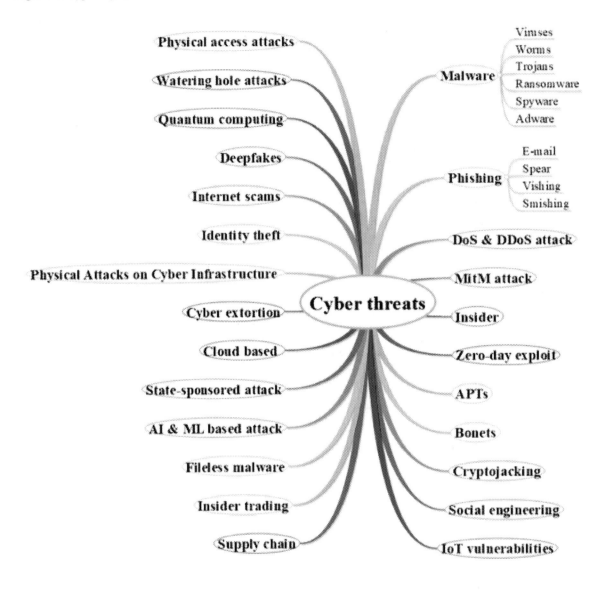

Email Phishing: Cybercriminals send fraudulent emails that appear to be from legitimate sources, typically with links to fake websites that capture login credentials.

Spear Phishing: A targeted form of phishing, where attackers tailor their messages to specific individuals or organizations, making them more convincing and harder to detect.

Vishing: Short for "voice phishing," this method involves attackers using phone calls to impersonate trusted entities, such as banks or tech support, to extract personal information.

Smishing: Phishing via SMS or text messages, where attackers send fraudulent messages containing malicious links or requests for personal information.[REMOVED INCLUDEPICTURE FIELD]

Denial of Service (DoS) and Distributed Denial of Service (DDoS) Attacks: Denial of Service attacks aim to disrupt a target's services, rendering them unavailable to users. DDoS attacks involve multiple compromised devices, coordinated to flood a target with traffic, overwhelming its capacity to respond (Eliyan & Di Pietro, 2021).

Man-in-the-Middle (MitM) Attacks: In MitM attacks, attackers secretly intercept and potentially alter communications between two parties without their knowledge. This can occur in unsecured Wi-Fi networks or through compromised routers (Cekerevac et al., 2017).

Insider Threats: Insider threats refer to malicious actions or data breaches initiated by individuals within an organization. These insiders can be employees, contractors, or business partners, who have accesssensitive data (Santosa et al., 2016).

Zero-Day Exploits: Zero-day exploits target vulnerabilities in software or hardware that are unknown to the vendor or lack available patches. Cybercriminals leverage these vulnerabilities before they are discovered and addressed (Santosa et al., 2016).

Advanced Persistent Threats (APTs): APTs are highly coordinated and sophisticated attacks, often state-sponsored. They involve long-term, stealthy intrusions into systems for data theft, espionage, or sabotage (Santosa et al., 2016).

Botnets: Botnets are networks of compromised devices, controlled by a central server. Cybercriminals use them for various malicious activities, including DDoS attacks and spam email distribution (Santosa et al., 2016).

Cryptojacking: Cryptojacking involves the illicit use of a victim's computing resources to mine cryptocurrencies. This often occurs through malware infections, slowing down affected devices (Tekiner et al., 2021).

Social Engineering: Social engineering tactics manipulate individuals into revealing confidential information or performing actions against their best interests. It includes techniques like pretexting, baiting, or tailgating.

Internet of Things (IoT) Vulnerabilities: Weak security in IoT devices can lead to unauthorized access and data breaches, as cybercriminals target these devices to gain entry into networks (Cekerevac et al., 2017; Madakam et al., 2015). There are many reasons for IoT vulnerabilities (Figure 2).

Figure 2. Reasons of IoT vulnerabilities

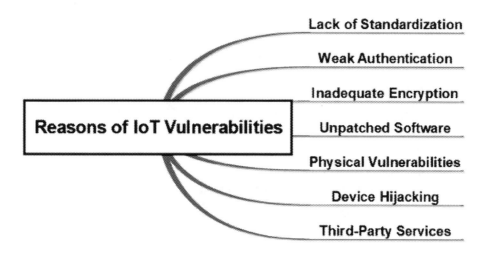

Supply Chain Attacks: Supply chain attacks exploit vulnerabilities in an organization's supply chain to compromise the security of the end product. Attackers may target software updates, third-party vendors, or hardware components to infiltrate systems.

Insider Trading: Insider trading involves illegally trading securities based on non-public information obtained from a data breach or data leak, potentially leading to financial fraud and legal consequences.

Fileless Malware: Fileless malware operates in memory without leaving traces on a victim's file system. This makes it challenging to detect with traditional antivirus software.

AI and Machine Learning-Based Attacks: Attackers employ AI and machine learning to enhance their tactics, creating more convincing phishing emails or automating attacks for greater efficiency (Yamin et al., 2021).

State-Sponsored Cyberattacks: Governments engage in cyber espionage, cyber warfare, or cybercrime to achieve political, economic, or military objectives, often using advanced techniques and resources (Prasad et al., 2020).

Cyber Extortion: Cyber extortion involves threatening to reveal sensitive information or launch a cyberattack unless a ransom is paid, exploiting fear and urgency.

Cloud-Based Threats: Cloud-based threats target vulnerabilities in cloud services or data stored in the cloud. These attacks can include data breaches or unauthorized access to cloud resources (Prasad et al., 2020).

Physical Attacks on Cyber Infrastructure: Physical attacks involve sabotaging data centers, servers, or networking equipment to disrupt services and compromise data security.

Identity Theft: Identity theft is the theft of personal information to commit fraud, open accounts, or conduct other criminal activities in the victim's name, often resulting in financial losses and reputational damage.

Internet Scams: Internet scams encompass a wide range of fraudulent schemes, including lottery scams, romance scams, and tech support scams, designed to deceive individuals for financial gain (Chiew et al., 2018).

Deepfakes: Deepfakes use AI to create convincing fake audio or video content, potentially damaging reputations or spreading misinformation (Yamin et al., 2021).

Quantum Computing Threats: Quantum computing threats are theoretical risks to current encryption methods posed by future quantum computers capable of breaking encryption algorithms (Denning, 2019).

Watering Hole Attacks: Watering hole attacks target websites or online platforms frequented by specific users. Malware is injected into these sites, infecting visitors (Alrwais et al., 2016).

Physical Access Attacks: Physical access attacks involve gaining unauthorized physical access to devices or systems, compromising security through direct tampering or theft.

NOTABLE CYBERSECURITY INCIDENTS AND BREACHES

Equifax (2017): In 2017, Equifax, one of the largest credit reporting agencies, suffered a massive data breach, considered one of the most significant in history. The breach exposed the personal information of approximately 147 million Americans. Attackers exploited a vulnerability in Equifax's web application software to gain unauthorized access to sensitive data, including Social Security numbers, birthdates, and credit card information. The fallout from this breach included numerous lawsuits, regulatory fines, and significant damage to Equifax's reputation, highlighting the dire consequences of lax cybersecurity measures (Wang & Johnson, 2018).

Yahoo (2013-2014): Yahoo, a prominent internet company, faced two major data breaches between 2013 and 2014, impacting more than a billion user accounts. These breaches, disclosed in 2016, involved stolen data such as names, email addresses, and hashed passwords. The incidents severely affected user trust and had financial repercussions, leading to a lower acquisition price when Verizon acquired Yahoo's core internet operations (Trautman & Ormerod, 2016).

Target (2013): In 2013, Target, a leading U.S. retailer, experienced a high-profile data breach that ultimately compromised the personal and financial information of over 40 million customers. Attackers gained access to Target's network through a third-party HVAC contractor, highlighting the risks posed by third-party vendors. The breach had severe financial and reputational consequences for the company, emphasizing the importance of robust cybersecurity practices in retail (Gray & Ladig, 2015).

Sony Pictures (2014): Attributed to North Korea, the cyberattack on Sony Pictures in 2014 was a watershed moment in the intersection of cybersecurity and geopolitics. The attack was launched in response to the release of a movie that depicted North Korea's leader unfavorably. Attackers leaked sensitive data, employee emails, unreleased movies, and more. The incident served as a stark reminder of the potential geopolitical implications of cybersecurity breaches and the importance of cybersecurity on a global scale (Tuttle, 2015).

WannaCry Ransomware (2017): The WannaCry ransomware attack in 2017 was a global cybersecurity crisis, affecting over 200,000 computers across 150 countries. Exploiting a Windows vulnerability, WannaCry encrypted files and demanded a ransom for decryption keys. The attack disrupted critical services, including healthcare systems in the United Kingdom, underscoring the real-world consequences of cyber threats (Mohurle & Patil, 2017).

NotPetya (2017): NotPetya, initially disguised as ransomware, emerged in 2017 as a destructive malware attack primarily targeting Ukraine. However, it quickly spread globally, causing widespread disruption and data loss. The attack is widely attributed to Russia, and its impact on critical infrastructure underscored the potential for state-sponsored cyberattacks to have far-reaching consequences (Greenberg, 2018).

SolarWinds (2020): The SolarWinds cyberattack in 2020 was a massive supply chain attack that affected thousands of organizations worldwide. Attackers compromised SolarWinds' software updates, allowing them to distribute malware to customers unknowingly. The breach exposed sensitive data, including government agencies and corporations, highlighting the vulnerabilities within complex supply chains (Alkhadra et al., 2021).

Colonial Pipeline (2021): In 2021, a ransomware attack on Colonial Pipeline, a major U.S. fuel pipeline operator, disrupted fuel supply to the East Coast. The company ultimately paid a multi-million-dollar ransom to regain control of its systems, sparking discussions about the ethical and strategic implications of paying ransoms to cybercriminals (Hobbs, 2021).

JBS (2021): JBS, one of the world's largest meat processing companies, fell victim to a ransomware attack in 2021. The attack temporarily shut down several processing plants, impacting the global food supply chain and emphasizing the vulnerabilities in critical infrastructure (Chundhoo et al., 2021).

Facebook (2019): In 2019, Facebook experienced a significant data breach that exposed over 500 million user records. The breach included sensitive data such as phone numbers, email addresses, and other personal information, underscoring the challenges in protecting user data on social media platforms (Choi, 2021).

Capital One (2019): Capital One, a major financial institution, faced a data breach in 2019 when a former employee exploited a vulnerability to access customer data. The breach compromised personal information of over 100 million individuals in the United States and Canada, highlighting the importance of robust internal security controls (Novaes Neto et al., 2020).

OPM (2015): The U.S. Office of Personnel Management (OPM) suffered a massive data breach in 2015, compromising sensitive data of government employees, including security clearance information. The breach exposed the vulnerabilities of government agencies to cyberattacks and raised concerns about national security (Gootman, 2016).

ESCALATING FREQUENCY AND SOPHISTICATION OF CYBER THREATS

In recent years, the digital landscape has witnessed an alarming trend: the escalating frequency and sophistication of cyber threats. The evolving tactics of cybercriminals, hacktivists, and nation-state actors have pushed the boundaries of cybersecurity, posing significant challenges for individuals, businesses, and governments worldwide.

Frequency of Attacks: The first notable trend is the sheer frequency of cyberattacks. Not long ago, major breaches were relatively infrequent and often made headline news due to their rarity. However, today, cyber incidents are an almost daily occurrence. This surge in attacks can be attributed to various factors, including the increasing attack surface created by the proliferation of digital devices, the growing interconnectedness of systems, and the ease of launching automated attacks (Mishra et al., 2022).

Sophistication of Malware: Cybercriminals have become increasingly adept at crafting sophisticated malware. Traditional viruses have given way to polymorphic and fileless malware that can adapt and change shape to evade detection. Ransomware has evolved from simple encryption to more complex attacks with data exfiltration and double extortion tactics. Such sophistication not only makes malware harder to detect but also increases its potential damage (Pachhala et al., 2021).

Advanced Persistent Threats (APTs): Nation-state actors have taken cyber espionage and warfare to new heights. APTs are long-term, highly orchestrated campaigns that often go undetected for extended periods. These attacks involve careful reconnaissance, zero-day exploits, and meticulous evasion techniques. Their objectives range from stealing sensitive data to disrupting critical infrastructure (Tatam et al., 2021).

Supply Chain Attacks: Cybercriminals have shifted their focus to supply chain attacks, targeting software providers, service providers, and third-party vendors. By compromising a trusted entity within an organization's supply chain, attackers can gain access to otherwise well-protected networks and systems. The SolarWinds breach serves as a prominent example, affecting numerous organizations worldwide (Miller, 2013).

Zero-Day Vulnerabilities: Zero-day vulnerabilities, previously rare and valuable commodities in the cyber underworld, are now being discovered and weaponized at an alarming rate. Attackers actively seek these unpatched vulnerabilities to exploit systems before patches can be deployed, leaving organizations vulnerable to rapidly evolving threats (Prasad et al., 2020).

Social Engineering: The art of manipulating individuals through social engineering techniques has evolved significantly. Phishing attacks, once characterized by obvious red flags, have become highly convincing, with attackers leveraging psychological manipulation, deep research, and spear-phishing tactics to deceive even vigilant users (Sukri et al., 2023).

Machine Learning and AI in Attacks: Cybercriminals have embraced machine learning and artificial intelligence (AI) to streamline their attacks. These technologies enable attackers to automate tasks, optimize attack vectors, and create convincing deepfake content for social engineering (Yamin et al., 2021).

Emerging Technologies: As technology advances, so do cyber threats. The proliferation of the Internet of Things (IoT) has expanded the attack surface, with insecure IoT devices becoming prime targets for botnets and entry points into networks. Quantum computing, while promising for many applications, poses a potential threat to current encryption methods (Madakam et al., 2015).

Extortion and Monetization: Cybercriminals have become increasingly focused on monetization. Ransomware attacks, in particular, have become lucrative criminal enterprises, with attackers demanding substantial ransoms in cryptocurrency. Double extortion tactics, where stolen data is threatened to be exposed, add to the pressure on victims (Li & Liu, 2021).

Nation-State Conflicts in Cyberspace: Nation-states are engaging in cyber conflicts that blur the lines between traditional warfare and digital attacks. These conflicts can disrupt critical infrastructure, manipulate elections, and compromise national security (Li & Liu, 2021).

Definition of Cyber Forensics

Cyber forensics can be defined as the scientific process of collecting, preserving, analyzing, and presenting electronic evidence in a way that is legally admissible in a court of law. It involves the systematic examination of digital devices, networks, and electronic data to uncover clues and evidence related to cybercrimes or other digital incidents. The primary goal of cyber forensics is to establish a clear and unambiguous chain of custody for digital evidence, ensuring its integrity and authenticity throughout the investigation process (Saharan & Yadav, 2022).

Scope of Cyber Forensics

The scope of cyber forensics is vast and continually evolving, reflecting the rapid advancement of technology and the ever-expanding digital landscape. Key areas within the scope of cyber forensics include (Marcella Jr & Menendez, 2010) (Figure 3):

Figure 3. Scope of Cyber Forensics

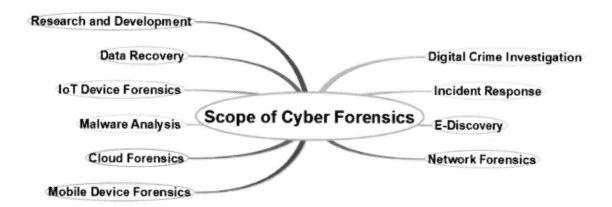

1. **Digital Crime Investigation:** Cyber forensics plays a pivotal role in investigating various digital crimes, including hacking, identity theft, online fraud, cyberbullying, and cyber espionage. It helps law enforcement agencies identify and apprehend cybercriminals, gather evidence, and build strong cases for prosecution.

2. **Incident Response:** Cyber forensics is essential for organizations to respond effectively to cyber-security incidents, such as data breaches, malware infections, and network intrusions. Forensic analysts investigate the source and extent of the breach, assess damage, and recommend remediation strategies.

3. **E-Discovery:** In legal contexts, e-discovery involves the identification, collection, and preservation of electronic evidence for litigation purposes. Cyber forensics experts assist legal professionals in locating and producing relevant digital evidence, ensuring compliance with legal requirements.

4. **Network Forensics:** Network forensics focuses on analyzing network traffic and logs to identify security incidents, intrusions, and malicious activities. It aids in understanding the scope of an attack, tracing its origins, and preventing future breaches.

5. **Mobile Device Forensics**: With the proliferation of smartphones and tablets, mobile device forensics has gained prominence. Forensic specialists extract data from mobile devices, including call records, text messages, GPS data, and application usage, to support investigations.

6. **Cloud Forensics:** As organizations migrate to cloud-based services, cloud forensics has become critical. Experts investigate cloud environments to recover data and ascertain if cloud services were used in cybercrimes.

7. **Malware Analysis:** Cyber forensics professionals analyze malware to understand its functionality, behavior, and impact. This aids in developing countermeasures, detecting infections, and attributing attacks.

8. **IoT Device Forensics:** The proliferation of Internet of Things (IoT) devices has introduced new forensic challenges. Forensic experts examine IoT devices to uncover evidence or vulnerabilities related to cybercrimes.

9. **Data Recovery:** Cyber forensics includes data recovery services to retrieve lost or deleted data from digital devices. This can be crucial in investigations and litigation where data is considered evidence.

10. **Research and Development:** Cyber forensics professionals engage in ongoing research and development to stay ahead of emerging threats and evolving technologies. They develop new tools and techniques to enhance forensic capabilities.

Core Principles and Methodologies

Cyber forensics, the systematic process of collecting, preserving, analyzing, and presenting digital evidence, is a cornerstone of modern cybersecurity. It plays a pivotal role in investigating cybercrimes, mitigating security incidents, and strengthening the overall security posture of organizations. The following core principles and methodologies underpin the discipline of cyber forensics, making it an invaluable asset in the ongoing battle against cyber threats (Brinson et al., 2006; Marcella Jr & Menendez, 2010; Prasanthi, 2016; Saharan & Yadav, 2022) (Figure 4).

1. Preserving Digital Evidence:

Figure 4. Core principles and methodologies

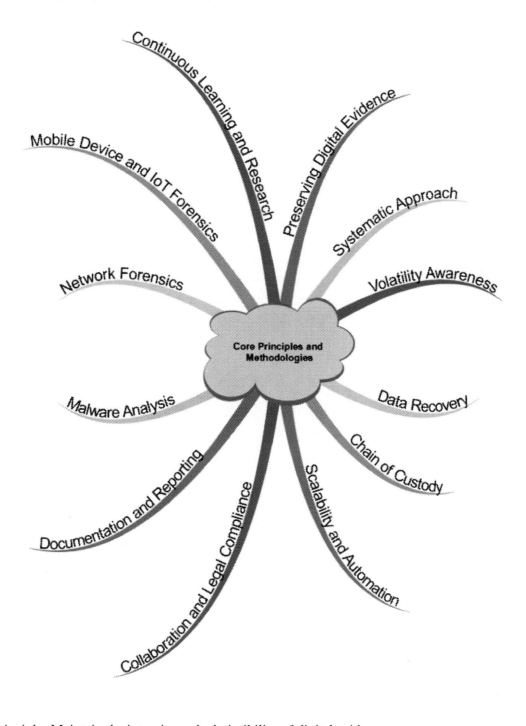

Principle: Maintain the integrity and admissibility of digital evidence.

Methodology: Establish a clear chain of custody, use write-blocking hardware and software, and create forensic copies of digital media to ensure that evidence remains untainted and legally sound.

2.   Systematic Approach:

Principle: Conduct investigations in a structured and methodical manner.

Methodology: Adhere to a well-defined investigative process, including identification, preservation, collection, examination, analysis, and presentation of digital evidence. Follow established protocols and standards.

3.   Volatility Awareness:

Principle: Recognize the transient nature of digital evidence.

Methodology: Prioritize volatile data sources, such as RAM, that can change or disappear quickly during an incident. Capture and analyze volatile data promptly to extract valuable insights.

4.   Data Recovery:

Principle: Strive to recover data even when it has been deleted or intentionally concealed.

Methodology: Employ specialized tools and techniques for data recovery, including file carving, file system analysis, and registry analysis. Explore unallocated space for remnants of deleted files.

5.   Chain of Custody:

Principle: Maintain a documented and unbroken chain of custody for digital evidence.

Methodology: Log all interactions with evidence, from its initial discovery to its presentation in court. Ensure that only authorized personnel have access to evidence and that it remains unaltered.

6.   Scalability and Automation:

Principle: Adapt to the scale and complexity of modern digital environments.

Methodology: Leverage automation and digital forensic tools to process large volumes of data efficiently. Implement workflows that can handle diverse devices and platforms.

7.   Collaboration and Legal Compliance:

Principle: Foster collaboration between forensic experts, legal teams, and other stakeholders.

Methodology: Work closely with legal counsel to ensure that forensic practices adhere to relevant laws and regulations. Respect individuals' rights to privacy and data protection.

8.   Documentation and Reporting:

Principle: Maintain comprehensive records and produce clear, concise reports.

Methodology: Document every step of the investigation, including methodologies, findings, and conclusions. Create well-structured reports suitable for legal proceedings.

9.   Malware Analysis:

Principle: Uncover the nature and scope of malicious software.

Methodology: Analyze malware samples to identify functionality, propagation mechanisms, and indicators of compromise. Reverse engineering may be required to understand advanced threats.

10. Network Forensics:

Principle: Investigate network traffic and logs to reconstruct events.

Methodology: Collect and analyze network data, including packet captures and logs, to trace the actions of attackers, detect anomalies, and identify intrusion points.

11. Mobile Device and IoT Forensics:

Principle: Extend forensic practices to encompass mobile devices and IoT devices.

Methodology: Apply specialized techniques for extracting and analyzing data from smartphones, tablets, and IoT devices. Recognize the unique challenges of these platforms.

12. Continuous Learning and Research:

Principle: Stay current with evolving technologies and threats.

Methodology: Engage in ongoing research, development, and training to keep pace with new cyber threats and forensic techniques. Collaborate with the cybersecurity community to share knowledge.

Digital Evidence and Its Significance

In the digital age, the role of digital evidence has become pivotal in various aspects of modern society, including law enforcement, cybersecurity, litigation, and beyond. Digital evidence refers to any information or data that is stored, transmitted, or processed in a digital form and can be used as proof in legal proceedings or investigations. Its significance lies in its ability to provide critical insights, establish facts, and support decision-making in a wide range of contexts. Here, we delve into the importance and significance of digital evidence (Raghavan, 2013):

1. **Crucial in Criminal Investigations:** Digital evidence plays a central role in solving and prosecuting cybercrimes and other criminal activities involving digital devices. It includes data from computers, mobile phones, emails, social media accounts, and more. This evidence can establish motive, intent, alibis, and connections between suspects and victims.
2. **Cybersecurity and Incident Response:** In the realm of cybersecurity, digital evidence is vital for understanding the scope and impact of security incidents. It helps incident response teams identify attack vectors, assess the extent of breaches, and determine the best strategies for containment and recovery.
3. **E-Discovery in Legal Proceedings:** In legal contexts, e-discovery relies heavily on digital evidence. Attorneys use it to gather, preserve, and present electronic information during litigation. This can include emails, documents, databases, and communication records.

4. **Ensuring Data Integrity:** Digital evidence is essential for ensuring the integrity of digital records and transactions. This is critical in industries like finance, healthcare, and government, where accurate and tamper-proof records are crucial for compliance and accountability.

5. **Proving Intellectual Property Theft:** In cases of intellectual property theft or corporate espionage, digital evidence can provide the necessary proof. It can reveal unauthorized access to proprietary data, the theft, or copyright infringement.

6. **Supporting Compliance and Regulations**: Many industries are subject to strict regulations governing data handling and security. Digital evidence is used to demonstrate compliance with these regulations, helping organizations avoid legal penalties.

7. **Preventing Insider Threats:** Organizations use digital evidence to identify and prevent insider threats, such as employees leaking sensitive data or engaging in malicious activities. Monitoring digital activities can uncover suspicious behavior.

8. **Detecting Fraud and Financial Crimes:** In the financial sector, digital evidence is crucial for detecting and preventing fraud and financial crimes. It can reveal fraudulent transactions, money laundering schemes, and unauthorized access to financial records.

9. **Documenting Human Rights Abuses:** Digital evidence has played a significant role in documenting human rights abuses, especially in situations where the media or government may attempt to suppress information. It empowers citizens to be vigilant watchdogs.

10. **Verifying Digital Identity**: In an age where identity theft and online fraud are prevalent, digital evidence helps verify individuals' digital identities. This is vital for online services, e-commerce, and secure access control.

11. **Enhancing Accountability and Transparency:** Public institutions and government bodies use digital evidence to ensure accountability and transparency in their operations. It can reveal cases of corruption, misconduct, or abuse of power.

12. **Supporting Scientific Research:** In scientific research, digital evidence can validate findings and experiments. It ensures that research data is accurate, replicable, and free from manipulation.

13. **Resolving Disputes:** In civil disputes and family law cases, digital evidence can provide critical information, such as communications, financial records, and electronic agreements, to help resolve conflicts.

Cyber Forensic Process

Cyber forensics, or digital forensics, involves collecting, preserving, analyzing, and presenting digital evidence in legal cases or cybersecurity investigations. The process includes identification, preservation, collection, examination, analysis, and reporting. It aims to uncover cybercrimes, determine their scope, and support legal action while maintaining the integrity of digital evidence (Saharan & Yadav, 2022).

Identification and Reporting of Cyber Incidents

Identification and reporting of cyber incidents are critical components of cybersecurity management. Timely recognition and effective reporting can help organizations mitigate the impact of cyber threats and enhance overall security (Figure 5).

Figure 5. Process of identification and reporting of cyber incidents

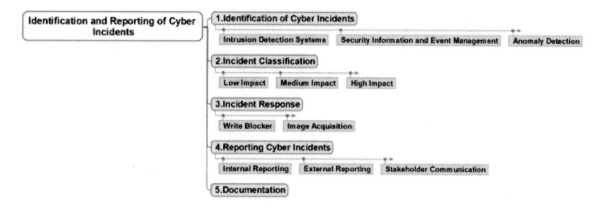

1. **Identification of Cyber Incidents:** Identifying cyber incidents involves monitoring networks, systems, and digital assets for signs of unauthorized access, unusual behavior, or security breaches. Common methods include (Gnatyuk et al., 2021):
   a. Intrusion Detection Systems (IDS): These tools monitor network traffic for suspicious patterns or signatures associated with known threats.
   b. Security Information and Event Management (SIEM): SIEM platforms collect and analyze log data from various sources to detect security events.
   c. Anomaly Detection: Machine learning and AI techniques can identify deviations from baseline behavior, signaling potential threats.
2. **Incident Classification:** After identification, incidents are classified based on severity and impact. This helps prioritize response efforts. Categories may include (Tsakalidis & Vergidis, 2017):
   a. Low Impact: Incidents with minor consequences.
   b. Medium Impact: Incidents that could disrupt operations or data integrity.
   c. High Impact: Incidents that pose a significant risk to the organization, including data breaches or system compromises.
3. **Incident Response:** Organizations must have an incident response plan outlining procedures for containment, eradication, and recovery. Key actions include isolating affected systems, removing threats, and restoring normal operations (Tsakalidis & Vergidis, 2017).
4. Reporting Cyber Incidents:
   a. Internal Reporting: Within the organization, employees and IT teams should promptly report incidents to the designated cybersecurity point of contact.
   b. External Reporting: Depending on the nature and impact of the incident, organizations may be legally obligated to report to regulatory authorities, such as data protection agencies or law enforcement.
   c. Stakeholder Communication: Communication with stakeholders, including customers, partners, and employees, is essential to maintain trust and transparency during and after an incident.
5. **Documentation:** All incident details, actions taken, and outcomes should be thoroughly documented. This documentation is valuable for post-incident analysis and regulatory compliance.

Preservation of Digital Evidence

Preserving digital evidence is a critical aspect of digital forensics and cybersecurity investigations. The integrity and admissibility of evidence depend on proper preservation techniques. Here's a concise overview of the key principles and practices in preserving digital evidence (Granja & Rafael, 2017):

1. **Maintaining Chain of Custody:** Establish a documented and unbroken chain of custody from the moment evidence is discovered. This ensures accountability and prevents tampering.
2. **Documentation:** Thoroughly document the discovery, handling, and storage of digital evidence. Detailed records include dates, times, locations, personnel involved, and the condition of the evidence.
3. **Write-Blocking:** Use write-blocking hardware or software to create forensic copies of digital media. This ensures that the original evidence remains untouched during examination.
4. **Hashing:** Calculate cryptographic hash values (e.g., MD5, SHA-256) of digital evidence at various stages. Hashes provide a unique fingerprint of the data, ensuring its integrity.
5. **Secure Storage:** Store digital evidence in a secure, controlled environment with limited access. Protection from physical and digital threats, such as theft, tampering, or data corruption, is essential.
6. **Chain-of-Custody Logs:** Maintain a detailed log of everyone who accesses the evidence and the purpose of their access. This log should be updated throughout the investigation.
7. **Redundancy:** Create multiple copies of digital evidence for backup purposes, ensuring that a pristine copy is available for examination and that no data is lost.
8. **Time Stamping:** Record the date and time of evidence collection and any subsequent actions. This information is crucial for establishing timelines during investigations.
9. **Forensic Tools:** Utilize specialized forensic software and hardware for evidence handling and analysis. These tools maintain data integrity and generate admissible reports.
10. **Evidence Bags and Seals:** Seal digital storage devices in tamper-evident evidence bags, and document the sealing process. Any tampering attempts will be evident upon inspection.
11. **Access Control:** Restrict access to digital evidence to authorized personnel only. Implement role-based access controls to ensure that only designated individuals can view or analyze evidence.
12. **Encryption:** If necessary, encrypt digital evidence during storage to protect sensitive information. Ensure that encryption keys are securely managed.
13. **Regular Verification:** Periodically verify the integrity of stored evidence by rehashing it. Any changes will be detected through a hash mismatch.
14. **Legal Considerations:** Comply with legal requirements for evidence preservation, including data retention regulations and chain-of-custody protocols.

Analysis and Interpretation of Evidence

The analysis and interpretation of digital evidence are fundamental steps in the field of digital forensics and cybersecurity investigations. These processes are pivotal for uncovering critical information, identifying patterns, and drawing conclusions relevant to a given case. The journey begins with data acquisition, where investigators carefully create forensic copies of digital devices, ensuring the original data remains intact and unaltered. This phase is executed using write-blocking tools to prevent any inadvertent changes or modifications to the evidence. Subsequently, the process advances to data recovery, where investigators employ specialized software and techniques to retrieve deleted or hidden data. This includes the examination of deleted files, unallocated space, and hidden partitions, which can provide valuable insights. Throughout the entire investigation, the preservation of data integrity is paramount. Regular calculations of hash values are conducted to confirm the consistency and authenticity of the data. Simultaneously, timeline analysis plays a pivotal role in reconstructing events. Investigators delve into timestamps, logs, and metadata to establish precise chronologies, aiding in piecing together the sequence of events leading to the incident. Keyword and string searches are employed to identify specific terms, phrases, or patterns within the digital evidence, facilitating the location of relevant documents, communications, or illicit activities (Sukri et al., 2023). Additionally, file carving techniques are applied to reconstruct deleted files or fragments that may not be accessible through standard methods. Digital artifacts left behind by operating systems and applications provide crucial insights into the investigation. Examinations of system registries, browser histories, and application logs can reveal significant information (Brinson et al., 2006; Marcella Jr & Menendez, 2010; Saharan & Yadav, 2022). In cybersecurity cases, network traffic analysis is a powerful tool to identify malicious activities, intrusion attempts, or unauthorized access. In cases involving malware, and in-depth analysis of the malicious code is performed to understand its behavior, purpose, and impact on the system. Pattern recognition within the data, such as access patterns, communication trends, or irregular behaviors, may unveil important insights that are critical to the investigation's progress. In instances of encrypted data, cryptanalysis techniques may be employed to decrypt the information and uncover its underlying content. Expert judgment is a fundamental aspect of digital evidence analysis. Forensic experts draw conclusions based on their specialized knowledge and the evidence they've gathered. This often involves identifying patterns, assessing the significance of findings, and forming hypotheses. Documentation at each step of the process is essential. Investigators maintain thorough records of their findings, methods, and procedures. This documentation serves as the foundation for comprehensive reports and can be vital in legal proceedings. Peer review is often employed to ensure the accuracy and reliability of findings, further bolstering the integrity of the investigation. Finally, a detailed and organized report is generated, summarizing the analysis, findings, and interpretations. These reports are meticulously crafted to be clear and concise, suitable for both technical and non-technical audiences when necessary. Throughout the entire process, investigators must adhere to legal standards, ensuring that evidence is admissible in court and that investigations are conducted with the utmost integrity and professionalism.

Legal and Ethical Framework for Cyber Forensics

Cyber forensics, the process of investigating digital and cybercrimes, operates within a legal and ethical framework to ensure that investigations are conducted responsibly, respect individual rights, and adhere to applicable laws and regulations. Here's an overview of the legal and ethical considerations that guide cyber forensic investigations (Ferguson et al., 2020):

1. Legal Authority:
   a. **Warrant Requirements:** In many jurisdictions, investigators must obtain legal authorization, such as search warrants or court orders, before conducting cyber forensic investigations. These documents specify the scope and purpose of the investigation.
   b. **Jurisdictional Considerations:** Investigators must operate within the legal boundaries of their jurisdiction, understanding the laws that apply to cybercrimes and digital evidence.

2. Privacy and Data Protection:
   a. **Data Privacy Laws:** Cyber forensic investigators must comply with data privacy laws, which vary by country and region. These laws govern the collection, storage, and handling of personal and sensitive data.
   b. **Informed Consent:** In some cases, obtaining informed consent from individuals before accessing their digital devices or data is required, particularly in non-criminal investigations.
3. Chain of Custody:
   a. **Evidence Handling:** Maintaining a secure and unbroken chain of custody is essential. Proper documentation of evidence handling is necessary to ensure that digital evidence is admissible in court.
4. Volatility and Preservation:
   a. **Volatility of Digital Evidence:** Cyber forensic investigators must be mindful of the volatile nature of digital evidence. Rapid preservation of evidence is critical to preventing data loss or alteration.
   b. **Forensic Imaging:** Creating a forensic copy (image) of digital media ensures that original evidence remains unchanged during analysis.
5. Ethical Conduct:
   a. **Professional Standards:** Cyber forensic professionals adhere to ethical standards set by industry associations and organizations, such as the International Association of Computer Investigative Specialists (IACIS) and the Digital Forensic Research Workshop (DFRWS).
   b. **Impartiality:** Investigators must remain impartial and unbiased throughout the investigation process, avoiding personal or organizational interests that could compromise the integrity of the investigation.
6. Transparency and Accountability:
   a. **Reporting:** Investigators are responsible for producing clear and comprehensive reports that accurately represent their findings. Transparency is crucial for maintaining trust in the investigative process.
   b. **Accountability:** Investigators are accountable for their actions and findings. Any errors or discrepancies must be addressed transparently.
7. Legal Privileges and Confidentiality:
   a. **Attorney-Client Privilege:** Cyber forensic investigators must respect attorney-client privilege when handling digital evidence in legal cases.
   b. **Medical Privilege:** In healthcare-related cases, investigators must safeguard medical records and respect doctor-patient confidentiality.
8. Admissibility of Evidence:
   a. **Expert Testimony:** In court proceedings, cyber forensic experts may be called upon to provide expert testimony to explain their findings and methodologies. They must present their findings clearly and truthfully.
9. Continuing Education:
   a. **Professional Development:** Cyber forensic professionals are encouraged to engage in ongoing education and training to stay updated on the latest technologies, legal developments, and ethical considerations.

Challenges in Cyber Forensics

Cyber forensics, the process of investigating digital and cybercrimes, faces several complex challenges that can complicate the collection and analysis of digital evidence. Here are explanations for some of the key challenges in cyber forensics:

1. **Encryption and Obfuscation Techniques:** Encryption is the process of converting data into a code to prevent unauthorized access. While encryption is a vital security measure, it poses a significant challenge in cyber forensics. Encrypted data, whether on storage devices or during transmission, is essentially indecipherable without the encryption keys. Obfuscation techniques are methods used to deliberately make data or code more difficult to understand, adding another layer of complexity. Investigators may encounter encrypted data or malicious code that is challenging or even impossible to decrypt or deobfuscate. This can hinder the retrieval of crucial evidence, especially in cases involving cybercrimes where the use of encryption is common (Boneh et al., 2015).

2. **Jurisdictional Challenges in Cross-Border Cases**: Cybercrimes often transcend national borders, making it challenging to determine which jurisdiction has authority over an investigation. Different countries have varying legal frameworks and extradition agreements, which can complicate the process of apprehending and prosecuting cybercriminals who operate across borders. Jurisdictional challenges can delay or hinder international cybercrime investigations. Coordinating efforts among multiple countries and navigating legal complexities require international cooperation and adherence to diplomatic agreements (Menon & Guan Siew, 2012).

3. **Evolving Digital Devices and Storage Media:** The rapid evolution of digital technology has led to a vast array of digital devices and storage media with varying formats, file systems, and proprietary technologies. Cyber forensic investigators must constantly adapt their methods and tools to accommodate new devices and storage technologies. The diversity of digital devices and storage media presents a challenge in terms of data acquisition, extraction, and analysis. Investigators must stay updated on the latest technologies to effectively handle evidence from a wide range of sources (Horsman, 2022).

4. **Anti-Forensic Techniques:** Cybercriminals are increasingly employing anti-forensic techniques to cover their tracks and make digital evidence more difficult to trace. These techniques include data wiping, file deletion, and the use of anonymization tools. Anti-forensic techniques can lead to the destruction or concealment of critical evidence. Investigators must develop countermeasures to detect and counteract these tactics to ensure the integrity of the investigation (Garfinkel, 2007).

5. **Privacy and Legal Considerations:** Balancing the need for cyber forensic investigations with individual privacy rights is a complex challenge. Investigative processes must comply with data protection laws and respect the privacy of individuals whose data is under examination. Failure to address privacy and legal considerations can lead to legal challenges and the inadmissibility of evidence in court. Investigators must carefully navigate these issues to maintain the legality of their actions (Tekiner et al., 2021).

The Future of Cyber Forensics

As technology continues to advance at a rapid pace, the field of cyber forensics is poised for significant developments and transformations. Here are elaborations on key aspects that represent the future of cyber forensics:

1. **Advancements in Technology and Automation:** The future of cyber forensics will be marked by advancements in technology and automation. This includes the development of more sophisticated forensic tools and techniques for extracting, analyzing, and preserving digital evidence. Automation will play a crucial role in streamlining routine tasks, such as data acquisition and preliminary analysis. These advancements will enhance the efficiency and effectiveness of cyber forensic investigations. Investigators will be able to process large volumes of data more quickly, identify relevant evidence with greater precision, and allocate their expertise to more complex tasks (Marcella Jr & Menendez, 2010).

2. **The Role of Machine Learning and Artificial Intelligence:** Machine learning (ML) and artificial intelligence (AI) are poised to revolutionize cyber forensics. These technologies can be used to develop intelligent algorithms that can detect patterns, anomalies, and trends within digital data. ML and AI can aid in automating the analysis of vast datasets, including those generated by the Internet of Things (IoT) devices. ML and AI will enable cyber forensic investigators to detect cyber threats, identify emerging attack vectors, and respond to incidents with greater speed and accuracy. These technologies will also be instrumental in predictive analysis, helping organizations anticipate and mitigate cyber risks (Yamin et al., 2021).

3. **Anticipating Challenges and Adaptations:** The future of cyber forensics will involve a proactive approach to anticipating challenges. As cybercriminals continually evolve their tactics and technologies, forensic experts will need to stay one step ahead. This entails ongoing education and training, as well as the development of new methodologies and tools. By proactively adapting to emerging threats and challenges, cyber forensic investigators will be better equipped to respond effectively. This adaptability will be crucial in addressing novel cybercrimes, including those involving quantum computing, 5G networks, and emerging technologies that cybercriminals may exploit (Brinson et al., 2006; Marcella Jr & Menendez, 2010; Saharan & Yadav, 2022).

4. **Cross-Disciplinary Collaboration:** The future of cyber forensics will likely involve greater collaboration with other fields such as data science, cybersecurity, and law enforcement. Cyber forensic experts will need to work hand in hand with professionals from these disciplines to tackle complex cybercrimes. Collaborative efforts will lead to a holistic approach to cybercrime prevention and investigation. By combining expertise from various domains, investigators can gain deeper insights into cyber threats and develop more effective countermeasures.

5. **Ethical and Legal Considerations:** As cyber forensic practices evolve, ethical and legal considerations will remain at the forefront. The responsible and lawful handling of digital evidence, along with respect for privacy rights, will continue to be paramount. Adhering to ethical and legal standards is essential for maintaining the integrity of cyber forensic investigations. It ensures that evidence is admissible in legal proceedings and upholds the trust of the public in the investigative process (Saharan & Yadav, 2022).

In conclusion, the future of cyber forensics promises significant advancements in technology, the integration of AI and ML, proactive adaptations to evolving threats, cross-disciplinary collaboration, and a steadfast commitment to ethical and legal considerations. These developments will empower cyber forensic investigators to address emerging cyber challenges effectively and contribute to a safer and more secure digital landscape.

REFERENCES

Alkhadra, R., Abuzaid, J., AlShammari, M., & Mohammad, N. (2021). Solar winds hack: In-depth analysis and countermeasures. *2021 12th International Conference on Computing Communication and Networking Technologies (ICCCNT)*.

Alrwais, S., Yuan, K., Alowaisheq, E., Liao, X., Oprea, A., Wang, X., & Li, Z. (2016). Catching predators at watering holes: finding and understanding strategically compromised websites. *Proceedings of the 32nd Annual Conference on Computer Security Applications*. ACM. 10.1145/2991079.2991112

Boneh, D., Lewi, K., Raykova, M., Sahai, A., Zhandry, M., & Zimmerman, J. (2015). Semantically secure order-revealing encryption: Multi-input functional encryption without obfuscation. *Annual International Conference on the Theory and Applications of Cryptographic Techniques*. Springer. 10.1007/978-3-662-46803-6_19

Brinson, A., Robinson, A., & Rogers, M. (2006). A cyber forensics ontology: Creating a new approach to studying cyber forensics. *digital investigation, 3*, 37-43.

Cekerevac, Z., Dvorak, Z., Prigoda, L., & Cekerevac, P. (2017). Internet of things and the man-in-the-middle attacks–security and economic risks. *MEST Journal, 5*(2), 15–25. doi:10.12709/mest.05.05.02.03

Chiew, K. L., Yong, K. S. C., & Tan, C. L. (2018). A survey of phishing attacks: Their types, vectors and technical approaches. *Expert Systems with Applications, 106*, 1–20. doi:10.1016/j.eswa.2018.03.050

Choi, Y. B. (2021). Organizational cyber data breach analysis of Facebook, Equifax, and Uber cases. [IJCRE]. *International Journal of Cyber Research and Education, 3*(1), 58–64. doi:10.4018/IJCRE.2021010106

Chundhoo, V., Chattopadhyay, G., Karmakar, G., & Appuhamillage, G. K. (2021). Cybersecurity risks in meat processing plant and impacts on total productive maintenance. 2021 International Conference on Maintenance and Intelligent Asset Management (ICMIAM). Research Gate.

Eliyan, L. F., & Di Pietro, R. (2021). DoS and DDoS attacks in Software Defined Networks: A survey of existing solutions and research challenges. *Future Generation Computer Systems, 122*, 149–171. doi:10.1016/j.future.2021.03.011

Ferguson, R., Renaud, K., Wilford, S., & Irons, A. (2020). PRECEPT: A framework for ethical digital forensics investigations. *Journal of Intellectual Capital, 21*(2), 257–290. doi:10.1108/JIC-05-2019-0097

Gnatyuk, S., Berdibayev, R., Avkurova, Z., Verkhovets, O., & Bauyrzhan, M. (2021). Studies on Cloud-based Cyber Incidents Detection and Identification in Critical Infrastructure. CPITS, Gootman, S. (2016). OPM hack: The most dangerous threat to the federal government today. *Journal of Applied Security Research, 11*(4), 517–525.

Granja, F. M., & Rafael, G. D. R. (2017). The preservation of digital evidence and its admissibility in the court. *International Journal of Electronic Security and Digital Forensics*, *9*(1), 1–18. doi:10.1504/IJESDF.2017.081749

Gray, D., & Ladig, J. (2015). The implementation of EMV chip card technology to improve cyber security accelerates in the US following target corporation's data breach. *International Journal of Business Administration*, *6*(2), 60. doi:10.5430/ijba.v6n2p60

Greenberg, A. (2018). The untold story of NotPetya, the most devastating cyberattack in history. *Wired*, (August), 22.

Hobbs, A. (2021). *The colonial pipeline hack: Exposing vulnerabilities in us cybersecurity*. SAGE Publications: SAGE Business Cases Originals.

Horsman, G. (2022). Digital evidence strategies for digital forensic science examinations. *Science & Justice*. PMID:36631176

Huang, X., Gong, P., Wang, S., White, M., & Zhang, B. (2022). Machine learning modeling of vitality characteristics in historical preservation zones with multi-source data. *Buildings*, *12*(11), 1978. doi:10.3390/buildings12111978

Li, Y., & Liu, Q. (2021). A comprehensive review study of cyber-attacks and cyber security; Emerging trends and recent developments. *Energy Reports*, *7*, 8176–8186. doi:10.1016/j.egyr.2021.08.126

Madakam, S., Lake, V., Lake, V., & Lake, V. (2015). Internet of Things (IoT): A literature review. *Journal of Computer and Communications*, *3*(05), 164–173. doi:10.4236/jcc.2015.35021

Marcella, A. Jr, & Menendez, D. (2010). *Cyber forensics: a field manual for collecting, examining, and preserving evidence of computer crimes*. Auerbach Publications. doi:10.1201/9780849383298

Menon, S., & Guan Siew, T. (2012). Key challenges in tackling economic and cyber crimes: Creating a multilateral platform for international co-operation. *Journal of Money Laundering Control*, *15*(3), 243–256. doi:10.1108/13685201211238016

Miller, E. A., & West, D. M. (2009). Where's the revolution? Digital technology and health care in the internet age. *Journal of Health Politics, Policy and Law*, *34*(2), 261–284. doi:10.1215/03616878-2008-046 PMID:19276318

Miller, J. F. (2013). *Supply chain attack framework and attack patterns*. The MITRE Corporation. doi:10.21236/ADA610495

Mishra, D. K., Ray, P. K., Li, L., Zhang, J., Hossain, M., & Mohanty, A. (2022). Resilient control based frequency regulation scheme of isolated microgrids considering cyber attack and parameter uncertainties. *Applied Energy*, *306*, 118054. doi:10.1016/j.apenergy.2021.118054

Mohurle, S., & Patil, M. (2017). A brief study of wannacry threat: Ransomware attack 2017. *International journal of advanced research in computer science*, *8*(5), 1938-1940.

Novaes Neto, N., Madnick, S., de Paula, M. G., & Malara Borges, N. (2020). *A case study of the capital one data breach*. Research Gate.

Prasad, R., Rohokale, V., Prasad, R., & Rohokale, V. (2020). Cyber threats and attack overview. *Cyber Security: The Lifeline of Information and Communication Technology*, 15-31.

Prasanthi, B. (2016). Cyber forensic tools: A review. [IJETT]. *International Journal of Engineering Trends and Technology*, *41*(5), 266–271. doi:10.14445/22315381/IJETT-V41P249

Raghavan, S. (2013). Digital forensic research: Current state of the art. *Csi Transactions on ICT*, *1*(1), 91–114. doi:10.1007/s40012-012-0008-7

Saharan, S., & Yadav, B. (2022). Digital and cyber forensics: A contemporary evolution in forensic sciences. In Crime Scene Management within Forensic Science: Forensic Techniques for Criminal Investigations (pp. 267-294). Springer. doi:10.1007/978-981-16-6683-4_11

Santosa, K. I., Lim, C., & Erwin, A. (2016). Analysis of educational institution DNS network traffic for insider threats. *2016 International Conference on Computer, Control, Informatics and its Applications (IC3INA)*. Research Gate.

Trautman, L. J., & Ormerod, P. C. (2016). Corporate directors' and officers' cybersecurity standard of care: The Yahoo data breach. *Am. UL Rev.*, *66*, 1231.

Tsakalidis, G., & Vergidis, K. (2017). A systematic approach toward description and classification of cybercrime incidents. *IEEE Transactions on Systems, Man, and Cybernetics. Systems*, *49*(4), 710–729. doi:10.1109/TSMC.2017.2700495

Tuttle, H. (2015). Sony faces lawsuits after data breach. *Risk Management*, *62*(2), 4.

Wang, P., & Johnson, C. (2018). Cybersecurity incident handling: A case study of the Equifax data breach. *Issues in Information Systems*, *19*(3).

Yamin, M. M., Ullah, M., Ullah, H., & Katt, B. (2021). Weaponized AI for cyber attacks. *Journal of Information Security and Applications*, *57*, 102722. doi:10.1016/j.jisa.2020.102722

Chapter 6
Does Technology Drive Supply Chain Visibility?
Evidence From the FMCG Sector in India

John Paul Raj V (44735c3a-ef57-4fe9-9689-58249c61c99a
Christ University, India

Kotapati Varshitha
Christ University, India

Sathish Pachiyappan
Christ University, India

Saravanan Vellaiyan
Christ University, India

ABSTRACT

Success and efficiency of today's business depends on many factors across various industries. Among the many factors, supply chain plays a crucial role. The well-functioning of distribution system may lead to customer satisfaction, cost reduction, risk management, competitive advantage, collaboration and integration, innovation and adoptability and sustainability. Adopting technology in supply chain systems is another way of increasing business growth in the present era. The technologies used in today's business organizations are blockchain, internet of things (IoT), cloud technology, etc. To what extent technology is used to improve supply chain visibility in business is a matter of concern. With this background, the study aims to explore the relationship and impact of different technology on supply chain visibility in fast moving consumer goods sector. To meet the objective of the study, the study chose the top 20 FMCG companies based on highest market share and collected the data from 20 supply chain managers. The variables considered for the study were internet of things (IoT), blockchain, artificial intelligence (AI), radio frequency identification (RFID), cloud technology and information technology. relevant statistical analysis was used to prove the results and it is evident that technology positively correlates with the supply chain visibility. Artificial Intelligence has the most significant impact on the supply chain visibility of a firm. Hence, there is a significant impact of technology on supply chain visibility and the extent impact is high.

DOI: 10.4018/978-1-6684-9576-6.ch006

INTRODUCTION

Supply chain visibility refers to the ability to track and monitor products, inventory, and information as they move through the various stages of the supply chain, from suppliers to manufacturers, distributors, retailers, and ultimately to customers. It involves real-time access to accurate and timely data on the status, location, and movement of goods, as well as the availability of relevant information related to orders, shipments, and demand (Mollenkopf et al., 2017). It allows organizations to gain insights into their supply chain operations, identify potential bottlenecks or disruptions, and make informed decisions to optimize performance, improve customer satisfaction, and enhance overall supply chain efficiency (Papathanasiou et al., 2017). Improved supply chain visibility leads to better inventory management (Chen et al., 2017). Supply chain visibility leads to higher customer satisfaction levels ((Lee & Tang, 2020). Real time supply chain visibility helps in early detection of potential disruptions (Wang et al., 2018). Increased supply chain visibility enhances collaboration, trust and information sharing (Zhang & Zhang, 2019). Enhanced visibility encourages transparency, traceability and environmental responsibility (Li et al., 2021) The technologies used in supply chain visibility are Internet of Things (IoT) (Chen & Paulraj, 2018), blockchain technology (Zhang et al., 2019), Artificial intelligence (AI) (Lee et al., 2020), Radio Frequency Identification (RFID) technology ((Wang et al., 2021), and cloud computing (Tseng et al., 2022). The fast-moving consumer goods (FMCG) sector is characterized by high product turnover, intense competition, and evolving customer preferences. Efficient Supply chain operations enable customer demands promptly (Verma et al., 2018). Agile supply chain practices enable FMCG companies adapt to market changes, reduce lead times, and improve responsiveness to customer needs (Agarwal et al., 2020). Effective integration of supply chain result in enhanced supply chain efficiency, reduced stockouts, and improved customer service levels (Saravanan & Ravi, 2019). Growing complexity of the FMCG supply chain: The FMCG supply chain is becoming increasingly complex, with multiple stakeholders and partners involved in the process. This complexity makes it more difficult to achieve visibility, and technology may be an important tool to help manage this complexity. Potential for cost savings: Technology has the potential to improve supply chain visibility, reduce inventory costs, and streamline the supply chain process. This can result in significant cost savings for FMCG companies. Improved customer service: Improved supply chain visibility can also result in better customer service, as companies can respond more quickly to customer demand and reduce delivery times. With these insights, the study aims to find the influence of each technology (such as Internet of Things (IoT), Blockchain, Artificial Intelligence (AI), Radio Frequency Identification (RFID), Cloud Technology and Information Technology) on Supply Chain Visibility (SCV) in Fast Moving Consumer Goods (FMCG) sector. In addition to this, the study provides opportunities to improve supply chain visibility in the FMCG sector.

LITERATURE REVIEW

By providing visibility across supply networks, supply chain visibility (SCV), a subset of supply chain management (SCM), aims to enhance business decision-making and operational effectiveness. Due to a number of issues with managing existing company supply chains as they change to meet the demands of the market, global megatrends towards globalisation have forced the study of supply chain visibility into the scientific spotlight. The ability to obtain precise and up-to-date information about a company's supply networks in relation to both internal and external activity is the basis of supply chain visibility.

This is accomplished by determining which aspects of the supply chain are most adversely affected by a lack of visibility and by putting in place (Caridi et al, 2014). According to (Wei & Wang, 2010), the main advantages of supply chain insight include a better basis for decision-making, both strategically and operationally, and an overall increase in business performance. As a result of ensuring effective supply chain visibility, a company may be able to improve its forecasting, planning, scheduling, and order execution, to mention a few benefits. On a strategic level, firms develop the ability to quickly and successfully reconfigure the supply chain, a skill that is increasingly important for gaining a competitive edge in environments where the business landscape is changing quickly.

The development of the block chain is one of the most significant advances in recent years, according to (Xu et al., 2021). Researchers claim that blockchains can specifically enhance SCM. They claim that because timestamped blocks can be generated for transactions, blockchain improves supply chain visibility and traceability. They also emphasise how each transaction on a public blockchain is by design permissionless, guaranteeing user anonymity and thus confidentiality. Hald and Kinra (2019) make the same assertion that blockchain can improve supply chain visibility and transparency by keeping unquestionable and corroded data about earlier transactions. Organisations should determine which stakeholders stand to profit the most from information security in order to ensure that the right amount of information security is started, planned, and implemented. According to (Chae et al., 2005), the adoption of innovative and disruptive technology is hastening the beginning of the fourth industrial revolution. In order to alert individuals and prevent terrible events, radio frequency identification (RFID) technology, for instance, can be used to automatically convey information. Thanks to the Internet of Things (IoT), the fourth industrial revolution has opened the door for a completely new degree of connectivity. The supply chain actors can now make better decisions for greater and communication, data analytics, and more visibility. In order to give insight into the supply chain and facilitate rapid decision-making, managers must take into account the utilisation of technologies and the necessity of developing a system of connected, integrated technologies. The cost of storing stockpiles and the labour required to maintain those stocks in the FMCG industry may be greatly reduced as a result of this technological fusion. According to (Li and Lin, 2006), as competition among FMCG companies rises and markets become more global, markets are becoming more international, dynamic, and customer-driven; customers are demanding more varieties, better quality, higher reliability, and faster delivery; product life is shortening and product proliferation is expanding; technological developments are occurring at a faster rate. Supply chain management is thus also distinguished by high degrees of difficulty because of the complexity of the multiple links and exchanges between trading partners. In addition to their volume and variety of operations, these interactions are further complicated by the complexity of the time and geographical relationships between the participants. Businesses are making headway in their efforts to improve the effectiveness and efficiency of their operations, as seen by the enormous number of companies that have already implemented supply chain technologies.

In order to make decisions for efficient supply chains, managers must be able to process the enormous amount of created data, according to (Williams et al., 2013). Visibility is a crucial enabler of inter-company collaboration, trust-building, and efficiency improvement, according to supply chain specialists, and it allows for integration between layers up to and including the consumer. Visibility allows for action in the supply chain, which reduces decision risk. This improves supply chain performance overall by giving organisations "capabilities to rearrange their supply chains and produce strategic value." Several SCM elements, including as cost, inventory management, and physical logistics, depend on visibility. Effective information use and, most importantly, information sharing with suppliers can have a positive impact on a number of factors, such as the responsiveness of supply chain partners, improved 17 measurement and design of key metrics, improved productivity, customer service, and overall firm performance. According to (Kim et al., 2006), blockchain technology may expose the user to a lot more data and information by enabling visibility and openness. Perfect visibility may not be advantageous over a SC. Sterman and Dogan (2015) conducted an experiment to demonstrate that, despite perfect visibility of the demand signal—which was known to be constant—and perfect knowledge of the orders at each instance of the supply chain, managers are unable to resist the urge to hoard, resulting in the destabilisation of the entire supply chain. Achieving sophisticated supply chains with high supply chain visibility is possible with the correct implementation and understanding. (Wu et al.,2017) Blockchain technology is flexible and may be applied to various SCM scenarios. As an illustration, tracking and visibility of the supply chain can streamline information flow and result in cost savings. Blockchain technology may improve information sharing throughout the supply chain, improving SCM's dependability and security. Blockchains offer a remedy for maintaining and enhancing security in intelligent transportation systems (Dorri et al., 2017). According to (Kharlamov & Parry, 2018), some examples of downstream or demand-related, partner-level information types include point-of-sale (POS) or real sales data, demand predictions, customer inventory levels, and customer promotional strategies. levels of supplier inventories, Upstream or supply-related information categories include supplier lead times/delivery dates, advanced shipping warnings, and distribution network inventory levels. Researchers claim that companies need to be aware of both supply and demand variables. These types of information are provided by the company's clients and suppliers (demand visibility and supply visibility). Additionally, corporations obtain information on market-level supply and demand from sources other than their partners (market visibility) in order to gain visibility into broader market conditions. According to (Dolgui and Ivanov, 2021), businesses that deal with FMCG products must adopt technologies like artificial intelligence to outperform their rivals in the market. In order to better understand the needs of their specific clientele, develop consumables that satisfy those needs, and improve organisational efficiency by lowering costs and maximising revenues, the FMCG sector is ready to integrate AI tools and technology. A change in the supply chain management system has been observed throughout time by organisations, particularly those dealing with FMCG products, as a result of technological improvements and the application of artificial intelligence and Big Data Analytics techniques. Real-time data collection made possible by AI helps companies maintain standards for the production of consumable goods while reducing resource waste. By incorporating AI technology throughout all of the organization's operational processes, results that are both profitable and appealing can be generated. Artificial intelligence (AI) can improve overall operational efficiency by measuring results through previous and present performances that would determine future prediction on the supply and demand activities. According to (Najafi et al., 2022), the use of AI in supply chain management is growing. quickly. One of the main benefits of AI is its ability to detect patterns in vast amounts of data. With the use of technology, supply chain managers may be able to find hidden links in large datasets. ability to recognise patterns. For instance, they could pinpoint the outside forces that regularly influence shifts in the seasonal demand for a certain commodity. Artificial intelligence and a fleet of IoT sensors can collaborate to increase supply chain transparency. AI may be able to stop human error in its tracks by assisting people with tedious and error-prone tasks. According to (Sharma et al., 2022), IoT enables real-time supply chain visibility. Whether the subject is availability of supplies, provider limits, or inventories, it has long been an interesting issue in respect to required supply chain upgrades, whether it be a manufacturing cap or other constraint. Innovation in the sensor industry can help to increase the visibility of the supply chain because sensors are actually well-suited for continuously gathering information. If supply chains have visibility into materials, inventory, how much provider limit is accessible, and how much manufacturing limit is accessible, they will be better able to design and execute within the supply chain and be better positioned to react and adjust to changes in the working conditions. IoT is also getting better and better at reducing supply chain risk. According to (Reyes et al., 2020), FMCG firms are focusing on achieving end-to-end visibility in order to make the most of their collaboration with logistics providers in this VUCA world (Volatility, Uncertainty, Complexity, and Ambiguity). For FMCG companies today, visibility and the flexibility that comes with end-to-end visibility are essential. In contrast to the past, when FMCG businesses focused primarily on delivery to retailers, supermarkets, and wholesalers, the expectation now is that brands will offer direct client service, typically through ecommerce. This calls for a radical redesign of the FMCG supply chain's visibility, which may be accomplished with the help of the right technical integration and intervention.

Research Model

Formulated six hypotheses which is given and highlighted in the research model. Outcome variable is supply chain visibility and explanatory variables are Internet of Things (IoT), Blockchain, Artificial Intelligence (AI), Radio Frequency Identification (RFID), Cloud Technology and Information Technology (IT)

Sample Collection Procedure and Measure

Total sample of 20 has been collected from supply chain manager in the 20 FMCG sector. Work experience and position of those respondents are different based on their companies. Structured questionnaire has been framed which consists of three part. First part of the questionnaire was demographic profile,

Figure 1.

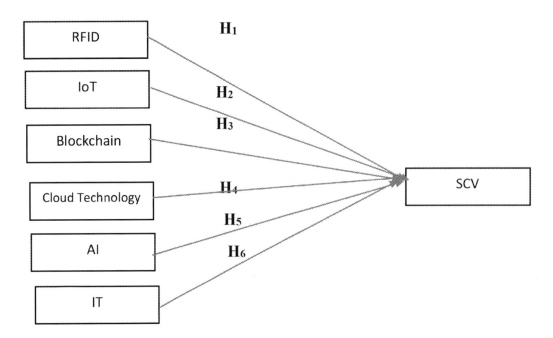

Technology related item in the second part and the final part is supply chain visibility. All the items used were five point likert scales (1="Strongly Disagree") to (5="Strongly Agree"). Snowball sampling method adopted under non probability sampling to collect the sample from each FMCG. Data were collected from the supply chain manager in selected FMCG companies in person between October 2022 to January 2023. The list of respondents, designation and year of experience given in Table 1.

Tools Used for Analysis

Using SPSS 24 version, reliability test has done to check the internal consistency of the items and found that the cronbach's alpha is 0.786 (Hair et al. 2012) which is acceptable to proceed further. Further, the study employed correlation analysis to establish the relationship exist and also used regression analysis to find the influence of technology on supply chain visibility.

Correlation Analysis

Table 2 provides the summary of correlation analysis. It could be observed that the chosen technology has positively correlated with the supply chain visibility except information technology. Among the different technology, AI has highly correlated with SCM (r=0.57, p<0.05) followed by CT (r=0.49, p<0.05),

Table 1. Description of the sample

Sample	Designation	Company Name	Year of Experience
1	Senior Manager -Supply Chain Excellence	Perfetti Van Melle	6
2	Manager	Britannia	8
3	Senior Manager	HUL	10
4	Head of Supply Chain	Britannia	13
5	Director	ITC	14
6	Senior Supply Chain Manager	P&G	6
7	Senior Manager	Parle	15
8	Sourcing Manager	Marico Ltd	9
9	Associate Manager	Dabur India	10
10	Purchasing Manager	Colgate Palmolive	14
11	Head of Supply Chain	Nestle India	13
12	Manager	Emami Ltd	15
13	Supply Chain Lead	GlaxoSmithKline Consumer Healthcare	10
14	Manager	Wipro Consumer Care and Lighting	10
15	Manager	Godrej & Boyce	9
16	Manager	Hersheys India	7
17	Manager	Amul	4
18	Senior Manager	Pepsico	5
19	Senior Manager	Coca-Cola	12
20	Director	Mondelez India	11

Table 2. Summary of correlation analysis

Variables	SCM	RFID	IoT	BT	CT	AI	IT
SCM	1						
RFID	0.39**	1					
IoT	0.30**	0.38**	1				
BT	0.40**	0.41**	0.39**	1			
CT	0.49**	0.39**	0.35**	0.31**	1		
AI	0.57**	0.37**	0.41**	0.38**	0.34**	1	
IT	0.06	0.41*	0.23*	0.31*	0.52*	0.29*	1

Note: * & ** indicates 1 percent and 5 percent respectively

BT (r=0.40, p<0.05), RFID (r=0.39, p<0.05) and IoT (r=0.30, p<0.05). But however, the information technology does not have correlated with the supply chain visibility since the p value is greater than 5 percent significance level.

Multiple Linear Regression Analysis

Used multiple linear regression since the number of explanatory variables is more than two and the summary of the output given in Table 3

Table 3 depicts the summary output of multiple linear regression. The overall model explained by R^2 is 0.49 percent which indicates changes in the supply chain visibility is clearly explained by changes in the Artificial Intelligence (AI), Internet of Things (IoT), Blockchain, Artificial Intelligence (AI), Radio Frequency Identification (RFID), Cloud Technology and Information Technology (IT). There are other factors also which would be influencing on supply chain visibility in the FMCG by 0.51 percent. Colum 2 shows the impact level of each variables represented by beta coefficient value. It is observed that only Artificial Intelligence (AI) does have positive and significant (B=0.588, P<0.01) influence on the supply chain visibility which indicates one percent change in the Artificial Intelligence (AI), increasing in the supply chain visibility in FMCG by 0.58 percent. Hence, H_5 is accepted. But, the contradictory result found in the previous studies (Xu et al., 2021, Hald and Kinra,2019 and Wu et al.,2017) claims

Table 3. Summary of multiple linear regression

Explanatory Variables	Coefficient	Std. Error	t statistics	p value	R^2	F-Stat
Constant	2.256	2.287	0.987	0.336		
RFID	0.095	0.186	0.513	0.613		
IoT	0.168	0.176	0.953	0.352		
BT	0.184	0.188	0.607	0.551	0.497	3.293**
CT	-0.032	0.230	-0.031	0.891		
AI	0.588	0.187	0.694	0.005*		
IT	-0.342	0.430	-0.131	0.436		

Dependent variable: SCV * &** Indicate 1 percent and 5 percent significance level that blockchain improves supply chain visibility and traceability. Though the result is contradictory with the previous results, the present study result is aligned with (Najafi et al., 2022) stated that the use of AI in supply chain management is growing. quickly. One of the main benefits of AI is its ability to detect patterns in vast amounts of data. However, the other chosen technologies such as RFID, IoT, BT, CT and IT does not have significant impact on the supply chain visibility in the FMCG sector and also the significant level of those variables are greater than five percent. Therefore, H_1 H_2 H_3 H_4 and H_6 rejected. A surprising learning here is that Artificial intelligence has the most significant impact than block chain whose application in the field of supply chain has been viewed crucial. However, IT and blockchain technologies might be very significant for other areas of supply chain and specifically for supply chain visibility the application of Artificial Intelligence is very significant for its enhancement.

CONCLUSION

Supply chain visibility can be considered as a process that captures and transfers accurate, timely, and complete information among business partners in supply chain. Based on an extensive literature review it is found that supply chain visibility literature assumes that technology has a direct impact on the supply chain visibility of an organization's supply chain. This study has proven it by performing statistical tests using the data collected from the supply chain managers from the top FMCG companies about the perception of the supply chain professionals about the supply chain visibility in their respective organizations. The study helped in understanding the direction of effect of technology on supply chain visibility. The study also gave insights into the main characteristics of supply chain visibility and the effect of technology on the key performance indicators of supply chain visibility. The impact of technology on supply chain visibility in the FMCG sector has been substantial. Especially, there was a greater impact of AI than the other technology on supply chain visibility. Apart from this, technology has enabled real-time tracking, data analytics, supply chain collaboration, and visibility, all of which have improved the efficiency and effectiveness of the supply chain. With the increasing demand for ethical and sustainable products, supply chain visibility has become more critical than ever before. Therefore, leveraging technology to improve supply chain visibility is crucial for companies operating in the FMCG sector to stay competitive and meet consumer expectations

Practical Implications

Though many technologies are available and adopted earlier by FMCG companies, the influence of Artificial Intelligence (AI) is much greater than the other technologies in the present study. AI technology contributes in many ways to supply chain visibility in the FMCG companies in the present scenario. AI algorithms can analyze the historical sales data, market trends and weather patterns for demand forecasting. Also, predictive analytics can be done with the help of machine learling algorithms to predict the potential supply chain issues. This would helps in reducing the risk, optimizing transportation issues and improve the overall efficiency of supply chain system. In addition to this, AI can also assist in evaluating and choosing the best suppliers based on various parameters such as quality, responsiveness and reliability. Route optimization also can be done wit help of AI to reducing the transportation cost, time saving etc. Hence, the FMCG companies can increase the customer satisfaction and can decrease the environmental impact. Overall, the adoption AI in supply chain visibility of FMCG companies would helps to take proactive decisions, improving operational efficiency, cost reduction and increasing customer satisfaction.

Limitation and Scope for Future Research

The present study examines the influence of technologies on supply chain visibility in FMCG sector, although the availability of data restricts its scope. Further research may take into the account of other sector such as energy, textiles, steel etc. The impact of technology on supply chain visibility may vary based on the nature of the product, market conditions, and the types of technology being used. Data availability may be a limitation, as some companies may not be willing to share their data due to confidentiality concerns. This could limit the scope of the research and make it difficult to draw conclusions that are representative of the entire FMCG sector. The successful integration of technology into the supply chain may require significant changes in the organizational structure, business processes, and cultural mindset of the companies involved. The research may not fully capture these complexities and may not provide a comprehensive understanding of the impact of technology on supply chain visibility. While supply chain collaboration has been recognized as a crucial factor for improving supply chain visibility, there is still much to learn about the most effective ways to collaborate among stakeholders. Future research can investigate how different collaboration models, such as vertical integration, horizontal collaboration, and platform-based collaboration, impact supply chain visibility in the FMCG sector. While technology has improved supply chain visibility, there is still a need to understand how it impacts sustainability in the FMCG sector. Future research can investigate how technology can be leveraged to improve the sustainability of the supply chain and reduce its environmental impact.

REFERENCES

Agarwal, P., Gupta, H., & Goyal, S. (2020). Impact of supply chain agility on FMCG sector: A comprehensive literature review. *Journal of Advances in Management Research*, *17*(1), 19–34.

Caridi, M., Moretto, A., Perego, A., & Tumino, A. (2014). The benefits of supply chain visibility: A value assessment model. *International Journal of Production Economics*, *151*, 1–19. doi:10.1016/j.ijpe.2013.12.025

Chen, F., Drezner, Z., Ryan, J. K., & Simchi-Levi, D. (2017). Quantifying the bullwhip effect in supply chains with high-frequency demand information. *Manufacturing & Service Operations Management*, *19*(3), 383–397.

Chen, I. J., & Paulraj, A. (2018). IoT in supply chain management. *Journal of Manufacturing Technology Management*, *29*(4), 658–666.

Dorri, A., Kanhere, S. S., Jurdak, R., & Gauravaram, P. (2017). Blockchain for IoT security and privacy: The case study of a smart home. *2017 IEEE International Conference on Pervasive Computing and Communications Workshops, PerCom Workshops 2017*, (pp. 618–623). IEEE. 10.1109/PERCOMW.2017.7917634

FMCG giant Marico's digital initiatives help them save ₹ 35 crore. (2018, January 19). CIO. https://www.cio.com/article/218437/fmcg-giant-marico-s-digital-initiatives-helpthem-save-35-crore.html

Gupta, R., Saxena, A., Singh, A. K., & Bhatia, M. (2022). Impact of technology adoption on supply chain performance in FMCG industry. *Journal of Enterprise Information Management*.

Hair, J. F., Sarstedt, M., Ringle, C. M., & Mena, J. A. (2012). An assessment of the use of partial least squares structural equation modeling in marketing research. *Journal of the Academy of Marketing Science*, *40*(3), 414–433. doi:10.1007/s11747-011-0261-6

Hald, K. S., & Kinra, A. (2019). How the blockchain enables and constrains supply chain performance. *International Journal of Physical Distribution & Logistics Management*, *49*(4), 376–397. doi:10.1108/IJPDLM-02-2019-0063

Hazen, B. T., Mollenkopf, D. A., & Wang, Y. (2017). Remanufacturing for the Circular Economy: An Examination of Consumer Switching Behavior. *Business Strategy and the Environment*, *26*(4), 451–464. doi:10.1002/bse.1929

How Block Chain Is Revolutionizing Supply Chain Industry. (2019, September 19). Gazelle Information Technologies. https://gazelle.in/how-block-chain-is-revolutionizing-supply-chain-industry

How FMCG companies benefit from supply chain visibility. (2022, June 9). Supply Chain Visibility for FMCG Companies| Maersk. https://www.maersk.com/insights/digitalisation/supply-chain-visibility-for-fmcgcompanies

Ivanov, D., & Dolgui, A. (2021). OR-methods for coping with the ripple effect in supply chains during COVID-19 pandemic: Managerial insights and research implications. *International Journal of Production Economics*, *232*, 107921. doi:10.1016/j.ijpe.2020.107921

Kharlamov, A., & Parry, G. (2018). Advanced Supply Chains: Visibility, Blockchain and Human Behaviour. *Contributions to Management Science*, 321–343. doi:10.1007/978-3-319-74304-2_15

Lee, C. Y., & Tang, C. S. (2020). Supply chain visibility and customer satisfaction: The moderating role of demand uncertainty. *Journal of Operations Management*, *65*(1), 32–48.

Lee, J. Y., Jeong, B., & Joo, Y. H. (2020). Artificial intelligence (AI) and machine learning (ML) in supply chain management: A comprehensive review. *Sustainability*, *12*(6), 2353.

Li, S., & Lin, B. (2006). Accessing information sharing and information quality in Supply chain management. *Decision Support Systems*, *42*(3), 1641–1656. doi:10.1016/j.dss.2006.02.011

Li, Y., Wang, Z., & Shang, J. (2021). Supply chain visibility and sustainability performance: Evidence from the fashion industry. *Journal of Business Ethics*, *169*(1), 85–101.

Machine Health & Supply Chain Reliability. (n.d.). Colgate-Palmolive. https://www.colgatepalmolive.com/enus/who-we-are/stories/machine-health-supply-chain-reliability

Mollenkopf, D., Stolze, H., & Tate, W. L. (2017). Supply chain visibility: Understanding the business value, components, and maturity levels. *Journal of Business Logistics*, *38*(1), 6–25.

Najafi, S. E., Nozari, H., & Edalatpanah, S. A. (2022, November 30). Artificial Intelligence of Things (AIoT) and Industry 4.0–Based Supply Chain (FMCG Industry). *A Roadmap for Enabling Industry 4.0 by Artificial Intelligence,* (pp. 31–41). Wiley. doi:10.1002/9781119905141.ch3

Next-gen Digital Supply Chain Planning & Optimization. (n.d.). ITC Infotech. https://www.itcinfotech.com/capabilities/supply-chain-management/

Papathanasiou, A., Gunasekaran, A., Dubey, R., & Fosso Wamba, S. (2017). Big data and analytics in operations and supply chain management: Managerial aspects and practical challenges. *Production Planning and Control, 28*(11-12), 929–932.

Reyes, P. M., Visich, J. K., & Jaska, P. (2020, March 1). Managing the Dynamics of New Technologies in the Global Supply Chain. *IEEE Engineering Management Review, 48*(1), 156–162. doi:10.1109/EMR.2020.2968889

Saravanan, R., & Ravi, V. (2019). Supply chain integration and performance in FMCG industry. *Journal of Advances in Management Research, 16*(3), 293–314.

Sharma, R., Shishodia, A., Gunasekaran, A., Min, H., & Munim, Z. H. (2022, February 9). The role of artificial intelligence in supply chain management: Mapping the territory. *International Journal of Production Research, 60*(24), 7527–7550. doi:10.1080/00207543.2022.2029611

Technologies, I. N. (2018, November 21). Blockchain and IoT Revolutionizing Supply Chain Management. How Blockchain and IoT Revolutionizing Supply Chain Management. https://www.indusnet.co.in/blockchain-and-iot-revolutionizing-supply-chainmanagement

Tests, S. (n.d.). *How to Test Validity questionnaire Using SPSS.* SPSS Tests. http://www.spsstests.com/2015/02/how-to-test-validity-questionnaire.htm

Tseng, S. H., Chen, S. M., & Yang, C. (2022). Cloud computing-enabled supply chain visibility: A systematic review and future research agenda. *Sustainability, 14*(2), 372.

Verma, A., Verma, P., & Verma, N. (2018). Supply chain management practices in FMCG industry: a literature review. *Journal of Advances in Management.*

Wang, H., Zhang, L., & Yeung, J. H. Y. (2018). The impact of supply chain visibility on supply chain disruption management: A structural equation modeling approach. *International Journal of Production Economics, 195*, 295–301.

Wang, Z., Zhao, L., & Duan, Y. (2021). Enhancing supply chain visibility: An RFID-enabled information system. *Journal of Intelligent Manufacturing, 32*(4), 825–838.

Wei, H. L., & Wang, E. T. (2010). The strategic value of supply chain visibility: Increasing the ability to reconfigure. *European Journal of Information Systems, 19*(2), 238–249. doi:10.1057/ejis.2010.10

Williams, B. D., Roh, J., Tokar, T., & Swink, M. (2013). Leveraging supply chain visibility for responsiveness: The moderating role of internal integration. *Journal of Operations Management, 31*(7-8), 543–554. doi:10.1016/j.jom.2013.09.003

Williams, B. D., Roh, J., Tokar, T., & Swink, M. (2013, October 4). Leveraging supply chain visibility for responsiveness: The moderating role of internal integration. *Journal of Operations Management*, *31*(7–8), 543–554. doi:10.1016/j.jom.2013.09.003

Wu, K. J., Liao, C. J., Tseng, M. L., Lim, M. K., Hu, J., & Tan, K. (2017). Toward sustainability: Using big data to explore the decisive attributes of supply chain risks and uncertainties. *Journal of Cleaner Production*, *142*, 663–676. doi:10.1016/j.jclepro.2016.04.040

Xu, P., Lee, J., Barth, J. R., & Richey, R. G. (2021, January 20). Blockchain as supply chain technology: Considering transparency and security. *International Journal of Physical Distribution & Logistics Management*, *51*(3), 305–324. doi:10.1108/IJPDLM-08-2019-0234

Zhang, M., Xu, L., & Zhang, J. (2019). Blockchain technology for enhancing supply chain visibility and traceability. *Industrial Management & Data Systems*, *119*(7), 1418–1437.

Zhang, X., & Zhang, Z. (2019). The impact of supply chain visibility on supply chain collaboration: A perspective of Chinese manufacturers. *Sustainability*, *11*(7), 1942.

Chapter 7
Enhancing Business Capabilities Through Digital Transformation, Upscaling, and Upskilling in the Era of Industry 5.0:
A Literature Review

Baranidharan Subburayan
https://orcid.org/0000-0002-7780-4045
Christ University, India

ABSTRACT

This literature review aims to understand the recent developments in the field of upscaling and upskilling in the digital transformation of business, from an Industry 5.0 prospective. It used a comprehensive search of relevant peer-reviewed journal articles, industry reports, and online sources to gather the relevant data. The findings indicate that upscaling is essential for industry 5.0, and that businesses should invest in upskilling and upscaling programs to meet the changing demands of the digital economy. This literature review provides a comprehensive analysis of the current state of upscaling and upskilling in the digital transformation of business and provides insights into the future direction of this field. It also highlights the importance of collaboration between businesses, governments, and educational institutions to ensure that the workforce is prepared for the future of work.

INTRODUCTION

The advent of Industry 5.0 has brought about a paradigm shift in the way businesses operate and compete. The integration of advanced technologies such as artificial intelligence, the Internet of Things, and robotics has revolutionized the traditional business landscape and has necessitated the need for organizations to

DOI: 10.4018/978-1-6684-9576-6.ch007

adapt to the new normal. Upscaling and upskilling are two crucial elements in ensuring that businesses remain competitive and relevant in the digital age. Upscaling involves the expansion of a company's operations, services, and offerings to meet the demands of the market. This requires organizations to invest in new technologies, infrastructure, and processes that can support the growth of their business. On the other hand, upskilling involves the development of new skills, knowledge, and competencies among employees to effectively implement new technologies and processes.

In recent years, there has been a growing body of literature that explores the relationship between upscaling and upskilling and the impact they have on business capabilities. The purpose of this literature review is to analyse and synthesize the existing research on upscaling and upskilling in the era of Industry 5.0, and to identify the key trends, challenges, and opportunities in this field.

The literature review methodology used in this study is based on the Preferred Reporting Items for Reviews and Meta-Analyses (PRISMA) guidelines, ensuring a comprehensive and rigorous examination of the relevant literature. The findings of this study will contribute to a deeper understanding of the role of upscaling and upskilling in digital transformation and will provide valuable insights for organizations seeking to enhance their business capabilities in the face of Industry 5.0.[1] Industry 5.0 represents a significant leap forward in terms of the integration of advanced technologies into businesses, compared to Industry 4.0. In Industry 4.0, the focus was primarily on digitizing operations and automating processes to increase efficiency. However, in Industry 5.0, the emphasis is on creating a fully interconnected and collaborative digital ecosystem, where all business operations, processes, and systems are interconnected and operate in real-time.

This shift has profound implications for upskilling and upscaling in digital transformation. In Industry 5.0, upskilling has become even more crucial, as employees must have a broader range of digital skills and competencies to effectively manage and implement advanced technologies. Upskilling in Industry 5.0 also involves developing new skills, such as data analysis, artificial intelligence, and cybersecurity, to support the integration of these technologies into businesses.

Upscaling in Industry 5.0 is also more comprehensive, as businesses must invest in the necessary technologies, infrastructure, and processes to fully leverage the benefits of Industry 5.0. This includes the implementation of cloud computing, the Internet of Things, and advanced data analytics systems. In addition, upscaling in Industry 5.0 also involves the creation of new business models and services, such as digital twins and the optimization of supply chains, to stay ahead of the competition.

Challenges and Opportunities Facing Industry 4.0 and Industry 5.0

Challenges:

1. Security concerns: As Industry 4.0 and Industry 5.0 rely heavily on the internet and digital technologies, the security of information and data is a major concern. The risk of cyberattacks, data breaches, and hacking is high.
2. High investment costs: The implementation of Industry 4.0 and Industry 5.0 requires a significant amount of investment in technology, equipment, and training. This is a major challenge for small and medium-sized enterprises.
3. Job displacement: Automation and digitalization may lead to job displacement as machines and robots replace human workers.

4. Resistance to change: The implementation of Industry 4.0 and Industry 5.0 requires a change in mindset, work culture, and business processes. Some organizations may resist the change due to their traditional work practices.

Opportunities:

1. Improved efficiency and productivity: Industry 4.0 and Industry 5.0 technologies can increase the efficiency and productivity of businesses by automating and streamlining processes.
2. Increased flexibility: Digitalization and automation can help businesses become more agile and flexible in responding to changing market demands.
3. Enhanced customer experience: Industry 4.0 and Industry 5.0 technologies enable businesses to better understand customer needs and provide personalized and efficient services.
4. New job opportunities: While Industry 4.0 and Industry 5.0 may lead to job displacement, they also create new job opportunities in areas such as data analysis, cybersecurity, and robotics.
5. Sustainable development: Industry 4.0 and Industry 5.0 can help businesses move towards sustainable development by reducing waste, optimizing energy consumption, and improving supply chain management.

LITERATURE REVIEW

Upskilling, Upscaling, AI, IoT, and Digital Transformation

The article "Scaling up Disruptive Agricultural Technologies in Africa" by Kim, J, Shah, P, Gaskell, JC, and Prasann (2020) focused on the importance of upskilling and upscaling in the implementation of modern technologies in the agricultural sector in Africa. The authors argue that supporting the development of the industry 5.0 requires the use of tools that can facilitate upskilling and upscaling. The authors found that the use of modern technologies, such as precision agriculture and data analytics, can help improve the productivity and efficiency of the agricultural sector in Africa. The digital transformation of SMEs was the focus of the article by Kergroach, S and Bianchini, MM (2021). The authors argued that SMEs must embrace the digital transformation to remain competitive and relevant in today's business environment. The authors found that upskilling and upscaling were crucial in the digital transformation of SMEs, as they must invest in advanced technologies and digital skills to compete in the industry 5.0.

The article "The Shifting Role of Accountants in the Era of Digital Disruption" by Mujiono, MN (2021) explored the impact of digital disruption on the role of accountants. The author argud that the industry 5.0 had led to significant changes in the role of accountants, and they must upskill and upscale to keep up with the latest technologies and processes. The author found that upskilling and upscaling can help accountants become more efficient, effective, and relevant in the era of digital disruption.

In "Digitalization and Social Dialogue: Challenges, Opportunities, and Responses" by Llorente, RM de Bustillo (2021), the author explored the impact of digitalization on social dialogue and the role of upskilling and upscaling in digital transformation. The author argues that digitalization presents both challenges and opportunities for social dialogue, and upskilling and upscaling were essential in ensuring that digital transformation benefits everyone. The author found that upskilling and upscaling can help overcome the challenges and take advantage of the opportunities presented by digitalization. The article "Stakeholders' Expectations of Graduates of a Work-Study Nursing Upskilling Programme in East Africa" by Brownie, S, Gatimu, S, Kambo, I, Mwizerwa, J, and ... (2020) focused on the importance of upskilling in the nursing sector in East Africa. The authors argude that upskilling was crucial for improving the quality of care and the competitiveness of the nursing sector in the era of industry 5.0. The authors found that upskilling can help meet the expectations of stakeholders, such as employers and patients, and improve the quality of care in the nursing sector.

These articles highlight the importance of upskilling and upscaling in the digital transformation of various industries and sectors in the era of industry 5.0. The authors found that upskilling and upscaling were essential in ensuring that businesses remain competitive and relevant in the era of digital disruption and can take advantage of the opportunities presented by the industry 5.0. Brownie, Gatimu, Kambo, et al. (2020) conducted a study on the stakeholders' expectations of nursing graduates following completion of a work-study upskilling programme in East Africa. The study revealed that the graduates were expected to possess a wide range of skills, including technical skills, interpersonal skills, and critical thinking skills. Yusif, Hafeez-Baig, Soar, and Teik (2020) used PLS-SEM path analysis to determined the predictive relevance of e-Health readiness assessment model. The results showed that the e-Health readiness model had a significant impact on the prediction of e-Health adoption in healthcare organizations. Kuriakose and Tiew (2022) conducted a review of the efficiency of the Malaysia-SME program. The review found that the program was successful in promoting the development of small and medium-sized enterprises in Malaysia and that there was room for improvement in terms of increasing the program's outreach and providing better support to participating companies.

Ngwa, Addai, Adewole, et al. (2022) wrote a commission on cancer in sub-Saharan Africa. The commission found that cancer was a growing health problem in the region, with a high burden of preventable cancers and a shortage of cancer care resources. Corsi (2002) wrote a book on exploring unemployment in the European Union. The book analysed the different factors that contribute to unemployment in the EU, including economic and labour market conditions, and provided policy recommendations for addressing the issue. Kamath, R, and Venumuddala, VR (2023) highlighted the impact of emerging technologies such as artificial intelligence, blockchain, and the Internet of Things (IoT) on the Indian IT sector. It outlines the opportunities and challenges posed by these technologies and provides recommendations for companies to adapt to the changing technology landscape.

Paula, D de, Marx, C, Wolf, and E, Dremel, C (2023) presented a managerial mental model to promote innovation in the context of digital transformation. The model emphasizes the importance of creativity, collaboration, and experimentation in the innovation process. The authors suggested that this model can help companies to achieve a competitive advantage in the digital economy. Fafunwa, T, and Odufuwa, F (2023) argued that digital transformation is essential for African micro, small, and medium enterprises (MSMEs) to take advantage of the Africa Continental Free Trade Area (AfCFTA). The authors outline the benefits of digital transformation for MSMEs and provided recommendations for policymakers to support the digitalization of these businesses.

Chowdhury, S, Dey, P, Joel-Edgar, S, et. al (2023) proposed an AI capability framework for human resource management that can unlock the value of artificial intelligence in this field. The authors suggested that this framework can help companies to automate routine tasks, improve decision-making, and enhance employee engagement. They also discuss the ethical implications of using AI in human resource management. Rajaram (2023) discussed the future of teaching and learning strategies in the context of digital transformation. The chapter highlighted the importance of understanding the characteristics of modern learners, including their preferences, learning styles, and knowledge acquisition methods.

Behrendt et al. (2021) focused on the use of Industrial IoT and other advanced technologies in digital transformation efforts. The authors highlight the importance of data-driven decision making and note that upskilling is necessary to enable organizations to make the most of these technologies. Mendoza and Ibarra (2023) explored technology-enabled circular business models for the hybridization of wind farms, focusing on integrated wind and solar energy, power-to-gas, and power-to-liquid systems. The authors identified the potential benefits of these technologies in enhancing energy efficiency and reducing environmental impacts.

Pelenkahu (2022) examined the challenges and opportunities associated with scaling up digital transformation in education. The paper revealed the importance of developing a comprehensive digital transformation strategy, leveraging emerging technologies, and providing training and education programs to support upskilling and reskilling. Kumar and Basu (2022) exhibited the role of end-user feedback in informing the policy landscape for agri-digital transition in India. The authors argued that participatory approaches to policymaking can help to foster greater engagement and trust between stakeholders and enable the development of more effective policies.

Wang and Pettit (2022) provided a primer on supply chain digital transformation, outlining key concepts and strategies for implementing digital technologies in the supply chain. The chapter highlights the potential benefits of digital transformation in enhancing supply chain visibility, agility, and responsiveness to changing market conditions. Rowan et al. (2022) explored the digital transformation of peatland eco-innovations, known as Paludiculture, to enable real-time sustainable production of green-friendly products. The article identified digital tools that can optimize Paludiculture production while reducing the ecological footprint of these products.

Klein et al. (2022) investigated how Portugal can maximize the benefits of the digital transformation. The authors suggested ways in which the country can leverage digital technology to improve its economic performance. Oeij et al. (2022) provided a policy paper on digital transformation and regional policy options for inclusive growth. The study highlighted the potential of digital transformation to promote regional economic growth and proposed policy measures that can facilitate this transformation. Nichols (2022) emphasized the need for professional services companies to fast-track their digital transformation efforts to keep up with the demands of the industry. The article proposed various strategies that can help these companies leverage digital technology to enhance their operations. Vide et al. (2022) examined how small and medium-sized enterprises can enhance their sustainable business practices through digitalization. The authors highlighted the benefits of digitalization, such as improved efficiency, reduced costs, and enhanced customer satisfaction, and provided a framework for SMEs to adopt digital technologies.

The selected articles provided insights into the digital transformation of various industries and domains. Chang-Richards et al. (2022) present a comprehensive review of technological advancements and their potential implications for the construction industry. Gamhewage et al. (2022) emphasized the use of digital tools to transform face-to-face focus group methodology in managing institutional change in global healthcare organizations. Ziozias and Anthopoulos (2022) explored the concept of smart governance and its role in the digital transformation of cities, while Mustafaoglu (2022) offered a case study of a local Turkish bank that implemented a digital transformation strategy. Ponnana and Uppalapati (2022) provided a case study and positive impact of the digital transformation of IKEA's supply chain during and after the pandemic. Stewart (2022) revealed that the transition from digitization to digital transformation for an undisclosed company, while Chakravorti (2022) offered a strategic framework for digital transformation implementation. Corbeil and Corbeil (2022) proposed a disruptive pedagogical approach to facilitate digital transformation in higher education. Finally, Mourtzis et al. (2022) survey enabling technologies and propose a framework for digital manufacturing based on extended reality, and Lang and Triantoro (2022) present a typology of digital skills initiatives to facilitate upskilling and reskilling for the future of work. Collectively, the articles suggested the need for a holistic approach to digital transformation that considers organizational culture, governance, and employee skills, among other factors.

Chang-Richards et al. (2022) evidenced that the future of technology implementation in construction, while Gamhewage et al. (2022) focused on the digital transformation of face-to-face focus group methodology in the healthcare sector. Ziozias and Anthopoulos (2022) presented a case study on forming smart governance under a city digital transformation strategy, while Mustafaoglu (2022) discussed the implementation of digital transformation in a local Turkish bank was effective. Lastly, Ponnana and Uppalapati (2022) studied the digital transformation of IKEA's supply chain was brunt during and after the pandemic.

In "HOW CAN COMPANY X EFFECTIVELY MAKE A TRANSITION FROM DIGITISATION TO DIGITAL TRANSFORMATION?", Stewart, L (2022) Stewart emphasized the importance of a holistic approach to digital transformation rather than just focusing on digitization. The study found that company X could improve its transition from digitization to digital transformation by increasing its investment in technology, prioritizing data security, engaging stakeholders, and implementing a culture of digital innovation. Chakravorti, N (2022) "Digital Transformation: A Strategic Structure for Implementation" is a comprehensive book that presents a strategic framework for implementing digital transformation in businesses. It explored the role of upskilling and upscaling in digital transformation and offered insights into how modern technologies and tools can support the process.

"Operator 5.0: A survey on enabling technologies and a framework for digital manufacturing based on extended reality" by Mourtzis et al (2022), giveaways insights into the concept of "Operator 5.0," which refers to a new type of worker enabled by emerging digital technologies. The study presents a framework for digital manufacturing based on extended reality (XR) and identifies several enabling technologies that can support the digital transformation of manufacturing processes. The article "Quality 4.0–a review of and framework for quality management in the digital era" by Kumar, R Ranjith, Ganesh, LS, et. al., (2022) provided a comprehensive review of Quality 4.0, a term used to refer to the integration of digital technologies into quality management. The article discussed the key principles and components of Quality 4.0 and provides a framework for implementing it in organizations. The authors concluded that Quality 4.0 has the potential to transform quality management by leveraging digital technologies to drive continuous improvement and enhance customer satisfaction.

The article "Digital innovations for transitioning to circular plastic value chains in Africa" Oyinlola, M, Schröder, P, Whitehead, T et. al (2022) focused on the potential of digital technologies to support the transition to circular plastic value chains in Africa. The authors highlight a range of digital innovations that can be used to improve the efficiency and sustainability of plastic value chains, including blockchain, data analytics, and IoT. The authors conclude that digital innovations have the potential to address the plastic waste challenge in Africa and create new economic opportunities. Johnston et al. (2022) revealed the barriers to the adoption of digital solutions by care homes in Scotland. Their findings highlighted the need for training and support for staff, adequate IT infrastructure, and clear governance frameworks to facilitate the adoption of digital solutions. Gyulai et al. (2022) proposed an operational structure for an Industry 4.0 oriented learning factory. Schreieck et al. (2022) provided an institutional perspective on the transformation of product platform ecosystems to innovation platform ecosystems. The authors identified the governance structures needed for successful ecosystem transformation.

The five articles presented cover a range of topics related to digital transformation, Industry 4.0, and organizational adoption of new technologies.

Al-Rashdi (2022) revealed based on a case study of the adoption of digital technologies in the petroleum industry in Oman, and proposed an adoption model to facilitate the implementation of such technologies. Auktor (2022) similarly presented a case study of Morocco's automotive and garment sectors, explored the opportunities and challenges presented by Industry 4.0. Dieste et al. (2022) examined organizational tensions that arise in Industry 4.0 implementation, applying a paradox theory approach. Rabiey et al. (2022) exhibited a different perspective, discussing the use of scaling-up methods to understand tree-pathogen interactions, demonstrating the diverse applications of digital technologies. Finally, Chugh et al. (2022) reviewed the grey literature on Robotic Process Automation (RPA) adoption in organizations.

Mitchell et al. (2022) reviewed the opportunities and challenges of artificial intelligence and robotics in the offshore wind sector. The authors highlighted the potential benefits of AI and robotics in enhancing the efficiency and safety of wind farms operations, as well as reducing the environmental impact. However, the study also emphasizes the need to address key challenges, such as the high costs of implementing AI and robotics and the need for skilled workers to operate and maintain them. Spohrer et al. (2022) provided a comprehensive review of service science in the AI era, focusing on science, logic, and architecture perspectives. The authors emphasize the importance of designing AI-based services that are not only efficient but also ethical, trustworthy, and user-cantered. The study provided useful insights for service designers, policymakers, and researchers interested in leveraging AI technologies to enhance service quality and customer experience.

Bellantuono et al. (2021) draw on change management literature to explore digital transformation models for the transition to Industry 4.0. The authors highlight the importance of change management strategies and upskilling to enable successful digital transformations, and emphasize the need for a focus on people, culture, and leadership alongside technology implementation. Casini (2021) focused on the construction industry and the potential for advanced technologies to support digital transformation. The author highlighted the importance of upskilling to ensure that workers are able to make the most of new tools and technologies, and notes the potential for digitalization to improve efficiency and sustainability in the construction sector.

Howie et al. (2022) examined the rapid rise of paediatric telehealth during the COVID-19 pandemic, highlighting the role of technology in enabling remote consultations and reducing barriers to care. The authors also note that upskilling was necessary to support the rapid implementation of telehealth services during the pandemic. Littlejohn and Pammer-Schindler (2022) explored the use of technology in professional learning, highlighting the potential for technology to support lifelong learning and enable more flexible, personalized learning experiences. They also noted the importance of ongoing upskilling to ensure that individuals can make the most of these technologies. The last five articles presented in this systematic literature review all focus on the digital transformation of various industries and sectors, and the role of technology and upskilling in enabling this transformation.

Potential Benefits and Challenges of Upscaling and Upskilling in the Digital Transformation of Business

In "A New Dawn for Global Value Chain Participation in the Philippines" (Arenas and Coulibaly, 2022), the authors analysed the potential for upscaling and upskilling in the Philippines' global value chain participation. They found that there was a need for improvement in infrastructure, skills development, and access to finance in order to increase the country's competitiveness in the global market. The authors suggested that government support and private sector investment were crucial for the successful implementation of upscaling and upskilling initiatives. In "Energy and Manufacturing" (2021), the author provided an overview of the role of energy and manufacturing in the industry 5.0 perspective. The paper highlighted the need for upskilling and upscaling in these sectors to support their growth and competitiveness in the modern digital landscape. The author also discusses the potential benefits of adopting new technologies and tools to increase efficiency and productivity.

In "High-touch and here-to-stay: Future skills demands in US low wage service occupations" (Gatta, Boushey, and Appelbaum, 2009), the authors analysed the skills demands in US low-wage service occupations. They found that despite technological advancements, there was still a high demand for human interaction and customer service skills in these occupations. The authors suggested that upskilling initiatives should focus on these high-touch skills to ensure the future competitiveness of the workers in these occupations. In "Skilling Tanzania: improving financing, governance and outputs of the skills development sector" (Andreoni, 2018), the author provided an overview of the skills development sector in Tanzania. The author argued that there was a need for improvements in financing, governance, and outputs to increase the effectiveness of upskilling initiatives in the country. The author suggested that these improvements would help Tanzania achieve its goal of becoming a middle-income country by 2025.

In "Measuring technical efficiency in Zimbabwe's manufacturing sector: a two-stage DEA Tobit approach" (Dube, 2021), the author investigated the technical efficiency of the manufacturing sector in Zimbabwe. The author found that there was a need for upscaling and upskilling initiatives in the sector to increase its competitiveness and productivity. The author suggested that the adoption of new technologies and tools would play a crucial role in achieving these goals. Implications of AI on the Indian Economy (Kathuria, Kedia, and Kapilavai, 2020) highlighted the potential benefits and challenges of the integration of AI in the Indian economy. The authors suggested that while AI could lead to increased productivity and efficiency, it could also lead to job losses and a skills gap in the workforce. Decarbonizing Energy Intensive Industries 2021: Country Study France (Serrano, 2021) focused on the challenges and opportunities in decarbonizing France's energy intensive industries. The author suggests that decarbonizing the industries could lead to significant reductions in greenhouse gas emissions, improved competitiveness, and job creation. Analysis of the FinTech Landscape in the Philippines (Quimba, Barral, and Carlos, 2021) provided an overview of the FinTech industry in the Philippines and its potential for growth and development. The authors suggested that the development of FinTech in the Philippines could increase financial inclusion and improve access to financial services for the unbanked population.

Project of Introducing a Supportive tool for Establishing and Growing Start-ups in the Environment of Secondary Schools in Zlín Region (Yatsenko, 2020) focused on the development of a tool to support start-ups in the Zlín region of the Czech Republic. The author suggests that the tool could lead to increased entrepreneurship and job creation in the region.

Pathways from VET Awards to Engineering Degrees: A Higher Education Perspective (King, Dowling, and Godfrey, 2011) focused on the pathways available for students with vocational education and training (VET) awarded to pursue engineering degrees. The authors suggested that these pathways could lead to increased access to higher education and improved career opportunities for students with VET awards.

Teaching and Education

Le, TT, Sit, HHW, and Chen, S (2023) examined the challenges faced by Vietnamese foreign language teachers during the COVID-19 pandemic and identifies the strategies that enabled them to succeed in online teaching. The authors highlighted the importance of adaptability, creativity, and collaboration in the online teaching environment. Corbeil, ME, and Corbeil, JR (2022) discussed the concept of "wrapping a course around a course" to promote learner agency in "Digital transformation of higher education through disruptive pedagogies." The paper focused on the use of disruptive pedagogies to enhance higher education institutions' digital transformation efforts, emphasized the need for innovative teaching methods to support learners' digital skills development.

Lang and Triantoro's (2022) "Upskilling and Reskilling for the Future of Work: A Typology of Digital Skills Initiatives" discussed the importance of upskilling and reskilling initiatives to address the skills gap in the digital age. The paper presents a typology of digital skills initiatives, including formal education, training programs, and digital skills certifications. The study highlights the need for a multidimensional approach to digital skills development to support the future of work. Stracke et al. (2022) discussed the international response to the COVID-19 pandemic in school and higher education, emphasizing the need for quick adaptation to digital solutions for remote learning. Finally, Arıker (2022) examined the role of massive open online course (MOOC) platforms in creating social value by reskilling and upskilling the unemployed, especially after COVID-19.

'EUvsVirus.' De Vries (2022) exhibited the ethical dimension of emerging technologies in engineering education, emphasizing the need to integrate ethical considerations into engineering education. Finally, Vujnovic and Foster (2022) explored the impact of online instruction and the "hyflex teaching 'shock doctrine'" on higher education and disaster capitalism. The authors argued that this mode of instruction has created a new opportunity for disaster capitalism, leading to further exploitation of students and instructors. Genelza, G (2022) examined the English language learning opportunities and competence of first-year BS-Criminology students under the new normal setting. The research highlighted the importance of English language proficiency in the global economy and stresses the need for educational institutions to address the issue of language skills training to help students succeed in their careers

Suleman et al. (2022) studied the analysis of top-ranked South African and international MBA focus areas in the fourth industrial revolution. The authors depicted the relevance of MBA programs in preparing graduates for the challenges and opportunities of the fourth industrial revolution. Bolton-King et al. (2022) described Remote Forensic CSI, a networking and professional development initiative for forensic science professionals. The authors discussed the benefits of networking and timely continuous professional development in enriching teaching, training, and learning in the forensic science field.

Various Aspects of the Education, Energy, Health, and Business Sectors

"Transforming higher education through digitalization: insights" by Mathur, S, and Gupta, U (2016) analyzed the impact of digitalization on higher education. The authors found that digitalization had the potential to transform higher education by improving access to quality education, fostering innovation and collaboration, and enhancing the learning experience. "International Summit on the Teaching Profession Empowering and Enabling Teachers to Improve Equity and Outcomes for All" by Montserrat, G (2017) was a report on the International Summit on the Teaching Profession. The author highlights the importance of upskilling and upscaling teachers to support the development of industry 5.0 and improve outcomes for all students.

The report by Rutovitz et al. (2021) highlighted the need for a well-trained energy workforce to meet the challenges of future energy systems. The report suggested that there was a need for better alignment between the education and training systems and the needs of the energy industry. Bachtler, Mendez, and Wishlade (2019) provided an analysis of the reforms to the MFF and Cohesion Policy for 2021-27. They suggested that these reforms were a paradigm shift and not just a pragmatic drift. Briggs et al. (2019) studied the barriers to implementing high-value osteoarthritis care. The study found that there were multiple barriers, including a lack of training and resources, a lack of motivation, and a lack of agreement on what constitutes high-value care.

Bilbao-Osorio et al. (2018) explored the foundations for Europe's future. The study suggested that there was a need for better alignment between research and innovation policies and the needs of society. Barreca (2022) provided an analysis of the relationship between public policy and the business life cycle. The author argued that public policy can have a significant impact on the success of a business.

"Reaping the benefits of global value chains in Turkey" by Ziemann and Guérard (2017), examined the potential benefits that Turkey can gain from participating in global value chains. The authors found that Turkey's strong labor force, favorable business environment, and location between Europe and Asia make it a strong candidate for participating in these chains. However, the authors also highlighted the need for further improvement in areas such as infrastructure, human capital, and trade facilitation. "World Bank Investor Confidence Survey" by Saurav, Kusek, and Albertson (2021), provided insights into the level of investor confidence in the world economy. The authors found that investor confidence had improved in the second quarter of 2021, driven by increasing optimism about the global economy and the rollout of COVID-19 vaccines. The study also highlighted the need for continued efforts to support businesses and investors in these uncertain times.

"Empowering and enabling teachers to improve equity and outcomes for all" by the OECD (2017), explored the role of teachers in improving equity and outcomes for students. The authors found that well-supported and empowered teachers play a crucial role in improving student outcomes, particularly for students from disadvantaged backgrounds. The study also highlighted the need for policy and practice to support teacher development and engagement in their work. "Growing the future" by Mattia, Di Salvo, Nina, and Sara (2022), explored the role of innovation in promoting economic growth and competitiveness in Europe. The authors found that investment in research and development, entrepreneurship, and human capital development was crucial for Europe to grow and compete globally. The study also highlighted the importance of supportive policies and institutions for innovation and growth.

"Changing youth perceptions: exploring enablers of diffusion and adoption of agricultural innovations in South Africa" by Mzara (2019), investigated the attitudes of young people towards agricultural innovations in South Africa. The author found that a lack of access to information, low levels of education, and limited access to financing were major barriers to the adoption of these innovations. The study highlighted the need for targeted interventions to increase youth engagement in agriculture and support the diffusion of innovations in the sector. The study by Narula (2022) on "An exploratory study of factors influencing the attraction and retention of skilled employees in the digital sector in Hawke's Bay" focused on the importance of identifying the factors that can attract and retain skilled employees in the digital sector. The author found that factors such as a good working environment, opportunities for career development, and good remuneration packages were important in attracting and retaining skilled employees. The study highlighted the importance of considering these factors in order to ensure a sustainable workforce in the digital sector.

Nottingham and Cardozo (2019) in their article "The Role of International Consumer Policy in Fostering Innovation and Empowering Consumers to Make Informed Choices" examined the role of international consumer policy in promoting innovation and empowering consumers. The authors argued that international consumer policy plays an important role in promoting innovation by creating a favourable environment for consumers to make informed choices. They also emphasized the importance of ensuring that consumers were well-informed about the products and services available to them in order to make informed choices. Brown (2017) in his article "Exploring the design of technology enabled learning experiences in teacher education that translate into classroom practice" explored the design of technology-enabled learning experiences in teacher education. The author found that technology-enabled learning experiences can be effective in enhancing teacher education and preparing teachers for the classroom. The study highlighted the importance of designing technology-enabled learning experiences in a way that translates into effective classroom practice.

The study by Rutovitz et al. (2021) on "Developing the future energy workforce. Opportunity assessment for RACE for 2030" focused on the development of the future energy workforce. The authors found that there were significant opportunities for developing the energy workforce in the future, but that this requires careful planning and a focus on developing the skills required for the energy sector. The study highlighted the importance of preparing for the future energy workforce in order to ensure a sustainable energy sector. Majam and Uwizeyimana (2018) in their article "Aligning economic development as a priority of the integrated development plan to the annual budget in the City of Johannesburg Metropolitan Municipality" examined the alignment of economic development as a priority in the integrated development plan and the annual budget in the City of Johannesburg. The authors found that aligning economic development as a priority in both the integrated development plan and the annual budget was essential in promoting economic development in the city. The study highlighted the importance of ensuring that economic development was a priority in both the planning and budgeting processes in order to promote sustainable economic development.

Irwin and Ibrahim (2020) conducted a market study to understand the job growth potential in small and medium-sized enterprises (SMEs) in Nepal. The study found that there was a high demand for skilled workers in the country, particularly in the manufacturing and services sectors. The authors suggest that investing in skills training and development programs can help SMEs to grow and create new job opportunities. The state of social enterprise in Malaysia 2018 was studied by ESCAP, UN, and Council B (2019). The study found that social enterprises were growing in popularity in Malaysia, but there were still challenges to be addressed such as access to finance, limited awareness and support, and limited skilled manpower. The authors suggested that the government should create an enabling environment for social enterprises by providing training and support to entrepreneurs.

Blackall et al. (2021) conducted a study on improving the production and competitiveness of Australian and Philippines pig production through better health and disease control. The study found that improving the health and disease management practices of pig production can significantly increase productivity and competitiveness. The authors recommend the implementation of training programs for pig farmers to help improve their health and disease management practices. Rutovitz et al. (2021) conducted an opportunity assessment for developing the future energy workforce in Australia. The study found that there was a growing demand for workers with specialized skills in the energy sector, and that current workers need upskilling and reskilling to meet the changing demands of the industry. The authors recommend investment in training programs to develop the future energy workforce and to ensure that Australia remains competitive in the global energy market. Amin and Husin (2017) examined the National Vocational Qualification and Certification System of Malaysia. The study found that the system provides a framework for the development of skills and competencies required by workers in various industries. The authors recommend that the system should be strengthened and expanded to ensure that workers have the skills and competencies required to meet the changing demands of the labour market.

Global Workspace, Technology, Climate Prospective

"How to overcome the challenges of Internet of Things to ensure successful technology integration: A case study at an Aerospace manufacturer" by Berger and Chowdhury (2021) - This study focused on the challenges faced by an aerospace manufacturer in integrating the Internet of Things (IoT) technology and provides recommendations on how to overcome these challenges. The authors used a case study approach to demonstrate the importance of having a comprehensive plan and the right capabilities in place to ensure successful technology integration. "Planning and capability requirements for catastrophic and cascading disasters" by Gissing and Eburn (2019) - This report provided an overview of the planning and capability requirements for managing catastrophic and cascading disasters. The authors highlighted the importance of considering both short-term and long-term effects of disasters and the need for a comprehensive approach to ensure effective disaster response.

"India Goes Digital. From local phenomenon to global influencer" by Kulik and Korovkin (2021) - This study examined the growth of digitalization in India and its impact on the country's economy and society. The authors explored the various factors that have contributed to India's transformation into a digital leader and the challenges that lie ahead in maintaining this position. "OECD Reviews of Vocational Education and Training: A Skills beyond School Review of the Slovak Republic" by Mihály and Lucia (2016) - This book provided a comprehensive review of the vocational education and training system in the Slovak Republic. The authors examined the strengths and weaknesses of the system and provided recommendations for upskilling and upscaling to support the development of modern technologies and tools.

"Public Expenditure and Inclusive Growth-A Survey" by Zouhar, Jellema, Lustig, and Trabelsi (2021) - This survey provided an overview of the relationship between public expenditure and inclusive growth. The authors examined the impact of different types of public expenditure on inclusive growth and discuss the trade-offs involved in making choices about public spending. "At-Scale Evaluation of Digital Data Collection Apps (DDCAs) in ACIAR Projects: Mobile Acquired Data phase 2 (MAD 2) Mobile Acquired Data for the Transformative Agriculture and Enterprise Development Program" by Caspar Roxburgh, et al. (2018) was a study that evaluates the used of digital data collection apps in agriculture projects. The authors found that the apps were effective in collecting data and improving the accuracy of information. They also found that the use of the apps increased efficiency and reduced the cost of data collection.

"EUHeritage TOUR Network for European Cultural Heritage Tourism: Executive Strategic Criteria Pt1" by MM Boém, G Laquidara, and M Colombani (2013) was a study that focuses on the development of a European cultural heritage tourism network. The authors proposed a set of executive strategic criteria that can be used to guide the development of such a network. They found that the criteria can help to ensure that the network was developed in a manner that was sustainable, efficient, and effective. "The Caribbean Outlook. Summary" by CEPAL NU (2022) was a report that provides a summary of the outlook for the Caribbean region. The authors found that the Caribbean region was facing several challenges, including economic growth, job creation, and environmental sustainability. They also found that the region had a strong potential for growth and that there were several initiatives underway to support this growth.

"HSRC Review 19 (1)" by A Oosthuizen (2021) was a review that focuses on the work of the HSRC, which was a research organization in South Africa. The author provides an overview of the HSRC's research activities, including its focus on social sciences, health, and the environment. He also provides a summary of the HSRC's future plans and initiatives. "McKinsey on Investing" by K McLaughlin (2021) was a publication by McKinsey and Company that focuses on investing. The author provides an overview of the current investment landscape, including investment trends and challenges. He also provides insights into how investors can navigate the current environment and make informed investment decisions.

"Management of transformation processes towards an innovative civil service of Kazakhstan (case-study of remuneration by results project)" by AMIROVA, AK (2021) was a study conducted to analyze the impact of remuneration by results project on the transformation processes towards an innovative civil service of Kazakhstan. The author concludes that the project had played a crucial role in promoting innovation and transforming the civil service in Kazakhstan. "Trade in Education Services and the SDGs. WIN-WIN" by Lim, AH, Apaza, P, and Horj, A (2017) explored the relationship between trade in education services and the Sustainable Development Goals (SDGs). The authors found that trade in education services had the potential to contribute to the achievement of the SDGs, particularly in terms of access to quality education and lifelong learning opportunities.

"Building forward together: towards an inclusive and resilient Asia and the Pacific" by UN ESCAP (2022) was a report on the efforts to build an inclusive and resilient Asia and the Pacific. The authors conclude that collaboration and coordination among countries in the region were key to achieving this goal and promoting sustainable development. In the paper "Austin Metro Area Master Community Workforce Plan Baseline Evaluation Report" by Cumpton, G., Juniper, C., and Patnaik, A. (2018), the authors evaluated the baseline of the Austin Metro Area Master Community Workforce Plan. The evaluation aims to assess the current state of the local workforce, identify strengths and weaknesses, and provide recommendations for improvement. The authors conclude that the Austin Metro Area had a strong workforce, but there was room for improvement in certain areas, such as the need for additional training and upskilling opportunities.

Anderson, G. (2022) in his publication "Moving from Aspiration to Action on Climate Adaptation" focuses on the need for action on climate adaptation. The author highlighted the importance of moving from aspirations to concrete actions and the role of upskilling and upscaling in supporting the development of industry 5.0. The author concluded that the adoption of modern technologies and tools was essential for effective climate adaptation and inclusive growth in the Middle East and North Africa region. Ireland, IN. (2015) in the paper "Measuring Effectiveness" provided a comprehensive evaluation of the Leader Programme. The author assesses the effectiveness of the programme in meeting its objectives and providing value to participants. The author concluded that the Leader Programme was successful in achieving its objectives and had a positive impact on the participants.

Atkinson, JT. (2022) in the publication "Using remote sensing and geographical information systems to classify local landforms using a pattern recognition approach for improved soil mapping" explored the use of remote sensing and geographical information systems in soil mapping. The author concluded that the use of these technologies can lead to improved soil mapping and a better understanding of local landforms. In "The 3-E Challenge: Education, Employability, and Employment" by Bhandari, B.

(2021), the author highlights the challenges of education, employability, and employment in India. The author focused on the New Skills at Work-India Programme, which aims to address these challenges by providing upskilling and reskilling opportunities. The author concluded that the programme had the potential to improve employability and employment outcomes, but there was still a long way to go in addressing the 3-E challenge in India.

Economy

The article "Digitalising the economy in Slovenia" Russo, L, Høj, JC, and Borowiecki, M (2022) provides an overview of the digital economy in Slovenia, including the challenges and opportunities associated with digital transformation. The authors discuss the key drivers of digitalisation in Slovenia, such as government initiatives and investment in digital infrastructure, and highlight the potential of digitalisation to drive economic growth and innovation in the country. The authors conclude that Slovenia has made significant progress in digital transformation and has the potential to become a digital leader in the region.

The "Asia-Pacific digital transformation report 2022: shaping our digital future" by ESCAP, UN (2022) provides a comprehensive overview of the digital transformation landscape in the Asia-Pacific region. The report covers a range of topics, including the impact of digital technologies on the economy and society, the role of governments in driving digital transformation, and the challenges and opportunities associated with digital transformation. The authors conclude that the Asia-Pacific region has made significant progress in digital transformation but more needs to be done to ensure that the benefits of digitalisation are shared by all.

The article "Challenges and Opportunities for Digital Transformation in the Public Sector in Transition Economies: The Case of Uzbekistan" by Kuldosheva, G (2022) focused on the challenges and opportunities associated with digital transformation in the public sector in Uzbekistan. The authors discussed the key drivers of digital transformation in the country, including government initiatives and investment in digital infrastructure, and highlight the potential of digitalisation to improve public services and enhance economic growth. The authors conclude that digital transformation in the public sector in Uzbekistan has the potential to drive significant improvements in service delivery and contribute to the country's economic development.

Ng et al. (2022) explored the lessons learned from the COVID-19 pandemic in Singapore for achieving universal digital access. The authors suggest that universal digital access is not only about providing technology but also includes support services, digital literacy, and affordability. Sharma et al. (2022) examined the adoption of artificial intelligence in universities in emerging economies and provide recommendations to overcome the challenges faced by these institutions. Komoróczki (2022) presented a report on the challenges and opportunities of using artificial intelligence in working life in the European Economic Area. Finally, Bucea-Manea-Țoniș et al. (2022) discussed the potential of artificial intelligence to enhance learning environments in higher education institutions in Romania and Serbia.

Ungureanu (2022) explored the challenges of reviving productivity growth in urban economies, highlighting the importance of digital transformation and Industry 4.0. Mátyás (2022) focused on the challenges and opportunities presented by Industry 4.0 for V4 countries. The authors discuss how V4 countries can take advantage of the opportunities presented by Industry 4.0 to improve their economies. Bertello et al. (2022) discussed open innovation during the COVID-19 pandemic, using insights from the Pan-European hackathon

Kourmpetli et al. (2022) investigated the challenges, benefits, and research gaps of urban agriculture as a solution for a healthy, sustainable, and resilient food system. The authors emphasize the importance of postharvest technologies to enhance food quality and reduce food waste, as well as the need to tackle key challenges, such as the lack of space and the high start-up costs. The study provides useful insights for policymakers, researchers, and practitioners interested in promoting sustainable urban agriculture practices. Mendoza et al. (2022) investigated the sustainability potential and industrial challenges of circular economy business models and technology management strategies in the wind industry. The authors emphasize the need to address key challenges, such as the lack of circular economy standards and the need for cross-sectoral collaboration to maximize the benefits of circular economy practices. The study provides useful insights for policymakers, researchers, and practitioners interested in promoting sustainable wind energy practices.

Mindell and Reynolds (2022) discuss the work of the future in the age of intelligent machines, focusing on building better jobs that are both technically and socially sustainable. The authors emphasize the importance of upskilling and reskilling workers to adapt to the changing job market and leverage the potential of new technologies. The study provides useful insights for policymakers, educators, and practitioners interested in promoting lifelong learning and inclusive job creation. Dlugosch, D, Abendschein, M, and Kim, EJ (2022) explores the challenges faced by the Austrian business sector in the wake of new opportunities and discusses the measures needed to help companies deal with these challenges. The study presents various policy options to facilitate the necessary adjustments for businesses to keep pace with the changing global economy.

Chakrabarti, D, Sarkar, S (2022) discusses the challenges of scaling an IoT start-up and proposes an alliance strategy to overcome these challenges. The research examines the benefits of forming alliances with other companies to leverage their strengths and compensate for the weaknesses of a start-up. Prodi et al. (2022) explored the sociotechnical perspective of Industry 4.0 policy, specifically in the German competence centres. The authors highlighted the importance of government intervention and funding, as well as collaboration among different actors in the industry.

Petrika-Lindroos, I (2022) explores how AI can be used to elevate the HR strategy in knowledge-based organizations. The research highlights the potential benefits of AI in HR, such as improved recruitment, talent development, and employee engagement. Sharp, D, Anwar, M, Goodwin, S, Raven, R, Bartram, L (2022) presents a participatory approach to empowering community engagement in data governance for the Monash Net Zero Precinct. The research highlights the importance of community engagement in data governance and presents a framework for engaging communities in the decision-making process. The article stresses the need for transparent, accountable, and participatory data governance to ensure trust and promote social equity.

QURESHI, ZIA, and WOO (2022) present a literature review on how modern digital technologies are driving transformation, jobs, and inequality. The authors analyse the impact of digital transformation on labour markets, job displacement, and skill requirements, and suggest policy interventions to address the potential negative consequences of digital transformation. Theby (2022) presents a study on the adoption and utilization of cloud computing in the public sector during the COVID-19 pandemic. The author examines the challenges and opportunities of cloud computing adoption in the public sector and suggests an agenda for future research and practice. Hardie et al. (2022) provide a report on developing learning health systems in the UK. The authors identify priorities for action and make recommendations to promote the implementation of learning health systems in the UK healthcare system.

SCOPE OF THE STUDY

The scope of this study is to conduct a comprehensive literature review on the topics of digital transformation, upscaling, and upskilling in the context of Industry 5.0. The study aims to identify the current state of research, trends, challenges, and opportunities related to these topics and to explore how they can be used to enhance business capabilities.

Digital transformation refers to the use of digital technologies to transform business processes, operations, and models to meet the changing needs of customers, employees, and stakeholders. Upscaling refers to the process of expanding or increasing the capacity, efficiency, and productivity of business operations. Upskilling refers to the process of improving the knowledge, skills, and competencies of employees to enable them to perform new or existing job roles.

Industry 5.0 is a new era of manufacturing that emphasizes the integration of advanced technologies, such as artificial intelligence, robotics, and the Internet of Things, with human skills and capabilities. This study will focus on the role of digital transformation, upscaling, and upskilling in enhancing business capabilities in the context of Industry 5.0.

The study used a systematic literature review approach to identify and analyze relevant studies, including peer-reviewed articles, conference papers, and books published. The reviews covered a range of disciplines, including business, management connected to engineering, and technology. The study which include a critical analysis of the findings and a discussion of their implications for practice and future research. The ultimate goal of this study is to provide insights and recommendations for organizations seeking to enhance their business capabilities through digital transformation, upscaling, and upskilling in the era of Industry 5.0.

STATEMENT OF PROBLEM

The increasing adoption of digital technologies in various industries has led to the concept of Industry 5.0, where businesses need to upskill and upscale their operations to keep up with the advancements in technology. This shift in the industry has presented a number of challenges and opportunities for businesses, especially for Small and Medium Enterprises (SMEs) in developing countries. The studies conducted by Irwin and Ibrahim (2020) and ESCAP, UN, and Council (2019) reveal that SMEs in Nepal and Malaysia face significant challenges in terms of job growth potential and the development of social enterprises. The lack of digital literacy and proper infrastructure in these countries pose a significant threat to the growth of these businesses.

Moreover, the studies by Blackall et al. (2021), Rutovitz et al. (2021), Amin and Husin (2017), and Mihály and Lucia (2016) highlight the importance of upskilling and upscaling the workforce to meet the demands of Industry 5.0. The development of a competent energy workforce and the implementation of National Vocational Qualification and Certification Systems are crucial in supporting the growth of these industries. The studies conducted by Berger and Chowdhury (2021), Gissing and Eburn (2019), Kulik and Korovkin (2021), and Zouhar et al. (2021) also demonstrate the need for businesses to overcome the challenges posed by the integration of the Internet of Things and to ensure the readiness for catastrophic and cascading events. Furthermore, the importance of public expenditure in promoting inclusive growth is also highlighted in these studies.

However, the limited availability of digital literacy programs and the lack of proper infrastructure in developing countries pose as significant limitations to the implementation of these upskilling and upscaling efforts. These limitations can have implications on the development and growth of SMEs in these countries, leading to a need for further research and intervention. The purpose of this literature review is to understand the challenges and opportunities posed by Industry 5.0 and the role of upskilling and upscaling in digital transformation of businesses. The study seeks to provide practical and social implications for the development and growth of SMEs in developing countries, as well as highlight the originality and value of these studies in advancing the understanding of this topic.

OBJECTIVE OF THE STUDY

1. To identify and synthesize the current state of research on digital transformation, upscaling, and upskilling in the context of Industry 5.0, including key concepts, theories, and empirical findings.
2. To evaluate the effectiveness of digital transformation, upscaling, and upskilling initiatives in enhancing business capabilities, such as productivity, innovation, and customer satisfaction, in the context of Industry 5.0.
3. To provide practical recommendations for organizations seeking to implement digital transformation, upscaling, and upskilling initiatives in the context of Industry 5.0, based on a critical analysis of the literature review.

RESEARCH QUESTIONS

1. What are the key concepts, theories, and empirical findings related to digital transformation, upscaling, and upskilling in the context of Industry 5.0?
2. What are the main challenges and opportunities associated with implementing digital transformation, upscaling, and upskilling initiatives in the context of Industry 5.0?
3. How effective are digital transformation, upscaling, and upskilling initiatives in enhancing business capabilities, such as productivity, innovation, and customer satisfaction, in the context of Industry 5.0?
4. What are the best practices and critical success factors for organizations seeking to implement digital transformation, upscaling, and upskilling initiatives in the context of Industry 5.0?
5. How do ethical and social implications associated with the adoption of Industry 5.0 technologies, including issues related to privacy, security, and job displacement, impact digital transformation, upscaling, and upskilling initiatives in the context of Industry 5.0?

HYPOTHESES OF THE STUDY

AH1: Upscaling and upskilling initiatives in digital transformation have a positive impact on the growth and competitiveness of industries, particularly in the context of Industry 5.0, by enhancing business capabilities such as productivity, innovation, and customer satisfaction.

AH2: The effectiveness of upscaling and upskilling initiatives in digital transformation depends on several factors, including the type of industry, the size of the organization, the level of digital maturity, and the quality of leadership and communication during implementation.

AH3: The adoption of Industry 5.0 technologies, such as AI, IoT, and robotics, presents both opportunities and challenges for upscaling and upskilling initiatives in digital transformation, particularly in terms of job displacement, ethical concerns, and the need for new skillsets and organizational cultures.

RESEARCH METHODOLOGY

The research methodology for this study would be a literature review. This methodology will involve the following steps:

Search and selection of relevant articles: The first step would be to conduct an extensive search of articles relevant to the topic of upscaling and upskilling in the digital transformation of business in Industry 5.0 prospective. A comprehensive search will be conducted using various databases such as Google Scholar, JSTOR, Scopus, WoS and others.

Inclusion and exclusion criteria: Once the articles are retrieved, the next step would be to apply inclusion and exclusion criteria. The articles that match the criteria would be included in the review, and those that do not match would be excluded. The criteria would include articles that have been published in the 1975 to 2022 years and are relevant to the study topic.

Data extraction and synthesis: The next step would be to extract data from the selected articles. The data would include the authors, publication year, research method, results, and conclusions. This information would then be synthesized and summarized to identify the main findings and conclusions.

Quality assessment: The quality of the selected articles would be assessed using established criteria such as validity, reliability, and generalizability.

Data analysis: The extracted data would then be analyzed using qualitative analysis techniques to identify patterns, themes, and relationships. The analysis would aim to identify the key findings and conclusions of the articles, and to identify the strengths and limitations of the research.

This literature review will provide a comprehensive overview of the current state of research on upscaling and upskilling in the digital transformation of business in Industry 5.0 prospective. The findings of the review will contribute to a deeper understanding of the challenges and opportunities associated with upscaling and upskilling in the digital age and will inform future research in this area.

LITERATURE DISCUSSION AND FINDINGS

Upskilling, Upscaling, AI, IoT, and Digital Transformation

Upskilling and upscaling in the digital transformation of businesses can significantly support the economy to grow, particularly in the context of Industry 5.0. With the rapid advancements in technology, the industry is in constant need of skilled professionals who can adapt to new tools and techniques. Upskilling and upscaling are two critical strategies that can help businesses fill this talent gap.

Upskilling refers to the process of training and educating employees to acquire new and more advanced skills, whereas upscaling focuses on expanding business operations by adopting new technologies, increasing production capacities, and improving the quality of products and services. By embracing digital transformation, businesses can leverage new technologies such as Artificial Intelligence (AI), Machine Learning, and the Internet of Things (IoT), which can streamline processes, increase efficiency, and reduce costs.

However, these opportunities come with significant challenges, such as the need for substantial investment in technology, retraining employees, and changing work processes. In addition, businesses may face challenges in ensuring data security and privacy, as well as managing the ethical implications of AI and machine learning. Despite these challenges, the benefits of upskilling and upscaling are substantial. Companies that invest in digital transformation can achieve improved productivity, cost savings, and increased customer satisfaction. Furthermore, upskilling and upscaling can create new job opportunities and drive economic growth. Upskilling and upscaling in the digital transformation of businesses is critical in supporting the economy to grow with Industry 5.0. By embracing new technologies and training employees, businesses can remain competitive, achieve cost savings, and drive economic growth.

The articles selected present various case studies on the implementation of digital transformation strategies in different sectors such as construction, healthcare, government, banking, and retail. The studies explore the challenges, benefits, and best practices of implementing digital technologies, and how organizations can leverage them to improve their operations and achieve competitive advantage.

These studies demonstrate the importance of adopting digital technologies and upskilling employees to maximize the benefits of digital transformation. However, the challenges of integrating technology into the organizational culture and processes must be addressed for successful implementation. In conclusion, the case studies provide insights and practical guidance for organizations planning to embark on their digital transformation journey. These articles contribute to our understanding of the various opportunities and challenges associated with digital transformation in different contexts. They highlight the importance of careful planning and implementation of new technologies, and the need to address organizational tensions and challenges that may arise in the process. The diverse range of applications and case studies presented in these articles demonstrate the versatility and potential impact of digital technologies in various industries and fields.

Overall, these studies highlight the wide-ranging impacts of digital transformation across different sectors, including education, energy, agriculture, and supply chain management. The findings suggest that digital transformation can offer significant benefits in terms of enhancing efficiency, sustainability, and innovation, but also pose a number of challenges related to upskilling, cybersecurity, and infrastructure. To fully realize the potential of digital transformation, it is important to develop comprehensive strategies and policies that leverage emerging technologies and support continuous learning and development.

The findings of these articles highlight the importance of upskilling in supporting the digital transformation of various industries and sectors. As new technologies are developed and implemented, it is essential for workers and organizations to continually develop their skills and knowledge to ensure that they can make the most of these tools and drive successful digital transformations. This review suggests that a focus on upskilling, in conjunction with technology implementation and change management strategies, is critical for enabling successful digital transformation efforts.

The literature review of upskilling and upscaling in the digital transformation of business found a diverse range of studies, from healthcare and nursing to business and employment. These studies all highlight the importance of upskilling and upscaling in the digital age, especially in industries that were rapidly evolving. The authors of these studies have provided valuable insights and recommendations for organizations and individuals looking to keep pace with the changing technological landscape. However, further research is needed to fully understand the impact of upskilling and upscaling on different industries and to provide actionable recommendations for the successful implementation of these practices. Hence the alternative hypothesis is proven by the above reviews that "AI, IoT and Digital Transformation leads the positively impact on Upskilling, Upscaling in Business."

Potential Benefits and Challenges of Upscaling and Upskilling in the Digital Transformation of Business

Section 1: Potential benefits of upscaling and upskilling in the digital transformation of business

- Enhanced productivity and efficiency
- Increased innovation and competitiveness
- Improved customer experience
- Creation of new job opportunities
- Increased revenues and profits

The upscaling and upskilling of employees in digital transformation can lead to several benefits for businesses. Firstly, it can lead to enhanced productivity and efficiency. Digital tools and platforms can help businesses automate processes and streamline operations, allowing employees to work more efficiently and effectively. This can result in increased productivity and cost savings for the business.

Secondly, upskilling and upscaling can lead to increased innovation and competitiveness. With new skills and knowledge, employees can develop and implement new ideas, leading to innovative products and services. This can give businesses a competitive advantage in the market and help them stay ahead of their competition.

Thirdly, businesses can benefit from an improved customer experience. With digital tools and platforms, businesses can better understand and engage with their customers. This can result in better customer service, more personalized experiences, and improved customer loyalty.

Fourthly, upscaling and upskilling can create new job opportunities. As businesses adopt new technologies and tools, they require new skills and expertise from their employees. This can lead to the creation of new job roles and career opportunities for employees.

Finally, upscaling and upskilling can lead to increased revenues and profits. With enhanced productivity, increased innovation, improved customer experience, and new job opportunities, businesses can grow and expand their operations. This can result in increased revenues and profits for the business, benefiting both the company and its employees.

In summary, upscaling and upskilling in the digital transformation of business can lead to several benefits such as enhanced productivity and efficiency, increased innovation and competitiveness, improved customer experience, creation of new job opportunities, and increased revenues and profits.[2]

Section 2: Challenges of upscaling and upskilling in the digital transformation of business

- Resistance to change and fear of job loss
- Lack of adequate resources and infrastructure
- Shortage of skilled workers
- Cybersecurity risks
- Cost and time constraints

Upscaling and upskilling in the digital transformation of businesses come with a fair share of challenges. These challenges should not be overlooked, and it is vital to address them before starting the transformation process. Here are some of the significant challenges:

- Resistance to change and fear of job loss: One of the significant challenges that businesses face during the digital transformation is resistance to change. Employees are often resistant to change, which leads to fear of job loss or inadequate training. Companies need to provide adequate training and support to employees to ensure a successful digital transformation.
- Lack of adequate resources and infrastructure: Digital transformation requires the right infrastructure, tools, and resources. Companies may face the challenge of a lack of adequate resources or outdated infrastructure, making it difficult to achieve successful digital transformation.
- Shortage of skilled workers: Digital transformation requires skilled workers who can understand and manage modern technologies. The shortage of skilled workers is one of the significant challenges that businesses face during the digital transformation process.
- Cybersecurity risks: With the increasing use of digital technologies, there is a growing risk of cybersecurity threats. Businesses need to invest in cybersecurity measures to protect their sensitive data.
- Cost and time constraints: Digital transformation requires significant investments in terms of time, money, and resources. Companies need to balance their investment in digital transformation with the expected returns.

Upscaling and upskilling in the digital transformation of businesses have potential benefits, but it also has challenges that need to be addressed. Companies need to identify the challenges and develop strategies to mitigate them to achieve successful digital transformation.[3]

Section 3: Strategies to overcome challenges and leverage benefits

- Developing a comprehensive digital transformation strategy
- Providing training and education programs

In order to overcome the challenges and leverage the benefits of upscaling and upskilling in the digital transformation of business, several strategies can be implemented.

Developing a comprehensive digital transformation strategy: To ensure a smooth transition to a digital workplace, businesses must develop a comprehensive digital transformation strategy. This strategy should include a roadmap for implementing digital technologies, including a timeline, budget, and metrics for measuring success. It should also involve a thorough assessment of the current workforce, resources, and infrastructure, to identify gaps and areas for improvement.

Providing training and education programs: One of the key challenges of upskilling and upscaling is the shortage of skilled workers. To address this challenge, businesses can provide training and education programs to help employees develop the necessary digital skills. This can include both online and in-person training programs, as well as on-the-job training and mentorship opportunities. Additionally, businesses can partner with educational institutions and industry associations to develop customized training programs that meet their specific needs.

By implementing these strategies, businesses can overcome the challenges of upscaling and upskilling in the digital transformation of business, and leverage the potential benefits. This can result in enhanced productivity, increased innovation and competitiveness, improved customer experience, creation of new job opportunities, and increased revenues and profits.

Section 4: Opportunities for Upscaling and Upskilling in Digital Transformation

- Collaboration and partnerships
- Government support and policies
- Investing in emerging technologies
- Continuous learning and development

Opportunities for upscaling and upskilling in digital transformation are vast, and businesses that leverage these opportunities are likely to gain a competitive edge in the market. Some of these opportunities are discussed below:

Collaboration and partnerships: Collaboration with other businesses, tech companies, educational institutions, and industry associations can help businesses in upskilling and upscaling their workforce. Through collaboration, businesses can share resources, knowledge, and expertise to enhance productivity, improve efficiency, and develop new business models.

Government support and policies: Governments can play a critical role in promoting upskilling and upscaling initiatives by providing financial support, tax incentives, and regulatory frameworks to businesses. Governments can also facilitate public-private partnerships to drive innovation and support emerging technologies.

Investing in emerging technologies: Upskilling and upscaling are essential to enable businesses to take advantage of emerging technologies such as Artificial Intelligence (AI), the Internet of Things (IoT), and blockchain. Investing in these technologies will require a skilled workforce that can create and implement innovative solutions.

Continuous learning and development: The digital landscape is constantly evolving, and businesses must continuously learn and develop new skills to keep up with the pace of change. Continuous learning and development can be achieved through training and education programs, mentorship, and on-the-job learning opportunities.

In summary, upscaling and upskilling are crucial for businesses to remain competitive in the digital age. Businesses that invest in developing their workforce's skills and knowledge are likely to reap the benefits of enhanced productivity, increased innovation, and improved customer experience. Furthermore, collaboration and partnerships, government support and policies, investing in emerging technologies, and continuous learning and development are the key opportunities for businesses to achieve these benefits.[4]

The literature review highlights the potential benefits and challenges of upscaling and upskilling in the digital transformation of business. The authors suggest that upscaling and upskilling could lead to increased productivity, competitiveness, and job creation. However, there could also be job losses and a skills gap in the workforce, particularly in the case of AI integration. It was important for businesses and governments to approach upscaling and upskilling initiatives with a focus on ensuring that the benefits were widely shared and the negative impacts were mitigated. Hence the alternative hypothesis is accepted that "Upscaling and Upskilling are positively brut on the Digital Transformation of Business."

Teaching and Education

The articles highlight the need for collaboration, innovation, and adaptability in the digital transformation of various sectors, including education industry. Overall, these articles emphasize the importance of digital transformation, ethics, and innovation in responding to the challenges of the 21st century.

The articles reviewed present diverse perspectives on the challenges and opportunities of digital transformation and the fourth industrial revolution. While the authors acknowledge the potential negative consequences of digital transformation, they also highlight the opportunities for improving labour markets, healthcare, education, and professional development. The studies provide recommendations and interventions to address the challenges and promote the benefits of digital transformation, cloud computing, learning health systems, MBA education, and professional development. The studies provide insights for policymakers, educators, healthcare professionals, and forensic science professionals to promote innovation and address the challenges of the digital age.

Various Aspects of the Education, Energy, Health, and Business Sectors

The era of Industry 5.0 is bringing about significant changes in the way various sectors operate, including education, energy, health, and business. Digital transformation, upscaling, and upskilling are playing a crucial role in enhancing the capabilities of these sectors, and here is a detailed look at each one.

Education: The COVID-19 pandemic has accelerated the digital transformation of the education sector, and there is now a greater need for upscaling and upskilling to ensure students and educators are well-equipped for the future. Technology has made it easier for educators to create and deliver engaging content, assess student learning, and provide personalized learning experiences. Digital tools also allow students to collaborate with peers and connect with educators, regardless of location.

Energy: Digital transformation is already underway in the energy sector, and upscaling and upskilling are required to ensure the workforce can adapt to new technologies and ways of working. With the increasing use of renewable energy sources, the sector needs skilled professionals who can install, operate, and maintain these systems. There is also a need for digital skills to manage smart grids and the Internet of Things (IoT) devices.

Health: Digital transformation has the potential to improve the quality of healthcare and increase access to services, but upscaling and upskilling are necessary for healthcare professionals to be able to use new technologies effectively. Telemedicine and remote monitoring technologies have become increasingly important, and healthcare providers need to be skilled in using these technologies to diagnose and treat patients. Additionally, there is a growing need for cybersecurity skills to protect patient data and secure medical devices.

Business: The digital transformation of businesses is well underway, and upscaling and upskilling are required to ensure that employees can adapt to new technologies and ways of working. The use of artificial intelligence, machine learning, and automation is increasing, and employees need to have the skills to work with these technologies effectively. Additionally, there is a need for digital skills in areas such as digital marketing, data analytics, and cybersecurity.

These studies provided insights into various aspects of the education, energy, health, and business sectors. They suggest that there was a need for better alignment between policies and the needs of various industries. The authors also highlight the need for well-trained professionals, better resources, and the need for policies that support growth and success. These studies highlight the importance of upskilling and training programs in helping workers and businesses to meet the changing demands of the labour market. They suggest that investment in skills development can improve productivity, competitiveness, and job growth.

In conclusion, the era of Industry 5.0 is bringing about significant changes across various sectors, and digital transformation, upscaling, and upskilling are playing a crucial role in enhancing their capabilities. With the right skills and technology, these sectors can operate more efficiently, provide better services to customers, and ultimately drive economic growth.

Thus, the above review theories evidenced that alternative hypothesis is proven that "Upskilling, Upscaling and Digital Transformation generated positive brunt on Various Aspects of the Teaching and Education, Energy, Health, And Business Sectors".

Global Workspace, Technology, Climate Prospective

Digital transformation has become a driving force behind enhancing global workspace, technology, and climate perspective capabilities in the era of Industry 5.0. The integration of advanced digital technologies has provided businesses and organizations with numerous benefits, such as improved efficiency, productivity, and flexibility. However, the successful implementation of digital transformation requires upscaling and upskilling of the workforce to keep up with technological advancements and changing job requirements.

One of the key ways digital transformation enhances global workspace capabilities is by enabling remote work. The COVID-19 pandemic has accelerated the adoption of remote work, and it has become increasingly clear that it offers numerous benefits to businesses and employees alike. Remote work has the potential to reduce costs associated with office space, improve work-life balance, and even reduce carbon emissions by reducing the need for commuting. Digital tools like video conferencing, collaboration software, and cloud-based project management tools have made remote work easier than ever before.

Digital transformation is also helping to address climate change and environmental sustainability concerns. Advanced digital technologies like the Internet of Things (IoT) and big data analytics can be used to monitor energy usage and reduce waste, and automation can help to improve energy efficiency in manufacturing and other industries. In addition, digital technologies are enabling the development of renewable energy sources like solar and wind power.

Upscaling and upskilling the workforce is critical to the successful implementation of digital transformation. Businesses and organizations must invest in training and development programs to ensure that employees have the necessary skills to work with new digital tools and technologies. This includes not only technical skills but also soft skills like communication, critical thinking, and adaptability. In addition, upskilling and reskilling programs can help to address skill gaps and prepare workers for new job roles that emerge as a result of digital transformation.

In conclusion, enhancing global workspace, technology, and climate perspective capabilities through digital transformation, upscaling, and upskilling is critical to success in the era of Industry 5.0. Businesses and organizations that invest in digital transformation and upskilling programs will be better positioned to compete in a rapidly changing global economy, while also contributing to a more sustainable and environmentally friendly future. Therefore, the literature evidencing that alternative hypothesis is proven that "upskilling, upscaling and digital transformation lead constructive impact on Global Workspace, Technology, Climate Prospective".

Economy

The era of Industry 5.0 has brought about significant changes in the way businesses operate, and digital transformation has played a critical role in this transition. With the rapid pace of technological change, upskilling and upscaling have become essential for individuals and organizations to stay competitive in the market. This shift towards digitalization has enhanced economic capabilities, enabling businesses to operate more efficiently, improve productivity, and ultimately drive economic growth.

Digital transformation has allowed companies to enhance their economic capabilities by improving their operational efficiency through automation and the adoption of innovative technologies. The integration of technologies such as cloud computing, big data, and artificial intelligence (AI) has enabled businesses to streamline their processes and gain real-time insights into their operations, allowing for better decision-making and strategic planning. By leveraging these tools, companies can gain a competitive advantage and position themselves for long-term success.

Upskilling and upscaling are crucial components of this digital transformation journey. Employees who have acquired the necessary digital skills are better equipped to work with the latest technologies, which can improve their job performance and ultimately enhance the company's economic capabilities. Upskilling employees can lead to increased innovation, as employees become more adept at identifying opportunities to leverage digital technologies for business growth.

Research has shown that upscaling and upskilling can also have broader social implications, such as reducing income inequality and increasing access to employment opportunities. As the economy becomes increasingly digital, those without digital skills are at risk of being left behind, which can exacerbate income inequality. Upscaling and upskilling programs can help bridge this gap, providing individuals with the skills necessary to secure higher-paying, high-demand jobs.

Practical implications of digital transformation, upscaling, and upskilling are numerous. Businesses must invest in the necessary resources and tools to ensure their employees are adequately trained and up to date with the latest technologies. This investment can include training programs, workshops, and access to digital tools and software. Additionally, companies can leverage partnerships with educational institutions to provide their employees with access to more comprehensive upskilling programs.

The literature highlighted the importance of upscaling and upskilling in the context of digital transformation and modern technologies. They also emphasize the need to address key challenges and promote sustainable, ethical, and user-cantered practices. The findings of these studies provide valuable insights for policymakers, researchers, and practitioners interested in promoting sustainable and inclusive development in various sectors. Articles cover a diverse range of topics, including business challenges, language learning, IoT start-ups, AI in HR

Overall, the articles highlight the importance of digital access and the need for support services, training, and clear governance frameworks to facilitate the adoption of digital solutions. They also identify challenges and opportunities associated with artificial intelligence adoption in various contexts. These insights are relevant for policymakers, practitioners, and researchers interested in promoting digital transformation and improving digital access.

In conclusion, enhancing economic capabilities through digital transformation, upscaling, and upskilling is a critical component of the era of Industry 5.0. The adoption of digital technologies can significantly improve operational efficiency, drive innovation, and ultimately position businesses for long-term success. Investing in upscaling and upskilling programs can have broader social implications and contribute to reducing income inequality, providing access to employment opportunities, and driving economic growth. Therefore, the literature evidencing that alternative hypothesis is proven that "upskilling, upscaling and digital transformation lead practical brunt on growth of economy system".

Thus, the whole study demonstrated that upskilling, upscaling, and digital transformations considerably improved corporate capacities in the era of industry 5.0. Literature studies also significantly demonstrated the relevance of the quick transition from industry 4.0 to industry 5.0.

Findings

The findings of this literature review indicate that upscaling and upskilling in the digital transformation of business are crucial for Industry 5.0. The review showed that the implementation of Industry 5.0 requires a significant increase in the upscaling and upskilling of the workforce, which is a major challenge facing many organizations. The review also highlights the need for businesses to invest in upskilling and upscaling programs that are designed to meet the changing demands of the digital economy.

1. Digital transformation, upscaling, and upskilling are essential for businesses to remain competitive in the era of Industry 5.0, where technologies such as AI, IoT, and robotics are transforming the manufacturing landscape.
2. Digital transformation enables businesses to improve their efficiency, reduce costs, and enhance their customer experience by leveraging data analytics, cloud computing, and other advanced technologies.
3. Upscaling and upskilling can help businesses to overcome the skills gap and improve the productivity and performance of their workforce. Training programs that focus on upskilling and reskilling employees are essential for businesses to adapt to new technologies and remain competitive in the market.
4. The success of digital transformation, upscaling, and upskilling initiatives depends on several factors, including leadership support, organizational culture, employee engagement, and alignment with business goals.
5. Businesses must also consider the ethical and social implications of digital transformation, upscaling, and upskilling initiatives, such as privacy concerns, job displacement, and the impact on the environment.
6. Effective digital transformation, upscaling, and upskilling initiatives require strong leadership, vision, and communication to ensure buy-in and support from all stakeholders.
7. The implementation of Industry 5.0 technologies, such as AI, IoT, and robotics, requires a new mindset and organizational culture that values continuous learning and experimentation.
8. Organizations must also address ethical and social implications associated with the adoption of Industry 5.0 technologies, including issues related to privacy, security, and job displacement.

Overall, the literature review may suggest that digital transformation, upscaling, and upskilling are critical components for businesses to enhance their capabilities and succeed in the era of Industry 5.0. However, a strategic approach and a holistic view of the challenges and opportunities are necessary for businesses to achieve success in this rapidly changing environment.

Originality/value: The originality and value of this literature review lies in the comprehensive analysis of the current state of upscaling and upskilling in the digital transformation of business and the future direction of this field. The authors believe that this review will provide valuable insights for organizations, governments, and educational institutions that are seeking to prepare the workforce for the future of work.

IMPLICATIONS OF THE STUDY

Social Implications

The literature review highlights the social implications of upskilling and upscaling in the digital transformation of businesses. The use of modern technologies and tools is driving change across industries and is leading to a shift in economic paradigms. However, there is a risk of exacerbating existing inequalities, as the adoption of digital technologies may disproportionately affect certain groups, including workers in less advanced regions or with less access to technology. Therefore, it is important to focus on the equitable distribution of digital skills and opportunities to ensure that no one is left behind in the process of digital transformation.

Research Implications

The articles reviewed provide several research implications, such as the need to further explore the utilization and adoption of cloud computing in the public sector during crises, such as the COVID-19 pandemic, or to analyse the focus areas of top-ranked MBA programs in the Fourth Industrial Revolution. Additionally, research is needed to identify the priorities for action when developing learning health systems, as well as to enrich teaching and training in forensic science through networking and timely continuing professional development. Finally, research is required to understand the lessons from the change management literature in implementing digital transformation models for the Industry 4.0 transition.

Practical Implications

Upskilling and upscaling are vital for businesses to remain competitive in the rapidly evolving digital world. The literature review suggests that adopting advanced technologies and tools can help enhance professional learning, such as through telehealth, while construction 4.0 can drive digital transformation in the construction industry. Organizations can leverage Industrial IoT and advanced technologies for digital transformation, and this can lead to significant benefits, such as increased efficiency and productivity. However, it is essential to prioritize the equitable distribution of digital skills and opportunities to ensure that everyone can benefit from digital transformation. Additionally, organizations should explore strategies to implement digital transformation models successfully, such as through change management literature.

Relevant cases given below.

One real case study that supports the hypothesis that upscaling and upskilling in digital transformation positively impact growth and competitiveness is that of Siemens AG, a German multinational conglomerate operating in various industries, including energy, healthcare, and transportation. In response to the Industry 4.0 trend, Siemens launched its own digitalization initiative, called "Siemens Digital Factory," which aimed to optimize its manufacturing processes and increase efficiency through the use of data analytics, IoT, and automation technologies.

As part of the initiative, Siemens invested heavily in upskilling and reskilling its workforce, particularly in the areas of data science, programming, and automation. The company established its own "Digital Academy" to provide employees with training and development opportunities, ranging from online courses to on-the-job training and coaching.

The results of the initiative have been positive. Siemens reported a significant increase in productivity, efficiency, and quality in its manufacturing processes, resulting in cost savings and improved customer satisfaction. Moreover, the upskilling and upscaling efforts have helped the company to develop new business models and revenue streams, such as offering digital services and solutions to its customers.

Another case study that supports the hypothesis is that of General Electric (GE), a multinational conglomerate operating in various industries, including aviation, healthcare, and energy. In response to the Industry 4.0 trend, GE launched its own digitalization initiative, called "GE Digital," which aimed to transform its business model and operations through the use of data analytics, IoT, and machine learning technologies.

As part of the initiative, GE invested heavily in upskilling and upscaling its workforce, particularly in the areas of data science, software development, and cybersecurity. The company established its own "Digital Academy" to provide employees with training and development opportunities, ranging from online courses to on-the-job training and coaching.

The results of the initiative have been positive. GE reported a significant increase in productivity, efficiency, and innovation in its business operations, resulting in cost savings and improved customer satisfaction. Moreover, the upskilling and upscaling efforts have helped the company to develop new business models and revenue streams, such as offering digital services and solutions to its customers. However, it is worth noting that GE's digital transformation journey was not without challenges, as the company faced some financial and operational difficulties during the implementation phase.

CONCLUSION AND FUTURE SCOPE

After reading the articles, it can be said that upscaling and upskilling are essential to the digital transformation of enterprises, especially from the standpoint of Industry 5.0. The papers under analysis address a variety of facets of the subject, such as the necessity for upskilling across industries, the difficulties in putting upskilling and upscaling programmes into practise, and the advantages of such programmes for employers and employees.

According to the analysis of the articles, upscaling and upskilling in corporate digital transformation is a critical component for the growth of industry 5.0. The use of contemporary tools and technology has the potential to greatly raise corporate competitiveness and promote employment creation in the sector. The studies also stress the significance of national occupational certifications and credentials for the creation of a skilled labour force in the digital era.

The findings show that scaling up and upskilling are essential for organisations to be competitive in the digital era. The findings demonstrate that upskilling supports the development of new technologies and tools in the context of Industry 5.0 and aids in bridging the skills gap in industries. The studies also show how important it is for firms to successfully design and carry out upskilling and upscaling projects, as well as to get beyond the difficulties involved in doing so.

The challenges in integrating technology, particularly in the aerospace industry, can be overcome through careful planning and addressing capability requirements. Public expenditure and inclusive growth play an important role in promoting the digital transformation of businesses and ensuring its sustainability in the long run.

Moreover, the articles highlight the importance of public-private partnerships in upskilling and upscaling programs, as well as the need for investment in vocational education and training to support the development of the future workforce. Additionally, the studies show that upskilling and upscaling have practical and social implications, including improved competitiveness and better job opportunities for employees. However, the studies also indicate that there is a need for further research to explore the social and practical implications of the digital transformation of businesses. Additionally, there is a need to address the limitations and implications of the existing studies, in order to arrive at more concrete and reliable conclusions.

Industry 5.0 represents a significant step forward in the integration of advanced technologies into businesses, and this has profound implications for upskilling and upscaling in digital transformation. The emphasis on creating a fully interconnected and collaborative digital ecosystem, as well as the need for a broader range of digital skills and competencies, make Industry 5.0 a more comprehensive and advanced approach to digital transformation compared to Industry 4.0.

In conclusion, the articles reviewed in this study provide valuable insights into the role of upskilling and upscaling in the digital transformation of businesses and the need for effective planning and implementation of these programs. The findings of the studies have implications for businesses, governments, and educational institutions in their efforts to support the development of the future workforce and promote competitiveness in the Industry 5.0 context. Overall, the review of the articles highlights the importance of upscaling and upskilling in digital transformation of business, and the need for continued research and development in this area.

The future scope of the study could be to conduct empirical research that tests and validates the theoretical findings of the literature review. This could involve case studies or surveys of organizations that have implemented digital transformation, upscaling, and upskilling initiatives in the context of Industry 5.0. The research could also explore the long-term effects of these initiatives on business performance and employee satisfaction. Additionally, the study could investigate emerging trends and technologies related to Industry 5.0 and their potential impact on digital transformation, upscaling, and upskilling in the future.

REFERENCES

Ajaram, K. (2023). Future of learning: Teaching and learning strategies. In *Learning Intelligence* (pp. 3–53). Innovative and Digital Transformative Learning Strategies., doi:10.1007/978-981-19-9201-8_1

Al-Rashdi, A. (2022). *Adoption Model for Digital Technologies: Case Study of Petroleum Development Oman* [Doctoral dissertation, University of Liverpool].

Amin, J. M., and Husin, M. A. National Vocational Qualification and Certification System of Malaysia. *Quality TVET in Asia Pacific Region: National Vocational Qualification Systems of CPSC Member Countries*, 99.

Amirova, A. (2021). *Management of transformation processes towards an innovative civil service of Kazakhstan (case-study of remuneration by results project).* APA. https://repository.apa.kz/handle/123456789/810

Anderson, G. (2022). Moving from Aspiration to Action on Climate Adaptation. *Inclusive Growth In The Middle East And North Africa*, 119.

Andreoni, A. (2018). *Skilling Tanzania: improving financing, governance and outputs of the skills development sector.* SOAS. https://eprints.soas.ac.uk/30117/1/Andreoni%20Skilling-Tanzania-ACE-Working-Paper-6.pdf

Arenas, G. (ed)., and Coulibaly, S. (ed). (2022). A new dawn for global value chain participation in the Philippines (G. Arenas and S. Coulibaly, Eds.). doi:10.1596/978-1-4648-1848-6

Arıker, Ç. (2022). Massive open online course (MOOC) platforms as rising social entrepreneurs: Creating social value through reskilling and upskilling the unemployed for after COVID-19 conditions. In Research Anthology on Business Continuity and Navigating Times of Crisis (pp. 607-629). IGI Global.

Atkinson, J. T. (2022). *Using remote sensing and geographical information systems to classify local landforms using a pattern recognition approach for improved soil mapping.* SUN. https://scholar.sun.ac.za/bitstream/handle/10019.1/124888/atkinson_remote_2022.pdf?sequence=1

Auktor, G. V. (2022). *The opportunities and challenges of Industry 4.0 for industrial development: A case study of Morocco's automotive and garment sectors* (No. 2/2022). Discussion Paper.

Bachtler, J., Mendez, C., & Wishlade, F. (2019). *Reforming the MFF and Cohesion Policy 2021-27: pragmatic drift or paradigmatic shift?* Strath. https://strathprints.strath.ac.uk/69563/1/Bachtler_etal_EPRC_2019_Reforming_the_MFF_and_cohesion_policy_2021_27_pragmatic_drift_or_paradigmatic_shift.pdf

Barreca, H. (2022). *Public Policy and the Business Life Cycle* [Doctoral dissertation, City University of New York]. https://search.proquest.com/openview/b62a8c65942e6d6d04db0dd40d3321e6/1?pq-origsite=gscholarand cbl=18750and diss=y

Behrendt, A., De Boer, E., Kasah, T., Koerber, B., Mohr, N., & Richter, G. (2021). *Leveraging Industrial IoT and advanced technologies for digital transformation.* McKinsey Co.

Bellantuono, N., Nuzzi, A., Pontrandolfo, P., & Scozzi, B. (2021). Digital transformation models for the I4. 0 transition: Lessons from the change management literature. *Sustainability (Basel)*, *13*(23), 12941. doi:10.3390/su132312941

Berger, V., & Chowdhury, S. (2021). *How to overcome the challenges of Internet of Things to ensure successful technology integration: A case study at an Aerospace manufacturer.* Diva. https://www.diva-portal.org/smash/record.jsf?pid=diva2:1567136

Bertello, A., Bogers, M. L., & De Bernardi, P. (2022). Open innovation in the face of the COVID-19 grand challenge: Insights from the Pan-European hackathon 'EUvsVirus'. *R & D Management*, *52*(2), 178–192. doi:10.1111/radm.12456

Bhandari, B. (2021). The 3-E Challenge: Education, Employability, and Employment (No. 122). National Council of Applied Economic Research.

Bilbao-Osorio, B., Burkhardt, K., Correia, A., Deiss, R., Lally, D., Martino, R., & Senczyszyn, D. (2018). *Science, Research and Innovation Performance of the EU 2018 Strengthening the Foundations for Europe's Future European Commission Directorate-General for Research and Innovation Directorate A—Policy Development and Coordination.* Riesal.

Blackall, P., Alawneh, J., Barnes, T., Meers, J., Palaniappan, G., Palmieri, C., & Turni, C. (2021). *Project Improving the production and competitiveness of Australian and Philippines pig production through better health and disease control.*

Boém, M. M., Laquidara, G., & Colombani, M. (2013). *Executive Strategic Criteria—Pt.*

Bolton-King, R. S., Nichols-Drew, L. J., & Turner, I. J. (2022). RemoteForensicCSI: Enriching teaching, training and learning through networking and timely CPD. *Science & Justice, 62*(6), 768–777. doi:10.1016/j.scijus.2022.01.004 PMID:36400498

Briggs, A. M., Houlding, E., Hinman, R. S., Desmond, L. A., Bennell, K. L., Darlow, B., Pizzari, T., Leech, M., MacKay, C., Larmer, P. J., Bendrups, A., Greig, A. M., Francis-Cracknell, A., Jordan, J. E., & Slater, H. (2019). Health professionals and students encounter multi-level barriers to implementing high-value osteoarthritis care: A multi-national study. *Osteoarthritis and Cartilage, 27*(5), 788–804. doi:10.1016/j.joca.2018.12.024 PMID:30668988

Brown, E. (2017). *Exploring the design of technology enabled learning experiences in teacher education that translate into classroom practice.* UCAL. https://prism.ucalgary.ca/handle/11023/4025

Brownie, S. M., Gatimu, S. M., Kambo, I., Mwizerwa, J., & Ndirangu, E. (2020). Stakeholders' expectations of nursing graduates following completion of a work-study upskilling programme. *Africa Journal of Nursing and Midwifery, 22*(2). doi:10.25159/2520-5293/5940

Brownie, S. M., Gatimu, S. M., Kambo, I., Mwizerwa, J., & Ndirangu, E. (2020). Stakeholders' expectations of nursing graduates following completion of a work-study upskilling programme. *Africa Journal of Nursing and Midwifery, 22*(2). doi:10.25159/2520-5293/5940

Bucea-Manea-Ţoniş, R., Kuleto, V., Gudei, S. C. D., Lianu, C., Lianu, C., Ilić, M. P., & Păun, D. (2022). Artificial intelligence potential in higher education institutions enhanced learning environment in Romania and Serbia. *Sustainability (Basel), 14*(10), 5842. doi:10.3390/su14105842

Casini, M. (2021). *Construction 4.0: Advanced Technology, Tools and Materials for the Digital Transformation of the Construction Industry.* Woodhead Publishing.

Cepal, N. (2022). *The Caribbean Outlook. Summary.* Cepal. https://repositorio.cepal.org/bitstream/handle/11362/48220/S2200950_en.pdf?sequence=1

Chakrabarti, D., Sarkar, S., & Mukherjee, A. (2022). Scaling an Internet of Things start-up: Can alliance strategy help? *Journal of Information Technology Teaching Cases, 12*(1), 43–49. doi:10.1177/2043886920986165

Chakravorti, N. (2022). *Digital Transformation: A Strategic Structure for Implementation.* CRC Press. doi:10.4324/9781003270904

Chang-Richards, A., Chen, X., Pelosi, A., & Yang, N. (2022). *Technology implementation: What does the future hold for construction?* BRANZ. https://prod.branz.co.nz/documents/3712/ER71_Technology_implementation_LR12069.pdf

Chowdhury, S., Dey, P., Joel-Edgar, S., Bhattacharya, S., Rodriguez-Espindola, O., Abadie, A., & Truong, L. (2023). Unlocking the value of artificial intelligence in human resource management through AI capability framework. *Human Resource Management Review*, *33*(1), 100899. doi:10.1016/j.hrmr.2022.100899

Chugh, R., Macht, S., & Hossain, R. (2022). Robotic Process Automation: A review of organizational grey literature. *International Journal of Information Systems and Project Management*, *10*(1), 5–26. doi:10.12821/ijispm100101

Corbeil, M. E., & Corbeil, J. R. (2022). Digital transformation of higher education through disruptive pedagogies: Wrapping a course around a course to promote learner agency. *Issues in Information Systems*. doi:10.48009/2_iis_2022_113

Council, B. (2019). The state of social enterprise in Malaysia 2018. *British Council. Retrieved June, 16,* 2020. https://repository.unescap.org/handle/20.500.12870/2885

Cumpton, G., Juniper, C., & Patnaik, A. (2018). *Austin Metro Area Master Community Workforce Plan Baseline Evaluation Report*. Ray Marshall Center for the Study of Human Resources.

De Paula, D., Marx, C., Wolf, E., Dremel, C., Cormican, K., & Uebernickel, F. (2023). A managerial mental model to drive innovation in the context of digital transformation. *Industry and Innovation*, *30*(1), 42–66. doi:10.1080/13662716.2022.2072711

de Vries, P. (2022). The Ethical Dimension of Emerging Technologies in Engineering Education. *Education Sciences*, *12*(11), 754. doi:10.3390/educsci12110754

Dieste, M., Sauer, P. C., & Orzes, G. (2022). Organizational tensions in industry 4.0 implementation: A paradox theory approach. *International Journal of Production Economics*, *251*, 108532. doi:10.1016/j.ijpe.2022.108532

Dlugosch, D., Abendschein, M., & Kim, E. J. (2022). *Helping the Austrian business sector to cope with new opportunities and challenges in Austria.*

Dube, R. (2021). *Measuring technical efficiency in Zimbabwe's manufacturing sector: a two-stage DEA Tobit approach* (Faculty of Commerce). https://open.uct.ac.za/handle/11427/33719

Fafunwa, T., & Odufuwa, F. (2022). African micro, small, and medium enterprises need to digitally transform to benefit from the Africa continental Free Trade area (AfCFTA). In Africa–Europe Cooperation and Digital Transformation (pp. 66–82). Taylor & Francis. doi:10.4324/9781003274322-5

Gamhewage, G., Mahmoud, M. E., Tokar, A., Attias, M., Mylonas, C., Canna, S., & Utunen, H. (2022). Digital transformation of face-to-face focus group methodology: Engaging a globally dispersed audience to manage institutional change at the World Health Organization. *Journal of Medical Internet Research*, *24*(5), e28911. doi:10.2196/28911 PMID:35617007

Gatta, M., Boushey, H., & Appelbaum, E. (2009). High-touch and here-to-stay: Future skills demands in US low wage service occupations. *Sociology*, *43*(5), 968–989. doi:10.1177/0038038509340735

Genelza, G. G. (2022). A case study research on Justin Herald's language development. *Journal of Languages. Linguistics and Literary Studies*, *2*(3), 133–141.

Gissing, A., & Eburn, M. (2019). *Planning and capability requirements for catastrophic and cascading disasters*. Bush Fire and Natural Hazards CRC. https://www.bnhcrc.com.au/sites/default/files/managed/downloads/cascading_and_catastrophic_events_final_report_2020_0.pdf

Gomendio, M., & the Organisation for Economic Co-operation and Development (OECD) Staff. (2017). *Empowering and enabling teachers to improve equity and outcomes for all*. OECD. https://www.oecd-ilibrary.org/content/publication/9789264273238-en?crawler=trueand mimetype=application/pdf

Gyulai, T., Wolf, P., Kása, F., & Viharos, Z. J. (2022). *Operational Structure for an Industry 4.0 oriented Learning Factory*. IMEKO.

Halvorsen, R. (1977). Energy substitution in US manufacturing. *The Review of Economics and Statistics*, *59*(4), 381–388. doi:10.2307/1928702

Hardie, T., Horton, T., Thornton-Lee, N., Home, J., & Pereira, P. (2022). Developing Learning Health Systems in the, UK: Priorities for Action. The Health Foundation, 10.

Howie, F., Kreofsky, B. L., Ravi, A., Lokken, T., Hoff, M. D., & Fang, J. L. (2022). Rapid rise of pediatric telehealth during COVID-19 in a large multispecialty health system. *Telemedicine Journal and e-Health*, *28*(1), 3–10. doi:10.1089/tmj.2020.0562 PMID:33999718

Irwin, D., & Ibrahim, N. (2020). *Market study to understand job growth potential in SMEs in Nepal*. Open Knowledge. https://openknowledge.worldbank.org/handle/10986/33952

Johnston, L., Koikkalainen, H., Anderson, L., Lapok, P., Lawson, A., & Shenkin, S. D. (2022). Foundation level barriers to the widespread adoption of digital solutions by care homes: Insights from three Scottish studies. *International Journal of Environmental Research and Public Health*, *19*(12), 7407. doi:10.3390/ijerph19127407 PMID:35742667

Kamath, R., & Venumuddala, V. R. (2023). *Emerging technologies and the Indian IT sector*. Taylor & Francis. doi:10.1201/9781003324355

Kathuria, R., Kedia, M., & Kapilavai, S. (2020). Implications of AI on the Indian Economy. https://www.think-asia.org/handle/11540/12242

Kim, J. (2020). *Scaling up disruptive agricultural technologies in Africa*. World Bank. doi:10.1596/978-1-4648-1522-5

King, R., Dowling, D., & Godfrey, E. (2011). *Pathways from VET awards to engineering degrees: a higher education perspective*. Australian Council of Engineering Deans. https://research.usq.edu.au/item/q0w4v/pathways-from-vet-awards-to-engineering-degrees-a-higher-education-perspective

Klein, C., Schwabe, M., Costa, H., & Sakha, S. (2022, February 11). *Getting the most of the digital transformation*. NIH. doi:10.1787/a74ff800-en

Komoróczki, I. (2022). *European Economic Area*. efta.int. https://www.efta.int/sites/default/files/images/22-43-Rev1.26-EEA%20CC%20resolution%20and%20report%20on%20the%20challenges%20and%20opportunities%20of%20greater%20use%20of%20artificial%20intelligence%20in%20working%20life.pdf

Kourmpetli, S., Falagán, N., Hardman, C., Liu, L., Mead, B., Walsh, L., & Davies, J. (2022). Scaling-up urban agriculture for a healthy, sustainable and resilient food system: The postharvest benefits, challenges and key research gaps. *International Journal of Postharvest Technology and Innovation*, 8(2-3), 145–157. doi:10.1504/IJPTI.2022.121791

Kuldosheva, G. (2022). Challenges and Opportunities for Digital Transformation in the Public Sector in Transition Economies: The Case of Uzbekistan. *Harnessing Digitalization for Sustainable Economic Development*, 365.

KulikL.KorovkinV. (2021). India Goes Digital. From local phenomenon to global influencer. SSRN 3829789.

Kumar, A., & Basu, S. (2022). Can end-user feedback inform 'Responsibilisation' of India's policy landscape for agri-digital transition? *Sociologia Ruralis*, 62(2), 305–334. doi:10.1111/soru.12374

Kuriakose, S., & Tiew, H. S. B. M. Z. (2022). *SME Program Efficiency Review.*, doi:10.1596/37137

Lang, G., & Triantoro, T. (2022). Upskilling and reskilling for the future of work: A typology of digital skills initiatives. *Information Systems Education Journal*, 20(4), 97–106. https://files.eric.ed.gov/fulltext/EJ1358297.pdf

Le, T. T., Sit, H. H. W., & Chen, S. (2023). How Vietnamese foreign language teachers survive and thrive: Tracing successful online teaching during the COVID-19 pandemic. In *The Post-pandemic Landscape of Education and Beyond* (pp. 112–136). Innovation and Transformation. doi:10.1007/978-981-19-9217-9_8

Lim, A. H., Apaza, P., and Horj, A. (2017). Trade in Education Services and the SDGs. *WIN–WIN*, 337.

Littlejohn, A., & Pammer-Schindler, V. (2022). Technologies for professional learning. In *Research Approaches on Workplace Learning: Insights from a Growing Field* (pp. 321–346). Springer International Publishing. doi:10.1007/978-3-030-89582-2_15

Majam, T., & Uwizeyimana, D. E. (2018). Aligning economic development as a priority of the integrated development plan to the annual budget in the City of Johannesburg Metropolitan Municipality. *African Journal of Public Affairs*, 10(4), 138–166.

Mathur, S., & Gupta, U. (Eds.). (2016). Transforming higher education through digitalization: insights. Learning, 3(1), 1-20.

Mátyás, T. B. (2022). *Industry 4.0: Challenges and Opportunities for V4 Countries*. v4cooperation.eu, https://v4cooperation.eu/wp-content/uploads/2022/05/Policy-Paper-3-Matyas.pdf

McLaughlin, K. (2021). *McKinsey on Investing.*, dln.jaipuria.ac.in, http://dln.jaipuria.ac.in:8080/jspui/bitstream/123456789/10841/1/Mckinsey-on-investing-issue-7-november-2021.pdf

Mendoza, J. M. F., & Ibarra, D. (2023). Technology-enabled circular business models for the hybridisation of wind farms: Integrated wind and solar energy, power-to-gas and power-to-liquid systems. *Sustainable Production and Consumption, 36*, 308–327. doi:10.1016/j.spc.2023.01.011

Mihály, F., & Lucia, M. K. (2016). *OECD Reviews of Vocational Education and Training A Skills beyond School Review of the Slovak Republic*. OECD Publishing.

Mindell, D. A., & Reynolds, E. (2022). *The work of the future: Building better jobs in an age of intelligent machines*. MIT Press.

Mitchell, D., Blanche, J., Harper, S., Lim, T., Gupta, R., Zaki, O., & Flynn, D. (2022). A review: Challenges and opportunities for artificial intelligence and robotics in the offshore wind sector. *Energy and AI*, 100146.

Montserrat, G. (2017). *International Summit on the Teaching Profession Empowering and Enabling Teachers to Improve Equity and Outcomes for All*. OECD Publishing.

Mourtzis, D., Angelopoulos, J., & Panopoulos, N. (2022). Operator 5.0: A survey on enabling technologies and a framework for digital manufacturing based on extended reality. *Journal of Machine Engineering, 22*(1), 43–69. doi:10.36897/jme/147160

Mujiono, M. N. (2021). The shifting role of accountants in the era of digital disruption. *International Journal of Multidisciplinary: Applied Business and Education Research, 2*(11), 1259–1274. doi:10.11594/10.11594/ijmaber.02.11.18

Mustafaoglu, A. (2022). *Imlementing digital transformation strategy the case of a local Turkish bank* [Master's thesis, Işık Üniversitesi]. https://acikerisim.isikun.edu.tr/xmlui/handle/11729/4848

Mzara, O. (2019). *Changing youth perceptions: exploring enablers of diffusion and adoption of agricultural innovations in South Africa* [Doctoral dissertation, University of Pretoria].

Narula, J. (2022). *An exploratory study of factors influencing the attraction and retention of skilled employees in the digital sector in Hawke's Bay* [Master's thesis, Research Bank]. https://researchbank.ac.nz/handle/10652/5783

Ng, I. Y., Lim, S. S., & Pang, N. (2022). Making universal digital access universal: Lessons from COVID-19 in Singapore. *Universal Access in the Information Society*, 1–11. PMID:35440934

Ngwa, W., Addai, B. W., Adewole, I., Ainsworth, V., Alaro, J., Alatise, O. I., Ali, Z., Anderson, B. O., Anorlu, R., Avery, S., Barango, P., Bih, N., Booth, C. M., Brawley, O. W., Dangou, J.-M., Denny, L., Dent, J., Elmore, S. N. C., Elzawawy, A., & Kerr, D. (2022). Cancer in sub-Saharan Africa: A lancet oncology Commission. *The Lancet. Oncology, 23*(6), e251–e312. doi:10.1016/S1470-2045(21)00720-8 PMID:35550267

Nichols, C. (2021). Professional services companies need to practise what they preach: the need to fast-track digital transformation in the industry. *Strategic HR Review*. doi:10.1108/SHR-09-2021-0046

Nottingham, K. D., & Cardozo, I. (2019). The Role of International Consumer Policy in Fostering Innovation and Empowering Consumers to Make Informed Choices. *Ind. Int'l and Comp. L. Rev., 30*, 1.

OECD. (2002). *Economic surveys and data analysis CIRET Conference proceedings, Paris 2000: CIRET Conference proceedings, Paris 2000*. OECD. https://books.google.at/books?id=CVTWAgAAQBAJ

Oeij, P., Hulsegge, G., Kirov, V., Pomares, E., Dhondt, S., Götting, A., & Deliverable, W. P. (2022). *Policy paper: digital transformation and regional policy options for inclusive growth.*

Oosthuizen, A. (2021). *HSRC Review 19 (1). March: 4-46.* HSRC. repository.hsrc.ac.za, https://repository.hsrc.ac.za/bitstream/handle/20.500.11910/18961/12807.pdf?sequence=1

Oyinlola, M., Schröder, P., Whitehead, T., Kolade, O., Wakunuma, K., Sharifi, S., Rawn, B., Odumuyiwa, V., Lendelvo, S., Brighty, G., Tijani, B., Jaiyeola, T., Lindunda, L., Mtonga, R., & Abolfathi, S. (2022). Digital innovations for transitioning to circular plastic value chains in Africa. *Africa Journal of Management*, 8(1), 83–108. doi:10.1080/23322373.2021.1999750

Petrika-Lindroos, I. (2022). *Unlocking the power of AI in HR: how Artificial Intelligence can elevate the HR strategy in knowledge-based organizations.*

Ponnana, R. K., & Uppalapati, N. (2022). *Digital Transformation of IKEA's Supply Chain during and after the pandemic.* Diva Portal. https://www.diva-portal.org/smash/record.jsf?pid=diva2:1673117

Prodi, E., Tassinari, M., Ferrannini, A., & Rubini, L. (2022). Industry 4.0 policy from a sociotechnical perspective: The case of German competence centres. *Technological Forecasting and Social Change*, *175*, 121341. doi:10.1016/j.techfore.2021.121341

Quimba, F. M. A., Barral, M. A. A., and Carlos, J. C. T. (2021). Analysis of the FinTech Landscape in the Philippines.

Qureshi, Z., & Woo, C. (2022). Economic paradigms are shifting. Digital technologies are driving trans. *Shifting Paradigms: Growth, Finance, Jobs, and Inequality in the Digital Economy*, 1.

Rabiey, M., Welch, T., Sanchez-Lucas, R., Stevens, K., Raw, M., Kettles, G. J., Catoni, M., McDonald, M. C., Jackson, R. W., & Luna, E. (2022). Scaling-up to understand tree–pathogen interactions: A steep, tough climb or a walk in the park? *Current Opinion in Plant Biology*, *68*, 102229. doi:10.1016/j.pbi.2022.102229 PMID:35567925

Ranjith Kumar, R., Ganesh, L. S., & Rajendran, C. (2022). Quality 4.0–a review of and framework for quality management in the digital era. *International Journal of Quality & Reliability Management*, *39*(6), 1385–1411. doi:10.1108/IJQRM-05-2021-0150

Rowan, N. J., Murray, N., Qiao, Y., O'Neill, E., Clifford, E., Barceló, D., & Power, D. M. (2022). Digital transformation of peatland eco-innovations ('Paludiculture'): Enabling a paradigm shift towards the real-time sustainable production of 'green-friendly' products and services. *The Science of the Total Environment*, *838*(Pt 3), 156328. doi:10.1016/j.scitotenv.2022.156328 PMID:35649452

Roxburgh, C., Gregory, A., Hall, J., Higgins, S., Titus, A., McGill, D., & Ross, C. (2018). Small research and development activity.

Russo, L., Høj, J. C., & Borowiecki, M. (2022). Digitalising the economy in Slovenia. https://www.oecd-ilibrary.org/economics/digitalising-the-economy-in-slovenia_9167aa58-en

Rutovitz, J., Visser, D., Sharpe, S., Taylor, H., Jennings, K., Atherton, A., & Mortimer, G. (2021). Developing the future energy workforce. *Opportunity assessment for RACE for, 2030*.

Rutovitz, J., Visser, D., Sharpe, S., Taylor, H., Jennings, K., Atherton, A., & Mortimer, G. (2021). Developing the future energy workforce. *Opportunity assessment for RACE for, 2030*.

Rutovitz, J., Visser, D., Sharpe, S., Taylor, H., Jennings, K., Atherton, A., & Mortimer, G. (2021). E3 Opportunity assessment: developing the future energy workforce-final report 2021. https://apo.org.au/sites/default/files/resource-files/2021-10/apo-nid314409.pdf

Saurav, A., Kusek, P., & Albertson, M. (2021). World Bank Investor Confidence Survey. https://openknowledge.worldbank.org/bitstream/handle/10986/36581/World-Bank-Investor-Confidence-Survey-Evidence-from-the-Quarterly-Global-Multinational-Enterprises-Pulse-Survey-for-the-Second-Quarter-of-2021.pdf?sequence=1

Schreieck, M., Wiesche, M., & Krcmar, H. (2022). From product platform ecosystem to innovation platform ecosystem: An institutional perspective on the governance of ecosystem transformations. *Journal of the Association for Information Systems, 23*(6), 1354–1385. doi:10.17705/1jais.00764

Serrano, J. (2021). Decarbonizing energy intensive industries: country study France. *etui.org*. https://www.etui.org/sites/default/files/2022-08/Decarbonizing%20energy%20intensive%20industries%20-%20France%20-%20Serrano.pdf

Sharma, H., Soetan, T., Farinloye, T., Mogaji, E., & Noite, M. D. F. (2022). AI adoption in universities in emerging economies: Prospects, challenges and recommendations. In *Re-imagining Educational Futures in Developing Countries: Lessons from Global Health Crises* (pp. 159–174). Springer International Publishing. doi:10.1007/978-3-030-88234-1_9

Sharp, D., Anwar, M., Goodwin, S., Raven, R., Bartram, L., & Kamruzzaman, L. (2022). A participatory approach for empowering community engagement in data governance: The Monash Net Zero Precinct. *Data & Policy, 4*, e5. doi:10.1017/dap.2021.33

Spohrer, J., Maglio, P. P., Vargo, S. L., & Warg, M. (2022). *Service in the AI Era: Science, Logic, and Architecture Perspectives*. Business Expert Press.

Stewart, L. (2022). *How Can Company X Effectively Make A Transition From Digitisation To Digital Transformation?* [Doctoral dissertation, University of Liverpool].

Stracke, C. M., Burgos, D., Santos-Hermosa, G., Bozkurt, A., Sharma, R. C., Swiatek Cassafieres, C., dos Santos, A. I., Mason, J., Ossiannilsson, E., Shon, J. G., Wan, M., Obiageli Agbu, J.-F., Farrow, R., Karakaya, Ö., Nerantzi, C., Ramírez-Montoya, M. S., Conole, G., Cox, G., & Truong, V. (2022). Responding to the initial challenge of the COVID-19 pandemic: Analysis of international responses and impact in school and higher education. *Sustainability (Basel), 14*(3), 1876. doi:10.3390/su14031876

Suleman, M. A., Meyer, N., & Nieuwenhuizen, C. (2022). *Analysis of Top-Ranked South African and International MBA Focus Areas in the 4th Industrial Revolution*. In *2022 INTERNATIONAL BUSINESS CONFERENCE*. TSHWANE UNIVERSITY OF TECHNOLOGY.

Theby, M. (2022). Public Sector Cloud Computing Adoption and Utilization during COVID-19: An Agenda for Research and Practice. [IJMPICT]. *International Journal of Managing Public Sector Information and Communication Technologies*, *13*(1), 1–11. doi:10.5121/ijmpict.2022.13101

Umar, M. A. (2022). Digital Transformation Strategies for Small Business Management. In *Handbook of Research on Digital Transformation Management and Tools* (pp. 435–452). IGI Global. doi:10.4018/978-1-7998-9764-4.ch019

UNESCAP. (2022). *Building forward together: towards an inclusive and resilient Asia and the Pacific*. UN. https://repository.unescap.org/handle/20.500.12870/4324

UNESCAP. (2022). *Asia-Pacific digital transformation report 2022: shaping our digital future*. https://repository.unescap.org/handle/20.500.12870/4725

Ungureanu, D. M. (2022). Reviving Productivity Growth in Urban Economies. *Annals of Spiru Haret University. Economic Series*, *22*(1), 169–182.

Vaughan-Whitehead, D., Ghellab, Y., and de Bustillo Llorente, R. (2021). *The new world of work*. doi:10.4337/9781800888050

Vide, R. K., Hunjet, A., & Kozina, G. (2022). Enhancing Sustainable Business by SMEs' Digitalization. *Journal of Strategic Innovation & Sustainability*, *17*(1).

Vujnovic, M., & Foster, J. E. (2022). Online Instruction and the "Hyflex Teaching 'Shock Doctrine. In *Higher Education and Disaster Capitalism in the Age of COVID-19* (pp. 167–180). Springer International Publishing. doi:10.1007/978-3-031-12370-2_7

Wang, Y., & Pettit, S. (2022). A Primer on Supply Chain Digital Transformation. *Digital Supply Chain Transformation*, *121*, 121–139. doi:10.18573/book8.g

Yatsenko, D. (2020). *Project of Introducing a Supportive tool for Establishing and Growing Start-ups in the Environment of Secondary Schools in Zlín Region*.

Yusif, S., Hafeez-Baig, A., Soar, J., & Teik, D. O. L. (2020). PLS-SEM path analysis to determine the predictive relevance of e-Health readiness assessment model. *Health and Technology*, *10*(6), 1497–1513. doi:10.1007/s12553-020-00484-9

Ziemann, V., & Guérard, B. (2017). *Reaping the benefits of global value chains in Turkey*. OECD. https://www.oecd-ilibrary.org/content/paper/d054af64-en

Ziozias, C., & Anthopoulos, L. (2022, June). Forming Smart Governance under a City Digital Transformation Strategy-findings from Greece and ICC. In *DG. O 2022: The 23rd Annual International Conference on Digital Government Research* (pp. 416-424). 10.1145/3543434.3543491

Zouhar, Y., Jellema, J., Lustig, N., & Trabelsi, M. (2021). *Public Expenditure and Inclusive Growth-A Survey*. International Monetary Fund. doi:10.5089/9781513574387.001

ENDNOTES

[1]   Preferred Reporting Items for Reviews and Meta-Analyses (PRISMA). (n.d.). Retrieved from https://www.prisma-statement.org/

[2]   Bughin, J., Hazan, E., Ramaswamy, S., Chui, M., Allas, T., Dahlström, P., ... and Kim, N. (2018). Skill shift: Automation and the future of the workforce. McKinsey Global Institute. Cheema, S. A., and Raza, S. A. (2021). Industry 5.0: A Review of Advanced Manufacturing Paradigm. In Industry 5.0 for Sustainable Future (pp. 1-22). Springer.

[3]   EY. (2019). Industry 4.0 and skills of the future: The road to 2020 and beyond. Hoque, R., and Chaudhury, N. (2018). Upskilling and Reskilling for the Future of Work. IEEE Technology and Society Magazine, 37(2), 11-15.

[4]   McQuarrie, E. F. (2020). Upskilling for Industry 4.0: An Empirical Analysis of the Canadian Automotive Sector. International Journal of Economics and Business Research, 20(3), 283-303. World Economic Forum. (2018). Towards a Reskilling Revolution: A Future of Jobs for All.

Chapter 8
Enhancing Organisational Intelligence Integration of Artificial Intelligence and Knowledge Management:
Frameworks in India

Deepa Sharma
https://orcid.org/0000-0003-4374-917X
Maharishi Markandeshwar University, India

Chauhan
Maharishi Markandeshwar University, India

Vinod Kumar
https://orcid.org/0000-0002-3578-8155
Maharishi Markandeshwar University, India

ABSTRACT

Knowledge is recognized as a central component for an organisation to remain competitive. In this current phase, the blend of artificial intelligence (AI) and knowledge management (KM) frameworks can upgrade and improve organizational success. The role of knowledge management (KM) frameworks has evolved because of fast changing environment technology and continuously upgrading technology. AI combining KM can become that thriving component for organizations to be more progressive. Application of AI can be used in different forms of KM, like creation, storage, share and usage of knowledge. Different forms of AI technologies such as expert systems, intelligent search, chatbots, Robotics process automation, machine learning (ML) and natural language processing (NLP), can help to process large data and extract valuable information. AI-enabled KM systems in organisations can bring transformation through improved organisation learning, better decision-making based on data analysis, upgraded technology and innovation, and can provide aid to be more informed, intelligent, and adaptable to respond quickly with unpredictable corporate settings. If a business were to leverage the power of AI in organisation

DOI: 10.4018/978-1-6684-9576-6.ch008

systems in India, they can gain competitive advantage, improve their innovation and agility in today's fast changing scenario. However, there are challenges in integrating AI and KM frameworks, such as data privacy and ethical concerns. This study explores the integration of KM frameworks and AI to increase organisation effectiveness also it examines how technologies of AI can help with creation of knowledge, its storage, knowledge sharing and application of knowledge. Though, it is also significant to consider challenges of using AI in KM frameworks, like data privacy and ethical concerns are particularly important, so that organization's sensitive information should not be compromised and can use AI technologies in transparent, accountable, and ethical manner.

INTRODUCTION

In today's fast-paced business environment, organizations are constantly looking for ways to improve their performance, maintain competitiveness, and overcome complex challenges. The approach which has gained significant attention is the incorporation of artificial intelligence (AI) and knowledge management (KM) frameworks to enhance or to maximize organizational intelligence Haleem et al (2022). This study focuses on how AI and KM frameworks can be united to improve organizational intelligence in India.

Organizational intelligence is an organization's capacity to acquire, process, and apply knowledge effectively in order to achieve its goals Kucharsk and Bedford (2023). AI, with its ability to simulate human intelligence and automate tasks, has emerged as a game-changing technology with vast potential in various industries. The evolving scenario, needs organizations to efficiently organize education among humans and artificial assistants (e.g., Berente et al., 2021; Young et al., 2021). (AI) has the power to greatly benefit Indian organizations in various industries. For example, AI can automate repetitive tasks, making things more efficient and freeing up employees to focus on important work. It can also improve customer experiences by using chatbots and virtual assistants to provide personalized help and recommendations. AI can analyze large amounts of data to find valuable insights, helping organizations make better decisions. Additionally, it can detect and prevent fraud in digital transactions, predict equipment failures to optimize maintenance, and revolutionize healthcare with improved diagnostics and access to services. Sutton and Barto, (2018) AI has the ability to optimize the network of supply chains, costs reduction, and also to boost the process of talent acquisition. Zalte (2023) supports the fact that artificial Intelligence (AI) has the power to bring great benefits to organizations in different industries. AI can benefit the organisation in so many ways and few of the are as follows:

- **Automation and Efficiency**: AI can do repetitive tasks automatically, making things faster and more efficient. For example, in manufacturing or logistics, AI can handle routine jobs, so people can focus on more important work.
- **Customer Experience**: AI can make customer service better. Chatbots and virtual assistants that use AI can talk to customers like humans and help them with their questions or give personalized recommendations. This makes customers happier and ensures they get help at any time.
- **Data Analytics and Insights**: Indian organizations have lots of data, and AI can help understand it better. AI can look at big amounts of data, find patterns, and make predictions. This helps organizations make smarter decisions based on data.

- **Fraud Detection and Security**: With more online transactions, AI can help catch fraud. AI can look at transactions in real-time and find strange patterns that might be fraud. This protects organizations from losing money and keeps sensitive information safe.
- **Predictive Maintenance**: AI can predict when machines might break down. By looking at data from sensors and past records, AI can tell when something is likely to go wrong. This helps fix problems before they happen, so things keep running smoothly.
- **Healthcare and Diagnostics**: AI can change healthcare in India. AI can help doctors diagnose diseases, look at medical images, and predict how patients will do. AI can also help people get healthcare in remote areas through chatbots and telemedicine.
- **Supply Chain Optimization**: AI can make supply chains work better. AI can predict what people will want to buy, manage how much stuff is in stock, and make delivery faster and better. This makes things cheaper, faster, and keeps customers happy.
- **Talent Acquisition and HR**: AI can make hiring easier and faster. AI can look at resumes, test candidates, and help HR teams make better decisions. AI can also help understand how happy employees are, see how well they do their jobs, and create personalized training programs.

At the same time, KM focuses on managing, sharing, and utilizing knowledge within an organization to drive innovation, learning, and decision-making. Knowledge Management (KM) is highly valuable for organizations Farooq (2023). Following facts illustrate the validation of KM in organisations:

1) **Preserving and Using Knowledge**: India has a rich cultural heritage and diverse knowledge traditions. KM helps organizations capture and preserve valuable knowledge from experts, employees, and external sources. This knowledge can be used to improve products, services, and processes, encouraging innovation and competitiveness.
2) **Collaboration and Sharing**: India has a large and diverse workforce. KM promotes collaboration and knowledge sharing among employees. By providing platforms and tools for sharing insights, best practices, and lessons learned, KM enables employees to learn from each other, solve problems together, and improve overall performance.
3) **Learning and Development:** Continuous learning is crucial in India. KM supports learning initiatives by providing access to learning resources, training materials, and communities of practice. This creates a culture of learning and helps employees acquire new skills and knowledge.
4) **Effective Decision-making**: In a complex business environment, KM helps organizations make informed decisions. By providing access to accurate and up-to-date information, KM allows managers and leaders to make decisions based on reliable data. This saves time, improves productivity, and leads to better outcomes.
5) **Innovation and Adaptability**: India is known for its innovation. KM captures ideas, lessons learned, and innovative practices. By encouraging knowledge sharing and collaboration, KM supports the development of new products, services, and processes, driving growth and adaptability in the Indian market.
6) **Customer Service**: KM enhances customer service and satisfaction. By capturing and organizing customer knowledge, organizations can provide personalized experiences. KM systems enable customer service representatives to access relevant information quickly, leading to faster issue resolution and improved customer relationships.

7) **Knowledge-based Economy**: India aims to become a knowledge-based economy. Effective KM helps manage and utilize knowledge assets, fueling economic growth and competitiveness. KM supports the creation, dissemination, and application of knowledge, driving innovation, entrepreneurship, and sustainable development.

8) **Government and Public Sector**: KM is crucial in the government and public sector in India. It facilitates efficient knowledge sharing across departments, improving policy-making, implementation, and citizen services.

Integration of AI and KM frameworks offers a synergistic approach to enhance organizational intelligence Raisch and Krakowski (2020). By combining AI technologies with KM practices, organizations can leverage advanced data analytics, machine learning, natural language processing, and other AI techniques to capture, analyze, and share knowledge throughout the organization. This integration enables the development of intelligent systems that facilitate informed decision-making, foster innovation, and promote continuous learning within the organization. Integrating AI and KM frameworks also poses challenges and considerations. Ethical and privacy concerns related to AI technologies must be addressed, such as responsible data use, privacy protection, and avoiding biases in decision-making algorithms. Organizations must also prioritize data security, protect intellectual property, and ensure transparency in AI algorithms to build trust in the integrated systems. Furthermore, successful integration of AI and KM frameworks relies on a supportive organizational culture that values knowledge sharing, collaboration, and continuous learning. Organizations must foster an environment where employees are encouraged to share their knowledge, collaborate across teams, and actively engage in learning activities. Investing in employee training and development is crucial to equip individuals with the necessary skills to effectively utilize AI-powered knowledge management systems. Integrating AI and KM frameworks holds great potential for enhancing organizational intelligence in India. By harnessing the capabilities of AI technologies, organizations can capture, analyse, and share knowledge more efficiently, leading to improved decision-making, enhanced innovation, and a culture of continuous learning. However, addressing ethical concerns, ensuring data security, and fostering a supportive organizational culture are critical for successful integration. This study will delve deeper into these aspects, examining real-world examples, case studies, and best practices to provide valuable insights for organizations seeking to leverage AI and KM frameworks to enhance their organizational intelligence within the Indian context.

LITERATURE REVIEW

Smith (2019) suggests that integrating AI and KM allows organizations to effectively utilize AI technologies to capture, organize, and leverage knowledge for better decision-making and innovation. According to Chen et al. (2020), AI can enhance KM processes by automating knowledge discovery, extraction, and representation, helping organizations effectively utilize their knowledge repositories. Brown and Jones (2018) emphasize the role of AI in supporting collaborative knowledge sharing. They discuss how AI technologies using natural language processing and machine learning algorithms can enable intelligent search and retrieval of relevant knowledge. In the healthcare sector, Park et al. (2021) explore the integration of AI and KM. They demonstrate how AI-powered systems can assist in knowledge-based diagnosis, treatment recommendations, and personalized healthcare delivery. Zhang and Li (2019) conducted a systematic review on AI and KM integration, highlighting the potential of AI in transforming

Figure 1. Benefits of AI for KM
Source: Taherdoost and Madanchain (2023)

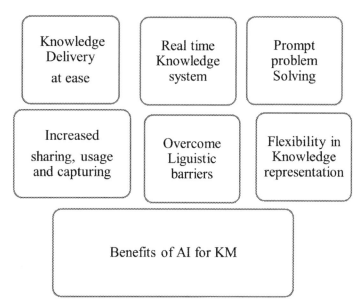

KM practices. They discuss how AI can improve knowledge acquisition, creation, sharing, and utilization, leading to enhanced organizational performance. Wang and Liang (2020) discuss the application of AI techniques, such as data mining and sentiment analysis, in extracting and analyzing tacit knowledge from various sources. Their research enriches organizational knowledge repositories. Choi and Kim (2019) examine the integration of AI and KM in supply chain management. They illustrate how AI algorithms can optimize knowledge-driven decision-making in areas like demand forecasting, inventory management, and logistics optimization. Li and Feng (2020) explore the use of AI in improving KM processes within multinational corporations. They discuss how AI-based recommendation systems can enhance knowledge sharing and collaboration among geographically dispersed teams.

Zhang et al. (2018) conducted a study on AI-enabled knowledge discovery. They emphasize the integration of AI techniques, such as natural language processing and machine learning, to extract valuable insights from unstructured data sources and enhance organizational knowledge bases. Hu et al. (2021) investigate the integration of AI and KM in talent management. They highlight how AI-powered tools can support knowledge sharing, competency assessment, and personalized learning and development programs. Chen and Huang (2019) focus on the integration of AI and KM in customer relationship management (CRM). They discuss how AI-driven analytics can enhance customer knowledge management, leading to improved customer satisfaction and loyalty. Liu et al. (2020) discuss the integration of AI and KM in project management. They highlight how AI technologies, such as intelligent chatbots and project knowledge repositories, can improve project collaboration, knowledge sharing, and decision-making. Gong et al. (2019) conducted a study on AI-assisted knowledge acquisition. They demonstrate how AI techniques, such as natural language processing and machine learning, can automate the extraction and classification of knowledge from unstructured data sources, enabling efficient knowledge capture and utilization. Li et al. (2021) explores the integration of AI and KM in organizational learning. They discuss how AI-powered tools can facilitate personalized and adaptive learning experiences, supporting employees in acquiring and applying knowledge effectively.

Zhao and Jiang (2020) conduct a literature review on the integration of AI and KM in innovation management. They highlight how AI techniques, such as data analytics and machine learning, can facilitate knowledge-driven innovation by identifying patterns, predicting trends, and supporting decision-making. Wang et al. (2019) discuss the integration of AI and KM in intellectual property management. They illustrate how AI technologies can assist in knowledge discovery, patent analysis, and intellectual asset management, enabling organizations to make informed strategic decisions.

Zhou et al. (2020) conducted a study on the integration of AI and KM in the context of e-commerce, illustrating how AI techniques, such as recommendation systems and personalized marketing, can enhance knowledge-driven customer engagement and improve business performance. Liang et al. (2019) projected AI and KM effectiveness in administrative decision-making, as AI algorithms has an ability to process and analyse big data and filter crucial knowledge for problem solving and strategic planning. Liu et al. (2021) also stressed upon the incorporation of AI and KM in area of human resource management highlighting AI-powered tools for employee development, talent acquisition and assessment programme leading to increased organisational performance and improved employee satisfaction. Chen et al. (2022) studied how AI and KM can improve customer support and service. They found that AI-powered chatbots and virtual assistants can enhance customer interactions by providing knowledge-based assistance, leading to higher customer satisfaction.

Wang and Zhang (2020) explored the integration of AI and KM in data analytics. They discovered that AI techniques can help organizations extract useful insights from large datasets, enabling them to make better decisions based on data. Li et al. (2022) investigated how AI and KM can facilitate knowledge discovery. They found that AI algorithms, such as machine learning and text mining, can help identify and extract valuable knowledge from various sources, improving knowledge management practices.

Huang et al. (2021) focused on the integration of AI and KM in cybersecurity. They highlighted how AI technologies can be utilized to detect and respond to security threats, protecting organizational knowledge assets and enhancing overall security. Zhou and Li (2021) studied the integration of AI and KM in smart cities. They found that AI-powered systems can support knowledge-driven urban planning, resource management, and service delivery, leading to more sustainable and efficient cities. Liu and Wang (2022) examined the integration of AI and KM in decision support systems. They emphasized how AI technologies can assist in knowledge-based decision-making, providing intelligent recommendations and predictions to support complex decision processes. Zhang et al. (2021) explored the integration of AI and KM in natural language processing. They discovered that AI techniques can be used to understand and extract knowledge from textual data, improving information retrieval and knowledge discovery processes. Wang et al. (2021) conducted a study on the integration of AI and KM in financial services. They found that AI-powered tools can enhance financial analysis, risk management, and personalized customer services by leveraging knowledge-based approaches.

FRAMEWORK OF ARTIFICIAL INTELLIGENCE

AI helps organizations make smarter decisions by analyzing large amounts of data from different sources. AI can create models that predict future trends and outcomes based on past data, helping organizations anticipate customer behavior and market trends. AI can also automate tasks like data entry and inventory management, freeing up employees to focus on more important work and improving efficiency. AI can provide personalized recommendations and targeted marketing campaigns to enhance customer satisfaction. AI can detect and prevent cybersecurity threats and fraud by analyzing data for suspicious activity. AI-powered robots can automate repetitive tasks in industries like manufacturing and logistics, improving productivity and accuracy. AI can be used to develop smart city solutions like intelligent traffic management and energy optimization, making cities more sustainable and efficient. From the above discussion we can draw following AI dimensions in order to gain organisational intelligence:

Expert Systems

Expert systems are a type of AI technology that helps organizations in India make better decisions and solve complex problems. They work by capturing the knowledge and expertise of human specialists and applying it to specific areas of the organization's operations. As an example, Apollo Hospitals, a leading healthcare provider in India, uses an expert system called "Apollo Expert" to improve patient care and diagnosis. This system mimics the knowledge and decision-making abilities of medical experts. It analyzes patient symptoms, medical history, and test results, and then suggests potential diagnoses, treatment options, and further tests. Apollo Expert helps doctors make informed decisions by providing access to the latest medical research and expert knowledge. It also serves as a training resource and can be used for second opinions. While expert systems have their limitations and cannot fully replicate human expertise, they are valuable tools for organizational intelligence in India. They leverage specialized knowledge and reasoning capabilities to support decision-making, automate tasks, and boost productivity

Figure 2. AI framework of organisational Intelligence
Source: Compiled through ROL by Author

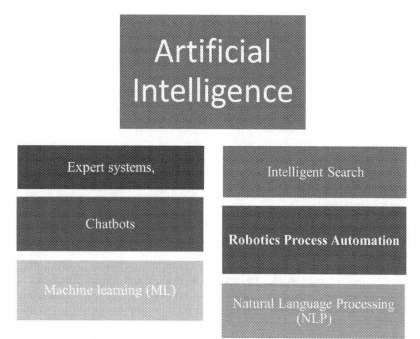

Intelligent Search

Intelligent search is a technology that uses artificial intelligence and machine learning to improve the search experience. It goes beyond simple keyword searches by understanding the context and meaning behind user queries. In the context of organizational intelligence in India, intelligent search can be highly effective.

Tata Consultancy Services (TCS), a large IT services company in India, uses intelligent search technology called "TCS Explorer." It helps their employees find information quickly and accurately. The system understands questions and context, even if they are asked in a conversational way. It can search through documents, project archives, and other sources to provide relevant results. By analyzing the content and extracting key information, intelligent search systems can surface valuable insights for users. This empowers employees to make more informed decisions and access relevant knowledge within the organization's databases, documents, and knowledge bases. Moreover, intelligent search utilizes natural language processing, enabling users to interact with the search engine using everyday language.

This eliminates the need for complex search queries and makes it easier for employees to find the information they seek. The system's ability to process and understand human language in a nuanced manner enhances the user experience and increases search efficiency. Furthermore, intelligent search systems offer recommendations and suggestions based on user behavior and past searches. By analyzing these patterns, the search engine can provide personalized recommendations for related content or relevant resources. This feature assists users in discovering new information and exploring additional resources that they may not have previously considered. In terms of collaboration and knowledge sharing, intelligent search plays a crucial role. It facilitates effective communication and knowledge sharing among employees by connecting them with experts, identifying relevant documents and resources, and providing access to valuable information. This fosters a collaborative work environment and ensures that knowledge is shared and utilized efficiently within the organization.

Chat Bots

Chatbots are computer programs that simulate human conversations using artificial intelligence. They can communicate with users through text or voice interfaces, providing automated responses to their questions or requests. In the context of organizational intelligence in India, chatbots have several important benefits. Chatbots greatly improve customer service. They can handle common inquiries, offer product information, troubleshoot problems, and guide users through various processes. For illustration Swiggy, a leading food delivery platform in India, utilizes chatbots to improve their customer experience. Customers can interact with the chatbot to place orders, track deliveries, inquire about offers or promotions, and address any concerns or issues they may have. The chatbot provides quick responses and ensures a seamless ordering process for users. By automating these interactions, chatbots provide quick and accurate responses to customers, resulting in better customer satisfaction. For example HDFC Bank, one of India's leading private banks, has integrated chatbots into their customer service operations. Their chatbot, known as "EVA" (Electronic Virtual Assistant), assists customers with various banking queries such as account balance inquiries, transaction history, credit card payments, and more. EVA is available 24/7 and provides personalized responses based on customer profiles and transaction history. Regardless of the hour, chatbots can promptly address customer queries and provide assistance, ensuring customers receive support whenever they need it. Chatbots also bring scalability and cost-effectiveness to organizations. They can engage in multiple conversations simultaneously, making them highly scalable. This means they can handle numerous user interactions concurrently, reducing the need for a large customer support team. Consequently, organizations can save costs while maintaining a high level of customer service.

Chatbots are valuable tools for organizational intelligence in India. They elevate customer service, provide round-the-clock availability, offer scalability and cost-effectiveness, enable data collection and analysis, support internal knowledge sharing, and act as virtual assistants. By leveraging chatbot technology, organizations can improve operational efficiency, enhance customer satisfaction, streamline internal processes, and ultimately achieve success.

Robotics Process Automation

Robotic Process Automation (RPA) is a technology that automates repetitive tasks using software robots. In India, RPA is an effective tool for improving organizational intelligence. For example, an Indian company like Flipkart, a leading e-commerce platform, utilizes RPA to streamline their order processing. RPA bots automatically handle tasks like order confirmation, inventory management, and shipping updates. This improves efficiency, reduces errors, and allows employees to focus on more strategic activities. By leveraging RPA, Flipkart gains valuable insights into customer purchasing patterns and can make data-driven decisions to enhance their business operations. Overall, RPA is a cost-effective solution that boosts productivity and enables organizations in India to make smarter, more informed choices.

Machine Learning (ML)

Machine learning, a subset of artificial intelligence, is a valuable tool for improving organizational intelligence in India. Machine learning teaches computers to learn from data and make predictions or decisions on their own. Instead of following specific instructions, computers use algorithms and models to analyze large amounts of data and find patterns. For instance, an Indian company like Ola, a prominent ride-hailing service, uses machine learning to analyze customer data and predict ride demand in different areas and at different times. This helps Ola efficiently allocate their drivers, reduce wait times for customers, and optimize their operations. By leveraging machine learning, Ola gains valuable insights and enhances their overall service quality and customer satisfaction.

Natural Language processing (NLP)

Natural Language Processing (NLP) is a branch of artificial intelligence that focuses on computer understanding and interaction with human language. In Indian companies, NLP can greatly enhance organizational intelligence. For instance, a company like Zomato, a popular food delivery platform, can use NLP to improve customer support. NLP algorithms can analyze and comprehend customer queries, enabling Zomato to respond accurately and promptly. This helps streamline customer service, automate routine inquiries, and create a smoother customer experience. Additionally, NLP can be applied by companies like Flipkart, an Indian e-commerce platform, to analyze customer reviews and extract valuable insights about customer sentiment. This information allows companies to identify trends and make data-driven decisions to improve their products and services. Overall, NLP empowers Indian companies to better understand and engage with their customers, leading to enhanced organizational intelligence.

INTEGRATED FRAMEWORK OF ARTIFICIAL INTELLIGENCE (AI) AND KNOWLEDGE MANAGEMENT (KM)

The integrated framework of Artificial Intelligence (AI) and Knowledge Management (KM) combines AI techniques with knowledge management practices to improve decision-making and organizational intelligence. While, Knowledge Management stands out as a crucial process in which how organizations capture, organize, share, and use knowledge to make better decisions and improve their performance. It involves managing information, expertise, and experiences in a systematic way. In India, where there is a diverse business environment, companies understand the importance of effectively managing knowledge to stay competitive. Knowledge management includes activities like collecting and organizing knowledge from different sources like employees, customers, and partners. The goal is to encourage sharing, collaboration, and learning within organizations. By managing knowledge well, Indian companies can make smarter decisions, improve their products and services, become more efficient, and drive innovation. Technology and digital tools play a big role in knowledge management in India. Organizations use platforms, intranets, and collaboration tools to share knowledge and make sense of large amounts of data. Furthermore, Knowledge management for organizational intelligence involves various aspects that help organizations make the most of their knowledge. Here are some key dimensions of knowledge management:

- Creating Knowledge: Organizations focus on generating new ideas, innovations, and insights within the company.
- Capturing and Acquiring Knowledge: They collect knowledge from different sources, including documents, databases, and the expertise and experiences of employees.
- Organizing Knowledge: They organize and categorize knowledge in a structured manner so that it is easy to find and use when needed.
- Storing and Retrieving Knowledge: Knowledge is stored in databases or repositories and can be easily accessed and retrieved when required.
- Sharing and Collaboration: Organizations foster a culture of knowledge sharing, encouraging employees to exchange ideas, expertise, and lessons learned.
- Transferring and Training: Knowledge is passed on from one individual or team to another through mentoring, training, and knowledge transfer programs.
- Applying and Utilizing Knowledge: Knowledge is used to solve problems, make informed decisions, and drive innovation within the organization.
- Measuring and Evaluating Knowledge: Organizations assess the effectiveness of their knowledge management efforts by measuring the impact of knowledge on performance and evaluating the value created.

By focusing on these dimensions of knowledge management, organizations can effectively leverage their knowledge resources, enhance their intelligence, and continuously improve their operations.

The framework of AI enabled KM practices focuses on knowledge capturing, organizing it in a discovering valuable insight from large datasets Taherdoost and Madanchain (2023). AI-enabled chatbots and virtual assistants helps to ease knowledge sharing among employees and expert systems, recommendation engines deliver intelligent visions.

The key components of this AI and KM enabled framework can be as follows:

Figure 3. Dimensions of Knowledge Management (KM)
Source: Compiled by Author

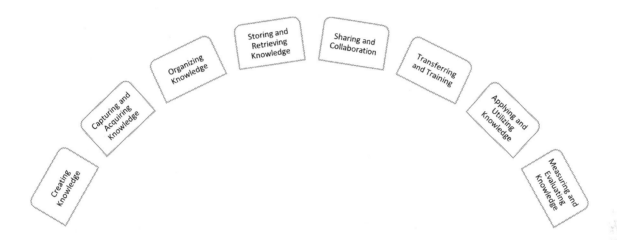

a. **AI-powered Knowledge Capture and Extraction**: Indian companies can use AI techniques, such as natural language processing and machine learning, to capture and extract knowledge from diverse sources. This includes documents, databases, websites, and even unstructured data like emails and social media content. By automatically extracting relevant information and insights, organizations can save time and effort in knowledge acquisition. For example, Indian e-commerce platform like Flipkart has the opportunity to harness AI algorithms for extracting valuable insights from customer reviews. Through the analysis of sentiments and opinions conveyed in these reviews, Flipkart can gather valuable information on customer preferences, pinpoint areas that need enhancement, and utilize data-driven strategies to improve its products and services.

b. **Knowledge Organization and Representation**: Once knowledge is captured, the integrated framework focuses on organizing and structuring it in a meaningful way. Indian companies can develop taxonomies, ontologies, and knowledge graphs to categorize and relate information. This helps in creating a hierarchical structure that facilitates easy navigation and retrieval of knowledge. For instance, an Indian pharmaceutical company may utilize AI-powered algorithms to automatically classify research papers, patents, and clinical trial data into specific therapeutic areas. This organized knowledge structure enables scientists and researchers to quickly access relevant information, accelerate the drug discovery process, and make informed decisions regarding new drug candidates.

c. **AI-based Knowledge Discovery and Analysis**: AI algorithms play a crucial role in uncovering patterns, trends, and insights within large volumes of data. Indian companies can leverage machine learning and data mining techniques to analyze knowledge repositories and extract valuable information.

d. **Knowledge Sharing and Collaboration** with AI-powered Tools: The integrated framework promotes knowledge sharing and collaboration within Indian companies by utilizing AI-powered tools. These tools include chatbots, virtual assistants, and collaborative platforms that facilitate communication, information exchange, and collaboration among employees. For instance, an Indian IT services company like Infosys can implement an AI-powered chatbot to assist employees in accessing knowledge resources, finding relevant information, and seeking answers to their queries.

This not only streamlines knowledge sharing but also improves employee productivity and reduces the time spent on searching for information.

e. **AI-driven Knowledge Application and Decision Support**: The integrated AI and KM framework enables Indian companies to apply and utilize knowledge effectively in decision-making processes. AI-based expert systems and recommendation engines can provide intelligent insights and suggestions based on the organizational knowledge. An example of this application is in supply chain management. An Indian manufacturing company like Tata Motors can leverage AI algorithms to analyze historical sales data, market trends, and production capacities. Based on these insights, the company can make accurate demand forecasts, optimize inventory levels, and improve supply chain efficiency.

f. **Continuous Learning and Improvement through AI and KM**: The integrated framework promotes a culture of continuous learning and improvement within Indian companies. AI technologies can automate knowledge updates, while KM practices capture lessons learned, best practices, and feedback from employees and customers.

g. **Data-driven Decision-Making**: By integrating AI and KM, Indian companies can leverage data-driven decision-making processes. AI algorithms can analyze vast amounts of structured and unstructured data, extract meaningful insights, and provide valuable recommendations. This enables organizations to make informed decisions based on accurate and up-to-date information. For example, an Indian retail company Reliance can utilize AI-powered analytics to analyze customer purchasing patterns, inventory levels, and market trends. Based on these insights, they can optimize their product assortment, pricing strategies, and marketing campaigns to better meet customer demands.

h. **Personalization and Customer Experience Enhancement:** The integration of AI and KM enables Indian companies to personalize customer experiences. By understanding customer preferences and behavior, organizations can provide tailored recommendations, offers, and support, resulting in improved customer satisfaction and loyalty. An Indian e-commerce platform like Amazon India can leverage AI algorithms to analyze customer browsing and purchasing history. This enables them to personalize product recommendations, offer targeted promotions, and enhance the overall shopping experience for their customers.

i. **Predictive Analytics and Risk Management**: The integrated framework empowers Indian companies to utilize predictive analytics for proactive risk management. By analyzing historical data and patterns, organizations can identify potential risks, anticipate future challenges, and take preventive measures. For instance, an insurance company in India, like ICICI Lombard, can leverage AI algorithms to analyze historical claims data, customer profiles, and market trends. This enables them to predict and mitigate risks, optimize underwriting processes, and offer customized insurance plans to customers.

j. **Innovation and New Product Development**: AI and KM integration can drive innovation in Indian companies by facilitating knowledge sharing, collaboration, and ideation. By leveraging AI-powered tools and KM practices, organizations can tap into the collective intelligence of their employees, identify market gaps, and develop innovative products and services. An Indian technology company like Infosys can implement AI-powered ideation platforms that enable employees to share ideas, collaborate on projects, and contribute to the innovation process. This promotes a culture of innovation, fosters creativity, and leads to the development of ground breaking solutions.

k. **Competitive Advantage and Market Differentiation**: The integration of AI and KM provides Indian companies with a competitive advantage in the marketplace. By effectively managing their knowledge assets and leveraging AI technologies, organizations can differentiate themselves by delivering unique products, services, and customer experiences. For example, an Indian telecommunications company like Jio can leverage AI-powered analytics to analyze customer usage patterns, network performance, and market trends. This enables them to optimize their network infrastructure, offer personalized services, and gain a competitive edge in the highly competitive telecom industry.

l. **Efficient Resource Allocation**: Indian companies can optimize resource allocation through the integrated framework. By leveraging AI-powered analytics and knowledge management techniques, organizations can better understand resource utilization patterns, identify areas of inefficiency, and allocate resources more effectively, resulting in cost savings and improved operational efficiency.

m. **Talent Management and Skill Development**: The integration of AI and KM facilitates talent management and skill development within Indian companies. AI-powered systems can assist in identifying skill gaps, recommending relevant training programs, and tracking employee progress. This enables organizations to nurture talent, enhance employee capabilities, and align skills with business objectives.

n. **Customer Sentiment Analysis**: Indian companies can leverage AI and KM to analyze customer sentiment and feedback. By applying natural language processing techniques to customer reviews, social media data, and customer service interactions, organizations can gain valuable insights into customer perceptions, preferences, and satisfaction levels, allowing them to make data-driven improvements to their products and services.

o. **Risk Prediction and Prevention**: The integrated framework enables Indian companies to predict and prevent potential risks. By analyzing historical data, industry trends, and external factors, AI algorithms can identify early warning signs of risks and support proactive risk mitigation strategies, helping organizations avoid costly disruptions and safeguard their operations.

p. **Efficient Knowledge Discovery**: Indian companies can leverage AI algorithms and KM practices to facilitate knowledge discovery. By automatically analyzing and linking relevant information from various sources, organizations can accelerate the process of discovering new knowledge, identifying emerging trends, and staying ahead of the competition.

q. **Improved Decision-making Speed**: The integration of AI and KM enables Indian companies to make faster and more accurate decisions. AI-powered algorithms can process vast amounts of data and provide real-time insights, empowering decision-makers with timely and relevant information, thereby reducing decision-making timeframes and enhancing organizational agility.

r. **Competitive Benchmarking**: Indian companies can utilize AI and KM to benchmark their performance against industry peers. By analyzing industry data, market trends, and best practices, organizations can gain a comparative understanding of their strengths and weaknesses, enabling them to identify areas for improvement and stay competitive in the market.

s. **Automation and Process Optimization**: The integrated framework supports automation and process optimization within Indian companies. By leveraging AI technologies like robotic process automation (RPA) and combining them with knowledge management practices, organizations can streamline and automate routine tasks, improve workflow efficiency, and reduce operational costs.

t. **Enhanced Collaboration and Knowledge Sharing**: The integration of AI and KM fosters collaboration and knowledge sharing among employees in Indian companies. AI-powered collaboration tools, such as virtual workspaces and document sharing platforms, facilitate seamless information exchange, idea generation, and collaborative problem-solving, leading to improved teamwork and innovation.

FINDINGS

The integration of Artificial Intelligence (AI) and Knowledge Management (KM) in Indian organizations for organizational intelligence brings both opportunities and challenges for the future. While there is immense potential, it is important to address certain implications and obstacles that may arise. One significant concern is the ethical and privacy implications of using AI and KM technologies. As these systems collect and analyze large amounts of data, organizations must ensure ethical practices, protect privacy, and comply with regulations to maintain trust among customers and stakeholders. Another challenge is the skill gap and workforce adaptation. Successfully integrating AI and KM requires a skilled workforce capable of effectively utilizing these technologies. Organizations need to invest in training programs to upskill employees and foster a culture of continuous learning to adapt to the changing nature of work. Implementing AI and KM initiatives also requires effective change management strategies.

Furthermore, the integration of AI and KM highlights the importance of robust technological infrastructure and seamless integration. Organizations by using scalable AI platforms, knowledge repositories, and analytics tools can derive maximum value from the integrated framework. Data quality and accessibility are also crucial factors. Relevance of data accuracy, completeness, and consistency to avoid biased or flawed outcomes. Providing easy access to relevant knowledge resources for employees is vital for effective knowledge management. Cultural and organizational barriers can impede the successful integration of AI and KM. Hierarchical structures, resistance to sharing knowledge, and lack of collaboration can hinder implementation. great promise for Indian organizations. It can lead to improved decision-making, enhanced customer experiences, increased operational efficiency, and innovation-driven growth. By effectively managing challenges, organizations can leverage AI and KM to stay competitive, drive sustainable growth, and navigate the changing business landscape with greater intelligence and agility.

CONCLUSION

The synergy between Artificial Intelligence (AI) and Knowledge Management (KM) offers substantial advantages to Indian enterprises, fostering organizational intelligence. Through the fusion of AI technologies and adept knowledge management strategies, Indian firms stand to uncover valuable insights, stimulate innovation, refine decision-making processes, elevate customer experiences, and secure a competitive advantage in the market. The utilization of AI empowers Indian businesses to analyze extensive datasets, extracting valuable insights that pave the way for well-informed decision-making. This data-driven approach allows organizations to better understand customer preferences, optimize resource allocation, identify potential risks, and discover new growth opportunities. Moreover, the integration of AI and KM promotes effective knowledge sharing and collaboration within Indian organizations. AI-powered tools such as chatbots and virtual assistants streamline access to knowledge resources, enhance employee productivity, and improve customer support services. Additionally, AI-powered ideation platforms and collaboration tools foster a culture of innovation, enabling companies to leverage the collective intelligence of their workforce and drive breakthrough solutions. The integration of AI and KM also facilitates continuous learning and improvement within Indian companies. By capturing and preserving knowledge, organizations can facilitate knowledge transfer, ensure compliance with regulations, and optimize processes. This fosters a culture of continuous improvement, enabling organizations to adapt to market trends, innovate in service delivery, and maintain a competitive advantage.

Several Indian companies across different industries have already embraced the integrated framework of AI and KM to drive organizational intelligence. Companies like Tata Consultancy Services (TCS), Apollo Hospitals, Reliance Retail, and Infosys have successfully implemented AI technologies and knowledge management practices to enhance their operations, improve customer experiences, and drive growth. However, it is important for Indian organizations to approach the integration of AI and KM strategically. This requires a supportive organizational culture that encourages knowledge sharing, collaboration across teams, and continuous learning. Strong leadership, effective change management, and investments in AI technologies and knowledge management infrastructure are also essential. By embracing the integrated framework of AI and KM, Indian companies can unlock the full potential of their knowledge assets, drive innovation, improve decision-making processes, and maintain a competitive position in the rapidly evolving Indian market. It is an opportunity for organizations to leverage the power of AI and tap into their collective knowledge to achieve sustainable growth, customer satisfaction, and overall organizational success in India's dynamic business landscape.

REFERENCES

Al-Jabri, I. M., & Roztocki, N. (2015). The impact of artificial intelligence on knowledge management systems: A literature review. *Journal of Enterprise Information Management*, *28*(5), 662–676.

Alavi, M. (2000). Knowledge management systems: Issues, challenges, and benefits. *Communications of the AIS*, *4*(6), 1–37.

Alavi, M., & Leidner, D. E. (2001). Review: Knowledge management and knowledge management systems: Conceptual foundations and research issues. *Management Information Systems Quarterly*, *25*(1), 107–136. doi:10.2307/3250961

Becerra-Fernandez, I., & Sabherwal, R. (2014). *Knowledge management: Systems and processes*. Routledge.

Bhattacharya, S., & Mandal, S. (2020). Artificial Intelligence and Knowledge Management: A Case Study of Indian Educational Institutions. In *Proceedings of International Conference on Education and Management Innovation* (pp. 192-199). IEEE.

Bouthillier, F., & Shearer, K. (2002). Understanding knowledge management and its relationship to artificial intelligence. *Journal of Knowledge Management*, *6*(3), 244–254.

Chalmeta, R., & Grangel, R. (2008). Knowledge management and organizational learning as competitive advantages in business environment: An overview. *Journal of Knowledge Management*, *12*(6), 124–137.

Chang, Y. H., & Tzeng, G. H. (2011). Evaluating intertwined effects in e-learning programs: A novel hybrid MCDM model based on factor analysis and DEMATEL. *Expert Systems with Applications*, *38*(5), 5600–5615.

Chen, H., Chiang, R. H., & Storey, V. C. (2012). Business intelligence and analytics: From big data to big impact. *Management Information Systems Quarterly*, *36*(4), 1165–1188. doi:10.2307/41703503

Chua, A. Y., & Goh, D. H. (2008). A study of knowledge management implementation in Singapore. *International Journal of Information Management*, *28*(2), 122–135.

Dalkir, K. (2011). *Knowledge management in theory and practice*. Routledge.

Davenport, T. H., & Prusak, L. (2000). *Working knowledge: How organizations manage what they know* (2nd ed.). Harvard Business Press.

Farooq, R. (2023). Knowledge management and performance: A bibliometric analysis based on Scopus and WOS data (1988–2021). *Journal of Knowledge Management*, *27*(7), 1948–1991. doi:10.1108/JKM-06-2022-0443

Goh, A. T., & Gunasekaran, A. (2001). Knowledge management: Approaches and policies. *Journal of Knowledge Management*, *5*(1), 33–46.

Grant, R. M. (1996). Toward a knowledge-based theory of the firm. *Strategic Management Journal*, *17*(S2), 109–122. doi:10.1002/smj.4250171110

Gupta, S. K., & Rastogi, R. (2019). Artificial Intelligence and Knowledge Management in Indian Organizations. In *Proceedings of International Conference on Computer Networks, Big Data and IoT* (pp. 1-5).

Haleem, A., Javaid, M., Qadri, M. A., Singh, R. P., & Suman, R. (2022). Artificial intelligence (AI) applications for marketing: A literature-based study. *International Journal of Intelligent Networks*, *3*, 119–132. doi:10.1016/j.ijin.2022.08.005

Holsapple, C. W., & Joshi, K. D. (2001). Knowledge management: A threefold framework. *The Information Society*, *17*(1), 15–28.

Kaur, A., & Singh, M. (2018). Artificial intelligence: A review of concepts, approaches, and applications. *International Journal of Advanced Scientific Research and Management*, *3*(1), 28–37.

Kucharska, W., & Bedford, D. A. D. (2023). *The KLC Cultures, Tacit Knowledge, and Trust Contribution to Organizational Intelligence Activation*. In proceedings of the 24th European Conference on Knowledge Management Lisbon, Portugal. https://ssrn.com/abstract=4440280 or doi:10.2139/ssrn.4440280

Kumar, A., & Sharma, V. (2021). Artificial Intelligence-Driven Knowledge Management for Competitive Advantage: A Study of Indian Companies. *Journal of Management Research*, *21*(3), 20–34.

Liebowitz, J., & Beckman, T. (Eds.). (1998). *Knowledge organizations: What every manager should know*. CRC Press.

Maier, R. (2007). *Knowledge management systems: Information and communication technologies for knowledge management*. Springer Science & Business Media.

Maier, R., & Peffers, K. (1998). The role of knowledge management systems in e-commerce. *Journal of Knowledge Management*, *2*(2), 79–90.

Mathur, A., & Agrawal, S. (2018). Artificial Intelligence and Knowledge Management in Indian Context. In *Proceedings of International Conference on Advances in Computer Engineering and Applications* (pp. 35-39). IEEE.

Mohapatra, S., & Misra, S. (2018). Artificial Intelligence and Knowledge Management: A Study of Indian Retail Sector. In *Proceedings of International Conference on Computer Science, Engineering and Applications* (pp. 31-36). IEEE.

Nonaka, I., & Takeuchi, H. (1995). *The knowledge-creating company: How Japanese companies create the dynamics of innovation.* Oxford University Press. doi:10.1093/oso/9780195092691.001.0001

Osterloh, M., & Frey, B. S. (2000). Motivation, knowledge transfer, and organizational forms. *Organization Science*, *11*(5), 538–550. doi:10.1287/orsc.11.5.538.15204

Parida, S., & Bhattacherjee, A. (2019). Artificial Intelligence and Knowledge Management in Indian Hospitals. In *Proceedings of International Conference on Advances in Computing and Communication Engineering* (pp. 361-368). IEEE.

Patra, S., & Rath, S. K. (2019). Artificial Intelligence and Knowledge Management: A Case Study of Indian Pharmaceutical Industry. In *Proceedings of International Conference on Computational Intelligence and Data Science* (pp. 183-190). IEEE.

Pattnaik, P. K., & Satpathy, M. (2020). Knowledge Management through Artificial Intelligence in Indian Organizations. *International Journal of Emerging Technologies in Engineering Research*, *8*(7), 1–5.

Ruggles, R. (1998). The state of the notion: Knowledge management in practice. *California Management Review*, *40*(3), 80–89. doi:10.2307/41165944

Sankar, C. S., & Sridevi, R. (2019). Artificial Intelligence and Knowledge Management: A Review. *International Journal of Information Dissemination and Technology*, *9*(4), 243–247.

Shadbolt, N., O'Hara, K., & Schraefel, M. C. (2006). The experimental evaluation of knowledge management system. *Journal of Knowledge Management*, *10*(4), 101–116.

Sharma, A., & Verma, R. (2020). Artificial Intelligence and Knowledge Management: An Exploratory Study in Indian IT Firms. In *Proceedings of International Conference on Intelligent Computing and Applications* (pp. 1067-1075). Research Gate.

Singh, A., & Mani, N. (2020). Leveraging Artificial Intelligence for Effective Knowledge Management: A Study of Indian IT Organizations. In *Proceedings of International Conference on Inventive Research in Computing Applications* (pp. 1155-1160). Research Gate.

Singh, P., & Singh, N. (2018). Artificial Intelligence and Knowledge Management: A Study of Indian Manufacturing Firms. In *Proceedings of International Conference on Computing, Power and Communication Technologies* (pp. 75-81).

Singh, S., & Mehrotra, D. (2020). Artificial Intelligence and Knowledge Management: A Study of Indian Banks. In *Proceedings of International Conference on Contemporary Computing and Informatics* (pp. 336-341). Research Gate.

Taherdoost, H., & Madanchian, M. (2023). Artificial Intelligence and Knowledge Management: Impacts, Benefits, and Implementation. *Computers*, *12*(4), 72. doi:10.3390/computers12040072

Tsui, E. (2005). Knowledge management in the era of artificial intelligence: Can machines really understand knowledge? *Journal of Knowledge Management*, *9*(2), 116–130.

Verma, V., & Singhal, S. (2019). Artificial Intelligence and Knowledge Management in Indian Public Sector Enterprises. In *Proceedings of International Conference on Machine Learning and Data Engineering* (pp. 619-625). IEEE.

Wang, Y. M., & Elhag, T. M. (2006). Fuzzy TOPSIS for multi-criteria decision making: A comparative study of fuzzy TOPSIS and fuzzy AHP. *European Journal of Operational Research*, *179*(1), 1–18. doi:10.1016/0377-2217(89)90055-6

Zack, M. H. (1999). Managing codified knowledge. *Sloan Management Review*, *40*(4), 45–58.

Chapter 9
Getting More Out of Software Prototypes:
A Systematic Literature Review

Alejandro Sánchez-Villarin
University of Seville, Spain

Alejandro E. Santos
University of Seville, Spain

José E. Gonzalez-Enriquez
University of Seville, Spain

Javier J. Gutierrez
University of Seville, Spain

Nicolas E. Sanchez-Gomez
https://orcid.org/0000-0001-9102-6836
University of Seville, Spain

Nora E. Koch
University of Seville, Spain

Maria Jose Escalona
https://orcid.org/0000-0002-6435-1497
University of Seville, Spain

ABSTRACT

Prototyping is a requirement technique frequently used for communication between customers and developers. Software prototypes help to understand users' expectations, but they are often seen as disposable artifacts because it is not easy to manage the transfer of knowledge from prototypes to software models or code. This chapter studies whether suitable solutions already exist for exploiting the knowledge acquired during the building of prototypes in the early phases of the lifecycle. The objective is addressed by means of a systematic literature review of approaches offering solutions for transforming software prototypes into analysis models. We propose a characterization schema for comparing them and describing the current state-of-the-art. The results reveal a need for more automated solutions that are more economical in terms of time and effort for transforming prototypes into models and thereby ensuring traceability between requirements and design artifacts.

INTRODUCTION

Prototypes can help to address what is unquestionably one of the most critical aspects of software engineering: requirements engineering, or the correct definition of end user[1] needs (Fernández et al., 2017).

DOI: 10.4018/978-1-6684-9576-6.ch009

The efficient acquisition, definition, validation, and maintenance of such needs are key to all software development and future maintenance (Escalona & Aragón, 2008).

Despite all the research and the importance that has been attached to requirements, this topic still has much room for improvement and has been the object of many studies (Fernández et al., 2017). Some works describe the development of different techniques. One of the most effective techniques for understanding the user has been found to be software prototyping (Canedo et al., 2020). In other engineering environments, such as aerospace or industry, the use of prototypes is not new (Jensen et al., 2016). This can clearly be seen in methodologies and references like Design Thinking (Plattner et al., 2009), Human Computer Interaction mechanisms (Yıldız, 2019) and User-centered Design (Dhandapani, 2016). In software development, however, prototyping is a somewhat controversial issue (Ali, 2017).

Prototype development usually facilitates user communication and is therefore often used precisely for that purpose (Beaudouin-Lafon & Mackay, 2003). In many cases, however, prototypes are discarded very early in the development process because work done on them is deemed to be "wasted" in the analysis and software design phase (Kuczenski et al., 2021). Proof of this are prototypes that are never looked at again, but just saved in repositories of old projects. These represent a waste of resources that could even be re-used for similar projects (Nguyen-Duc et al., 2017).

This paper presents a study into the use of prototypes in the software development process, both in research and in industry. It also looks at solutions that allow the effective use of prototypes (knowledge provided by prototypes) and analyzes problems associated with this practice. We call this technique "reusing" prototypes.

In industry, where it is necessary to reduce project costs, prototyping tends to be seen as a negligible activity. This should not surprise us. In many cases, prototypes are produced in external environments (mockup or interface design tools) which, once validated, are discarded and the information passed to development environments. In other words, a team develops and validates the prototypes and the information collected is then manually passed to analysis or even design or implementation models, leaving the prototype as something that can be destroyed. This causes several major problems:

1. Since prototypes are destined to be destroyed, no importance is attached to their design and construction. As a result, in many cases, not enough resources are allocated to produce a prototype of high quality.
2. Precisely because of this lack of quality and precision in prototype development, definitions may be established which are either ambiguous or incomplete, covering only part of the development.
3. If the prototype is destroyed, it is difficult to trace the origins of customers' and users' requirements for future changes or problems. Here, one recommended procedure guided by good practice is that of the CMMI model (Aggarwal et al., 2014; Gupta, 2011).

In view of the above concerns, a need has arisen to investigate whether mechanisms exist which allow us to conceive prototypes as something that is "usable" in subsequent phases and consequently supportive to the development of a tool. If a development team could automatically (or semi-automatically) use all the knowledge that a prototype provides, more effort should be devoted to it, with the guarantee that it is an investment for the future. Improving prototypes would allow us to improve communication with users and increase the quality of requirements models.

This work addresses this premise and aims to analyze the solutions that have been proposed in the literature for using prototypes efficiently and effectively. The objective is to find out how analysis artifacts can be generated as automatically as possible from a prototype. To do so, the Systematic Literature Review (SLR) method proposed by Barbara Kitchenham et al. (2009) was followed. The first step of this method is to define a set of research questions (RQs) that will guide the investigation towards the proposed objective. These research questions are linked to different dimensions. Dimensions are characteristics of the solutions being researched. A set of indicators are also selected for classifying solutions in order to achieve the best results. Once the research questions have been established, keywords are defined which are used to search for potential solutions in different databases. Finally, a characterization map is defined. The solutions found are evaluated according to this map and final conclusions are obtained, answering the RQs.

To summarize, the SLR reported in this paper attempts to answer the following question: "Does any solution exist which automatically generates analysis artifacts as models from prototypes?" The question is directly related to the relevance of the knowledge obtained through user participation and the transfer of such knowledge. If no such solution exists, the objective is to demonstrate current shortcomings and lay the groundwork for the provision of new solutions. The following sections offer some insight into different approaches to these problems, evaluating whether they respond to the question posed above.

The results obtained in this study indicate that even though the topic is of some interest to the research community, a solution for getting more out of prototypes—i.e., using the valuable information they provide in requirements models, as we propose— does not yet exist. To solve this problem, we plan to develop such an approach as part of a future project.

The rest of the paper is organized as follows: Section II presents the research method and the background and related work. Section III explains the process of identifying and selecting papers and analyzes the selected studies using a characterization map. Section IV discusses the information obtained; and Section V includes some conclusions and suggestions for future work, stating the need for a solution that will allow analysis elements to be generated from prototypes.

METHODOLOGY

Research Method

The Systematic Literature Review (SLR) proposed by Barbara Kitchenham et al. (2009) was selected as the research method for analyzing existing mechanisms for "reusing" prototypes. Kitchenham's process comprises three main phases (see Figure 1).

1. Planning the review. In this phase, open questions related to the problems to be addressed are defined. These are the so-called research questions (RQ). Keywords and digital libraries also need to be selected.
2. Conducting the review. Based on the decisions taken in the previous phase, the most relevant publications are identified and a classification schema is developed for comparing them.
3. Reporting the review. A report is generated detailing the main conclusions obtained from the analysis and the comparison of the selected publications.

The process outlined above is refined by dividing each phase into sub-phases, and defining corresponding tasks for implementation.

Figure 1. Systematic literature review process

Figure 2. Phase one: Planning the review

Figure 2 shows the steps of the "Planning the Review" phase. The following tasks are needed to establish the basis of the research:

- Justification of the need for the review: in our case, the relevance of knowledge acquired from user participation in the development of prototypes and the transfer of such knowledge to subsequent software development phases.
- The most relevant questions posed in the SLR should be answered through the formulation of research questions.

The review protocol will then be defined and validated. Search strings, digital libraries, and keywords for the searches to be performed will also be defined in this step.

Phase 2 "Conducting the Review" focuses on the analysis of the selected publications. The process is shown in Figure 3.

- Identification of the most relevant publications based on the searches defined in the planning phase.
- Selection of papers subject to inclusion and exclusion criteria.
- Evaluation and summary of the results of all the selected papers.
- Elaboration of a characterization schema for the selected publications. Full comparison and analysis based on the schema.
- In the last step of this phase, the information extracted is synthesized, obtaining data and objectives to be used in subsequent research.

Figure 3. Phase two: Conducting the review

Figure 4. Phase three: Reporting the review

As shown in Figure 4, the third phase "Reporting the Review" consists of writing and validating the report.

BACKGROUND

The information and communications technology (ICT) industry uses prototyping sparingly to reduce development times. The hypothesis underlying this SLR is that it is possible to develop software by reusing prototyping: i.e., software that can be fed back the development team with new elements, thus engaging users or clients in reducing the final costs and durations of projects.

Present-day software development strives to be as agile and user-oriented as possible (Torrecilla-Salinas et al., 2015). The user is the main factor in this field, so it is important to understand what the user wants and is able to provide. Prototyping is the way development teams show users the shape of a possible desired solution. Prototypes are directly based on users' requirements. One user-empathetic technique aimed at identifying requirements is Design Thinking (Corral & Fronza, 2018; Surma-Aho et al., 2018). The relationship between user-orientation and prototyping is therefore also within the scope of this study.

The other incentive driving this SLR is the cost & time aspect of prototyping. Designing prototypes requires a lot of work, and may therefore slow down development (Oran et al., 2019). Depending on whether their development is vertical or horizontal, prototypes may be discarded and not used in other phases of development. The reuse problem is of particular interest to the research community for its impact on agile methodologies and the development of tools capable of integrating the use of prototypes (Hoyos & Restrepo-Calle, 2017).

If prototypes could be generated automatically through a process of reverse engineering based on user requirements and if they were reusable, teams would gain in time and efficiency and obtain better results in their projects (Miao et al., 2018).

In the search for previous SLRs with themes and objectives similar to those proposed here, the results obtained were not very encouraging.

The study performed by Strmečki et al. (2018) proposes a search for the reuse of software and its prototypes involving ontologies and software development tools and, finally, obtaining the source code of the software. This differs greatly from the objective of our SLR, as it does not focus on reverse engineering from prototypes, although it does address their reuse.

In our previous survey (Sánchez-Villarín et al., 2019), we compared commercially available tools for automatically reusing prototypes in software engineering. In this article, a set of industry-defined requirements are used to analyze the tools: requirements such as the possible exports that they enable, if the exported labels are correct, if the tools provide an API or a multiplatform, among others. After our study, we conclude that no tools are available which satisfy all industrial requirements.

We found that many papers focus on the development of theoretical or practical tools—that is, tools designed to create, but not to reuse, prototypes. Surveys conducted pertaining to prototyping tools, such as the comparison of academic and commercial tools performed by Rocha Silva et al. (2017), do not consider user involvement and the reuse or final transfer of prototypes. As far as we know, no other studies, papers, surveys or SLRs have been found with the same approach as the current SLR.

RESULTS

Planning the Review

This section describes the process followed for planning our SLR. The first step was to establish the context and objectives of the review and to identify the open questions related to the research problem. In this case, the main objective was:

- To investigate whether any approaches exist which allow us to automatically generate reusable analysis documents from software prototypes.
- To identify the advantages and disadvantages of each approach.

The main question relating to the objective was established as: "Do approaches exist which allow analysis models to be automatically generated from prototypes?". Considering that this question is quite general, it was divided up into the following sub-questions—the so-called research questions (RQs). These RQs allowed us to classify results based on the different approaches' capacities for automating and reusing prototypes and on the type of elements they can generate:

- RQ1: What are the existing software development techniques for using prototypes in later phases of software development?
- RQ2: How capable are these approaches of using prototypes as analysis products?
- RQ3: Is the prototype reuse supported by tools that automate the process?
- RQ4: Have these approaches been empirically validated?
- RQ5: What is the range of automation covered by these approaches (mainly in tools)?
- RQ6: How do these approaches that provide prototype reuse involve users? And in which phases of the development process?

Each one of these questions was associated with a dimension, which was a characteristic of the solution being searched for. The dimension is used to classify the characteristics. The dimensions are listed in Table 1, together with short descriptions.

In Table 2, each research question is linked to a dimension of the problem under analysis, thus covering all the characteristics.

After formulating these questions, a systematic search strategy was designed involving the use of search tools to identify papers published in conferences, and journals, as defined below. The search strategy was limited to three specific digital libraries: IEEE Xplore, ACM Digital Library and Scopus. These

Table I. Dimensions

Dimension	Description
User interaction	is used to establish the level of interaction of the end user (customer, end user,..) in the development approach.
Degree of automation	establishes how automatable the approach is. A high degree of automation is desirable.
Support tool	indicates whether the approach is supported by a tool and, if so, establishes the maturity of the tool, which may be undeveloped, partially developed or fully developed.
Degree of validation	establishes whether the approach has been tested in companies or only in the academic environment. If it has been tested, there will be feedback about its use in companies.
Results	tells us the type of results the approach generates. It is important to differentiate between approaches that generate specific types of results and generic tools that present general pattern-based products, for instance general UML models (activity diagrams, etc.).
Degree of reusability	indicates the level of reuse of an approach: i.e., the approach's degree of adaptability to different environments

Table 2. Research questions

Nº.	Description	Dimension
RQ1	aims to ascertain whether there are any approaches currently being used that allow for prototype "reuse".	Results
RQ2	aims to establish whether the prototype reuse technique can be used again in other steps of the development process or in another environment.	Degree of reusability
RQ3	aims to demonstrate the existence of tools that support an approach and if they are accessible in the market.	Support tool
RQ4	aims to identify whether the approaches have been validated.	Degree of validation
RQ5	aims to determine the level of automation, how the solution interacts with the user. The higher the interaction, the lower the automation, and vice versa.	Degree of automation
RQ6	aims to find out how much the user is involved.	User interaction

digital libraries provide wide coverage and offer the largest, most varied databases. Search strings were selected for the search strategy. The search strings had three parts, each one defining a set of keywords corresponding to the following parts of the papers:

- Title: words or sets of words that had to be found in the title of the paper, such as prototype, prototyping, generation, etc..
- Abstract: words or sets of words that had to be found in the abstract of the paper, like automatic, automated, transformation rules, etc.
- Keywords: words or sets of words that had to be included in the papers' lists of keywords, mainly software prototyping, automatic generation, model-driven, etc..

This strategy was selected in accordance with the SLR structure described by Torrecilla et al. (2015), in which the search is defined by different parts.

Table 3, shows the keyword packages used in the search:

The above search chain was structured as a (A1 OR A2 OR ...) AND (B1 OR B2 OR ...) AND (C1 OR C2 OR ...) pattern, designed to cover the largest number of papers related to this SLR. The first segment was searched for in the title, the second in the abstract and the third in the list of keywords. Some words in Table III are separated by "/". This broadened the search by allowing for variants of the words used.

Table 3. Keyword packages

Title	Abstract	Keyword
prototype / prototypes	automatic	software prototyping
prototyping	automated	automatic generation
generation	transformation rules	model driven
generating	user interface /user interfaces	UI prototyping
model driven / model-driven	generating prototypes	user interface prototypes user interface models

Inclusion and exclusion criteria were also added. Since this SLR focused on software engineering, one of the inclusion criteria was that the papers' stated area of study had to be Computer Science. We also stipulated that the year of publication should be later than 2005, because we were focusing on recent research results that could be replicated and studied using current technologies. In addition, the language of the paper had to be English. Finally, we excluded papers catalogued as belonging to the field of mathematics, as papers related to formal methods were not relevant for our SLR.

The inclusion and exclusion criteria described above could only be applied in their entirety in Scopus, producing the following query:

TITLE (prototype OR prototypes OR prototyping OR generation OR generating OR "model driven" OR "model-driven") AND ABS (automatic OR automated OR "transformation rules" OR "user interface" OR "user interfaces" OR "generating prototypes") AND KEY ("software prototyping" OR "automatic generation" OR "model driven" OR "ui prototyping" OR "user interface prototypes" OR "user interface models") AND PUBYEAR > 2005 AND (LIMIT-TO (PUBSTAGE, "final")) AND (LIMIT-TO (SUBJAREA, "COMP") OR EXCLUDE (SUBJAREA, "MATH")) AND (LIMIT-TO (LANGUAGE, "English"))

In IEEE Xplore it was not possible to include such criteria, although once the search had been carried out we could check that the publication date of the papers was later than 2005 or filter the papers by topic, eliminating those focusing on subjects like "power generation control", "frequency control", "power system interconnection", and "three-term control". The query used for IEEE Xplore was:

"Document Title": prototype OR prototypes OR prototyping OR generation OR generating OR "Model driven" OR "Model-Driven") AND ("Abstract": automatic OR automated OR "Transformation Rules" OR "User Interface" OR "User interface" OR "User Interfaces" OR "User interfaces" OR "Generating prototypes") AND ("Author Keywords": "Software prototyping" OR "Automatic Generation" OR "Model driven" OR "UI prototyping" OR "User interface prototypes" OR "User interface models")

In the ACM Digital Library, the search could be conducted by parts, specifying title, keywords or abstract. Date of publication was included in the same query, but it was impossible to include the other criteria described above, although the number of papers obtained was relatively small. The query used in this case was:

[[Publication Title: prototype] OR [Publication Title: prototypes] OR [Publication Title: prototyping] OR [Publication Title: generation] OR [Publication Title: generating] OR [Publication Title: "model driven"] OR [Publication Title: "model-driven"]] AND [[Abstract: automatic] OR [Abstract: automated] OR [Abstract: "transformation rules"] OR [Abstract: "user interface"] OR [Abstract: "user interfaces"] OR [Abstract: "generating prototypes"]] AND [[Keywords: "software prototyping"] OR [Keywords: "automatic generation"] OR [Keywords: "model driven"] OR [Keywords: "ui prototyping"] OR [Keywords: "user interface prototypes"] OR [Keywords: "user interface models"]] AND [Publication Date: (01/01/2005 TO 28/02/2021)]

CONDUCTING THE REVIEW

The review process comprised a series of steps involving the collection and selection of papers. During this process, the papers were collected on the JabRef (JabRef Web, n.d.) tool, using the BibTeX format to organize the information.

The process followed to select the papers comprised three steps. The first was to execute the search automatically in the abovementioned search engines: IEEE Xplore, ACM Digital Library and Scopus. After this first search, two improvements were included. The first one, called the *quasi-gold standard*, was proposed by Zhang et al. (2011). It consisted of reviewing other papers, obtained by other vias related with our approach. Our previous studies provided us the information that was no need to add additional papers. The second step, called *snowball*, consisted of reviewing the selected papers and checking their references in order to locate other studies. Table 4 shows the results of the first automatic search and the improvements.

In the next step, duplicates were removed automatically using the JabRef tool, leaving 3352 papers. JabRef allows the papers identified in the proposed databases to be imported as BibTeX entries. Before importing new papers, the tool checks whether there are any completely identical entries, removing any duplicates. However, two or more entries may exist that correspond to the same paper but in databases with slightly differing formats. These would constitute two different entries. If slightly different duplicates existed, they were removed using a duplicate detection option, which analyzes similar entries and allows the user to decide if they correspond to the same paper, choose one, or keep both of them.

The protocol described in Torrecilla-Salinas et al. (2015) was then applied to the remaining papers. This involved the following two steps: (1) Papers were analyzed by title, keywords and abstract. This review was carried out by two different researchers. A paper could be accepted by both, rejected by both, or accepted by only one of them. In the last case, the paper was read in detail by both reviewers and a consensus meeting was held. The papers selected in this step were called "*preliminary accepted papers*" and in our case totaled 219 papers. (2) The preliminary accepted papers were then reviewed in detail by three researchers in order to eliminate those falling outside the scope of our SLR. The papers included in our SLR had to be clearly related to prototype-based transformations or generation. If this was not the case, the paper in question was not chosen. There were also a lot of completely theoretical papers lacking practical components that would allow us to validate their applicability in the industrial context—a crucial aspect in our study. A high number of papers were discarded after the detailed reading due to their theoretical content. After this second review, and based on consensus between all the researchers, there remained 23 "*selected papers*". They are listed in Table 5.

A summary of each paper can be found In Table 6.

Table 4. Initial Search

		#Search Results
Automatic	**IEEE Xplore**	1872
	ACM Digital Library	172
	Scopus	1766
Quasi-gold standard		0
Snowball		35
Total		**3845**

Table 5. Selected papers

	Title	Databases	Year
A1	Mockup-driven development: providing agile support for model-driven web engineering (Rivero et al., 2014)	Scopus	2014
A2	A metamodel-based approach for automatic user interface generation (Rocha Silva et al., 2017)	Scopus, ACM DL	2010
A3	A model-driven approach for creating storyboards of web-based user interfaces (Rasheed et al., 2019)	Scopus, ACM DL	2019
A4	A model-driven approach for generating interfaces from user interaction diagrams (Zeferino & Vilain, 2014)	Scopus, ACM DL	2014
A5	A model-driven approach for the semi-automated generation of web-based applications from requirements (Fatolahi et al., 2008)	Scopus	2008
A6	Algorithm of interface generation for model-driven data consolidation system (Korobko, 2018)	IEEE Xplore	2018
A7	Automated generation of user-interface prototypes based on controlled natural language description (Juárez-Ramirez et al., 2014)	Scopus, IEEE Xplore	2014
A8	Automated prototyping of user interfaces based on UML scenarios (Elkoutbi et al., 2006)	Scopus	2006
A9	Automatic generation of feature models from UML requirement models (Casalánguida & Durán, 2012)	Scopus, ACM DL	2012
A10	Evaluation of a use-case-driven requirements analysis tool employing web UI prototype generation (Ogata & Matsuura, 2010)	Scopus	2010
A11	From formal requirements to automated web testing and prototyping (de Matos & Sousa, 2010)	Scopus	2010
A12	Fully automatic user interface generation from discourse models (Escalona et al., 2021; Falb et al., 2009)	Scopus, ACM DL	2009
A13	Generating a language-independent graphical user interface from UML models (Shatnawi & Shatnawi, 2016)	Scopus	2016
A14	Generating essential user interface prototypes to validate requirements (Juárez-Ramirez et al., 2014)	Scopus, IEEE Xplore	2011
A15	Model driven development by separating concerns in UML requirements specification (Kawai & Matsuura, 2015)	IEEE Xplore	2015
A16	Modeling and generating graphical user interface for MVC Rich Internet Application using a model driven approach (Roubi et al., 2016)	Scopus, IEEE Xplore	2016
A17	Research on the interaction process in use case for automatic generation of user interface prototype (Ren & Wei, 2008)	IEEE Xplore	2008
A18	Research on user interface transformation method based on MDA (Miao et al., 2018)	IEEE Xplore	2017
A19	RM2PT: A tool for automated prototype generation from requirements model (Yang et al., 2019)	Scopus	2019
A20	Scenario-based automatic prototype generation (Ogata & Matsuura, 2008)	Scopus, IEEE Xplore	2008
A21	System prototype generation tool for requirements review (Saito & Hagiwara, 2012)	Scopus	2012
A22	User interface prototype generation from agile requirements specifications written in Concordia (Pinto et al., 2019)	Scopus, ACM DL	2019
A23	Validation of requirement models by automatic prototyping (Li et al., 2008)	Scopus	2008

Reporting

Once the papers had been read and analyzed, in the next step of the SLR process a characterization map was defined to allow comparison of the selected papers as proposed in Escalona et al. (2011). A characterization map is a schema for normalizing the information found about each approach. The main objective of this map was to make it possible to answer and quantify the research questions defined in Table II. The map was based on the dimensions shown in Table I, and the selection of one or more indicators.

Table 6. Summary of fully-analyzed papers

	Summary
A1	This paper proposes an iterative process based on agile prototypes, but exploiting the advantages of Model-Driven Web Engineering (MDWE). In this case, the development process is reversed, taking interface mockups as a starting point, and software specifications are obtained at different levels.
A2	This paper describes a model-driven development to automatically generate user interfaces based on domain models with entities and triggers, use case models with interactions, and user interface models containing the distribution of the elements in the interface. These elements are automatically transformed, generating a prototype that provides action flows.
A3	This paper proposes transforming functional and non-functional requirements into storyboards based on MDSE principles. The proposal is partially automated and involves the user in several phases, including ideation and design. The results generated are prototypes.
A4	This paper presents a model-driven approach to generate a user interface from user interaction diagrams. The proposal starts with the transformation of a model representing the interaction between a user and a system into a conceptual model of a generic user interface. This is then transformed into a platform-independent model, and subsequently into a technology-specific models and real user interfaces that can be validated by the user.
A5	This paper describes a semi-automated method for generating web-based applications from high-level requirements in accordance with model-driven architecture (MDA). A series of state-machine-like steps are given, allowing use cases to be transformed into executable code automatically and semi-automatically. The resulting UI model can be refined manually into a more concrete UI model
A6	This paper presents a theoretical description of a meta-metamodel for a model-oriented data consolidation system. An algorithm is used to automatize the client-part of the system and construct the interface of a model-driven system in which the client can select different groups and options to control the metamodel and change its functions.
A7	This paper talks about the importance of the language of requirements, requirements being the basis of software construction. It describes a proposal for automating the generation of user interface prototypes, mainly to minimize task overload and make the best use of work already done in the development cycle.
A8	This paper presents an interesting idea for our SLR, since it seeks to automate requirements engineering through user interfaces (UI) and UML models. The static and dynamic aspects of the user interface are derived from the dynamic specifications obtained from its objects, providing prototypes with which to perform validation through the implementation of a tool. This allows reverse engineering and the automatic modification of scenarios using UI prototypes.
A9	This paper introduces the importance of UML and feature models in a software project, indicating the inconsistences that can exist between both. Automatic generation of feature models from UML would be more efficient, so the paper proposes a way of transforming requirements into UML diagrams, and UML into feature models. Once UML diagrams have been generated from requirements, following process automation mechanisms, the feature model can be generated automatically using transformations based on model-driven development (MDD).
A10	This paper presents the functionality of a tool which transforms a requirements analysis (RA) model into a UI prototype. The RA model comprises different elements: an interaction activity diagram, a class diagram, an object diagram, scenarios, and navigation models. With these elements, the tool can obtain a UI prototype with those requirements. This has been tested and it could improve prototype creation times, although some aspects, like non-functional requirements, will be implemented in the future using OCL.
A11	This paper shows a method and a tool for the automatic generation of web testing and prototypes from formal requirements. The approach uses use cases, a glossary and user interface specifications in XML format. Using an XML parser of XML and a tool developed by the authors, it is possible to automatically generate a prototype in HTML and test cases in Selenium. This solution therefore speeds up the first stages of development.
A12	This paper presents a tool that automatically generates UI from discourse models. First of all, the discourse model has to be created manually using communicative acts. From this model an automatic model-driven transformation derives a structural UI model using a GUI toolkit like Swing.
A13	This paper presents a tool that automates the creation of user interfaces based on UML models. The aim is similar to the one followed in this SLR: that is, the reduction of development costs. The tool generates a prototype that is coded using an extensible markup language (XML) called User Interface Markup Language (UIML), obtaining reusable code that can be used during development.
A14	This paper describes a tool for capturing requirements like Essential Use Cases and translating them into low-fidelity, rapid "Essential User Interface" prototypes. The tool follows a process that starts with requirements in natural language and carries out several transformations to obtain a prototype. The prototype has low-fidelity but would be improved in future versions.

continued on following page

Table 6. Continued

	Summary
A15	This paper is based on the premise that model-driven development has great potential for generating software efficiently, but that it is difficult to generate consistent models with requirements traceability. It therefore proposes a method in which requirements specifications can be modeled separating UI, internal logic, and exceptions, allowing the systematic generation of design models.
A16	This paper presents a model-based-architecture approach to building a Rich Internet Application (RIA). To do this, a transformation process has to be designed in which code can be generated from design templates. An example of a use case on RIA product searches is also presented in the paper. A final tool is not presented, but theoretical knowledge is addressed for its possible generation in the future.
A17	This paper describes a study of the automatic generation of a user interface based on use cases. The authors focus on analyzing the interaction process between actors and the system in use cases, finally applying an MVC pattern and a hierarchical interface structure mode. Future works will improve the current structure and implement a tool that supports this process.
A18	This paper presents a method of transforming prototypes or user interfaces designed for multiplatform systems, allowing the reuse and sharing of prototypes and code. For this purpose, it defines a metamodel of platform-specific main models (PSM) and mapping rules between platform-independent models (PIM). A user interface development tool is available that allows such transformations.
A19	This paper proposes the development of a tool which makes it possible to generate automated prototypes from requirements. It is based on the generation of different views and rules allowing prototype generation. Generation is based on OCL (Object Constraint Language) and MVC (Model View Controller). The proposal has a high degree of reusability, and is therefore closely aligned with this study.
A20	This paper proposes a systematic approach for automatically generating prototypes, using concrete examples of requirements analysis in UML. The tool developed facilitates the generation of scenarios for validating the product, obtaining activity diagrams for the specified workflows.
A21	This paper proposes a system prototyping tool that transforms three requirement artifacts into system prototypes, also using requirements elicitation. The tool represents an interesting approach for this SLR due to its integration with different business processes and its validation in a use case, despite its still being in a development stage.
A22	This paper presents a backward approach to the objective pursued in this SLR: that is to say, the automatic generation of prototypes and user interfaces based on system requirements. Here, the authors use Concordia, an agile requirements specification metalanguage, and its prototyping tool. The paper validates the saving of time invested in the development task and the possible reuse of the code, two aspects on which we also focus in our research.
A23	This paper presents a tool for the automatic generation and analysis of prototypes in order to validate system requirements at an early stage of development. The proposed operation consists of describing a use case using UML and OML specifications that are transformed into executable prototypes, in order to improve user validation.

These indicators allowed us to provide measures for the dimensions of each paper: i.e., the dimensions were evaluated quantitatively. The indicators and their corresponding values are explained below:

- Interaction (I1): This indicator for the User Interaction dimension establishes the level of interaction the user has during the development process proposed by the approach: i.e., whether the user interacts during the whole process or only in certain parts of it.
- Parts (I2): This second indicator for the User Interaction dimension tells us about the specific phases in which the user is involved. For example, empathy indicates the possibility of using techniques like design thinking.
- Involvement (I3): This indicator for the Degree of Automation dimension tells us in which phases of the process the software developer is involved. A higher level of involvement means low automation and vice versa.
- Development (I4): This indicator for the Support Tools dimension shows whether a support tool is already available for the approach and indicates the degree of development of that tool.

- Validation (I5): This indicator for the Degree of Validation dimension establishes whether the approach is validated and how it is being validated, distinguishing between validation in academic and enterprise environments.
- Transfer (I6): This indicator for the Results dimension establishes the extent to which the approach is used by enterprises. Zero to full integration in an enterprise environment is possible.
- Type (I7): This second indicator for the Results dimension provide information on the different kinds of results that the approach generates. These results can be prototypes, codes, use cases, etc. Code and user interfaces are the most important things due to closeness to the final product.
- Reusability (I8): This indicator for the Degree of Reusability dimension shows the implicit reusability of the generated artifacts. If the level is high, all the artifacts are reusable.

Table 7 specifies the characterization map: i.e., the characteristics and their derived indicators. It also describes the possible values for each indicator.

Tables 8 and 9, show the results of each paper's evaluation against the defined characterization schema. The tables were compiled by completely reading and reviewing all 23 papers. Some questions, such as the number of tools, parts of involvement, type of results and degree of transfer, were purely objective and could be answered by reading the papers and identifying any of those elements that may have appeared in the document. To answer the question about the degree of transfer, the authors of the

Table 7. Indicators

	Indicators		
	N	**Description**	**Values**
User interaction	**Interaction (I1)**	**Degree of interaction required by the user.**	**Low (L): no interaction** **Medium (M): interaction takes place in some parts of the process.** **High (H): interaction during the whole process.**
	Phases (I2)	**Degree of user intervention in the different phases of Design Thinking.**	**Low (L): intervention in empathy or ideation.** **Medium (M): intervention in design.** **High (H): intervention in prototyping or validation.**
Degree of automation	Involvement (I3)	Degree of developer involvement in the software design process.	Low (L): involvement in all stages of the development. Medium (M): involvement in some stages of the development. High (H): involvement in a minimal number of stages of the development.
Support tool	Tool Maturity (I4)	Degree of completion of tool development.	Low (L): early stage of development. Medium (M): partially developed. High (H): fully developed.
Degree of validation	Validation (I5)	Degree of validation of the approach.	Low (L): no validation, either at companies or at universities. Medium (M): partial validation mainly at universities. High (H): validation in the industrial environment.
Technology transfer	Transfer (I6)	Degree of results transfer to companies.	Low (L): not used at companies. Medium (M): partially transferred to companies. High (H): used at companies.
	Result types (I7)	Types of results generated	Low (L): use cases or activity diagrams. Medium (M): prototypes or mockups. High (H): user interfaces or code.
Degree of reusability	Reusability(I8)	Degree of reusability of the generated results.	Low (L): the resulting models cannot be reused. Medium (M): some of the results are reusable. High (H): all models resulting from transfers are reusable.

papers were contacted. For other, more subjective, questions, the value of each indicator was decided by consensus, based on the opinion of the authors of this SLR.

DISCUSSION

The characterization scheme presented in the previous section was applied to those papers selected as the most relevant for this study. It provided an overview of the state-of-the-art, addressing the dimensions listed in Table 1 and the indicators in Table 7.

In this section, each of those dimensions is analyzed using the results obtained. Table 10 provides an overview of the results for each indicator.

Figure 5 displays the same results as a chart. The length of each value depicts the resulting evaluation of the indicators for the selected papers based on the characterization schema.

User interaction

The User Interaction dimension has to do with the roles users play in the development process. We considered two indicators for this dimension—Interaction and Phases—which helped us to answer RQ6:

Table 8. Evaluation of papers with the characterization schema (1)

	A1	A2	A3	A4	A5	A6	A7	A8	A9	A10	A11	A12
Interaction	**H**	**L**	**L**	**M**	**M**	**M**	**L**	**L**	**L**	**H**	**L**	**L**
Phases	M	L	L	M	L	H	L	M	L	H	L	M
Involvement	M	M	M	M	L	H	L	M	H	L	M	M
Tool maturity	M	L	L	H	M	L	M	H	L	M	H	H
Validation	M	L	L	M	L	L	L	M	L	L	L	L
Transfer	L	L	L	M	L	L	L	L	L	L	L	L
Result types	H	M	M	H	H	H	L	H	H	M	H	H
Reusability	M	M	M	H	H	H	M	H	H	H	H	M

Table 9. Evaluation of papers with the characterization schema (2)

	A1	A2	A3	A4	A5	A6	A7	A8	A9	A10	A11	A12
Interaction	**L**	**L**	**L**	**L**	**M**	**L**	**L**	**M**	**M**	**L**	**L**	**L**
Phases	L	L	L	L	L	L	M	H	L	L	L	L
Involvement	M	H	L	M	M	L	M	M	M	M	L	M
Tool maturity	H	M	L	H	L	H	H	M	M	H	H	H
Validation	L	L	M	M	L	L	M	L	M	M	L	L
Transfer	L	L	L	L	L	L	L	L	L	L	L	L
Result types	M	H	L	H	H	H	M	M	M	H	H	M
Reusability	H	M	L	L	M	M	H	M	L	H	M	H

Table 10. Overview of results for each indicator

Indicator	Total Low	Total Medium	Total High
Interaction	15	6	2
Phases	15	5	3
Involvement	6	14	3
Tool maturity	6	7	9
Validation	15	8	0
Transfer	22	1	0
Result types	2	7	14
Reusability	3	10	10

i.e., How do these approaches that provide prototype reuse involve users? And in which phases of the development process?

We differentiated three levels of user interaction. Low (L) means that the user does not participate in the process: he/she provides the requirements at the beginning and then plays no part in the process. Medium (M) means that the user sometimes participates in the process, for example by checking or validating the results that are being generated. High (H) means that the user is an active stakeholder during the process or is constantly informed of its evolution.

Figure 5. Overview of results

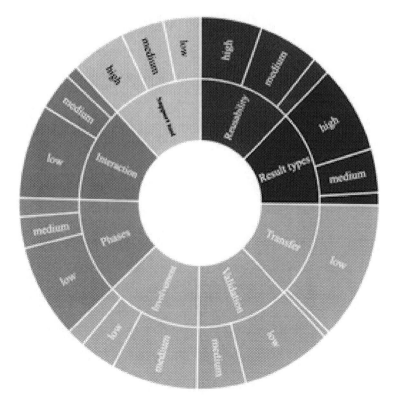

Figure 6A shows the number of papers found for each level of user interaction. In this figure, we can see that 15 of the 23 analyzed papers have a Low level of User Interaction, 6 have a Medium level and 2 a High Level. Papers such as A1 entitled "Mockup-driven development: providing agile support for model-driven web engineering" (Rivero et al., 2014) and A10 entitled "Evaluation of a use-case-driven requirements analysis tool employing web UI prototype generation" (Ogata & Matsuura, 2010) show higher end user interaction as the user is involved in the whole process. In many of the selected papers, however, the user is only a frequently interactive stakeholder in the first stage of development.

The second indicator of the User Interaction dimension is called Phases and indicates the kind of involvement the end user has during the process. We differentiated three levels. Low (L) means the user intervenes only in empathy or ideation. Medium (M) means that the user intervenes also in design. High (H) means the user intervenes directly in the process of prototyping and in validation.

Figure 6B shows a column chart for the number of papers with each different level of the Phases indicator. In this figure, we can see that 15 of the 23 analyzed papers have a Low level, 5 have a Medium level and 3 a High level. In papers like A6 "Algorithm of interface generation for model-driven data consolidation system" [25], A10 "Evaluation of a use-case-driven requirements analysis tool employing web UI prototype generation" [30] and "A20 Scenario-based automatic prototype generation" [31], users are directly involved not only in the elicitation of requirements but also in the prototyping process.

In the last of the three papers mentioned above, the user validates the prototype and provides input for its development throughout the entire process, but in the rest of the papers the user only participates in the basic elicitation of the requirement right at the beginning and later plays a less relevant role. We can thus conclude that the user normally intervenes only in ideation. Users only have a high level of involvement, validating results and participating in prototyping, in three of the selected papers.

Figure 6. Results for interaction, phases, involvement, and tool support

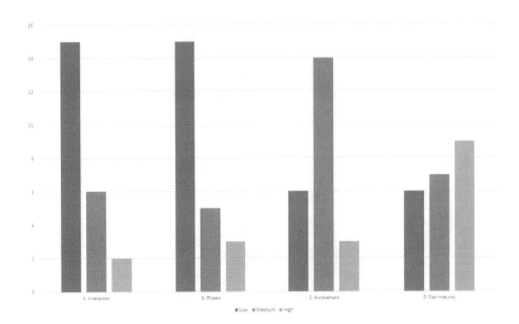

Degree of Automation

The Degree of Automation dimension has to do with the degree of developer involvement in the prototype generation process and helps answer RQ5. The indicator for this dimension is Involvement.

Involvement represents the degree of user involvement, the extent to which the user is involved in the process of prototyping. We differentiated three levels: Low (L) means that users, developers, and clients are present during the whole process, and automation is therefore very low. Medium (M) means that users or developers have to perform part of the process manually. High (H) means that the whole process is automatic, and users are therefore not directly involved.

Figure 6C shows the number of papers with each different level of Involvement in the form of a column chart. We can see that 14 of the 23 analyzed papers have a Medium level of Involvement, 6 have a Low level and 3 a High level. Most of them have a medium level of involvement because their solutions are not automated due to the manual work done by humans during the process. Some are completely manual; others are partially automated. Only three of them are completely automated, thanks to the fact that their solutions have well defined processes, with tasks like transformations coded, and almost the entire process is therefore executed without any human involvement. We can therefore conclude that the user is normally partially involved in development, and that most of the solutions are partially automated but very few of them are completely automated.

Support Tools

The Support Tools dimension has to do with the existence of a tool that makes it possible to support and implement a solution. The indicator for this dimension is Tool maturity and allow us to respond to RQ3.

Tool maturity shows an existing tool's degree of development. We differentiated three levels. Low (L) means that the tool is in an early stage of development, or does not yet exist. Medium (M) means that the tool is partially developed: it has some functions but major improvements have to be made in the future. High (H) means that the tool is fully developed and performs all the functions of the solution.

Figure 6D shows the number of papers with each different level of Tool maturity in the form of a column chart. This figure shows that 6 of the 23 analyzed papers have a Low level, 7 have a Medium level and 9 a High level. The solutions with a high level have fully developed tools that perform all the functions proposed in the papers. However, since nearly half of the papers present this level of tool maturity, we can conclude that there is a tendency to build tools capable of supporting given solutions. Many solutions are completely theoretical, making it rather difficult to test their real effectivity.

Degree of Validation

The Degree of Validation dimension has to do with the solution's degree of validation, meaning how and where it was tested. The indicator for this dimension is Validation and it helps us to provide an answer to RQ4.

Validation shows the extent to which the solution, or the tool (if one has been developed), has been validated. We differentiated three levels. Low (L) means that users, including developers and clients, are present in the whole process, and the solution has therefore not been validated in any environment. Medium (M) means that the solution has been tested only in a university environment, usually by students. High (H) means that the solution has been tested in companies or by real customers.

Figure 7. Results for validation, transfer, result types, and reusability

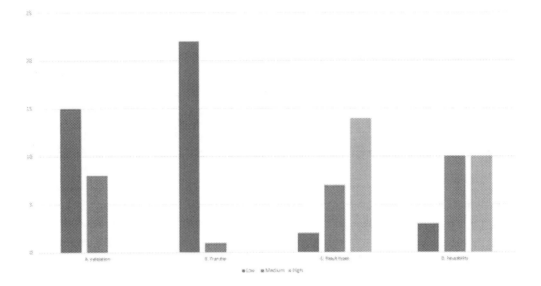

Figure 7A shows the number of papers with each different level of Validation in the form of a column chart. This figure shows that 15 of the 23 analyzed papers have a Low level, 8 have a Medium level and 0 a High level. Most of the solutions have not been subjected to any kind of testing in an industrial environment. However, seven of the solutions have been tested in universities. These studies carried out by groups of people in an academic environment test the solutions locally, but none of them describe validation in enterprises. We can conclude that most of the solutions are not tested or have been tested only partially by universities and students. This indicates a lack of testing in real enterprises, which would provide a business vision and make it possible to evaluate whether the solution is applicable in enterprises.

Technology Transfer

The Technology Transfer dimension has to do with the solution's efficiency, whether it has been transferred to companies and the types of results generated. There are two indicators for this dimension—Transfer and Result— and they provide an answer to RQ1.

Transfer shows the degree of transfer, indicating whether the solution has been partially or completely transferred to companies. We differentiated three levels. Low (L) means that the solution has not been transferred to companies. Medium (M) means that the solution has been transferred to companies but only partially, so it is not being used actively in their processes. High (H) means the solution has been transferred completely and it is being used by the company.

Figure 7B shows the number of papers with each different level of Transfer in the form of a column chart. Here, we can see that 22 of the 23 analyzed papers have a Low level of Transfer and only 1 of them has a Medium level. None of solutions has been transferred to companies. Only paper A4, "A model-driven approach for generating interfaces from user interaction diagrams," mentions that the proposal was presented to a team of analysts and developers at a software company, but the company in question is not specified. We can conclude that the solutions in the literature have not been transferred to companies, the main reason being that since this research is carried out in a university environment any transfer takes place within the university itself.

Result is the second indicator of the Technology transfer dimension. It shows the kinds of results that are generated. We differentiated three levels: Low (L) means that the only things generated are uses cases or activity diagrams, which are of the lowest level of importance for research. Medium (M) means that the solutions generated are prototypes or mockups, this being the main focus of the research. High (H) means that user interfaces or code have been generated. User interfaces are like prototypes but since they implement real functionality, they are more efficient.

Figure 7C shows the number of papers with each different level of generated result types. In this figure, we can see that 2 of the 23 analyzed papers have a Low level, 7 have a Medium level and 14 a High level. More than half of the solutions generate user interfaces, normally using code. These are like prototypes, but as they are made with code they allow better interaction, sometimes using unique formats for the solution. There are also many solutions that generate only prototypes. This is the main focus of this SLR, but the importance of those solutions is relative: the really important solutions are those that generate prototypes using code. We can conclude that the solutions focus on the generation of prototypes and mockups. Many of them do this through code, thus demonstrating their importance.

Degree of Reusability

The Degree of Reusability dimension has to do with the solution's degree of reusability, with whether the results generated can be used for other projects or works. The indicator for this dimension is Reusability, and helps us answer RQ2.

Reusability shows how reusable the solution is. We differentiated three levels. Low (L) means that the solution is not reusable and cannot be used to generate resources in other works. Medium (M) means that some results are reusable, while other results are not. High (H) means that all the solution's results are reusable and can be used in other projects. Figure 7D shows the number of papers with each different level of Reusability in the form of a column chart.

Here, we can see that 3 of the 23 analyzed papers have a Low level, 10 have a Medium level and 10 a High level. Half of the studies reuse part of the solutions they generate. This happens because some of the studies generate intermediate elements that are used in the process to generate final elements, and which are not therefore useful for reuse. In contrast, other solutions directly generate final elements because the whole process, including the intermediate elements, is transparent to the user. These solutions are therefore fully reusable. We can conclude that most of the solutions have a medium or high level of reusability, meaning that their results can be considered reusable.

CONCLUSION AND FUTURE WORKS

The objective of this SLR was to evaluate the current state of the literature regarding how analysis artifacts can be generated as automatically as possible from a prototype. To do this, the steps described in Section 2 were followed, the main objectives being:

- To specify research questions
- To identify related works
- To define a characterization schema
- To perform a detailed analysis

For the first objective, six research questions were established (see Section 4.1 and Table 1). These were used to define the lines of research in which the subsequent literature search would be conducted. Related papers were then identified from different sources, and twenty-three of them—all closely related to this approach—were selected.

Those 23 articles were used to create a characterization map that reflected their similarity to the objectives being addressed in this SLR (third objective). Most of the papers are recent, reflecting recent interest in this field, so this study can be considered a starting point for future research.

Finally, the results obtained were analyzed. The main conclusion was that the tools currently proposed do not establish the user as their main focus, address development phases, allow for the real reuse of prototypes, or include the real transfer of information to companies. This can be seen in Section III, where the papers and their characteristics are evaluated. In many of the papers, user interaction is low, meaning that the user is not sufficiently considered. Automation is generally medium, with very few completely automated solutions. Companies are not sufficiently taken into account for validation and transfer, so the solutions tend to remain in an academic environment. However, most of the solutions focus on prototypes and code and most of their elements can be reused.

This study, then, presents some bases from which further research needs to be done to create new tools capable of overcoming the deficiencies referenced above and improving prototyping in all its phases.

Rapid and effective prototyping and code automation is today a real challenge in the software world. Clients need technology that will not only meet their needs but will also cover those needs efficiently, effectively, and rapidly. In the real world, this causes companies to focus on development.

The current proposals are not capable of solving all the problems mentioned in this study because none of them provide an optimal answer to the six requirement questions. All the proposals are lacking in one or more characteristics. More specifically, the main problems are that there are no proposals in which interaction with the user is a relevant aspect and no proposals capable of generating requirements, code, or other type of models from prototypes. Each proposal focusses on generating just one of those elements.

We can therefore conclude that prototype generation and reuse is still a problem in the software world, and there is a need for a better solution. We are considering using Model-Driven Development (MDD) to create a process of transformation between prototypes, requirements, and code, applying Design Thinking to understand users' needs (Escalona et al., 2021). This idea has been validated with an industrial partner (Sanchez-Villarín et al., 2020) and we are currently defining a complete methodological environment around this idea.

Finally, it has to be possible to validate the approach described in this study in an industrial environment since the tool developed in the future must be transferable, subject to a proof of concept program (Sánchez-Villarín et al., 2020). It is therefore necessary to consider previous studies into the validation of works in MDE (such as Lopez et al., 2020), which lay the groundwork for an effective transfer.

ACKNOWLEDGMENT

This research was supported by projects SocietySoft (AT17_5904_USE), NDT4.0 (US-1251532) and SmarAuditor Project (P20/00644) of the Andalusian Regional Government's. Department of Economy, Knowledge, Business, and Universities (Spain) and NICO project (PID2019-105455GB-C31), funded by MCIN/AEI/10.13039/501100011033/ and by the European Union.

REFERENCES

Aggarwal, S. K., Deep, V., & Singh, R. (2014). Speculation of CMMI in agile methodology. In *Proc of International Conference on Advances in Computing, Communications and Informatics*. IEEE.

Ali, K. (2017). Study of Software Development Life Cycle Process Models. *International Journal of Advanced Research in Computer Science*, 8(1).

Anjum, R., Azam, F., Anwar, M. W., & Amjad, A. (2019) A meta-model to automatically generate evolutionary prototypes from software requirements. *ACM International Conference Proceeding Series*. ACM. 10.1145/3348445.3351304

Beaudouin-Lafon, M., & Mackay, W. (2003). *Prototyping tools and techniques*. Human Computer Interaction-Development Process.

Canedo, E. D., Dos Santos Pergentino, A. C., Calazans, A. T. S., Almeida, F. V., Costa, P. H. T., & Lima, F. (2020). Design thinking use in agile software projects: Software developers' perception. *ICEIS 2020 – Proc. of the 22nd International Conference on Enterprise Information Systems*. Research Gate.

Casalánguida, H., & Durán, J. E. (2012). Automatic generation of feature models from UML requirement models. *ACM International Conference Proceeding Series*, (vol. 2, pp. 10-17). ACM. 10.1145/2364412.2364415

Corral, L., & Fronza, I. (2018). Design thinking and agile practices for software engineering an opportunity for innovation. *Proc. of the 19th Annual SIG Conference on Information Technology Education*, (pp. 26-31). ACM. 10.1145/3241815.3241864

de Matos, E. C. B., & Sousa, T. C. (2010). From formal requirements to automated web testing and prototyping. *Innovations in Systems and Software Engineering*, 6(1), 163–169. doi:10.1007/s11334-009-0112-5

Dhandapani, S. (2016). Integration of User Centered Design and Software Development Process. *7th IEEE Annual Information Technology, Electronics and Mobile Communication Conference, IEEE IEMCON 2016*. IEEE. 10.1109/IEMCON.2016.7746075

Elkoutbi, M., Khriss, I., & Keller, R. K. (2006). Automated prototyping of user interfaces based on UML scenarios. *Automated Software Engineering*, 13(1), 5–40. doi:10.1007/s10515-006-5465-5

Escalona, M. J., & Aragón, G. (2008). NDT. A model-driven approach for web requirements. *IEEE Transactions on Software Engineering*, 34(3), 377–390. doi:10.1109/TSE.2008.27

Escalona, M. J., García-Borgoñón, L., & Koch, N. (2021). Don't Throw your Software Prototypes Away. Reuse them! *International Conference on Information System Development*. IEEE.

Escalona, M. J., Gutierrez, J. J., Mejías, M., Aragón, G., Ramos, I., Torres, J., & Domínguez, F. J. (2011). An overview on test generation from functional requirements. *Journal of Systems and Software, 84*(8), 1379–1393. doi:10.1016/j.jss.2011.03.051

Falb, J., Kavaldjian, S., Popp, R., Raneburger, D., Arnautovic, E., & Kaindl, H. (2009) Fully automatic user interface generation from discourse models. *International Conference on Intelligent User Interfaces, Proceedings IUI*, (pp. 475-476). IEEE. 10.1145/1502650.1502722

Fatolahi, A., Somé, S. S., & Lethbridge, T. C. (2008). A model-driven approach for the semi- automated generation of web-based applications from requirements. *20th International Conference on Software Engineering and Knowledge Engineering,* (pp. 619-624). IEEE.

Fernández, D. M., Wagner, S., Kalinowski, M., Felderer, M., Mafra, P., Vetrò, A., Conte, T., Christiansson, M.-T., Greer, D., Lassenius, C., Männistö, T., Nayabi, M., Oivo, M., Penzenstadler, B., Pfahl, D., Prikladnicki, R., Ruhe, G., Schekelmann, A., Sen, S., & Wieringa, R. (2017). Naming the pain in requirements engineering: Contemporary problems, causes, and effects in practice. *Empirical Software Engineering, 22*(5), 2298–2338. doi:10.1007/s10664-016-9451-7

Gupta, P. (2011). Best Practices to Achieve CMMI Level 2 Configuration Management Process Area through VSS tool. *International Journal of Computer Technology and Applications., 2*(3), 542–558.

Hoyos, J. P. A., & Restrepo-Calle, F. (2017). Fast Prototyping of Web-Based Information Systems Using a Restricted Natural Language Specification. In *International Conference on Evaluation of Novel Approaches to Software Engineering*. Springer.

JabRef Web. (n.d.). *Home*. JabRefWeb. https://www.jabref.org/

Jensen, L. S., Özkil, A. G., & Mortensen, N. H. (2016). Prototypes in engineering design: Definitions and strategies. *Proceedings of International Design Conference* (pp. 821-839). IEEE.

Juárez-Ramirez, R., Huertas, C., & Inzunza, S. (2014). Automated generation of user-interface prototypes based on controlled natural language description. *Proceedings - IEEE 38th Annual International Computers, Software and Applications. Conference Workshops*. IEEE. 10.1109/COMPSACW.2014.44

Kamalrudin, M., & Grundy, J. (2011). Generating essential user interface prototypes to validate requirements. *26th IEEE/ACM International Conference on Automated Software Engineering, ASE 2011, Proceedings*. IEEE. 10.1109/ASE.2011.6100126

Kawai, S., & Matsuura, S. (2015). Model driven development by separating concerns in UML requirements specification. *Proceedings – International Computer Software and Applications Conference, 3*.

Kitchenham, B., Pearl Brereton, O., Budgen, D., Turner, M., Bailey, J., & Linkman, S. (2009). Systematic Literature Reviews in Software Engineering – A Systematic Literature Review. *Information and Software Technology, 51*(1), 7–15. doi:10.1016/j.infsof.2008.09.009

Korobko, A. A. (2018). Algorithm of interface generation for model-driven data consolidation system. *RPC 2018. Proceedings of the 3rd Russian-Pacific Conference on Computer Technology and Applications, art. no. 8482134*. IEEE. 10.1109/RPC.2018.8482134

Kuczenski, B., Mutel, C., Srocka, M., Scanlon, K., & Ingwersen, W. (2021). Prototypes for automating product system model assembly. *The International Journal of Life Cycle Assessment*, *26*(3), 1–14. doi:10.1007/s11367-021-01870-9 PMID:34017158

Li, D., Li, X., Liu, J., & Liu, Z. (2008). Validation of requirement models by automatic prototyping. *Innovations in Systems and Software Engineering*, *4*(3), 241–248. doi:10.1007/s11334-008-0062-3

Lopez, G., García-Borgoñon, L., Vegas, S., Escalona, M. J., & Juristo, N. (2020). Cultivating Practitioners for Software Engineering Experiments in industry. Best Practices learned from the experience" Advancements in Model-Driven Architecture in Software Engineering. IGI Global.

Miao, G., Hongxing, L., Songyu, X., & Juncai, L. (2018). Research on User Interface Transformation Method Based on MDA. *Proceedings – 2017 16th Int. Symposium on Distributed Computing and Applications to Business, Engineering and Science, DCABES 2017*, (pp. 150-153). IEEE.

Nguyen-Duc, A., Wang, X., & Abrahamsson, P. (2017). What influences the speed of prototyping? An empirical investigation of twenty software startups. In *International Conference on Agile Software Development*. Springer. 10.1007/978-3-319-57633-6_2

Ogata, S., & Matsuura, S. (2008). Scenario-based automatic prototype generation. *Proceedings – International Computer Software and Applications Conference*. IEEE.

Ogata, S., & Matsuura, S. (2010). "Evaluation of a use-case-driven requirements analysis tool employing web UI prototype generation" WSEAS. *Transactions on Information Science and Applications*, *7*(2), 273–282.

Oran, A. C., Valentim, N., Santos, G., & Conte, T. (2019). Why use case specifications are hard to use in generating prototypes? *IET Software*, *13*(6), 510–517. doi:10.1049/iet-sen.2018.5239

Pinto, T. D., Gonçalves, W. I., & Costa, P. V. (2019). User interface prototype generation from agile requirements specifications written in Concordia. *Proceedings of the 25th Brazilian Symposium on Multimedia and the Web, WebMedia 2019*, (pp. 61-64). ACM. 10.1145/3323503.3360639

Plattner, H., Meinel, C., & Weinberg, U. (2009). Design-thinking. *Landsberg am Lech*. Mi-Fachverlag.

Rasheed, Y., Azam, F., Anwar, M. W., & Tufail, H. (2019). A model-driven approach for creating storyboards of web-based user interfaces. *ACM International Conference Proceeding Series*, (pp. 169-173). ACM. 10.1145/3348445.3348465

Ren, X., & Wei, C. (2008). Research on the interaction process in use case for automatic generation of user interface prototype. *Proceedings of the International Conference on Computer and Electrical Engineering*. Research Gate.

Rivero, J. M., Grigera, J., Rossi, G., Luna, E. R., Montero, F., & Gaedke, M. (2014). Mockup-driven development: Providing agile support for model-driven web engineering. *Information and Software Technology*, *56*(6), 670–687. doi:10.1016/j.infsof.2014.01.011

Rocha Silva, T., Hak, J.-L., Winkler, M., & Nicolas, O. (2017). A Comparative Study of Milestones for Featuring GUI Prototyping Tools. *Journal of Software Engineering and Applications, 10*(6).

Rosado da Cruz, A. M., & Pascoal-Faria, J. (2010). A metamodel-based approach for automatic user interface generation. *13th International Conference on Model Driven Engineering Languages and Systems.* Springer. 10.1007/978-3-642-16145-2_18

Roubi, S., Erramdani, M., & Mbarki, S. (2016). Modeling and generating graphical user interface for MVC Rich Internet Application using a model driven approach. *International Conference on Information Technology for Organizations Development.* Research Gate.

Saito, S., & Hagiwara, J. (2012). System prototype generation tool for requirements review. *Frontiers in Artificial Intelligence and Applications, 240,* 81–87.

Sánchez-Villarín, A., Santos-Montano, A., & Enríquez, J. G. (2019). Automatic reuse of prototypes in software engineering: A survey of available tools. *Proceedings of the 15th International Conference on Web Information Systems and Technologies,* (pp. 144-150). ACM. 10.5220/0008352900002366

Sánchez-Villarín, A., Santos-Montano, A., Koch, N., & Lizcano-Casas, D. (2020). Prototypes as starting point in MDE: Proof of concept. *Proceedings of the 16th International Conference on Web Information Systems and Technologies.* ACM. 10.5220/0010213403650372

Shatnawi, A., & Shatnawi, R. (2016). Generating a language-independent graphical user interfaces from UML models. *The International Arab Journal of Information Technology, 13*(3), 291–296.

Strmečki, D., Magdalenić, I., & Radosević, D. (2018). A Systematic Literature Review on the Application of Ontologies in Automatic Programming. *International Journal of Software Engineering and Knowledge Engineering, 28*(5), 559–591. doi:10.1142/S0218194018300014

Surma-Aho, A. O., Björklund, T. A., & Holtta-Otto, K. (2018). Assessing the development of empathy and innovation attitudes in a project-based engineering design course. *Annual Conference and Exposition, Conference Proceedings.* ACM. 10.18260/1-2--29826

Torrecilla-Salinas, C. J., Sedeño, J., Escalona, M. J., & Mejías, M. (2015). Estimating, planning and managing Agile Web development projects under a value-based perspective. *Information and Software Technology, 61,* 124–144. doi:10.1016/j.infsof.2015.01.006

Yang, Y., Li, X., Liu, Z., & Ke, W. (2019). RM2PT: A tool for automated prototype generation from requirements model. *IEEE/ACM 41st International Conference on Software Engineering: Companion, ICSE-Companion 2019.* ACM. 10.1109/ICSE-Companion.2019.00038

Yıldız, T. (2019). Human-Computer Interaction Problem in Learning: Could the Key Be Hidden Somewhere Between Social Interaction and Development of Tools? *Integrative Psychological & Behavioral Science, 53*(3), 541–557. doi:10.1007/s12124-019-09484-5 PMID:30826986

Zeferino, N. V., & Vilain, P. (2014). A model-driven approach for generating interfaces from user interaction diagrams. *ACM International Conference Proceeding Series,* (pp. 474-478). ACM. 10.1145/2684200.2684326

Zhang, H., Babar, M., & Tell, P. (2011, June). Identifying relevant studies in software engineering. *Information and Software Technology*, *53*(6), 625–637. doi:10.1016/j.infsof.2010.12.010

ENDNOTE

[1]   In the rest of the text "user" will be used instead of "end user."

Chapter 10
Impact of 5G Security on Smart Cities' Internet of Things Implementation

Wasswa Shafik

 https://orcid.org/0000-0002-9320-3186

School of Digital Science, Universiti Brunei Darussalam, Uganda

Kassim Kalinaki

Islamic University in Uganda, Uganda

ABSTRACT

Smart cities are imperative in terms of smart buildings, transportation, parking, healthcare, agriculture, traffic systems, and public safety aided by the fifth generation (5G) computation standards. They are entirely capable of controlling real-time devices and delivering relevant smart information to the citizens. However, different architectural stages experience privacy and security concerns. Therefore, in this survey, an internet of things (IoT) based architecture is proposed, showing the critical layers that are key to ensure secure smart IoT implementation. The study further covers the recent approaches to security applications for information centric SCs. 5G security solutions have been highlighted in SCs' settings and proposed. Comparably, a comprehensive SC current 5G security and numerous open security concerns are demonstrated. Lastly, offer potential research directions and motivations mainly in academia and industry, outlining these concerns that need to be considered to enhance smart daily operations.

INTRODUCTION

The United Nations report demonstrated that over half of the global population resides in urban centers and cities, therefore making the urban population grow faster than in the past few decades (Cui et al., 2018). As a result of its stringent standards and feasible urbanized environment, the definition of "smart city" (SC) has attracted the interest of industry and academia (Jain et al., 2022). Different smart strategies and infrastructures have been adopted by several SCs across the globe to enhance people's standards

DOI: 10.4018/978-1-6684-9576-6.ch010

of living and services. Some notable countries with large populations are investing money in initiatives connected to SCs. China is reported to be engaged in more than 200 projects that support the concept of SCs. Urban municipals are managing their daily operations to increase the quality of life for people due to technologies related to SCs (Xu et al., 2022). Smart, healthcare, transit, and traffic systems are a few examples of the myriad gadgets and interconnected systems that make up the infrastructure of SCs.

The 5G (fifth-generation) security and integration in SC operates using the Internet of Things (IoT), where physical devices are evolving into smart devices in daily life. This has increased because of the combination of numerous low-charge devices, for instance, actuators and sensors, and the quick advancement of wireless communication tech. Information-centric networking (ICN) solutions can be used to advance the rise of IoT and its implementation. In addition, internet protocol (IP)-based strategies like the one described instead of relying on Internet Protocol (IP) host identification address, ICNs are defined as a strategy that places information at the core of the design (Yang et al., 2021). ICNs can serve numerous 5G IoT circumstances and get based on their existing constraints. In the IoT context, it can be applied as a framework to connect multiple sensor-equipped items and provide a range of services, as demonstrated in Figure 1. In the IoT era, using ICN can also reduce energy consumption.

Cities are growing smarter, which might put people at serious risk for security and privacy at all operation levels. Resource-constrained devices make the SC susceptible to many types of 5G security threats. These weaknesses could make SCs vulnerable to several cyberattacks. For instance, malevolent

Figure 1. Smart city situation using internet of things submission (smart healthcare, smart transportation, smart building, and other IoT devices), as adopted by Jun et al., 2021

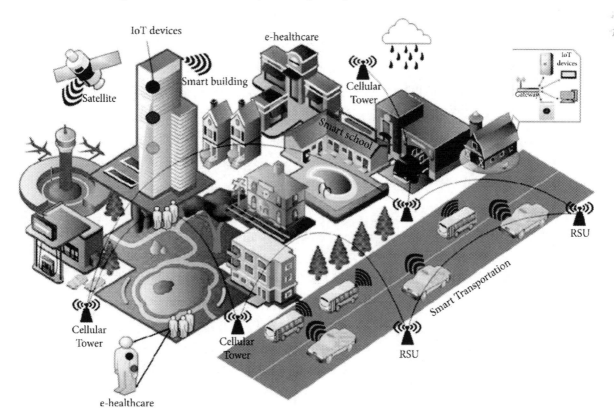

attackers may manipulate sensor data to produce false data, thus leading to the loss of control in smart systems (Jain et al., 2022). For instance, in early 2015, a denial-of-service (DoS) attack by hackers on the smart grid caused a significant power outage that affected 230,000 people in Ukraine. Residents' security and privacy in SCs may be jeopardized by cyberattacks and cyber threats from a variety of resource-based devices, for instance, cameras and sensors, that collect and share sensitive data in SCs (Xu et al., 2022). As a result of these cyberattacks, information about a person's home gathered and managed by smart homes can reveal a person's lifestyle in terms of privacy and even cause financial and other related damage.

The market for smart cities will gradually grow to $1.5 trillion by 2020, and some governments are attracting significant funds to realize the vision of SCs. Figure 2 illustrates the public engagement in smart city acceptance using IoT and non-IoT connections globally. This enormous development includes sensor node implementation within the city to require people to access information in real-time. They provide information about a variety of services, including traffic patterns on the water and air quality, public transportation, and energy consumption, among others (Preuveneers & Joosen, 2016). To safeguard sensitive data from the existence of illegal entities, processing and analyzing massive amounts of sensitive data presents several privacy and security concerns.

Within this period of artificial intelligence (AI) and in SCs with 5G security, cloud computing can provide relatively inexpensive data processing and storage services. The fog computing paradigm can aid in the resolution of several issues with cloud-to-based IoT applications, including reduced latency, location awareness, security, and mobility support. Fog computing addresses these issues by making resource computation available to users by using the network (Maamar et al., 2018). The differences between fog and cloud computing present difficult security and privacy challenges, making it impossible for consumers to use cloud security solutions for fog computing services.

Different cryptography methods can defend against 5G security breaches. These methods are ineffective for resource-to-constrained IoT devices in SCs. Offloading is another security-related task; the fog node, which enables security and privacy data processing at the edge of the network, is one way to address this issue. Moreover, publications are distributed utilizing a group of brokers who can gather sensitive user data through subscription and publishing systems, which transfer data from the subscriber to the publisher. The system is supposed to protect subscription and publication confidentiality while attackers attempt to gain access to publishing tags and subscriber interests.

Existing Similar Survey Comparisons

Despite the benefits of SCs described above, a few privacy and security concerns are emerging because of the vast array of wireless-based cameras and sensors that collect and transfer data to other connected devices to the internet for resource sharing. Data is considered the most appreciated resource for humans in today's intelligent world. Hardware and software manage all data, both of which have security and privacy flaws, such as infrastructure security flaws and cyberattacks. As a result of these security concerns, the services provided by high-tech systems may perform less well. It is vital to solve security concerns to make highly sophisticated systems safer and more beneficial for users in the future (Butte et al., 2019).

Several surveys on the privacy and security of SCs and IoT 5G security perspectives have been published. For instance, regarding privacy and security in SCs' applications (Zhang et al., 2017), The study also reviewed various privacy and security challenges in the application context. The authors recognized the methods applied for data privacy and security and examined the existing technologies making SCs

Figure 2. Global total IoT and non-IoT active devices between 2015 to 2025 connections

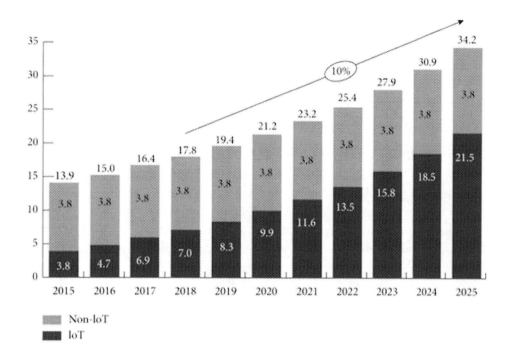

a reality (Gharaibeh et al., 2017). Eckhoff and Wagner presented various types of privacy, the needed resources, and potential attackers in SCs. They additionally examined several forms of citizen privacy in SCs and contemporary privacy-improving techniques (Eckhoff & Wagner, 2018). Like the above, the primary research difficulties and the most recent security concerns for 5G IoT security contexts were discussed (Sicari et al., 2015). According to the examined literature, all existing surveys miss out on the point of impact of 5G security on SC implementation. This approach to examining the possible impacts on the SC implementation will provide a clear context on the challenges and open future trends to reduce security flaws in SC development.

The Chapter Contributions

This study mainly contributes the following, as summarized below concerning the current literature:

- The study presents the key uses of SCs, which also discusses the important 5G security concerns in the design of SC implementation.
- The study avails a variety of resolutions to address significant security threats in smart setups.
- Within the same study, a secure 5G IoT-based architecture for SCs is proposed.
- The study also discusses security approaches dealing with the implementation process of secure techniques.
- Finally, it presents several open research concerns that should be considered when improving SCs in terms of privacy and security.

The Chapter Contributions

Section 2 discusses an Internet of Things-based architecture focusing on the SCs' 5G privacy and security concerns. Section 3 presents 5G Security solutions for SCs. Section 4 examines privacy and 5G security issues and resolution in SCs' settings correspondingly. Section 5 provides a comprehensive recommended state-of-the-art 5G security from an SC perspective. Section 6 demonstrates a discussion of various open research concerns and offers potential research directions and conclusions in Section 7.

5G SECURITY ARCHITECTURE FOR SMART CITIES

Within this section, a proposed Internet of Internet-based architecture focusing on SC privacy and 5G security concerns in layer format is presented. The vision is grand, the challenges are intricate, but the rewards are transformative. Figure 3 depicts the increase in urbanization from 1990 to 2014 and a projection for 2050. Moreover, the sections provide a concise explanation of every layer of the proposed architecture.

The Physical Layer

The physical layer contains heterogeneous devices (for example, actuators and sensors), and its sole duty is to gather and communicate information from it to the architecture's next layer. For further processing, the physical layer passes the collected information to the network layer (Tan & Wang 2010).

Figure 3. Population increase in smart cities

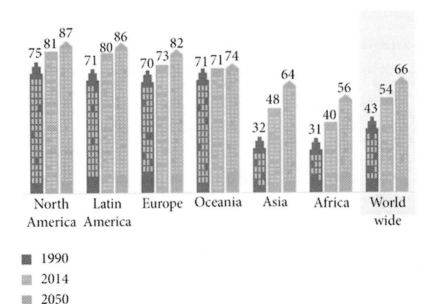

It mostly used wearable devices at this layer, including MPEG Audio Layer 3 players, smart watches, digital cameras, activity trackers, digital books, tablet computers, smartphones, health care devices, and running watches, among others.

The Network Layer

It is sometimes called the communication layer and is considered the foundation of this architecture. The layer is dependent relatively on the networks, for instance, the internet and wireless sensor networks, as well as communication networks. The network layer's major responsibility is to transfer the data acquired from the physical layer and to link various network-based peripheral devices, the main layers as presented in Figure 4

The Database Layer

This is a support layer since it cooperates with the architecture's top levels. It is made up of intelligent computer systems and database servers. This layer's primary duty is to meet application requirements using advanced computing techniques including cloud and edge computing.

The Virtualization Layer

It offers an integration of a virtual network that unifies hardware or network and software capabilities into a single software-centered, logically configurable entity. Platform virtualization and resource virtualization may be necessary for network virtualization to be successful. Utilizing the virtualization layer is accomplished.

Figure 4. Smart city layers

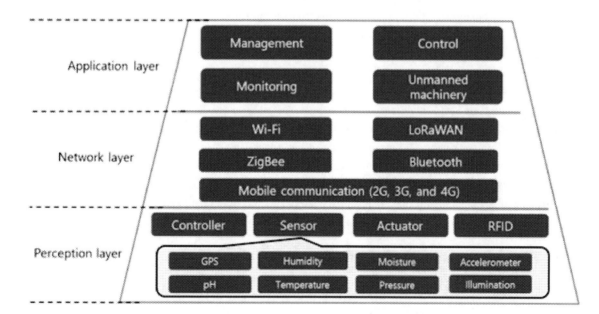

The Mining Layer and Data Analytics

Unprocessed data is transformed into useful information in the mining layer and data analytics, which can assist in increasing network performance and forecasting future occurrences, including system breakdown. To examine the data, this layer utilizes a variety of data analytics and mining approaches, including machine learning (ML) systems.

Application Layer

This layer supervises by providing users with smart implementation and services based on their specific needs. Some common notable examples of the applications include smart grid, transportation, environment, living, health, and energy, among others; the next section presents 5G security solutions for SCs.

5G SECURITY SOLUTIONS FOR SMART CITIES

The expected tremendous increase in the plethora of connected IoT devices, together with the volume of connectivity traffic because of the convergence of 5G and IoT, poses security challenges. Such challenges are poised to slow down the adoption of smart cities in most parts of the world as 5G becomes fully embraced. A brief description of the recommended 5G security solutions for smart cities is provided in this section.

Blockchain

Because the current mobile networks, along with the implemented IoT systems, are solely based on centralized models, it's expected that numerous security challenges will be prevalent as they try to catch up with the future 5G-enabled IoT smart city requirements. Blockchain, therefore, becomes a viable solution to such security problems with offerings that include non-repudiation, immutability, integrity, proof of provenance, privacy, accelerated data change, trust building, improved security, lower costs, decentralization, and automation via smart contracts (Hewa et al., 2020). Several blockchain-based frameworks have been proposed to solve different security problems in 5G-enabled SCs. In their study (Deebak & AL-Turjman, 2022), a robust & lightweight distributed framework for a 5G-enabled smart city network using blockchain was proposed.

This architecture restricts security key exposure by authenticating smart city device access that publicizes genuine data possession. Upon experimental analysis, the proposed framework was found to be capable of achieving better privacy against trusted third-party applications. Authors further proposed a safe and secure blockchain-based authentication scheme that stores security credentials on IoT devices in a decentralized fashion (Goswami & Choudhury, 2022). Upon analyzing its experimental performance, the scheme achieved minimized communication latency compared to the existing protocols.

5G-IoT Standardization and Regulation

Due to the diversity of devices, networks, and applications running in 5G-enabled smart cities, challenges of standardization and consistency for both applications and IoT devices are abounding (Banafa, 2020).

5G-IoT-enabled standardization is categorized into four sections that include IoT devices, connectivity, business models, and IoT applications (Li et al., 2018). IoT Technology standards and regulation standards will have to be out of place to solve different security and privacy challenges in 5G-enabled smart cities. The military and hospitals use unprotected smart devices, and the devices can be easily hacked, resulting in novel attacks at every layer of the protocol stack (Park et al., 2021). Recent hacks on IoT devices, like the one detailed in (Saleem et al., 2018), have raised awareness of the need for strong security procedures and procedures for internet-connected devices. Economic sustainability is another imperative. Figure 5 demonstrates the application of AI and IoT. Smart city initiatives entail significant investments; to be viable, they must demonstrate straightforward economic returns.

Artificial Intelligence

AI has emerged as one of the most important promising technological revolutions for 5G-IoT security aimed at managing IoT systems to ensure they can identify network anomalies and predict future behaviors, especially for smart cities. Its associated technologies, such as deep learning (DL) and ML algorithms, allow 5G-IoT-enabled networks to provide reliable services by being proactive in predicting future network events in an automated and programmed manner.

Through learning and mastering the historical activity patterns and scrutinizing the current connectivity traffic within the smart city network, AI for 5G security helps in identifying and tracking malicious activities such as man-in-the-middle attacks and radio jamming, among others, to prevent similar attacks in the future (Salahdine et al., 2022). ML algorithms such as support vector machines, decision trees, and Naive Bayes have the potential to enhance the security resistance over the Software Defined Networks (SDN) control plane as well as detect intrusions/attacks with limited intelligence capabilities (Li et al., 2018; Kuadey et al., 2022). DL frameworks such as DeepSecure have been proposed to detect

Figure 5. Application artificial intelligence and internet of things in smart cities

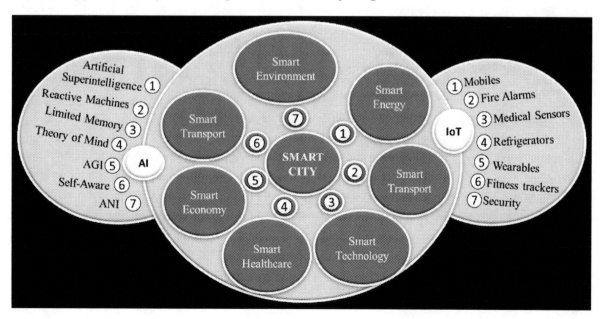

distributed DoS attacks on 5G network slicing using long short-term memory. Their results indicated exceptional performance in Distributed Denial-of-Service (DDoS) detection with an accuracy of up to 99.9% (Kuadey et al., 2022).

Cryptography

For 5G-enabled smart city IoT networks, creative cryptographic techniques will have to be adopted to cope with the new threat dimensions. The emergence of quantum computers and their associated technologies is threatening the existence of traditional cryptographic techniques, which are the current standards for 5G communication security (Ajtai, 2005; Shafik et al., 2023a). To safeguard 5G-IoT-enabled smart cities from quantum attacks, quantum cryptographic techniques capable of providing more secure communications that are tough to intercept will have to be adopted. The Lattice-based technique of cryptography, which has been proven effective against quantum attacks has been proposed. Quantum key distribution (QKD) is another solution to quantum attacks that has proven effective after its deployment by SK Telekom in 2016 (Park et al., 2021).

Nevertheless, post-quantum cryptographic techniques will have to be created to cope with future threats beyond techniques. As mentioned earlier, standardization for such emerging cryptographic methods will have to be developed to ensure consistency and preserve confidentiality, non-repudiation, integrity, and availability in 5G-IoT-enabled smart cities. Lightweight elliptic curve cryptography (ECC) and a biometric-based framework for authorization, authentication, and session key agreement were proposed for 5G-IoT-enabled smart city security (Nyangaresi, 2022). Furthermore, the scheme was able to offer anonymity and untraced ability as well as demonstrate resilience against most of the current 5G-IoT security attacks and privacy violations that include, among others, conspiracy, privileged insiders, side-channeling, man-in-the-middle, replay ephemeral secret leakages and offline password guessing.

Biometrics

In IoT-based infrastructures, biometric authentication is becoming increasingly prevalent. This technology is highly dependent on human behavior and can detect an individual using biodata collected from their face, fingerprints, handwritten signatures, voice, and other distinguishing features. Brainwave-based authentication is one of the most precise technologies currently known, with the potential to attain both high precision and efficiency. In a similar vein, a mutual authentication mechanism is a means of protecting the privacy of users' personally identifiable information kept on storage devices (Singandhupe, 20218; Shafik et al., 2023b). Please be warned that there is the potential for a breach of privacy in case the offered bio-based methodologies are not employed responsibly. Wang and others contended that it is essential to develop biometric systems that protect privacy comparable to the one presented in the work (Wang et al., 2018; Bauspieß et al., 2022). In addition, scientists observed that these biometrics may have future applications in a range of fields, including online commerce. Others further developed a safety system for UAVs based on biometrics and employed low-cost resources in the case that detected attacks (Amin et al., 2017).

5G SECURITY REQUIREMENTS

This section provides the security requirements that 5G-IoT-enabled smart city networks that are needed to ensure safety for users, devices, and applications; these include secrete sharing, privacy, and security in design, system security, testing and verification, access control, multiparty, and computation as explained below.

Secret Sharing (SS)

This strategy permits the provision of confidential information to several individuals. Typically, it is allocated into *m* shares with every member receiving one. The recovery of the secret requires at least n shares using this procedure (Li et al., 2016). Consequently, it provides system dependability and confidentiality. SS is mainly used for allocated data storage and aggregation in smart sensor networks and meters105 and information-centric SCs.

Privacy by Modelling

This strategy addresses information-on-centric SC privacy and safety concerns [34]. This method has some guidelines for designing a new system (Eckhoff & Wagner, 2018; Wang et al., 2011; Ståhlbröst et al., 2015; Shafik et al., 2023c). Proactive privacy protection should replace reactive responses to infringement. Privacy should be a default setting and considered during system development. Data should be protected forever. The system should be open and private. Several studies have built novel privacy-protecting technologies using these ideas. Proactively designing a remote health monitoring system was the focus of studies that introduced transparency and visibility to SC Systems (Cavoukian, 2009; Preuveneers & Joosen, 2016).

System Security

Information-driven smart cities require system and component safety to protect residents' privacy. If the system is vulnerable, attackers might easily get access to smart devices and steal data, compromising users' privacy. To prevent hacker attacks, system security is essential. Data is protected by access control. It would also reduce system control to prevent data misuse (Barth et al., 2022; Randall et al., 2022). Internet-connected autonomous systems with remotely monitored intelligent devices need access management.

Verification and Testing (VaT)

This is a critical component of designing a privacy and security-friendly system to guarantee that its implementation meets their needs. Privacy-connected VaTs are supposed to add to existing testing processes because they are similar (Li et al., 2022; Shafik et al., 2023d; Rani et al., 2022). These verification methodologies, such as black box differential testing, find application information leaks. Any new information-centric smart city system architecture must include testing and verification.

Privacy Architecture

Numerous protective measures must be incorporated into the privacy architecture to prevent system-caused privacy breaches. A broker would mediate access to users' data stores, and dependable remote data storage would be utilized (Sowmiya & Poovammal, 2022; Aski et al., 2022). To ensure user privacy, the research employed many cryptographic techniques.

Data Minimizations

The authors demonstrated that data reduction is one of the crucial parts of the security-by-design approach. The electronic toll pricing system in information-centric SCs uses this method to evaluate architectural options (Monreale, 2014; Shafik et al., 2023e). It can also be used to analyze large data to develop privacy measures. Smart city system design should avoid duplication (Shashidhara et al., 2022). ITS cameras may record unrelated data, while smart environment sensors may accumulate more secure data than required. Consequently, data-reduction algorithms can overcome such barriers.

Protected Multiparty Computing

A cryptographic system that enables various users to evaluate the performance deprived of disclosing the secret inputs of any party or varying to the trusted third party (TTP). This method is known as "multiparty computation." The Rivest Shamir Adleman security group is credited for the creation of this cryptographic technology. This technology can be utilized to establish a healthcare system in smart cities to review the findings of genomic testing (Wan et al., 2022).

RECOMMENDED STATE-OF-THE-ART 5G SECURITY FROM A SMART CITY PERSPECTIVE

An architecture for a smart city that is built on the Internet of Things runs on heterogeneous networks (HetNets), and it is made up of millions of devices with limited resources. The fundamental building blocks of an IoT–centered SC architecture are depicted in Figure 6 (Shafik et al., 2024a). These components include trusted software-defined networks (SDN) controllers referred to as the TTP and unified black networks (BNs). The registry is also known as the Key Management System (KMS) and the Unified Registry (UR).

These four components each have a unique function within the architecture, and together, they are accountable for authenticated communication and secure transmission across HetNets. Data privacy, data integrity, data secrecy, and data authentication are the responsibilities of black networks. A trusted third party oversees effective routing between IoT node(s), whereas UR is utilized for a database of diverse devices (Al-Turjman et al., 2022; Shafik et al., 2024b). Both functions are related to the IoTs; in the end, KMS oversees the IoT networks. The four identified recommendations are explained below.

The Black Market

Black networks are utilized to protect the data that is associated with each packet in an Internet of Things protocol. They have access to a variety of encryption techniques, one of which is the advanced encryption standard, which can be implemented in the environmental audio extensions (EAX) (Chakrabarty et al., 2015). Authentication and encrypted communication can be achieved by the link and network layers with black networks, respectively (Bhardwaj & Panda, 2022. This is because BNs can reduce the number of communication hops essential for an attack to complete.

Trusted Software-Defined Network Controller

A paradigm known as software-defined networking (SDN) offers various options to improve the effectiveness of network protection in a few different ways. The communication of network devices in this architecture is handled by an SDN controller, which makes use of a variety of different protocols (Shafik et al., 2024c). Regarding the communication that occurs between the many devices that make up a network and controller, OpenFlow is by far the most used protocol (Chakrabarty et al., 2015). The

Figure 6. A summary of secure IoTs' architecture in implementation

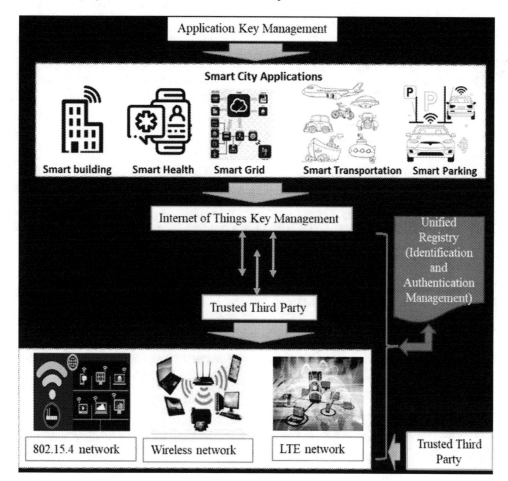

primary objective of the SDN controller is to address the difficulties associated with routing in the context of the preservation of security for IoT-centered BNs. The OpenFlow protocol makes it possible for the controller to initiate a safe connection with the various devices that are connected to the network as well as maintain an IoT-based network view globally.

Unified Registry

The Unified Registry (UR) unifies diverse technologies to construct IoT networks for SCs. Mobile IoT nodes or cross-systems can have a visiting UR. The wireless interaction of fixed nodes in IoT networks is crucial for network security. Wi-Fi and LTE wireless connections are utilized in SCs (Kavitha et al., 2022; Shafik et al., 2024d). UR simplifies the technology and protocol and addresses the conversion of wireless communication. Implementing UR is difficult because of regulatory, practical, and security restrictions. The SCs can build a highly dispersed logical entity that focuses on the data and attributes of IoT node traits (Shivraj et al., 2015).

Key Management Systems (KMS)

KMS manages cryptographic key duties for cryptosystem features. Every security system needs it. Asymmetric shared key secures low-resource IoT devices. Safely generate, store, and use keys. Symmetric keys in mobile dispersed systems must be disseminated. Hierarchical KMSs distribute symmetric keys efficiently in smart cities (Kelly & Hammoudeh, 2021; Shafik, 2024e). IoT communications must be authenticated. Due to security issues, IoT applications require different security procedures and standards. A secure socket layer can increase security for restricted application protocols and other protocols (Carlin et al., 2015). This suggests that IoT device communication is unsafe with single-factor authentication. A KMS with two-factor authentication reduces risk and secures IoT networks (Sookhak et al., 2018). As an example, KMS also lets IoT nodes securely connect using a shared key via external key management.

OPEN RESEARCH CONCERNS AND POTENTIAL RESEARCH DIRECTIONS

Despite the numerous studies and rapid advancements regarding the privacy and security of SCs, there are still unresolved concerns that should be taken into consideration concerning the 5G security implementation in SCs in terms of privacy and security.

Fog or Cloud Technology Application

Cloud computation offers a way for storage and massive data organization collected locally by 5G IoT devices. Nevertheless, transmitting such massive data necessitates a substantial amount of storage, bandwidth, latency, and connection resources (Shafik & Kalinaki, 2023). To avoid transmitting such a high volume of data to the cloud, IBM proposed employing fog computing to process data at the network's edge. Fog computing can be used in a variety of ways to suit the needs of constructing sustainable SCs, including smart agriculture. Various security and privacy challenges, for instance, web or data security and virtualization, must be addressed despite the enormous advantages of SC fog computation (Sookhak et al., 2018). In addition, because fog nodes are frequently more accessible, cyberattacks against them are more likely than those against cloud data centers.

Integrity and Availability

In SCs, services should always be available. Besides, when they are being attacked, they must be able to continue operating effectively. Furthermore, smart systems in SCs must be able to recognize unusual conditions to prevent future system damage (Shafik et al., 2022). To combat increasingly sophisticated attacks, research into dependable protection solutions is required. Moreover, the privacy of IoT and the data shared between them and the cloud is critical (Anwar & Saqib, 2022; He et al., 2017). Thus, it is crucial to investigate realistic approaches for ensuring data integrity during transmission across SC devices.

Confidentiality and Authentication

Confidentiality is a prerequisite for SC protection. It protects knowledge from erroneous sources and passive attacks. Attackers gain access to gadgets in IoT networks and can listen in to communications invisibly. To guarantee the security of data transfer between nodes, research into encryption-based methods is critical. This, in turn, makes it easier to have a dependable communication system (Anwar & Saqib, 2022; Shafik et al., 2024). Moreover, SC devices can authenticate messages from control stations, the network, and other network nodes.

Lightweight Security

Several techniques have recently been established to address SC privacy and security challenges. Meanwhile, some of the applications of these methods are impractical. Due to the existence of energy and resource-constrained devices in SC infrastructure, it is complex to apply intricate and effective security algorithms (He et al., 2017; Shokoor et al., 2022). To save coinage while still providing adequate protection, research must be conducted to develop lightweight security systems.

IoTs-Based Network Security

IoTs have capabilities operating as a heterogeneous network in which various networks, for instance, social networks, smartphones, internet, and industrial networks, are merged and linked together to give greater services to consumers (Jun et al., 2021; Shafik et al., 2023). This complicated security situation is necessary to propose efficient frameworks to tackle the most recent issues in SC privacy and security. Consequently, the development of effective Preventive strategies is crucial (Yu et al., 2015). Furthermore, modeling data dispersion patterns in wireless sensor networks is crucial as well.

Big Data

The increasing proliferation of smart devices and big data raises concerns about privacy and security in SC implementation applications like intelligent systems (Yang et al., 2021; Shafik et al., 2021). Cyber attackers exploit cognitive abilities and obtain access to large amounts of data to violate data owners' privacy. Cryptographic methodologies can be employed to identify these attackers (Alam, 2022). Furthermore, it is critical to achieving integrity, data privacy, availability, and authentication to safeguard large volumes of data.

Mobile Crowd Sensing (MCS)

Crowdsensing (CS) is an approach in which a group of people using mobile devices extracts and exchanges relevant information on their interests. MCS has the potential to vastly improve people's lives in a wide range of applications, like healthcare and transportation (Hilal et al., 2022). Notwithstanding MCS's advantages, user reliability and data privacy are important issues that may be encountered.

CONCLUSION

To conclude, the 5G security and privacy concerns have grown significantly because of the adoption of numerous smart devices that are not security or privacy vigilance. Therefore, smart devices require an effective privacy and security mechanism for the public during daily operations. Furthermore, it is essential to take privacy and security issues into account at the designing and implementation stages for the fourth-coming smart systems. In this study, an investigation of privacy and security concerns in the implementation of information-centric SCs has been examined. We began by proposing an IoT-based architecture with a brief explanation of every layer, followed by 5G security solutions, and 5G security requirements, and recommended high-tech 5G security from a smart city perspective. Ultimately, a discussion between some unresolved research questions that should be carefully considered when implementing and improving smart city privacy and security. We are more motivated to develop frameworks that facilitate and encamp security and privacy aspects the academia, industries, and manufacturers during design, password, or key management systems need as the technology keeps on advancing.

REFERENCES

Ajtai, M. (2005, May). Representing hard lattices with O (n log n) bits. In *Proceedings of the thirty-seventh annual ACM symposium on Theory of computing* (pp. 94-103). ACM. 10.1145/1060590.1060604

Al-Turjman, F., Zahmatkesh, H., & Shahroze, R. (2022). An overview of security and privacy in smart cities' IoT communications. *Transactions on Emerging Telecommunications Technologies, 33*(3), e3677. doi:10.1002/ett.3677

Alam, T. (2022). Blockchain cities: The futuristic cities driven by Blockchain, big data and internet of things. *GeoJournal, 87*(6), 5383–5412. doi:10.1007/s10708-021-10508-0

Amin, R., Sherratt, R. S., Giri, D., Islam, S. H., & Khan, M. K. (2017). A software agent enabled biometric security algorithm for secure file access in consumer storage devices. *IEEE Transactions on Consumer Electronics, 63*(1), 53–61. doi:10.1109/TCE.2017.014735

Anwar, R. W., & Ali, S. (2022). Smart Cities Security Threat Landscape: A Review. *Computer Information, 41*(2), 405–423.

Aski, V. J., Dhaka, V. S., Kumar, S., & Parashar, A. (2022). IoT Enabled Elderly Monitoring System and the Role of Privacy Preservation Frameworks in e-health Applications. In *Intelligent Data Communication Technologies and Internet of Things.* Springer.

Banafa, A. (2020). IoT Standardization and Implementation Challenges. *IEEE Internet of Things.* IEEE. https://iot.ieee.org/newsletter/july-2016/iot-standardization-and-imple mentation-challenges.html.

Barth, S., Ionita, D., & Hartel, P. (2022). Understanding online privacy—A systematic review of privacy visualizations and privacy by design guidelines. *ACM Computing Surveys, 55*(3), 1–37. doi:10.1145/3502288

Bauspieß, P., Kolberg, J., Drozdowski, P., Rathgeb, C., & Busch, C. (2022). Privacy-Preserving Preselection for Protected Biometric Identification Using Public-Key Encryption with Keyword Search. *IEEE Transactions on Industrial Informatics.*

Bhardwaj, S., & Panda, S. N. (2022). Performance evaluation using RYU SDN controller in software-defined networking environment. *Wireless Personal Communications, 122*(1), 701–723. doi:10.1007/s11277-021-08920-3

Butt, T. A., & Afzaal, M. (2019). Security and privacy in smart cities: issues and current solutions. In *Smart Technologies and Innovation for a Sustainable Future: Proceedings of the 1st American University in the Emirates International Research Conference—Dubai, UAE* 2017 (pp. 317-323). Springer International Publishing. 10.1007/978-3-030-01659-3_37

Carlin, A., Hammoudeh, M., & Aldabbas, O. (2015). Intrusion detection and countermeasure of virtual cloud systems-state of the art and current challenges. *International Journal of Advanced Computer Science and Applications, 6*(6). doi:10.14569/IJACSA.2015.060601

Cavoukian, A. (2009). Privacy by design: The 7 foundational principles. Information and privacy commissioner of Ontario, Canada, 5, 12.

Chakrabarty, S., Engels, D. W., & Thathapudi, S. (2015, October). Black SDN for the Internet of Things. In *2015 IEEE 12th International Conference on Mobile Ad Hoc and Sensor Systems* (pp. 190-198). IEEE. 10.1109/MASS.2015.100

Cui, L., Xie, G., Qu, Y., Gao, L., & Yang, Y. (2018). Security and privacy in smart cities: Challenges and opportunities. *IEEE Access : Practical Innovations, Open Solutions, 6*, 46134–46145. doi:10.1109/ACCESS.2018.2853985

Deebak, B. D., & Fadi, A. T. (2022). A robust and distributed architecture for 5G-enabled networks in the smart blockchain era. *Computer Communications, 181*, 293–308. doi:10.1016/j.comcom.2021.10.015

Eckhoff, D., & Wagner, I. (2017). Privacy in the smart city—Applications, technologies, challenges, and solutions. *IEEE Communications Surveys and Tutorials, 20*(1), 489–516. doi:10.1109/COMST.2017.2748998

Gharaibeh, A., Salahuddin, M. A., Hussini, S. J., Khreishah, A., Khalil, I., Guizani, M., & Al-Fuqaha, A. (2017). Smart cities: A survey on data management, security, and enabling technologies. *IEEE Communications Surveys and Tutorials, 19*(4), 2456–2501. doi:10.1109/COMST.2017.2736886

Goswami, B., & Choudhury, H. (2022). A blockchain-based authentication scheme for 5g-enabled IoT. *Journal of Network and Systems Management, 30*(4), 61. doi:10.1007/s10922-022-09680-6

He, D., Zeadally, S., Kumar, N., & Lee, J. H. (2016). Anonymous authentication for wireless body area networks with provable security. *IEEE Systems Journal*, *11*(4), 2590–2601. doi:10.1109/JSYST.2016.2544805

Hewa, T. M., Kalla, A., Nag, A., Ylianttila, M. E., & Liyanage, M. (2020, October). Blockchain for 5G and IoT: Opportunities and challenges. In *2020 IEEE Eighth International Conference on Communications and Networking* (ComNet) (pp. 1-8). IEEE. 10.1109/ComNet47917.2020.9306082

Hilal, H. A., Hilal, N. A., Hilal, T. A., & Hilal, T. A. (2022). Crowdsensing application on coalition game using GPS and IoT parking in smart cities. *Procedia Computer Science*, *201*, 535–542. doi:10.1016/j.procs.2022.03.069

Jain, S., Gupta, S., Sreelakshmi, K. K., & Rodrigues, J. J. (2022). Fog computing in enabling 5G-driven emerging technologies for development of sustainable smart city infrastructures. *Cluster Computing*, *25*(2), 1–44. doi:10.1007/s10586-021-03496-w

Jun, Y., Craig, A., Shafik, W., & Sharif, L. (2021). Artificial intelligence application in cybersecurity and cyberdefense. *Wireless Communications and Mobile Computing*, *2021*, 1–10. doi:10.1155/2021/3329581

Jun, Y., Craig, A., Shafik, W., & Sharif, L. (2021). Artificial intelligence application in cybersecurity and cyberdefense. *Wireless Communications and Mobile Computing*, *2021*, 1–10. doi:10.1155/2021/3329581

Kelly, D., & Hammoudeh, M. (2018, June). Optimisation of the public key encryption infrastructure for the internet of things. In *Proceedings of the 2nd International Conference on Future Networks and Distributed Systems* (pp. 1-5). ACM. 10.1145/3231053.3231098

Kuadey, N. A. E., Maale, G. T., Kwantwi, T., Sun, G., & Liu, G. (2021). DeepSecure: Detection of distributed denial of service attacks on 5G network slicing—Deep learning approach. *IEEE Wireless Communications Letters*, *11*(3), 488–492. doi:10.1109/LWC.2021.3133479

Li, J., Gan, W., Gui, Y., Wu, Y., & Yu, P. S. (2022, October). Frequent itemset mining with local differential privacy. In *Proceedings of the 31st ACM International Conference on Information & Knowledge Management* (pp. 1146-1155). ACM. 10.1145/3511808.3557327

Li, J., Zhao, Z., & Li, R. (2018). Machine learning-based IDS for software-defined 5G network. *IET Networks*, *7*(2), 53–60. doi:10.1049/iet-net.2017.0212

Li, L., Lu, R., Choo, K. K. R., Datta, A., & Shao, J. (2016). Privacy-preserving-outsourced association rule mining on vertically partitioned databases. *IEEE Transactions on Information Forensics and Security*, *11*(8), 1847–1861. doi:10.1109/TIFS.2016.2561241

Li, S., Da Xu, L., & Zhao, S. (2018). 5G Internet of Things: A survey. *Journal of Industrial Information Integration*, *10*, 1–9. doi:10.1016/j.jii.2018.01.005

Maamar, Z., Baker, T., Sellami, M., Asim, M., Ugljanin, E., & Faci, N. (2018). Cloud vs edge: Who serves the Internet-of-Things better? *Internet Technology Letters*, *1*(5), e66. doi:10.1002/itl2.66

Monreale, A., Rinzivillo, S., Pratesi, F., Giannotti, F., & Pedreschi, D. (2014). Privacy-by-design in big data analytics and social mining. *EPJ Data Science*, *3*(1), 1–26. doi:10.1140/epjds/s13688-014-0010-4

Nyangaresi, V. O. (2022). Terminal independent security token derivation scheme for ultra-dense IoT networks. *Array (New York, N.Y.), 15*, 100210. doi:10.1016/j.array.2022.100210

Park, J. H., Rathore, S., Singh, S. K., Salim, M. M., Azzaoui, A. E., Kim, T. W., & Park, J. H. (2021). A comprehensive survey on core technologies and services for 5G security: Taxonomies, issues, and solutions. *Hum.-Centric Comput. Inf. Sci, 11*(3).

Preuveneers, D., & Joosen, W. (2016). Privacy-enabled remote health monitoring applications for resource constrained wearable devices. In *Proceedings of the 31st Annual ACM Symposium on Applied Computing* (pp. 119-124). ACM. 10.1145/2851613.2851683

Randall, N., Šabanović, S., Milojević, S., & Gupta, A. (2022). Top of the class: Mining product characteristics associated with crowdfunding success and failure of home robots. *International Journal of Social Robotics, 14*(1), 1–15. doi:10.1007/s12369-021-00776-8

Rani, S., Kataria, A., Chauhan, M., Rattan, P., Kumar, R., & Sivaraman, A. K. (2022). Security and privacy challenges in the deployment of cyber-physical systems in smart city applications: State-of-art work. *Materials Today: Proceedings, 62*, 4671–4676. doi:10.1016/j.matpr.2022.03.123

Salahdine, F., Han, T., & Zhang, N. (2023). Security in 5G and beyond recent advances and future challenges. *Security and Privacy, 6*(1), e271. doi:10.1002/spy2.271

Saleem, J., Hammoudeh, M., Raza, U., Adebisi, B., & Ande, R. (2018, June). IoT standardisation: Challenges, perspectives and solution. In *Proceedings of the 2nd international conference on future networks and distributed systems* (pp. 1-9).ACM.

Shafik, W. (2023a). A Comprehensive Cybersecurity Framework for Present and Future Global Information Technology Organizations. In *Effective Cybersecurity Operations for Enterprise-Wide Systems* (pp. 56–79). IGI Global. doi:10.4018/978-1-6684-9018-1.ch002

Shafik, W. (2023b). Cyber Security Perspectives in Public Spaces: Drone Case Study. In Handbook of Research on Cybersecurity Risk in Contemporary Business Systems (pp. 79-97). IGI Global.

Shafik, W. (2023c). *Artificial intelligence and Blockchain technology enabling cybersecurity in telehealth systems. Artificial Intelligence and Blockchain Technology in Modern Telehealth Systems*. IET.

Shafik, W. (2023d). IoT-Based Energy Harvesting and Future Research Trends in Wireless Sensor Networks. Handbook of Research on Network-Enabled IoT Applications for Smart City Services, 282-306.

Shafik, W. (2023e). Making Cities Smarter: IoT and SDN Applications, Challenges, and Future Trends. In Opportunities and Challenges of Industrial IoT in 5G and 6G Networks (pp. 73-94). IGI Global.

Shafik, W. (2024a). *Wearable Medical Electronics in Artificial Intelligence of Medical Things. Handbook of Security and Privacy of AI-Enabled Healthcare Systems and Internet of Medical Things*. CRC Press.

Shafik, W. (2024b). Introduction to ChatGPT. In *Advanced Applications of Generative AI and Natural Language Processing Models* (pp. 1–25). IGI Global.

Shafik, W. (2024c). Artificial intelligence and Blockchain technology enabling cybersecurity in telehealth systems. In Artificial Intelligence and Blockchain Technology in Modern Telehealth Systems (pp. 285-326).

Shafik, W. (2024d). Navigating Emerging Challenges in Robotics and Artificial Intelligence in Africa. In *Examining the Rapid Advance of Digital Technology in Africa* (pp. 124–144). IGI Global. doi:10.4018/978-1-6684-9962-7.ch007

Shafik, W. (2024e). Predicting Future Cybercrime Trends in the Metaverse Era. In *Forecasting Cyber Crimes in the Age of the Metaverse* (pp. 78–113). IGI Global.

Shafik, W., & Kalinaki, K. (2023). Smart City Ecosystem: An Exploration of Requirements, Architecture, Applications, Security, and Emerging Motivations. In Handbook of Research on Network-Enabled IoT Applications for Smart City Services (pp. 75-98). IGI Global.

Shafik, W., & Matinkhah, S. M. (2021). Unmanned aerial vehicles analysis to social networks performance. The *CSI. Journal of Computing Science and Engineering : JCSE, 18*(2), 24–31.

Shafik, W., Matinkhah, S. M., & Shokoor, F. (2022). Recommendation system comparative analysis: internet of things aided networks. *EAI Endorsed Transactions on Internet of Things, 8*(29).

Shafik, W., Matinkhah, S. M., & Shokoor, F. (2023). Cybersecurity in unmanned aerial vehicles: A review. *International Journal on Smart Sensing and Intelligent Systems, 16*(1), 20230012. doi:10.2478/ijssis-2023-0012

Shafik, W., Tufail, A., Liyanage, C. D. S., & Apong, R. A. A. H. M. (2024). Medical Robotics and AI-Assisted Diagnostics Challenges for Smart Sustainable Healthcare. In AI-Driven Innovations in Digital Healthcare: Emerging Trends, Challenges, and Applications (pp. 304-323). IGI Global. doi:10.4018/979-8-3693-3218-4.ch016

Shashidhara, R., Lajuvanthi, M., & Akhila, S. (2022). A secure and privacy-preserving mutual authentication system for global roaming in mobile networks. *Arabian Journal for Science and Engineering, 47*(2), 1435–1446. doi:10.1007/s13369-021-05940-w

Shivraj, V. L., Rajan, M. A., Singh, M., & Balamuralidhar, P. (2015, February). One time password authentication scheme based on elliptic curves for Internet of Things (IoT). In *2015 5th National Symposium on Information Technology: Towards New Smart World (NSITNSW)* (pp. 1-6). IEEE.

Shokoor, F., Shafik, W., & Matinkhah, S. M. (2022). Overview of 5G & beyond security. *EAI Endorsed Transactions on Internet of Things, 8*(30).

Sicari, S., Rizzardi, A., Grieco, L. A., & Coen-Porisini, A. (2015). Security, privacy and trust in Internet of Things: The road ahead. *Computer Networks, 76*, 146–164. doi:10.1016/j.comnet.2014.11.008

Singandhupe, A., La, H. M., & Feil-Seifer, D. (2018). Reliable security algorithm for drones using individual characteristics from an EEG signal. *IEEE Access : Practical Innovations, Open Solutions, 6*, 22976–22986. doi:10.1109/ACCESS.2018.2827362

Sookhak, M., Yu, F. R., & Zomaya, A. Y. (2017). Auditing big data storage in cloud computing using divide and conquer tables. *IEEE Transactions on Parallel and Distributed Systems*, *29*(5), 999–1012. doi:10.1109/TPDS.2017.2784423

Sowmiya, B., & Poovammal, E. (2022). A heuristic K-anonymity based privacy preserving for student management hyperledger fabric blockchain. *Wireless Personal Communications*, *127*(2), 1359–1376. doi:10.1007/s11277-021-08582-1

Ståhlbröst, A., Padyab, A., Sällström, A., & Hollosi, D. (2015). Design of smart city systems from a privacy perspective. *IADIS International Journal on WWW/Internet*, *13*(1), 1-16.

Tan, L., & Wang, N. (2010, August). Future internet: The internet of things. In *2010 3rd international conference on advanced computer theory and engineering (ICACTE)*. IEEE.

Wan, Z., Hazel, J. W., Clayton, E. W., Vorobeychik, Y., Kantarcioglu, M., & Malin, B. A. (2022). Socio-technical safeguards for genomic data privacy. *Nature Reviews. Genetics*, *23*(7), 429–445. doi:10.1038/s41576-022-00455-y PMID:35246669

Wang, Q., Ren, K., Yu, S., & Lou, W. (2011). Dependable and secure sensor data storage with dynamic integrity assurance. [TOSN]. *ACM Transactions on Sensor Networks*, *8*(1), 1–24. doi:10.1145/1993042.1993051

Wang, Y., Wan, J., Guo, J., Cheung, Y. M., & Yuen, P. C. (2017). Inference-based similarity search in randomized montgomery domains for privacy-preserving biometric identification. *IEEE Transactions on Pattern Analysis and Machine Intelligence*, *40*(7), 1611–1624. doi:10.1109/TPAMI.2017.2727048 PMID:28715325

Xu, N., Ding, Y., & Guo, J. (2022). Do Smart City policies make cities more innovative: Evidence from China. *Journal of Asian Public Policy*, *15*(1), 1–17. doi:10.1080/17516234.2020.1742411

Yang, Z., Jianjun, L., Faqiri, H., Shafik, W., Talal Abdulrahman, A., Yusuf, M., & Sharawy, A. M. (2021). Green internet of things and big data application in smart cities development. *Complexity*, *2021*, 1–15. doi:10.1155/2021/4922697

Yu, S., Gu, G., Barnawi, A., Guo, S., & Stojmenovic, I. (2014). Malware propagation in large-scale networks. *IEEE Transactions on Knowledge and Data Engineering*, *27*(1), 170–179. doi:10.1109/TKDE.2014.2320725

Zhang, K., Ni, J., Yang, K., Liang, X., Ren, J., & Shen, X. S. (2017). Security and privacy in smart city applications: Challenges and solutions. *IEEE Communications Magazine*, *55*(1), 122–129. doi:10.1109/MCOM.2017.1600267CM

Chapter 11

Impact of Artificial Intelligence, Machine Learning, and IoT in 5G Wireless Communications on the Smarter World:
A Review

Sumit Kumar
 https://orcid.org/0000-0002-4092-385X
Rajan Mamta Degree College, India

Samta Jain Goyal
Amity University, India

Ipseeta Nanda
Gopal Narayan Singh University, Sasaram, India

Rajeev Goyal
Amity University, India

Chandra Shekhar Azad
National Institute of Technology, Jamshedpur, India

ABSTRACT

With the prompt evolution of the internet, the growth of the data rate is increasing day by day. Most of the current technologies, including 5G, provide high data rate services to handle and process those data. For this reason, machine learning came into its role. Machine learning is quite different from the traditional programming paradigm. Machine learning takes a massive, huge amount of data and results to produce such programs or models used for prediction purposes. The key enabling technologies with 5G are IoT and ML, which are used to change the picture of the real world, change their trends, and explore their applications worldwide. This review chapter starts with relating 5G with the opportunities of machine learning, and its techniques to manage these challenges.

DOI: 10.4018/978-1-6684-9576-6.ch011

INTRODUCTION

There is the major implementation of the machine learning field is Neural Networks (NN). NN is the best way to show that how machine learning works. In General, NN contains three consecutive layers. One is Input Layer; the Second is the Hidden Layer and the Third Layer is the Output Layer. The main element of NN is artificial neurons. At present, 'the internet of things (IoT) has revolutionized based on sensor and their activities. As per today's conditions till the year 2025, almost all IoT-based devices will be used by many people in their day-to-day life. Cyber-physical and device-to-device communication systems (D2D) are the systems these devices are used with. As per the condition these devices are expected to form a major platform for the 5G network paradigm (Cui et al., 2018; Santos et al., 2020, pp 1-34; Kumar et al., 2017, pp 32-52; Jagannath et al., 2019). The landscape of various industries is expected to change drastically due to some of the IoT techniques. The major three amazing trends in the present scenario in terms of technologies are:-

1). The rapid growth of IoT (i.e.), "Internet of Things".
2). The rapid growth of Artificial intelligence (AI)/Machine learning (ML).
3). The rapid growth and demand of 5G for communications.

Now a day's people are transferring manual work to automatic work with smart techniques. Due to adopting new technologies, work has been taken a very little amount of time. This innovation generates new ways for business growth.

Artificial Intelligence (AI)

Artificial Intelligence (AI) refers to design the machine as a human being who understands and reacts according to situations or past experiences.AI is a concept used to perform tasks that or-

Figure 1. Application areas of IoT
(Pathak S 2013)

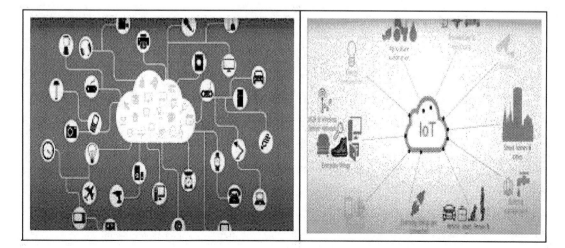

Figure 2. Architecture of Neural Network helps to learn the concept of Machine Learning (https://medium. com/data-science-365/overview-of-a-neural-networks-learning-process-61690a502fa)

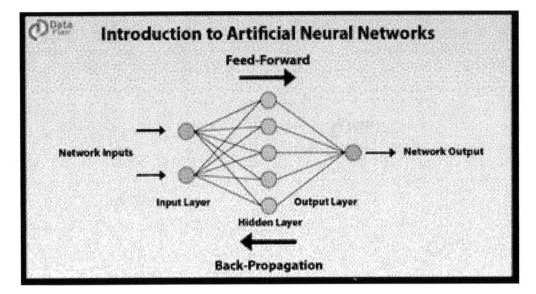

dinarily require human intelligence. Many of these artificial intelligence systems are powered by machine learning, some of them are powered by deep learning and some of them are powered by some logic-like programs. A driverless car has several sensors and actuators to drive the car, to find out the path, shortest, safe path to reach onto the destination. So overall we can say that the AI concept uses mathematics, common sense, neuroscience, psychology, sociology, philosophy, biology, etc. All these information in terms of knowledge feeds into a system to create intelligent or smart agents. These agents are known as efficient engines. These engines help in automating repetitive learning, achieve incredible accuracy in comparison to human calculations, adapts through progressive learning algorithms, analyses more and deeper data using neural networks. These intelligent agents adaptively improve their patience level and they should be able to provide much and more deep understanding and information.While the IoT connects "dumb" devices to the internet, artificial intelligence gives them a "brain." Together, they're capable of changing the world as we know it. In Post-Event processing, Pattern recognition is the process of recognizing patterns by using a machine learning algorithm (Mamdouh et al., 2018, pp 215-218; Bagaa et al., 2020, pp 1-12; Shafin et al., 2019; S. Patnaik, 2020; Hussain et al., 2020, pp 8-10).

Types of Analysis With the Combination of AI and IoT

There is predictive analysis to knowabout what will happen next Then Prescriptive Analysis is used to say about that what should we do.IoT-Sensors sense the acquired data. But that data is valuable or not, this is taken care of through AI- ML techniques. This combination helps us to take appropriate actions on acquired data (C. Technology, 2020).

Figure 3. Role of Artificial Intelligence in IoT
(Phifer L, 2017)

Levels of Artificial Intelligence

There are the following levels of AI with its features (Pagani, 2018, pp 1-17):

- Assisted Intelligence
- Augmented Intelligence
- Autonomous Intelligence

Types of AI Applications

There are mainly two categories of AI. In the first category, they focus on one task i.e. not being able to channelize many tasks at a moment. The other category of AI works on many processes at the same time to mimic human behavior (P. Magazine, 2018).

MACHINE LEARNING

Machine learning is a type of artificial intelligence used by software applications to learn automatically and become more accurate at pretending outcomes (Alsamiri et al., 2019; Mohammadi et al., pp 1-40; Xie et al., 2021).

Types of Machine Learning

There are three types of machine learning:

Figure 4. Application areas for the combination of IoT and ML
(Pathak S, 2013)

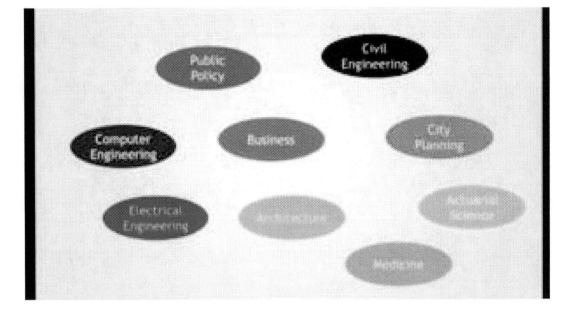

1. Supervised learning
2. Unsupervised/self-learning
3. Reinforcement learning

Seven Steps of Machine Learning for Prediction the Result Based on Acquired Data

STEP-1 Gathering Data

STEP-2 Data Preparation (Training & Evaluation)

STEP-3 Choosing a Model

STEP-4 Training (Training Data gives some model to give prediction results. This result Evaluation (Evaluate the data with some new data)

STEP-5 Hyper parameter Tuning with Learning Rate

STEP-6 Prediction

STEP-7 test and update the parameters of the model)

Future Aspects of AI/ML

Figure 5. Future prospects of AI/ML and IoT based applications

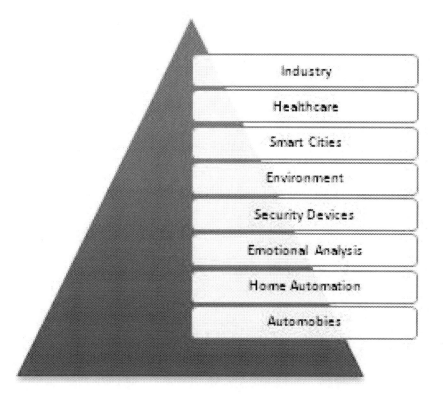

IoT Domain Works With AI/ML

To deal with IoT and AI/ML the following steps are used to carry. First of all, we all need to know (Mohammadi et al., pp 1-40; Xie et al., 2021; Moore, et al., 2020, pp 147-163; Al-dhief et al., 2020):

Step-1. The details of Sensors, how to program the devices.

Step-2. Which network (how to connect the network to share data) and cloud (how the data should store on to the cloud) programming is required

Step-3. UI (User Interface) Programming

Step-4. AI/ML Programming (playing a huge role, where all these things can be made useful)

Step-5. Data structure & Algorithm

Step-6. The optimization process for the time, space, CPU, memory, energy

Figure 6. AI/ML-based IoT applications areas

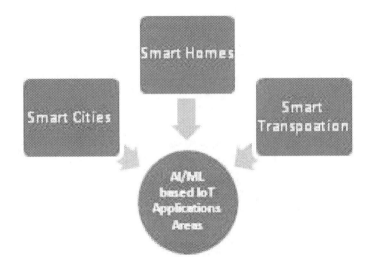

Figure 7. Step by step procedure to deal with IoT based application through ML/AI

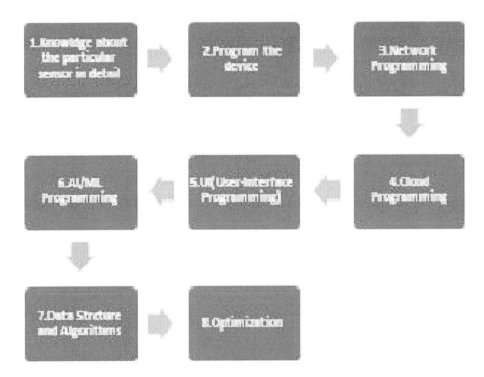

AI/ML-Based IoT Applications Areas

Figure 8. Detailed application areas of smart transportation

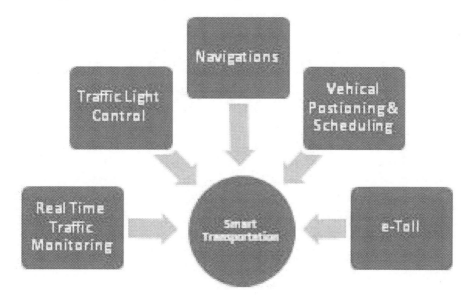

Figure 9. Detailed application areas of smart city

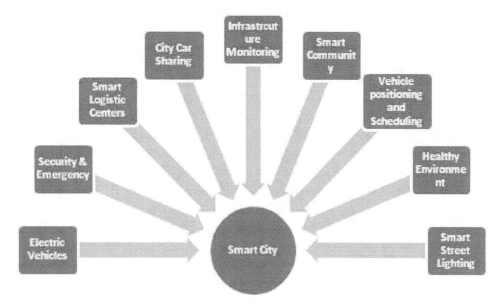

Figure 10. Detailed application areas of smart home

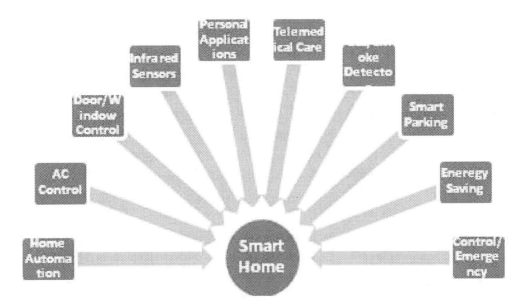

ML and IoT Work Together to get Effective Results in Terms of Output

IoT-based devices are small hardware devices whereas AI/ML techniques play the role of Software or brain for them. There are the following steps for the data analysis to get decisions-

STEP-1 Import data sets
STEP-2 Clean and prepare data for analysis
STEP-3 Manipulate or update data
STEP-4 Summarize the data
STEP-5 Build ML-models

INTERNET OF THINGS (IOT)

The Internet of Things (IoT) describes the network of physical objects which are embedded with sensor software, and other technologies to connect and exchange data with other devices and systems over the internet. The benefits of using IoT is to more productive in terms of time .Through the help of IoT sensors, easy to track the conditions of physical things. The data are transmitted, stored, and can be retrieved at any time. It helps users to save their times in many aspects (Kumar et al., 2017, pp 32-52; Kuzlu et al., 2021). There are numerous and effective benefits of using IoT such as efficient resource utilization, improved security, saving time, minimizing human efforts, etc.

Current IoT Market

Figure 11. Current IoT based market growth
(Rappaport et al., 2014)

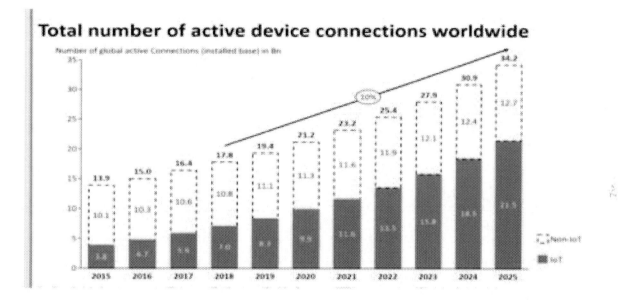

Figure 12. Growth chart of AI in IoT market
(Rossi et al., 2015)

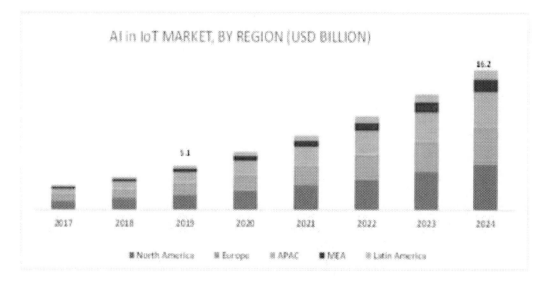

Figure 13. Stakeholders in IoT-based market

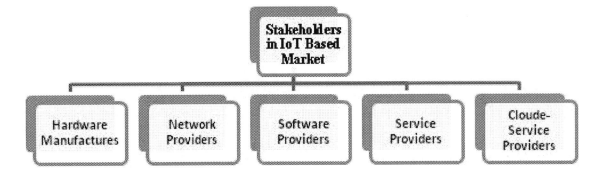

3.2 Challenges With IoT (Kumar et al., 2017, pp 32-52; Jagannath et al., 2019; Pathak S, 2013)

a. Low CPU Capabilities
b. Security of Data
c. Lots of sensors, its cost, its maintenance
d. Generating high frequencies of data

5G-CELLULAR WIRELESS NETWORK TECHNOLOGY (5G)

With the advancement of the new technology, the expectation of the people is growing regarding their mobile and its networkcoverages.5G network will consist of a lot of new, reliable, and affordable features as well. The networking standards of the 5G network will be divided mainly into two types (Rong et al., 2020; Nguyen et al., 2021, pp. 1984–1986; Kusuma et al., 2018, pp. 164–167; Ejaz et al., 2017; Saha et al., 2016, pp 87–112; Zhang et al., 2015, pp 35–41; Pham et al., 2020; Rao et al., 2018, pp: 161–176; Shafi et al., 2017, pp: 1201–1221; Sharma et al., 2020; Shi et al., 2019, pp: 109–116):

1. Non-standalone (NSA)
2. Standalone (SA)

The 5G is used to transmit large number of small cell stations. 5G will expand the mobile ecosystem into new realms with its high speeds, superior reliability, and negligible latency. There are many ways and areas where 5G technology can do much better, faster, and more reliable solutions for societies & industries which are (Rong et al., 2020; Nguyen et al., 2021, pp. 1984–1986; Kusuma et al., 2018, pp. 164–167; Ejaz et al., 2017; Saha et al., 2016, pp 87–112; Zhang et al., 2015, pp 35–41; Pham et al., 2020; Rao et al., 2018, pp: 161–176; Shafi et al., 2017, pp: 1201–1221; Sharma et al., 2020; Shi et al., 2019, pp: 109–116):

- Improving safety and sustainability.
- Smarter electricity grids to reduce carbon emissions effectively

- Smart vehicles to prevent road accidents
- Drones accelerate and support emergency responses

AI improves the capabilities of 5G technology to understand and take actions on input data. 5G Technology uses a fast and low latency connection to provide extremely high quality from the wireless devices just because of its speed. For public safety and infrastructure, smart cities use 5G Technology for convention monitoring, parking sensors, and smart waste management (Rong et al., 2020; Nguyen et al., 2021, pp. 1984–1986; Kusuma et al., 2018, pp. 164–167; Ejaz et al., 2017; Saha et al., 2016, pp 87–112; Zhang et al., 2015, pp 35–41; Pham et al., 2020; Rao et al., 2018, pp: 161–176; Shafi et al., 2017, pp: 1201–1221; Sharma et al., 2020; Shi et al., 2019, pp: 109–116).

CONCLUSION AND FUTURE WORK

In the present era, a huge amount of data is generated due to many advanced internet-based technologies. Machine Learning Algorithms gives solution for processing and these solutions should be embedded with new technologies such as IoT to get much more effective solutions for society's real-time issues.5G Technology turning a future with high-powered connectivity in the communications among the devices and is used to provide a facility for the rapid increase of IoT-based devices.5G networks-based technology help in reliable connections improved accessing at the high speed, best bandwidth range, low latency, and response time.

REFERENCES

Al-dhief, F. T., Member, S., Mu, N., & Abdul, A. (2020). *A Survey of Voice Pathology Surveillance Systems Based on Internet of Things and Machine Learning Algorithms* (Vol. XX). doi:10.1109/ACCESS.2020.2984925

Alsamiri, J., & Alsubhi, K. (2019). Internet of Things Cyber Attacks Detection using. *Machine Learning*, *10*(12).

Bagaa, M., Taleb, T., & Bernabe, J. B. (2020). *for IoT Systems*. IEEE. doi:10.1109/ACCESS.2020.2996214

Cui, L., Yang, S., Chen, F., Ming, Z., Lu, N., & Qin, J. (2018). A survey on application of machine learning for Internet of Things. *International Journal of Machine Learning and Cybernetics*, *9*(8), 1399–1417. Advance online publication. doi:10.1007/s13042-018-0834-5

Ejaz, W., Imran, M., & Jo, M. (2016). *Internet of Things (IoT) in 5G Wireless Communications*. IEEE. . doi:10.1109/ACCESS.2016.2646120

Hussain, F., Hussain, R., Hassan, S. A., & Hossain, E. (2020). Machine Learning in IoT Security. *IEEE Communications Surveys and Tutorials*, *22*(April), 8–10. doi:10.1109/COMST.2020.2986444

Jagannath, J., Polosky, N., & Jagannath, A. (2019). *Machine Learning for Wireless Communications in the Internet of Things : A Comprehensive Survey*. Cornell University. https://arxiv.org/abs/1901.07947

Kusuma, S., & Viswanath, D. K. (2018). IOT And Big Data Analytics In E-Learning : A Technological Perspective and Review. Research Gate.

Kuzlu, M., Fair, C., & Guler, O. (2021). *Discover Internet of Things Role of Artificial Intelligence in the Internet of Things (IoT) cybersecurity.* Discov. Internet Things. . doi:10.1007/s43926-020-00001-4

Mamdouh, M., Elrukhsi, M. A. I., & Khattab, A. (2018). Securing the Internet of Things and Wireless Sensor Networks via Machine Learning : A Survey. *Int. Conf. Comput. Appl.*, (pp. 215–218). IEEE. 10.1109/COMAPP.2018.8460440

Mohammadi, M., Member, G. S., Al-fuqaha, A., & Member, S. (2018). Deep Learning for IoT Big Data and Streaming Analytics. *Survey (London, England)*, *X*(X), 1–40. doi:10.1109/COMST.2018.2844341

Moore, S. J., Nugent, C. D., Zhang, S., & Cleland, I. (2020). IoT reliability : A review leading to 5 key research directions. *CCF Trans. Pervasive Comput. Interact.*, *2*(3), 147–163. doi:10.1007/s42486-020-00037-z

Nguyen, V., Duong, T. Q., & Vien, Q. (2021). Editorial : Emerging Techniques and Applications for 5G Networks and Beyond, (pp. 1984–1986). Research Gate.

Pagani, S. (2018). S. M. P. D, A. Jantsch, and S. Member, "Machine Learning for Power, Energy, and Thermal Management on Multi-core Processors. *Survey (London, England)*, *0070*(JULY), 1–17. doi:10.1109/TCAD.2018.2878168

Pathak, S. (2013). *Evolution in generations of cellular mobile communication.* Master of Science in Cyber Law and Information Security. https://medium.com/data-science-365/overview-of-a-neural-networks-learning-process-61690a502fa

Pham, Q., Fang, F., Ha, V. N., Piran, M. J., Le, M., Le, L. B., Hwang, W.-J., & Ding, Z. (2020). A survey of multi-access edge computing in 5G and beyond: Fundamentals, technology integration, and state-of-the-art. *IEEE Access : Practical Innovations, Open Solutions*, *8*, 116974–117017. doi:10.1109/ACCESS.2020.3001277

Phifer, L. (2017) What's the diference between licensed and unlicensed wireless? *TechTarget.* https://searchnetworking.techtarget.com/answer/Whats-the-difference-between-licensed-and-unlicensed-wireless

Rao, S. K., & Prasad, R. (2018). Impact of 5G technologies on smart city implementation. *Wireless Personal Communications*, *100*(1), 161–176. doi:10.1007/s11277-018-5618-4

Rappaport, T. S., Daniels, R. C., Heath, R. W., & Murdock, J. N. (2014). Introduction. In *Millimeter wave wireless communication*. Pearson Education.

Rong, B., Han, S., Kadoch, M., Chen, X., & Jara, A. (2020). Integration of 5G Networks and Internet of Things for Future Smart City. Hindawi. doi:10.1155/2020/2903525

Rossi, R., & Hirama, I. L. (2015). Characterizing big data management. *Issues Inf Sci Inf Technol*, *12*, 165–180.

Saha, R. K., Saengudomlert, P., & Aswakul, C. (2016). Evolution towards 5G mobile networks—A survey on enabling technologies. *Engineering Journal (New York)*, *20*(1), 87–112. doi:10.4186/ej.2016.20.1.87

Santos, G. L., Endo, P. T., Sadok, D., & Kelner, J. (2020). When 5G Meets Deep Learning. *Algorithms*, *13*(9), 1–34. doi:10.3390/a13090208

Shafi, M., Molisch, A. F., Smith, P. J., Haustein, T., Zhu, P., De Silva, P., Tufvesson, F., Benjebbour, A., & Wunder, G. (2017). 5G: a tutorial overview of standards, trials, challenges, deployment, and practice. *IEEE Journal on Selected Areas in Communications*, *35*(6), 1201–1221. doi:10.1109/JSAC.2017.2692307

ShafinR.LiuL.ChandrasekharV.ChenH.ReedJ.ZhangJ. (2019). *Artificial intelligence-enabled cellular networks: a critical path to beyond-5G and 6G*. arXiv 1907.07862. doi:10.1109/MWC.001.1900323

Sharma, S. K., Woungang, I., Anpalagan, A., & Chatzinotas, S. (2020). Toward tactile internet in beyond 5G era: Recent advances, current issues, and future directions. *IEEE Access : Practical Innovations, Open Solutions*, *8*, 56948–56991. doi:10.1109/ACCESS.2020.2980369

Shi, Y., Han, Q., Shen, W., & Zhang, H. (2019). Potential applications of 5G communication technologies in collaborative intelligent manufacturing. *IET Collaborative Intelligent Manufacturing*, *1*(4), 109–116. doi:10.1049/iet-cim.2019.0007

Xie, F., Wei, D., & Wang, Z. (2021). Traffic analysis for 5G network slice based on machine learning. *EURASIP Journal on Wireless Communications and Networking*, *2021*(1), 108. doi:10.1186/s13638-021-01991-7

Zhang, Q., & Fitzek, F. H. P. (2015). Mission critical IoT communication in 5G. In *Future access enablers for ubiquitous and intelligent infrastructures* (Vol. 159, pp. 35–41). Springer International Publishing. doi:10.1007/978-3-319-27072-2_5

Chapter 12
Measures and Preventions of Cyber Policies in Smart Cities

Dipti Chauhan

https://orcid.org/0000-0003-1665-7587

Department of Artificial Intelligence & Data Science, Prestige Institute of Engineering Management and Research, Indore, India

Jay Kumar Jain

https://orcid.org/0000-0002-9590-0006

Department of Mathematics, Bioinformatics and Computer Applications, Bhopal, India

ABSTRACT

Smart cities are gradually becoming a reality rather than a distant vision. Governments, companies, and everyday people are using technology more and more these days to boost productivity at work and at home. On the one hand, smart cities have enacted a number of modifications in an effort with the goal of revolutionizing people's lives. On the other side, while smart cities offer improved quality of life and more convenience, there are also increased hazards to cyber security, including data leaks and malicious cyberattacks. As smart cities are evolving with more connected, as well as enhanced digital infrastructures becoming more sophisticated, these services will become increasingly exposed to cyber intrusions. Cities can only be as strong as their weakest link, and even the tiniest flaws can be used to deadly advantage. Governments must invest more money in cyber security and threat reduction as a result. In this proposed chapter we will be discussing about the measures need to be taken for the development of Smart city and what are the preventions of cyber policies in smart cities.

INTRODUCTION

The Indian government's daring new project, the Smart Cities Mission, aims to boost economic growth and enhance peoples' quality of life by promoting local development and using technology to provide intelligent outcomes for citizens. A smart city is an urbanized area where several sectors collaborate to produce sustainable results through analysis of contextual real-time information shared among sector-

DOI: 10.4018/978-1-6684-9576-6.ch012

specific information and operational technology systems. In order to boost the city's collective intelligence, it connects the social, business, and physical infrastructures as well as the information technology and information infrastructure (Solanki, Patel, and Doshi, 2019). By 2024, 1.3 billion smart city wide-area network connections are anticipated, according to ABI Research. The cybersecurity infrastructure investment forecast for the same year, according to the same study, was 135 billion dollars. This may seem like a lot of money, but just 44% of it will be spent to protect the transportation, water, health care, energy, and public safety sectors. It's only $59.4 billion, after all. Despite the fact that this is merely an estimate, it is insufficient in light of the importance of those regions. In fact, the ABI Research recommended that the state proclaim municipal cybersecurity's future to be "extremely gloomy", this can be highly applicable in smart cities where a lot of infrastructure development is taking place.

The Smart Communities Mission aims to promote cities that offer basic infrastructure, a respectable standard of living for its residents, a clean and sustainable environment, and the application of "Smart" Solutions. In order to produce a repeatable model that will serve as a guide for other aspirant cities, the focus is on sustainable and equitable growth. A daring new project is the government's Smart Cities Mission. In order to spur the creation of comparable Smart Cities in other areas and portions of the country, it is aimed to provide models that can be applied both inside and outside the Smart City. A smart city's core infrastructure components would include the following facilities as illustrated in table-1

A list of Smart Solutions is provided below as an illustration in figure-1. This is not an exhaustive list, and cities are free to add additional applications.

Smart cities are vast, complex, and greater reliance on technology solutions that face a plethora of technological, financial, political, and societal factors (Al-Saidi and Zaidan, 2020). Some of the issues

Table 1. Infrastructure elements in smart city

Sufficient water supply	Sanitation, including solid waste management	Affordable housing, especially for the poor	e-Governance and citizen participation,	Safety and security of citizens, especially women, children and the elderly
Electricity supply in all areas	Efficient urban mobility and public transport	Robust IT connectivity and digitalization	Sustainable environment	Education & Healthcare

Figure 1. Smart city solutions

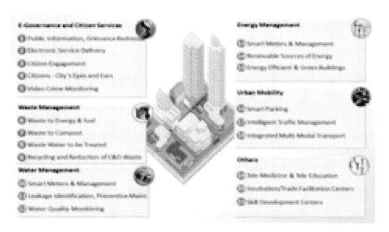

and challenges that smart cities face are economic and investment issues, individuals' ever-changing needs, stakeholder co - operation, user-friendly jointing, security and safety (Aghajani and Ghadimi, 2018). Smart cities can be smarter in six ways: smart administration, creative individuals, smart economic system, infrastructure, smart environment, and intelligent transportation (Razmjoo et al., 2021). Smart cities met the needs of businesses, citizens, and institutions by providing appropriate and efficient services. Urban services can be expanded in the following areas: environment, transportation, health, tourism, energy management, and home safety (Vitunskaite et al., 2019). Despite the benefits of smart cities for citizens, businesses, the environment, and so on, these cities are vulnerable to a wide range of cyber-security threats, making security maturity difficult to achieve (Atitallah et al., 2020). In a smart city, a vulnerable action by an individual or organization can put the entire city at risk (Zhou et al., 2021). This complicated city is also a significant challenge for digital court investigations. Data protection from attacks and malicious behavior is part of ensuring security in a smart city (Sengan et al., 2021). The software and technology for smart cities are rarely cyber-secure according to vendors. Therefore, utilizing such unsecure items puts the system at risk of being hacked, having bogus data added to it, and being stopped. In addition to cyber security, the privacy of citizens and their relationships with the government are also issues. The usage of this technology by consumers will be questioned by the potential for user privacy invasion and the absence of cyber security in smart cities.

There is no denying that the idea of smart cities has the potential to raise our standard of living. To ensure safety, security, and data privacy, organizations that are or will be in charge of designing and constructing smart cities must overcome a variety of obstacles. This is challenging to accomplish since smart cities are a special amalgamation of cyber hazards that must all be taken into account throughout the design phase. The following list includes some of the more serious cyber security issues linked to the difficulties facing smart cities:

The idea of smart cities isn't far off any more; it's actually getting closer. In order to boost productivity and efficiency at home and at work, governments, businesses, and individuals are embracing technology more and more frequently these days. As public expectations rise and urban populations grow, it is anticipated that the pace of development and the need for innovation will not slow down (Campisi et al., 2021).

1. Providing safety-critical services will include smart cities: These services must be provided in a way that is "fail safe" (i.e., safeguards people from harm in the event of a disruption) and guarantees high availability.
2. Sensitive data volumes and extensive sharing necessitate strong data management and protection measures in smart cities.
3. Environments that are highly networked but distributed: Security measures are needed to reduce the risk of targeted cyberattacks on the infrastructure of smart cities.

Cyber Security in Smart Cities

Cities need to adopt new smart technologies to become smart. Every new technology or urban system gives a new opportunity to cyber attackers. For example, many communications between traffic control systems and traffic lights in intelligent traffic control systems take place without any encryption or authentication, allowing the attacker to modify or forge data. One of the most important attacks on the smart grid is the denial of service through channel congestion, computational flooding of equipment with low computing power (such as smart meters), distributed denial of service to SCADA, or delaying a time-critical message that may cause widespread shutdown. Forgery of data from various sensors is another potential threat in the urban area; For example, forging sensors to detect earthquakes, floods, shootings, etc. can cause erroneous warnings and cause public fear. Eavesdropping on consumer data reported from a smart building to a smart meter by an attacker is a major risk to customer privacy. In addition, forging a customer identity by an attacker to remotely control building equipment can cause various damages to the customer.

High dependence on the information network certainly exposes the smart grid to possible vulnerabilities related to communications and grid equipment. In traditional power grids, grid control systems were kept isolated from insecure environments such as the Internet. However, in the smart grid, cyber-attacks on the grid infrastructure can be easily carried out from different parts of the infrastructure. For example, an attacker does not need to access enclosed sites or systems (such as generators, substations, command centers, etc.) to damage the power delivery process. An attacker can easily launch an attack from anywhere on the smart grid. Malicious intrusion into the grid will have various severe consequences for the smart grid. These consequences include leaks of customer information, sequences of failures such as massive shutdowns, and failure of generators and infrastructure. The smart distribution grid is a set of new technologies whose main purpose is to modernize the electricity distribution grid by integrating telecommunication systems and information technology in it. Smart distribution grid information infrastructure consists of a set of software and databases. Smart grid information infrastructure software needs to communicate with each other in order to function properly and coordinate. Millions of vital equipment is used in smart grid, and this equipment is related to SCADA server. Cyber-attacks on SCADA systems such as STUXNET are rigid threats to that system. Currently, the Open-Source Vulnerability Database contains 1096 vulnerabilities related to industrial control systems. Table 2 describes the security threats of this subsystem.

One of the security challenges of smart buildings is privacy breaches. User privacy is a major concern in the smart grid. To optimize smart grid performance and maximize user benefits, high-frequency user power consumption data is transferred from users' smart meters to other smart grid entities. This compromises user privacy. Sensitive information about the user may be disclosed, such as the user's power consumption patterns, the type of electrical equipment used, whether the building is empty or full, etc. In addition, traces left by electric vehicle charges can be used by various entities such as charging stations and suppliers to profile the consumption and location of electric vehicles and violate the privacy of users. Furthermore, by eavesdropping the attacker may obtain private information about the client and violate privacy. Another security challenge of smart buildings is change or repeats the message. An attacker could challenge the security of a smart building by changing or repeating various messages. An attacker could change messages containing smart meter measurement data. Since measurement data is used for a variety of purposes (such as managing power flows in the grid, planning future grid development, building new generation capacity, and billing), manipulation of valid data can cause financial losses to smart grid entities and undermine grid stability. An attacker could insert new consumption messages or repeat old consumption messages of a device into the smart meter and impose a financial charge on the customer for energy that has not been consumed. The customer sells electricity to the grid by installing distributed energy sources in the building if needed. It also imports energy from the smart grid by using an electric vehicle in an emergency to protect the grid from overload breakdowns. Any message sent from the smart grid to the smart building can be manipulated by the attacker and cause large-scale instability of the smart grid. The malicious customer can change the message containing the building consumption data from the smart meter to the electricity company and refuse to pay for electricity consumption. Changing the messages containing dynamic electricity price signals from the electricity market to the customer causes receiving wrong prices from the customer and as a result inappropriate decisions for when to use high-consumption electrical appliances by the customer and finally impose a financial burden on the customer and increase load on the smart grid. In addition, an attacker could act as a smart meter and report incorrect amounts of energy consumption to the smart grid, and incorrectly request/enter energy signals to be distributed to energy sources and electric vehicles, or receive signals from the smart grid. The attacker can also position himself as a customer and remotely control the building's electrical equipment. In the impersonation of the device by the attacker, the customer makes a mistake in remote control and does not control the considered device. Fig. 2 shows the basic items of the security challenges of smart buildings.

The types of security challenges in a smart transportation system can be divided into suspend message, fake information, denial of service, forgery of identity, eavesdropping, and hardware manipulation. Fake information occurs when information sent by an attacker, such as certificates, alerts, security messages, and IDs, is incorrect. The attacker alters, falsifies, or repeats data to mislead other drivers. Denial of service occurs when attackers send large volumes of irrelevant messages, clogging the communication channel and consuming computing resources of other nodes. The purpose of this attack type is to disable the case network of a vehicle that can have vital consequences in the event of an emergency. Also, forgery of identity occurs when an attacker pretends to be an authenticated vehicle or a roadside unit. Attackers use malicious IDs that have been hacked to inject malicious information into the network and mislead other vehicles. Eavesdropping also occurs when an attacker in a car or on a fake roadside unit eavesdrops on wireless communications in a car network. An attacker could gain access to the confidential data of the target vehicles, including the real identity of the drivers, their priorities or even their credit card information, and seriously infringe on the drivers privacy. Message suspension occurs as an attacker holds messages for a while before sending. An attacker electively holds messages packets from the system that may contain vital data for specific recipients. One purpose of attack could be to forbid insurance authorities from being aware of the accident involving the attacking vehicle or to avoid reporting the accident to roadside access points. Eventually, hardware manipulation occurs when

Table 2. Security threats to power grid subsystems

Type of security threat	Description
Denial of Service	One of the main goals of the attackers is to disrupt the monitoring and control activities of the SCADA Center. Traffic flood attacks from various systems connected to SCADA can prevent the service of this center. Attackers try to disrupt the smart grid by consuming computing resources and bandwidth.
Forgery of identity	An attacker can disrupt the identity of any of the control and monitoring devices. For example, if an attacker poses as an intelligent electronic monitoring device, it can send fake open/close messages to the switches, disrupting the subscribers' power protection and power outage systems.
Delay	Some of the messages exchanged in the transmission and distribution system are time-critical and must be transmitted within a short period of time (3 to 500 ms). It is enough for the attacker to delay sending these messages a little, to have the effect of denial of service attack.
Distort the message	Targeted change of messages sent to the control centers causes incorrect view of the grid status to the control center. As a result, incorrect control messages are sent to various devices and the normal operation of the grid is disturbed.
Eavesdropping	Eavesdropping on information sent from various equipment and sensors to the SCADA center gives the attacker sufficient knowledge of the power situation and provides the potential for further attacks such as change or repetition.

Figure 2. Basic items of the security challenges of smart buildings

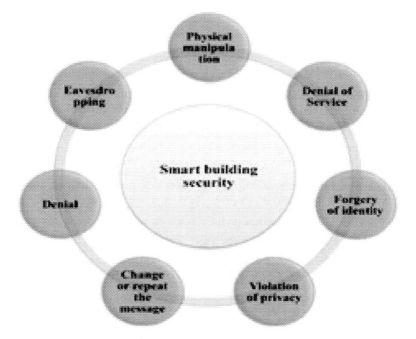

in-vehicle sensors or roadside unit hardware are tampered with by attackers. For example, an attacker could manipulate traffic lights in front of him that are always green.

Security vulnerabilities in smart healthcare technologies will have different outcomes for sick. Security vulnerabilities in service procurers can result in legal penalties, financial losses, or loss of reputation. Since wearable medical devices determine health status of an individual they can easily violate a person's privacy. In addition, because the device is accompanied by the patient, the capability to show the system can easily determine the absence or presence of a person in a specific place and violate the spatial privacy of the user. Moreover, by tracking the connections between the source and <u>destination nodes</u>, it is easy to locate patients and service providers and thus violate their location. Today, most applications of private health have been expanded for tablets and smartphones. Conservation approaches are mostly not sufficient for these applications. Many <u>smartphone applications</u> send information to third parties without the user's notice, including the unique device ID, phone location, and even personal information such as age and gender. <u>Malware</u> may access a variety of information, including text messages, calls, videos, and call history, as part of a health care program. Malware can forward fake messages to people in the contact list or record audio. On the other hand, online health-based social networks are widely used by users. There are several vulnerabilities in various components of these social networks including client side code, server side code, web server, etc. These vulnerabilities allow an attacker to perform various attacks, including stealing a user's session, changing a website, publishing a worm, accessing unauthorized resources, stealing an ID, etc. The communication channel that connects the nodes may be implemented by physical media and various routing and communication protocols. The physical layer of the network must be resistant to a variety of attacks, including congestion, eavesdropping, and blocking. Most communications between monitoring devices, body sensors, and medical care providers are wireless. Therefore, security issues of wireless communications in medical care networks are also raised. Bluetooth, for example, which is widely used in medical applications, is prone to man-in-the-middle attacks and <u>battery discharge</u>. Finally, an attacker could exploit vulnerabilities in the hardware of medical devices to launch attacks.

As opposed to the flaws of a single technology or system, it is obvious that many issues relate to the interoperability of several organizations and technologies, which means that a large portion of the "problem" is not physically present. In order to provide the guardrails required to ensure that the likelihood and impact of key security risks are addressed, while also allowing government and local authorities the flexibility to tailor their approach specifically to given circumstances, a principles-based approach to securing their design is required. It is essential to address these issues up front to avoid having to implement security controls later on, which is less efficient and frequently more expensive (Ghazal et al., 2021). The rest of the paper is organized as follows- Section 1 is the introduction of the paper, Section 2 discusses about the Protection of Smart Cities from Cyber Security threats, Section 3 discusses about the Vulnerabilities in the Cyber World, Section 4 is discussion about the Factors affecting influence cyber risk in smart cities, Section 5 discusses about the status of work done in this area, Section 6 explains about the Smart City Security Solutions, Section 7 explains about the Best Cyber Security Practices in Smart Cities, Section 8 focuses on the Security Challenges in Smart Cities, Section 9 Concludes the paper.

PROTECTION OF SMART CITIES FROM CYBER SECURITY THREATS

Government entities can follow the appropriate steps to establish digitally secured smart city initiatives:

Every month, millions of pieces of malware are created, as well as computer security like scamming and ransom will become more prevalent in the coming years. As a result, governments should be aware of security vulnerabilities and identify which are even more likely to be dangerous to smart urban cities. Government agencies can work with cyber security specialists to better understand the anatomy of cyberattacks and build mitigation techniques for this goal (Cheng and Wang, 2022). As a result, government agencies may devise plans for dealing with various sorts of cyber risks and take the required precautions to avoid them.2

Developing policies that safeguard data security and privacy is one of the most effective approaches to construct a cyber-secure smart city (Konstantinou, 2021). Urban areas are coming up in different places, including the United States, Europe, Singapore, Australia, among many other places, have established successful cyber security policies to address cyber security concerns. With the correct laws and policies in place cities that are smart have the ability to oversee the use of IoT, AI, and Big Data are examples of modern technology that can be used, as well as prepare for cyber threats (Chauhan and Jain, 2019). These policies should be updated on a regular basis to keep up with changing technologies, cyber dangers, and public perception.

Two-factor authentication and authorization is required for online services such as digital identity, management of water resources, energy management, transit apps, and surveillance systems. To authenticate a user's identity, two-factor authentication comprises employing a username and password authentication, along with a biometric input or an OTP (one-time password). Governments can utilise this mechanism for authentication to get beyond the limitations of ordinary username and password with special authentication. As a result, governments have the ability to utilize two-factor authentication to prevent unauthorised access to essential services and sensitive data, opening the path for cyber-secure smart cities to emerge.

Encrypting data is one of the most effective ways to keep information safe. Encryption can be used to protect confidential files by constructing a cryptographic hash code which could only be only be confirmed with the public key of an authorised user. Unauthorized access to encrypted data prevents an attacker from decrypting, seeing, or changing the data's contents (William et al., 2022). As a result, data encryption can aid governments and citizens in safeguarding sensitive information.

Educating leaders and citizens is another crucial part of creating a cyber-secure smart city. By educating citizens, governments may ensure that they can recognise phishing emails, viruses, and unethical internet habits and execute mitigation techniques by educating them. Governments can also educate citizens on online and offline activities that can help them protect themselves against cyber-attacks (Turan, 2021). In this approach, citizens will be able to stop computer hackers at their source.

Besides these initiatives, government agencies and network security specialists will need to build automated cyber-attack prevention and mitigation systems. Creating such ways to automate and many other cyber risks, on the other hand can indeed be time-consuming and inconvenient and costly. Additionally, as cyber criminals develop more sophisticated attacks, government entities will need to use modern technologies like AI and blockchain to create cyber-secure smart cities.

VULNERABILITIES IN THE CYBER WORLD

In a variety of ways, smart cities are vulnerable to cyber attacks. APTs (Advanced Persistent Threats) are among the most deadly threats. These threats rely on a combination of attacks to impair city services, with malware and "zero-day" software vulnerabilities frequently used. Internet of Things (IoT) devices are extremely vulnerable, and while it is easy to patch any exposed areas, hackers can do irreversible damage. This damage may need the repair of both physical and digital infrastructure. Here are a few examples of assaults that could cause harm to smart city infrastructure.

Data theft is the most well-known type of cybercrime. Hackers have the ability to break into data banks and obtain Personally Identifiable Information (PII) (Edwards, 2021). Smart city infrastructure is especially vulnerable, as hackers have been known to steal personal information from public payment systems, with disastrous results.

One of the most sinister forms of cybercrime is device hijacking. Attackers can take control of a device and use it to intercept a process by exploiting security flaws. Street signs and traffic signals are especially susceptible.

A man-in-the-middle (MITM) attack happens when a hacker intercepts communication between two devices and pretends to be the sender, transmitting bogus data to cause havoc (Pakhare, Krishnan, and Charniya, 2021). For example, A hacker could obtain access to a mobility platform and report delays in public transportation, allowing more people to drive to work, resulting in an inflow of traffic that can bring a city to a halt.

DDoS (Distributed Denial of Service) attacks are straightforward. By flooding a system with requests, a hacker can disable a service for those who require it. City systems will fail to support their citizens if real-life users are unable to access a service.

All of the aforementioned can be used to pay a ransom to a city. Hackers, sometimes known as hacktivists, utilise them to compromise a system or expose sensitive information until particular demands are met (Falco and Rosenbach, 2022). If the ransom is paid, it will set a dangerous precedent.

Physical power can also be utilised to compromise a complicated network. Physical damage to just one component can generate a chain reaction of damage since many systems rely on complicated operations and data from a network of sensors.

These are just a few examples of how evil actors can target smart cities. The Harvard Business Review was correct when they stated that "smart cities are going to be a security nightmare." It isn't all doom and gloom, either (Nasif, Othman, and Sani, 2021). Cities can reduce security concerns to a minimum if the necessary preparations are taken and local leaders act carefully.

FACTORS AFFECTING INFLUENCE CYBER RISK IN SMART CITIES

The evolution of smart cities is taking place on a global scale. These are brought about by developments in information technology, which while they open up new economic and social possibilities also put our security and privacy expectations in jeopardy. With the help of technology like smartphones, people are already connected. In many cities, smart appliances, security systems, and energy meters are in use. The "Internet of Things" is currently on its way to fully connecting homes, cars, public spaces, and other social systems (Jain and Chauhan, 2021). For all of these potentially interconnected systems, standards are developing. They will result in life quality enhancements that have never been seen before. New networked systems for monitoring, controlling, and automating are being added to city infrastructures and services to take use of them. Both public and private intelligent transportation will have access to a web of interconnected data, ranging from GPS location to weather and traffic updates.

Three elements are shown in Figure 3 as potential cyber risks in an ecosystem of smart cities (Deloitte, 2019): It is helpful to look into each of these variables in more detail in order to start managing the cyber risk landscape.

This phenomenon rapidly broadens the range of cyber threats while also enabling cities to monitor and control technical systems via remote cyber operations. In smart cities, it might be difficult to distinguish between the real and online worlds. Both operational technology (OT) systems for monitoring events, processes, and devices and information technology (IT) systems for data-centric computing are used to integrate people, processes, and locations in this context (Martínez et al., 2021). Because of this convergence, cities may now manage and control technology systems through remote cyber operations. This convergence, where various edge devices may present cyber threat vectors, exponentially increases the risk of bad actors penetrating the system and interfering with ground operations. The proliferation of IoT devices has given attackers a wide range of access points through which they may now penetrate a city's infrastructure and take advantage of the corresponding vulnerabilities.

Companies/Organizations pursuing digital transformation frequently have a need for the integration of digital technology with existing systems, which can present difficult problems and hazards. The ecosystem for smart cities is plagued by hidden security vulnerabilities as a result of these issues, which also include uneven security policies and processes and diverse technological platforms. This problem is made worse by the fact that more and more cities are adopting IoT technologies, but only as retrofits. Large, well-established gas and water networks within a city, for instance, have widely used sensors. These sensors need to be a part of a bigger network in order for the data to be gathered and evaluated centrally. These sensors do, however, contain very basic security measures. Retrofitting might not be a practical option in the long term because many gadgets might stop being able to accommodate improvements on a physical level. The absence of widely recognized standards controlling the operation of IoT enabled devices

Figure 3. Potential cyber risks in an ecosystem of smart cities

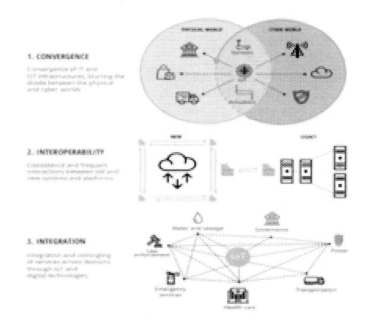

presents another difficulty. Typically, city departments and agencies use sensor technology from many vendors, which produce data in various forms and employ various communication protocols (Chauhan, Jain, and Sharma, 2016). In such circumstances, establishing interoperability might be challenging, and cities might have to choose between security and interoperability. Every additional device that is added to an IoT ecosystem expands its attack surface or provides new opportunities.

Integration of diverse city services and supporting infrastructural facilities: This blending of services and systems gives cities the chance to offer new services and increase efficiencies, but it also presents a unique set of obstacles. A problem in one service area might easily spread to other sectors due to the increasing levels of integration, connectivity, and data sharing, which could possibly cause extensive and catastrophic disruptions. Cities must also re-evaluate their legal obligations, make sense of their numerous security precautions, and deal with concerns regarding data usage and ownership. Additionally, the privacy of residents may be impacted by the misuse of data held across several systems. One common approach is to hide or remove personal identifiers from data. The tools and strategies used by malevolent attackers to compare several datasets and re-identify a person, however, are growing more complex. Therefore, a breach that affects numerous systems and datasets might cause major privacy issues for cities. In the upcoming years, cyber risk will continue to change as many cities combine a range of services and infrastructure, linking even more data, systems, and devices.

LITERATURE REVIEW

Researchers have generally examined cyber security concerns and dangers to users' privacy in smart cities from diverse points of view. The most significant of these are highlighted below.

Infrastructure security was highlighted as an important component on information and data security in smart cities by AlDairi (2017) in their extensive evaluation of research on significant security concerns and contemporary solutions. The advantages of urban intelligence come with several hazards and vulnerabilities in the physical-cyber substructure. Numerous security vulnerabilities exist in the primary physical-cyber systems that affect urban infrastructure, such as the delivery of electricity and water, as well as streets, buildings, etc. Cameras, communication networks, building management systems, and transportation management systems are just a few of these parts and systems.

Ijaz et al. (2016) has separated commercial privacy issues from communication privacy issues. Eavesdropping, denial of service, malicious manipulation and attacks, channel attacks, detection, and secondary usage were among the difficulties to communication privacy. In addition, scams and attacks on data integrity were presenting company privacy challenges. Arabo (2015) looked into the purposes and difficulties of cyber-security for linked smart buildings' smart devices. He researched some of the historical contexts around the creation and desire for interconnecting smart gadgets to provide users various capabilities. Then he demonstrated that despite their advantages, these technologies can pose risks and difficulties. Finally, he covered concerns about cyber-security relating to connected smart buildings and smart devices. In that study, the primary problems facing smart buildings were determined to be information theft, manipulation of data, loss of data, and viruses. Thing (2014) looked into the possibility of already-existing global smart cities as well as any security issues or obstacles in their key locations. He talked about the possibilities utilizing cyber security to build a smart, secure, and safe city. He listed the dangers to the security and difficulties that the smart city's key industries are facing, including those in banking, healthcare, governance, energy, and general security.

Khatoun and Zeadally (2017) analyzed new plans for the smart city and explained the fundamental concepts of smart city design. They explored several solutions, ideas, and standards connected to these concerns applications after describing numerous privacy subjects and security vulnerabilities in smart cities. Additionally, they looked at the major difficulties that smart cities face from the viewpoints of the cyber-security architecture of smart cities as well as security and privacy issues in various smart city components.

To maintain cyber-security and privacy in smart cities, Alibasic et al. (2017) suggested three architecture and use procedures for encrypted communications, access privileges, authorization, and software updates when working on new developments, manual and ensure security cancellation in all urban systems, and creation of operational plans and procedures to handle cyber-attacks. Among the most useful concepts for smart city cyber-security was offered by Cerrudo, Hasbini, and Russell (2015). In that research, infrastructures were given recommendations for selecting and evaluating technology connected to smart cities. Their research focused on offering appropriate evaluation and testing approaches for choosing these technologies and associated providers.

Based on six deep learning classifications, Chen, Wawrzynski, and Lv (2021) offered an overview of the cyber security options. They discussed the prospective research areas in cyber-security. The multi-view ensemble method that Fard et al. (2020) suggested integrated the results of individual classifiers. Their research changed a cheap, lazy method of threat hunting using different points.

Habibzadeh et al. (2019) came to the conclusion that security flaws could be created by smart city applications. Additionally, system and governmental agencies were active in eliminating security flaws. Smart cities could be regarded as a level of security. Said and Tolba (2021) offered a deep learning model that predicts the performance of IoT communication systems using a dynamic neural network technique. They discovered that the strategy significantly improved sustainable smart cities and removed IoT communication system flaws.

In Khan et al. (2021) the prediction and absorption of traffic information, authors presented a mixed deep learning approach. The results revealed improvements in accuracy, time, and errors. In Ghiasi et al. (2021) the Hilbert-Huang transform method was looked into as a way to stop fake data injection assaults in the micro-grid. They used block-chain ledger technology in their study of the current and voltage signals in sensors. They discovered that the suggested strategy might improve the micro-data grid's interchange security and provide a more accurate and reliable detection mechanism.

The indexes of the switching surface in the sliding mode controllers were computed by the authors Dehghani et al. (2021) based on the union of singular value decomposition and Fourier transform. The proposed approach was also tested against various bogus data injection attacks. The outcomes demonstrated that the suggested approach can shorten the time it takes to identify an attack. Additionally, their system detected attacks with a 96% accuracy rate.

SMART CITY SECURITY SOLUTIONS

Cities can lower the risks associated with cyber security by implementing a number of safeguards and obtaining the appropriate help. Two choices are available. The first entails paying a security company to break into a network and look for vulnerabilities. In essence, outside companies will replicate assaults and look for vulnerabilities. The security company will identify any flaws and provide workable defences after an attack. While building infrastructure that is impenetrable from the beginning is desirable, this kind of penetration testing is fantastic. Making ensuring that their linked infrastructure is safe from hackers even if they obtain access is the second security precaution that cities may put in place (Ma, 2021).

- To make smart cities secure, the following aspects should be a regular component of every city's cyber security program:
- Data that is encrypted – All data should be encrypted. Data can be scrambled via encryption, making it useless and unreadable to everyone save those with access to the encryption key that can decode it. The encryption key ought to be protected with two-factor authentication as well. Because the infrastructure of smart cities deals with extremely sensitive data, encryption should be adopted as a standard. Hackers won't be able to use sensitive PII data if they get access to it.
- Constant security surveillance - Security surveillance requires a specialized crew that can watch traffic and search for irregularities. Security tools that can analyze massive volumes of data and hunt for indicators of compromise can automate this. Once identified, potential risk regions can be separated to avoid data breaches.
- A wide range of supported environments and devices – Any new supported environment or device should be able to secure a wide range of linked environments and objects. An all-encompassing security system should be implemented to safeguard the many components of an interconnected city because smart cities are composed of various networks, SaaS, IaaS, and cloud environments.

A smart city can be protected with the help of these straightforward security solutions. These services aren't free, though. Cost is an issue, and many local governments do not currently have a budget set up specifically for cyber security.

THE BEST CYBER SECURITY PRACTICES FOR SMART CITIES

One option to ensure the security of smart city services is to invest in expensive security measures, however there are several less expensive procedures that can promote safer interconnection. This means, the people in power determine how smart a city is, by maintaining the integrity of a city's smart systems, you may protect both yourself and your fellow people. Cybersecurity must be taken more seriously now more than ever. Here are some concepts to think about:

- Research new technologies thoroughly before putting it into use: Instead of rushing to deploy a fresh, cutting-edge technology, spend some time researching it and looking for any potential weaknesses.
- Start small - Test a tiny proof-of-concept to check if it can withstand a simulated cyber-attack before implementing a larger system. It is not ready for city-wide implementation if it doesn't hold up.
- Assemble a committed security team by hiring IT spec.ialists with security experience. The ideal team will be able to do penetration tests, check for vulnerabilities, develop fail-safe and override tools, and ensure the integrity of encryption.
- Avoid leaning too heavily on smart technology - It's simple to be caught up in the trap of sticking to just one way of doing things.
- Always be ready for the worst because preparation pays off. To make sure you are prepared in the event that your city is the target of a cyber-assault, always prepare for the worst-case scenario.

SECURITY CHALLENGES IN SMART CITIES

Data Privacy and protection issues: Privacy is seen as a fundamental human right and is shielded in various ways by national laws. Concerns concerning privacy include the proper procedures for accessing and sharing a person's sensitive and personal information (Nair and Tyagi, 2021). Sensitive information can relate to a wide range of characteristics of a person's life, including any information that can be used either on its own or in combination with other information to locate, identify, or contact a particular person, or to place that person in a certain situation.

The volume, scope, and level of detail of the data being collected about people and places are dramatically increased by smart city technologies, which also collect data relating to all types of privacy. Several behaviours that are typically seen as inappropriate yet are common in the functioning of a smart city eco system might threaten and violate privacy.

- **Surveillance**: Observing, following, hearing, or recording someone's movements
- **Aggregation**: Combining different data points on a person to find a pattern or trend in their behaviour.
- **Data leakage**: a lack of data protection policies may cause sensitive information to be improperly accessed or leaked.
- **Extended usage**: the use of data gathered without the subject's consent for a longer period of time than stated or for purposes other than those stated.

8.1 Insecure Hardware: One of the main issues with smart cities is the insecurity and lack of thorough testing of the sensors in the infrastructure, buildings, etc. The sensors are vulnerable to hacking since IoT devices are not standardized. False data can be sent into the sensors by notorious people, leading to signal failures, system shutdowns, etc.

Greater attack surface: Smart city operations administer diverse services using a complex, networked assemblage of ICT equipment. Any gadget that is linked to the internet is susceptible to hacking, and smart cities have more access points than usual. A system or network can be attacked by taking control of just one device. Numerous problems, including inadequate encryption and security, the usage of susceptible legacy technologies, poor maintenance, cascade consequences, and human mistake, increase the susceptibility of systems.

More Consumption of bandwidth: When a large number of actuators or sensors attempt to connect with a single server, the server may crash due to a surge in data flow. Furthermore, most sensors communicate through an unencrypted channel, which increases the risk of security issues. The megahertz frequencies used for other wireless communications, such as radio, television, emergency services, etc., will be strained by the bandwidth usage from billions of devices (Chauhan and Sharma, 2015).

Risks Related to the usage of Applications: Apps have sped up the process of integrating mobile devices into our daily lives. Applications, such as social networking, productivity tools, gaming, and mapping apps, have mostly been responsible for the smartphone revolution. This has contributed to the size and scope of the current smartphone revolution. Applications present capability that seems to be only constrained by developer ingenuity, but they also increase the danger of enabling Bring Your Own Device in a work environment. Employees who are permitted to bring their own devices to work may unavoidably need to access work-related data using those same devices. This presents two security risks specifically:

Adware-containing applications: As the number of installed apps grows, the likelihood that some of them have security holes or dangerous malware increases.

App vulnerabilities: The organization may have security issues in applications it has developed or utilized to give customers access to business data.

Simple software bugs can have a significant negative effect. A single software fault can have a significant impact since Smart Cities will be powered by hundreds of devices and systems that will manage key services. For instance, the Bay Area Rapid Transit (BART) experienced a significant software issue in November 2013 that caused 19 trains carrying between 500 and 1,000 passengers to be halted in their tracks .

Securing urban areas for expansion: Realizing the potential of smart cities will depend on striking a balance between the cyber threats that could arise and the promise of smart cities, as well as on how well those risks are managed. Cities should start by involving all the participants and organizations in the larger ecosystem. The following are some further actions that cities should think about:

Integrating a cyber-strategy with a smart city: The continuous fusion, interoperability, and interconnection of local systems and activities provide challenges that cities should address by developing a comprehensive cybersecurity strategy that supports their overall smart city strategy. For the purpose of identifying, evaluating, and mitigating the risks related to technological processes, policies, and solutions, cities should take into consideration while assessment of their data, systems, and cyber assets (Turk et al., 2022). Cities may be able to create a thorough cybersecurity strategy with an integrated perspective of the risks and understanding of the interdependencies of the vital assets. For instance, Singapore introduced a new cyber security law in 2016 after launching its National Cyber Security Master plan in 2013. Both programs were essential components of Singapore's.

Establishing formal data and cyber governance: The control of data, assets, infrastructure, and other technological components needs to be formalized in cities. Each essential part of the ecosystem for smart cities should have clear roles and duties defined in a complete governance model. Several organizations will have to collaborate in order to put into practice an ecosystem approach to dealing with cyber challenges, with a solid governance model acting as the cornerstone. To exchange threat information, capabilities, and contracts and to bolster their cyber defenses, cities can create networks with other cities, state agencies, academic institutions, and businesses.

Data Management: Additionally, a key component of this governance is data management, which includes strong data sharing and privacy regulations, data analytics expertise, and monetization models that make it easier to get and use "city data." To ensure the proper balance of protection, privacy, transparency, and utility, policies, legislation, and technology must be consistently aligned. The city's comprehensive cyber strategy must develop together with the governance, regulations, and procedures. For instance, the "Hague Security Delta," a network of more than 200 businesses specializing in forensics, critical infrastructure, cyber and urban security, and national security, is located in the city of Hague.

Create strategic alliances to expand your cyber capabilities: Cities need to be creative and proactive in closing the cyber skills gap in their areas because it is not going away any time soon (Badran 2023). This strategy might necessitate that the municipal government look into unconventional ways to access cyber talent, such as crowdsourcing, rewards, and challenges to address cyber-related concerns. New abilities and competencies across the multiple ecosystem layers are needed for a smart city. By forming strategic alliances and signing agreements with service providers, cities can increase their current capabilities.

Recognizing that protecting cities from cyber risk is not a one-time exercise where cyber strategy changes in reaction to changes in cyber threats is just as crucial for municipal leadership as being able to recover from cyberattacks. Cities should also collaborate with a network of local institutions, corporations, start-ups, and companies rather than battling this struggle on their own. A cybersecurity solution can benefit from technology, but it also needs a thorough asset and data control framework. The need for a comprehensive plan for controlling cyber risk in cities that incorporates cybersecurity concepts into every stage of the creation of smart cities is more crucial (i.e., from strategy and design to implementation and operations).

CONCLUSION

Cities have shifted in recent years toward utilizing more technologies and becoming smarter. Cities can better utilize their resources, save money, and provide top-notch services to their inhabitants thanks to new technologies and quick, easy communications. Offering a great quality of life and a vibrant economic environment has become more important as cities compete to draw capital, new residents, and tourists. Governments have come to the conclusion that although their objectives are frequently hampered by tight budgets, scare resources, and antiquated systems, innovative technologies may turn such obstacles into possibilities. A smart city, by definition, is one that uses technology to automate, change, and improve the lives of its residents. Digital systems are advantageous in smart cities because they may be used to improve the performance and delivery of urban services, reduce resource consumption and financial load, and engage citizens in effective and active communication. With the development of smart city technology, industries like government services and traffic, transportation, electricity, water, health, and waste management have emerged. Governments have become more serious in recent years about cyber security. The GDPR is a shining example of how requiring businesses doing business in the EU to adhere to stringent EU regulations has helped to drastically reduce the number of data breaches. Deep learning implementation in smart cities has a number of intriguing avenues. It is obvious that an educational technique yields precise outcomes when the information from the teaching and testing is identical to the results of the set. The second study area, learning transfer, deals with how teaching and testing are distributed or transferred from one system to another. Researchers might also look into how to use semantic systems in smart city applications to improve performance. This paper mainly focus upon the measures and preventions taken in the area for the development of smart cities..

REFERENCE

Aghajani, G., & Ghadimi, N. (2018). Multi-objective energy management in a micro-grid. *Energy Reports*, *4*, 218–225. doi:10.1016/j.egyr.2017.10.002

Al-Saidi, M., & Zaidan, E. (2020). Gulf futuristic cities beyond the headlines: Understanding the planned cities megatrend. *Energy Reports*, *6*, 114–121. doi:10.1016/j.egyr.2020.10.061

AlDairi, A., & Tawalbeh, L. (2017). Cyber security attacks on smart cities and associated mobile technologies. *Procedia Computer Science*, *109*, 1086–1091. doi:10.1016/j.procs.2017.05.391

Alibasic, A., Al Junaibi, R., Aung, Z., Woon, W. L., & Omar, M. A. (2017). Cybersecurity for smart cities: A brief review. In *Data Analytics for Renewable Energy Integration: 4th ECML PKDD Workshop, DARE 2016, Riva del Garda, Italy, September 23, 2016, Revised Selected Papers 4* (pp. 22-30). Springer International Publishing. 10.1007/978-3-319-50947-1_3

Arabo, A. (2015). Cyber security challenges within the connected home ecosystem futures. *Procedia Computer Science*, *61*, 227–232. doi:10.1016/j.procs.2015.09.201

Atitallah, S. B., Driss, M., Boulila, W., & Ghézala, H. B. (2020). Leveraging Deep Learning and IoT big data analytics to support the smart cities development: Review and future directions. *Computer Science Review*, *38*, 100303. doi:10.1016/j.cosrev.2020.100303

Badran, A. (2023). Developing smart cities: Regulatory and policy implications for the State of Qatar. *International Journal of Public Administration*, *46*(7), 519–532. doi:10.1080/01900692.2021.2003811

Campisi, T., Severino, A., Al-Rashid, M. A., & Pau, G. (2021). The development of the smart cities in the connected and autonomous vehicles (CAVs) era: From mobility patterns to scaling in cities. *Infrastructures*, *6*(7), 100. doi:10.3390/infrastructures6070100

Cerrudo, C., Hasbini, A., & Russell, B. (2015). *Cyber security guidelines for smart city technology adoption*. Cloud Security Alliance.

Chauhan, D., & Jain, J. K. (2019). A Journey from IoT to IoE. [IJITEE]. *International Journal of Innovative Technology and Exploring Engineering*, *8*(11).

Chauhan, D., Jain, J. K., & Sharma, S. (2016, December). An end-to-end header compression for multihop IPv6 tunnels with varying bandwidth. In *2016 Fifth international conference on eco-friendly computing and communication systems (ICECCS)* (pp. 84-88). IEEE. 10.1109/Eco-friendly.2016.7893247

Chauhan, D., & Sharma, S. (2015). Addressing the bandwidth issue in end-to-end header compression over ipv6 tunneling mechanism. *International Journal of Computer Network and Information Security*, *7*(9), 39–45. doi:10.5815/ijcnis.2015.09.05

Chen, D., Wawrzynski, P., & Lv, Z. (2021). Cyber security in smart cities: A review of deep learning-based applications and case studies. *Sustainable Cities and Society*, *66*, 102655. doi:10.1016/j.scs.2020.102655

Cheng, E. C., & Wang, T. (2022). Institutional strategies for cybersecurity in higher education institutions. *Information (Basel)*, *13*(4), 192. doi:10.3390/info13040192

Dehghani, M., Niknam, T., Ghiasi, M., Siano, P., Haes Alhelou, H., & Al-Hinai, A. (2021). Fourier singular values-based false data injection attack detection in AC smart-grids. *Applied Sciences (Basel, Switzerland)*, *11*(12), 5706. doi:10.3390/app11125706

Deloitte. (2019). *Making Smart Cities Cybersecurity, Deloitte Center for Government Insights*. Deloitte. https://www2.deloitte.com/us/en/insights/focus/smart-city/making-smart-cities-cyber-secure.html

Edwards, G. (2021, June). Cybercrime: Targeting your intellectual property. In Intellectual Property Forum: Journal of the Intellectual Property Society of Australia and New Zealand (No. 124, pp. 35-40). IEEE.

Falco, G. J., & Rosenbach, E. (2022). *Confronting Cyber Risk: An Embedded Endurance Strategy for Cybersecurity*. Oxford University Press. doi:10.1093/oso/9780197526545.001.0001

Fard, S. M. H., Karimipour, H., Dehghantanha, A., Jahromi, A. N., & Srivastava, G. (2020). Ensemble sparse representation-based cyber threat hunting for security of smart cities. *Computers & Electrical Engineering*, *88*, 106825. doi:10.1016/j.compeleceng.2020.106825

Ghazal, T. M., Hasan, M. K., Alshurideh, M. T., Alzoubi, H. M., Ahmad, M., Akbar, S. S., Al Kurdi, B., & Akour, I. A. (2021). IoT for smart cities: Machine learning approaches in smart healthcare—A review. *Future Internet*, *13*(8), 218. doi:10.3390/fi13080218

Ghiasi, M., Dehghani, M., Niknam, T., Kavousi-Fard, A., Siano, P., & Alhelou, H. H. (2021). Cyber-attack detection and cyber-security enhancement in smart DC-microgrid based on blockchain technology and Hilbert Huang transform. *IEEE Access : Practical Innovations, Open Solutions*, *9*, 29429–29440. doi:10.1109/ACCESS.2021.3059042

Habibzadeh, H., Nussbaum, B. H., Anjomshoa, F., Kantarci, B., & Soyata, T. (2019). A survey on cybersecurity, data privacy, and policy issues in cyber-physical system deployments in smart cities. *Sustainable Cities and Society*, *50*, 101660. doi:10.1016/j.scs.2019.101660

Ijaz, S., Shah, M. A., Khan, A., & Ahmed, M. (2016). Smart cities: A survey on security concerns. *International Journal of Advanced Computer Science and Applications*, *7*(2). doi:10.14569/IJACSA.2016.070277

Jain, J. K., & Chauhan, D. (2021). An Energy-Efficient Model For Internet Of Things Using Compressive Sensing. *Journal of Management Information and Decision Sciences*, *24*, 1–7.

Khan, S., Nazir, S., García-Magariño, I., & Hussain, A. (2021). Deep learning-based urban big data fusion in smart cities: Towards traffic monitoring and flow-preserving fusion. *Computers & Electrical Engineering*, *89*, 106906. doi:10.1016/j.compeleceng.2020.106906

Khatoun, R., & Zeadally, S. (2017). Cybersecurity and privacy solutions in smart cities. *IEEE Communications Magazine*, *55*(3), 51–59. doi:10.1109/MCOM.2017.1600297CM

Konstantinou, C. (2021). Toward a secure and resilient all-renewable energy grid for smart cities. *IEEE Consumer Electronics Magazine*, *11*(1), 33–41. doi:10.1109/MCE.2021.3055492

Ma, C. (2021). Smart city and cyber-security; technologies used, leading challenges and future recommendations. *Energy Reports*, *7*, 7999–8012. doi:10.1016/j.egyr.2021.08.124

Martínez, P. L., Dintén, R., Drake, J. M., & Zorrilla, M. (2021). A big data-centric architecture metamodel for Industry 4.0. *Future Generation Computer Systems*, *125*, 263–284. doi:10.1016/j.future.2021.06.020

Nair, M. M., & Tyagi, A. K. (2021). Privacy: History, statistics, policy, laws, preservation and threat analysis. *Journal of information assurance & security, 16*(1).

Nasif, A., Othman, Z. A., & Sani, N. S. (2021). The deep learning solutions on lossless compression methods for alleviating data load on IoT nodes in smart cities. *Sensors (Basel)*, *21*(12), 4223. doi:10.3390/s21124223 PMID:34203024

Pakhare, P. S., Krishnan, S., & Charniya, N. N. (2021). A survey on recent advances in cyber assault detection using machine learning and deep learning. *Innovative Data Communication Technologies and Application: Proceedings of ICIDCA 2020*, (pp. 571-582). IEEE.

Razmjoo, A., Østergaard, P. A., Denai, M., Nezhad, M. M., & Mirjalili, S. (2021). Effective policies to overcome barriers in the development of smart cities. *Energy Research & Social Science*, *79*, 102175. doi:10.1016/j.erss.2021.102175

Said, O., & Tolba, A. (2021). Accurate performance prediction of IoT communication systems for smart cities: An efficient deep learning based solution. *Sustainable Cities and Society*, *69*, 102830. doi:10.1016/j.scs.2021.102830

Sengan, S., Subramaniyaswamy, V., Indragandhi, V., Velayutham, P., & Ravi, L. (2021). Detection of false data cyber-attacks for the assessment of security in smart grid using deep learning. *Computers & Electrical Engineering*, *93*, 107211. doi:10.1016/j.compeleceng.2021.107211

Solanki, A. S., Patel, C., & Doshi, N. (2019). Smart cities-A case study of Porto and Ahmedabad. *Procedia Computer Science*, *160*, 718–722. doi:10.1016/j.procs.2019.11.021

Thing, V. L. (2014, December). Cyber security for a smart nation. In *2014 IEEE International Conference on Computational Intelligence and Computing Research* (pp. 1-3). IEEE.

Turan, S. G. (2021). Deepfake and digital citizenship: A long-term protection method for children and youth. In *Deep fakes, fake news, and misinformation in online teaching and learning technologies* (pp. 124–142). IGI Global. doi:10.4018/978-1-7998-6474-5.ch006

Turk, Ž., de Soto, B. G., Mantha, B. R., Maciel, A., & Georgescu, A. (2022). A systemic framework for addressing cybersecurity in construction. *Automation in Construction*, *133*, 103988. doi:10.1016/j. autcon.2021.103988

Vitunskaite, M., He, Y., Brandstetter, T., & Janicke, H. (2019). Smart cities and cyber security: Are we there yet? A comparative study on the role of standards, third party risk management and security ownership. *Computers & Security*, *83*, 313–331. doi:10.1016/j.cose.2019.02.009

William, P., Choubey, A., Chhabra, G. S., Bhattacharya, R., Vengatesan, K., & Choubey, S. (2022, March). Assessment of hybrid cryptographic algorithm for secure sharing of textual and pictorial content. In *2022 International conference on electronics and renewable systems (ICEARS)* (pp. 918-922). IEEE. 10.1109/ICEARS53579.2022.9751932

Zhou, X., Li, S., Li, Z., & Li, W. (2021). Information diffusion across cyber-physical-social systems in smart city: A survey. *Neurocomputing*, *444*, 203–213. doi:10.1016/j.neucom.2020.08.089

Chapter 13
Optimizing Integrated Spatial Data Management Through Fog Computing:
A Comprehensive Overview

Munir Ahmad
https://orcid.org/0000-0003-4836-6151
Survey of Pakistan, Pakistan

Asmat Ali
https://orcid.org/0000-0002-8804-2285
Survey of Pakistan, Pakistan

Hassan Nawaz
Huawei MiddleEast Cloud, Pakistan

Muhammad Arslan
Chenab College of Advance Studies, Faisalabad, Pakistan

Nirmalendu Kumar
Survey of India, India

ABSTRACT

Fog computing offers key features such as real-time communication, physical distribution, position awareness, compatibility, scalability, and energy efficiency, which collectively enhance the management of integrated spatial data. It provides benefits such as real-time data processing, seamless data sharing, improved efficiency, enhanced data security and privacy, and effective resource utilization. The distributed architecture and edge processing capabilities of fog computing enable real-time spatial data processing, faster insights, and localized decision-making. It presents opportunities for web-based analytics, real-time analysis, fault tolerance, event-triggered actions, and context-aware applications. However, challenges exist in terms of user needs and requirements, collaboration and partnership, data quality and interoperability, technical infrastructure, and policy and governance. Future work should focus on addressing these challenges and exploring new opportunities.

INTRODUCTION

The management of integrated spatial data has brought about a significant transformation in the utilization of spatial data across government, academia, the private sector, and the general public. This

DOI: 10.4018/978-1-6684-9576-6.ch013

practice has profoundly altered how we access and incorporate data by facilitating the easy sharing, discovery, and utilization of spatial data (Hendriks et al., 2012). However, the rapid expansion of spatial data from diverse sources, such as remote sensing, social media, and the Internet of Things (IoT), presents new challenges in terms of data processing and analysis. The sheer volume and diversity of data pose difficulties for conventional methods, particularly when real-time processing is required. Therefore, there is a growing need to explore innovative approaches to enhance the efficiency and effectiveness of integrated spatial data management. To enhance the efficiency and effectiveness of integrated spatial data management, innovative approaches like fog computing are increasingly sought after (Das et al., 2021). These strategies aim to address the evolving needs of integrated spatial data management and optimize the utilization of spatial data in the face of expanding data sources and processing requirements.

A distributed computing paradigm called fog computing has gained attention as a potential solution to overcome these obstacles. Fog computing extends cloud computing to the network edge, enabling efficient processing and storage capabilities with low latency and high bandwidth for real-time and location-based applications. By deploying fog nodes closer to the data sources, data can be filtered and preprocessed before transmission to the cloud for further analysis. This approach minimizes network traffic and processing time, improving overall system performance. Therefore, there is a growing interest in exploring the opportunities and challenges of using fog computing in integrated spatial data management (R. K. Barik et al., 2017, 2019).

To this effect, this chapter investigated the potential of fog computing to support integrated spatial data management and address their challenges. The objectives of this chapter are:

1. To evaluate the potential of fog computing for integrated spatial data management.
2. To examine the benefits and opportunities offered by fog computing in enhancing spatial data management systems.
3. To identify the challenges and obstacles associated with the integration of fog computing and spatial data management.

To achieve these objectives, the structure of this chapter follows a logical progression to explore the potential of fog computing for integrated spatial data management. Firstly, an overview is provided, highlighting the key features and benefits of fog computing in supporting spatial data management systems. This sets the foundation for understanding the significance of fog computing in this context. Subsequently, the chapter delves into the various opportunities and applications where fog computing can be applied, including emergency response systems, navigation applications, precision agriculture systems, real-time monitoring systems, and context-aware applications. The chapter then addresses the challenges and obstacles that arise in the integration of fog computing and spatial data management, such as user needs, collaboration, data quality, technical infrastructure, and policy and governance issues. Finally, the chapter concludes by proposing future directions and research opportunities that can address the challenges and explore new possibilities in fog computing for spatial data management.

KEY FEATURES OF FOG COMPUTING

Figure 1 summarizes key fog computing features, which have the potential to bring significant advancements in integrated geospatial data management. Further discussion of these features is provided in the upcoming subsections.

Real-Time Communications

Real-time communication is an important feature of fog computing that facilitates fast and real-time data analysis. Fog computing refers to the deployment of devices and sensors close to data sources and end users, thereby bringing processing resources closer to the network edge. This proximity of devices reduces the time consumed to transfer data to distant centralized data centers or cloud servers for processing and analysis tasks (Nguyen et al., 2020). The data generated by sensors and other network edge devices are locally acquired by fog nodes at the network edge, where they are processed and stored by network edge devices (Bonomi et al., 2012).

The real-time communication offered by fog computing is highly beneficial in the context of integrated spatial data management, especially in situations where time-sensitive data is required for immediate actions in real-world events. The closeness of devices facilitates the swift transmission of large amounts of spatial data to nearby cloud servers. By leveraging fog computing, spatial data can be processed and analyzed close to its source. Real-time communication also enables the fetching of immediate feedback on events, which can be promptly sent to the data sources or end users if immediate action is warranted based on the feedback.

Physical Distribution

The physical distribution of fog computing is a key component that refers to the dispersal of computing power across several edge devices deployed in close proximity to data sources and end users. This distribution of devices in fog computing facilitates more effective and efficient processing of spatial data while easing the pressure on centralized data centers. It empowers data processing to take place at the network's edge, near to place where the data is generated, by decentralizing computational resources. Due to the closeness of devices, there is less need to spend significant amounts of geographical data for processing to distant data centers or cloud servers (Sabireen & Neelanarayanan, 2021).

These characteristics of fog computing offer various advantages for integrated spatial data management. Due to the reduced round-trip time for data transmission, response times decrease. This is especially helpful for time-sensitive spatial applications such as autonomous vehicles or real-time monitoring systems, where quick response and action are required. Scalability is also improved due to the distributed nature of devices. Processing capacity scales up by dispersing computational resources among several edge devices. Each edge device adds to the overall computer capacity, enabling parallel processing and supporting the increasing demand for spatial data. Through this scalability, the growing volume of spatial data can be handled without running into performance bottlenecks.

Less Latency

Fog computing effectively reduces network latency by minimizing the distance between data sources and processing resources. In traditional cloud computing, spatial data is typically transferred across the network to centralized data centers for processing and analysis. However, this transmission from data sources to centralized cloud centers increases latency due to the long distances the data must travel. In contrast, fog computing brings computational power closer to the edge, where the data sources are located. This proximity of devices in fog computing significantly reduces latency during data transfer (Ahmed & Zeebaree, 2021; Sabireen & Neelanarayanan, 2021).

In integrated spatial data management, rapid and nearly real-time analysis is crucial. Spatial data often contains time-sensitive information, such as tracking moving objects, monitoring events as they occur, or making quick judgments based on changing circumstances. Fog computing ensures that location-based services and applications can operate with minimal delays, resulting in more accurate and up-to-date information.

Position Awareness

Position awareness is also another key feature of fog computing for the management of spatial data. The geographical distribution of fog nodes and edge devices empowers them to have contextual awareness of their particular location (Sabireen & Neelanarayanan, 2021). This position awareness makes it possible to handle spatial data while being aware of the location where it was collected. In this way, fog computing can assist in developing various context-aware applications by utilizing the feature of position awareness. Fog nodes, for example, can process and analyze sensor data inside their zones in a smart city environment (Songhorabadi et al., 2023).

This localized analysis can provide personalized and accurate decision-making in many real-life applications such as energy management, risk prediction, and traffic flow optimization. Additionally, by employing position awareness in fog computing, location-based services and applications can be developed for many different purposes. For example, spatial data from surrounding sources along with the user's real-time position can be utilized to deliver precise and customized route assistance in navigation applications.

Compatibility

Compatibility is also a key component of fog computing that enables its easy integration with current cloud infrastructure and spatial data management systems. This compatibility feature of fog computing made it possible to enable interoperability between fog nodes and cloud servers for effective and efficient spatial data processing and analysis. Fog nodes can interact and exchange data with cloud-based systems by making use of their capabilities and resources. Due to their compatibility, the tools, frameworks, and technologies created for cloud-based spatial data management systems can be used by fog computing networks. In this way, fog computing can access the enormous computing power and storage capacity offered by cloud-based spatial data management systems (Mahmud et al., 2018).

Fog computing and cloud infrastructure's compatibility boost data synchronization and consistency as well. In this way, the processed spatial data is made accessible to all segments of integrated spatial data management. This data consistency and synchronization ability enables easy data sharing and collaboration between fog nodes and cloud servers to help comprehensive spatial data analysis and thus decision-making as well. Compatibility features also ease the development and deployment of fog computing applications. Developers can employ already-existing knowledge and skills in cloud-based technologies, to develop fog computing systems. In this way, developers can lessen the development time by reusing existing software components, libraries, and frameworks created for cloud-based spatial data management.

Heterogeneity

Another essential trait of fog computing is heterogeneity which makes it possible to handle a variety of platforms, devices, and sensors used in the integrated management of spatial data. Fog computing offers a platform to support a wide variety of hardware and software capabilities, embracing the heterogeneity of devices. The devices used for fog computing may include edge devices, gateways, routers, IoT sensors, and even mobile devices. With the ability to handle a variety of devices, a fog computing system, is well-suited for managing and integrating spatial data generated for multiple devices (Ometov et al., 2022).

Geospatial data, sensor data, and IoT data are just a few examples of data sources that can be integrated and managed by fog computing. Maps, satellite images, and GPS coordinates are examples of the types of information included in geospatial data. Data gathered by various sensors, such as weather sensors, traffic sensors, or temperature sensors, is referred to as sensor data. IoT data is information produced by networked devices, such as smart home appliances and commercial sensors. Fog computing network provides standardized data formats, protocols, and interfaces that provide easy connection between various hardware and data sources. This guarantees that spatial data may be handled, exchanged, and analyzed within the fog computing ecosystem regardless of its source or format.

Interoperability

In the context of fog computing, interoperability refers to the capacity of fog nodes and end devices to easily communicate, work together, and support a variety of services. Fog nodes and end devices may have different hardware, operating systems, communication protocols, and data formats due to the heterogeneous nature of manufacturers and providers. However, by defining common standards, protocols, and interfaces, various elements of fog computing networks cooperate. This also facilitates the utilization of common spatial data formats and standards for communication between fog nodes and end devices (Karthika et al., 2020). For instance, adopting widely used geographical data formats like GeoJSON or s Open Geospatial Consortium (OGC) standards can boost the interoperability feature of the fog computing networks.

Fog computing solutions may smoothly incorporate spatial data from various sources and providers by providing interoperability. Through this integration, spatial data resources may be used more effectively, cross-domain collaborations are made possible, and the creation of creative location-based services is made easier. Additionally, interoperability enables the sharing of spatial data among fog nodes, endpoints, and cloud systems, improving the scalability, dependability, and performance of the entire system.

Scalability

Fog computing's capacity to provide a flexible and scalable infrastructure suitable for the specific requirements of the assorted nature of applications is one of its primary features. This fog computing characteristic is particularly beneficial in the context of integrated spatial data management, for example, real-time location-based services, environmental monitoring services, and smart city solutions. Fog computing provides localized processing and analysis of spatial data by carefully positioning fog nodes close to the data sources, such as sensors, GPS devices, or IoT devices (R. Barik et al., 2017). Fog nodes are simple to add to or remove from the fog computing network, allowing the infrastructure to scale up or down dependent on the changing requirements of tasks related to spatial data processing and analysis. This scalability makes it possible to distribute and use resources effectively, guaranteeing that computational resources are deployed where they are most needed.

Fog computing architecture's modular design also makes simple alterations and upgrades possible to accommodate changing needs of various spatial data applications. Fog nodes, for instance, can be outfitted with specialized software modules or machine learning algorithms specially designed for spatial analysis if an application requires high-end spatial analytics capabilities. Fog computing's customizability allows for customized solutions that address particular application needs, and its scalability guarantees that the infrastructure can keep up with rising data volumes and processing needs.

Privacy and Confidentiality

Integrating spatial data management requires careful consideration of data privacy and confidentiality, particularly when working with sensitive data such as healthcare, finance, and defense-related data. By offering a highly secure infrastructure, fog computing enables the deployment of critical applications and assures the protection of sensitive data transferred between devices and the cloud. End-to-end encryption, which ensures that data remains encrypted during transmission from the edge devices to the fog nodes and then to the cloud, is one of the fundamental security measures used in a fog computing network. By using encryption, the data is protected against unauthorized access and network eavesdropping (Mukherjee et al., 2017).

By ensuring that spatial data is safeguarded throughout its lifecycle, integrated spatial data management takes advantage of the security features of fog computing. Fog computing lessens the risk of transferring data over long distances and minimizes the exposure of sensitive data to external threats by processing data locally at the edge. Additionally, this localized processing facilitates quicker reaction times and lessens reliance on a single vulnerable central location.

Energy Efficiency

Processing and generating enormous amounts of spatial data require an energy efficiency mechanism. By processing data closer to the network's edge, the fog computing network significantly contributes to increasing energy efficiency through lower energy usage and more effective data transfer. Fog computing eliminates the need for lengthy data transfers by bringing data processing capabilities closer to the edge of the network, where the data is generated (Mukherjee et al., 2018). In this way, the system's total energy efficiency is improved by the decreased energy use.

Fog computing also makes it possible to intelligently process data and allocate resources according to proximity and relevance. Fog nodes can filter and analyze incoming spatial data by processing it locally, negating the need to send unnecessary or duplicated data to the cloud. By maximizing resource utilization, this selective data processing lowers the computing workload and further improves energy efficiency.

BENEFITS OF FOG COMPUTING IN INTEGRATED SPATIAL DATA MANAGEMENT

Figure 2 outlines the primary advantages of utilizing fog computing for integrated spatial data management. These advantages are discussed in detail in the subsequent subsections. According to the studies (Hu et al., 2017; Mouradian et al., 2018), the following are the key benefits of fog computing:

Realtime Spatial Data Processing

Faster spatial data processing is essential for integrated spatial data management to assist businesses and governments get timely insights and decisions. Distributed architecture and edge processing capabilities of fog computing make it suitable to assist quicker spatial data processing and hence increase the effectiveness of spatial data management systems. A fog computing system places fog nodes adjacent to data sources to process data rather than depending entirely on centralized cloud servers. In this way, fog computing accelerates the processing of spatial data by reducing data transfer times. Even fog nodes can carry out computations locally if sending the data to centralized cloud servers is not required. This local processing capacity reduces data transfer latency and speeds up the analysis of spatial data (Kumari et al., 2018).

Fog nodes can work together and run in parallel to process portions of spatial data at once. Due to the ability to analyze data in parallel, vast amounts of spatial data may be efficiently analyzed, cutting down on processing time. Additionally, edge caching is used in fog computing to accelerate the processing of spatial data. Spatial data that is often accessed or computationally demanding might be cached closer to the data sources, at the edge. By removing the need for frequent data transfers to centralized

Figure 1. Key features of fog computing

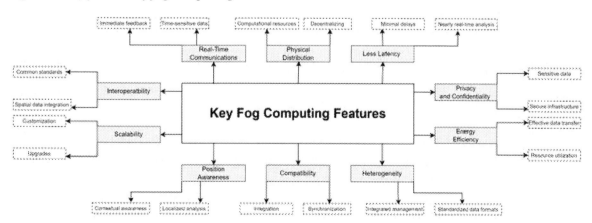

servers, this caching approach speeds up processing and enhances the responsiveness of spatial data management systems.

Handling Large Volumes of Spatial Data

Given the growing accessibility of sensors, satellites, and other data sources that provide massive volumes of spatial information, managing the volume of spatial data is a key problem for integrated spatial data management. With its distributed design and edge processing capabilities, fog computing provides a productive way to handle massive amounts of spatial data. Fog computing, which moves data processing closer to the edge of the network, is essential for handling the vast volume of spatial data in integrated spatial data management (Kumari et al., 2018).

Fog computing places fog nodes close to data sources rather than depending entirely on centralized cloud servers. Due to the localization of data processing, there is less of a need to send vast quantities of spatial data over great distances to centralized servers, reducing network traffic and capacity restrictions. Fog computing is distributed in nature and allows parallel processing and distributed computing techniques to effectively handle the massive amount of spatial data (Kumari et al., 2018). Fog computing also makes use of edge analytics and clever filtering to efficiently handle the vast amount of spatial data. Data reduction methods like data filtering, aggregation, or compression can be carried out by fog nodes at the edge. Before sending spatial datasets to centralized servers for additional analysis, this preparation procedure helps to reduce their size.

Seamless Data Sharing

Spatial data sharing is an essential component of integrated spatial data management. By addressing issues with data transfer, latency, and network connectivity, fog computing, with its distributed architecture and edge processing capabilities, plays a critical role in supporting smooth spatial data sharing. Fog computing uses its distributed design to enable easy spatial data sharing. Fog nodes serve as data exchange mediators by being placed close to data sources and users. These nodes act as localized data centers, facilitating efficient and direct contact between various stakeholders involved in the exchange of spatial data (Saidi et al., 2022).

The amount of data that needs to be shared over the network can be decreased by enabling data filtering, aggregation, or transformation techniques at the edge. In this way, fog computing enhances the effectiveness of spatial data sharing and lessens network congestion by minimizing the amount of data delivered. Fog computing also provides standardized interfaces and protocols for smooth spatial data sharing. It encourages system, device, and platform interoperability, allowing them to smoothly connect and share spatial data (Dang et al., 2018; Saidi et al., 2022).

Integration of Different Types of Spatial Data

Another aspect of integrated spatial data management is the integration of various types of spatial data, which enables stakeholders to combine and analyze heterogeneous spatial datasets from numerous sources. By addressing data heterogeneity, interoperability, and processing efficiency, fog computing, with its distributed architecture and edge processing capabilities, significantly contributes to the integration of various forms of spatial data (Badidi et al., 2020).

By enabling localized data processing and transformation at fog nodes, various types of spatial data can be seamlessly integrated and analyzed while also undergoing on-the-fly data translation, format conversion, and data harmonization. Moreover, fog nodes serve as translators and adapters of data formats or protocols across various systems and data sources thus enabling seamless integration of various types of spatial data such as IoT, Sensors, and many more (Badidi et al., 2020).

Improved Spatial Data Security and Privacy

Integrating spatial data management must address improved privacy and security challenges, especially when working with sensitive data. Fog computing plays a crucial role in increasing data security and privacy due to its decentralized design and emphasis on local data processing. Fog computing's decentralized structure makes it possible to handle and analyze sensitive geographic data locally, closer to the data source. Because of this proximity, less data must be transmitted across vast distances, lowering the possibility of transmission-related data breaches. Fog computing improves the security of spatial data by keeping it in the local environment of the fog nodes, making it less susceptible to interception or unauthorized access while in transit.

Furthermore, by using strong encryption and authentication systems, fog computing offers improved data security. End-to-end encryption methods can be used to encrypt spatial data sent within a fog computing environment, guaranteeing that only authorized parties can access and decrypt the data. By preventing unauthorized access or tampering, this encryption helps safeguard the confidentiality and integrity of geographical information. Fog computing also makes it possible for authorized parties to share geographical data securely and confidentially (Anand & Khemchandani, 2020).

Increased Availability and Accessibility of Spatial Data

In the context of integrated spatial data management, fog computing is essential in boosting the availability and accessibility of geospatial data. Fog computing provides local caching and processing of spatial data by dispersing computing resources to the network's edge, minimizing dependency on central servers, and boosting data availability and accessibility (Badidi et al., 2020). Frequently accessible or crucial spatial datasets can be stored on fog nodes set up at the network's edge, allowing for quicker and more dependable access to the data. In this way, spatial data is kept accessible even in networks with poor connectivity or sporadic service. This is especially advantageous for applications that need constant access to spatial data, such as in disaster management systems, where the ability to retrieve data in real time is crucial for making prompt decisions.

Fog computing also supports offline access to vital data because spatial data is locally accessible and available. Users can access and work with crucial datasets even when they are cut off from the centralized network because fog nodes can locally cache and analyze geospatial data. In this way, fog computing improves the dependability and usability of spatial information in difficult or resource-constrained contexts by enabling offline access to crucial data (Badidi et al., 2020; Dang et al., 2018).

Promotes Spatial Data Consistency

Integrating spatial data management requires promoting the synchronization and consistency of spatial datasets to keep them coherent, up-to-date, and consistent across various systems and platforms. Fog computing plays a crucial role in attaining spatial data consistency and synchronization due to its distributed design and real-time data processing capabilities. By carrying out data transformation and harmonization activities, fog nodes installed at the network's edge can serve as data mediators, assuring uniform data formats, properties, and definitions. To align and standardize spatial data from many sources, these nodes can apply predetermined data integration rules or algorithms, assuring data consistency across various systems and platforms (Badidi et al., 2020).

Fog computing lowers the latency associated with data transfers and processing by dispersing computer resources closer to the data sources. As a result, data synchronization is made quicker and more responsive, guaranteeing that spatial datasets are consistently updated across many systems, even in dynamic or quickly changing contexts. Fog computing also enables strategies for data caching and replication that improve the consistency and synchronization of spatial data. It is possible to retain duplicate copies of spatial data across numerous fog nodes to guarantee data availability and consistency in the event of node failures or network disruptions.

Enables Spatial Data Interoperability

Another key component of integrated spatial data management is spatial data interoperability to enable spatial data exchange and utilization between various systems and applications to resolve issues of data formats, structures, and semantics (Badidi et al., 2020). Fog computing is essential for promoting spatial data interoperability because of its distributed architecture and support for standardized protocols. To promote the interoperability of spatial data, fog computing can also carry out data transformation and harmonization operations at the edge. Fog computing also supports real-time data processing and streaming, which improves spatial data interoperability.

Fog computing also encourages the seamless fusion of sensor data with other geographic information, furthering the interoperability of spatial data. Fog nodes can connect to a variety of sensors, including Internet of Things (IoT) gadgets or remote sensing platforms, and aggregate their data with that of other sources of spatial data. The value and usefulness of integrated spatial data management systems are increased due to interoperability between real-time sensor observations and current spatial datasets.

Reduced Spatial Data Transmission Costs

Reduced spatial data transmission costs allow to use resources effectively and save money, which is a significant benefit of integrated spatial data management. With its distributed design and local data processing capabilities, fog computing is essential in reducing the cost of transmitting spatial data. Fog computing moves data processing and storage closer to the network edge, which lowers the cost of spatial data transmission. The amount of data that needs to be transferred across the network is drastically decreased by this localized data processing method, which lowers the cost of transmission (Sadri et al., 2022).

Fog computing also enables data filtering and aggregation at the edge, enabling communication with only the pertinent and condensed data rather than the complete raw data set. By further reducing the quantity of data that must be communicated, this data reduction approach lowers the cost of bandwidth and data transfer fees. Additionally, fog computing makes it possible for edge data replication and caching, which eliminates the need for constant data transfers. Fog nodes can locally store geographic data that is regularly used, making it easier to obtain and eliminating the need for constant data exchanges.

Figure 2. Benefits of fog computing

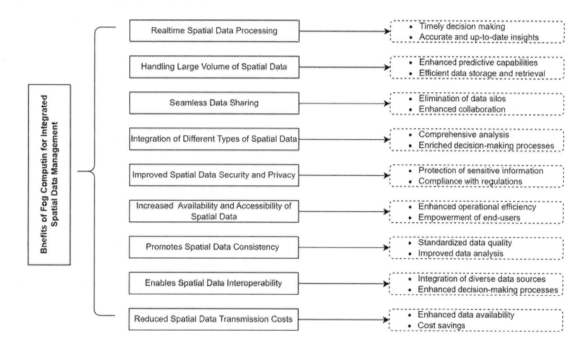

OPPORTUNITIES

In this section, a concise overview of how fog computing can enhance integrated spatial data management is provided, as summarized and depicted in Figure 3.

Web-Based Analytics

Web-based analytics is a method of data analysis that makes use of the internet and web technologies to process, look over, and display data. It involves collecting, analyzing, and gaining insights from a variety of data sources, including spatial data, utilizing web-based tools or platforms. Fog computing can enable real-time analytics and data visualization on edge devices or in close proximity to data sources. It allows quick insights and decision-making based on spatial data without sending large amounts of data to the cloud. Web-based analytics applications can be hosted on edge devices using fog computing, enabling instant processing, examination, and visualization of spatial data. Edge devices can use web-based analytics for localized decision-making, and fog computing facilitates immersive and interactive visualization of data on edge devices. Users can interact with spatial data in real-time and gain deeper insights through dynamic filtering and aggregation (Bebortta et al., 2020; Sabireen & Neelanarayanan, 2021).

Localized Decision-Making

Localized decision-making is greatly facilitated by Integrated Spatial Data Management. Location-based information, maps, satellite imagery, and other geospatial datasets are all included in the category of spatial data. Fog nodes can use the amount of data to make context-specific decisions by integrating and making this data easily accessible (Kang et al., 2017; Pandit et al., 2018). Fog nodes are given the ability to make localized decisions based on the particular requirements and limits of certain applications or domains due to the merging of integrated spatial data management and fog computing. In situations where quick answers, low-latency interactions, or autonomous actions are necessary, this feature becomes especially useful.

Real-Time Analysis

The processing and analysis of data in real-time means doing so without waiting around for a while. This entails instantaneously deriving useful insights, patterns, and trends from geospatial data in the context of spatial data management. By utilizing the integrated spatial data that is available to them, fog nodes that are situated closer to the data source can carry out this analysis locally. Organizations can obtain precise and up-to-date information about the environment by analyzing the data in real-time, giving them the ability to base their decisions on the most recent information available (Pareek et al., 2021). Fog nodes can rapidly analyze the combined spatial data and produce results or start actions depending on the learned information. This quick reaction time is especially important for time-sensitive applications like emergency response systems, where quick action is required to reduce risks or handle urgent situations.

Improves Fault Tolerance and Reliability

A system's fault tolerance is its capacity to continue operating normally in the face of mistakes or failures. Fog computing lessens reliance on centralized infrastructure by distributing computational capabilities to edge devices or fog nodes. By reducing single points of failure, this decentralized architecture enhances fault tolerance (Grover & Garimella, 2018). In case one fog node fails, the other nodes will still duplicate and spread spatial data. Reducing dependency on external networks, fog computing, and integrated data management also improves system dependability. Fog nodes' proximity to data sources lowers latency, allowing for real-time processing and quicker responses for applications like autonomous vehicles. Systems become more resilient in dynamic situations because of these technologies, which improve fault tolerance, reliability, and responsiveness.

Support Event-Triggered Action

Fog nodes can take action in response to events based on real-time data monitoring. They enable rapid decision-making by immediately analyzing event data without centralized processing or human involvement. By recognizing patterns or irregularities that demand immediate attention, this talent permits quick responses to important occurrences or circumstances. Fog nodes, for instance, can change traffic flow in real time based on congestion events or accidents in a smart city scenario, providing effective traffic management. In addition to providing real-time feedback via notifications, warnings, or visualizations, event-triggered actions also keep stakeholders updated on important events as they happen.

Figure 3. Opportunities offered by fog computing

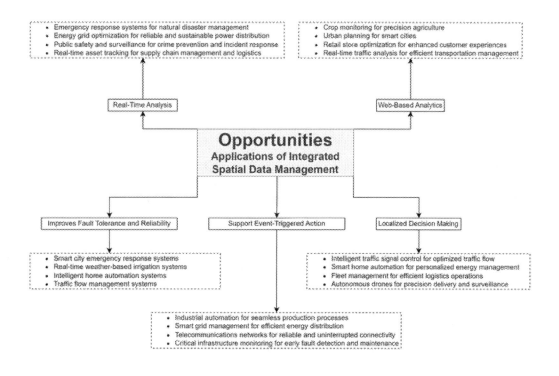

APPLICATIONS

In this section, a concise overview of some potential applications of integrated spatial data management where fog computing can be beneficial is provided.

Emergency Response Systems

By supplying real-time data processing, analysis, and transmission capabilities at the edge of the network, fog computing plays a significant role in improving the effectiveness of Emergency Response Systems. In an emergency, this facilitates quicker decision-making, better situational awareness, and effective resource allocation. Fog computing can be used to create a distributed network of fog nodes nearby the affected area in the event of a natural disaster, such as a hurricane or earthquake. These fog nodes can gather and analyze real-time data from a variety of devices, including sensors, drones, and satellite imaging, to produce insights that can be put to use. The integration and accessibility of pertinent spatial data, such as maps, information about the infrastructure, or population density, are ensured through integrated spatial data management at the fog nodes. As a result, emergency responders can have access to the most recent spatial information and make decisions that take into account the particular qualities and needs of the impacted area.

Navigation Applications

By providing real-time data processing, increased accuracy, and effective route optimization, fog computing can improve the performance and capabilities of navigation systems. For instance, computational processing from centralized cloud infrastructure to edge devices or fog nodes can be distributed to assist the operations of navigation applications. This reduces latency and improves the application's overall performance by enabling quicker data processing and response times. To produce real-time traffic updates, route suggestions, or alerts for hazardous road conditions, fog nodes can perform real-time analysis of data from a variety of sources, including GPS signals, traffic sensors, or crowd-sourced data. Because decisions are made locally at the fog nodes, they may be tailored to the specific needs of each user and the present state of the road network to provide context-sensitive and individualized navigation guidance. Fog nodes, for instance, might analyze real-time traffic information and recommend alternate routes to steer clear of jams or accidents. To enhance the navigation experience, they can also take into account elements like weather conditions, special events, or road closures. Fog computing also makes it possible to navigate while offline by storing pertinent map data and routing details at the edge devices, or fog nodes. By doing this, consumers are guaranteed access to navigation services even when there is little to no network connectivity.

Precision Agriculture System

By facilitating real-time data processing, localized decision-making, and effective resource allocation, fog computing can also improve the capabilities of Precision Agriculture Systems. Fog computing, for instance, can be used in a Precision Agriculture System to deliver computing power to edge devices or fog nodes situated inside the agricultural field. To produce useful insights, these fog nodes can gather and interpret real-time data from multiple sources, including sensors, weather stations, or drones.

Field boundaries, soil maps, or statistics on crop yields are just a few examples of the pertinent spatial data that must be integrated and made available at fog nodes. As a result, decisions can be made locally, taking into account the particular traits and needs of each field. Farmers can get real-time information about crop health, soil moisture levels, pest infestations, and nutrient deficits from the fog nodes by analyzing sensor data, satellite imagery, and historical records. With the help of this localized analysis, farmers may select the best irrigation, fertilization, pesticide treatment, or planting techniques for each area of the field.

Real-Time Monitoring Systems

By facilitating effective data processing, analysis, and decision-making at the edge of the network, fog computing can expand the potential of real-time monitoring systems and increase their responsiveness and accuracy. The fog nodes are capable of real-time data analytics, employing models and algorithms to find patterns, anomalies, or noteworthy events. Fog nodes, for instance, can analyze data from multiple sensors in a smart city monitoring system to find aberrant trends in energy usage, air pollution levels, or traffic congestion. Fog nodes eliminate the requirement for data transmission to a centralized cloud infrastructure by processing data locally, which leads to quicker reaction times and less network congestion. This enables the speedier detection of important events or circumstances that call for quick action.

Context-Aware Applications

Fog nodes or edge devices that are geographically dispersed and located closer to the users or devices can be deployed using fog computing in a context-aware application. To produce contextual insights, these fog nodes may gather and interpret real-time data from numerous sources, including sensors, wearables, and mobile devices. The acquired data can be analyzed by the fog nodes to derive pertinent contexts, such as location, climate, user preferences, or social interactions. The application can offer individualized and situation-specific services or recommendations thanks to its context awareness feature. Fog nodes, for instance, might leverage information about a user's location within a business, past purchases, and current inventory levels to give tailored product recommendations or targeted advertisements in real-time.

CHALLENGES

In this section, an overview of some potential challenges is provided, as summarized and depicted in Figure 4.

User Needs and Requirements

Understanding and satisfying the various demands and requirements of users is one of the main issues in fog computing for integrated spatial data management. Fog computing systems must be customized to meet the unique spatial data management needs of various applications and industries. To create fog computing architectures that successfully handle these issues, it is necessary to pinpoint the precise spatial data requirements, performance specifications, and application limitations (Javadzadeh & Rahmani, 2020).

Collaboration and Partnership

Integrated spatial data management using fog computing frequently entails partnerships between a variety of stakeholders, including data producers, service providers, infrastructure providers, and end users (de Moura Costa et al., 2020; Gomes et al., 2021; Mouradian et al., 2018). This is especially necessary in the case of spatial data infrastructure established for integrated spatial data management. For implementation to be successful, these stakeholders must establish strong alliances and teamwork. Roles and duties be established, resources and knowledge be shared, and coordination and communication between the various parties involved need to be effective (R. K. Barik et al., 2019; Ghosh & Mukherjee, 2022).

Data Quality and Interoperability

The availability of high-quality and interoperable data from many sources is essential for integrated geographic data management. When working with geographical data from many sensors, devices, and platforms, it can be difficult to ensure data quality, including correctness, completeness, and timeliness (R. K. Barik et al., 2019; Indrajit et al., 2021). Although fog computing offers some form of data interoperability, it is insufficient for some spatial data types. Reliable data integration and transformation techniques are needed to provide interoperability among heterogeneous spatial data sources, such as various data formats, standards, and schemas (Badidi et al., 2020; R. K. Barik et al., 2018).

Technical Infrastructure and Capabilities

To properly enable integrated geographic data management, fog computing requires a strong technical infrastructure. Fog nodes, edge devices, communication networks, and storage systems are all included in this, along with their deployment and control. Technical issues in terms of scalability, dependability, and resource management arise when creating and maintaining such infrastructure that can handle the volume, velocity, and variety of spatial data (Chen et al., 2017; Mouradian et al., 2018). To enhance the availability and accessibility of fog computing resources, investment in technical infrastructure and capabilities, such as hardware, software, and network resources, are required (R. K. Barik et al., 2018; Bhusan Dash et al., 2023; Da Silva et al., 2022).

Policy and Governance

Clear policies and governance frameworks are required for fog computing for integrated geographic data management in order to address concerns about data privacy, security, ownership, and usage rights (de Moura Costa et al., 2020; Gomes et al., 2021; Indrajit et al., 2021). Spatial data collection, processing, and sharing need to be done responsibly and ethically through appropriate regulations and governance structures. It entails resolving legal and regulatory issues, developing frameworks for data governance, and putting in place systems for keeping track of and enforcing compliance (R. K. Barik et al., 2019; Ghosh & Mukherjee, 2022; Saber et al., 2022).

Figure 4. Challenges associated with fog computing

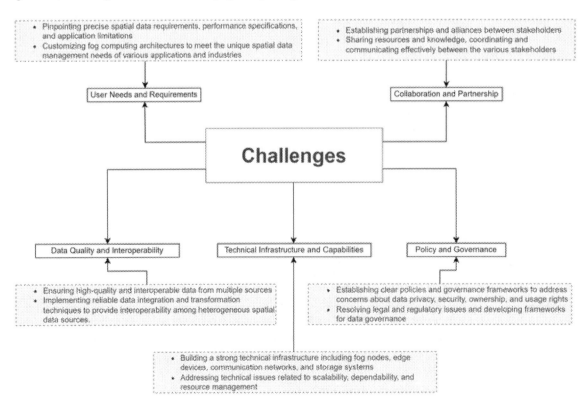

CONCLUSION

This chapter evaluated the potential of fog computing integrated spatial data management. Fog computing offers a range of key features to support integrated spatial data management. Fog computing's key features, include real-time communication, physical distribution, less latency, position awareness, compatibility, heterogeneity, interoperability, scalability, privacy and confidentiality, and energy efficiency, collectively enhancing the management and analysis of integrated spatial data. These features enable swift data processing, accurate decision-making, seamless integration, and improved resource utilization, making fog computing a valuable framework for spatial data management in various domains.

Fog computing offers numerous benefits to various dimensions of integrated spatial data management. Its distributed architecture and edge processing capabilities enable real-time spatial data processing, faster insights, and more effective decision-making. By handling large volumes of spatial data through localized processing, fog computing reduces data transfer times and network congestion, leading to improved efficiency. It facilitates seamless data sharing by minimizing data transmission and enhancing interoperability between different systems and stakeholders. Fog computing supports the integration of various types of spatial data, ensuring compatibility and harmonization across multiple sources. Moreover, it enhances data security and privacy by keeping sensitive information closer to the source and employing robust encryption measures. Fog computing improves the availability and accessibility of spatial data, even in resource-constrained environments, while promoting consistency, synchronization, and interoperability of spatial datasets. Lastly, fog computing reduces spatial data transmission costs through localized processing, data filtering, aggregation, and caching, resulting in effective resource utilization and cost savings.

Fog computing also presents various opportunities for enhancing integrated spatial data management. Web-based analytics can leverage fog computing to enable real-time data processing, visualization, and decision-making without extensive data transfers to the cloud. Localized decision-making is facilitated by integrating spatial data management and fog computing, allowing fog nodes to make context-specific decisions based on geospatial datasets. The real-time analysis becomes possible by processing data locally on fog nodes, providing up-to-date insights and enabling prompt decision-making. Fog computing's distributed architecture improves fault tolerance and reliability by reducing reliance on centralized infrastructure and minimizing single points of failure. Event-triggered actions can be performed by fog nodes in response to real-time data monitoring, enabling quick responses to important occurrences or circumstances. These opportunities offered by fog computing enhance the effectiveness, efficiency, and responsiveness of integrated spatial data management systems.

Fog computing has diverse applications across various domains. In emergency response systems, fog computing enables real-time data processing and analysis, enhancing decision-making, situational awareness, and resource allocation. Navigation applications benefit from fog computing by providing accurate and real-time route optimization, traffic updates, and personalized navigation guidance. Precision agriculture systems leverage fog computing for local data processing and decision-making, optimizing farming practices based on real-time insights. Real-time monitoring systems utilize fog nodes for efficient data analytics, enabling quick detection of anomalies or events requiring immediate action. Context-aware applications leverage fog computing to provide personalized and situation-specific services by gathering and analyzing real-time data from various sources. Fog computing plays a crucial role in enhancing the effectiveness and capabilities of these applications, improving their responsiveness, accuracy, and user experience.

Fog computing for integrated spatial data management faces several challenges that need to be addressed for successful implementation. Understanding and meeting diverse user needs and requirements is crucial for customizing fog computing systems to specific applications and industries. Collaboration and partnerships between stakeholders are essential for effective implementation, requiring strong alliances, resource sharing, and effective communication. Ensuring data quality and interoperability is a challenge when dealing with heterogeneous spatial data sources, requiring reliable integration and transformation techniques. The technical infrastructure and capabilities of fog computing systems must be robust and scalable to handle the volume and variety of spatial data. Clear policies and governance frameworks are necessary to address privacy, security, ownership, and usage rights concerns, ensuring responsible and ethical data collection, processing, and sharing. Overcoming these challenges is vital for the successful integration of fog computing and spatial data management.

In conclusion, fog computing offers significant potential for integrated spatial data management. Its key features, including real-time communication, physical distribution, and compatibility, enhance the management and analysis of spatial data across various domains. Fog computing provides benefits such as swift data processing, seamless integration, improved resource utilization, and enhanced data security. It presents opportunities for real-time analytics, localized decision-making, and event-triggered actions, leading to more effective and responsive spatial data management systems. Applications in emergency response, navigation, precision agriculture, real-time monitoring, and context-aware services demonstrate the practical value of fog computing. However, challenges remain in understanding user needs, establishing collaborations, ensuring data quality and interoperability, developing robust technical infrastructure and implementing appropriate policies and governance frameworks. Addressing these challenges is crucial for the successful integration of fog computing and spatial data management, enabling the realization of its full potential.

Future work in the field of fog computing for integrated spatial data management should focus on addressing the identified challenges and exploring new opportunities for application. Efforts should be directed toward customizing fog computing systems to meet the diverse needs and requirements of users in different domains. Collaboration and partnerships among stakeholders should be strengthened to ensure effective implementation and resource sharing. Research should also aim to improve data quality and interoperability by developing reliable integration techniques for heterogeneous spatial data sources. Additionally, advancements in the technical infrastructure, scalability, and resource management of fog computing systems are needed. Policy and governance frameworks should be developed to address privacy and security concerns. Furthermore, exploring new applications and evaluating the performance and cost-effectiveness of fog computing in real-world scenarios is crucial for its wider adoption and success in spatial data management.

REFERENCES

Ahmed, K. D., & Zeebaree, S. R. M. (2021). Resource Allocation in Fog Computing : A Review. *International Journal of Science and Business*, 5(2).

Anand, D., & Khemchandani, V. (2020). Data Security and Privacy Functions in Fog Computing for Healthcare 4.0. In Studies in Big Data (Vol. 76). Springer. doi:10.1007/978-981-15-6044-6_16

Badidi, E., Mahrez, Z., & Sabir, E. (2020). Fog computing for smart cities' big data management and analytics: A review. In Future Internet, 12(11). doi:10.3390/fi12110190

Barik, R., Dubey, H., Sasane, S., Misra, C., Constant, N., & Mankodiya, K. (2017). Fog2Fog: Augmenting Scalability in Fog Computing for Health GIS Systems. *Proceedings - 2017 IEEE 2nd International Conference on Connected Health: Applications, Systems and Engineering Technologies, CHASE 2017.* IEEE. 10.1109/CHASE.2017.83

Barik, R. K., Dubey, H., Mankodiya, K., Sasane, S. A., & Misra, C. (2019). GeoFog4Health: A fog-based SDI framework for geospatial health big data analysis. *Journal of Ambient Intelligence and Humanized Computing, 10*(2), 551–567. doi:10.1007/s12652-018-0702-x

Barik, R. K., Dubey, H., Misra, C., Borthakur, D., Constant, N., Sasane, S. A., Lenka, R. K., Mishra, B. S. P., Das, H., & Mankodiya, K. (2018). Fog Assisted Cloud Computing in Era of Big Data and Internet-of-Things: Systems, Architectures, and Applications. In Studies in Big Data (Vol. 39). Springer. doi:10.1007/978-3-319-73676-1_14

Barik, R. K., Dubey, H., Samaddar, A. B., Gupta, R. D., & Ray, P. K. (2017). FogGIS: Fog Computing for geospatial big data analytics. *2016 IEEE Uttar Pradesh Section International Conference on Electrical, Computer and Electronics Engineering, UPCON 2016.* IEEE. 10.1109/UPCON.2016.7894725

Bebortta, S., Das, S. K., Kandpal, M., Barik, R. K., & Dubey, H. (2020). Geospatial serverless computing: Architectures, tools and future directions. In ISPRS International Journal of Geo-Information, 9(5). doi:10.3390/ijgi9050311

Bhusan Dash, B., Shekhar Patra, S., Nanda, S., Rani Jena, J., Rout, S., & Kumar Barik, R. (2023). *SFA4SDI: A Secure Fog Architecture for Spatial Data Infrastructure.* IEEE. doi:10.1109/iSSSC56467.2022.10051572

Bonomi, F., Milito, R., Zhu, J., & Addepalli, S. (2012). Fog computing and its role in the internet of things. *MCC'12 - Proceedings of the 1st ACM Mobile Cloud Computing Workshop.* ACM. 10.1145/2342509.2342513

Chen, N., Chen, Y., Ye, X., Ling, H., Song, S., & Huang, C. T. (2017). Smart City Surveillance in Fog Computing. In Studies in Big Data (Vol. 22). Springer. doi:10.1007/978-3-319-45145-9_9

Da Silva, T. P., Batista, T., Lopes, F., Neto, A. R., Delicato, F. C., Pires, P. F., & Da Rocha, A. R. (2022). Fog Computing Platforms for Smart City Applications: A Survey. *ACM Transactions on Internet Technology, 22*(4), 1–32. doi:10.1145/3488585

Dang, L., Dong, M., Ota, K., Wu, J., Li, J., & Li, G. (2018). Resource-Efficient Secure Data Sharing for Information Centric E-Health System Using Fog Computing. *IEEE International Conference on Communications, 2018-May.* IEEE. 10.1109/ICC.2018.8422844

Das, J., Ghosh, S. K., & Buyya, R. (2021). Geospatial Edge-Fog Computing: A Systematic Review, Taxonomy, and Future Directions. In Mobile Edge Computing. doi:10.1007/978-3-030-69893-5_3

de Moura Costa, H. J., da Costa, C. A., da Rosa Righi, R., & Antunes, R. S. (2020). Fog computing in health: A systematic literature review. In Health and Technology, 10(5). doi:10.1007/s12553-020-00431-8

Ghosh, S., & Mukherjee, A. (2022). STROVE: Spatial data infrastructure enabled cloud–fog–edge computing framework for combating COVID-19 pandemic. *Innovations in Systems and Software Engineering*. doi:10.1007/s11334-022-00458-2 PMID:35677629

Gomes, E., Costa, F., De Rolt, C., Plentz, P., & Dantas, M. (2021). A Survey from Real-Time to Near Real-Time Applications in Fog Computing Environments. In Telecom, 2(4). doi:10.3390/telecom2040028

Grover, J., & Garimella, R. M. (2018). Reliable and Fault-Tolerant IoT-Edge Architecture. *Proceedings of IEEE Sensors, 2018-October*. doi:10.1109/ICSENS.2018.8589624

Hendriks, P. H. J., Dessers, E., & van Hootegem, G. (2012). Reconsidering the definition of a spatial data infrastructure. In International Journal of Geographical Information Science, 26(8). doi:10.1080/13658816.2011.639301

Hu, P., Dhelim, S., Ning, H., & Qiu, T. (2017). Survey on fog computing: architecture, key technologies, applications and open issues. In Journal of Network and Computer Applications, 98. doi:10.1016/j.jnca.2017.09.002

Indrajit, A., van Loenen, B., Suprajaka, Jaya, V. E., Ploeger, H., Lemmen, C., & van Oosterom, P. (2021). Implementation of the spatial plan information package for improving ease of doing business in Indonesian cities. *Land Use Policy*, *105*, 105338. doi:10.1016/j.landusepol.2021.105338

Javadzadeh, G., & Rahmani, A. M. (2020). Fog Computing Applications in Smart Cities: A Systematic Survey. *Wireless Networks*, *26*(2), 1433–1457. Advance online publication. doi:10.1007/s11276-019-02208-y

Kang, J., Yu, R., Huang, X., & Zhang, Y. (2017). Privacy-preserved pseudonym scheme for fog computing supported internet of vehicles. *IEEE Transactions on Intelligent Transportation Systems*, *19*(8), 2627–2637. doi:10.1109/TITS.2017.2764095

Karthika, P., Ganesh Babu, R., & Karthik, P. A. (2020). Fog Computing using Interoperability and IoT Security Issues in Health Care. In Lecture Notes in Networks and Systems. Springer doi:10.1007/978-981-15-2329-8_10

Kumari, A., Tanwar, S., Tyagi, S., & Kumar, N. (2018). Fog computing for Healthcare 4.0 environment: Opportunities and challenges. *Computers & Electrical Engineering*, *72*, 1–13. doi:10.1016/j.compeleceng.2018.08.015

Mahmud, R., Kotagiri, R., & Buyya, R. (2018). Fog Computing: A taxonomy, survey and future directions. In Internet of Things (Vol. 0, Issue 9789811058608). doi:10.1007/978-981-10-5861-5_5

Mouradian, C., Naboulsi, D., Yangui, S., Glitho, R. H., Morrow, M. J., & Polakos, P. A. (2018). A Comprehensive Survey on Fog Computing: State-of-the-Art and Research Challenges. In IEEE Communications Surveys and Tutorials, 20(1). IEEE. doi:10.1109/COMST.2017.2771153

Mukherjee, M., Matam, R., Shu, L., Maglaras, L., Ferrag, M. A., Choudhury, N., & Kumar, V. (2017). Security and Privacy in Fog Computing: Challenges. *IEEE Access : Practical Innovations, Open Solutions*, *5*, 19293–19304. doi:10.1109/ACCESS.2017.2749422

Mukherjee, M., Shu, L., & Wang, D. (2018). Survey of fog computing: Fundamental, network applications, and research challenges. *IEEE Communications Surveys and Tutorials, 20*(3), 1826–1857. doi:10.1109/COMST.2018.2814571

Nguyen, N. D., Phan, L. A., Park, D. H., Kim, S., & Kim, T. (2020). ElasticFog: Elastic resource provisioning in container-based fog computing. *IEEE Access : Practical Innovations, Open Solutions, 8*, 183879–183890. Advance online publication. doi:10.1109/ACCESS.2020.3029583

Ometov, A., Molua, O. L., Komarov, M., & Nurmi, J. (2022). A Survey of Security in Cloud, Edge, and Fog Computing. In Sensors (Vol. 22, Issue 3). doi:10.3390/s22030927

Pandit, M. K., Naaz, R., & Chishti, M. A. (2018). Distributed iot analytics across edge, fog and cloud. *2018 Fourth International Conference on Research in Computational Intelligence and Communication Networks (ICRCICN)*, (pp. 27–32). IEEE. 10.1109/ICRCICN.2018.8718738

Pareek, K., Tiwari, P. K., & Bhatnagar, V. (2021). Fog Computing in Healthcare: A Review. *IOP Conference Series. Materials Science and Engineering, 1099*(1), 012025. doi:10.1088/1757-899X/1099/1/012025

Saber, W., Eisa, R., & Attia, R. (2022). *Efficient Geospatial Data Analysis Framework in Fog Environment*. IEEE., doi:10.1109/ACCESS.2022.3231787

Sabireen, H., & Neelanarayanan, V. (2021). A Review on Fog Computing: Architecture, Fog with IoT, Algorithms and Research Challenges. *ICT Express, 7*(2), 162–176. doi:10.1016/j.icte.2021.05.004

Sadri, A. A., Rahmani, A. M., Saberikamarposhti, M., & Hosseinzadeh, M. (2022). Data reduction in fog computing and internet of things: A systematic literature survey. *Internet of Things : Engineering Cyber Physical Human Systems, 20*, 100629. Advance online publication. doi:10.1016/j.iot.2022.100629

Saidi, A., Nouali, O., & Amira, A. (2022). SHARE-ABE: An efficient and secure data sharing framework based on ciphertext-policy attribute-based encryption and Fog computing. *Cluster Computing, 25*(1), 167–185. doi:10.1007/s10586-021-03382-5

Songhorabadi, M., & Rahimi, M. MoghadamFarid, A. M., & Haghi Kashani, M. (2023). Fog computing approaches in IoT-enabled smart cities. In Journal of Network and Computer Applications, 211. doi:10.1016/j.jnca.2022.103557

Chapter 14
Revenge Porn and Blackmailing on the Internet

Nayanika Nandy
Illinois Institute of Technology, USA

ABSTRACT

In the era of technological advancements and widespread internet access, numerous issues have emerged, including cyber bullying, cyber extortion, and the disturbing trend of revenge pornography. Revenge pornography, also known as non-consensual pornography, involves the malicious act of sharing explicit photos or videos of individuals without their consent, aimed at compromising their sexual integrity. While the term "revenge porn" may suggest that the content is leaked by vengeful ex-intimate partners, it is important to note that many cases involve the illegal acquisition of explicit material through means such as hacking, with perpetrators seeking personal gain, amusement, or notoriety.

THESIS STATEMENT

Revenge pornography is on the rise these days, and there is no legislation to regulate it. The government should enact laws that prevent revenge pornography and cyber-blackmail. During the pandemic, sextortion and revenge porn cases have increased dramatically. Is revenge porn and blackmail on the Internet against the law?

INTRODUCTION

In this modern era, technology has advanced quite significantly. With just a swipe on the screen, you can access data and information from the remotest corner of the globe. This ease of access to information has promoted trade, communication, peace, and entertainment. However, technology and the Internet have proved to be a double-edged sword that cuts two ways. The Internet has been abused n many ways; for example, it has promoted cyberterrorism, identity crimes, revenge pornography, and blackmail.

DOI: 10.4018/978-1-6684-9576-6.ch014

Revenge porn, also referred to as nonconsensual pornography, refers to obtaining and sharing sexually explicit materials to cause embarrassment, annoy or emotionally distress the victim. In this era, cases of revenge pornography have been on the rise, a fact that can be attributed to the absence of strict laws against those who seek to infringe on another person's peace and safety. Blackmail, on the other, refers to the extortion of another person by holding something incrimination on them to manipulate them to do your will. The effects of these activities are quite adverse to the victims resulting in depression, low esteem, loss of employment, paranoia, social out casting, anxiety and, in some cases, it has resulted in suicide.

An example of cyberbullying and revenge pornography is the highly publicized case of Rutgers University in 2010(Kamal & Newman, 2016).In this particular case, Dharun Ravi secretly placed a web camera inside his dormitory when his roommate Tyler Clementi requested privacy for a night. When Clementi started getting intimate with another male, he live-streamed them on Twitter when he actively encouraged others to join in and watch. Two days later, Mr. Ravi tried to make another recording. This breach of privacy was the death of Mr. Clementi, who killed himself by jumping off the George Washington Bridge. In 2012, Mr. Ravi was found guilty on the charge of invasion of privacy, intimidation, and tampering with evidence, and he was sentenced to serve thirty days in jail and three years of probation.

According to research conducted, ten percent of ex-intimate partners have threatened to expose nudity pictures or videos of their partners, with up to sixty percent following through with this threat (McAfee, 2013). According to the Cyber Civil Rights Initiative, ninety percent of the victims are women. It is troubling the ease at which people can access explicit information once it has been electronically disseminated. The real challenge lies in removing eliminating their digital trail once uploaded on social media. Another challenge concerning revenge pornography is that pornography websites post the victim's identifying information such as the name, residence, and phone number, place of work or email accounts. The victim's sexual integrity gets damaged, which leads to lifelong mental health repercussions such as anxiety, depression, damaged relationships, and social out casting.

However, some of the cases of revenge pornography are not actual cases of revenge. In some cases, the perpetrator is usually out to make a profit or just to humiliate the victim just for their fun and notoriety. One of such cases was the 'revenge porn king' in 2010. The perpetrator, Hunter Moore, began the website isanyoneup.com, which featured explicit content about its victim and most of the time; it contained links to the victim's social media profile. Victims usually claimed that an ex-intimate partner trying to get intimidate them, and in some other cases released the explicit content, victims claimed that their computers and other devices had been hacked into. In 2014, the Federal Bureau of Investigations on several counts of identity theft, and fifteen counts of conspiracy indicted Mr. Moore. After pleading guilty, he was sentenced to two and a half years in penitentiary institution and a fine of two thousand dollars (Kamal & Newman, 2016).

Objective Statement

This paper's primary and core aim is to explain how to tackle a blackmailing case and the best practices to avoid being a victim of revenge porn.

What does the term revenge porn and blackmailing on the Internet mean?

Revenge porn has been a matter of deep contention in the academic world. The terms that have been actively suggested to define its true meaning include involuntary porn("Burns,2015"), nonconsensual pornography("Citron &Franks,2014:Franks,2015"),image-based sexual exploitation ("Powell,2009,2010") and image-based sexual abuse ("Mcglynn & Rackley,2017:Dekeseredy & Dragiewicz,2018")All these terms suggested can be used to collectively refer to the release of explicit sexual content with or without the consent of the victim.

However, scholars argue that labeling the release of the explicit content on the Internet as revenge pornography is imprecise and inaccurate since not all cases are due in pursuit of revenge("Franks,2015; Flynn, Henry & Powell,2016"). Some perpetrators can release the explicit content for coercion intentions, blackmailing the victims into doing their bidding, for fun and entertainment, for sexual gratification for the perpetrator, to earn a social status or for financial gain ("Henry & Powel, 2016").

Why Is Revenge Porn a Prevalent Issue on the Internet?

The Internet and the World Wide Web have been cutting-edge technology that has advanced the development of humanity at least by a couple of light-years. The Internet has fostered trade relationships, motivating cooperation and treaties between nation-states, which has promoted global peace; it has promoted unity in the globe where someone can interact with another person across the globe while in their living room. However, not every item on the Internet is worth rating a five star, revenge porn also known as the nonconsensual pornography refers to the distribution of images and videos taken with or without the consent of the victim either for fun and entertainment, for financial gain, for sexual gratification, to cause humiliation and embarrassment to the victim in the cases failed intimate relationship or to gain coercion advantage over the victim.

Revenge pornography has been termed as Technology-facilitated abuse. Currently, several interactive websites offer open platforms for such abuses to happen. According to the cyber Civil Rights Initiatives (CCRI), ninety percent of the victims of revenge porn are usually women or girls. These interactive websites offer the perpetrator's audiences social validation for their vile actions and reputational support in the same capacity, where these perpetrators end up being famous at the emotional expense of the victims. In other cases, these interactive websites offer money incentives to the perpetrators, a factor that has further increased the abuse on the Internet. A common misconception if someone gets abused online, they can press the log out button, and everything will magically be fixed. Easier said than done; the line between our digital lives and real life is very faint in this modern era. Today everyone is on the Internet and social media, where they can say anything without the fear of any legal consequences. What happens in the virtual world can cast its gloomy shadow over the victim's real life.

Until recently, very few laws have been governing the use of internet resources, which has provided violators with the capacity to abuse and blackmail victims without the fear of legal repercussions. Only after a public outburst and social outcry did some of the social media platforms try to enact measures to protect people from social media victimization by revenge pornography perpetrators. For example, Facebook enacted the Community Standards that warn any content deemed as a threat to promote sexual violence and exploitation will be removed. However, these social sites are yet to put action to their words as some of the victims have argued that the accounts of the offenders most of the time were not being brought down, which gave them future allowance to redo the action again.

One out of every ten women or girls is a victim of revenge pornography (Reynolds, 2017 p 2) another challenge that actively hinders proper mitigation of unsolicited revenge pornography on the Internet is the anonymity afforded to the perpetrators by the interactive websites. 'When there is no evidence, there is no case is a common phrase within the law enforcement agencies. In the cases of hacking, the victim is not acquitted with the perpetrator; therefore, with the anonymity afforded by these sites, it becomes challenging for law agencies to apprehend the offender successfully, and in most cases, the offender gets to walk away free as a bird but on the other hand leaving scars that will take an entire lifetime to heal. Sadly, victims suffer too much depression in some cases, which results in committing suicide. The biggest challenge that faces revenge pornography victims is the social stigmatization. The stigmatization has resulted in the end of marriages and the loss of family and friends, people who could have been the pillar of support for the victim crumble and become void of the expected support.

Rise and Development of Revenge Pornography and Cyberblackmail

As asserted earlier in the paper, academic scholars have termed revenge pornography as a technology-facilitated abuse or violation of another person's privacy. Earlier in the century, the cases of revenge pornography and cyber blackmailing were not many; however, with the advancement of technology, smart devices such as mobile phones, smart televisions, computers, and smartwatches can now access the Internet. However, with the ease of access can the freedom to abuse them. People have actively used these as tools of terror and invaded other people's privacy through hacking and cyber trolling to obtain information that can be used as leverage. Nonconsensual pornography refers to the distribution of sexual images and videos of another person without their due consent ("Citron & Franks, 2014; Stroud & Henson, 2017"). This trend has been a major issue among the millennials who have vast access and knowledge on using technology, especially with women as the victims (Citron). One out of every twenty-five people experiences the threat of someone posting their explicit material without prior consent ("Nonconsensual Image Sharing," 2016).

Nonconsensual pornography is a developing dimension of sexual violence that has been further promoted through Computer-Mediated Communication (CMC) such as social-networking sites and the Internet. In 2010, ESPN reporter Erin Andrews was secretly recorded while coming out of the shower nude. The aim of this unknown perpetrator was a financial incentive; after failing to receive any offers on the video, he still released the video anyway. From 2014 to 2017, several celebrities have had their explicit photos and videos leaked on the Internet, which has opened the public eye that it could be any of the next being targeted. One of the first mainstream instances of revenge pornography released featured celebrities Paris Hilton in 2004 and Kim Kardashian in 2007 (Beato,2010).In these cases, revenge pornography was an act of getting revenge for a relationship that ended badly for their ex-intimate partners. However, not all cases of revenge pornography are cases of hacking or celebrities. Research estimates that around eighty percent of nonconsensual

pornography is acquired through the voluntary sharing of explicit images through a practice referred to as sexting ("Henry & Powel, 2015; Meyer, 2016: Winkelman et al., 2014")

OVERVIEW

Types of Pornography

One of the challenges plaguing the fight against revenge pornography is the lack of knowledge of this topic, where consensual pornography can be mistaken for nonconsensual pornography. This paper will address four common types of pornography on the Internet; consensual pornography, uninvolved pornography, on-voluntary pornography and edited portrayals.

1. **Uninvolved Pornography:** In this kind of pornography, neither the victim nor the person entrusted with the explicit content was responsible for the leak by giving their consent. The factors that lead to such occurrences include cybercrimes such as trolling, hacking, or theft of devices. This kind of pornography is not made to acquire revenge on the victim, and it is either financially driven or just for the fun and amusement of the perpetrator with the intent to gain popularity and reputation among their online fanatics. Another developing issue with uninvolved pornography is using these explicit materials as leverage for blackmailing uses. These videos and memes are being used to make memes; while the intent of the memes could be casual, the damage it does to the victim can be quite traumatizing. The issue with uninvolved pornography has been made worse by the existence of media sharing social platforms such as WhatsApp, Facebook, and Instagram (Law Audience, 2020).

2. **Non-Voluntary Pornography:** Non-voluntary pornography is a subtype of nonconsensual pornography where sexually explicit images or videos are taken or distributed without the victim's knowledge. In this case, the victims are completely unaware they are being watched or filmed; for example, in the case of ESPN journalist Erin Andrews in 2010 where she was filmed across the peeping hole by an unknown offender while she was coming out of the shower with absolutely no knowledge she was being recorded. Later the video was distributed on the Internet (Law Audience, 2020).

3. **Edited Portrayals:** In this case, a different person's body is edited and matched with the victim's face in a process referred to as morphing when shared with the intent to defame the target, blackmail them or simply for fun; it is referred to as nonconsensual pornography (Law Audience, 2020).

4. **Non-consensual Pornography:** When it comes to sexual violence, nonconsensual pornography is a topic that has constantly been looked down on sadly; this shows how lowly the society regards women and their morals; according to research, ninety percent of revenge pornography is usually women or girls. The moral decadence of the community has to be stopped to help empower the female gender to better themselves. This cannot be achieved when one gender is constantly perceived as better and actively tries to the other under their heel. Ninety-three percent of victims suffer significant emotional distress after this experience, with up to eighty-two percent losing their jobs and alternatively finding it difficult to secure jobs in other areas. Apart from the financial blow that is struck on the victim, they also end up in a estranged relationship or, in some scenarios, completely lose them.

Reasons for Lack of Well-Thought Laws Prohibiting Revenge Pornography

One of the challenges that face revenge pornography is the lack of laws and regulations to govern the distribution of explicit images and videos without the victims' consent. The lack of well-established and harsh laws that prohibit cyberbullying and the distribution of explicit images and videos on the Internet have motivated offenders to pursue their vile activities constantly. This article addresses how the public and the private aspects affect the formulation of these laws, the unnoticed difference between consensual and nonconsensual pornography and how to address blackmail issues.

1. **The Public and Private Aspects:** Revenge pornography is a developing problem in this modern-day era. People generally assume that the posts can be assumed for fun, but the truth is that these images and videos have the potency to leave deep scars on the victim that could take a very long

time to heal, and in other extreme cases, the victims end up committing suicide. It was not until a few years ago that this was openly viewed as a threat. However, well-thought laws are yet to get established to prohibit the public from sharing the explicit content of the victims. One of the reasons for this is that those interactive websites that host these vile actions are immune to prosecution. Moreover, in cases where civil lawsuits manage to get the website to bring down the posted content, several other websites will pop in their place and post the content again. The one true way for the public to beat this counter-measure of these websites is by campaigning and advocating for the formulation of laws to safeguard the privacy of people who have not given consent for their explicit content to be shared. However, the major problem is that some of the active audiences on these sites find sexual thrill when viewing these images or videos or when they are insulting the victims. Lack of unity among the public in fighting this scourge is one of the reasons there are no strict rules prohibiting revenge pornography.

2. **Unrecognized Difference between Consensual and Non-consensual:** Pornography and Cyberblackmail: Limited research and established laws have posed a challenge for the public to differentiate between consensual and nonconsensual pornography. Nonconsensual pornography refers to the distribution of explicit sexual images or videos without the victim's consent. On the other hand, consensual pornography refers to explicit images and videos shared with the consent and knowledge of the person in them. However, with little research on this topic, the public is not educated; therefore, to them, pornography is pornography in general, where people are objectified as items of sex. According to research, ninety percent of the time, women tend to be on the receiving end under which they are labeled as 'sluts,' and their sexual integrity is damaged. These comments and trolls lead to the victims having low self-esteem and confidence, depression, and induced anxiety attacks, leading to suicide. Research has to be encouraged in this field to provide more knowledge regarding revenge pornography, which can be utilized to pursue justice for the victims of nonconsensual pornography.

3. **Tackling blackmail:** Cyber blackmail and extortion refer to the act where cybercriminals demand payment or make other similar demands using the threat of data compromise or the denial of service ((Cyber Extortion: An Industry Hot Topic, 2016). When it comes to handling these situations, paying them or falling in line with their demands most probably never stops them. In some situations, the cybercriminals are usually bluffing, trying to get you to have self-doubt and therefore benefit from it, while in other cases, the cyber-criminal is serious with the full intent to inflict damage. The following strategies can be followed in the case of cyber blackmail.

   ◦ **End your contact with the cyber-criminal;** by maintaining further contact with the criminal, chances are they will find a weak link within you to convince you to fall into their demand. If you follow their will, at best, you can get them to delay further demand failure, to which they will release the material they are holding over you. It is advisable to log out of your internet presence and cut off the communication chain with the offender.

   ◦ **Place filters and another protective measure on your email accounts;** when you sever their connection link to you on the Internet, they will follow you back to the email and further on with their demands and threats. Therefore, you should block and report that offender as spam to prevent this. Thereby he will have no access to you at all. You can further change your privacy settings such that the offender cannot access the list of your friends and try to reach you through a proxy.

○ **Contacting Authorities is another very crucial measure to take**. A few years ago, contacting the authorities or the law enforcement agencies would not have changed anything. However, several laws have been enacted to protect people from cyberbullying and ensure that offenders are held responsible. An example of such systems placed to offer online protection includes the Cyber Civil Rights Initiative, the White House Task Force, which protects students from assault and the Federal Legislative Bill. The challenge facing this measure is when the perpetrator is located in a different state, which could bring a case of jurisdiction complication.

○ **Another measure to take if you find yourself a victim of cyber blackmail is to address the damage**. When it comes to blackmailing, some cyber-criminals are usually bluffing while others are serious, and most of the time, they usually go through with the threat. When you get blackmailed, the chance is that damage will get done regardless of whether you pay the criminal or not. One of the strategies is removing the blackmail content; you can do this by requesting the website to take down the incriminating information. Another strategy that can be used is rebuilding your online reputation to cover up the negative results that come up when your name is searched. Another tactic that can be used is to register your image with the national copyright office, thereby cementing your case in case of blackmail; you can sue the offender on the legal grounds of copyright infringement.

○ **Password encryption and protection of devices are usually a strategy to protect yourself from hacking**. A process from which a hacker can obtain information and use t as leverage to make you bend to their will. A strong password should eliminate the chance of an educated guesser or be hacked.

○ **Putting a sticker over your web camera**, nowadays hackers are getting more creative in inventing new ways to obtain information illegally. For example, they can hack into the web camera of a computer and monitor a person's activity using the real-time video feed, which they can later use to blackmail and extort them if they were to record something private or intimate. Putting a stick or any object to deter their vision could go a long way to ensure there is leverage to use.

Effects of Revenge Pornography and Cyberblackmail

Revenge pornography and cyber blackmail have adverse effects on the victims. What you would consider a joke or just a casual meme could be the reason someone else remains scarred for the rest of his or her life and, in some cases lifelong mental health repercussions. Apart from health, revenge pornography can lead to estranged marriages and relationships, social out casting and shaming, induced levels of anxiety and depression, and high levels of emotional imbalance due to guilt and paranoia. Moreover, when these cases are not handled professionally with measures such as therapy, depression could lead to suicide.

1. **Breach of Trust:** Trust is a critical tool in addressing the interaction between individuals in society. Lack of trust directly translates to poor interactions since everyone operates with the assumption that everyone is out to get them. Apart from the mental and psychological torment, the victim has to go through, revenge pornography, the will to trust gets broken. Trust is at the root of an individual's ability to share personal information with other people. When this is broken, everyone in the society is suspicious and hence the ability to communicate and help each other solve problems in the

society gets severed. Therefore, trust can be considered a social norm that is critical to ensuring continuity within the society. Victims of revenge pornography lost their trust after formally putting their trust in their ex-partners, believing they would observe their privacy. According to studies conducted, when people lose trust in each other, chances are they will not trust in the government and other governing institutions used to control society, which could result in a state of anarchy and lawlessness.

2. **Coercive Control:** Coercive Control refers to the situation where the person you feel you are personally or emotionally connected to constantly makes you feel controlled, isolated and dependent on them. Usually, these are the dominating signs in a toxic relationship where one person feels they own their partner and there is nothing they can do about it. The most common signs of coercion control include the other person isolating you from your friends or family, usually pointing out that they do not like him, they tend to get control of the other person's finances, usually limiting them to how they make or use the money, threatening to reveal private or explicit material s about you, these could be sexual image or videos. Revenge porn can be used to exert control over the victim where the offender threatens to expose the explicit images to the Internet if the victim fails to follow the directions offered by the perpetrator. Using this as the leverage, they can control the dressing code of the victim, how they relate to friends and family, how they earn and use their finances, being jealous and insecure or threatening to physically harm the victim and release those items if the victim were to report the issue.

3. **Social Impact:** Nudity and explicit content are considered highly repulsive in society, and when revenge porn is leaked on the Internet and made available to everyone, these social and cultural morals tend to erode. One social impact of revenge pornography is the erosion of societal morals; in the modern era, where children can access mobile phones as early as the age of ten, the prevalence of revenge porn impacts the growth negatively.

Another negative impact of revenge pornography is the loss of trust in the systems that control society. Victims of Revenge pornography had argued that when they tried to seek the help of law enforcement agencies, they were told that a crime had not yet been committed. Usually, this is because the interactive websites hosting these vile activities are protected from legal lawsuits, making them immune to the scrutiny of law. When the victims cannot access the help they desperately need, they tend to lose their trust in the government and its protection capacity. When society loses its interest in social institutions, maintaining peace and order tends to become a challenge since no one is willing to conform to a weak system.

Best Practices to Avoid Being Victim to Revenge Porn and Cyberblackmail

The development of regulations, rules and laws that safeguard and protect the society against threats posed by revenge porn and blackmail can prove quite slow due to obstacles that block the road to this achievement, such as the protection of interactive websites that host the distribution of the explicit materials, the unwillingness of the public to openly protest against revenge pornography due to the belief that one should not be sending those unsolicited images in the first place. To avoid being a statistic being counted among the toll of victims, you can start by practicing these simple precautionary measures.

1. **Stop sharing and capturing nude photos**: The safest way to prevent and end the cycle of revenge pornography is by not taking the pictures at all in the first place. Even if you were to exercise the precaution of not sending the pictures to anyone, the risk still lies with them being located in your phone. In case of theft or hacking, there is still a big chance they will be leaked or used to blackmail you. When photos are taken, a copy automatically uploads itself in the cloud, and when devices are synced, for example, computers and your mobile phones, more copies are generated, which increases your chances of being a victim. The second and very important rule to ensuring you are not a victim is refusing to share nude pictures or videos with anyone. Bonds get severed, and trust gets broken; even in the cause of love, it is advisable to exercise some amount of precaution. Once those pictures are sent, you are technically under the control of that person if the relationship was to go south.

2. **Protect your Devices:** In this modern era, hackers have innovated more cunning and smart ways to trick people into releasing personal information, which can be later used to hack into your devices and retrieve personal information, which can blackmail and coerce other individuals. Sometimes technology can frustrate by leaving tiny loopholes that can be used to trick the systems into releasing personal information; therefore, to avoid the occurrence of this scenario, it is advisable to ensure your devices are fully encrypted and protected with strong passwords and logins that would take much more than a simple guess to crack. When the level of hacking rises, it is up to the individual to rise to the occasion and set necessary precautionary measures for their protection. "Do not wait for the disease to infect so you can try to administer the cure instead avoid contracting the disease all along" this metaphorically means instead of having to undergo through the torment of trying to contact websites to pull down explicit image and videos, it is advisable to use protect the devices and deter the cybercriminal from accessing those explicit materials.Do not be scared to tell someone to delete a picture you feel is explicit.When someone takes a picture that you do not feel comfortable with, it is critical to tell them to delete it and check to confirm it has been deleted. No one should feel scared to safeguard his or her privacy and mental serenity regardless of how you feel about that person. Sixty percent of victims of revenge pornography are a result of an angry ex-partner who seeks to cause emotional distress to the other person due to the relationship that ended badly. Therefore, it is advisable to keep in mind that emotions that you could be feeling now could fade, and when necessary precautions have not been set in place, you could get embarrassed greatly. If a professional photographer has taken a photo, it is advisable to ensure that you own the copyrights; this way, that person cannot distribute that image or video without your consent.

3. **Cover identifying features and the face**: If you have to send that explicit image or video, the least one can cover their face or any other features that could identify you, such as tattoos, birthmarks, or the face. It is critical to remember that friendships do not last forever, and relationships too can end. Statistically, victims of revenge porn fall due to ex-partners; therefore, if you have to send a photo or video that could later affect your mental health, you can block or crop out identifying features.

Pros, Cons of Revenge Porn and Cyber Blackmailing

Cons

Revenge porn, also known as nonconsensual pornography, refers to the distribution of explicit images or videos of another person without their consent. The key aim of this action is to damage the sexual integrity of the victim and by it manages to annoy, embarrass, and humiliate the target.

1. **Mental Health and well-being:** Once the explicit materials are leaked, the victims undergo immerse stigmatization by the society, usually referred to as'sluts' even in the cases where the victim is a male. According to research conducted, ninety-three percent of the victims suffer significant emotional distress. The resulting disgrace, social cutting off, and mocking of the victim are enough to induce anxiety, paranoia, and depression. There is a common myth that the effects of revenge pornography can only last as long as it is trending, and when the public finds something else to induce their amusement, the chances are that revenge pornography will be forgotten. However, the effects of revenge pornography and the negative comments that follow, especially if the interactive website attached the victim's contact information, can leave lifelong scars that can be quite challenging ever to get over.

2. **Financial Challenges:** Coupled with the disturbing mental health, the victims have to undergo financial problems where they cannot access employment opportunities due to their already tarnished public image. In the long run, these victims abuse drugs until they get addicted to the point of no return or, in other cases, due to anxiety and depression, the victims commit suicide. The shadow cast by the revenge pornography is very dark and long that the only way to escape it is by changing their names, altering their physical appearances, and relocating to other places. In short, the victim's mental, emotional, and physical strain and torment do not end easily.

3. **Estranged Marriages and relationships:** Victims of revenge pornography end up losing their relationships due to shaming and the loss of their sexual and moral integrity.

Pros

1. **Swallowing the bitter pill**: The severity of lifelong mental health repercussions coupled with several other negative effects of revenge pornography and cyber blackmail do not merit this topic any pros. The aftermath effects of revenge pornography have no end and can pursue the victim their whole lifetime.

CONCLUSION

Increasing general awareness of this topic is critical in ending revenge pornography in modern society. Revenge pornography is a repulsive reflection of society's views that women are an inferior gender and can be objectified as sex objects. There is a need to create more organizations that serve in the capacity of the Cyber Civil Rights Initiatives (CCRI), which campaign and raise public awareness on nonconsensual pornography via the information provided on its website, journals, and media interventions. This organization further provides emotional and technical support to the victims of such atrocities. In the field of practitioning and law, there is a need to devise more ways to curb the spread and promotion of the distribution of explicit materials despite the elusive nature of the interactive websites that host platforms that permit the posting of pictures and videos.

Finally, to avoid being a victim of revenge pornography, it is critical to exercise precaution at a personal level by encrypting the phone to dodge hackers and, even more importantly, to ensure you do not capture or send explicit photos at all.

REFERENCES

Bates, S. (2016). Revenge Porn and Mental Health. *Feminist Criminology*, *12*(1), 22–42. doi:10.1177/1557085116654565

Coercive control and the law - Rights of Women. (2016). Rights of Women. https://rightsofwomen.org.uk/get-information/violence-against-women-and-international-law/coercive-control-and-the-law/

Cyber Extortion: An Industry Hot Topic. (2016, November 23). CIS. https://www.cisecurity.org/insights/blog/cyber-extortion-an-industry-hot-topic

Extortion: Strategies. (2014, November 22). Take Back the Tech. https://takebackthetech.net/be-safe/extortion-strategies

Guggisberg, M. (2017, April 3). *Revenge Porn: A Growing Contemporary Problem*. ResearchGate. https://www.researchgate.net/publication/316075558_Revenge_Porn_A_Growing_Contemporary_Problem

Hadwin, J. (2015). *Victim Blaming And Third-Person Effect: A Comparative Analysis Of Attitudes For Revenge Porn And Sexual Assault*. Shareok. https://shareok.org/bitstream/handle/11244/54533/Hadwin_okstate_0664M_15165.pdf?sequence=1

Henry, N., Mcglynn, C., Powell, A., Scott, A. J., Johnson, K., & Flynn, A. (2020). *Image-based sexual abuse: a study on the causes and consequences of non-consensual nude or sexual imagery*. Routledge.

Kamal, M., & Newman, W. J. (2016). Revenge Pornography: Mental Health Implications and Related Legislation. *The Journal of the American Academy of Psychiatry and the Law*, *44*(3), 359–367. https://jaapl.org/content/44/3/359 PMID:27644870

Kirchengast, T., & Crofts, T. (2019). The legal and policy contexts of "revenge porn" criminalisation: The need for multiple approaches. *Oxford University Commonwealth Law Journal*, *19*(1), 1–29. doi:10.1080/14729342.2019.1580518

Law Audience. (2020, June 6). *Volume 2 & Issue 2» The Crime of Privacy Invasion-An Intricate Analysis*. Lawaudience.com. https://www.lawaudience.com/the-crime-of-privacy-invasion-an-intricate-analysis/

Mania, K. (2020). The Legal Implications and Remedies Concerning Revenge Porn and Fake Porn: A Common Law Perspective. *Sexuality & Culture*, *24*(6), 2079–2097. doi:10.1007/s12119-020-09738-0

Mania, K. (2020). The Legal Implications and Remedies Concerning Revenge Porn and Fake Porn: A Common Law Perspective. *Sexuality & Culture*, *24*(6), 2079–2097. doi:10.1007/s12119-020-09738-0

Revenge Pornography. (2013). Mtsu.edu. https://www.mtsu.edu/first-amendment/article/1532/revenge-pornography

Reynolds, E. (2017, March 16). Revenge porn: what it is and how can it be stopped? *Wired*. https://www.wired.co.uk/article/revenge-porn-facebook-social-media

Šepec, M. (2019). *Revenge Pornography or Nonconsensual Dissemination of Sexually Explicit Material as a Sexual Offence or as a Privacy Violation Offence*. Zenoob. doi:10.5281/zenodo.3707562

Understanding revenge porn and how to get justice if affected - People Daily. (2019, September 30). PD. https://www.pd.co.ke/lifestyle/understanding-revenge-porn-and-how-to-get-justice-if-affected-7464/

Chapter 15
Role of Quantum Computing in Government and the Defence Sector

Vivek Topno
Amity University, India

Tannisha Kundu
Amity University, India

Mohan Kumar Dehury
Amity University, India

ABSTRACT

Quantum computing is a revolutionary technology that has the potential to transform various industries, including government operations, defence strategies, and national security. The chapter discusses its fundamental principles, advantages, limitations, and applications in cryptography, optimization, resource allocation, quantum sensing, and metrology. It highlights the need for quantum-resistant cryptography and post-quantum cryptographic algorithms to safeguard sensitive information. Quantum algorithms can improve decision-making processes, enhance efficiency, and address logistical challenges in defense strategy planning and disaster management. Quantum communication and secure networks are crucial for secure communication among government agencies, military units, and allied nations. Challenges include high costs, skilled personnel, and ethical and legal implications. The chapter concludes with a discussion on the future outlook of quantum computing in these sectors, emphasizing the need for continued research and investment.

INTRODUCTION

Quantum Computing in Government and Defense

In the ever-evolving realm of technology, quantum computing stands out as a groundbreaking field poised to bring about substantial transformations across numerous sectors, including government and

DOI: 10.4018/978-1-6684-9576-6.ch015

defence (Couteau et al., 2023). The established norms of computing face profound challenges from the distinctive attributes of quantum mechanics, such as superposition and entanglement, which quantum computers harness to execute intricate computations at unparalleled velocities. This study delves into the captivating domain of quantum computing, with a particular emphasis on its utilization within the contexts of government and defense.

Problem Domain

As computational demands continue to escalate, classical computers face limitations in solving complex problems efficiently. This prompts a need for alternative computing paradigms that can outpace classical computers in tackling intricate tasks. Quantum computing harnesses the principles of quantum mechanics to process information in a fundamentally different manner, enabling it to address challenges that were previously insurmountable using classical methods.

Statement

The central thesis of this research paper is to explore how quantum computing intersects with the domains of government and defense, uncovering the potential applications, challenges, and ethical considerations associated with its integration. By understanding the implications of quantum computing in these sectors, we aim to provide insights into the transformative power it holds for shaping the future of national security and strategic planning.

Objectives

- To elucidate the foundational principles of quantum computing and their departure from classical computing
- To analyse key quantum computing technologies and their relevance to government and defense applications.
- To examine quantum computing algorithms that have the potential to impact cryptography, optimization, and simulation.
- To investigate the role of quantum communication in ensuring secure information exchange within governmental and military contexts.
- To evaluate the potential applications of quantum computing in enhancing defense strategies, resource allocation, and logistics.
- To discuss ethical and security considerations arising from the integration of quantum computing in sensitive sectors.
- To highlight ongoing government initiatives and collaborations aimed at advancing quantum computing research and development.

WHAT IS QUANTUM COMPUTING?

Layman's Explanation

Imagine you have a very powerful computer that doesn't work like the regular computers you know. Instead of using bits that can only be 0 or 1, this special computer uses "quantum bits" or "qubits." These qubits can be 0, 1, or both 0 and 1 at the same time, thanks to the strange rules of quantum physics (Knight and Walmsley, 2019; Inglesant et al., 2018). This allows the computer to handle incredibly complex tasks way faster than normal computers. It's like having a supercharged calculator that can solve problems that were previously impossible or took a very long time to solve.

Technical Explanation

Quantum computing is a computational paradigm based on the principles of quantum mechanics. At its core, it utilizes quantum bits (qubits) which can represent both 0 and 1 simultaneously due to a phenomenon called superposition. This property allows quantum computers to explore multiple solutions in parallel, offering the potential for significant speedup in certain computations.

In the mathematical model, a qubit can be described using a vector in a two-dimensional complex vector space (Pan et al., 2017; Zhang et al., 2019). Mathematically, a qubit state $|\psi\rangle$ can be represented as a linear combination of basis states $|0\rangle$ and $|1\rangle$: $|\psi\rangle = \alpha|0\rangle + \beta|1\rangle$

where α and β are complex numbers that represent the probability amplitudes of the qubit being in states $|0\rangle$ and $|1\rangle$ respectively. The probability of measuring a qubit in state $|0\rangle$ is $|\alpha|^2$, and the probability of measuring it in state $|1\rangle$ is $|\beta|^2$. Importantly, because of superposition, the qubit can be in a combination of both states until measured.

Quantum gates are the building blocks of quantum circuits. They manipulate qubits, changing their states through unitary transformations. Quantum operations can be described using matrices or gate diagrams. For example, the Pauli-X gate, which acts as a classical NOT gate, flips the amplitudes of the basis states: Pauli-X $|0\rangle = |1\rangle$ Pauli-X $|1\rangle = |0\rangle$

Quantum algorithms leverage the properties of qubits to perform certain computations more efficiently than classical counterparts. Notable examples include Shor's algorithm for factoring large numbers and Grover's algorithm for searching an unsorted database (Herman and Friedson, 2018).

Quantum computing exploits the principles of quantum mechanics, like superposition and entanglement, to process information in ways that classical computers cannot. While its mathematical model can be intricate, the fundamental concept is harnessing the unique properties of qubits to perform powerful computations.

JOURNEY OF QUANTUM COMPUTING

Timeline of Quantum Computing (Mavroeidis et al., 2018; Dumitrescu et al., 2018; Krelina, 2021)

1980s: The concept of quantum computing begins to take shape, with physicist Richard Feynman proposing that quantum systems could simulate quantum physics more efficiently than classical computers.

1994: Peter Shor devises Shor's algorithm, demonstrating that a quantum computer could efficiently factor large numbers, which has implications for breaking classical encryption schemes.

1996: Lov Grover introduces Grover's algorithm, showcasing the potential of quantum computers to search unsorted databases faster than classical methods.

2000s: Experimental progress in controlling qubits leads to the development of rudimentary quantum computers capable of performing basic operations.

2010s: Companies like IBM, Google, and Rigetti build and announce their own quantum computers, focusing on increasing qubit coherence and error correction.

2019: Google claims to achieve quantum supremacy, performing a task that a classical computer would struggle to accomplish within a reasonable timeframe.

2020s: Quantum computing technology continues to advance, with increased emphasis on error correction, fault tolerance, and expanding qubit counts.

APPLICATIONS OF QUANTUM COMPUTING

Some fields in which quantum computing is applied is as follows (Basset et al., 2023; Kappe et al., 2023; Berendsen, 2019; Ningsih, Wadjdi, and Budiyanto, 2022).

Cryptography: Quantum computers have the potential to break classical encryption schemes, leading to the need for quantum-resistant cryptography.

Optimization: Quantum algorithms like the Quantum Approximate Optimization Algorithm (QAOA) can provide solutions to optimization problems in fields such as finance, logistics, and supply chain management.

Drug Discovery: Quantum computing can simulate complex molecular interactions, aiding in the discovery of new drugs and materials.

Machine Learning: Quantum machine learning algorithms could provide faster solutions for pattern recognition and data analysis tasks.

Financial Modelling: Quantum computers can perform rapid simulations for risk assessment and portfolio optimization in finance.

Materials Science: Quantum simulations can aid in understanding materials' properties and designing new materials with specific characteristics.

Supply Chain Optimization: Quantum computing's ability to handle complex optimization problems could revolutionize supply chain management.

Climate Modelling: Quantum simulations can contribute to more accurate climate models and advance our understanding of environmental changes.

Logistics and Routing: Quantum algorithms can optimize routes for delivery and transportation networks.

Artificial Intelligence: Quantum computing could enhance AI capabilities by improving training of complex machine learning models.

APPLICATIONS OF QUANTUM COMPUTING IN GOVERNMENT

Quantum computing holds promise for various governmental sectors, offering the potential to solve complex problems faster and more efficiently than classical computers. Here are some key areas where quantum computing can be applied in government, along with examples (Ningsih, Wadjdi, and Budiyanto, 2022; Arraoui et al., 2023; Al-Hawawreh and Hossain, 2023; Guillame, Vrain, and Wael, 2020).

Data Analysis and Policy Formulation

Quantum computing's advanced processing capabilities enable efficient analysis of vast datasets, aiding government agencies in identifying trends, making informed decisions, and formulating effective policies. Quantum algorithms can unravel insights from complex data, enhancing the understanding of social, economic, and environmental factors that influence policy direction.

For instance, quantum computing can rapidly analyse demographic data to optimize social welfare programs, ensuring resources are allocated where they are needed most. This capability extends to economic forecasting, allowing governments to make well-informed budget allocations and policy adjustments. Quantum-enhanced data analysis empowers policymakers to respond swiftly and effectively to dynamic challenges, fostering more responsive and evidence-based governance.

Example: Quantum algorithms can help analyze demographic data for more effective social welfare programs.

Secure Communication and Encryption

Quantum computing offers revolutionary solutions for secure communication and encryption in government. Quantum communication protocols leverage the principles of quantum mechanics to establish unbreakable encryption methods. Quantum Key Distribution (QKD) ensures that data exchange between government agencies remains confidential and tamper-proof. By utilizing the properties of entanglement and superposition, quantum encryption provides a new level of data security, safeguarding sensitive information from potential quantum-based cyberattacks. This application has the potential to reshape the way classified information is exchanged, ensuring privacy and integrity in government communication.

Example: Quantum key distribution (QKD) ensures confidential communication among government agencies.

Financial Modelling and Taxation

Quantum computing's potential in the domain of financial modeling and taxation lies in its ability to revolutionize economic forecasting, risk assessment, and tax optimization strategies. Quantum algorithms can efficiently handle complex calculations inherent in financial markets, offering insights that go beyond classical computational capabilities. This advancement holds promise for governments in optimizing tax collection, budget allocation, and economic policies by providing more accurate predictions of market trends, helping manage risks, and enhancing fiscal planning for greater economic stability.

Example: Quantum algorithms can optimize tax rates to maximize revenue while considering economic indicators.

Public Health and Epidemiology

In the realm of government applications, the integration of quantum computing into public health and epidemiology holds immense potential. Quantum simulations can provide a new level of accuracy in modeling disease spread and analyzing complex interactions within biological systems. By harnessing the computational power of quantum systems, researchers can rapidly simulate various scenarios of disease outbreaks, aiding in the formulation of effective public health strategies and interventions. This capability not only enhances our understanding of disease dynamics but also contributes to proactive measures for disease prevention and management, ultimately strengthening national healthcare systems and response capabilities.

Example: Quantum computers can simulate the impact of various intervention strategies during disease outbreaks.

Infrastructure Optimization

Quantum computing's potential in government extends to optimizing critical infrastructure such as transportation networks, energy distribution systems, and urban planning. By leveraging quantum algorithms, governments can efficiently solve complex optimization problems, leading to enhanced resource allocation, reduced congestion, and improved overall efficiency within cities. Quantum computing's ability to process multiple possibilities simultaneously enables the exploration of optimal solutions, addressing challenges such as traffic flow, energy consumption, and environmental sustainability. As urban populations grow and resource demands increase, quantum-powered infrastructure optimization offers the prospect of more resilient and sustainable government systems. *Example:* Quantum computing can optimize traffic flow and reduce congestion in urban areas.

Environmental Conservation

Quantum computing's application in government extends to environmental conservation through advanced simulations that model climate change scenarios. Quantum simulations enable highly accurate predictions of environmental changes, aiding in the formulation of effective policies to mitigate climate impacts (Patel et al., 2019). By analysing intricate interactions in ecosystems and simulating the effects of policy changes on greenhouse gas emissions, quantum-enhanced simulations contribute to informed decision-making that addresses critical environmental challenges. This has the potential to guide sustainable resource management, preserve biodiversity, and shape strategies to combat climate change, ultimately fostering a more resilient and ecologically balanced future.

Example: Quantum computers can simulate the effects of policy changes on greenhouse gas emissions.

Resource Allocation and Disaster Response

Quantum computing's unique ability to solve complex optimization problems efficiently holds significant potential in the domain of resource allocation during emergencies and disaster response. Quantum algorithms can rapidly analyze vast datasets, considering multiple variables and constraints to optimize the allocation of critical resources such as medical supplies, personnel, and equipment. This capability enhances the agility and effectiveness of disaster response efforts, ensuring that resources are distributed in a timely and targeted manner to mitigate the impact of natural disasters, humanitarian crises, and emergency situations.

Example: Quantum computing can optimize distribution of supplies and aid during humanitarian crises (Hareshbhai et al., 2023).

Digital Governance and e-Government Services

In the realm of digital governance and e-government services, quantum computing holds the potential to revolutionize how governments interact with citizens and manage public services. Quantum-enhanced encryption ensures the security and integrity of sensitive citizen data, paving the way for secure online transactions and e-services. Additionally, quantum algorithms can streamline complex administrative tasks, optimizing resource allocation and decision-making processes. From secure data sharing to efficient service delivery, quantum computing promises to enhance transparency, efficiency, and security in the digital government landscape.

Example: Quantum-enhanced encryption ensures secure access to citizen records and sensitive information (Rani et al., 2023).

Energy and Resource Management

Quantum algorithms have the potential to revolutionize the way energy grids are managed by efficiently balancing supply and demand, leading to reduced energy wastage and enhanced sustainability. Moreover, these algorithms can provide insights into resource distribution for critical infrastructure projects, enabling more effective utilization of resources and contributing to greener and more efficient urban planning strategies.

Example: Quantum computing can optimize energy grids to balance supply and demand (Hareshbhai et al., 2023; Kumar et al., 2021).

Public Safety and Law Enforcement

Law enforcement organizations may proactively address crime hotspots, optimize resource deployment, and maintain public safety thanks to quantum machine learning algorithms' ability to scan enormous volumes of data to find trends, abnormalities, and potential security risks. Quantum cryptography can also improve the security of data sharing and communication among law enforcement organizations, protecting sensitive data from interception by hackers or unauthorized parties. With the use of this application, law enforcement operations should be able to operate in a more secure and effective setting, ultimately making communities safer and enhancing crime prevention tactics. As an illustration, quantum algorithms are capable of locating crime hotspots and more efficiently allocating police resources.

Government Surveillance and Privacy Protection

Quantum computing introduces new dimensions to government surveillance and privacy protection. On one hand, quantum-enhanced machine learning enables the analysis of vast data streams for pattern recognition, enhancing threat detection and intelligence gathering capabilities. On the other hand, quantum cryptography offers a unique opportunity to strike a balance between surveillance needs and individual privacy rights. Quantum secure communication protocols can safeguard classified government information while ensuring that citizens' private data remains secure from potential breaches, making it a pivotal tool in preserving both national security and civil liberties.

Example: Quantum secure communication protocols protect classified government information (Hareshbhai et al., 2023).

Election Security and Voter Privacy

Within the applications of quantum computing in government, ensuring the integrity of democratic processes and protecting voter privacy is paramount. Quantum cryptography can fortify electronic voting systems, rendering them resilient to advanced cyber threats that could compromise election results. Quantum-enhanced encryption techniques can secure voter data, guaranteeing the anonymity and confidentiality of citizens' choices while maintaining the transparency and accuracy of electoral outcomes. This quantum-powered approach addresses the critical concerns of election security and voter privacy, contributing to the foundation of trustworthy democratic governance.

Example: Quantum-enhanced encryption ensures voter anonymity and secure vote counting (Patel et al., 2019).

APPLICATIONS OF QUANTUM COMPUTING IN DEFENSE

Cryptography and Codebreaking

Cryptography and codebreaking represent a pivotal application of quantum computing in defense. Quantum computers possess the potential to break classical encryption methods, threatening the security of sensitive defense communications and classified data. Algorithms like Shor's algorithm exploit quantum parallelism to efficiently factor large numbers, rendering classical encryption techniques vulnerable. This capability compels defense agencies to explore and develop quantum-resistant encryption methods that can withstand the computational power of quantum adversaries, ensuring the confidentiality and integrity of critical defense information in an era of evolving threats.

Example: Shor's algorithm can break widely used encryption schemes, posing a threat to secure communication and data protection (Pan et al., 2017; Mavroeidis et al., 2018; Dumitrescu et al., 2018).

Secure Communication and Encryption

Secure Communication and Encryption: With impenetrable secure communication protocols, quantum computing's use in defense reaches its pinnacle. Quantum communication uses the concepts of quantum mechanics to offer an unmatched level of encryption that is unbreakable from prying eyes. Since any attempt to intercept the sent information disturbs the quantum state and makes the attempt identifiable, Quantum Key Distribution (QKD) ensures the exchange of encryption keys with unbreakable security. This capability ensures private communication between government and military organizations, protecting sensitive data from quantum-based attacks and online threats. In a period of growing cyber vulnerabilities, quantum-enhanced secure communication becomes the cornerstone of confidential data sharing, guaranteeing the integrity of classified information.

Example: Quantum cryptography prevents eavesdropping, safeguarding sensitive defense communications (Couteau et al., 2023; Inglesant et al., 2018).

Optimization for Military Planning

Optimization for military planning stands as a pivotal application of quantum computing in defense, promising to revolutionize resource allocation, strategic decision-making, and operational efficiency. Quantum algorithms possess the unique ability to process numerous scenarios simultaneously, enabling rapid analysis of complex logistical challenges encountered in military campaigns. From troop deployment to supply distribution and mission planning, quantum optimization algorithms hold the potential to offer optimal solutions that minimize costs, enhance troop safety, and streamline critical resource allocation, thus providing a formidable tool for military planners to navigate the complexities of modern warfare.

Example: Quantum computing can streamline troop movement, resource distribution, and mission planning (Mavroeidis et al., 2018; Dumitrescu et al., 2018; Kappe et al., 2023).

Cybersecurity

Quantum computers have the potential to revolutionize cryptographic techniques by rapidly breaking traditional encryption methods, necessitating the development of quantum-resistant cryptographic protocols. This shift enables defense agencies to fortify data protection, thwart cyber threats, and ensure the confidentiality of classified information against adversaries equipped with quantum capabilities. Quantum-enhanced encryption mechanisms offer unprecedented security, fostering resilient communication channels and safeguarding critical defense networks from emerging quantum-based cyberattacks.

Example: Quantum-safe encryption protocols protect defense networks from quantum-based attacks (Arraoui et al., 2023; Al-Hawawreh and Hossain, 2023).

Sensor and Radar Systems

Quantum computing has the potential to revolutionize sensor and radar systems in defense. By leveraging quantum algorithms, these systems could achieve enhanced accuracy and sensitivity in target detection, identification, and tracking. Quantum-enhanced sensing technologies could enable radar systems to identify stealth aircraft, submarines, and other advanced threats more effectively. Quantum-based algorithms could also optimize sensor data processing, reducing false positives and improving the overall efficiency of defense surveillance systems. This application holds the promise of significantly advancing the capabilities of military intelligence and reconnaissance efforts.

Example: Quantum sensors can improve the accuracy of detecting stealth aircraft or submarines (Kappe et al., 2023; Berendsen, 2019).

Nuclear Modelling and Simulation

Nuclear modelling and simulation, as an application of quantum computing in defense, offers a transformative approach to understanding the intricacies of nuclear reactions. By harnessing the unique capabilities of quantum computers, accurate simulations of nuclear interactions can be achieved, contributing to advancements in defense research, nuclear policy formulation, and non-proliferation efforts. Quantum simulations provide insights into the behaviours of atomic nuclei, facilitating the design and evaluation of nuclear weapons and reactors without the need for real-world tests. This application has the potential to enhance national security by ensuring the reliability of nuclear technologies while minimizing the risks associated with physical experimentation.

Example: Quantum computers can simulate nuclear weapon behaviours to ensure reliability without real-world testing (Herman and Friedson, 2018; Ningsih, Wadjdi, and Budiyanto, 2022).

Complex System Simulation

Quantum computing offers a transformative approach to simulating intricate defense scenarios involving chemical reactions, biological processes, and material properties. By exploiting quantum parallelism, quantum simulations can provide more accurate and detailed insights into the behavior of complex systems, enabling better understanding of the effects of chemical agents, the performance of advanced materials, and the interactions within biological processes. This capability has the potential to revolutionize defense research, leading to optimized strategies, enhanced material design, and improved preparedness against chemical and biological threats.

Example: Quantum simulations can model the effects of chemical agents or evaluate the performance of new materials (Pan et al., 2017; Patel et al., 2019).

AI and Machine Learning for Threat Detection

AI and Machine Learning for Threat Detection: Quantum computing's application in defense extends to leveraging its computational power for enhancing AI and machine learning algorithms in threat detection. Quantum machine learning enables the analysis of vast and complex datasets, identifying patterns and anomalies in radar systems, cybersecurity networks, and intelligence data. By harnessing quantum parallelism and superior data processing, quantum-enhanced AI can offer faster and more accurate recognition of emerging threats, aiding defense agencies in proactive identification and mitigation of potential security risks.

Example: Quantum algorithms can improve threat detection in radar systems by identifying unusual patterns in data (Zhang et al., 2019).

Image and Signal Processing

In the realm of defense, quantum computing's impact on image and signal processing holds promise for enhancing reconnaissance, surveillance, and intelligence gathering. Quantum algorithms have the potential to process large and complex datasets from satellite imagery, radar systems, and encrypted signals more efficiently than classical methods. This could lead to sharper image analysis, improved target identification, and enhanced signal decryption, ultimately bolstering defense capabilities by providing quicker and more accurate insights from sensor data.

Example: Quantum algorithms can sharpen satellite imagery or analyze encrypted signals more efficiently (Hareshbhai et al., 2023).

Nuclear Non-Proliferation

Quantum computing holds the potential to significantly advance nuclear non-proliferation efforts by enabling more accurate and efficient simulations of nuclear reactions and weapon behaviors. These simulations, performed with quantum algorithms, can verify disarmament agreements and assess the reliability of existing nuclear arsenals without the need for actual testing. Quantum-enhanced modeling enhances the international community's ability to monitor and enforce nuclear non-proliferation agreements while maintaining confidentiality regarding sensitive weapon designs and materials. This application contributes to global security by promoting transparency and bolstering efforts to prevent the spread of nuclear weapons.

Example: Quantum simulations can validate the dismantlement of nuclear weapons without revealing sensitive information (Rani et al., 2023; Kumar et al., 2021).

Resource Allocation in Defense Logistics

Resource Allocation in Defense Logistics: Quantum computing's applications extend to optimizing resource allocation in defense logistics, where complex scenarios necessitate efficient distribution of personnel, equipment, and supplies. Quantum algorithms can tackle large-scale combinatorial optimization problems inherent in military campaigns, leading to enhanced operational effectiveness, minimized costs, and improved decision-making. By leveraging quantum parallelism, these algorithms explore multiple allocation strategies simultaneously, yielding solutions that classical computers would struggle to attain within reasonable timeframes. This capability holds the potential to revolutionize the way resources are managed in military contexts, ensuring that critical assets reach their destinations promptly, aiding troop deployment, and optimizing strategic planning.

Example: Quantum computing can optimize fuel and ammunition distribution for military campaigns (Guillame, Vrain, and Wael, 2020; Rani et al., 2023).

Battlefield Simulation and Strategy Planning

Quantum computing offers a paradigm shift in battlefield simulation and strategy planning by enabling highly accurate and complex simulations of various scenarios. Quantum simulations can factor in numerous variables and interactions, providing military strategists with unparalleled insights into the outcomes of different courses of action. This capability allows for the rapid development and refinement of optimal strategies, enhancing decision-making for military operations, resource allocation, and mission success. Quantum-enabled simulations have the potential to revolutionize how defense agencies analyze and anticipate outcomes in dynamic and high-stakes situations on the battlefield.

Example: Quantum simulations can help in planning complex military operations by considering multiple variables (Herman and Friedson, 2018; Dumitrescu et al., 2018).

CASE STUDY:

Case Study One: Quantum Computing in Secure Communication – Government

Application: Quantum Key Distribution (QKD) for Secure Government Communication

Description: Quantum Key Distribution (QKD), a method that makes use of quantum entanglement to create secure communication between ground stations, was demonstrated by the Chinese satellite "Micius". QKD offers unrivaled security for the exchange of encryption keys. Any attempt to intercept the information being transferred would cause the quantum state to change, making eavesdropping obvious. This is made possible via quantum entanglement. This technique has implications for highly secure government data transmission and communication, offering a way to guard against illegal access and guarantee the integrity of private data (Knight and Walmsley, 2019; Zhang et al., 2019).

Case Study Two: Quantum Computing in Defense - Simulating Nuclear Reactions

Application: Quantum Simulations for Nuclear Reactor Design

Description: A quantum computer was used by Los Alamos National Laboratory researchers to simulate nuclear processes. In comparison to conventional computers, quantum simulations offer a more effective method for simulating intricate nuclear interactions. By providing knowledge on the behavior and features of nuclear processes, these simulations aid in the design of safer and more effective nuclear reactors. In order to optimize reactor designs and comprehend nuclear phenomena, it is important to be able to accurately simulate nuclear behavior. This has consequences for both national security and energy production (Herman and Friedson, 2018; Dumitrescu et al., 2018; Krelina, 2021).

Case Study Three: Quantum Computing in Defense - Military Logistics Optimization

Application: Quantum Algorithms for Military Resource Allocation

Description: The defense sector often faces complex logistical challenges, such as optimizing troop deployment, supply distribution, and mission planning. Quantum algorithms have the potential to efficiently solve large-scale optimization problems that are crucial for military operations. By leveraging quantum computing's ability to explore multiple possibilities simultaneously, defense agencies can improve resource allocation, minimize costs, and enhance operational efficiency (Kappe et al., 2023; Arraoui et al., 2023; Guillame, Vrain, and Wael, 2020).

Case Study Four: Quantum Computing in Government - Public Health Forecasting

Application: Quantum Simulations for Epidemic Spread Prediction

Description: Public health agencies require accurate models to predict the spread of diseases and plan effective interventions. Quantum simulations offer the potential to simulate complex disease transmission dynamics more efficiently than classical methods. Quantum computers can handle large datasets and intricate interactions, enabling quicker simulations and more precise predictions for public health authorities (Herman and Friedson, 2018; Patel et al., 2019; Kumar et al., 2021).

MERITS AND DEMERITS OF QUANTUM COMPUTING

Merits

Speed: Quantum computers leverage the unique properties of qubits to perform multiple calculations simultaneously. This inherent parallelism allows them to solve complex problems much faster than classical computers, revolutionizing fields like cryptography, optimization, and scientific simulations. *Example:* Quantum computers can factor large numbers much faster using Shor's algorithm, impacting encryption and cryptography.

Optimization: Quantum algorithms excel at solving optimization problems by exploring multiple solutions in parallel. This capability is invaluable for industries like finance and logistics, where efficient resource allocation and decision-making are critical for success. *Example:* Quantum computing can optimize supply chain logistics, allocating resources for military operations efficiently.

Cryptography: Quantum computers have the ability to break classical encryption methods, driving the development of quantum-resistant cryptography. This transition ensures that data remains secure in the face of evolving computational capabilities. *Example:* Quantum computers threaten traditional encryption, necessitating advanced cryptographic techniques like lattice-based encryption.

Simulation: Quantum simulations enable accurate modeling of intricate interactions at the molecular and atomic levels. This aids in understanding complex systems, like chemical reactions and climate patterns, that are essential for scientific research and informed policy decisions. *Example:* Quantum simulations enable precise understanding of molecular interactions for drug development and advanced material design.

Machine Learning: Quantum machine learning algorithms process and analyze data more efficiently, enhancing pattern recognition and enabling AI systems to learn from complex datasets faster, thereby advancing fields like medical diagnosis and data analysis. *Example:* Quantum computers can speed up training complex AI models, improving pattern recognition in medical image analysis.

Communication: Quantum communication protocols provide unbreakable encryption through the principles of quantum mechanics. These protocols ensure secure data transmission, protecting sensitive information from interception or tampering. *Example:* Quantum key distribution (QKD) guarantees secure communication between government agencies by preventing eavesdropping.

Demerits:

Qubit Stability: Quantum computers are sensitive to external factors like temperature fluctuations and electromagnetic interference. This instability can cause qubits to lose their quantum states, leading to computation errors. *Example:* Environmental noise disrupting qubits' delicate quantum states, resulting in inaccurate calculations.

Error Correction: Due to the susceptibility of qubits to errors, error correction techniques are required. These techniques involve redundant qubits to detect and correct errors, which can significantly increase hardware and computational demands. *Example:* Implementing error correction consumes a substantial number of additional qubits, making quantum computations more complex and resource-intensive.

Hardware Complexity: Quantum computers require advanced technologies and precise control mechanisms to maintain qubit coherence. Building and maintaining such complex hardware setups can be challenging and expensive. *Example:* Creating and sustaining stable qubits that remain in their quantum states demands sophisticated equipment and expertise.

Limited Applicability: Quantum computers excel in specific types of problems, such as cryptography and optimization, but they are not universally advantageous. Some tasks are better suited for classical computers. *Example*: Quantum computers are not necessarily faster at tasks like simple arithmetic calculations that classical computers handle efficiently.

Resource Intensive: Quantum computations often require a significant number of qubits to achieve meaningful results. This demand for resources can strain hardware capabilities and complicate scaling efforts. *Example:* Complex quantum algorithms may require hundreds or thousands of qubits, which is currently challenging to achieve and maintain.

Scaling Challenges: Scaling up the number of qubits while maintaining their coherence is a formidable challenge. As qubit counts increase, managing interactions between qubits becomes more intricate. *Example:* As qubit numbers rise, it becomes increasingly difficult to suppress errors and maintain the quantum state of all qubits, hindering large-scale quantum computations.

FUTURE SCOPE

Secure Communication and Encryption: Quantum computing offers a transformative approach to secure communication and encryption by harnessing the principles of quantum mechanics. Quantum key distribution (QKD) ensures unbreakable encryption, as any eavesdropping attempt disrupts the quantum state, alerting both sender and receiver to potential tampering. In the future, quantum communication networks could establish ultra-secure channels for classified government communications, secure financial transactions, and confidential data exchange. With advancements in quantum technologies, the integration of quantum encryption methods into mainstream communication systems holds the potential to redefine the concept of data security, rendering traditional cryptographic methods obsolete and safeguarding sensitive information against quantum-powered threats.

Military Logistics Optimization: Quantum algorithms can navigate the complex variables of troop deployment, supply distribution, and mission planning with unparalleled efficiency, resulting in optimized resource utilization, reduced costs, and enhanced strategic outcomes. By leveraging quantum parallelism, these algorithms can evaluate numerous possibilities simultaneously, providing military planners with real-time insights that lead to more agile and effective decision-making. This quantum-powered approach to military logistics optimization promises to reshape the way resources are managed in defense operations, streamlining deployments and bolstering overall operational readiness.

Nuclear Modeling and Simulation: Quantum simulations offer the ability to precisely model complex nuclear reactions, behavior of isotopes, and even nuclear fusion processes. With quantum computers' computational power, scientists can gain deeper insights into nuclear phenomena, enabling safer and more efficient nuclear reactor designs, accurate assessment of nuclear weapon behaviors without actual testing, and enhanced nuclear non-proliferation efforts. As quantum technology advances, its role in simulating and understanding nuclear interactions is set to reshape how we approach energy production, national security, and international nuclear agreements.

Resource Allocation in Defense: Quantum algorithms can tackle complex optimization challenges that arise in military logistics, such as troop deployment, supply distribution, and mission planning. By simultaneously exploring multiple solutions, quantum computing can efficiently determine optimal resource allocation, leading to cost reduction, enhanced operational efficiency, and better-informed strategic decisions. This advancement aligns with the evolving nature of modern defense, where precision and agility in resource management play a pivotal role in maintaining readiness and effectively responding to dynamic security scenarios.

Intelligence and Surveillance: In the future scope of quantum computing, the field of intelligence and surveillance stands to benefit significantly. Quantum-enhanced machine learning and data analysis can revolutionize how vast amounts of information are processed and patterns are detected. Quantum algorithms can swiftly identify anomalies in data streams, aiding in the identification of potential threats or unusual activities. This technology can enhance predictive analysis and facilitate proactive measures in counterterrorism efforts, cybersecurity, and law enforcement. Quantum computing's ability to handle complex data sets with remarkable speed offers the potential to elevate the precision and efficiency of intelligence and surveillance operations, ensuring the safety and security of nations.

National Security Policy Formulation: In the future scope of quantum computing, the intricate modeling capabilities of quantum simulations can play a pivotal role in shaping national security policies. Quantum simulations can analyze complex geopolitical scenarios, provide insights into potential security threats, and assist in devising informed strategies. By harnessing quantum-enhanced computational power, governments can gain deeper understanding and predictive insights into global dynamics, enabling more effective policy responses and preemptive measures. This quantum-driven approach ensures that national security policies are founded on data-driven intelligence, enhancing a nation's preparedness and strategic decision-making prowess in an increasingly complex and interconnected world.

Election Security: Quantum computing has the potential to transform election security in the future by overcoming complicated problems that are difficult to solve with current techniques. Electronic voting systems can benefit from quantum cryptography's uncrackable encryption, which protects voter data and hinders tampering or illegal access. As adversaries using quantum computers attempt to crack conventional encryption, quantum-resistant cryptography approaches will become increasingly important. Additionally, voters' authentication can be strengthened by quantum-enhanced verification mechanisms, ensuring the accuracy and integrity of electoral procedures. Election security can be strengthened against new threats by utilizing the special qualities of quantum systems, strengthening the basis of democratic government and preserving public confidence in voting processes.

Financial and Economic Intelligence: Quantum-enhanced algorithms can analyse vast financial datasets and complex economic models much faster than classical methods. This speed enables more accurate economic forecasts, risk assessments, and real-time tracking of financial transactions relevant to national security interests. Quantum computers can optimize investment portfolios, identify market trends, and simulate various economic scenarios with unprecedented precision. By enhancing financial and economic intelligence, quantum computing could aid governments and defense organizations in making informed decisions to ensure economic stability and security in an increasingly interconnected world.

Public Health and Biological Defense: Quantum simulations can model the complex behaviours of diseases, aiding in predicting disease spread patterns and evaluating potential interventions. These simulations enable rapid analysis of various scenarios, aiding in preparedness for pandemics and bioterrorism threats. Quantum computing's ability to process vast amounts of biological data efficiently enhances our understanding of pathogens and drug interactions, accelerating drug discovery and vaccine development. This future scope aligns with the imperative of bolstering global health resilience and strengthening national security against biological threats.

CONCLUSION

The exploration of quantum computing's potential in the realms of government and defense unveils a transformative horizon of possibilities. From enhancing secure communication through unbreakable encryption to optimizing military logistics and policy formulation, quantum computing holds the promise of revolutionizing the way nations safeguard their interests, make informed decisions, and address complex challenges. The merits of quantum computing, including its unparalleled speed, optimization capabilities, and cryptographic prowess, intersect with the challenges of qubit stability, error correction, and hardware complexity. As we venture into the future, collaboration between researchers, industries, and governments will be essential to address these challenges and fully leverage quantum computing's capabilities. With the ever-evolving landscape of security threats and strategic imperatives, quantum computing emerges as a beacon of innovation, empowering nations to navigate the complexities of the modern world while upholding data security, optimizing resources, and ensuring a secure future for generations to come.

REFERENCES

Al-Hawawreh, M., & Hossain, M. S. (2023). A privacy-aware framework for detecting cyber attacks on internet of medical things systems using data fusion and quantum deep learning. *Information Fusion*, *99*, 101889. doi:10.1016/j.inffus.2023.101889

Arraoui, R., El-Bakkari, K., Limame, K., Ed-Dahmouny, A., Jaouane, M., Fakkahi, A., Azmi, H., & Sali, A. (2023). Pressure and temperature influences on the nonlinear optical rectification of an impurity in a symmetrical double quantum dot. *The European Physical Journal Plus*, *138*(3), 292. doi:10.1140/epjp/s13360-023-03892-8

Basset, F. B., Valeri, M., Neuwirth, J., Polino, E., Rota, M. B., Poderini, D., & Trotta, R. (2023). Daylight entanglement-based quantum key distribution with a quantum dot source. *Quantum Science and Technology*, *8*(2), 025002. doi:10.1088/2058-9565/acae3d

Berendsen, R. G., & US Army School of Advanced Military Studies Fort Leavenworth United States. (2019). *The Weaponization of Quantum Mechanics: Quantum Technology in Future Warfare*.

Couteau, C., Barz, S., Durt, T., Gerrits, T., Huwer, J., Prevedel, R., Rarity, J., Shields, A., & Weihs, G. (2023). Applications of single photons to quantum communication and computing. *Nature Reviews. Physics*, *5*(6), 1–13. doi:10.1038/s42254-023-00583-2

Dumitrescu, E. F., McCaskey, A. J., Hagen, G., Jansen, G. R., Morris, T. D., Papenbrock, T., Pooser, R. C., Dean, D. J., & Lougovski, P. (2018). Cloud quantum computing of an atomic nucleus. *Physical Review Letters*, *120*(21), 210501. doi:10.1103/PhysRevLett.120.210501 PMID:29883142

Guillaume, A., Vrain, C., & Wael, E. (2020). Predictive maintenance on event logs: Application on an ATM fleet. *arXiv preprint arXiv:2011.10996*.

Hareshbhai, B. S., Valiveti, S., Kothari, D., & Raval, G. (2023, March). Generating near-ideal nonces for cryptographic processes using Quantum Cryptography. In *2023 First International Conference on Microwave, Antenna and Communication (MAC)* (pp. 1-6). IEEE. 10.1109/MAC58191.2023.10177098

Herman, A., & Friedson, I. (2018). *Quantum computing: how to address the national security risk*. Hudson Institute.

Inglesant, P., Jirotka, M., & Hartswood, M. (2018). *Responsible Innovation in Quantum Technologies applied to Defence and National Security*. *NQIT*. Networked Quantum Information Technologies.

Kappe, F., Karli, Y., Bracht, T. K., da Silva, S. F. C., Seidelmann, T., Axt, V. M., & Remesh, V. (2023). Collective excitation of spatio-spectrally distinct quantum dots enabled by chirped pulses. *Mathematics of Quantum Technologies*, *3*(2), 025006. doi:10.1088/2633-4356/acd7c1

Knight, P., & Walmsley, I. (2019). UK national quantum technology programme. *Quantum Science and Technology*, *4*(4), 040502. doi:10.1088/2058-9565/ab4346

Krelina, M. (2021). Quantum technology for military applications. *EPJ Quantum Technology*, *8*(1), 24. doi:10.1140/epjqt/s40507-021-00113-y

Kumar, A., Bhatia, S., Kaushik, K., Gandhi, S. M., Devi, S. G., Diego, A. D. J., & Mashat, A. (2021). Survey of promising technologies for quantum drones and networks. *IEEE Access : Practical Innovations, Open Solutions*, *9*, 125868–125911. doi:10.1109/ACCESS.2021.3109816

Mavroeidis, V., Vishi, K., Zych, M. D., & Jøsang, A. (2018). The impact of quantum computing on present cryptography. *arXiv preprint arXiv:1804.00200*.

Ningsih, S. J., Wadjdi, A. F., & Budiyanto, S. (2022). The Importance of Quantum Technology in National Defense in the Future. *The International Journal of Business Management and Technology, 6*(1).

Pan, J. W., Yuan, Z. S., Zhang, Y., Zhang, C., Zhao, Y. A., & Zeng, B. (2017). Experimental quantum secure direct communication with single photons. *Light, Science & Applications*, *7*(1), 17117.

Patel, O. P., Bharill, N., Tiwari, A., Patel, V., Gupta, O., Cao, J., Li, J., & Prasad, M. (2019). Advanced quantum based neural network classifier and its application for objectionable web content filtering. *IEEE Access : Practical Innovations, Open Solutions*, *7*, 98069–98082. doi:10.1109/ACCESS.2019.2926989

Rani, S., Pareek, P. K., Kaur, J., Chauhan, M., & Bhambri, P. (2023, February). Quantum Machine Learning in Healthcare: Developments and Challenges. In *2023 IEEE International Conference on Integrated Circuits and Communication Systems (ICICACS)* (pp. 1-7). IEEE. 10.1109/ICICACS57338.2023.10100075

Zhang, Q., Xu, F., Li, L., Liu, N. L., & Pan, J. W. (2019). Quantum information research in China. *Quantum Science and Technology*, *4*(4), 040503. doi:10.1088/2058-9565/ab4bea

Chapter 16
The Role of Artificial Intelligence (AI) in Improving Product Development Efficiency

Cagla Ozen
https://orcid.org/0000-0003-1817-9806
Yeditepe University, Turkey

Zehra Mine Tas
Yeditepe University, Turkey

ABSTRACT

When examining domestic and foreign literature, surprisingly, very few studies examining the effects of AI on product efficiency have been observed in the domestic literature. Therefore, this study aims to contribute to domestic literature by focusing on the effects AI on product development efficiency. When the studies in foreign literature are examined, it is seen that AI increases the efficiency in product development, data analysis, management, control, and supply process. The overall result of this study shows that AI, which plays an important role in the design of high scalable algorithms that analyze complex and large-scale data, increases the efficiency of product development from the production process to supply chains.

INTRODUCTION

Within the fast-paced, competitive world of business, product advancement could be a critical aspect that decides the victory and development of companies. Companies got to persistently enhance, adjust, and refine their products to remain ahead of the bend. Artificial Intelligence (AI) has risen as a system to quicken this handle, advertising transformative capabilities in different businesses, from fabricating and healthcare to fund and retail.

Artificial intelligence has a large database, and it analyzes and processes this data. By making use of the statistics, it gives the closest result to accuracy. In this way, it provides a fast and easy business

DOI: 10.4018/978-1-6684-9576-6.ch016

process for companies in decision making and forecasting. To completely saddle the potential of AI in product improvement, it is pivotal to distinguish the key variables that contribute to its efficient integration. These basic victory variables include a wide run of viewpoints, such as information quality and accessibility, well-defined issue explanations, intrigue collaboration, and vital venture in AI foundation and ability. By tending to these components, companies can successfully use AI to optimize their product improvement forms and accomplish prevalent results.

The execution of artificial insights in product advancement forms has the potential to altogether upgrade proficiency, drive advancement, and move companies to unused statures of victory. In this chapter, questions such as how companies may take advantage of AI in product development and integrate AI into processes of improving efficiency will be answered.

This study, which examines the role of AI in increasing product development efficiency, consist of five parts. The definition and basic functions of AI in the first part, the key technologies and components associated with AI in the second part, the efficiency of product development in the third part, the roles and effects of AI on product development efficiency in the fourth part, and the general findings of studies examining the effects of AI on product development efficiency in the fifth and final part were examined.

METHOD

In the context of examining "The Role of Artificial Intelligence in Enhancing Efficiency in Product Development," the research approach encompassed an exploration of the multifaceted dimensions inherent in integrating AI into the product development landscape. Through a systematic analysis of various sources, including academic journals, industry reports, and technological databases, a comprehensive understanding of AI's impact on improving product development efficiency was garnered. Key aspects such as AI-driven predictive modeling, automated quality control, and data-driven decision-making were scrutinized. By synergizing these insights, this chapter aims to shed light on how AI's infusion into product development processes has led to accelerated iteration cycles, reduced resource wastage, and ultimately, heightened overall efficiency.

UNDERSTANDING ARTIFICIAL INTELLIGENCE (AI)

Definition and Scope of AI

The field of artificial intelligence (AI), which is used to perform tasks similar to human intelligence, can be defined as an area developed by computer systems. Computer systems aim to acquire abilities such as learning, problem-solving, reasoning, and making decisions by developing algorithms and models that mimic specific characteristics of human intelligence. There is a wide range of subfields and applications in artificial intelligence. A field called "machine learning" is one of them. Jordan and Mitchell explain that in artificial intelligence, machine learning has taken over as the preferred method for developing practical software for tasks like speech recognition, computer vision, robot control, natural language processing, and other uses. (Jordan & Mitchell, 2015) Machine learning aims to train computer systems to gradually raise their performance and make more out of information. The processing of "natural languages" is a major area that enables computers to recognize and reproduce human language. Applications such as speech assistants, chatbots, and language translation systems rely on it. In the area of artificial intelligence, image processing allows computers to interpret and analyze visual information. It shall include techniques such as the identification of objects, recognition of faces, and the understanding of a scene. Autonomous vehicles, security systems, and medical imaging are some of the areas where this field is used. Another crucial area of artificial intelligence is "robotics". Robotics aims to create intelligent machines that can physically interact with their environment by combining artificial intelligence techniques with mechanical systems. Robots, which are used in many areas, from the manufacturing industry to healthcare and logistics management, can perform tasks in collaboration with humans.

In the product development process, artificial intelligence also has significant effects. Artificial intelligence at the design and concept creation stages can increase creativity and innovation. Artificial intelligence may contribute to evaluating product performance and optimizing production processes during simulation and prototype testing. Moreover, AI can help product development teams to gain valuable insights about market trends, analyze customer feedback and predict consumer preferences with the use of Big Data Analytics.

An acceleration of product time to market, improvement in the quality of products, decreasing costs, and increasing customer satisfaction could be possible benefits from artificial intelligence. However, there are also specific difficulties and limits to the development of AI. Consideration should be given to issues such as ethical concerns, data protection problems, algorithm bias, and the need for supervision by humans. For AI to be properly and efficiently incorporated into product development processes, these problems must be addressed.

Among the technological developments that are taking place today, AI plays an important role and is predicted to become more common in the future. It is, therefore, possible to combine AI with the computer sciences and business management fields that you have learned in your classroom for a comprehensive understanding of it. AI may be regarded as an area in which computer systems that can imitate human intelligence are developed. To simulate the intelligence capabilities of human beings, such as solving problems, learning, decision-making, and reasoning, AI uses algorithms and models.

Artificial intelligence is used in many fields and applications. The focus of machine learning is on the training algorithms which learn from data and are continuously improving their performance. A type of machine learning called deep learning enables the processing of complicated data and the creation of sophisticated predictions or classifications based on artificial neural networks.

A computer's ability to read and analyze visual information is a function of image processing. Techniques related to image recognition, object detection, facial recognition, and scene understanding are also included. In a variety of areas, e.g., self-walking vehicles, security systems, and medical imaging applications, it is in use.

There is also an overlap with robotics in the scope of AI. Robotics is attempting to create intelligent machines that are physically capable of interacting with the environment through a combination of AI techniques and physical systems. Robots can accomplish activities that humans can in numerous fields, including manufacturing, healthcare, and logistics management.

Artificial intelligence should also contribute to the process of product development. AI technologies could provide an opportunity for improvements in product development processes through better design ideation, reduction of production cycles and improved precision testing with regard to the products (Dwivedi et al, 2020, p.1026). The performance of the product may be assessed, and production processes optimized through the use of this technology in simulation and prototype techniques. AI can also be useful for identifying market trends, analyzing customer feedback, and predicting product preferences by means of Big Data Analytics. Decreased product sales time, improvement of quality and cost reduction, as well as increased customer satisfaction could also be potential benefit from artificial intelligence. However, there are some issues and constraints in the area of artificial intelligence that need to be addressed, like ethics concerns, data protection problems, or human's responsibility. Responsible and effective integration of artificial intelligence within product development processes must be addressed.

With regard to the development of today's technology, AI plays a very important role and is expected to become increasingly widespread over time. For this reason, you will be able to combine computer science and business management topics from your course with artificial intelligence in order to build a complete understanding.

Key Technologies and Components

AI is increasingly reaching a broader audience in today's world. The presence of such sectors can be seen in many more areas: engineering, health care, education, and so on. Some technologies and efficiency are behind the evolution of artificial intelligence during this process. Data, algorithms, and human feedback are typically included in AI applications. It is crucial to ensure that the various components are properly structured and validated in order for AI applications to be developed and implemented. Here are five technologies and components of AI:

- **Data and Data Storage:** By associating the creation of AI with human development, it is possible to understand its formation. The baby learns by accumulating what he hears and sees from the outside, starting at an early age. Data taken from outside is accepted and kept in memory until childhood. Data collected are questioned, analyzed, and predicted in the course of childhood to adulthood. Based on this cycle, it can be called one of the building blocks of data and data storage in artificial intelligence applications. Data sets are frequently used to train AI algorithms. This data can be anything from customers' contact information, social media postings, weather reports, or biostatistics. Such information may be in structured formats, e.g., databases or unparsed formats like text files or social media posts. This data is analyzed, and patterns and relationships are determined by AI for particular tasks like identifying objects in the photograph or classifying an emotional tone in a text; this information is used to do those tasks. (Provost & Fawcett, 2013)

Data has to be stored as soon as data collection or flows have been set up that enable it to take place in real-time on the AI-enabled system. The AI data may be structured or unstructured, and it may be large data that requires a lot of storage space and needs to be accessed quickly. The data storage process covers a number of technologies, such as databases, cloud storage systems, and distributed file systems. The security, privacy, and compliance of data shall also be ensured by data storage solutions. (Chen, Chiang & Storey, 2012)

- **Machine Learning (ML) and Deep Learning (DL):** AI analyzes data, observes situations, learns from past experiences, and acts on these outputs. What makes AI so powerful is its ability to learn. This skill is accomplished with machine learning technology. To perform complex tasks, such as human problem solving, machine learning is a subfield of artificial intelligence that aims to imitate intelligent people's behavior. For the purposes of providing training data on a ML model, data are collected and retained. A ML system is constructed in such a way as to enhance the efficiency of its tasks by using data models and algorithms. The more data you have got, the faster your program is. In this case, ML is said to happen when the system has been able to correct errors and better solve a particular problem (Jordan &Mitchell,2015).

Deep learning is the technique of machine learning which teaches computers how to naturally do things that humans are capable of doing and solve more complex problems. It teaches computers to process information like the human brain's thinking processes. Complex language, image, and sound patterns can be picked up by dense learning models that are able to make accurate inferences and predictions.

- **Natural Language Processing (NLP):** NLP is essential as a field that provides the ability of computers to understand and produce human language. Hirschberg and Manning state that natural language generation, natural language understanding, and speech recognition are NLP applications in AI that allow technologies like voice-assistant platforms and automated customer care bots. (Hirshberg & Manning, 2022)
- **Computer Vision:** Computer vision is an artificial intelligence technology that assesses visual inputs, such as images and videos, to infer information about the results. This technology sees the digital image as a sequence of numbers, and when it analyses these elements, it shows its effect by understanding the images. Medical imaging, automation systems, and video analysis are some of the applications for which it is used.
- **Artificial Neural Network (ANN):** Artificial neural networks are an AI technology developed on the basis of human brain. For the purpose of analyzing and interpreting a wide range of data, such networks have been effectively used (Schmidhuber, 2015). For instance, it can collect a large amount of data on users' shopping history and browsing patterns for the purpose of an e-commerce company's marketing strategy. The neural network is able to anticipate users' preferences and what they may buy in the future by analyzing this data.

PRODUCT DEVELOPMENT EFFICIENCY

Definition and Importance

Product development is the process of creating new, innovative products to improve a company's market position. (Cooper & Sommer, 2016) All steps that start with identifying a product idea and making it available to end users are part of the product development process. Not only physical products must be taken into account when the product is referred to here. The product development process also involves digital products manufactured by a technology company. Indeed, this process develops other aspects of the product as well as a service and business model established by an organization. As an example, although AirBnB provides services to users, it's actually a product. The process of producing a new product concurrently with an existing one is also included. User experience and behavior change on a daily basis. On the other hand, new products enter into the market. In light of this situation, companies are endeavoring to catch up with market conditions to adapt or develop their products accordingly. For example, Netflix was by far the strongest app on the market when it first became available to its users. Netflix has been given an opportunity to expand the functionality of its Mobile app in view of new providers entering the Streaming Services market over recent years. The most effective way to use resources in the management of products is through product development efficiency. The speed, costs, and quality of product development are evaluated in order to measure its effectiveness. Positive results such as increasing the quality of products, decreasing costs, and raising sales can be obtained through an increase in product development efficiency. Businesses need to continuously improve and optimize their processes in view of increased competition in the market (Langerak & Hultink, 2006).

Efficiency in product development enables businesses to innovate and expand sustainably. Companies grow their client base as they develop more efficiently, which has a significant impact on their profitability. They do this by presenting new concepts and goods to the market. The business can expand and have long-term success in this way (Pisano, 2019).

As a result, it is obvious that an organization is a process to be considered when considering the importance of product development efficiency. It plays a critical role in order to be one step ahead of the market and to achieve success. It is not easy to optimize a process that is so important, of course. The continuous review of business practices and the use of technology in digitalization is unavoidable for companies.

Existing Challenges

Product development efficiency has a positive impact on companies' ability to achieve substantial results, but this feedback is not easy to obtain. Difficulties for companies may arise in this process. These problems can be identified as a series of the rapid growth of the market and the increase in the competition making it difficult to stand out with change, rapidly evolving technology, the complexity of interprocess, changes and growth in customer needs or quality, and appropriate resources at their disposal.

The process of creating a product begins with ideation. Once an idea and business model are in place, the prospect of a customer base is established. As indicated by the prospective audience, this idea is starting to take shape. Consideration of consumers' requirements and preferences is necessary to make that notion relevant. It may not be entirely distinctive, but if it is to succeed in the marketplace, making an impact must be taken into account when reaching a specific audience. Resources of money, energy, and time tend to be consumed by the search for an idea. It is not easy to find a new and distinctive idea due to the rapid growth of trading volumes day by day. In addition, when taking action for potential users and products, problems such as a lack of resources or equipment may exist. Legal obstacles may also exist in order to develop an idea. Constraints like international regulations, privacy, and data protection rules, or intellectual property rights must be taken into account.

The quick growth of technology in the modern digital era allows businesses to grow. Yet, as technology improves, businesses can find it becoming increasingly difficult to adapt. Adopting and integrating new technology into the procedures used to manufacture products might cost businesses more money. The need for this integrated process to be quick can complicate commercial operations for firms and make management challenging. Recruiting and integrating human resources who are informed about these technologies, nevertheless, may be costly and time-consuming.

The product development process is complicated as it covers all business processes from idea finding to final user adoption. These processes develop in an integrated manner within themselves. For example, in order to ensure the most effective delivery of a strategy for marketing and sales at the end user level, financial and marketing processes come together. This complexity may also be increased by the speed at which technology changes occur. Businesses can apply different strategies, such as effective project management, process automation, cross-functional teams, and continuous training for their business in order to avoid the complexity of processes (Eppinger & Ulrich, 2011).

It is crucial to adjust during the product development process to client requests because all businesses create their goods to satisfy the wants and desires of the consumers. With the effect of technological developments and social media, the tastes and needs of users are changing rapidly. This rate of change may cause businesses to see their products in demand below their expectations when they lunch. Companies have to keep their products dynamic to meet ever-changing needs. This dynamism can further complicate processes and increase costs. In order to manage this process in the most effective and fastest way, businesses should receive continuous feedback from users and test the product frequently. Another management strategy is to introduce the product as a Minimum Viable Product (MVP). MVP is the version of a product that contains the most basic features that will meet the needs of the users. MVP allows businesses to get quick feedback from users and evaluate the potential success of the product by publishing it with the most basic version before developing the product fully and making big investments (Blank, 2018).

Undoubtedly, solid resources are needed to develop a product. These resources include finance, skilled labor, and technological tools and equipment. Accessing these resources can be both difficult and costly. Finding financial investment when developing a product from scratch is often a long and challenging time. This process is risky and full of uncertainties. Companies are required to contribute these funds and administer them wisely. (Hall, 2002) Employment is an additional resource. A crucial and difficult aspect of the product development process is having qualified and skilled employees in several divisions. Finding and hiring these people makes recruitment long, costly, and painful for operators in markets where competition is high and talent is scarce. (Manyika et al., 2012) Quality and powerful tools are needed to ensure the production process is fast and smooth. Access to these resources can again force companies. Access to technological resources and integrating them into the product development is a cost-increasing factor for operators. In addition, after having these resources, it is necessary to have regular maintenance. At this point, operators must develop certain methods to manage the most reliable and appropriate supply chain.

Businesses that want to be successful in product development efficiency implement a variety of measures and create objectives in response to the challenges that they anticipate. By using these methods and procedures, they maximize efficiency by reducing obstacles to efficient management. Operators might occasionally collaborate with consultants who are authorities in the appropriate subject in addition to establishing a strategy to reduce the complexity of management and to have a quicker, higher-quality production. Despite the fact that these consultants are expensive, businesses ultimately benefit from their services.

ROLE OF AI IN PRODUCT DEVELOPMENT EFFICIENCY

As a result of AI's recent rapid progress, it is clear that its utilization has risen. AI is used by businesses and people in every industry and procedure. Employees save time through AI's ability to make work simpler and faster. In this way, people can concentrate on tasks that require more manpower and creativity, rather than doing things that AI can do very quickly. This enables them to produce a better-quality end product.

The use of AI to enhance the effectiveness of product generation has also grown to a point at which it cannot be ignored. AI has developed into a potent tool that can be used to identify answers to issues businesses have during the product development process. Businesses are now required to utilize technology and even artificial intelligence in everything, and everywhere they generate. AI not only slows down the time to market but also lowers costs, expands client reach, improves profit margins, and results in higher-quality products. Evaluation of these benefits demonstrates that increasing production efficiency is successful. The application of AI to various stages of the product development process will be discussed in this section.

AI Design and Concept Generation

As in many areas, the use of AI is becoming widespread in design industry, and many time-consuming design processes can be done easily and by saving time thanks to AI. In the researchers, it is thought that most of the effort of the designers can be easily automated and done with AI. For this reason, large software companies are working on approaches that can product solutions to design problems. The solutions of software companies enable even people who have never designed before in their lives design without the need for any training. Some of the solutions offered by software companies in the field of design using AI are as flows;

- Sensei, a product of Adobe and using AI and machine learning technologies, identifies image patterns to help designers fix, edit, or even completely a reinvent particular scene as seen in Figure 1.
- As seen in Figure 2, Adobe's Photoshop program can successfully select objects. On the other hand, has the ability to automatically fill the edges of a cropped image with matching content with artificial intelligence-supported cropping tool, and it fulfills its task quite successfully.
- Nowadays, mobile applications such as Prisma, which apply smart filters to photos and videos based on image recognition technology, are also very popular. These technologies can automatically select and animate the best visual effect to be applied photograph, as seen in Figure 3. Such mobile applications enable people who do not have a computer, to create design elements on devices such as smartphones and tablets.
- As seen in Figure 4, Logo design software such as Vectorstock, Inkscape, Wix Logo Maker offers many logo alternatives after choosing company's name, favorite styles and color chart.
- An example of software that automatically creates visual elements is the AutoDraw application developed by Google as seen in Figure 5. The artificial intelligence application automatically completes drawings and can transform drawings with the mouse into more advanced shapes. The more people interact with the tool using machine learning technology, the more accurately the artificial intelligence learns what users are trying to draw and offers suggestions accordingly.
- As seen Figure 6 the Uizard application uses AI to convert drawings into mobile applications in seconds and does not require writing code. This application provides opportunities for those who do not know the software but also allows companies to view an application or feature that is desired to be published as a demo without wasting time.
- As seen Fig. 7, AI products such as Generated Photos and Fake AI Face Generator can create human faces that do not belong to anyone, so users or companies can use these people, created without any copyright, in places such as presentations. For example, such AI tools can be used in an advertisement or blog content, thus saving companies from copyright costs and extra efforts.

Figure 1. The process of selecting an object in the Adobe Source: Adobe announces Premiere and Photoshop elements 2020—Adding powerful adobe sensei "AI" features
(slrlounge.com)

Figure 2. A feature of Adobe's Photoshop CC with AI Source: Adobe Photoshop CC now makes selecting objects a one-click affair
TechCrunch

Thanks to these features supported by artificial intelligence technology, designers do not have to do manual operations and save time. The processes that graphic designers struggle with for minutes can be solved in seconds without any problems. With the artificial intelligence logical decision system, the works that people spend a lot of time thinking creatively and logically and producing design ideas that have already started to facilitate the work of the design world. It is predicted that the world of visual arts will encounter a significant change and transformation with the development of technology.

Figure 3. A logo design software with AI
(Source: Lensa AI's Avatars Return Startup Prisma to the Limelight — The Information)

Figure 4. Logo maker applications
(Source: Ai Logo Maker - Generate your free logo online in minutes!LogoAi.com)

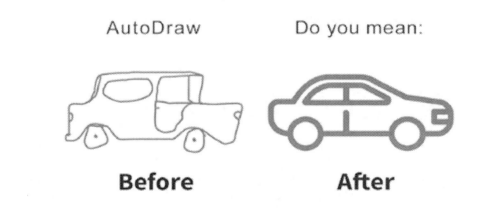

AI in Simulation and Prototyping

Nearly every endeavor to design a product, system, or service involves prototyping. A prototype is a depiction of an idea or final design in pre-production form. The success of design projects is typically influenced by prototyping, which often decides a significant amount of resource deployment throughout development. Prototyping and design have always been intertwined (Camburn et al., 2017).

Despite the introduction of several intriguing new tools for the creation of machine learning models, there is not much that focuses directly on the design of the behaviors and interactions that make up the human experience surrounding AI models. AI interactions have a complex and unique nature, due to the independence of these systems as well as their development that entails continuous care and maintenance by end users. In order to go above the cliches of AI and create new interactions that are meaningful,

Figure 5. Google Autodraw application source: Google AutoDraw instantly transforms your terrible scribbles into awesome icons for free
Bored Panda

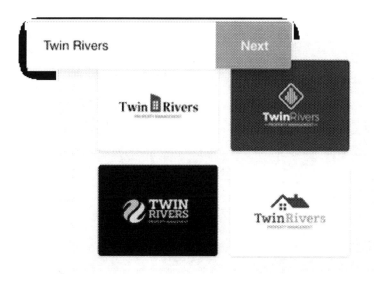

Figure 6. AI-Powered design assistant
Source: Uizard's AI-Powered Design Assistant | Uizard

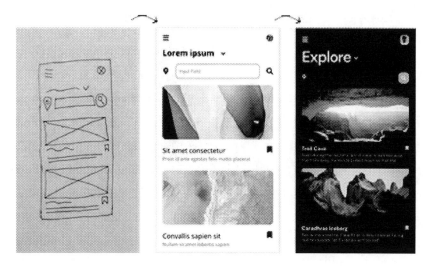

gratifying, and ethically acceptable, designers must find effective methods to construct a sophisticated style for the design of acts, interactions, and storylines that AI systems need (Van Allen, 2018).

Figure 8 show how to use a wireless tablet to replicate an act in reacting to simulated speech recognition. In this case, the designer presses a button from a distance away from the person performing the testing to simulate a vocal command even if a speech-to-text technology is not actually being used (robot makes backwards when user says Goodbye).

According to Van Allen (2018), a puppet system that enables the designer to replace AI in the early design phase is included in the AI simulation toolkit. As shown in Figure 4.8, by using a toolkit the

Figure 7. Generated photos and fake AI face generator source: Fake faces created by AI look more trustworthy than real people
New Scientist

Figure 8. A Prototype for simulated voice recognition
Source: (Van Allen, 2018)

designer is able to control prototype's behavior directly and observe what people are experiencing and interacting with. This is driven by an open standard protocol (OSC) for a remote control that simulates artificial intelligence and uses a tablet or phone to wirelessly activate specified actions.

As Dash et al. (2019) highlighted, contemporary robots made possible by the AI platform can learn about their environment and decide how to operate in a way that has the best chance of success. Machines do this by employing logic and probability to make their decisions. This is done by machines that take their decisions on the basis of logic and probability. These devices, based on large datasets, are designed to distinguish objects and sounds with extreme accuracy and to learn and behave in an intelligent manner.

AI in Data Analytics and Decision Support

Artificial intelligence has the potential to make decisions in real-time by using already set-up computer technologies and algorithms created through data analysis to automatically adapt and learn to deliver increasingly complex answers to circumstances (Rodgers et al., 2023).

The development of highly scalable algorithms and system for integrating data and finding hidden figures in datasets that are different, complex, and massively scaled presents a huge challenge to Big Data Analytics. Data is first put into the AI engine to increase its intelligence. Additionally, less human involvement is required for the AI to function correctly. Furthermore, as fewer humans are needed to manage this continual AI/big data loop, society will also be closer to realizing its full potential. To take part in that evolution, humans with skills in building AI algorithms and analyzing data will be required (Manimozhi et al., 2023).

Manimozhi et al. (2023), focuses on six ultimate goals in AI's data analytics and decision support:

- General Intelligence
- Reasoning
- Natural Language processing (the capacity to comprehend spoken human language)
- Machine Learning
- Automated Learning and Scheduling
- Robotics
- Computer vision (reliable information extraction from a single or a set of photos)

AI algorithms will need enormous volumes of data in order to develop and become specialists in the aims. For instance, natural language processing would not have been feasible rather than the vast number of human voice samples that have been captured and divided into a form that artificial intelligence systems are able to simply handle. It is anticipated that AI will maintain its present control in big data analytics and decision support systems in the coming years as it becomes a more viable choice to automate more tasks.

Figure 9 depicts the three branches of AI's decision-making and data analysis components. According to Pournader et al. (2021), the first branch includes techniques for perceiving and engaging with diverse types of text, including speech, vision, and natural language processing. The second branch consists of programs and applications for data-driven learning. The majority of machine learning approaches, including deep learning, can utilize this categorization. The third branch covers decision-making applications and procedures, such as planning, expert systems, modeling, simulation, optimization, and scheduling.

Rath et al. (2022) states that human skills such as understanding, reasoning, planning, communication and observation are also possessed in AI technology. However, these are just a few of the many advantages of AI, such as enhanced decision-making and automatic synthesis of data. Better decision-making is made possible by the use of AI in fields like autonomous automobiles, automatic medical diagnosis, voice input for interfaces between humans and computers, and automatic data synthesis.

AI in Manufacturing

The basic needs of most manufacturing operations in industries are to provide a safe working environment for all and meet efficiency, cost, and quality objectives. However, these targets have become increasingly

Figure 9. All components of AI
(Source: (Pournader et al., 2021)).

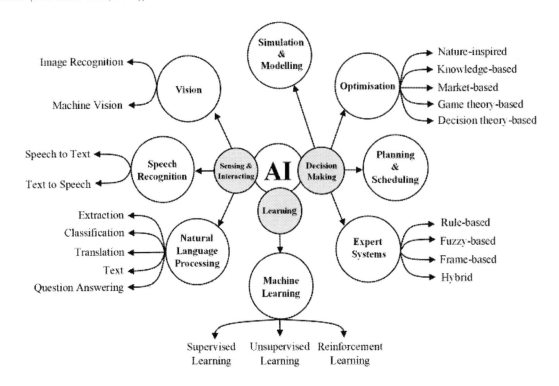

difficult to achieve due to the myriad demands arising from increasing product and process complexity, and the ever-changing demands of customers and competitive pressures in the market to remain profitable. In the challenging business environment facing most manufacturers, AI's unique capabilities over traditional tools and approaches present an opportunity. Artificial intelligence has become an indispensable technology in order to finding the main source of the problem with its function of finding and classifying multivariate, nonlinear patterns in operational and performance data in the production process. Using artificial intelligence, huge amounts of data are constantly generated about machines, environmental sensors, controllers, and labor records. Thanks to the data produced, the importance of the parameters that affect each other is understood, but the main sources of the problems can be seen more clearly. Artificial intelligence is able to interpret the vast amounts of complicated production data that are frequently seen in today's factories and convert this data into informative and insightful information because of its high-dimensional data processing capacity (Arinez et al., 2020).

The idea of "intelligent manufacturing" is one that is always changing, but it can be categorized into three major paradigms: "digital manufacturing", which is the first generation of the concept, "digital-networked manufacturing," which is the second generation, and "new-generation intelligent manufacturing." An examination of the progress of smart manufacturing shows that the transition from traditional manufacturing to smart manufacturing is unmistakably a process of development through the initial human-physical systems (HPS) to human-cyber-physical systems (HCPS). An HCPS is the conceptual foundation for the advancement of new-generation smart manufacturing, which is depicted in Fig 10. It shows the fundamental principles of intelligent manufacturing development (Buchmeister et al., 2019).

Figure 10. Intelligent manufacturing: from human-psychical system (HPS) to human-cyber-physical system (HCPS)
Source:(Buchmeister et al., 2019)

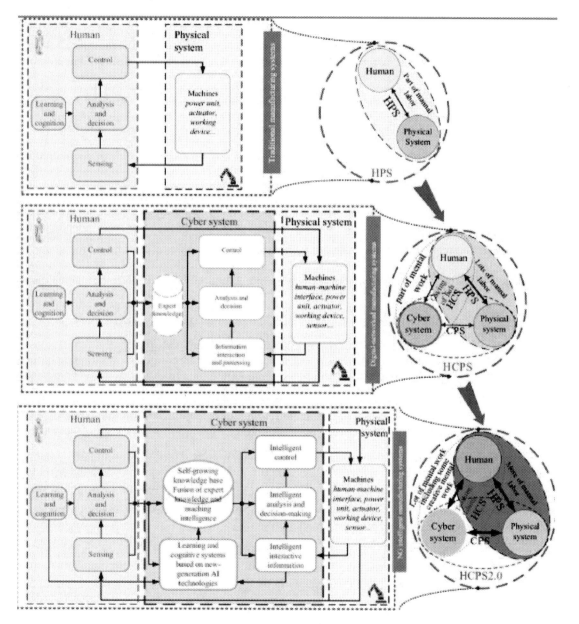

Given the crucial role that technology plays in creating intelligent systems, artificial intelligence has drawn substantial interest from almost every region of the world. AI is useful in the manufacturing industry, particularly during the product design phase. Smart manufacturing is an essential component of industry 4.0 and is vital for the global economy. The full integration of diverse technologies to boost flexibility through real-time reactions and partnerships is vital for the future of smart manufacturing. All elements work toward meeting client expectations with customization by delivering goods to consumers quickly and efficiently. In order to achieve high performance, every manufacturing process, particularly the development and design of products, needs to dramatically increase its effectiveness. (Aphirakmethawong et al., 2022).

Since the majority of manufacturing procedures use a data-based approach, it is essential to gather a lot of data when a production process is in operation. Aphirakmethawong et al. (2022) state that AI is applied to analyze data to decide on operating systems in order to minimize impacts that affects quality and cost in manufacturing operations. The aim of AI systems is to respond to process problems in a timely manner. In addition, Arinez et al. (2020) states that the vast amounts of complicated production data that are common in today's factories may be transformed into useful knowledge thanks to AI's capacity to comprehend high-dimensional data.

Buchmeister et al. (2019) emphasized that a common and deep-learning AI process may subsequently be developed using a company's data, automatically perform simulations of viable futures, and construct the algorithms required to produce desired business efficiency. In order to preserve maximum efficiency, AI can utilize well-known operational research techniques, implement them in newly developed circumstances, and then reevaluate their results. It can create methods that improve the distribution of consumer goods for a single device maker by figuring out which method is best to get per product from manufacturing to the retail shelves or to the consumer's house.

AI in Supply Chain and Distribution

To be successful, each organization in business requires a functional supply chain. An important edge over competitors can be provided by definite inventory projection. The performance of the supply chain is affected by a variety of internal and external elements, including changes in customer perception, excessive seasonality, weather, and media attention, as well as new product launch and distribution network development. Supply chain management (SCM), a field centered on interactions between numerous industries, including marketing, logistics, and production, is a challenging discipline. Artificial intelligence advances have been shown to be of enormous use to supply chain management in recent years. Artificial intelligence refers to computational instruments that are made to act, reason, sense, and learn appropriately. With the development of mobile computing, it is possible to store huge quantities of data through the internet, algorithms for information processing, cloud-based machine learning, etc. It has been demonstrated that AI can save costs, boost income, and improve asset utilization in many different business areas (Dash et al., 2019).

One can create information on how certain phenomena may influence the whole chain over time using AI-based technologies' visibility capabilities. During the pandemic, demand patterns continue to fluctuate, making it tough for supply chains to adhere to their current service-level agreements with chain participants. This is an additional area where AI may help the supply chain with regard to routes, production, and other linking points. In the supply chain, mapping and network planning are significant issues. The collaboration between vendors and contractors in defining the supply chain in these unusual times may be further improved by AI. It provides route visibility so that commitments to customers may be made. To manage the amount, pace, value, variability, diversity, truthfulness, and data visualization for crucial insight, AI uses principles of data science. AI also assists in measuring the effectiveness of warehouses in terms of shelf and demand lives. AI offers a complete analysis of inventory levels and effectively organizes relevant operations (Modgil et al., 2022).

According to Dash et al. (2019), AI can help companies estimate client demand with almost 100% accuracy, maximize their research and development efforts, and boost production at a cheaper cost and higher standard.

AI in Testing and Quality Assurance

Software quality, according to Felderer & Ramler (2021), is a software product's capacity to satisfy explicit and implicit demands when employed in a particular setting. They (2021) described software quality assurance as the methodical assessment of how well a software product satisfies both explicit and implicit needs.

Testing continues to be one of the most developed and focused approaches for evaluating and improving software quality, despite years of academics and specialists working on various software qualities. But going beyond the continuous testing approach is now unavoidable. The requirement to anticipate customer wants and create a framework that is adaptable and prescient enough to take into account future changes is at an all-time high as the globe moves toward digital transformation. In the current environment, testing needs help to speed up delivery. To that end, artificial intelligence in quality assurance will contribute (Ramchand et al., 2022a).

As a result of recent advances in artificial intelligence, notably in deep learning and machine learning, and the integration of them into software-based systems of all dominants, modern AI-based systems meet major technological challenges. Because of their inherent nondeterminism and data intensiveness, these systems are constantly changing and self-adapting, and as a result, their behavior demonstrates some ambiguity. These features need innovative and improved constructive and analytical quality assurance approaches from the discipline of software engineering (SE) to be able to ensure quality throughout development and operation in real-world contexts (Felderer & Ramler, 2021).

According to Ramchand et al. (2022b), 64% of businesses will employ AI for their Software Quality Assurance (SQA) procedures, and in the very near future, SQA engineers are unlikely to test it manually. AI also makes the processes more accurate and learnable. It is crucial to the software testing process. They assert (2022b) that the power of AI will rule the new era of quality assurance since it will drastically cut down on time and boost a company's productivity in creating more complex software.

For the goal of quality assurance, Felderer & Ramler (2021) emphasize the need of taking into account a number of characteristics when describing AI-based systems. These are the dimension of the artifact, the dimension of the process, and the dimension of the quality characteristics. Fig. 4.11 displays the dimensions and their associated values.

DISCUSSION

This section will focus on the findings of studies examining the role of AI in increasing product development efficiency.

Camburn et al. (2017) contend that prototyping defines a significant portion of resource allocation throughout development and influences the success of the design projects in their study that looked at literature sources in the domains of engineering, design science, architecture, and management.

In his study, in which he examines the effects of AI simulation on product development, Van Allen (2018) highlights the need fort he puppet system in the toolkit to support AI simulation, which allows

Figure 11. Dimensions of AI-based System and Quality Assurance
Source: (Felderer & Ramler, 2021)

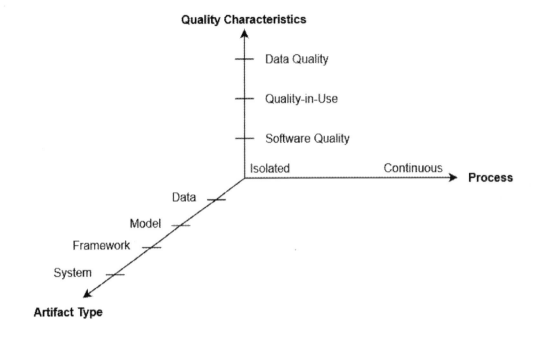

the designer to replace AI at the preliminary design stages. The toolset allows the designers to modify the prototype's functionality in real time while seeing how users engage with it. A standard protocol (OSC) for a remote control that simulates AI and uses a phone or tablet to wirelessly activate specified actions supports this. The puppet may be programmed to perform pre-written or spontaneous movements, sound, speech, perception, and lighting sequences.

Dash et al. (2019) suggest that the use of AI creates a competitive advantage in supply chains in their study, in which they examine the effects of AI in the supply chain. Nowadays, large e-commerce enterprises have the ability to predict trends, store and logistic to set prices and personalize promotions etc. They (2019) argue that they use AI for their purpose and that these companies are one step ahead, such as predicting orders and delivering products before even waiting for purchase approval using AI.

Rodgers et al. (2023) suggest that the time and inefficiency associated with managing activities are decreased with AI software, but employees and management continue to have trust questions about AI in their study, in which they examine the effectiveness and effect of AI in management processes. They also emphasize that if the management of organizations cannot maintain up with the future developments in AI technology, firms will not expect to be able to successfully compete in luring and employing workers in useful professions. They argue that in order to be successful, organizations should allocate resource based on cost estimates influenced by AI, rather than funding management development based solely on previous corporate income.

Manimozhi et al. (2023) argue that AI plays an important role in creating extremely scalable systems and algorithms to reveal large hidden values from complex and large scale data sets in their study, in which AI examines the effects of big data analysis on product development. They are analyzing the most effective applications for various types of AI in solving issues. In addition, the report predicts that the global AI Sunday will grow like an avalanche over the next few years and will reach a market value of

$ 190.61 billion in 2025. They estimate that international AI chip by 2027, Sunday sales are anticipated to reach $83.25 billion, and by 2030, AI is predicted to contribute to a $15.7 trillion or 26% growth in the global GDP.

Pournader et al. (2021) divide AI into three categories: a) perception and interaction, b) learning and, c) decision-making in their study, in which they give a thorough analysis of research on artificial intelligence applications in supply chain management (SCM). They find that learning techniques are gradually gaining momentum while sensing and interaction techniques provide new study opportunities. As a general result of their study, they suggest that it does not provide an in-depth analysis of AI methods and their adoption techniques in SCM.

Arinez et al. (2020) have extensively studied the current use of AI and its potential to create more opportunities in production systems and processes at multiple hierarchical levels in their study, which shows that traditional machine learning methods rely on high-quality data to extract product-related characteristics, so AI-based diagnostic has found a popular use for formulating classifications and associating data with corresponding error types and severity levels, therefore, in relation to process monitoring, diagnostic and prognostics, processes, they argue that the deployment of AI tools has become more comprehensive due to rich flow of data emanating from sensors and equipment. In addition, in the study, they argue that AI facilitates a better understanding of the material properties used in manufacturing process monitoring and modeling.

Buchmeister et al. (2019) argue that AI will drastically change the production and management, from the production and design process to the supply chain and management, in their study examining the effects of AI in the manufacturing industry, In general findings of the study, they show that AI can be effective in creating, improving and making new products cheaper in the manufacturing industry, AI technology is urgently needed to solve the main problems of information production, efficient use and large-scale application in the production processes and the further realize the talent and value in the entire production system.

Dash et al. (2019) examined the effects of AI on supply chain method in their study; artificial neural networks, mobile computing, robotics, big data storage on the cloud-based machine learning, internet, and information processing algorithms, etc technological process in the fields have suggested that it encourages the implementation of AI in diverse industries. They also argue that since AI provides significant competitive advantages, many enterprises use AI in large parts of their supply chain.

Modgil et al. (2022) argue that AI strengthens durability of the supply chain through the use of AI in their study, in which they investigate the impacts of AI on the supply chain. They have suggested that assuring last-mile delivery of necessary household supplies, maintaining a dynamic strategy, offering individualized solutions, and minimizing the disruption brought on by Covid 19 are just a few of the important supply chain challenges that AI can help with.

Ramchand et al. (2022a) argue that artificial intelligence will guide the new generation of quality assurance, which significantly reduces times and increases the efficiency of a company's development of more sophisticated software in their study, in which they discuss how AI influences in the software testing industry. Thus, they suggested that they except AI to assume a vital role in software testing in the long term, and the tester's new job will be gain to expertise in verifying AI models and computational strategies in order to become more intelligent. AI methodologies similarly claim that they will then interface with new developments (such as Big Data, he Internet of Things, Cloud-Based Technologies, and others) and extract accepted procedural techniques that to perform more accurate and insightful tests and produce excellent findings, meet the customer requirement.

CONCLUSION

This study, which examines the role of AI in increasing product development efficiency, consist of five parts. The definition and basic functions of AI in the firs part, the key technologies and components associated with AI in the second part, the efficiency of product development in the third part, the roles and effects of AI on product development efficiency in the fourth part, and the general findings of studies examining the effects of AI on product development efficiency in the fifth and final part were examined.

As a general result of this thesis, it can be clearly stated that artificial intelligence has significantly increased product development efficiency. Thanks to the features developed in many areas such as artificial intelligence product design, prototype preparation, market analysis, and production processes such as quality control and testing, it has been documented that it accelerates the product development process, increases product quality, and reduces costs.

In systems where artificial intelligence is integrated, it has been observed that the rate of catching future forecasts increases by analyzing the market dynamics and consumer demands in the closest way, and the success of the products in reaching the end user increases at a high rate. To take full advantage of all the AI capabilities, users need to be more aware and develop their skills. The capacity and areas of influence of AI shall continue to develop at a similar rate, as regards the development of artificial intelligence technologies like Machine Learning and Deep Learning. Capturing this development is one of the main sources for systems to gain maximum efficiency and success. A product is useless in the hands of those who do not know how to utilize it, even if it is a good product. As the employees involved in the system process realized the success of artificial intelligence, their demands on this technology began to increase. Artificial intelligence has actually brought new perspectives, workflow, and lines of business to the industry. As artificial intelligence started to do the work that most employees do easily and quickly, instead of the workers who will do the related work, the employees who will make these jobs done by artificial intelligence have started to be hired. Some business lines such as Prompt Engineering are now in rematch. As companies that have not benefited from these blessings of technology begin to fall behind in the market, they hire teams and employees who will integrate artificial intelligence and the like into their systems, and organize and develop their organizational structures according to this integration, regardless of their salaries.

To utilize AI to create increasingly complicated and specialized goods and commercial processes, technological hurdles include the creation of algorithms and AI components. For instance, a deeper comprehension and advancement of cutting-edge AI techniques like deep learning and artificial neural networks may more successfully incorporate these techniques into product creation. Strategies to better incorporate these technologies into the processes of product creation may be the main subject of future research in this area.

However, concerns about security and ethics are raised with the widespread use of AI. There are concerns around the ethics and security implications of artificial intelligence, especially in relation to privacy and personal data. It is necessary to investigate further the effects of automation on the labor market and how it may alter employment. These issues could be the subject of subsequent studies that can help us better understand what an AI has to do with morality and society.

The influence of artificial intelligence on product development will grow and become more pervasive in the next years. Making product development predictable, for instance, will enable forecasting of the product's performance in the market and raise the product's investment. Greater usage of AI in product creation would speed up manufacturing procedures and make it possible to create goods that are more specialized and more matched to consumer requirements. However, further research, invention, and education are necessary to fully utilize this technology. To better comprehend the constantly evolving nature and ramifications of this technology, future research will need to be updated and expanded on regularly. In addition, it is important for societies, policy makers and technology developers to collaborate in understanding and managing the ethical and societal impacts of AI. (see at: Ramchand et al. (2022a); Modgil et al. (2022); Dash et al. (2019); Buchmeister et al. (2019); Manimozhi et al. (2023) etc.)

REFERENCES

Aphirakmethawong, J., Yang, E., & Mehnen, J. (2022). An Overview of Artificial Intelligence in Product Design for Smart Manufacturing. *2022 27th International Conference on Automation and Computing: Smart Systems and Manufacturing, ICAC 2022, 1018*, (pp. 1–6). IEEE. 10.1109/ICAC55051.2022.9911089

Arinez, J. F., Chang, Q., Gao, R. X., Xu, C., & Zhang, J. (2020). Artificial Intelligence in Advanced Manufacturing: Current Status and Future Outlook. *Journal of Manufacturing Science and Engineering, 142*(11), 1–16. doi:10.1115/1.4047855

Buchmeister, B., Palcic, I., & Ojstersek, R. (2019). Artificial Intelligence in Manufacturing Companies and Broader: An Overview. İçinde *DAAAM INTERNATIONAL SCIENTIFIC BOOK* (Sayı 7). doi:10.2507/daaam.scibook.2019.07

Camburn, B., Viswanathan, V., Linsey, J., Anderson, D., Jensen, D., Crawford, R., Otto, K., & Wood, K. (2017). Design prototyping methods: State of the art in strategies, techniques, and guidelines. *Design Science, 3*(Schrage 1993), 1–33. doi:10.1017/dsj.2017.10

Chen, H., Chiang, R. H., & Storey, V. C. (2012). Business Intelligence and Analytics: From Big Data to Big Impact. *Management Information Systems Quarterly, 36*(4), 1165–1188. doi:10.2307/41703503

Cooper, R. G., & Kleinschmidt, E. J. (1995). Benchmarking the firm's critical success factors in new product development. *Journal of Product Innovation Management, 12*(5), 374–391. doi:10.1111/1540-5885.1250374

Dash, R., Rebman, C., & Kar, U. K. (2019). Application of Artificial Intelligence in Automation of Supply Chain Management. *Journal of Strategic Innovation and Sustainability, 14*(3), 43–53. doi:10.33423/jsis.v14i3.2105

Dwivedi, Y. K., Hughes, L., Coombs, C., Constantiou, I., & Duan, Y. (2020). Artificial Intelligence (AI): Multidisciplinary perspectives on emerging challenges, opportunities, and agenda for research, practice and policy. *International Journal of Information Management, 57*, 101994. doi:10.1016/j.ijinfomgt.2019.08.002

Eppinger, S. D., & Ulrich, K. T. (2011). Product design and development. New York, NY: McGraw-Hill.

FeldererM.RamlerR. (2021). *Quality Assurance for AI-based Systems: Overview and Challenges*. 1–10. http://arxiv.org/abs/2102.05351

Hall, B. H. (2002). The financing of research and development. *Oxford Review of Economic Policy, 18*(1), 35–51. doi:10.1093/oxrep/18.1.35

Hirschberg, J., & Manning, C. D. (2022). Advances in natural language processing. *Science, 349*(6245), 261–266. doi:10.1126/science.aaa8685 PMID:26185244

Jordan, M. I., & Mitchell, T. M. (2015). Machine learning: Trends, perspectives, and prospects. *Science, 349*(6245), 255–260. doi:10.1126/science.aaa8415 PMID:26185243

Langerak, F., & Jan Hultink, E. (2006). The impact of product innovativeness on the link between development speed and new product profitability. *Journal of Product Innovation Management, 23*(3), 203–214. doi:10.1111/j.1540-5885.2006.00194.x

Manimozhi, N., Suganya, R., Pandian, P. S., Suguna, G., Devi, R. S., & Ramya, S. (2023). A Compressive Review Models For Big Data Analytics Relies On. *Artificial Intelligence, 01*, 415–420.

Mehnen, J. (2022). An Overview of Artificial Intelligence in Product Design for Smart Manufacturing. *2022 27th International Conference on Automation and Computing: Smart Systems and Manufacturing, ICAC 2022, 1018*, (pp. 1–6). IEEE. 10.1109/ICAC55051.2022.9911089

Modgil, S., Singh, R. K., & Hannibal, C. (2022). Artificial intelligence for supply chain resilience: Learning from Covid-19. *International Journal of Logistics Management, 33*(4), 1246–1268. doi:10.1108/IJLM-02-2021-0094

Pisano, G. P. (2019). The hard truth about innovative. *Harvard Business Review, 97*(1), 62–71.

Pournader, M., Ghaderi, H., Hassanzadegan, A., & Fahimnia, B. (2021). Artificial intelligence applications in supply chain management. *International Journal of Production Economics, 241*(July), 108250. doi:10.1016/j.ijpe.2021.108250

Provost, F., & Fawcett, T. (2013). Data Science and its Relationship to Big Data and Data-Driven Decision Making. *Big Data, 1*(1), 51–59. doi:10.1089/big.2013.1508 PMID:27447038

Ramchand, S., Shaikh, S., & Alam, I. (2022a, April). Role of Artificial Intelligence in Software Quality Assurance. *Lecture Notes in Networks and Systems, 295*, 125–136. doi:10.1007/978-3-030-82196-8_10

Rath, R. C., Baral, S. K., Singh, T., & Goel, R. (2022). Role of Artificial Intelligence and Machine Learning in Product Design and Manufacturing. *2022 International Mobile and Embedded Technology Conference, MECON 2022*, (pp. 571–575). IEEE. 10.1109/MECON53876.2022.9752455

Rodgers, W., Murray, J. M., Stefanidis, A., Degbey, W. Y., & Tarba, S. Y. (2023). An artificial intelligence algorithmic approach to ethical decision-making in human resource management processes. *Human Resource Management Review, 33*(1), 100925. doi:10.1016/j.hrmr.2022.100925

Schmidhuber, J. (2015). Deep learning in neural networks: An overview. *Neural Networks, 61*, 85–117. doi:10.1016/j.neunet.2014.09.003 PMID:25462637

Van Allen, P. (2018). Prototyping Ways of Prototyping AI. *INTERACTIONS*, 46–51. https://github.

Zeba, G., Dabić, M., Čičak, M., Daim, T., & Yalcin, H. (2021). Technology mining: Artificial intelligence in manufacturing. *Technological Forecasting and Social Change, 171*(February), 120971. doi:10.1016/j.techfore.2021.120971

Zeba, G., Dabić, M., Čičak, M., Daim, T., & Yalcin, H. (2021). Technology mining: Artificial intelligence in manufacturing. *Technological Forecasting and Social Change*, *171*(February), 120971. doi:10.1016/j. techfore.2021.120971

Chapter 17
The Role of Internet of Things (IoT) in Disaster Management

Cagla Ozen

https://orcid.org/0000-0003-1817-9806
Yeditepe University, Turkey

İremnaz Yolcu
Yeditepe University, Turkey

ABSTRACT

The purpose of this book chapter is to delve into the role of the internet of things (IoT) in disaster management. Specifically, this chapter will address the following research questions and subjects: How can IoT be utilized in early warning systems for natural disasters? How does big data analytics contribute to disaster management when combined with IoT? Furthermore, a review of literature on the analysis of case studies involving IoT-based disaster management approaches will also be discussed.

INTRODUCTION

Disasters are events that can occur due to natural causes or man-made causes. Regardless of the cause, disasters often result in devastating outcomes in terms of human lives and the economy (Ray et al., 2017). The report by CRED (2023) states that a total of 387 natural hazards and disasters has been recorded worldwide, which resulted in the loss of 30,704 human lives along with 185 million affected individuals and an economic loss with the amount of US$223.8 billion, according to the data Emergency Event Database EM-DAT has been collected.

Disaster management primarily involves developing strategies for decreasing the impact and consequences of the disasters, rather than eliminating the underlying threats, since disaster management is not solely concerned with the averting potential disasters but also with preparing for and responding to them when they occur (Wellington & Ramesh, 2017).

The Internet of Things (IoT) is an emerging paradigm which is a concept itself regarding to everyday objects will be enabling to communicate among each other along with the users, integrating into

DOI: 10.4018/978-1-6684-9576-6.ch017

the Internet (Bhosle et al., 2018). IoT has emerged as a promising solution for addressing challenges in various fields, thanks to its appealing features such as heterogeneity, interoperability, lightweight, and flexibility (Ray et al., 2017).

IoT has demonstrated its capability to offer solutions that are more substantial, scalable, portable and energy efficient in addressing a range of issues in disaster management. Driven by these issues, it becomes essential to have a solid understanding of how IoT is currently being utilized to monitor and manage disasters (Ray et al., 2017). Although IoT can't prevent disasters, it has the capability to assist in recognizing life-threatening hazards, provide early warning to authorities, and aid in rescue operations for those affected, resulting in saving lives, resources, and money. Emergency management and response can be improved by the utilization of IoT technologies, leading to significantly better results (Lembke, 2021).

The purpose of this book chapter is to explore the role of IoT in disaster management. Specifically, this book chapter will address the following research questions: How can IoT be used in early warning systems for natural disasters? How does big data analytics contribute to disaster management when combined with IoT? Furthermore, a review of literature on the analysis of case studies involving IoT-based disaster management approaches will be discussed.

METHODS

For this book chapter, the research involved collecting and analyzing existing literature reviews to gather relevant articles and publications to explore the role of IoT in disaster management. To ensure that multiple academic resources such as IEEE Xplore, Google Scholar, Yeditepe University Knowledge Center were used. The search terms used were "IoT in disaster management", "Role of IoT in disaster management", "IoT early in warning" and similar variations. The content of the selected articles and publications primarily focused on the usage, role, benefits, challenges, and overall contributions of IoT in disaster management.

DISASTER MANAGEMENT

Definition of Disaster Management

Coppola (2015) emphasizes what drives the idea of disaster management is to minimize the effects of disasters on human life, properties, and environment. It consists of actions as such mitigation of aftermath of disasters, making sure of people will be prepared for scenarios where disasters occur, plans the response to disasters, and assists people with recovery from disasters. Even though, disaster management cycle has been described in a range of terminology, it can be presented in an overall manner as the following:

Mitigation: The mitigation phase refers to actions that include programs specifically designed to mitigate the impact of disasters on a nation or community (Carter, 1991).

Carter (1991) describes mitigation actions as following:

- Implementation of construction regulations.
- Enforcement of regulations related to land use.

- Agricultural initiatives targeting the reduction of hazards' impact on crops.
- Systems designed to safeguard critical installations like power supplies and essential communication networks.

Preparedness: The preparedness phase refers to actions that make it possible for communities and individuals to effectively respond to disasters. It especially carries importance in regard to individuals being prepared for survival, as there are many scenarios where resources and services are limited (Carter, 1991).

Carter (1991) describes preparedness actions as following:

- Creating and keeping up-to-date disaster response strategies that can be implemented as needed.
- Establishing systems for issuing warnings.
- Developing emergency communication methods.
- Implementing training programs, including drills and assessments.

Response: The response phase refers to actions that are taken right before and immediately after a disaster occurs. These actions specifically aim for preventing casualties, protecting property along with addressing the immediate consequences resulting from the disaster (Carter, 1991).

Carter (1991) describes response actions as following:

- carrying out strategies
- conducting search and recovery operations
- supplying urgent provisions like food, shelter, and medical aid
- evaluating and analyzing the situation

Recovery: The recovery phase refers to actions taken such as restoration, rehabilitation, and reconstruction for the purpose of helping communities to return to their normal life after a disaster (Carter, 1991).

Carter (1991) describes recovery actions as following:

- Reestablishing vital services;
- Implementing measures to support the physical and psychological recovery of individuals affected by the disaster;
- Implementing long-term reconstruction measures, including replacing buildings and infrastructure destroyed by the disaster.

Key Challenges in Disaster Management

Disaster management does not come without its challenges. Those challenges can be grouped specifically into disaster response phase and therefore can be given as coordination challenges, communication challenges, information challenges, and logistics challenges. Coordination challenges refer to difficulties occurring while agencies attempt to coordinate with one another across different agencies. This can be especially challenging for agencies, for the cases when they are not able to develop, maintain, and share information, resulting in delays in disaster response efforts. For example, this occurred as an such a major issue during Hurricane Katrina when the other teams searched for the same area more than once, and this information was not shared with other rescue teams. Communication challenges go hand in hand with coordination challenges. In the context of disaster management, establishing seamless communication with one agency to another can be challenging. At this step, interoperable radios can be a game changer. These radios provide the teams with easy communication within each other and make sharing information easier. Information challenges refer to difficulty to obtain key information that is accurate and timely during the disasters. In these situations, there are also rumors that prevail concerning the disaster itself. Logistical challenges refer to difficulties occurring during the moving of large number of people and supplies. It has been seen that supplies did not reach the teams at their designated locations, resulting in responders having to buy the supplies themselves or manage without them. There have also been cases where valuable resources could not be used due to logistical issues (Oden et al., 2012).

Other key challenges in disaster management can be grouped into two groups: infrastructures and facilities, and human negligence challenges. infrastructures and facilities challenges refer to challenges such as the investment in disaster management being too expensive, disaster alert systems being weak, and infrastructures can be destroyed during the disasters, communication problems, and most important of them existence of excessive amount of information which makes responding phase of disasters extra challenging. On the other hand, human negligence refers to the lack of knowledge, preparation, skills, and awareness when it comes to disaster management (Ghasemi & Karimian, 2020).

INTERNET OF THINGS (IOT)

Definition of Internet of Things (IoT)

Internet of Things (IoT) is a paradigm that refers to a network of physical collection of objects that are capable of sensing, communicating, and sharing information amongst each other while interconnected over Internet Protocol (IP) networks. IoT makes it possible for these interconnected objects to collect and analyze data to take specific actions, resulting in enhanced insight for planning, management and decision making. The internet has evolved into a specific point where it is not only consists of network of computers but also network of devices of a wide range of variety such as vehicles, home appliances, people, industrial systems that are all connected which also capable of communicating and sharing information amongst each other based on specific protocols for specific purposes (Patel & Patel, 2016).

IoT has emerged as a promising solution recently for addressing challenges in various fields, thanks to its appealing features such as heterogeneity, interoperability, lightweight, and flexibility (Ray et al., 2017).

IoT has emerged as a benchmark in the realm of communication, connecting billions of devices and optimizing their efficiency by using sensors. Therefore a considerable amount of information is generated by these sensors which are processed to gain cognitive knowledge, and new technologies certainly have been benefiting from that since the past few years. With the continuous increase in the number of devices connected to the internet, new methodologies associated with IoT devices are continuously born. IoT devices have found applications in various areas such as smart homes, public safety, agriculture, healthcare, and more (Sharma et al., 2021).

An Overview of IoT Architecture

IoT refers to the interconnection of objects, which enables the administration, mining, and access of data generated by these connected objects. Its primary function is to connect objects, actuators, and sensors to execute specific tasks such as environmental monitoring (Esposito et al., 2022).

Esposito et al. (2022) describes a fundamental architecture for IoT consists of three tiers as the following:

- the local environment, there exists a network of smart objects or sensors that possess the capability to communicate, interact, and perceive data from the surrounding environment.
- a transport layer that facilitates communication between end-nodes in the lower layer and higher layers as well as infrastructure.
- a cloud-based layer is responsible for storage, data mining, and processing tasks, potentially incorporating systems and interfaces that provide users with access to and visualization of the data.

Key Challenges in IoT

- **Architecture Challenge:** The IoT concept includes interconnected devices and sensors that offer transparency and invisibility. Communication methods within these devices involve wireless, autonomic, and ad hoc connections. Services have become increasingly complex. It will become a necessity for systems to establish infrastructure solutions that combine data obtained from different sources, identify relevant patterns, and provide decision-making support. One single blueprint architecture cannot be applicable for all applications, and for that reason, heterogeneous architectures are needed in IoT. IoT architectures should possess flexibility when it comes to scenarios involving identification, such as RFID tags, intelligent devices, and smart objects (Chen et al., 2014).
- **Technical Challenge:** Usage of heterogeneous architectures in IoT solutions poses as a challenge in regard to requiring different applications, different networking technologies are needed by environments, usage of cellular and wireless area networks along with RFID technologies vary significantly from one another. Also communication technologies should be affordable and provide dependable connectivity for both simple and complex fixed and mobile devices. All of these factors may be posing as a challenge for IoT to connect with as many "Things" as possible (Chen et al., 2014).
- **Hardware Challenge:** With smart devices communicating among each other, smart systems with superior intelligence will be born. Hence, the deployment of IoT applications and the emergence of new services are on the horizon. Therefore, the development of hardware that focuses on wireless identifiable systems that are compact, affordable, and possess adequate functionality is essential. However, two main requirements carry the utmost importance: the need for low power consumption in sleep mode and ultra-low cost, respectively (Chen et al., 2014).
- **Privacy and Security Challenge:** In comparison to traditional networks IoT solutions are posing more challenges in regard to security and privacy since private information of users is mostly included. When it comes to security of IoT, it should be more comprehensive in comparison to security of traditional networks since it uses combinations of things, services, and networks. Current security architectures might not be applicable to IoT systems due to being designed based

on human communication aspects and will hinder the logical connection between objects within IoT. Hence, implementing cost-effective and machine-to-machine (M2M) focused solutions is necessary to ensure privacy and security in IoT (Chen et al., 2014).

- **Standard Challenge:** Standards are an important aspect in IoT. They are necessary for providing equal access and usage among all participants. Standards will contribute to the overall IoT solutions and components. Additionally, protocols within standards, along with the development process of standards, should be open for free public access (Chen et al., 2014).

IOT IN DISASTER MANAGEMENT

Usage of Internet of Things (IoT) in Early Warning Systems for Disaster Management

The integration of IoT technologies plays a crucial role in early warning (EW) systems and overall disaster management. By leveraging IoT, these systems enable the monitoring of expansive environmental areas by collecting data from diverse sources. With low-latency communication and real-time data processing, IoT facilitates the generation of precise and timely warnings in response to disaster events. Notably, IoT, Cloud Computing, and Artificial Intelligence play crucial roles in monitoring, forecasting, and generating alarms within EW systems. These technologies provide tools for sensing, cleaning, processing, and analyzing environmental data, enhancing the overall effectiveness of the system (Esposito et al., 2022).

IoT Architectures for Early Warning Systems

A common architecture for most basic IoT solutions consists of three layers: the perception layer, the communication layer, and the application layer. These layers serve as a general framework for describing IoT-based systems. In addition to this, specific architectures may incorporate additional. Nonetheless, the fundamental IoT architectures follow a systematic approach that involves the following steps: data collection from the environment, data processing, and transmission to a central server. The central servers employ various techniques to generate real-time alarms using both stored and current data (Esposito et al., 2022).

IoT-Enabled Early Warning Systems for Different Natural Disasters

Floods

Floods are among the most perilous natural disasters, causing numerous casualties and significant environmental damage. They can be triggered by heavy rainfall, thunderstorms, or snow melts, while hydro-geological and soil-related factors also contribute to the risk. Several EW systems for floods already exist, such as the European Flood Awareness Systems, which utilizes rainfall detection to generate alarms based on the observed rainfall levels. The advent of IoT systems has provided immediate access to data, enabling real-time warning applications. These systems leverage hydro-geological models, statistics, and machine learning algorithms to predict and mitigate floods by collecting real-time data from WSNs. Then, collected data is sent to a remote server for further processing, resulting in alarm generations (Esposito et al., 2022).

EXPLORING IoT-BASED FLOOD EARLY WARNING: PREVIOUS STUDIES / CASE STUDIES

Jayashree et al. (2017) introduces a simple IoT system designed for floods in dams. The system aims to address issues encountered in previous solutions, including handling heterogeneous data, power consumption issues and the lack of cellular coverage. The proposed architecture consists of flow and water level sensors. These sensors will only send the data to a server if the data obtained by them surpasses a certain threshold. To overcome the problem of cellular network failure, the researchers suggest the usage of Zigbee technology. This involves the utilization of Zigbee hardware, which necessitates the use of an Android app for mobile users. The Zigbee hardware is connected through a USB On-The-Go module to facilitate communication, ensuring that users can receive alarms even in areas with no cellular coverage. However in exchange, users will be required to use Zigbee hardware (Esposito et al., 2022).

In a separate study conducted by Ibarreche et al. (2020), the researchers employed the 3G network and the MQTT protocol for transmitting data to a Cloud server, where it is processed and stored. Furthermore, the system incorporates mobile sensor nodes equipped with LoRa modules to relay data to the nodes connected to the 3G network. The solution proves itself successful in delivering timely warnings thanks to the volume of data collected from various sources and the reliable network. However, this success comes at a significant cost (Esposito et al., 2022).

Thekkil and Prabakaran (2017) present an EW system that combines feature extraction and image comparison algorithms. The system uses images captured by CMOS cameras and an image database to apply image comparison techniques, enabling the generation of danger rankings for flooding events. The images are acquired through Zigbee from the cameras, then transmitted to a GSM gateway, and finally forwarded to a processing server for comprehensive analysis. One notable advantage of this system is its cost-effectiveness and economic viability (Esposito et al., 2022).

Earthquakes

IoT can also play a significant role in earthquake early warning systems. Vibrations and ground movements are being monitored by the use of sensors which generate alarms to alert people before an earthquake strikes. Even a few seconds or minutes of advance warning can make a significant difference in saving lives. In the context of earthquake early detection, P-wave detection is commonly employed. During an earthquake, compression P-waves and transverse S-waves are released from the epicenter. P-waves propagate faster than S-waves and are less destructive. Their ability to travel swiftly with minimal damage makes them valuable for issuing early warnings before the more destructive S-waves arrive at a specific location (Esposito et al., 2022).

Alphonsa and Ravi (2016) introduce a fundamental IoT system that adopts a similar approach. The system employs accelerometers connected to microcontrollers to gather and analyze ground vibration measurements. These measurements are then transmitted to a receiver using Zigbee, which is connected to a PC responsible for forwarding warnings to users. Additionally, GSM modules can be employed to alert mobile phone users through a base transceiver station (Esposito et al., 2022).

Exploring IoT-Based Earthquake Early Warning: Previous Studies / Case Studies

In a study conducted by Tariq et al. (2019), it was demonstrated that the Seismic Wave Event Detection Algorithm (SWEDA) is a highly effective method for early earthquake warnings. This system harnesses the power of IoT technologies, including inclinometer nodes for Industry 4.0 and the CANOpen communication protocol. SWEDA is designed to detect various wave types, including P-waves, S-waves, Rayleigh waves, and Love waves, by strategically positioning sensors according to the specific wave characteristics. This approach minimizes computational requirements while maximizing detection accuracy. To enhance the system's performance and reduce false alarms, the data processing algorithm was optimized. The results of the study demonstrated the system's effectiveness, as it successfully detected the initial trigger of P-waves 11 seconds before the occurrence of the second trigger for S-waves, highlighting its early warning capabilities (Esposito et al., 2022).

Klapez et al. (2018) initiated Earthcloud as a cost-effective, energy-efficient, and cloud-based earthquake EW system. In Earthcloud, geophones are utilized instead of Micro Electronic Mechanical Systems (MEMS) accelerometers, as geophones are known for producing lower noise levels when operated at lower sampling frequencies. The system operates by detecting ground motion through the sensors, which then transmit the data to a server. If the detected motion surpasses a certain threshold, an alarm is generated. The data is encapsulated into MQTT packets and sent to Amazon Web Services (AWS) IoT Core for processing. Then, the data is forwarded to Amazon Kinesis, a platform for pre-processing and real-time data forwarding to connected devices. In case the first alarm fails to generate, a second alarm is ensured to be triggered. Amazon S3 is utilized as a data storage service. The effectiveness of the developed solution was validated in Modena, Italy, using a three-unit network. Only one out of the three sensors encountered a failure in detecting an earthquake, indicating the overall success of the system (Esposito et al., 2022).

In their work, Fauvel et al. (2020) present a novel approach that integrates data from GPS stations and seismometers into a machine learning algorithm for earthquake EW systems. The efficacy of this algorithm has been demonstrated through the use of real-world datasets. To optimize data transmission on the network, the approach employs Edge/Fog computing techniques, leveraging machine learning classification at each sensor to minimize the volume of excessive data. The study demonstrates that the use of classifiers leads to noteworthy reductions in transmission effort, lower latency, and improved communication. As an outcome, the combination of GPS stations and seismometers demonstrates a synergistic effect, showcasing the importance of a multi-parametric model for achieving enhanced accuracy in earthquake early warning systems (Esposito et al., 2022).

Tsunamis

Tsunamis are another form of natural disaster. Tsunamis occur in the water in the shape of large waves. Tsunamis can be caused by various events such as earthquakes, volcanic eruptions, or underwater explosions. EW systems designed for tsunamis utilize methods such as seismic event detections, hydro-acoustic waves measurement, pressure measurements, and camera-based observation. In the cases where tsunamis are caused by seismic events, earthquake measurements can be of use by the location of epicenter which can help to make a prediction on the arrival of tsunamis. When underwater movements are caused by earthquakes, they generate hydro-acoustic waves, that can be of use by using underwater acoustic sensors since they assist with the prediction of arrival of tsunamis. Underwater pressure sensors are commonly employed for the detection of tsunami waves. To cover extensive geographical areas, it is typical to deploy Underwater Wireless Sensor Networks (UWSN) for data collection. The collected data is transmitted to a central hub for subsequent processing, which facilitates the generation of early warnings. In underwater environments, the preferred communication method is acoustic modems rather than radio units (Esposito et al., 2022).

Exploring IoT-Based Tsunami Early Warning: Previous Studies / Case Studies

S-Net is a comprehensive underwater observation network strategically positioned along the Japan Trench. This advanced network encompasses a total of 150 observation units, equipped with seismometers and bottom pressure sensors. These units are meticulously connected by cables, maintaining a consistent interval of 30 kilometers between them. Optic fiber communications enable the real-time transmission of all the collected data to the land-based stations (Esposito et al., 2022).

In their study, Inoue et al. (2019) propose a specialized method for real-time tsunami forecasting utilizing the S-Net sensor network. This method focuses on analyzing the recorded pressure waveforms captured by the sensors, classifying them based on their proximity to the uplift region caused by the earthquake. By calculating the distance between the sensors and the uplift region, the method determines the extent of the affected area. The approach is applicable for estimating both tsunamis and earthquakes, as it can detect seismic events and hydro-acoustic waves. However, it requires appropriate filtering of the pressure data. The sensor classification process takes only 1 minute, while computing the source area of the tsunami following an earthquake typically takes around 10 minutes, without the need for complex simulations. The effectiveness of this method has been successfully demonstrated in two major earthquakes that occurred in the region previously (Esposito et al., 2022).

According to Darmawan et al. (2020), a proposed design for an IoT device incorporates Fuzzy Logic to accurately predict abnormal wave behaviors and generate EWs. The sensor nodes of this device comprise a gyroscope, accelerometer, and a LoRa module for data transmission. Placed on the water's surface, the sensor effectively detects and analyzes data to gather information on wave height and speed. Employing Fuzzy Logic embedded within the sensor unit, the waves are classified based on these parameters. The collected data is subsequently transmitted to a server utilizing the LoRa module. This classification algorithm enables the generation of danger labels ranging from safe to dangerous, with corresponding danger levels from 0 to 100 based on the computed wave height and speed. During testing, the Fuzzy Logic algorithm exhibited an accuracy level of 98% to 100%, the LoRa communication revealing a delay of approximately 4.6279 seconds and a minimal error rate (Esposito et al., 2022).

Gardner-Stephen et al. (2019) proposes a cost-effective model that addresses the potential deterrent of high costs, especially for certain countries, in implementing an Early Warning (EW) system for tsunamis. The model aims to improve upon existing EW systems by considering communication challenges in compromised situations. The designed solution includes an EW system integrated with a platform called the "Warning Decision Support System." This integration allows the solution to operate offline in the event of internet connection disruptions during a disaster. The system utilizes low-cost, low-mobility vehicles with minimal power consumption. These vehicles employ acoustic detection to detect tsunamis before they occur. The vehicle network is equipped with GPS units and satellite connectivity, serving as a valuable addition to the conventional fixed tsunami sensors. Additionally, satellite communications are integrated into the Alert Distribution and Support System as a backup option to ensure continuous connectivity in case standard IP-based connections become unavailable during a disaster (Esposito et al., 2022).

Landslides

Landslides are another form of natural disaster that occurs when there is downward movement of land. However, they can also be triggered by factors such as rainfall, heavy snow melts, and earthquakes. EW systems that are designed for landslides can be implemented on various levels, such as regional, national, or even within a specific locality. Also it is possible to lower expenses and enable the installation of sensor networks with a higher density by the utilization of IoT. For scenarios where rainfall is triggering factor of landslides, on-site sensors can be a great use when the weather data obtained from forecasts get combined with them (Esposito et al., 2022).

Exploring IoT-Based Landslide Early Warning: Previous Studies / Case Studies

Gamperl et al. (2021) propose a system that utilizes MEMS technology and LoRa communication for an EW system designed for landslides.

The system operates in the following manner: it comprises a multi-sensor LoRa network with three types of sensor nodes, each equipped with a minimum of two LoRa Gateways to ensure redundancy. In comparison to other systems like Continuous Shear Monitor, piezometers, and extensometers, which require more space and encounter installation challenges, the compact LoRa nodes offer advantages such as wider area coverage and cost-effective monitoring of various environmental factors. Data collected from both the LoRa nodes and other systems are consolidated at a central station and transmitted to a Cloud server named Inform@Risk. This Cloud server manages and integrates data from different sensors to generate early warnings and determine danger levels, although the specific thresholds for danger levels are yet to be determined. When an early warning is triggered, alerts are disseminated through a mobile application, and local sirens are installed to notify nearby individuals. However, immediate alarms are only dispatched if at least two neighboring nodes simultaneously detect significant accelerations and a data analysis algorithm has been executed. In cases where these conditions are not met, an expert is required to monitor the data and prevent false alarms from being triggered (Esposito et al., 2022).

In a previous study conducted by Hemalatha et al. (2020), a landslide EW system was introduced, integrating machine learning techniques for prediction purposes. The researchers also performed an analysis of multiple factors to enhance the overall reliability of the system. The system is organized into five main components, which are as follows:

- data collection,
- data transmission,
- forecasting,
- warning,
- response.

The utilization of ML algorithms in the system enables the generation of accurate predictions even in cases where the first two components encounter failures. The researchers emphasized the significance of reliable and redundant data transmission in landslide EW systems, as current systems often do not give enough attention to this aspect. The proposed system employs two types of predictions: "nowcasting" and "forecasting." The nowcasting prediction utilizes rainfall forecast information to generate warnings even in situations where sensor data is unavailable. On the other hand, the forecasting prediction utilizes data from the first two components, when accessible, to produce advanced warnings and offer additional lead time for early warning purposes (Esposito et al., 2022).

Li et al. (2021) conducted a study in China where they develop an EW system for landslides in China. This system utilizes 5G technology and incorporates monitoring of various factors such as rainfall, ground fissure, and real-time tracking of surface deformations. The warning system classifies alerts into four levels, determined by the tangent angle of the slope deformation. To ensure dependable data transmission, the system utilizes two complementary modes: mesh mode, which improves fault tolerance and reliability, and linear mode, which enables efficient long-range communication. This dual communication approach incorporates the BeiDou satellite module and GPRS, enhancing the reliability of data transmission. Surface displacement tracking is performed using GNSS stations, and the data collected from these stations, along with data from ground monitoring stations and weather stations, is continually transmitted to a central server. Real-time monitoring of the data is also possible through a web interface developed by the researchers (Esposito et al., 2022).

BIG DATA ANALYTICS (BDA) AND INTERNET OF THINGS (IoT) IN DISASTER MANAGEMENT

Big Data Analytics (BDA) is employed to analyze extensive datasets obtained from disaster areas, aiming to enhance our understanding and perspective of the situation, thereby enabling effective management of rescue operations and logistics. BDA provides data scientists with the advantage of analyzing large volumes of data from various sources that may not be feasible with conventional tools. To conduct data analysis on massive and diverse datasets encompassing structured, semi-structured, and unstructured data, BDA relies on a range of technologies and tools. Furthermore, current research trends in BDA involve analyzing both the contextual/textual aspects and spatial characteristics of data to generate valuable insights (Shah et al., 2019).

In a different earlier study conducted by Avvenuti et al. (2018), Kafka and Spark were employed to collect and analyze Twitter data using a specially designed system. The system gathered disaster-related information and geo-tagged tweets, which were then subjected to classification techniques. The resulting information was visualized on a web-based dashboard to create early awareness during disaster events (Shah et al., 2019).

In another earlier study conducted by Asencio-Cortés et al. (2017), a large dataset of earthquake events was analyzed using Spark. The study yielded successful results, showcasing promising outcomes in accurately predicting earthquake magnitudes, particularly in California (Shah et al., 2019).

In yet another earlier study conducted by Liu et al. (2018), it was demonstrated that a real-time algorithm, utilizing stream processing environments like Kafka and Spark, collected, and classified mobile phone position data. The objective of this algorithm was to generate a precise heat map illustrating the population affected by an earthquake (Shah et al., 2019).

Another study conducted by Wang et al. (2017) proposed a system that is a combination of Hadoop and Spark that uses large datasets in regard to spatial and temporals perspectives and conduct risk analytics to optimize the allocation of resources and plan evacuations for fire response (Shah et al., 2019).

From Wireless Sensor Networks (WSN) to Internet of Things (IoT) for Disaster Management

Wireless Sensor Networks (WSNs) are a type of low-power sensor technology designed to measure and report various environmental conditions, including factors such as smoke, temperature, vibration, and location. WSNs have been extensively employed in disaster monitoring and management for a considerable period of time. These networks play a crucial role in gathering real-time data, enabling rapid response, and providing valuable insights for effective disaster mitigation and response strategies. However, WSNs alone do not fully address the social, technical, and economic aspects of disaster management. Integrating WSNs with the IoT can enhance data management, processing, and decision-making, resulting in more meaningful insights from the collected data. In recent years, the field of disaster management has been undergoing a transformation to embrace the potential of IoT. IoT offers significant advantages in data gathering in disaster-affected areas, providing alternative communication options through low-power IoT-enabled wireless devices. It acts as a game changer by facilitating timely decision-making through the availability of multi-sourced information. Moreover, IoT greatly enhances situational awareness by enabling smart aggregation, integration, and analysis of multidimensional and diverse data sources (Shah et al., 2019).

A study conducted by Xu et al. (2018) shows that evacuation of large crowds after disaster is made through an IoT based system. Crows lives oriented track and help optimization system (CLOTHO) uses mobile cloud computing platform to decrease the loss of lives by the usage of IoT based solution. The solution consists of a mobile terminal for collecting data which is backed by IoT, and a cloud backed system is used for storage and data analytics parts (Shah et al., 2019).

Another noteworthy study conducted by Arbia et al. (2017) highlights the monitoring of emergency and disaster relief systems through an IoT-based cloud platform. The CROW^2 system, short for Critical and Rescue Operations using Wearable Wireless Sensor Networks, combines a diverse range of wireless devices, including smartphones and sensors, that utilize different communication technologies like Wi-Fi or Bluetooth. These devices work together to establish network connectivity for critical and rescue operations. This system enables seamless connectivity for emergency responders with operational networks or the internet, enhancing their effectiveness in critical situations (Shah et al., 2019).

Post-Disaster Communication Networks

In post-disaster situations, traditional communication infrastructures often become inaccessible due to physical damage or network congestion. Wireless communication technologies offer excellent solutions in such scenarios, as they are easily deployable and scalable. They provide crucial access to data and communication support for rescue and response operations through their robust network capabilities (Shah et al., 2019).

Ali et al. (2018) introduced a D2D (Device-to-Device) communication architecture in their previous study. The study focused on leveraging radio frequency signals through the user equipment relay at the base station. The primary goal of this approach is to prolong the lifespan of networks with limited energy resources (Shah et al., 2019).

Thomas and Raja (2019) conducted a previous study that introduced FINDER (Finding Isolated Nodes using D2D for Emergency Response), a framework aimed at locating and connecting disconnected mobile devices in disaster-stricken areas. The study employed multi-hop D2D communication to increase the chances of successful message delivery, while also extending the network's lifespan and improving energy efficiency for the devices involved (Shah et al., 2019).

A Mobile Ad-Hoc Network (MANET) refers to a temporary network comprising a collection of mobile nodes characterized by features such as infrastructure-less connectivity and dynamic topology. MANETs also play a crucial role in post-disaster communication scenarios (Shah et al., 2019).

Another study conducted by Mahiddin et al. (2017) reveals that, in post-disaster scenarios, an approach incorporates routing and gateway load balancing techniques for MANETs. This innovative approach aims to improve communication in affected regions by mitigating network congestion (Shah et al., 2019).

In post-disaster scenarios, Unmanned Aerial Vehicles (UAVs) serve as a valuable tool. They have the capability to swiftly deploy cellular base stations as secondary communication infrastructure (Shah et al., 2019).

Another research conducted by Peng et al. (2018) presents the utilization of UAVs as Aerial Base Stations (ABSs) in situations where the communication infrastructure has failed. The study showcases that deploying ABSs in strategic locations can significantly enhance the probability of effective communication (Shah et al., 2019).

Crowdsourcing

Crowdsourcing refers to the idea of using "people as sensors". It is a relatively new concept in disaster management that aims to generate more insight with the information that is in hand due to processing big datasets. It can either be active or passive. Active crowdsourcing refers to people participating in providing data, while passive crowdsourcing refers to obtaining the data from the social media whether it is in contributor's knowledge or not. With Government or Non-Governmental Organizations (NGOs)/ Civil Society Organizations (CSOs) platforms can be used to real-time information from disaster affected areas which contributes to emergency response and resource allocations, this is an example of active crowdsourcing. There are some other platforms that make it possible to active crowdsourcing for disaster affected areas, one of them is Ushahidi platform. Ushahidi platform has been in use when it comes to disasters since a long time, 2010 Haiti earthquake and 2011 Japan tsunami is included in such scenarios. With active crowdsourcing more credible data can be obtained in comparison to passive crowdsourcing. Yet, current research is leaning towards passive crowdsourcing when it comes to disaster management since a massive amount of data is generated with it through the use of social media such as tweets, descriptions, images, videos, audios, locations which are sources coming from people. Therefore analyzing that data can result in enhanced situational awareness along with rescue and response operations. Additionally, social media also acts as a bridge between people who are affected by disasters and concerned authorities, since it establishes communication between them. In that regard, social media has emerged as an important data source for disaster management due to increasing use of smartphones and geospatial data obtained from social media platforms being more in demand in comparison to traditional data sources (Shah et al., 2019).

Volunteered Geographical Information (VGI) is a concept that is frequently used in disaster management since citizen engagement during disaster response started to increase as well (Shah et al., 2019).

In a study conducted by Kusumo et al. (2017), the advantages of employing Volunteered Geographic Information (VGI) are highlighted. The research specifically focuses on the use of VGI in the context of evacuation during Jakarta floods. The findings reveal that 35.6% of the shelter locations preferred by residents align with the government evacuation shelters, as observed in the case study (Shah et al., 2019).

However, the reliability of passive crowdsourcing still remains challenging to evaluate. Especially, extracting meaningful information from such huge sets of data that is obtained from social media within limited timeframes poses an issue. To counter such issues, BDA becomes the key player (Shah et al., 2019).

Another study conducted by Toujani et al. (2018) shows that through the usage of Hadoop platform and ML techniques analyzation can be performed on vast amounts of social media data. By utilizing algorithms designed to classification and visualization, timely decision-making information is possible to do (Shah et al., 2019).

DISCUSSION

Wherever we are in the world, unfortunately, disasters are a harsh reality and a part of our lives. In the very recent past, on February 6, 2023, an earthquake in Kahramanmaraş, Turkey resulted in a tragic scene, causing 50,783 fatalities, 107,204 injuries, and $104 billion in material loss for Turkey. This event joined many other disasters in the history of humanity. As mentioned, disasters are an inevitable part of our lives, but being prepared for them and managing the aftermath is possible.

This book chapter aims to present a general study and research based on existing literature and case studies on questions such as: What are the key challenges and benefits of implementing IoT solutions in disaster management? How can IoT be used in early warning systems for natural disasters? How does big data analytics contribute to disaster management when combined with IoT?

The concept called IoT, which stands for the Internet of Things, refers to the ability of interconnected sensors within a specific network to communicate with each other and exchange data, enabling them to monitor their environment and conditions. The range of applications for IoT extends from home automation to healthcare, smart agriculture, and smart cities. Due to the interconnected nature of IoT devices, the services it provides have become complex. Therefore, IoT faces certain challenges in the field of disaster management. These challenges include the lack of a single applicable architectural structure for all applications, the need for heterogeneous architectures, the requirement for different applications and network technologies, low power consumption, low cost, and the presence of more private data compared to traditional networks, which raises security and privacy concerns. These points can provide ideas and guidance for future research and work in this or similar areas. Additionally, among the reasons for IoT being a revolutionary concept are its contributions to disaster management.

First of all, IoT can play a significant role in every phase of disaster management. However, the most prominent aspect of IoT lies in early warning systems. Regardless of the type of disaster we face, early warning systems are crucial, regardless of how much time in advance they provide warnings. IoT-based systems can monitor their environments by collecting data from various sources and perform real-time data processing. As a result, precise and timely warnings can be issued in response to disasters. Early warning systems also play important roles in monitoring and generating alarms through cloud computing and artificial intelligence. Early warning system architectures may include additional layers, but the basic principles of operation progress as follows: they collect data from their environment, process this data, apply various methods to a central server, and generate alarms using real-time and stored data. In this part of the thesis, existing studies and case studies in the literature have been examined to synthesize how early warning systems can be implemented for different natural disasters such as floods, earthquakes, tsunamis, and landslides, as well as the requirements and limitations encountered during the implementation of these systems, including the use of different sensors, protocols, and similar systems. In current IoT-based disaster management solutions, there are several main challenges, such as the high cost of IoT solutions, the lack of standardized data acquisition, uncertainty about how to effectively control vast amounts of data, and the presence of personal information within this data, leading to security and privacy issues. These points have the potential to provide insights and ideas for future research and development in these or similar fields.

The situation formed by the vast amount of data collected and generated by IoT devices and sensors has been framed. In this context, another concept that has emerged with IoT is Big Data Analytics (BDA). When BDA is combined with IoT, it has the potential to make significant contributions to disaster management. In this section of the thesis, existing studies in the literature and case studies are examined to explore how BDA can be used in combination with IoT for disaster management, the benefits it offers, the different technologies, methods, and requirements used in this context are synthesized. When BDA is used together with IoT for disaster management, some fundamental benefits that emerge include connectivity, data storage, real-time analytics, cost-effectiveness, and multiple data sources. One impressive method is the concept of crowdsourcing, which allows BDA to use people as sensors, resulting in more meaningful insights from the massive amounts of data being dealt with. It is also worth noting the benefits this brings to NGOs and CSOs. Furthermore, BDA applications, combined with IoT, have the capability to be a complementary actor in disaster management by enabling alerting, reporting, monitoring, and detecting disaster situations such as early warning systems or response and relief systems. Through a review of the literature, it has been observed that data processing techniques particularly contribute significantly to evacuation efforts. For example, data processing can direct people to the safest and least congested routes. The combination of BDA and IoT plays an important role in disaster monitoring by collecting data from different sources and having the ability to monitor. Another important point is that BDA and IoT can predict disasters in advance using machine learning techniques. Therefore, real-time predictions of disasters stand out as a significant area where BDA plays a role.

In general, it is undeniable that the more effective and efficient improvements made by IoT technologies in disaster management are of great importance, and IoT can be clearly used as an important tool for disaster management. In today's world and in the literature, it has been observed how IoT, especially in early warning systems, when used together with BDA, can provide inclusive benefits to the overall disaster management process. Although this book chapter provides answers to these issues, it is also evident that these topics are presented with challenges, aiming to provide inspiration for future studies in these or similar areas. In addition to the mentioned aspects, the following area may provide ideas and inspiration for potential future research: How can IoT-based disaster management systems be designed and implemented to ensure they are inclusive and accessible for all populations, including those with disabilities or language barriers? This question is also closely related to other IoT challenges highlighted throughout the book chapter. Universal design principles, which refer to interfaces accessible to disabled individuals and features available in multiple formats such as voice commands or gesture controls, can be considered. Additionally, alternative communication channels can be developed to overcome the barriers faced by individuals who may not have access to IoT devices or applications. Designing and implementing IoT systems that are accessible to the needs of all populations, including people with disabilities or language barriers, has the potential to contribute to the literature.

REFERENCES

Ali, K., Nguyen, H. X., Vien, Q., Shah, P., & Chu, Z. (2018). Disaster Management Using D2D Communication With Power Transfer and Clustering Techniques. *IEEE Access : Practical Innovations, Open Solutions, 6*, 14643–14654. doi:10.1109/ACCESS.2018.2793532

Alphonsa, A., & Ravi, G. (2016). *Earthquake early warning system by IOT using Wireless sensor networks*. IEEE. doi:10.1109/WiSPNET.2016.7566327

Arbia, D. B., Alam, M. A., Kadri, A., Hamida, E. B., & Attia, R. (2017). Enhanced IoT-Based End-To-End Emergency and Disaster Relief System. *Journal of Sensor and Actuator Networks, 6*(3), 19. doi:10.3390/jsan6030019

Asencio–Cortés, G., Morales–Esteban, A., Shang, X., & Martínez–Álvarez, F. (2017). Earthquake prediction in California using regression algorithms and cloud-based big data infrastructure. *Computers & Geosciences, 115*, 198–210. doi:10.1016/j.cageo.2017.10.011

Avvenuti, M., Cresci, S., Del Vigna, F., Fagni, T., & Tesconi, M. (2018). CrisMap: A Big Data Crisis Mapping System Based on Damage Detection and Geoparsing. *Information Systems Frontiers, 20*(5), 993–1011. doi:10.1007/s10796-018-9833-z

Bhosle, S. (2018). *Disaster Management System using IoT, 3*. 148-154.

Carter, W. N. (1991). *Disaster management: A disaster manager's handbook*. Bitstream. https://think-asia.org/bitstream/11540/5035/1/disaster-management-handbook.pdf

Chen, S., Xu, H., Liu, D., Hu, B., & Hucheng, W. (2014). A Vision of IoT: Applications, Challenges, and Opportunities With China Perspective. *IEEE Internet of Things Journal, 1*(4), 349–359. doi:10.1109/JIOT.2014.2337336

Coppola, D. P. (2015). Introduction to International Disaster Management. In Elsevier eBooks. Elsevier. doi:10.1016/C2014-0-00128-1

CRED. (2023). *2022 Disasters in numbers*. CRED. https://cred.be/sites/default/files/2022_EMDAT_report.pdf

Darmawan, S., Irawan, B., Setianingsih, C., & Murty, M. A. (2020). *Design of Detection Device for Sea Water Waves with Fuzzy Algorithm Based on Internet of Things*. IEEE. doi:10.1109/IAICT50021.2020.9172018

De Assis, L. F. F. G., Horita, F., De Freitas, E. P., Ueyama, J., & De Albuquerque, J. P. (2018). A Service-Oriented Middleware for Integrated Management of Crowdsourced and Sensor Data Streams in Disaster Management. *Sensors (Basel), 18*(6), 1689. doi:10.3390/s18061689 PMID:29794979

Disaster management cycle. (n.d.). ELRHA. https://higuide.elrha.org/humanitarian-parameters/disaster-management-cycle/

Esposito, M., Palma, L., Belli, A., Sabbatini, L., & Pierleoni, P. (2022). Recent Advances in Internet of Things Solutions for Early Warning Systems: A Review. *Sensors (Basel)*, *22*(6), 2124. doi:10.3390/s22062124 PMID:35336296

Fauvel, K., Balouek-Thomert, D., Melgar, D., Silva, P., Simonet, A., Antoniu, G., Costan, A., Masson, V., Parashar, M., Rodero, I., & Termier, A. (2020). A Distributed Multi-Sensor Machine Learning Approach to Earthquake Early Warning. *Proceedings of the AAAI Conference on Artificial Intelligence*, *34*(01), 403–411. doi:10.1609/aaai.v34i01.5376

Fruhlinger, J. (2022, August 7). *What is IoT? The internet of things explained*. Network World. https://www.networkworld.com/article/3207535/what-is-iot-the-internet-of-things-explained.html

Gamperl, M., Singer, J. N., & Thuro, K. (2021). Internet of Things Geosensor Network for Cost-Effective Landslide Early Warning Systems. *Sensors (Basel)*, *21*(8), 2609. doi:10.3390/s21082609 PMID:33917752

Gao, H., Luo, H., & Ding, S. X. (2014). Real-Time Implementation of Fault-Tolerant Control Systems With Performance Optimization. *IEEE Transactions on Industrial Electronics*, *61*(5), 2402–2411. doi:10.1109/TIE.2013.2273477

Gardner-Stephen, P., Wallace, A., Hawtin, K., Al-Nuaimi, G., Tran, A. T., Mozo, T. L., & Lloyd, M. D. (2019). *Reducing cost while increasing the resilience & effectiveness of tsunami early warning systems*. https://doi.org/ doi:10.1109/GHTC46095.2019.9033084

Ghasemi, P., & Karimian, N. (2020). *A Qualitative Study of Various Aspects of the Application of IoT in Disaster Management*. IEEE. doi:10.1109/ICWR49608.2020.9122323

Gold, J. (2017, October 30). *IoT standards, protocols and technologies explained*. Network World. https://www.networkworld.com/article/3235124/internet-of-things-definitions-a-handy-guide-to-essential-iot-terms.html

Hemalatha, T., Ramesh, M. V., & Rangan, V. P. (2020). Enhancing the reliability of landslide early warning systems by machine learning. *Landslides*, *17*(9), 2231–2246. doi:10.1007/s10346-020-01453-z

Ibarreche, J., Aquino, R., Edwards, R., Rangel, V., Pérez, I., Martinez, M. A., Castellanos, E., Álvarez, E., Jimenez, S., Rentería, R. G., Edwards, A. H., & Álvarez, O. (2020). Flash Flood Early Warning System in Colima, Mexico. *Sensors (Basel)*, *20*(18), 5231. doi:10.3390/s20185231 PMID:32937798

Inoue, M., Tanioka, Y., & Yamanaka, Y. (2019). Method for Near-Real Time Estimation of Tsunami Sources Using Ocean Bottom Pressure Sensor Network (S-Net). *Geosciences*, *9*(7), 310. doi:10.3390/geosciences9070310

Jayashree, S., Sarika, S., L, S. A., & Prathibha, S. (2017). *A novel approach for early flood warning using android and IoT*. IEEE. doi:10.1109/ICCCT2.2017.7972302

Jo. (2022, December 3). *The Disaster Management Cycle: 5 Key Stages UCF Online*. UCF Online. https://www.ucf.edu/online/leadership-management/news/the-disaster-management-cycle/

Klapez, M., Grazia, C. A., Zennaro, S., Cozzani, M., & Casoni, M. (2018). *First Experiences with Earthcloud, a Low-Cost*. Cloud-Based IoT Seismic Alert System. doi:10.1109/WiMOB.2018.8589155

Kusumo, A., Reckien, D., & Verplanke, J. (2017). Utilising volunteered geographic information to assess resident's flood evacuation shelters. Case study: Jakarta. *Applied Geography (Sevenoaks, England), 88,* 174–185. doi:10.1016/j.apgeog.2017.07.002

Lee, I., & Lee, K. (2015). The Internet of Things (IoT): Applications, investments, and challenges for enterprises. *Business Horizons, 58*(4), 431–440. doi:10.1016/j.bushor.2015.03.008

Lembke, J. (2021, December 7). *The Role of IoT in Disaster Management & Emergency Planning - Tele2 IoT*. Tele2 IoT. https://tele2iot.com/article/the-role-of-iot-in-disaster-management-emergency-planning/

Li, Z., Fang, L., Sun, X., & Peng, W. (2021). 5G IoT-based geohazard monitoring and early warning system and its application. *Eurasip Journal on Wireless Communications and Networking, 2021*(1). doi:10.1186/s13638-021-02033-y

Liu, X., Li, X., Chen, X., Liu, Z., & Li, S. (2018). Location correction technique based on mobile communication base station for earthquake population heat map. *Geodesy and Geodynamics, 9*(5), 388–397. doi:10.1016/j.geog.2018.01.003

Mahiddin, N. A., Sarkar, N. I., & Cusack, B. (2017). An Internet Access Solution: MANET Routing and a Gateway Selection Approach for Disaster Scenarios. *The Review of Socionetwork Strategies, 11*(1), 47–64. doi:10.1007/s12626-017-0004-3

Oden, R. V., Militello, L. G., Ross, K. G., & Lopez, C. E. (2012). Four Key Challenges in Disaster Response. *Proceedings of the Human Factors and Ergonomics Society . . . Annual Meeting, 56*(1), 488–492. 10.1177/1071181312561050

Patel, K. K., Patel, S. M., & Scholar, P. (2016). Internet of things-IOT: definition, characteristics, architecture, enabling technologies, application & future challenges. *International journal of engineering science and computing, 6*(5).

Peng, G., Xia, Y., Zhang, X., & Bai, L. (2018). UAV-Aided Networks for Emergency Communications in Areas with Unevenly Distributed Users. *Journal of Communications and Information Networks, 3*(4), 23–32. doi:10.1007/s41650-018-0034-1

Pratt, M. K. (2022). Top 12 most commonly used IoT protocols and standards. *IoT Agenda.* https://www.techtarget.com/iotagenda/tip/Top-12-most-commonly-used-IoT-protocols-and-standards

Ray, P. P., Mukherjee, M., & Shu, L. (2017). Internet of Things for Disaster Management: State-of-the-Art and Prospects. *IEEE Access : Practical Innovations, Open Solutions, 5,* 18818–18835. doi:10.1109/ACCESS.2017.2752174

Saha, H. N., Auddy, S., Pal, S., Kumar, S., Pandey, S., Singh, R., Singh, A. K., Banerjee, S., Ghosh, D., & Saha, S. (2017). Disaster management using Internet of Things. *2017 8th Annual Industrial Automation and Electromechanical Engineering Conference (IEMECON).* IEEE. 10.1109/IEMECON.2017.8079566

Shah, S. A., Seker, D. Z., Hameed, S., & Draheim, D. (2019). The Rising Role of Big Data Analytics and IoT in Disaster Management: Recent Advances, Taxonomy and Prospects. *IEEE Access : Practical Innovations, Open Solutions, 7,* 54595–54614. doi:10.1109/ACCESS.2019.2913340

Sharma, K., Anand, D., Sabharwal, M., Tiwari, P. K., Cheikhrouhou, O., & Frikha, T. (2021). A Disaster Management Framework Using Internet of Things-Based Interconnected Devices. *Mathematical Problems in Engineering, 2021*, 1–21. doi:10.1155/2021/9916440

Sinha, A., Kumar, P., Rana, N. P., Islam, R., & Dwivedi, Y. K. (2019). Impact of internet of things (IoT) in disaster management: A task-technology fit perspective. *Annals of Operations Research, 283*(1–2), 759–794. doi:10.1007/s10479-017-2658-1

Tariq, H., Touati, F., Al-Hitmi, M., Crescini, D., & Mnaouer, A. B. (2019). A Real-Time Early Warning Seismic Event Detection Algorithm Using Smart Geo-Spatial Bi-Axial Inclinometer Nodes for Industry 4.0 Applications. *Applied Sciences (Basel, Switzerland), 9*(18), 3650. doi:10.3390/app9183650

Thekkil, T. M., & Prabakaran, N. (2017). *Real-time WSN based early flood detection and control monitoring system*. IEEE. doi:10.1109/ICICICT1.2017.8342828

Thomas, A. A., & Raja, G. (2019). FINDER: A D2D based critical communications framework for disaster management in 5G. *Peer-to-Peer Networking and Applications, 12*(4), 912–923. doi:10.1007/s12083-018-0689-2

Toujani, R., Chaabani, Y., Dhouioui, Z., & Bouali, H. (2018). The Next Generation of Disaster Management and Relief Planning: Immersive Analytics Based Approach. In Communications in computer and information science (pp. 80–93). Springer Science+Business Media. doi:10.1007/978-3-319-93596-6_6

Wang, Z., Vo, H. N. P., Salehi, M., Rusu, L. C., Reeves, C. E., & Phan, A. (2017). *A large-scale spatiotemporal data analytics system for wildfire risk management*. ACM. doi:10.1145/3080546.3080549

Wellington, J. J., & Ramesh, P. (2017). Role of Internet of Things in disaster management. *International Conference on Innovations in Information, Embedded and Communication Systems*. IEEE. 10.1109/ICIIECS.2017.8275928

Xu, X., Zhang, L., Sotiriadis, S., Asimakopoulou, E., Li, M., & Bessis, N. (2018). CLOTHO: A Large-Scale Internet of Things-Based Crowd Evacuation Planning System for Disaster Management. *IEEE Internet of Things Journal, 5*(5), 3559–3568. doi:10.1109/JIOT.2018.2818885

Compilation of References

Ngwa, W., Addai, B. W., Adewole, I., Ainsworth, V., Alaro, J., Alatise, O. I., Ali, Z., Anderson, B. O., Anorlu, R., Avery, S., Barango, P., Bih, N., Booth, C. M., Brawley, O. W., Dangou, J.-M., Denny, L., Dent, J., Elmore, S. N. C., Elzawawy, A., & Kerr, D. (2022). Cancer in sub-Saharan Africa: A lancet oncology Commission. *The Lancet. Oncology*, *23*(6), e251–e312. doi:10.1016/S1470-2045(21)00720-8 PMID:35550267

Adamopoulou, E., & Moussiades, L. (2020). An Overview of Chatbot Technology. In IFIP Advances in Information and Communication Technology (Vol. 584 IFIP). Springer International Publishing. doi:10.1007/978-3-030-49186-4_31

Adams, V., Burger, S., Crawford, K., & Setter, R. (2018). Can you escape? Creating an escape room to facilitate active learning. *Journal for Nurses in Professional Development*, *34*(2), E1–E5. doi:10.1097/NND.0000000000000433 PMID:29481471

Adelaar, T., Chang, S., Lancendorfer, K. M., Lee, B., & Morimoto, M. (2003). Effects of media formats on emotions and impulse buying intent. *Journal of Information Technology*, *18*(4), 247–266. doi:10.1080/0268396032000150799

Adi, K., Widodo, C. E., Widodo, A. P., & Margiati, U. (2022). Detection of foreign object debris (Fod) using convolutional neural network (CNN). *Journal of Theoretical and Applied Information Technology*, *100*(1), 184–191.

Adner, R., & Helfat, C. E. (2003). Corporate effects and dynamic managerial capabilities. *Strategic Management Journal*, *24*(10), 1011–1025. doi:10.1002/smj.331

Agarwal, P., Gupta, H., & Goyal, S. (2020). Impact of supply chain agility on FMCG sector: A comprehensive literature review. *Journal of Advances in Management Research*, *17*(1), 19–34.

Aggarwal, S. K., Deep, V., & Singh, R. (2014). Speculation of CMMI in agile methodology. In *Proc of International Conference on Advances in Computing, Communications and Informatics*. IEEE.

Aghajani, G., & Ghadimi, N. (2018). Multi-objective energy management in a micro-grid. *Energy Reports*, *4*, 218–225. doi:10.1016/j.egyr.2017.10.002

Ahlawat, S., Choudhary, A., Nayyar, A., Singh, S., & Yoon, B. (2020). Improved handwritten digit recognition using convolutional neural networks (CNN). *Sensors (Basel)*, *20*(12), 3344. doi:10.3390/s20123344 PMID:32545702

Ahmed, K. D., & Zeebaree, S. R. M. (2021). Resource Allocation in Fog Computing : A Review. *International Journal of Science and Business*, *5*(2).

Ai, C. (n.d.). *The New wave of customer and employee experiences*. Deloitte Digital.

Ajaram, K. (2023). Future of learning: Teaching and learning strategies. In *Learning Intelligence* (pp. 3–53). Innovative and Digital Transformative Learning Strategies., doi:10.1007/978-981-19-9201-8_1

Ajtai, M. (2005, May). Representing hard lattices with O (n log n) bits. In *Proceedings of the thirty-seventh annual ACM symposium on Theory of computing* (pp. 94-103). ACM. 10.1145/1060590.1060604

Alam, T. (2022). Blockchain cities: The futuristic cities driven by Blockchain, big data and internet of things. *GeoJournal*, *87*(6), 5383–5412. doi:10.1007/s10708-021-10508-0

Alavi, M. (2000). Knowledge management systems: Issues, challenges, and benefits. *Communications of the AIS*, *4*(6), 1–37.

Alavi, M., & Leidner, D. E. (2001). Review: Knowledge management and knowledge management systems: Conceptual foundations and research issues. *Management Information Systems Quarterly*, *25*(1), 107–136. doi:10.2307/3250961

AlDairi, A., & Tawalbeh, L. (2017). Cyber security attacks on smart cities and associated mobile technologies. *Procedia Computer Science*, *109*, 1086–1091. doi:10.1016/j.procs.2017.05.391

Al-dhief, F. T., Member, S., Mu, N., & Abdul, A. (2020). *A Survey of Voice Pathology Surveillance Systems Based on Internet of Things and Machine Learning Algorithms* (Vol. XX). doi:10.1109/ACCESS.2020.2984925

Al-Hawawreh, M., & Hossain, M. S. (2023). A privacy-aware framework for detecting cyber attacks on internet of medical things systems using data fusion and quantum deep learning. *Information Fusion*, *99*, 101889. doi:10.1016/j.inffus.2023.101889

Alibasic, A., Al Junaibi, R., Aung, Z., Woon, W. L., & Omar, M. A. (2017). Cybersecurity for smart cities: A brief review. In *Data Analytics for Renewable Energy Integration: 4th ECML PKDD Workshop, DARE 2016, Riva del Garda, Italy, September 23, 2016, Revised Selected Papers 4* (pp. 22-30). Springer International Publishing. 10.1007/978-3-319-50947-1_3

Ali, K. (2017). Study of Software Development Life Cycle Process Models. *International Journal of Advanced Research in Computer Science*, *8*(1).

Ali, K., Nguyen, H. X., Vien, Q., Shah, P., & Chu, Z. (2018). Disaster Management Using D2D Communication With Power Transfer and Clustering Techniques. *IEEE Access : Practical Innovations, Open Solutions*, *6*, 14643–14654. doi:10.1109/ACCESS.2018.2793532

Al-Jabri, I. M., & Roztocki, N. (2015). The impact of artificial intelligence on knowledge management systems: A literature review. *Journal of Enterprise Information Management*, *28*(5), 662–676.

Alkhadra, R., Abuzaid, J., AlShammari, M., & Mohammad, N. (2021). Solar winds hack: In-depth analysis and countermeasures. *2021 12th International Conference on Computing Communication and Networking Technologies (ICCCNT)*.

Alphonsa, A., & Ravi, G. (2016). *Earthquake early warning system by IOT using Wireless sensor networks*. IEEE. doi:10.1109/WiSPNET.2016.7566327

Al-Rashdi, A. (2022). *Adoption Model for Digital Technologies: Case Study of Petroleum Development Oman* [Doctoral dissertation, University of Liverpool].

Alrwais, S., Yuan, K., Alowaisheq, E., Liao, X., Oprea, A., Wang, X., & Li, Z. (2016). Catching predators at watering holes: finding and understanding strategically compromised websites. *Proceedings of the 32nd Annual Conference on Computer Security Applications*. ACM. 10.1145/2991079.2991112

Al-Saidi, M., & Zaidan, E. (2020). Gulf futuristic cities beyond the headlines: Understanding the planned cities megatrend. *Energy Reports*, *6*, 114–121. doi:10.1016/j.egyr.2020.10.061

Alsamiri, J., & Alsubhi, K. (2019). Internet of Things Cyber Attacks Detection using. *Machine Learning*, *10*(12).

Altun, M., Gürüler, H., Özkaraca, O., Khan, F., Khan, J., & Lee, Y. (2023). Monkeypox detection using CNN with transfer learning. *Sensors (Basel)*, *23*(4), 1783. doi:10.3390/s23041783 PMID:36850381

Al-Turjman, F., Zahmatkesh, H., & Shahroze, R. (2022). An overview of security and privacy in smart cities' IoT communications. *Transactions on Emerging Telecommunications Technologies*, *33*(3), e3677. doi:10.1002/ett.3677

Amin, J. M., and Husin, M. A. National Vocational Qualification and Certification System of Malaysia. *Quality TVET in Asia Pacific Region: National Vocational Qualification Systems of CPSC Member Countries*, 99.

Amin, R., Sherratt, R. S., Giri, D., Islam, S. H., & Khan, M. K. (2017). A software agent enabled biometric security algorithm for secure file access in consumer storage devices. *IEEE Transactions on Consumer Electronics*, *63*(1), 53–61. doi:10.1109/TCE.2017.014735

Amirova, A. (2021). *Management of transformation processes towards an innovative civil service of Kazakhstan (case-study of remuneration by results project)*. APA. https://repository.apa.kz/handle/123456789/810

Analytics, C. (2020). *Key Factors Driving the Growth of Conversational AI in Retail*. Uniphore. https://www.uniphore.com/key-factors-driving-the-growth-of-conversational-ai-in-retail/

Anand, D., & Khemchandani, V. (2020). Data Security and Privacy Functions in Fog Computing for Healthcare 4.0. In Studies in Big Data (Vol. 76). Springer. doi:10.1007/978-981-15-6044-6_16

Anderson, G. (2022). Moving from Aspiration to Action on Climate Adaptation. *Inclusive Growth In The Middle East And North Africa*, 119.

Andreoni, A. (2018). *Skilling Tanzania: improving financing, governance and outputs of the skills development sector*. SOAS. https://eprints.soas.ac.uk/30117/1/Andreoni%20Skilling-Tanzania-ACE-Working-Paper-6.pdf

Anjum, R., Azam, F., Anwar, M. W., & Amjad, A. (2019) A meta-model to automatically generate evolutionary prototypes from software requirements. *ACM International Conference Proceeding Series*. ACM. 10.1145/3348445.3351304

Anwar, R. W., & Ali, S. (2022). Smart Cities Security Threat Landscape: A Review. *Computer Information*, *41*(2), 405–423.

Aphirakmethawong, J., Yang, E., & Mehnen, J. (2022). An Overview of Artificial Intelligence in Product Design for Smart Manufacturing. *2022 27th International Conference on Automation and Computing: Smart Systems and Manufacturing, ICAC 2022, 1018*, (pp. 1–6). IEEE. 10.1109/ICAC55051.2022.9911089

Arabo, A. (2015). Cyber security challenges within the connected home ecosystem futures. *Procedia Computer Science*, *61*, 227–232. doi:10.1016/j.procs.2015.09.201

Arbia, D. B., Alam, M. A., Kadri, A., Hamida, E. B., & Attia, R. (2017). Enhanced IoT-Based End-To-End Emergency and Disaster Relief System. *Journal of Sensor and Actuator Networks*, *6*(3), 19. doi:10.3390/jsan6030019

Arenas, G. (ed)., and Coulibaly, S. (ed). (2022). A new dawn for global value chain participation in the Philippines (G. Arenas and S. Coulibaly, Eds.). doi:10.1596/978-1-4648-1848-6

Arıker, Ç. (2022). Massive open online course (MOOC) platforms as rising social entrepreneurs: Creating social value through reskilling and upskilling the unemployed for after COVID-19 conditions. In Research Anthology on Business Continuity and Navigating Times of Crisis (pp. 607-629). IGI Global.

Arinez, J. F., Chang, Q., Gao, R. X., Xu, C., & Zhang, J. (2020). Artificial Intelligence in Advanced Manufacturing: Current Status and Future Outlook. *Journal of Manufacturing Science and Engineering*, *142*(11), 1–16. doi:10.1115/1.4047855

Arora, R., Parashar, A., & Transforming, C. C. I. (2013). Secure user data in cloud computing using encryption algorithms. *International Journal of Engineering Research and Applications*, *3*(4), 1922-1926.

Arraoui, R., El-Bakkari, K., Limame, K., Ed-Dahmouny, A., Jaouane, M., Fakkahi, A., Azmi, H., & Sali, A. (2023). Pressure and temperature influences on the nonlinear optical rectification of an impurity in a symmetrical double quantum dot. *The European Physical Journal Plus, 138*(3), 292. doi:10.1140/epjp/s13360-023-03892-8

Asencio–Cortés, G., Morales–Esteban, A., Shang, X., & Martínez–Álvarez, F. (2017). Earthquake prediction in California using regression algorithms and cloud-based big data infrastructure. *Computers & Geosciences, 115*, 198–210. doi:10.1016/j.cageo.2017.10.011

Aski, V. J., Dhaka, V. S., Kumar, S., & Parashar, A. (2022). IoT Enabled Elderly Monitoring System and the Role of Privacy Preservation Frameworks in e-health Applications. In *Intelligent Data Communication Technologies and Internet of Things*. Springer.

Atitallah, S. B., Driss, M., Boulila, W., & Ghézala, H. B. (2020). Leveraging Deep Learning and IoT big data analytics to support the smart cities development: Review and future directions. *Computer Science Review, 38*, 100303. doi:10.1016/j.cosrev.2020.100303

Atkinson, J. T. (2022). *Using remote sensing and geographical information systems to classify local landforms using a pattern recognition approach for improved soil mapping*. SUN. https://scholar.sun.ac.za/bitstream/handle/10019.1/124888/atkinson_remote_2022.pdf?sequence=1

Auktor, G. V. (2022). *The opportunities and challenges of Industry 4.0 for industrial development: A case study of Morocco's automotive and garment sectors* (No. 2/2022). Discussion Paper.

Avis, E. (2015). The Rise of Digital Challengers. *Independent Banker, 65*(11), 28–30. http://search.ebscohost.com/login.aspx?direct=true%7B&%7Ddb=bth%7B&%7DAN=111109565%7B&%7Dsite=ehost-live

Avvenuti, M., Cresci, S., Del Vigna, F., Fagni, T., & Tesconi, M. (2018). CrisMap: A Big Data Crisis Mapping System Based on Damage Detection and Geoparsing. *Information Systems Frontiers, 20*(5), 993–1011. doi:10.1007/s10796-018-9833-z

Bachtler, J., Mendez, C., & Wishlade, F. (2019). *Reforming the MFF and Cohesion Policy 2021-27: pragmatic drift or paradigmatic shift?* Strath. https://strathprints.strath.ac.uk/69563/1/Bachtler_etal_EPRC_2019_Reforming_the_MFF_and_cohesion_policy_2021_27_pragmatic_drift_or_paradigmatic_shift.pdf

Badidi, E., Mahrez, Z., & Sabir, E. (2020). Fog computing for smart cities' big data management and analytics: A review. In Future Internet, 12(11). doi:10.3390/fi12110190

Badran, A. (2023). Developing smart cities: Regulatory and policy implications for the State of Qatar. *International Journal of Public Administration, 46*(7), 519–532. doi:10.1080/01900692.2021.2003811

Bagaa, M., Taleb, T., & Bernabe, J. B. (2020). *for IoT Systems*. IEEE. doi:10.1109/ACCESS.2020.2996214

Baker, C. M., Crabtree, G., & Anderson, K. (2020). Student pharmacist perceptions of learning after strengths-based leadership skills lab and escape room in pharmacy practice skills laboratory. *Currents in Pharmacy Teaching & Learning, 12*(6), 724–727. doi:10.1016/j.cptl.2020.01.021 PMID:32482276

Banafa, A. (2020). IoT Standardization and Implementation Challenges. *IEEE Internet of Things*. IEEE. https://iot.ieee.org/newsletter/july-2016/iot-standardization-and-imple mentation-challenges.html.

Barik, R. K., Dubey, H., Misra, C., Borthakur, D., Constant, N., Sasane, S. A., Lenka, R. K., Mishra, B. S. P., Das, H., & Mankodiya, K. (2018). Fog Assisted Cloud Computing in Era of Big Data and Internet-of-Things: Systems, Architectures, and Applications. In Studies in Big Data (Vol. 39). Springer. doi:10.1007/978-3-319-73676-1_14

Barik, R., Dubey, H., Sasane, S., Misra, C., Constant, N., & Mankodiya, K. (2017). Fog2Fog: Augmenting Scalability in Fog Computing for Health GIS Systems. *Proceedings - 2017 IEEE 2nd International Conference on Connected Health: Applications, Systems and Engineering Technologies, CHASE 2017*. IEEE. 10.1109/CHASE.2017.83

Barik, R. K., Dubey, H., Mankodiya, K., Sasane, S. A., & Misra, C. (2019). GeoFog4Health: A fog-based SDI framework for geospatial health big data analysis. *Journal of Ambient Intelligence and Humanized Computing*, 10(2), 551–567. doi:10.1007/s12652-018-0702-x

Barik, R. K., Dubey, H., Samaddar, A. B., Gupta, R. D., & Ray, P. K. (2017). FogGIS: Fog Computing for geospatial big data analytics. *2016 IEEE Uttar Pradesh Section International Conference on Electrical, Computer and Electronics Engineering, UPCON 2016*. IEEE. 10.1109/UPCON.2016.7894725

Barreca, H. (2022). *Public Policy and the Business Life Cycle* [Doctoral dissertation, City University of New York]. https://search.proquest.com/openview/b62a8c65942e6d6d04db0dd40d3321e6/1?pq-origsite=gscholarandcbl=18750anddiss=y

Barth, S., Ionita, D., & Hartel, P. (2022). Understanding online privacy—A systematic review of privacy visualizations and privacy by design guidelines. *ACM Computing Surveys*, 55(3), 1–37. doi:10.1145/3502288

Basset, F. B., Valeri, M., Neuwirth, J., Polino, E., Rota, M. B., Poderini, D., & Trotta, R. (2023). Daylight entanglement-based quantum key distribution with a quantum dot source. *Quantum Science and Technology*, 8(2), 025002. doi:10.1088/2058-9565/acae3d

Bates, S. (2016). Revenge Porn and Mental Health. *Feminist Criminology*, 12(1), 22–42. doi:10.1177/1557085116654565

Bauspieß, P., Kolberg, J., Drozdowski, P., Rathgeb, C., & Busch, C. (2022). Privacy-Preserving Preselection for Protected Biometric Identification Using Public-Key Encryption with Keyword Search. *IEEE Transactions on Industrial Informatics*.

Beaudouin-Lafon, M., & Mackay, W. (2003). *Prototyping tools and techniques*. Human Computer Interaction-Development Process.

Bebortta, S., Das, S. K., Kandpal, M., Barik, R. K., & Dubey, H. (2020). Geospatial serverless computing: Architectures, tools and future directions. In ISPRS International Journal of Geo-Information, 9(5). doi:10.3390/ijgi9050311

Becerra-Fernandez, I., & Sabherwal, R. (2014). *Knowledge management: Systems and processes*. Routledge.

Beguin, E., Besnard, S., Cros, A., Joannes, B., Leclerc-Istria, O., Noel, A., Roels, N., Taleb, F., Thongphan, J., Alata, E., & Nicomette, V. (2019). Computer-security-oriented escape room. *IEEE Security and Privacy*, 17(4), 78–83. doi:10.1109/MSEC.2019.2912700

Behrendt, A., De Boer, E., Kasah, T., Koerber, B., Mohr, N., & Richter, G. (2021). *Leveraging Industrial IoT and advanced technologies for digital transformation*. McKinsey Co.

Belay, A. J., Salau, A. O., Ashagrie, M., & Haile, M. B. (2022). Development of a chickpea disease detection and classification model using deep learning. *Informatics in Medicine Unlocked*, 31, 100970. doi:10.1016/j.imu.2022.100970

Bellantuono, N., Nuzzi, A., Pontrandolfo, P., & Scozzi, B. (2021). Digital transformation models for the I4. 0 transition: Lessons from the change management literature. *Sustainability (Basel)*, 13(23), 12941. doi:10.3390/su132312941

Berendsen, R. G., & US Army School of Advanced Military Studies Fort Leavenworth United States. (2019). *The Weaponization of Quantum Mechanics: Quantum Technology in Future Warfare*.

Berger, V., & Chowdhury, S. (2021). *How to overcome the challenges of Internet of Things to ensure successful technology integration: A case study at an Aerospace manufacturer*. Diva. https://www.diva-portal.org/smash/record.jsf?pid=diva2:1567136

Bertello, A., Bogers, M. L., & De Bernardi, P. (2022). Open innovation in the face of the COVID-19 grand challenge: Insights from the Pan-European hackathon 'EUvsVirus'. *R & D Management*, *52*(2), 178–192. doi:10.1111/radm.12456

Bhandari, B. (2021). The 3-E Challenge: Education, Employability, and Employment (No. 122). National Council of Applied Economic Research.

Bhardwaj, S., & Panda, S. N. (2022). Performance evaluation using RYU SDN controller in software-defined networking environment. *Wireless Personal Communications*, *122*(1), 701–723. doi:10.1007/s11277-021-08920-3

Bhattacharya, S., & Mandal, S. (2020). Artificial Intelligence and Knowledge Management: A Case Study of Indian Educational Institutions. In *Proceedings of International Conference on Education and Management Innovation* (pp. 192-199). IEEE.

Bhosle, S. (2018). *Disaster Management System using IoT, 3*. 148-154.

Bhusan Dash, B., Shekhar Patra, S., Nanda, S., Rani Jena, J., Rout, S., & Kumar Barik, R. (2023). *SFA4SDI: A Secure Fog Architecture for Spatial Data Infrastructure*. IEEE. doi:10.1109/iSSSC56467.2022.10051572

Bilbao-Osorio, B., Burkhardt, K., Correia, A., Deiss, R., Lally, D., Martino, R., & Senczyszyn, D. (2018). *Science, Research and Innovation Performance of the EU 2018 Strengthening the Foundations for Europe's Future European Commission Directorate-General for Research and Innovation Directorate A—Policy Development and Coordination*. Riesal.

Blackall, P., Alawneh, J., Barnes, T., Meers, J., Palaniappan, G., Palmieri, C., & Turni, C. (2021). *Project Improving the production and competitiveness of Australian and Philippines pig production through better health and disease control*.

Bloomberg, J. (2018). Digitization, digitalization, and digital transformation: confuse them at your peril. *Forbes*.

Boém, M. M., Laquidara, G., & Colombani, M. (2013). *Executive Strategic Criteria—P*t.

Bolognese, A. F. (2002). *Employee resistance to organizational change*. Research Gate.

Bolton-King, R. S., Nichols-Drew, L. J., & Turner, I. J. (2022). RemoteForensicCSI: Enriching teaching, training and learning through networking and timely CPD. *Science & Justice*, *62*(6), 768–777. doi:10.1016/j.scijus.2022.01.004 PMID:36400498

Boneh, D., Lewi, K., Raykova, M., Sahai, A., Zhandry, M., & Zimmerman, J. (2015). Semantically secure order-revealing encryption: Multi-input functional encryption without obfuscation. *Annual International Conference on the Theory and Applications of Cryptographic Techniques*. Springer. 10.1007/978-3-662-46803-6_19

Bonomi, F., Milito, R., Zhu, J., & Addepalli, S. (2012). Fog computing and its role in the internet of things. *MCC'12 - Proceedings of the 1st ACM Mobile Cloud Computing Workshop*. ACM. 10.1145/2342509.2342513

Borrego, C., Fernández, C., Blanes, I., & Robles, S. (2017). Room escape at class: Escape games activities to facilitate the motivation and learning in computer science. *JOTSE*, *7*(2), 162–171. doi:10.3926/jotse.247

Botturi, L., & Babazadeh, M. (2020). Designing educational escape rooms: Validating the star model. *International Journal of Serious Games*, *7*(3), 41–57. doi:10.17083/ijsg.v7i3.367

Bouthillier, F., & Shearer, K. (2002). Understanding knowledge management and its relationship to artificial intelligence. *Journal of Knowledge Management*, *6*(3), 244–254.

Brandtzaeg, P. B., & Følstad, A. (2017). Why people use chatbots. Lecture Notes in Computer Science (Including Subseries Lecture Notes in Artificial Intelligence and Lecture Notes in Bioinformatics). Springer. doi:10.1007/978-3-319-70284-1_30

Briggs, A. M., Houlding, E., Hinman, R. S., Desmond, L. A., Bennell, K. L., Darlow, B., Pizzari, T., Leech, M., MacKay, C., Larmer, P. J., Bendrups, A., Greig, A. M., Francis-Cracknell, A., Jordan, J. E., & Slater, H. (2019). Health professionals and students encounter multi-level barriers to implementing high-value osteoarthritis care: A multi-national study. *Osteoarthritis and Cartilage*, 27(5), 788–804. doi:10.1016/j.joca.2018.12.024 PMID:30668988

Brinson, A., Robinson, A., & Rogers, M. (2006). A cyber forensics ontology: Creating a new approach to studying cyber forensics. *digital investigation, 3*, 37-43.

Brown, E. (2017). *Exploring the design of technology enabled learning experiences in teacher education that translate into classroom practice*. UCAL. https://prism.ucalgary.ca/handle/11023/4025

Brownie, S. M., Gatimu, S. M., Kambo, I., Mwizerwa, J., & Ndirangu, E. (2020). Stakeholders' expectations of nursing graduates following completion of a work-study upskilling programme. *Africa Journal of Nursing and Midwifery, 22*(2). doi:10.25159/2520-5293/5940

Brynjolfsson, E., & Collis, A. (2019). How should we measure the digital economy. *Harvard Business Review, 97*, 140–148.

Bucea-Manea-Țoniș, R., Kuleto, V., Gudei, S. C. D., Lianu, C., Lianu, C., Ilić, M. P., & Păun, D. (2022). Artificial intelligence potential in higher education institutions enhanced learning environment in Romania and Serbia. *Sustainability (Basel), 14*(10), 5842. doi:10.3390/su14105842

Buchmeister, B., Palcic, I., & Ojstersek, R. (2019). Artificial Intelligence in Manufacturing Companies and Broader: An Overview. İçinde *DAAAM INTERNATIONAL SCIENTIFIC BOOK* (Sayı 7). doi:10.2507/daaam.scibook.2019.07

Butt, T. A., & Afzaal, M. (2019). Security and privacy in smart cities: issues and current solutions. In *Smart Technologies and Innovation for a Sustainable Future: Proceedings of the 1st American University in the Emirates International Research Conference—Dubai, UAE* 2017 (pp. 317-323). Springer International Publishing. 10.1007/978-3-030-01659-3_37

Cain, J. (2019). Exploratory implementation of a blended format escape room in a large enrollment pharmacy management class. *Currents in Pharmacy Teaching & Learning, 11*(1), 44–50. doi:10.1016/j.cptl.2018.09.010 PMID:30527875

Camburn, B., Viswanathan, V., Linsey, J., Anderson, D., Jensen, D., Crawford, R., Otto, K., & Wood, K. (2017). Design prototyping methods: State of the art in strategies, techniques, and guidelines. *Design Science, 3*(Schrage 1993), 1–33. doi:10.1017/dsj.2017.10

Campisi, T., Severino, A., Al-Rashid, M. A., & Pau, G. (2021). The development of the smart cities in the connected and autonomous vehicles (CAVs) era: From mobility patterns to scaling in cities. *Infrastructures, 6*(7), 100. doi:10.3390/infrastructures6070100

Canedo, E. D., Dos Santos Pergentino, A. C., Calazans, A. T. S., Almeida, F. V., Costa, P. H. T., & Lima, F. (2020). Design thinking use in agile software projects: Software developers' perception. *ICEIS 2020 – Proc. of the 22nd International Conference on Enterprise Information Systems*. Research Gate.

Caridi, M., Moretto, A., Perego, A., & Tumino, A. (2014). The benefits of supply chain visibility: A value assessment model. *International Journal of Production Economics, 151*, 1–19. doi:10.1016/j.ijpe.2013.12.025

Carlin, A., Hammoudeh, M., & Aldabbas, O. (2015). Intrusion detection and countermeasure of virtual cloud systems-state of the art and current challenges. *International Journal of Advanced Computer Science and Applications, 6*(6). doi:10.14569/IJACSA.2015.060601

Carrigan, M. (2020). *2019 Small Business Failure Rate: Startup Statistics by Industry*. National Biz. https://www.national.biz/2019-small-business-failure-rate-startup-statistics-industry/

Carter, W. N. (1991). *Disaster management: A disaster manager's handbook.* Bitstream. https://think-asia.org/bitstream/11540/5035/1/disaster-management-handbook.pdf

Casalánguida, H., & Durán, J. E. (2012). Automatic generation of feature models from UML requirement models. *ACM International Conference Proceeding Series,* (vol. 2, pp. 10-17). ACM. 10.1145/2364412.2364415

Casini, M. (2021). *Construction 4.0: Advanced Technology, Tools and Materials for the Digital Transformation of the Construction Industry.* Woodhead Publishing.

Cavallo, J. J., & Forman, H. P. (2020). The economic impact of the COVID-19 pandemic on radiology practices. *Radiology, 296*(3), 201495. doi:10.1148/radiol.2020201495 PMID:32293225

Cavoukian, A. (2009). Privacy by design: The 7 foundational principles. Information and privacy commissioner of Ontario, Canada, 5, 12.

Ceker, E., & Ozdamh, F. (2017). What "gamification" is and what it's not. *European Journal of Contemporary Education, 6*(2), 221–228.

Cekerevac, Z., Dvorak, Z., Prigoda, L., & Cekerevac, P. (2017). Internet of things and the man-in-the-middle attacks–security and economic risks. *MEST Journal, 5*(2), 15–25. doi:10.12709/mest.05.05.02.03

Cepal, N. (2022). *The Caribbean Outlook. Summary.* Cepal. https://repositorio.cepal.org/bitstream/handle/11362/48220/S2200950_en.pdf?sequence=1

Cepel, M., Gavurova, B., Dvorský, J., & Belas, J. (2020). The impact of the COVID-19 crisis on the perception of business risk in the SME segment. *Journal of International Students, 13*(3), 248–263. doi:10.14254/2071-8330.2020/13-3/16

Cerrudo, C., Hasbini, A., & Russell, B. (2015). *Cyber security guidelines for smart city technology adoption.* Cloud Security Alliance.

Chakrabarti, D., Sarkar, S., & Mukherjee, A. (2022). Scaling an Internet of Things start-up: Can alliance strategy help? *Journal of Information Technology Teaching Cases, 12*(1), 43–49. doi:10.1177/2043886920986165

Chakrabarty, S., Engels, D. W., & Thathapudi, S. (2015, October). Black SDN for the Internet of Things. In *2015 IEEE 12th International Conference on Mobile Ad Hoc and Sensor Systems* (pp. 190-198). IEEE. 10.1109/MASS.2015.100

Chakravorti, N. (2022). *Digital Transformation: A Strategic Structure for Implementation.* CRC Press. doi:10.4324/9781003270904

Chalmeta, R., & Grangel, R. (2008). Knowledge management and organizational learning as competitive advantages in business environment: An overview. *Journal of Knowledge Management, 12*(6), 124–137.

Chandralekha, M., & Shenbagavadivu, N. (2017). AN INSIGHT INTO THE USAGE OF BIG DATA ANALYTICS. *International Journal of Advanced Research in Computer Science, 8*(9).

Chang-Richards, A., Chen, X., Pelosi, A., & Yang, N. (2022). *Technology implementation: What does the future hold for construction?* BRANZ. https://prod.branz.co.nz/documents/3712/ER71_Technology_implementation_LR12069.pdf

Chang, Y. H., & Tzeng, G. H. (2011). Evaluating intertwined effects in e-learning programs: A novel hybrid MCDM model based on factor analysis and DEMATEL. *Expert Systems with Applications, 38*(5), 5600–5615.

Chapman, J., & Rich, P. (2018). Does educational gamification improve students' motivation? If so, which game elements work best? *Journal of Education for Business, 93*(7), 314–321. doi:10.1080/08832323.2018.1490687

Charlton, G. (2013). *Consumers Prefer Live Chat For Customer Service: Stats.* Econsultancy. https://econsultancy.com/blog/63867-consumers-prefer-live-chat-for-customer-service-stats#i.1nockyz1cffd8a

Chatterjee, D., Grewal, R., & Sambamurthy, V. (2002). Shaping up for e-commerce: Institutional enablers of the organizational assimilation of web technologies. *Management Information Systems Quarterly, 26*(2), 65–89. doi:10.2307/4132321

Chattopadhyay, A., & Maitra, M. (2022). *MRI-based brain tumor image detection using CNN based deep learning method.* Neuroscience Informatics.

Chauhan, D., Jain, J. K., & Sharma, S. (2016, December). An end-to-end header compression for multihop IPv6 tunnels with varying bandwidth. In *2016 Fifth international conference on eco-friendly computing and communication systems (ICECCS)* (pp. 84-88). IEEE. 10.1109/Eco-friendly.2016.7893247

Chauhan, D., & Jain, J. K. (2019). A Journey from IoT to IoE. [IJITEE]. *International Journal of Innovative Technology and Exploring Engineering, 8*(11).

Chauhan, D., & Sharma, S. (2015). Addressing the bandwidth issue in end-to-end header compression over ipv6 tunneling mechanism. *International Journal of Computer Network and Information Security, 7*(9), 39–45. doi:10.5815/ijcnis.2015.09.05

Chen, N., Chen, Y., Ye, X., Ling, H., Song, S., & Huang, C. T. (2017). Smart City Surveillance in Fog Computing. In Studies in Big Data (Vol. 22). Springer. doi:10.1007/978-3-319-45145-9_9

Chen, D., Wawrzynski, P., & Lv, Z. (2021). Cyber security in smart cities: A review of deep learning-based applications and case studies. *Sustainable Cities and Society, 66*, 102655. doi:10.1016/j.scs.2020.102655

Chen, F., Drezner, Z., Ryan, J. K., & Simchi-Levi, D. (2017). Quantifying the bullwhip effect in supply chains with high-frequency demand information. *Manufacturing & Service Operations Management, 19*(3), 383–397.

Cheng, E. C., & Wang, T. (2022). Institutional strategies for cybersecurity in higher education institutions. *Information (Basel), 13*(4), 192. doi:10.3390/info13040192

Chen, H., Chiang, R. H., & Storey, V. C. (2012). Business intelligence and analytics: From big data to big impact. *Management Information Systems Quarterly, 36*(4), 1165–1188. doi:10.2307/41703503

Chen, I. J., & Paulraj, A. (2018). IoT in supply chain management. *Journal of Manufacturing Technology Management, 29*(4), 658–666.

Chen, K., Wang, M., Huang, C., Kinney, P. L., & Anastas, P. T. (2020). Air pollution reduction and mortality benefit during the COVID-19 outbreak in China. *The Lancet. Planetary Health, 4*(6), e210–e212. doi:10.1016/S2542-5196(20)30107-8 PMID:32411944

Chen, S., Xu, H., Liu, D., Hu, B., & Hucheng, W. (2014). A Vision of IoT: Applications, Challenges, and Opportunities With China Perspective. *IEEE Internet of Things Journal, 1*(4), 349–359. doi:10.1109/JIOT.2014.2337336

Chen, Y. Y. K., Jaw, Y. L., & Wu, B. L. (2016). Effect of digital transformation on organisational performance of SMEs. *Internet Research, 26*(1), 186–212. doi:10.1108/IntR-12-2013-0265

Chiew, K. L., Yong, K. S. C., & Tan, C. L. (2018). A survey of phishing attacks: Their types, vectors and technical approaches. *Expert Systems with Applications, 106*, 1–20. doi:10.1016/j.eswa.2018.03.050

Chitra, A., & Rajkumar, A. (2016). Plagiarism detection using machine learning-based paraphrase recognizer. *Journal of Intelligent Systems, 25*(3), 351–359. doi:10.1515/jisys-2014-0146

Choi, Y. B. (2021). Organizational cyber data breach analysis of Facebook, Equifax, and Uber cases. [IJCRE]. *International Journal of Cyber Research and Education*, *3*(1), 58–64. doi:10.4018/IJCRE.2021010106

Chowdhury, S., Dey, P., Joel-Edgar, S., Bhattacharya, S., Rodriguez-Espindola, O., Abadie, A., & Truong, L. (2023). Unlocking the value of artificial intelligence in human resource management through AI capability framework. *Human Resource Management Review*, *33*(1), 100899. doi:10.1016/j.hrmr.2022.100899

Chua, A. Y., & Goh, D. H. (2008). A study of knowledge management implementation in Singapore. *International Journal of Information Management*, *28*(2), 122–135.

Chugh, R., Macht, S., & Hossain, R. (2022). Robotic Process Automation: A review of organizational grey literature. *International Journal of Information Systems and Project Management*, *10*(1), 5–26. doi:10.12821/ijispm100101

Chundhoo, V., Chattopadhyay, G., Karmakar, G., & Appuhamillage, G. K. (2021). Cybersecurity risks in meat processing plant and impacts on total productive maintenance. 2021 International Conference on Maintenance and Intelligent Asset Management (ICMIAM). Research Gate.

Clarke, S., Peel, D. J., Arnab, S., Morini, L., Keegan, H., & Wood, O. (2017). escapED: A framework for creating educational escape rooms and Interactive Games For Higher/Further Education. *International Journal of Serious Games*, *4*(3), 73–86. doi:10.17083/ijsg.v4i3.180

Coercive control and the law - Rights of Women. (2016). Rights of Women. https://rightsofwomen.org.uk/get-information/violence-against-women-and-international-law/coercive-control-and-the-law/

Cohen, C. J., & Kahne, J. (2011). *Participatory politics. New media and youth political action*.

Cohen, J. P., Morrison, P., & Dao, L. 2020. COVID-19 image data collection. *arXiv preprint arXiv:2003.11597*.

Cooper, R. G., & Kleinschmidt, E. J. (1995). Benchmarking the firm's critical success factors in new product development. *Journal of Product Innovation Management*, *12*(5), 374–391. doi:10.1111/1540-5885.1250374

Coppola, D. P. (2015). Introduction to International Disaster Management. In Elsevier eBooks. Elsevier. doi:10.1016/C2014-0-00128-1

Corbeil, M. E., & Corbeil, J. R. (2022). Digital transformation of higher education through disruptive pedagogies: Wrapping a course around a course to promote learner agency. *Issues in Information Systems*. doi:10.48009/2_iis_2022_113

Corral, L., & Fronza, I. (2018). Design thinking and agile practices for software engineering an opportunity for innovation. *Proc. of the 19th Annual SIG Conference on Information Technology Education,* (pp. 26-31). ACM. 10.1145/3241815.3241864

Correani, A., De Massis, A., Frattini, F., Petruzzelli, A. M., & Natalicchio, A. (2020). Implementing a digital strategy: Learning from the experience of three digital transformation projects. *California Management Review*, *62*(4), 37–56. doi:10.1177/0008125620934864

Council, B. (2019). The state of social enterprise in Malaysia 2018. *British Council. Retrieved June, 16*, 2020. https://repository.unescap.org/handle/20.500.12870/2885

Couteau, C., Barz, S., Durt, T., Gerrits, T., Huwer, J., Prevedel, R., Rarity, J., Shields, A., & Weihs, G. (2023). Applications of single photons to quantum communication and computing. *Nature Reviews. Physics*, *5*(6), 1–13. doi:10.1038/s42254-023-00583-2

CRED. (2023). *2022 Disasters in numbers*. CRED. https://cred.be/sites/default/files/2022_EMDAT_report.pdf

Cui, L., Xie, G., Qu, Y., Gao, L., & Yang, Y. (2018). Security and privacy in smart cities: Challenges and opportunities. *IEEE Access : Practical Innovations, Open Solutions, 6*, 46134–46145. doi:10.1109/ACCESS.2018.2853985

Cui, L., Yang, S., Chen, F., Ming, Z., Lu, N., & Qin, J. (2018). A survey on application of machine learning for Internet of Things. *International Journal of Machine Learning and Cybernetics, 9*(8), 1399–1417. Advance online publication. doi:10.1007/s13042-018-0834-5

Cumpton, G., Juniper, C., & Patnaik, A. (2018). *Austin Metro Area Master Community Workforce Plan Baseline Evaluation Report*. Ray Marshall Center for the Study of Human Resources.

Cyber Extortion: An Industry Hot Topic. (2016, November 23). CIS. https://www.cisecurity.org/insights/blog/cyber-extortion-an-industry-hot-topic

Da Silva, T. P., Batista, T., Lopes, F., Neto, A. R., Delicato, F. C., Pires, P. F., & Da Rocha, A. R. (2022). Fog Computing Platforms for Smart City Applications: A Survey. *ACM Transactions on Internet Technology, 22*(4), 1–32. doi:10.1145/3488585

Dale, R. (2016). The return of the chatbots. *Natural Language Engineering, 22*(5), 811–817. doi:10.1017/S1351324916000243

Dalkir, K. (2011). *Knowledge management in theory and practice*. Routledge.

Dang, L., Dong, M., Ota, K., Wu, J., Li, J., & Li, G. (2018). Resource-Efficient Secure Data Sharing for Information Centric E-Health System Using Fog Computing. *IEEE International Conference on Communications, 2018-May*. IEEE. 10.1109/ICC.2018.8422844

Darmawan, S., Irawan, B., Setianingsih, C., & Murty, M. A. (2020). *Design of Detection Device for Sea Water Waves with Fuzzy Algorithm Based on Internet of Things*. IEEE. doi:10.1109/IAICT50021.2020.9172018

Das, J., Ghosh, S. K., & Buyya, R. (2021). Geospatial Edge-Fog Computing: A Systematic Review, Taxonomy, and Future Directions. In Mobile Edge Computing. doi:10.1007/978-3-030-69893-5_3

Dash, R., Rebman, C., & Kar, U. K. (2019). Application of Artificial Intelligence in Automation of Supply Chain Management. *Journal of Strategic Innovation and Sustainability, 14*(3), 43–53. doi:10.33423/jsis.v14i3.2105

Davenport, T. H., & Prusak, L. (2000). *Working knowledge: How organizations manage what they know* (2nd ed.). Harvard Business Press.

De Assis, L. F. F. G., Horita, F., De Freitas, E. P., Ueyama, J., & De Albuquerque, J. P. (2018). A Service-Oriented Middleware for Integrated Management of Crowdsourced and Sensor Data Streams in Disaster Management. *Sensors (Basel), 18*(6), 1689. doi:10.3390/s18061689 PMID:29794979

de Matos, E. C. B., & Sousa, T. C. (2010). From formal requirements to automated web testing and prototyping. *Innovations in Systems and Software Engineering, 6*(1), 163–169. doi:10.1007/s11334-009-0112-5

de Moura Costa, H. J., da Costa, C. A., da Rosa Righi, R., & Antunes, R. S. (2020). Fog computing in health: A systematic literature review. In Health and Technology, 10(5). doi:10.1007/s12553-020-00431-8

De Paula, D., Marx, C., Wolf, E., Dremel, C., Cormican, K., & Uebernickel, F. (2023). A managerial mental model to drive innovation in the context of digital transformation. *Industry and Innovation, 30*(1), 42–66. doi:10.1080/13662716.2022.2072711

de Vries, P. (2022). The Ethical Dimension of Emerging Technologies in Engineering Education. *Education Sciences, 12*(11), 754. doi:10.3390/educsci12110754

Deebak, B. D., & Fadi, A. T. (2022). A robust and distributed architecture for 5G-enabled networks in the smart block-chain era. *Computer Communications*, *181*, 293–308. doi:10.1016/j.comcom.2021.10.015

Dehghani, M., Niknam, T., Ghiasi, M., Siano, P., Haes Alhelou, H., & Al-Hinai, A. (2021). Fourier singular values-based false data injection attack detection in AC smart-grids. *Applied Sciences (Basel, Switzerland)*, *11*(12), 5706. doi:10.3390/app11125706

Deloitte. (2019). *Making Smart Cities Cybersecurity, Deloitte Center for Government Insights*. Deloitte. https://www2.deloitte.com/us/en/insights/focus/smart-city/making-smart-cities-cyber-secure.html

Deng, J., Shi, S., Li, P., Zhou, W., Zhang, Y., & Li, H. (2021, May). Voxel r-cnn: Towards high performance voxel-based 3d object detection. *Proceedings of the AAAI Conference on Artificial Intelligence*, *35*(2), 1201–1209. doi:10.1609/aaai.v35i2.16207

Dhandapani, S. (2016). Integration of User Centered Design and Software Development Process. *7th IEEE Annual Information Technology, Electronics and Mobile Communication Conference, IEEE IEMCON 2016*. IEEE. 10.1109/IEMCON.2016.7746075

Dhumne, K. M. (2017). Paperless Society in Digital Era. *International Journal of Library and Information Studies*, *7*(4), 317–319.

Diaz-Saenz, H. R. (2011). Transformational leadership. The SAGE handbook of leadership, 5(1), 299-310.

Dieste, M., Sauer, P. C., & Orzes, G. (2022). Organizational tensions in industry 4.0 implementation: A paradox theory approach. *International Journal of Production Economics*, *251*, 108532. doi:10.1016/j.ijpe.2022.108532

Dietrich, N. (2018). Escape classroom: The leblanc process—an educational "Escape Game". *Journal of Chemical Education*, *95*(6), 996–999. doi:10.1021/acs.jchemed.7b00690

Disaster management cycle. (n.d.). ELRHA. https://higuide.elrha.org/humanitarian-parameters/disaster-management-cycle/

Dlugosch, D., Abendschein, M., & Kim, E. J. (2022). *Helping the Austrian business sector to cope with new opportunities and challenges in Austria*.

Dorri, A., Kanhere, S. S., Jurdak, R., & Gauravaram, P. (2017). Blockchain for IoT security and privacy: The case study of a smart home. *2017 IEEE International Conference on Pervasive Computing and Communications Workshops, PerCom Workshops 2017*, (pp. 618–623). IEEE. 10.1109/PERCOMW.2017.7917634

Dua, N., Singh, S. N., & Semwal, V. B. (2021). Multi-input CNN-GRU based human activity recognition using wearable sensors. *Computing*, *103*(7), 1461–1478. doi:10.1007/s00607-021-00928-8

Dube, R. (2021). *Measuring technical efficiency in Zimbabwe's manufacturing sector: a two-stage DEA Tobit approach* (Faculty of Commerce). https://open.uct.ac.za/handle/11427/33719

Duggins, R. (2019). Innovation and problem-solving teaching case: The breakout box–a desktop escape room. *Journal of Organizational Psychology*, *19*(4).

Dumitrescu, E. F., McCaskey, A. J., Hagen, G., Jansen, G. R., Morris, T. D., Papenbrock, T., Pooser, R. C., Dean, D. J., & Lougovski, P. (2018). Cloud quantum computing of an atomic nucleus. *Physical Review Letters*, *120*(21), 210501. doi:10.1103/PhysRevLett.120.210501 PMID:29883142

Dwivedi, Y. K., Hughes, L., Coombs, C., Constantiou, I., & Duan, Y. (2020). Artificial Intelligence (AI): Multidisciplinary perspectives on emerging challenges, opportunities, and agenda for research, practice and policy. *International Journal of Information Management*, *57*, 101994. doi:10.1016/j.ijinfomgt.2019.08.002

Ebert, C., & Duarte, C. H. C. (2018). Digital Transformation. *IEEE Software*, *35*(4), 16–21. doi:10.1109/MS.2018.2801537

Eckhoff, D., & Wagner, I. (2017). Privacy in the smart city—Applications, technologies, challenges, and solutions. *IEEE Communications Surveys and Tutorials*, *20*(1), 489–516. doi:10.1109/COMST.2017.2748998

Edwards, G. (2021, June). Cybercrime: Targeting your intellectual property. In Intellectual Property Forum: Journal of the Intellectual Property Society of Australia and New Zealand (No. 124, pp. 35-40). IEEE.

Ejaz, W., Imran, M., & Jo, M. (2016). *Internet of Things (IoT) in 5G Wireless Communications*. IEEE. . doi:10.1109/ACCESS.2016.2646120

Elevating customer experience excellence in the next normal . (n.d.). McKinsey. https://www.mckinsey.com/business-functions/operations/our-insights/elevating-customer-experience-excellence-in-the-next-normal#

Eliyan, L. F., & Di Pietro, R. (2021). DoS and DDoS attacks in Software Defined Networks: A survey of existing solutions and research challenges. *Future Generation Computer Systems*, *122*, 149–171. doi:10.1016/j.future.2021.03.011

Elkoutbi, M., Khriss, I., & Keller, R. K. (2006). Automated prototyping of user interfaces based on UML scenarios. *Automated Software Engineering*, *13*(1), 5–40. doi:10.1007/s10515-006-5465-5

Eppinger, S. D., & Ulrich, K. T. (2011). Product design and development. New York, NY: McGraw-Hill.

Escalona, M. J., & Aragón, G. (2008). NDT. A model-driven approach for web requirements. *IEEE Transactions on Software Engineering*, *34*(3), 377–390. doi:10.1109/TSE.2008.27

Escalona, M. J., García-Borgoñón, L., & Koch, N. (2021). Don't Throw your Software Prototypes Away. Reuse them! *International Conference on Information System Development*. IEEE.

Escalona, M. J., Gutierrez, J. J., Mejías, M., Aragón, G., Ramos, I., Torres, J., & Domínguez, F. J. (2011). An overview on test generation from functional requirements. *Journal of Systems and Software*, *84*(8), 1379–1393. doi:10.1016/j.jss.2011.03.051

Esposito, M., Palma, L., Belli, A., Sabbatini, L., & Pierleoni, P. (2022). Recent Advances in Internet of Things Solutions for Early Warning Systems: A Review. *Sensors (Basel)*, *22*(6), 2124. doi:10.3390/s22062124 PMID:35336296

Eukel, H., & Morrell, B. (2021). Ensuring educational escape-room success: The process of designing, piloting, evaluating, redesigning, and re-evaluating educational escape rooms. *Simulation & Gaming*, *52*(1), 18–23. doi:10.1177/1046878120953453

Extortion: Strategies. (2014, November 22). Take Back the Tech. https://takebackthetech.net/be-safe/extortion-strategies

Fafunwa, T., & Odufuwa, F. (2022). African micro, small, and medium enterprises need to digitally transform to benefit from the Africa continental Free Trade area (AfCFTA). In Africa–Europe Cooperation and Digital Transformation (pp. 66–82). Taylor & Francis. doi:10.4324/9781003274322-5

Fairlie, R. W., Couch, K., & Xu, H. (2020). The impacts of covid-19 on minority unemployment: First evidence from april 2020 cps microdata (No. w27246). National Bureau of Economic Research.

Falb, J., Kavaldjian, S., Popp, R., Raneburger, D., Arnautovic, E., & Kaindl, H. (2009) Fully automatic user interface generation from discourse models. *International Conference on Intelligent User Interfaces, Proceedings IUI*, (pp. 475-476). IEEE. 10.1145/1502650.1502722

Falco, G. J., & Rosenbach, E. (2022). *Confronting Cyber Risk: An Embedded Endurance Strategy for Cybersecurity*. Oxford University Press. doi:10.1093/oso/9780197526545.001.0001

Fard, S. M. H., Karimipour, H., Dehghantanha, A., Jahromi, A. N., & Srivastava, G. (2020). Ensemble sparse representation-based cyber threat hunting for security of smart cities. *Computers & Electrical Engineering, 88*, 106825. doi:10.1016/j.compeleceng.2020.106825

Farooq, R. (2023). Knowledge management and performance: A bibliometric analysis based on Scopus and WOS data (1988–2021). *Journal of Knowledge Management, 27*(7), 1948–1991. doi:10.1108/JKM-06-2022-0443

Fatolahi, A., Somé, S. S., & Lethbridge, T. C. (2008). A model-driven approach for the semi- automated generation of web-based applications from requirements. *20th International Conference on Software Engineering and Knowledge Engineering,* (pp. 619-624). IEEE.

Fauvel, K., Balouek-Thomert, D., Melgar, D., Silva, P., Simonet, A., Antoniu, G., Costan, A., Masson, V., Parashar, M., Rodero, I., & Termier, A. (2020). A Distributed Multi-Sensor Machine Learning Approach to Earthquake Early Warning. *Proceedings of the AAAI Conference on Artificial Intelligence, 34*(01), 403–411. doi:10.1609/aaai.v34i01.5376

FeldererM.RamlerR. (2021). *Quality Assurance for AI-based Systems: Overview and Challenges.* 1–10. http://arxiv.org/abs/2102.05351

Ferguson, R., Renaud, K., Wilford, S., & Irons, A. (2020). PRECEPT: A framework for ethical digital forensics investigations. *Journal of Intellectual Capital, 21*(2), 257–290. doi:10.1108/JIC-05-2019-0097

Fernández, D. M., Wagner, S., Kalinowski, M., Felderer, M., Mafra, P., Vetrò, A., Conte, T., Christiansson, M.-T., Greer, D., Lassenius, C., Männistö, T., Nayabi, M., Oivo, M., Penzenstadler, B., Pfahl, D., Prikladnicki, R., Ruhe, G., Schekelmann, A., Sen, S., & Wieringa, R. (2017). Naming the pain in requirements engineering: Contemporary problems, causes, and effects in practice. *Empirical Software Engineering, 22*(5), 2298–2338. doi:10.1007/s10664-016-9451-7

Fitriasari, F. (2020). How do Small and Medium Enterprise (SME) survive the COVID-19 outbreak?. *Jurnal Inovasi Ekonomi, 5*(02).

FMCG giant Marico's digital initiatives help them save ₹ 35 crore . (2018, January 19). CIO. https://www.cio.com/article/218437/fmcg-giant-marico-s-digital-initiatives-helpthem-save-35-crore.html

Fotaris, P., & Mastoras, T. (2019, October). Escape rooms for learning: A systematic review. In *Proceedings of the European Conference on Games Based Learning* (pp. 235-243). IEEE.

Froehle, C. M. (2006). Service personnel, technology, and their interaction in influencing customer satisfaction. *Decision Sciences, 37*(1), 5–38. doi:10.1111/j.1540-5414.2006.00108.x

Fruhlinger, J. (2022, August 7). *What is IoT? The internet of things explained.* Network World. https://www.networkworld.com/article/3207535/what-is-iot-the-internet-of-things-explained.html

Gamhewage, G., Mahmoud, M. E., Tokar, A., Attias, M., Mylonas, C., Canna, S., & Utunen, H. (2022). Digital transformation of face-to-face focus group methodology: Engaging a globally dispersed audience to manage institutional change at the World Health Organization. *Journal of Medical Internet Research, 24*(5), e28911. doi:10.2196/28911 PMID:35617007

Gamperl, M., Singer, J. N., & Thuro, K. (2021). Internet of Things Geosensor Network for Cost-Effective Landslide Early Warning Systems. *Sensors (Basel), 21*(8), 2609. doi:10.3390/s21082609 PMID:33917752

Gantz, J. F., Reinsel, D., Turner, V., & Minton, S. (2014). The Digital Universe of Opportunities: Rich Data and the Increasing Value of the Internet of Things. *IDC iView: IDC Analyze the Future.*

Gao, H., Luo, H., & Ding, S. X. (2014). Real-Time Implementation of Fault-Tolerant Control Systems With Performance Optimization. *IEEE Transactions on Industrial Electronics, 61*(5), 2402–2411. doi:10.1109/TIE.2013.2273477

Gardner-Stephen, P., Wallace, A., Hawtin, K., Al-Nuaimi, G., Tran, A. T., Mozo, T. L., & Lloyd, M. D. (2019). *Reducing cost while increasing the resilience & effectiveness of tsunami early warning systems.* https://doi.org/ doi:10.1109/GHTC46095.2019.9033084

Gatta, M., Boushey, H., & Appelbaum, E. (2009). High-touch and here-to-stay: Future skills demands in US low wage service occupations. *Sociology*, *43*(5), 968–989. doi:10.1177/0038038509340735

Gefen & Straub. (2003). Managing User Trust in B2C e-Services. E-Service Journal, 2(2), 7. https://doi.org/ doi:10.2979/esj.2003.2.2.7

Genelza, G. G. (2022). A case study research on Justin Herald's language development. *Journal of Languages. Linguistics and Literary Studies*, *2*(3), 133–141.

Gerald, C. (2015). *Research Report Strategy, Not Technology, Drives Digital Transformation.* Research Gate.

Gharaibeh, A., Salahuddin, M. A., Hussini, S. J., Khreishah, A., Khalil, I., Guizani, M., & Al-Fuqaha, A. (2017). Smart cities: A survey on data management, security, and enabling technologies. *IEEE Communications Surveys and Tutorials*, *19*(4), 2456–2501. doi:10.1109/COMST.2017.2736886

Ghasemi, P., & Karimian, N. (2020). *A Qualitative Study of Various Aspects of the Application of IoT in Disaster Management.* IEEE. doi:10.1109/ICWR49608.2020.9122323

Ghazal, T. M., Hasan, M. K., Alshurideh, M. T., Alzoubi, H. M., Ahmad, M., Akbar, S. S., Al Kurdi, B., & Akour, I. A. (2021). IoT for smart cities: Machine learning approaches in smart healthcare—A review. *Future Internet*, *13*(8), 218. doi:10.3390/fi13080218

Ghiasi, M., Dehghani, M., Niknam, T., Kavousi-Fard, A., Siano, P., & Alhelou, H. H. (2021). Cyber-attack detection and cyber-security enhancement in smart DC-microgrid based on blockchain technology and Hilbert Huang transform. *IEEE Access : Practical Innovations, Open Solutions*, *9*, 29429–29440. doi:10.1109/ACCESS.2021.3059042

Ghosh, S., & Mukherjee, A. (2022). STROVE: Spatial data infrastructure enabled cloud–fog–edge computing framework for combating COVID-19 pandemic. *Innovations in Systems and Software Engineering*. doi:10.1007/s11334-022-00458-2 PMID:35677629

Gill, H. S., Khalaf, O. I., Alotaibi, Y., Alghamdi, S., & Alassery, F. (2022). Multi-Model CNN-RNN-LSTM Based Fruit Recognition and Classification. *Intelligent Automation & Soft Computing*, *33*(1).

Gissing, A., & Eburn, M. (2019). *Planning and capability requirements for catastrophic and cascading disasters.* Bush Fire and Natural Hazards CRC. https://www.bnhcrc.com.au/sites/default/files/managed/downloads/cascading_and_catastrophic_events_final_report_2020_0.pdf

Glavaš, A., & Stašcik, A. (2017). Enhancing positive attitude towards mathematics through introducing Escape Room games. *Mathematics Education as a Science and a Profession*, *281*, 293.

Gnatyuk, S., Berdibayev, R., Avkurova, Z., Verkhovets, O., & Bauyrzhan, M. (2021). Studies on Cloud-based Cyber Incidents Detection and Identification in Critical Infrastructure. CPITS, Gootman, S. (2016). OPM hack: The most dangerous threat to the federal government today. *Journal of Applied Security Research*, *11*(4), 517–525.

Gnewuch, U., Morana, S., Adam, M., & Maedche, A. (2017). This is the author's version of a work that was published in the following source Please note : Copyright is owned by the author and / or the publisher. Commercial use is not allowed. Institute of Information Systems and Marketing (IISM) The psychop. *Thirty Eighth International Conference on Information Systems*, South Korea.

Gobble, M. M. (2018). Digitalization, digitization, and innovation. *Research Technology Management*, *61*(4), 56–59. doi:10.1080/08956308.2018.1471280

Goh, A. T., & Gunasekaran, A. (2001). Knowledge management: Approaches and policies. *Journal of Knowledge Management*, *5*(1), 33–46.

Gold, J. (2017, October 30). *IoT standards, protocols and technologies explained*. Network World. https://www.networkworld.com/article/3235124/internet-of-things-definitions-a-handy-guide-to-essential-iot-terms.html

Gomendio, M., & the Organisation for Economic Co-operation and Development (OECD) Staff. (2017). *Empowering and enabling teachers to improve equity and outcomes for all*. OECD. https://www.oecd-ilibrary.org/content/publication/9789264273238-en?crawler=trueand mimetype=application/pdf

Gomes, E., Costa, F., De Rolt, C., Plentz, P., & Dantas, M. (2021). A Survey from Real-Time to Near Real-Time Applications in Fog Computing Environments. In Telecom, 2(4). doi:10.3390/telecom2040028

Gómez-Urquiza, J. L., Gómez-Salgado, J., Albendín-García, L., Correa-Rodríguez, M., González-Jiménez, E., & Cañadas-De la Fuente, G. A. (2019). The impact on nursing students' opinions and motivation of using a "Nursing Escape Room" as a teaching game: A descriptive study. *Nurse Education Today*, *72*, 73–76. doi:10.1016/j.nedt.2018.10.018 PMID:30453202

Goswami, B., & Choudhury, H. (2022). A blockchain-based authentication scheme for 5g-enabled IoT. *Journal of Network and Systems Management*, *30*(4), 61. doi:10.1007/s10922-022-09680-6

Gourinchas, P. O., Kalemli-Özcan, Ş., Penciakova, V., & Sander, N. (2020). COVID-19 and SME Failures (No. w27877). National Bureau of Economic Research.

Goyal, H., Sidana, K., Singh, C., Jain, A., & Jindal, S. (2022). A real time face mask detection system using convolutional neural network. *Multimedia Tools and Applications*, *81*(11), 14999–15015. doi:10.1007/s11042-022-12166-x PMID:35233179

Granja, F. M., & Rafael, G. D. R. (2017). The preservation of digital evidence and its admissibility in the court. *International Journal of Electronic Security and Digital Forensics*, *9*(1), 1–18. doi:10.1504/IJESDF.2017.081749

Grant, R. M. (1996). Toward a knowledge-based theory of the firm. *Strategic Management Journal*, *17*(S2), 109–122. doi:10.1002/smj.4250171110

Gray, D., & Ladig, J. (2015). The implementation of EMV chip card technology to improve cyber security accelerates in the US following target corporation's data breach. *International Journal of Business Administration*, *6*(2), 60. doi:10.5430/ijba.v6n2p60

Greenberg, A. (2018). The untold story of NotPetya, the most devastating cyberattack in history. *Wired*, (August), 22.

Groarke, J. M., Berry, E., Graham-Wisener, L., McKenna-Plumley, P. E., McGlinchey, E., & Armour, C. (2020). Loneliness in the UK during the COVID-19 pandemic: Cross-sectional results from the COVID-19 Psychological Wellbeing Study. *PLoS One*, *15*(9), e0239698. doi:10.1371/journal.pone.0239698 PMID:32970764

Grover, J., & Garimella, R. M. (2018). Reliable and Fault-Tolerant IoT-Edge Architecture. *Proceedings of IEEE Sensors, 2018-October*. doi:10.1109/ICSENS.2018.8589624

Guerrieri, V., Lorenzoni, G., Straub, L., & Werning, I. (2020). *Macroeconomic Implications of COVID-19: Can Negative Supply Shocks Cause Demand Shortages?* (No. w26918). National Bureau of Economic Research.

Guggisberg, M. (2017, April 3). *Revenge Porn: A Growing Contemporary Problem.* ResearchGate. https://www.research-gate.net/publication/316075558_Revenge_Porn_A_Growing_Contemporary_Problem

Guigon, G., Humeau, J., & Vermeulen, M. (2018, March). A model to design learning escape games: SEGAM. In *10th International Conference on Computer Supported Education* (pp. 191-197). SCITEPRESS-Science and Technology Publications. 10.5220/0006665501910197

Guillaume, A., Vrain, C., & Wael, E. (2020). Predictive maintenance on event logs: Application on an ATM fleet. *arXiv preprint arXiv:2011.10996.*

Gupta, P. (2011). Best Practices to Achieve CMMI Level 2 Configuration Management Process Area through VSS tool. *International Journal of Computer Technology and Applications., 2*(3), 542–558.

Gupta, R., Saxena, A., Singh, A. K., & Bhatia, M. (2022). Impact of technology adoption on supply chain performance in FMCG industry. *Journal of Enterprise Information Management.*

Gupta, S. K., & Rastogi, R. (2019). Artificial Intelligence and Knowledge Management in Indian Organizations. In *Proceedings of International Conference on Computer Networks, Big Data and IoT* (pp. 1-5).

Gyulai, T., Wolf, P., Kása, F., & Viharos, Z. J. (2022). *Operational Structure for an Industry 4.0 oriented Learning Factory.* IMEKO.

H˝ogberg, J., Hamari, J., & W¨astlund, E. (2019). Gameful Experience Questionnaire (GAMEFULQUEST): An instrument for measuring the perceived gamefulness of system use. *User Modeling and User-Adapted Interaction, 29*(3), 619–660. doi:10.1007/s11257-019-09223-w

Habibzadeh, H., Nussbaum, B. H., Anjomshoa, F., Kantarci, B., & Soyata, T. (2019). A survey on cybersecurity, data privacy, and policy issues in cyber-physical system deployments in smart cities. *Sustainable Cities and Society, 50,* 101660. doi:10.1016/j.scs.2019.101660

Hadwin, J. (2015). *Victim Blaming And Third-Person Effect: A Comparative Analysis Of Attitudes For Revenge Porn And Sexual Assault.* Shareok. https://shareok.org/bitstream/handle/11244/54533/Hadwin_okstate_0664M_15165.pdf?sequence=1

Hainey, T., Connolly, T., Boyle, E., Azadegan, A., Wilson, A., Razak, A., & Gray, G. (2014, October). A systematic literature review to identify empirical evidence on the use of games-based learning in primary education for knowledge acquisition and content understanding. In *8th European Conference on Games Based Learning: ECGBL* (p. 167). IEEE.

Hair, J. F., Sarstedt, M., Ringle, C. M., & Mena, J. A. (2012). An assessment of the use of partial least squares structural equation modeling in marketing research. *Journal of the Academy of Marketing Science, 40*(3), 414–433. doi:10.1007/s11747-011-0261-6

Hald, K. S., & Kinra, A. (2019). How the blockchain enables and constrains supply chain performance. *International Journal of Physical Distribution & Logistics Management, 49*(4), 376–397. doi:10.1108/IJPDLM-02-2019-0063

Haleem, A., Javaid, M., Qadri, M. A., Singh, R. P., & Suman, R. (2022). Artificial intelligence (AI) applications for marketing: A literature-based study. *International Journal of Intelligent Networks, 3,* 119–132. doi:10.1016/j.ijin.2022.08.005

Hall, B. H. (2002). The financing of research and development. *Oxford Review of Economic Policy, 18*(1), 35–51. doi:10.1093/oxrep/18.1.35

Halvorsen, R. (1977). Energy substitution in US manufacturing. *The Review of Economics and Statistics, 59*(4), 381–388. doi:10.2307/1928702

Hamari, J., Shernoff, D. J., Rowe, E., Coller, B., Asbell-Clarke, J., & Edwards, T. (2016). Challenging games help students learn: An empirical study on engagement, flow and immersion in game-based learning. *Computers in Human Behavior*, *54*, 170–179. doi:10.1016/j.chb.2015.07.045

Hardie, T., Horton, T., Thornton-Lee, N., Home, J., & Pereira, P. (2022). Developing Learning Health Systems in the, UK: Priorities for Action. The Health Foundation, 10.

Hareshbhai, B. S., Valiveti, S., Kothari, D., & Raval, G. (2023, March). Generating near-ideal nonces for cryptographic processes using Quantum Cryptography. In *2023 First International Conference on Microwave, Antenna and Communication (MAC)* (pp. 1-6). IEEE. 10.1109/MAC58191.2023.10177098

Hazen, B. T., Mollenkopf, D. A., & Wang, Y. (2017). Remanufacturing for the Circular Economy: An Examination of Consumer Switching Behavior. *Business Strategy and the Environment*, *26*(4), 451–464. doi:10.1002/bse.1929

He, D., Zeadally, S., Kumar, N., & Lee, J. H. (2016). Anonymous authentication for wireless body area networks with provable security. *IEEE Systems Journal*, *11*(4), 2590–2601. doi:10.1109/JSYST.2016.2544805

He, K., Zhang, X., Ren, S., & Sun, J. (2016). Deep residual learning for image recognition. In *Proceedings of the IEEE conference on computer vision and pattern recognition* (pp. 770-778). IEEE.

Helfat, C. E., & Martin, J. A. (2015). Dynamic managerial capabilities: Review and assessment of managerial impact on strategic change. *Journal of Management*, *41*(5), 1281–1312. doi:10.1177/0149206314561301

Helfat, C. E., & Winter, S. G. (2011). Untangling dynamic and operational capabilities: Strategy for the (n)ever-changing world. *Strategic Management Journal*, *32*(11), 1243–1250. doi:10.1002/smj.955

Hemalatha, T., Ramesh, M. V., & Rangan, V. P. (2020). Enhancing the reliability of landslide early warning systems by machine learning. *Landslides*, *17*(9), 2231–2246. doi:10.1007/s10346-020-01453-z

Hendriks, P. H. J., Dessers, E., & van Hootegem, G. (2012). Reconsidering the definition of a spatial data infrastructure. In International Journal of Geographical Information Science, 26(8). doi:10.1080/13658816.2011.639301

Henry, N., Mcglynn, C., Powell, A., Scott, A. J., Johnson, K., & Flynn, A. (2020). *Image-based sexual abuse: a study on the causes and consequences of non-consensual nude or sexual imagery*. Routledge.

Herman, A., & Friedson, I. (2018). *Quantum computing: how to address the national security risk*. Hudson Institute.

Hess, T., Matt, C., Benlian, A., & Wiesböck, F. (2016). Options for formulating a digital transformation strategy. *MIS Quarterly Executive*, *15*(2).

Hewa, T. M., Kalla, A., Nag, A., Ylianttila, M. E., & Liyanage, M. (2020, October). Blockchain for 5G and IoT: Opportunities and challenges. In *2020 IEEE Eighth International Conference on Communications and Networking* (ComNet) (pp. 1-8). IEEE. 10.1109/ComNet47917.2020.9306082

Hilal, H. A., Hilal, N. A., Hilal, T. A., & Hilal, T. A. (2022). Crowdsensing application on coalition game using GPS and IoT parking in smart cities. *Procedia Computer Science*, *201*, 535–542. doi:10.1016/j.procs.2022.03.069

Hirschberg, J., & Manning, C. D. (2022). Advances in natural language processing. *Science*, *349*(6245), 261–266. doi:10.1126/science.aaa8685 PMID:26185244

Hobbs, A. (2021). *The colonial pipeline hack: Exposing vulnerabilities in us cybersecurity*. SAGE Publications: SAGE Business Cases Originals.

Holsapple, C. W., & Joshi, K. D. (2001). Knowledge management: A threefold framework. *The Information Society*, *17*(1), 15–28.

Horsman, G. (2022). Digital evidence strategies for digital forensic science examinations. *Science & Justice*. PMID:36631176

Horzyk, A., Magierski, S., & Miklaszewski, G. (2009). An Intelligent Internet Shop-Assistant Recognizing a Customer Personality for Improving Man-Machine Interactions. *Recent Advances in Intelligent Information Systems*, 13–26.

Hossain, T., Shishir, F. S., Ashraf, M., Al Nasim, M. A., & Shah, F. M. (2019, May). Brain tumor detection using convolutional neural network. In *2019 1st international conference on advances in science, engineering and robotics technology (ICASERT)* (pp. 1-6). IEEE. 10.1109/ICASERT.2019.8934561

How Block Chain Is Revolutionizing Supply Chain Industry. (2019, September 19). Gazelle Information Technologies. https://gazelle.in/how-block-chain-is-revolutionizing-supply-chain-industry

How FMCG companies benefit from supply chain visibility. (2022, June 9). Supply Chain Visibility for FMCG Companies| Maersk. https://www.maersk.com/insights/digitalisation/supply-chain-visibility-for-fmcgcompanies

Howie, F., Kreofsky, B. L., Ravi, A., Lokken, T., Hoff, M. D., & Fang, J. L. (2022). Rapid rise of pediatric telehealth during COVID-19 in a large multispecialty health system. *Telemedicine Journal and e-Health*, 28(1), 3–10. doi:10.1089/tmj.2020.0562 PMID:33999718

Hoyos, J. P. A., & Restrepo-Calle, F. (2017). Fast Prototyping of Web-Based Information Systems Using a Restricted Natural Language Specification. In *International Conference on Evaluation of Novel Approaches to Software Engineering*. Springer.

Hu, P., Dhelim, S., Ning, H., & Qiu, T. (2017). Survey on fog computing: architecture, key technologies, applications and open issues. In Journal of Network and Computer Applications, 98. doi:10.1016/j.jnca.2017.09.002

Huang, X., Gong, P., Wang, S., White, M., & Zhang, B. (2022). Machine learning modeling of vitality characteristics in historical preservation zones with multi-source data. *Buildings*, 12(11), 1978. doi:10.3390/buildings12111978

Hussain, F., Hussain, R., Hassan, S. A., & Hossain, E. (2020). Machine Learning in IoT Security. *IEEE Communications Surveys and Tutorials*, 22(April), 8–10. doi:10.1109/COMST.2020.2986444

Ianenko, M., Ianenko, M., Huhlaev, D., & Martynenko, O. (2019, March). Digital transformation of trade: Problems and prospects of marketing activities. [). IOP Publishing.]. *IOP Conference Series. Materials Science and Engineering*, 497(1), 012118. doi:10.1088/1757-899X/497/1/012118

Ibarreche, J., Aquino, R., Edwards, R., Rangel, V., Pérez, I., Martinez, M. A., Castellanos, E., Álvarez, E., Jimenez, S., Rentería, R. G., Edwards, A. H., & Álvarez, O. (2020). Flash Flood Early Warning System in Colima, Mexico. *Sensors (Basel)*, 20(18), 5231. doi:10.3390/s20185231 PMID:32937798

Ijaz, S., Shah, M. A., Khan, A., & Ahmed, M. (2016). Smart cities: A survey on security concerns. *International Journal of Advanced Computer Science and Applications*, 7(2). doi:10.14569/IJACSA.2016.070277

Indrajit, A., van Loenen, B., Suprajaka, Jaya, V. E., Ploeger, H., Lemmen, C., & van Oosterom, P. (2021). Implementation of the spatial plan information package for improving ease of doing business in Indonesian cities. *Land Use Policy*, 105, 105338. doi:10.1016/j.landusepol.2021.105338

Inglesant, P., Jirotka, M., & Hartswood, M. (2018). *Responsible Innovation in Quantum Technologies applied to Defence and National Security. NQIT*. Networked Quantum Information Technologies.

Inoue, M., Tanioka, Y., & Yamanaka, Y. (2019). Method for Near-Real Time Estimation of Tsunami Sources Using Ocean Bottom Pressure Sensor Network (S-Net). *Geosciences*, 9(7), 310. doi:10.3390/geosciences9070310

Ioffe, S., & Szegedy, C. (2015, June). Batch normalization: Accelerating deep network training by reducing internal covariate shift. In *International conference on machine learning* (pp. 448-456). PMLR.

Irwin, D., & Ibrahim, N. (2020). *Market study to understand job growth potential in SMEs in Nepal.* Open Knowledge. https://openknowledge.worldbank.org/handle/10986/33952

Ivanov, D., & Dolgui, A. (2021). OR-methods for coping with the ripple effect in supply chains during COVID-19 pandemic: Managerial insights and research implications. *International Journal of Production Economics, 232,* 107921. doi:10.1016/j.ijpe.2020.107921

JabRef Web. (n.d.). *Home.* JabRefWeb. https://www.jabref.org/

Jagannath, J., Polosky, N., & Jagannath, A. (2019). *Machine Learning for Wireless Communications in the Internet of Things : A Comprehensive Survey.* Cornell University. https://arxiv.org/abs/1901.07947

Jain, M., Kumar, P., Kota, R., & Patel, S. N. (2018). Evaluating and informing the design of chatbots. *DIS 2018 - Proceedings of the 2018 Designing Interactive Systems Conference, 895–906.* ACM. 10.1145/3196709.3196735

Jain, J. K., & Chauhan, D. (2021). An Energy-Efficient Model For Internet Of Things Using Compressive Sensing. *Journal of Management Information and Decision Sciences, 24,* 1–7.

Jain, S., Gupta, S., Sreelakshmi, K. K., & Rodrigues, J. J. (2022). Fog computing in enabling 5G-driven emerging technologies for development of sustainable smart city infrastructures. *Cluster Computing, 25*(2), 1–44. doi:10.1007/s10586-021-03496-w

Jambhekar, K., Pahls, R. P., & Deloney, L. A. (2020). Benefits of an escape room as a novel educational activity for radiology residents. *Academic Radiology, 27*(2), 276–283. doi:10.1016/j.acra.2019.04.021 PMID:31160173

Jamil, M. I. M., & Almunawar, M. N. Importance of Digital Literacy and Hindrance Brought About by Digital Divide. In *Encyclopedia of Information Science and Technology* (5th ed., pp. 1683–1698). IGI Global.

Javadzadeh, G., & Rahmani, A. M. (2020). Fog Computing Applications in Smart Cities: A Systematic Survey. *Wireless Networks, 26*(2), 1433–1457. Advance online publication. doi:10.1007/s11276-019-02208-y

Jayashree, S., Sarika, S., L, S. A., & Prathibha, S. (2017). *A novel approach for early flood warning using android and IoT.* IEEE. doi:10.1109/ICCCT2.2017.7972302

Jensen, L. S., Özkil, A. G., & Mortensen, N. H. (2016). Prototypes in engineering design: Definitions and strategies. *Proceedings of International Design Conference* (pp. 821-839). IEEE.

Jo. (2022, December 3). *The Disaster Management Cycle: 5 Key Stages UCF Online.* UCF Online. https://www.ucf.edu/online/leadership-management/news/the-disaster-management-cycle/

Johnston, L., Koikkalainen, H., Anderson, L., Lapok, P., Lawson, A., & Shenkin, S. D. (2022). Foundation level barriers to the widespread adoption of digital solutions by care homes: Insights from three Scottish studies. *International Journal of Environmental Research and Public Health, 19*(12), 7407. doi:10.3390/ijerph19127407 PMID:35742667

Jordan, M. I., & Mitchell, T. M. (2015). Machine learning: Trends, perspectives, and prospects. *Science, 349*(6245), 255–260. doi:10.1126/science.aaa8415 PMID:26185243

Juárez-Ramirez, R., Huertas, C., & Inzunza, S. (2014). Automated generation of user-interface prototypes based on controlled natural language description. *Proceedings - IEEE 38th Annual International Computers, Software and Applications. Conference Workshops.* IEEE. 10.1109/COMPSACW.2014.44

Jun, Y., Craig, A., Shafik, W., & Sharif, L. (2021). Artificial intelligence application in cybersecurity and cyberdefense. *Wireless Communications and Mobile Computing*, *2021*, 1–10. doi:10.1155/2021/3329581

Kaczorowska-Spychalska, D. (2019). How chatbots influence marketing. *Management*, *23*(1), 251–270. doi:10.2478/manment-2019-0015

Kamal, M., & Newman, W. J. (2016). Revenge Pornography: Mental Health Implications and Related Legislation. *The Journal of the American Academy of Psychiatry and the Law*, *44*(3), 359–367. https://jaapl.org/content/44/3/359 PMID:27644870

Kamalraj, R., Neelakandan, S., Kumar, M. R., Rao, V. C. S., Anand, R., & Singh, H. (2021). Interpretable filter based convolutional neural network (IF-CNN) for glucose prediction and classification using PD-SS algorithm. *Measurement*, *183*, 109804. doi:10.1016/j.measurement.2021.109804

Kamalrudin, M., & Grundy, J. (2011). Generating essential user interface prototypes to validate requirements. *26th IEEE/ACM International Conference on Automated Software Engineering, ASE 2011, Proceedings*. IEEE. 10.1109/ASE.2011.6100126

Kamath, R., & Venumuddala, V. R. (2023). *Emerging technologies and the Indian IT sector*. Taylor & Francis. doi:10.1201/9781003324355

Kane, G. C., Palmer, D., Phillips, A. N., Kiron, D., & Buckley, N. (2015). Strategy, not technology, drives digital transformation. *MIT Sloan Management Review and Deloitte University Press*, *14*, 1–25.

Kang, J., Yu, R., Huang, X., & Zhang, Y. (2017). Privacy-preserved pseudonym scheme for fog computing supported internet of vehicles. *IEEE Transactions on Intelligent Transportation Systems*, *19*(8), 2627–2637. doi:10.1109/TITS.2017.2764095

Kappe, F., Karli, Y., Bracht, T. K., da Silva, S. F. C., Seidelmann, T., Axt, V. M., & Remesh, V. (2023). Collective excitation of spatio-spectrally distinct quantum dots enabled by chirped pulses. *Mathematics of Quantum Technologies*, *3*(2), 025006. doi:10.1088/2633-4356/acd7c1

Karageorgiou, Z., Mavrommati, E., & Fotaris, P. (2019, October). Escape room design as a game-based learning process for STEAM education. In *ECGBL 2019 13th European Conference on Game-Based Learning* (p. 378). Academic Conferences and publishing limited.

Karthika, P., Ganesh Babu, R., & Karthik, P. A. (2020). Fog Computing using Interoperability and IoT Security Issues in Health Care. In Lecture Notes in Networks and Systems. Springer doi:10.1007/978-981-15-2329-8_10

Kathuria, R., Kedia, M., & Kapilavai, S. (2020). Implications of AI on the Indian Economy. https://www.think-asia.org/handle/11540/12242

Katoch, S., Singh, V., & Tiwary, U. S. (2022). Indian Sign Language recognition system using SURF with SVM and CNN. *Array (New York, N.Y.)*, *14*, 100141. doi:10.1016/j.array.2022.100141

Kaur, A., & Singh, M. (2018). Artificial intelligence: A review of concepts, approaches, and applications. *International Journal of Advanced Scientific Research and Management*, *3*(1), 28–37.

Kaur, G., Sinha, R., Tiwari, P. K., Yadav, S. K., Pandey, P., Raj, R., Vashisth, A., & Rakhra, M. (2022). Face mask recognition system using CNN model. *Neuroscience Informatics (Online)*, *2*(3), 100035. doi:10.1016/j.neuri.2021.100035 PMID:36819833

Kawai, S., & Matsuura, S. (2015). Model driven development by separating concerns in UML requirements specification. *Proceedings – International Computer Software and Applications Conference, 3*.

Kelly, D., & Hammoudeh, M. (2018, June). Optimisation of the public key encryption infrastructure for the internet of things. In *Proceedings of the 2nd International Conference on Future Networks and Distributed Systems* (pp. 1-5). ACM. 10.1145/3231053.3231098

Khan, S., Nazir, S., García-Magariño, I., & Hussain, A. (2021). Deep learning-based urban big data fusion in smart cities: Towards traffic monitoring and flow-preserving fusion. *Computers & Electrical Engineering, 89*, 106906. doi:10.1016/j.compeleceng.2020.106906

Kharlamov, A., & Parry, G. (2018). Advanced Supply Chains: Visibility, Blockchain and Human Behaviour. *Contributions to Management Science*, 321–343. doi:10.1007/978-3-319-74304-2_15

Khatoun, R., & Zeadally, S. (2017). Cybersecurity and privacy solutions in smart cities. *IEEE Communications Magazine, 55*(3), 51–59. doi:10.1109/MCOM.2017.1600297CM

Khitskov, E. A., Veretekhina, S. V., Medvedeva, A. V., Mnatsakanyan, O. L., Shmakova, E. G., & Kotenev, A. (2017). Digital transformation of society: Problems entering in the digital economy. *Eurasian Journal of Analytical Chemistry, 12*(5), 855–873. doi:10.12973/ejac.2017.00216a

Kim, J. (2020). *Scaling up disruptive agricultural technologies in Africa*. World Bank. doi:10.1596/978-1-4648-1522-5

Kim, J., Kim, J., Kim, H., Shim, M., & Choi, E. (2020). CNN-based network intrusion detection against denial-of-service attacks. *Electronics (Basel), 9*(6), 916. doi:10.3390/electronics9060916

King, R., Dowling, D., & Godfrey, E. (2011). *Pathways from VET awards to engineering degrees: a higher education perspective*. Australian Council of Engineering Deans. https://research.usq.edu.au/item/q0w4v/pathways-from-vet-awards-to-engineering-degrees-a-higher-education-perspective

Kirchengast, T., & Crofts, T. (2019). The legal and policy contexts of "revenge porn" criminalisation: The need for multiple approaches. *Oxford University Commonwealth Law Journal, 19*(1), 1–29. doi:10.1080/14729342.2019.1580518

Kitchenham, B., Pearl Brereton, O., Budgen, D., Turner, M., Bailey, J., & Linkman, S. (2009). Systematic Literature Reviews in Software Engineering – A Systematic Literature Review. *Information and Software Technology, 51*(1), 7–15. doi:10.1016/j.infsof.2008.09.009

Klapez, M., Grazia, C. A., Zennaro, S., Cozzani, M., & Casoni, M. (2018). *First Experiences with Earthcloud, a Low-Cost*. Cloud-Based IoT Seismic Alert System. doi:10.1109/WiMOB.2018.8589155

Klein, C., Schwabe, M., Costa, H., & Sakha, S. (2022, February 11). *Getting the most of the digital transformation*. NIH. doi:10.1787/a74ff800-en

Knight, P., & Walmsley, I. (2019). UK national quantum technology programme. *Quantum Science and Technology, 4*(4), 040502. doi:10.1088/2058-9565/ab4346

Komoróczki, I. (2022). *European Economic Area*. efta.int. https://www.efta.int/sites/default/files/images/22-43-Rev1.26-EEA%20CC%20resolution%20and%20report%20on%20the%20challenges%20and%20opportunities%20of%20greater%20use%20of%20artificial%20intelligence%20in%20working%20life.pdf

Konstantinou, C. (2021). Toward a secure and resilient all-renewable energy grid for smart cities. *IEEE Consumer Electronics Magazine, 11*(1), 33–41. doi:10.1109/MCE.2021.3055492

Korachi, Z., & Bounabat, B. (2020). General Approach for Formulating a Digital Transformation Strategy. *Journal of Computational Science, 16*(4), 493–507. doi:10.3844/jcssp.2020.493.507

Korobko, A. A. (2018). Algorithm of interface generation for model-driven data consolidation system. *RPC 2018. Proceedings of the 3rd Russian-Pacific Conference on Computer Technology and Applications, art. no. 8482134*. IEEE. 10.1109/RPC.2018.8482134

Kourmpetli, S., Falagán, N., Hardman, C., Liu, L., Mead, B., Walsh, L., & Davies, J. (2022). Scaling-up urban agriculture for a healthy, sustainable and resilient food system: The postharvest benefits, challenges and key research gaps. *International Journal of Postharvest Technology and Innovation, 8*(2-3), 145–157. doi:10.1504/IJPTI.2022.121791

Krelina, M. (2021). Quantum technology for military applications. *EPJ Quantum Technology, 8*(1), 24. doi:10.1140/epjqt/s40507-021-00113-y

Kroski, E. (2020). What is a digital breakout game? *Library Technology Reports, 56*(3), 5–7.

Kuadey, N. A. E., Maale, G. T., Kwantwi, T., Sun, G., & Liu, G. (2021). DeepSecure: Detection of distributed denial of service attacks on 5G network slicing—Deep learning approach. *IEEE Wireless Communications Letters, 11*(3), 488–492. doi:10.1109/LWC.2021.3133479

Kucharska, W., & Bedford, D. A. D. (2023). *The KLC Cultures, Tacit Knowledge, and Trust Contribution to Organizational Intelligence Activation*. In proceedings of the 24th European Conference on Knowledge Management Lisbon, Portugal. https://ssrn.com/abstract=4440280 or doi:10.2139/ssrn.4440280

Kuczenski, B., Mutel, C., Srocka, M., Scanlon, K., & Ingwersen, W. (2021). Prototypes for automating product system model assembly. *The International Journal of Life Cycle Assessment, 26*(3), 1–14. doi:10.1007/s11367-021-01870-9 PMID:34017158

Kuldosheva, G. (2022). Challenges and Opportunities for Digital Transformation in the Public Sector in Transition Economies: The Case of Uzbekistan. *Harnessing Digitalization for Sustainable Economic Development, 365*.

KulikL.KorovkinV. (2021). India Goes Digital. From local phenomenon to global influencer. SSRN 3829789.

Kumar, A., & Basu, S. (2022). Can end-user feedback inform 'Responsibilisation' of India's policy landscape for agri-digital transition? *Sociologia Ruralis, 62*(2), 305–334. doi:10.1111/soru.12374

Kumar, A., Bhatia, S., Kaushik, K., Gandhi, S. M., Devi, S. G., Diego, A. D. J., & Mashat, A. (2021). Survey of promising technologies for quantum drones and networks. *IEEE Access : Practical Innovations, Open Solutions, 9*, 125868–125911. doi:10.1109/ACCESS.2021.3109816

Kumar, A., & Sharma, V. (2021). Artificial Intelligence-Driven Knowledge Management for Competitive Advantage: A Study of Indian Companies. *Journal of Management Research, 21*(3), 20–34.

Kumari, A., Tanwar, S., Tyagi, S., & Kumar, N. (2018). Fog computing for Healthcare 4.0 environment: Opportunities and challenges. *Computers & Electrical Engineering, 72*, 1–13. doi:10.1016/j.compeleceng.2018.08.015

Kuriakose, S., & Tiew, H. S. B. M. Z. (2022). *SME Program Efficiency Review.*, doi:10.1596/37137

Kusuma, S., & Viswanath, D. K. (2018). IOT And Big Data Analytics In E-Learning : A Technological Perspective and Review. Research Gate.

Kusumo, A., Reckien, D., & Verplanke, J. (2017). Utilising volunteered geographic information to assess resident's flood evacuation shelters. Case study: Jakarta. *Applied Geography (Sevenoaks, England), 88*, 174–185. doi:10.1016/j.apgeog.2017.07.002

Kuzlu, M., Fair, C., & Guler, O. (2021). *Discover Internet of Things Role of Artificial Intelligence in the Internet of Things (IoT) cybersecurity*. Discov. Internet Things. . doi:10.1007/s43926-020-00001-4

Lafreni'ere, M. A. K., Verner-Filion, J., & Vallerand, R. J. (2012). Development and validation of the gaming motivation scale (GAMS). *Personality and Individual Differences, 53*(7), 827–831. doi:10.1016/j.paid.2012.06.013

Land, R., Beetham, H., Sharpe, R., DeNoyelles, A., Zydney, J., Chen, B., Sendall, P., Shaw, R., Round, K., Larkin, J., Barczyk, C. C., Duncan, D. G., Abes, E. S., Jones, S. R., McEwen, M. K., Boon, S., Sinclair, C., Borup, J., West, R. E., & Tu, C.-H. (2013). Social Presence and Cognitive Engagement in Online Learning Environments. *Language Learning & Technology, 10*(1), 1–22. doi:10.1111/j.1467-8527.2008.00397_1.x

Langerak, F., & Jan Hultink, E. (2006). The impact of product innovativeness on the link between development speed and new product profitability. *Journal of Product Innovation Management, 23*(3), 203–214. doi:10.1111/j.1540-5885.2006.00194.x

Lang, G., & Triantoro, T. (2022). Upskilling and reskilling for the future of work: A typology of digital skills initiatives. *Information Systems Education Journal, 20*(4), 97–106. https://files.eric.ed.gov/fulltext/EJ1358297.pdf

LaPaglia, J. A. (2020). Escape the evil professor! Escape room review activity. *Teaching of Psychology, 47*(2), 141–146. doi:10.1177/0098628320901383

Law Audience. (2020, June 6). *Volume 2 & Issue 2» The Crime of Privacy Invasion-An Intricate Analysis*. Lawaudience.com. https://www.lawaudience.com/the-crime-of-privacy-invasion-an-intricate-analysis/

Lee, C. Y., & Tang, C. S. (2020). Supply chain visibility and customer satisfaction: The moderating role of demand uncertainty. *Journal of Operations Management, 65*(1), 32–48.

Lee, I., & Lee, K. (2015). The Internet of Things (IoT): Applications, investments, and challenges for enterprises. *Business Horizons, 58*(4), 431–440. doi:10.1016/j.bushor.2015.03.008

Lee, J. Y., Jeong, B., & Joo, Y. H. (2020). Artificial intelligence (AI) and machine learning (ML) in supply chain management: A comprehensive review. *Sustainability, 12*(6), 2353.

Lee, S. (2022). A study on classification and detection of small moths using CNN model. *Computers, Materials & Continua, 71*(1), 1987–1998. doi:10.32604/cmc.2022.022554

Leiblein, M. J. (2011). *What do resource-and capability-based theories propose?* Research Gate.

Lembke, J. (2021, December 7). *The Role of IoT in Disaster Management & Emergency Planning - Tele2 IoT*. Tele2 IoT. https://tele2iot.com/article/the-role-of-iot-in-disaster-management-emergency-planning/

Le, T. T., Sit, H. H. W., & Chen, S. (2023). How Vietnamese foreign language teachers survive and thrive: Tracing successful online teaching during the COVID-19 pandemic. In *The Post-pandemic Landscape of Education and Beyond* (pp. 112–136). Innovation and Transformation. doi:10.1007/978-981-19-9217-9_8

Letheren, K., & Glavas, C. (2017). Embracing the bots: How direct to consumer advertising is about to change forever. QUT Business School, 11–13. https://eprints.qut.edu.au/107945/

Li, Z., Fang, L., Sun, X., & Peng, W. (2021). 5G IoT-based geohazard monitoring and early warning system and its application. *Eurasip Journal on Wireless Communications and Networking, 2021*(1). doi:10.1186/s13638-021-02033-y

Liao, Q. V., Davis, M., Geyer, W., Muller, M., & Shami, N. S. (2016). What can you do? Studying social-agent orientation and agent proactive interactions with an agent for employees. *DIS 2016 - Proceedings of the 2016 ACM Conference on Designing Interactive Systems: Fuse*, (pp. 264–275). ACM. 10.1145/2901790.2901842

Li, D., Li, X., Liu, J., & Liu, Z. (2008). Validation of requirement models by automatic prototyping. *Innovations in Systems and Software Engineering, 4*(3), 241–248. doi:10.1007/s11334-008-0062-3

Liebowitz, J., & Beckman, T. (Eds.). (1998). *Knowledge organizations: What every manager should know.* CRC Press.

Li, J., Gan, W., Gui, Y., Wu, Y., & Yu, P. S. (2022, October). Frequent itemset mining with local differential privacy. In *Proceedings of the 31st ACM International Conference on Information & Knowledge Management* (pp. 1146-1155). ACM. 10.1145/3511808.3557327

Li, J., Zhao, Z., & Li, R. (2018). Machine learning-based IDS for software-defined 5G network. *IET Networks, 7*(2), 53–60. doi:10.1049/iet-net.2017.0212

Li, L., Lu, R., Choo, K. K. R., Datta, A., & Shao, J. (2016). Privacy-preserving-outsourced association rule mining on vertically partitioned databases. *IEEE Transactions on Information Forensics and Security, 11*(8), 1847–1861. doi:10.1109/TIFS.2016.2561241

Li, L., Su, F., Zhang, W., & Mao, J. Y. (2018). Digital transformation by SME entrepreneurs: A capability perspective. *Information Systems Journal, 28*(6), 1129–1157. doi:10.1111/isj.12153

Lim, A. H., Apaza, P., and Horj, A. (2017). Trade in Education Services and the SDGs. *WIN–WIN*, 337.

Li, S., Da Xu, L., & Zhao, S. (2018). 5G Internet of Things: A survey. *Journal of Industrial Information Integration, 10*, 1–9. doi:10.1016/j.jii.2018.01.005

Li, S., & Lin, B. (2006). Accessing information sharing and information quality in Supply chain management. *Decision Support Systems, 42*(3), 1641–1656. doi:10.1016/j.dss.2006.02.011

Littlejohn, A., & Pammer-Schindler, V. (2022). Technologies for professional learning. In *Research Approaches on Workplace Learning: Insights from a Growing Field* (pp. 321–346). Springer International Publishing. doi:10.1007/978-3-030-89582-2_15

Liu, R. W., Yuan, W., Chen, X., & Lu, Y. (2021). An enhanced CNN-enabled learning method for promoting ship detection in maritime surveillance system. *Ocean Engineering, 235*, 109435. doi:10.1016/j.oceaneng.2021.109435

Liu, X., Li, X., Chen, X., Liu, Z., & Li, S. (2018). Location correction technique based on mobile communication base station for earthquake population heat map. *Geodesy and Geodynamics, 9*(5), 388–397. doi:10.1016/j.geog.2018.01.003

Li, Y., & Liu, Q. (2021). A comprehensive review study of cyber-attacks and cyber security; Emerging trends and recent developments. *Energy Reports, 7*, 8176–8186. doi:10.1016/j.egyr.2021.08.126

Li, Y., Wang, Z., & Shang, J. (2021). Supply chain visibility and sustainability performance: Evidence from the fashion industry. *Journal of Business Ethics, 169*(1), 85–101.

Li, Z., Wang, F., & Wang, N. (2021). Lidar r-cnn: An efficient and universal 3d object detector. In *Proceedings of the IEEE/CVF Conference on Computer Vision and Pattern Recognition* (pp. 7546-7555). IEEE. 10.1109/CVPR46437.2021.00746

Lopez, G., García-Borgoñon, L., Vegas, S., Escalona, M. J., & Juristo, N. (2020). Cultivating Practitioners for Software Engineering Experiments in industry. Best Practices learned from the experience" Advancements in Model-Driven Architecture in Software Engineering. IGI Global.

López-Pernas, S., Gordillo, A., Barra, E., & Quemada, J. (2019). Analyzing learning effectiveness and students' perceptions of an educational escape room in a programming course in higher education. *IEEE Access : Practical Innovations, Open Solutions, 7*, 184221–184234. doi:10.1109/ACCESS.2019.2960312

López-Pernas, S., Gordillo, A., Barra, E., & Quemada, J. (2019b). Examining the use of an educational escape room for teaching programming in a higher education setting. *IEEE Access : Practical Innovations, Open Solutions, 7*, 31723–31737. doi:10.1109/ACCESS.2019.2902976

Lucia, P., Schmid, B. F., Wolfgang, M., & Müller, J. P.LUCIA. (2003). Editorial: Software Agents. *Electronic Markets*, *13*(1), 1–2. doi:10.1080/1019678032000062195

Maamar, Z., Baker, T., Sellami, M., Asim, M., Ugljanin, E., & Faci, N. (2018). Cloud vs edge: Who serves the Internet-of-Things better? *Internet Technology Letters*, *1*(5), e66. doi:10.1002/itl2.66

Ma, C. (2021). Smart city and cyber-security; technologies used, leading challenges and future recommendations. *Energy Reports*, *7*, 7999–8012. doi:10.1016/j.egyr.2021.08.124

Machine Health & Supply Chain Reliability . (n.d.). Colgate-Palmolive. https://www.colgatepalmolive.com/enus/who-we-are/stories/machine-health-supply-chain-reliability

Madakam, S., Lake, V., Lake, V., & Lake, V. (2015). Internet of Things (IoT): A literature review. *Journal of Computer and Communications*, *3*(05), 164–173. doi:10.4236/jcc.2015.35021

Mahiddin, N. A., Sarkar, N. I., & Cusack, B. (2017). An Internet Access Solution: MANET Routing and a Gateway Selection Approach for Disaster Scenarios. *The Review of Socionetwork Strategies*, *11*(1), 47–64. doi:10.1007/s12626-017-0004-3

Mahmud, R., Kotagiri, R., & Buyya, R. (2018). Fog Computing: A taxonomy, survey and future directions. In Internet of Things (Vol. 0, Issue 9789811058608). doi:10.1007/978-981-10-5861-5_5

Maier, R. (2007). *Knowledge management systems: Information and communication technologies for knowledge management*. Springer Science & Business Media.

Maier, R., & Peffers, K. (1998). The role of knowledge management systems in e-commerce. *Journal of Knowledge Management*, *2*(2), 79–90.

Majam, T., & Uwizeyimana, D. E. (2018). Aligning economic development as a priority of the integrated development plan to the annual budget in the City of Johannesburg Metropolitan Municipality. *African Journal of Public Affairs*, *10*(4), 138–166.

Makri, A., Vlachopoulos, D., & Martina, R. A. (2021). Digital escape rooms as innovative pedagogical tools in education: A systematic literature review. *Sustainability (Basel)*, *13*(8), 4587. doi:10.3390/su13084587

Mamdouh, M., Elrukhsi, M. A. I., & Khattab, A. (2018). Securing the Internet of Things and Wireless Sensor Networks via Machine Learning : A Survey. *Int. Conf. Comput. Appl.*, (pp. 215–218). IEEE. 10.1109/COMAPP.2018.8460440

Mania, K. (2020). The Legal Implications and Remedies Concerning Revenge Porn and Fake Porn: A Common Law Perspective. *Sexuality & Culture*, *24*(6), 2079–2097. doi:10.1007/s12119-020-09738-0

Manimozhi, N., Suganya, R., Pandian, P. S., Suguna, G., Devi, R. S., & Ramya, S. (2023). A Compressive Review Models For Big Data Analytics Relies On. *Artificial Intelligence*, *01*, 415–420.

Mao, J., Niu, M., Bai, H., Liang, X., Xu, H., & Xu, C. (2021). Pyramid r-cnn: Towards better performance and adaptability for 3d object detection. In *Proceedings of the IEEE/CVF International Conference on Computer Vision* (pp. 2723-2732). IEEE. 10.1109/ICCV48922.2021.00272

Marcella, A. Jr, & Menendez, D. (2010). *Cyber forensics: a field manual for collecting, examining, and preserving evidence of computer crimes*. Auerbach Publications. doi:10.1201/9780849383298

Martínez, P. L., Dintén, R., Drake, J. M., & Zorrilla, M. (2021). A big data-centric architecture metamodel for Industry 4.0. *Future Generation Computer Systems*, *125*, 263–284. doi:10.1016/j.future.2021.06.020

Mathur, S., & Gupta, U. (Eds.). (2016). Transforming higher education through digitalization: insights. Learning, 3(1), 1-20.

Mathur, A., & Agrawal, S. (2018). Artificial Intelligence and Knowledge Management in Indian Context. In *Proceedings of International Conference on Advances in Computer Engineering and Applications* (pp. 35-39). IEEE.

Matt, C., Hess, T., & Benlian, A. (2015). Digital transformation strategies. *Business & Information Systems Engineering*, *57*(5), 339–343. doi:10.1007/s12599-015-0401-5

Mátyás, T. B. (2022). *Industry 4.0: Challenges and Opportunities for V4 Countries*. v4cooperation.eu, https://v4cooperation.eu/wp-content/uploads/2022/05/Policy-Paper-3-Matyas.pdf

Mavroeidis, V., Vishi, K., Zych, M. D., & Jøsang, A. (2018). The impact of quantum computing on present cryptography. *arXiv preprint arXiv:1804.00200.*

McLaren, P. G., Mills, A. J., & Durepos, G. (2009). Disseminating Drucker. *Journal of Management History*, *15*(4), 388–403. doi:10.1108/17511340910987310

McLaughlin, K. (2021). *McKinsey on Investing.*, dln.jaipuria.ac.in, http://dln.jaipuria.ac.in:8080/jspui/bitstream/123456789/10841/1/Mckinsey-on-investing-issue-7-november-2021.pdf

McTear, M., Callejas, Z., & Griol, D. (2016). The conversational interface: Past and. *The Conversational Interface: Talking to Smart Devices*, 1–422.

Medhi Thies, I., Menon, N., Magapu, S., Subramony, M., & O'Neill, J. (2017). How do you want your chatbot? An exploratory Wizard-of-Oz study with young, Urban Indians. Lecture Notes in Computer Science (Including Subseries Lecture Notes in Artificial Intelligence and Lecture Notes in Bioinformatics). Springer. doi:10.1007/978-3-319-67744-6_28

Mendoza, J. M. F., & Ibarra, D. (2023). Technology-enabled circular business models for the hybridisation of wind farms: Integrated wind and solar energy, power-to-gas and power-to-liquid systems. *Sustainable Production and Consumption*, *36*, 308–327. doi:10.1016/j.spc.2023.01.011

Menon, S., & Guan Siew, T. (2012). Key challenges in tackling economic and cyber crimes: Creating a multilateral platform for international co-operation. *Journal of Money Laundering Control*, *15*(3), 243–256. doi:10.1108/13685201211238016

Merx, S., Veldkamp, A., & van Winden, J. (2020). *Educational escape rooms: Challenges in aligning game and education.*

Meuter, M. L., Bitner, M. J., Ostrom, A. L., & Brown, S. W. (2005). Choosing among alternative service delivery modes: An investigation of customer trial of self-service technologies. *Journal of Marketing*, *69*(2), 61–83. doi:10.1509/jmkg.69.2.61.60759

Miao, G., Hongxing, L., Songyu, X., & Juncai, L. (2018). Research on User Interface Transformation Method Based on MDA. *Proceedings – 2017 16th Int. Symposium on Distributed Computing and Applications to Business, Engineering and Science, DCABES 2017*, (pp. 150-153). IEEE.

Michiels, E. (2017). Modelling Chatbots with a cognitive system allows for a differentiating user experience. *CEUR Workshop Proceedings*, *2027*, 70–78.

Mihály, F., & Lucia, M. K. (2016). *OECD Reviews of Vocational Education and Training A Skills beyond School Review of the Slovak Republic*. OECD Publishing.

Miller, E. A., & West, D. M. (2009). Where's the revolution? Digital technology and health care in the internet age. *Journal of Health Politics, Policy and Law*, *34*(2), 261–284. doi:10.1215/03616878-2008-046 PMID:19276318

Miller, J. F. (2013). *Supply chain attack framework and attack patterns*. The MITRE Corporation. doi:10.21236/ADA610495

Mindell, D. A., & Reynolds, E. (2022). *The work of the future: Building better jobs in an age of intelligent machines*. MIT Press.

Mishra, D. K., Ray, P. K., Li, L., Zhang, J., Hossain, M., & Mohanty, A. (2022). Resilient control based frequency regulation scheme of isolated microgrids considering cyber attack and parameter uncertainties. *Applied Energy, 306*, 118054. doi:10.1016/j.apenergy.2021.118054

Mitchell, D., Blanche, J., Harper, S., Lim, T., Gupta, R., Zaki, O., & Flynn, D. (2022). A review: Challenges and opportunities for artificial intelligence and robotics in the offshore wind sector. *Energy and AI, 100146*.

Modgil, S., Singh, R. K., & Hannibal, C. (2022). Artificial intelligence for supply chain resilience: Learning from Covid-19. *International Journal of Logistics Management, 33*(4), 1246–1268. doi:10.1108/IJLM-02-2021-0094

Moffitt, K. C., Rozario, A. M., & Vasarhelyi, M. A. (2018). Robotic process automation for auditing. *Journal of Emerging Technologies in Accounting, 15*(1), 1–10. doi:10.2308/jeta-10589

Mohammadi, M., Member, G. S., Al-fuqaha, A., & Member, S. (2018). Deep Learning for IoT Big Data and Streaming Analytics. *Survey (London, England), X*(X), 1–40. doi:10.1109/COMST.2018.2844341

Mohapatra, S., & Misra, S. (2018). Artificial Intelligence and Knowledge Management: A Study of Indian Retail Sector. In *Proceedings of International Conference on Computer Science, Engineering and Applications* (pp. 31-36). IEEE.

Mohurle, S., & Patil, M. (2017). A brief study of wannacry threat: Ransomware attack 2017. *International journal of advanced research in computer science, 8*(5), 1938-1940.

Mollenkopf, D., Stolze, H., & Tate, W. L. (2017). Supply chain visibility: Understanding the business value, components, and maturity levels. *Journal of Business Logistics, 38*(1), 6–25.

Monaghan, S. R., & Nicholson, S. (2017). Bringing escape room concepts to pathophysiology case studies. *HAPS Educator, 21*(2), 49–65. doi:10.21692/haps.2017.015

Monreale, A., Rinzivillo, S., Pratesi, F., Giannotti, F., & Pedreschi, D. (2014). Privacy-by-design in big data analytics and social mining. *EPJ Data Science, 3*(1), 1–26. doi:10.1140/epjds/s13688-014-0010-4

Monshi, M. M. A., Poon, J., Chung, V., & Monshi, F. M. (2021). CovidXrayNet: Optimizing data augmentation and CNN hyperparameters for improved COVID-19 detection from CXR. *Computers in Biology and Medicine, 133*, 104375. doi:10.1016/j.compbiomed.2021.104375 PMID:33866253

Montserrat, G. (2017). *International Summit on the Teaching Profession Empowering and Enabling Teachers to Improve Equity and Outcomes for All*. OECD Publishing.

Moore, S. J., Nugent, C. D., Zhang, S., & Cleland, I. (2020). IoT reliability : A review leading to 5 key research directions. *CCF Trans. Pervasive Comput. Interact., 2*(3), 147–163. doi:10.1007/s42486-020-00037-z

Morvan, L. (2016). Data: The Fuel of the Digital Economy and SME Growth. *Accenture Report*.

Mouradian, C., Naboulsi, D., Yangui, S., Glitho, R. H., Morrow, M. J., & Polakos, P. A. (2018). A Comprehensive Survey on Fog Computing: State-of-the-Art and Research Challenges. In IEEE Communications Surveys and Tutorials, 20(1). IEEE. doi:10.1109/COMST.2017.2771153

Mourtzis, D., Angelopoulos, J., & Panopoulos, N. (2022). Operator 5.0: A survey on enabling technologies and a framework for digital manufacturing based on extended reality. *Journal of Machine Engineering, 22*(1), 43–69. doi:10.36897/jme/147160

Muhammad, K., Ullah, A., Imran, A. S., Sajjad, M., Kiran, M. S., Sannino, G., & de Albuquerque, V. H. C. (2021). Human action recognition using attention based LSTM network with dilated CNN features. *Future Generation Computer Systems, 125*, 820–830. doi:10.1016/j.future.2021.06.045

Mujiono, M. N. (2021). The shifting role of accountants in the era of digital disruption. *International Journal of Multidisciplinary: Applied Business and Education Research*, 2(11), 1259–1274. doi:10.11594/10.11594/ijmaber.02.11.18

Mukherjee, M., Matam, R., Shu, L., Maglaras, L., Ferrag, M. A., Choudhury, N., & Kumar, V. (2017). Security and Privacy in Fog Computing: Challenges. *IEEE Access : Practical Innovations, Open Solutions*, 5, 19293–19304. doi:10.1109/ACCESS.2017.2749422

Mukherjee, M., Shu, L., & Wang, D. (2018). Survey of fog computing: Fundamental, network applications, and research challenges. *IEEE Communications Surveys and Tutorials*, 20(3), 1826–1857. doi:10.1109/COMST.2018.2814571

Mustafaoglu, A. (2022). *Imlementing digital transformation strategy the case of a local Turkish bank* [Master's thesis, Işık Üniversitesi]. https://acikerisim.isikun.edu.tr/xmlui/handle/11729/4848

Mzara, O. (2019). *Changing youth perceptions: exploring enablers of diffusion and adoption of agricultural innovations in South Africa* [Doctoral dissertation, University of Pretoria].

Nair, M. M., & Tyagi, A. K. (2021). Privacy: History, statistics, policy, laws, preservation and threat analysis. *Journal of information assurance & security, 16*(1).

Najafi, S. E., Nozari, H., & Edalatpanah, S. A. (2022, November 30). Artificial Intelligence of Things (AIoT) and Industry 4.0–Based Supply Chain (FMCG Industry). *A Roadmap for Enabling Industry 4.0 by Artificial Intelligence,* (pp. 31–41). Wiley. doi:10.1002/9781119905141.ch3

Narula, J. (2022). *An exploratory study of factors influencing the attraction and retention of skilled employees in the digital sector in Hawke's Bay* [Master's thesis, Research Bank]. https://researchbank.ac.nz/handle/10652/5783

Nasif, A., Othman, Z. A., & Sani, N. S. (2021). The deep learning solutions on lossless compression methods for alleviating data load on IoT nodes in smart cities. *Sensors (Basel)*, 21(12), 4223. doi:10.3390/s21124223 PMID:34203024

Next-gen Digital Supply Chain Planning & Optimization. (n.d.). ITC Infotech. https://www.itcinfotech.com/capabilities/supply-chain-management/

Ng, I. Y., Lim, S. S., & Pang, N. (2022). Making universal digital access universal: Lessons from COVID-19 in Singapore. *Universal Access in the Information Society*, 1–11. PMID:35440934

Nguyen, V., Duong, T. Q., & Vien, Q. (2021). Editorial : Emerging Techniques and Applications for 5G Networks and Beyond, (pp. 1984–1986). Research Gate.

Nguyen-Duc, A., Wang, X., & Abrahamsson, P. (2017). What influences the speed of prototyping? An empirical investigation of twenty software startups. In *International Conference on Agile Software Development*. Springer. 10.1007/978-3-319-57633-6_2

Nguyen, N. D., Phan, L. A., Park, D. H., Kim, S., & Kim, T. (2020). ElasticFog: Elastic resource provisioning in container-based fog computing. *IEEE Access : Practical Innovations, Open Solutions*, 8, 183879–183890. Advance online publication. doi:10.1109/ACCESS.2020.3029583

Nichols, C. (2021). Professional services companies need to practise what they preach: the need to fast-track digital transformation in the industry. *Strategic HR Review*. doi:10.1108/SHR-09-2021-0046

Nicholson, S. (2015). *Peeking behind the locked door: A survey of escape room facilities.*

Nicole Radziwill and Morgan Benton. (2017). *Evaluating Quality of Chatbots and Intelligent Conversational Agents.* Arxiv.Org.

Ningsih, S. J., Wadjdi, A. F., & Budiyanto, S. (2022). The Importance of Quantum Technology in National Defense in the Future. *The International Journal of Business Management and Technology, 6*(1).

Nonaka, I., & Takeuchi, H. (1995). *The knowledge-creating company: How Japanese companies create the dynamics of innovation.* Oxford University Press. doi:10.1093/oso/9780195092691.001.0001

Nottingham, K. D., & Cardozo, I. (2019). The Role of International Consumer Policy in Fostering Innovation and Empowering Consumers to Make Informed Choices. *Ind. Int'l and Comp. L. Rev., 30*, 1.

Novaes Neto, N., Madnick, S., de Paula, M. G., & Malara Borges, N. (2020). *A case study of the capital one data breach.* Research Gate.

Nyangaresi, V. O. (2022). Terminal independent security token derivation scheme for ultra-dense IoT networks. *Array (New York, N.Y.), 15*, 100210. doi:10.1016/j.array.2022.100210

Oden, R. V., Militello, L. G., Ross, K. G., & Lopez, C. E. (2012). Four Key Challenges in Disaster Response. *Proceedings of the Human Factors and Ergonomics Society . . . Annual Meeting, 56*(1), 488–492. 10.1177/1071181312561050

OECD. (2002). *Economic surveys and data analysis CIRET Conference proceedings, Paris 2000: CIRET Conference proceedings, Paris 2000.* OECD. https://books.google.at/books?id=CVTWAgAAQBAJ

OECD. (2018). *Maintaining competitive conditions in the era of digitalisation.* OECD. https://www.oecd.org/g20/Maintaining-competitive-conditions-in-era-of-digitalisation-OECD.pdf

Oeij, P., Hulsegge, G., Kirov, V., Pomares, E., Dhondt, S., Götting, A., & Deliverable, W. P. (2022). *Policy paper: digital transformation and regional policy options for inclusive growth.*

Ogata, S., & Matsuura, S. (2008). Scenario-based automatic prototype generation. *Proceedings – International Computer Software and Applications Conference.* IEEE.

Ogata, S., & Matsuura, S. (2010). "Evaluation of a use-case-driven requirements analysis tool employing web UI prototype generation" WSEAS. *Transactions on Information Science and Applications, 7*(2), 273–282.

Ometov, A., Molua, O. L., Komarov, M., & Nurmi, J. (2022). A Survey of Security in Cloud, Edge, and Fog Computing. In Sensors (Vol. 22, Issue 3). doi:10.3390/s22030927

Oosthuizen, A. (2021). *HSRC Review 19 (1). March: 4-46.* HSRC. repository.hsrc.ac.za, https://repository.hsrc.ac.za/bitstream/handle/20.500.11910/18961/12807.pdf?sequence=1

Oran, A. C., Valentim, N., Santos, G., & Conte, T. (2019). Why use case specifications are hard to use in generating prototypes? *IET Software, 13*(6), 510–517. doi:10.1049/iet-sen.2018.5239

Osterloh, M., & Frey, B. S. (2000). Motivation, knowledge transfer, and organizational forms. *Organization Science, 11*(5), 538–550. doi:10.1287/orsc.11.5.538.15204

Ouichka, O., Echtioui, A., & Hamam, H. (2022). Deep Learning Models for Predicting Epileptic Seizures Using iEEG Signals. *Electronics (Basel), 11*(4), 605. doi:10.3390/electronics11040605

Oyinlola, M., Schröder, P., Whitehead, T., Kolade, O., Wakunuma, K., Sharifi, S., Rawn, B., Odumuyiwa, V., Lendelvo, S., Brighty, G., Tijani, B., Jaiyeola, T., Lindunda, L., Mtonga, R., & Abolfathi, S. (2022). Digital innovations for transitioning to circular plastic value chains in Africa. *Africa Journal of Management, 8*(1), 83–108. doi:10.1080/23322373.2021.1999750

Paffenholz, G. (1998). Krisenhafte Entwicklungen in mittelständischen *Unternehmen: Ursachenanalyse und Implikationen für die Beratung.* Ifm.

Pagani, S. (2018). S. M. P. D, A. Jantsch, and S. Member, "Machine Learning for Power, Energy, and Thermal Management on Multi-core Processors. *Survey (London, England), 0070*(JULY), 1–17. doi:10.1109/TCAD.2018.2878168

Pakhare, P. S., Krishnan, S., & Charniya, N. N. (2021). A survey on recent advances in cyber assault detection using machine learning and deep learning. *Innovative Data Communication Technologies and Application: Proceedings of ICIDCA 2020*, (pp. 571-582). IEEE.

Pandit, M. K., Naaz, R., & Chishti, M. A. (2018). Distributed iot analytics across edge, fog and cloud. *2018 Fourth International Conference on Research in Computational Intelligence and Communication Networks (ICRCICN)*, (pp. 27–32). IEEE. 10.1109/ICRCICN.2018.8718738

Panetta, K. (2016). *Artificial intelligence, machine learning, and smart things promise an intelligent future.* Gartner. https://www.gartner.com/smarterwithgartner/gartners-top-10-technology-trends-2017/

Pan, J. W., Yuan, Z. S., Zhang, Y., Zhang, C., Zhao, Y. A., & Zeng, B. (2017). Experimental quantum secure direct communication with single photons. *Light, Science & Applications, 7*(1), 17117.

Papathanasiou, A., Gunasekaran, A., Dubey, R., & Fosso Wamba, S. (2017). Big data and analytics in operations and supply chain management: Managerial aspects and practical challenges. *Production Planning and Control, 28*(11-12), 929–932.

Pareek, K., Tiwari, P. K., & Bhatnagar, V. (2021). Fog Computing in Healthcare: A Review. *IOP Conference Series. Materials Science and Engineering, 1099*(1), 012025. doi:10.1088/1757-899X/1099/1/012025

Parida, S., & Bhattacherjee, A. (2019). Artificial Intelligence and Knowledge Management in Indian Hospitals. In *Proceedings of International Conference on Advances in Computing and Communication Engineering* (pp. 361-368). IEEE.

Park, J. H., Rathore, S., Singh, S. K., Salim, M. M., Azzaoui, A. E., Kim, T. W., & Park, J. H. (2021). A comprehensive survey on core technologies and services for 5G security: Taxonomies, issues, and solutions. *Hum.-Centric Comput. Inf. Sci, 11*(3).

Patel, K. K., Patel, S. M., & Scholar, P. (2016). Internet of things-IOT: definition, characteristics, architecture, enabling technologies, application & future challenges. *International journal of engineering science and computing, 6*(5).

Patel, O. P., Bharill, N., Tiwari, A., Patel, V., Gupta, O., Cao, J., Li, J., & Prasad, M. (2019). Advanced quantum based neural network classifier and its application for objectionable web content filtering. *IEEE Access : Practical Innovations, Open Solutions, 7*, 98069–98082. doi:10.1109/ACCESS.2019.2926989

Pathak, S. (2013). *Evolution in generations of cellular mobile communication.* Master of Science in Cyber Law and Information Security. https://medium.com/data-science-365/overview-of-a-neural-networks-learning-process-61690a502fa

Patra, S., & Rath, S. K. (2019). Artificial Intelligence and Knowledge Management: A Case Study of Indian Pharmaceutical Industry. In *Proceedings of International Conference on Computational Intelligence and Data Science* (pp. 183-190). IEEE.

Pattnaik, P. K., & Satpathy, M. (2020). Knowledge Management through Artificial Intelligence in Indian Organizations. *International Journal of Emerging Technologies in Engineering Research, 8*(7), 1–5.

Paymode, A. S., & Malode, V. B. (2022). Transfer learning for multi-crop leaf disease image classification using convolutional neural network VGG. *Artificial Intelligence in Agriculture, 6*, 23–33. doi:10.1016/j.aiia.2021.12.002

Pearson, A. (2019). Personalisation the artificial intelligence way. *Journal of Digital and Social Media Marketing, 7*(3), 245–269.

Peleg, R., Yayon, M., Katchevich, D., Moria-Shipony, M., & Blonder, R. (2019). A lab-based chemical escape room: Educational, mobile, and fun! *Journal of Chemical Education, 96*(5), 955–960. doi:10.1021/acs.jchemed.8b00406

Peng, G., Xia, Y., Zhang, X., & Bai, L. (2018). UAV-Aided Networks for Emergency Communications in Areas with Unevenly Distributed Users. *Journal of Communications and Information Networks, 3*(4), 23–32. doi:10.1007/s41650-018-0034-1

Pereira, M. J., Coheur, L., Fialho, P., & Ribeiro, R. (2019). Chatbots' greetings to human-computer communication. *CEUR Workshop Proceedings, 2390*(1994), 61–66.

Petrika-Lindroos, I. (2022). *Unlocking the power of AI in HR: how Artificial Intelligence can elevate the HR strategy in knowledge-based organizations.*

Pham, Q., Fang, F., Ha, V. N., Piran, M. J., Le, M., Le, L. B., Hwang, W.-J., & Ding, Z. (2020). A survey of multi-access edge computing in 5G and beyond: Fundamentals, technology integration, and state-of-the-art. *IEEE Access : Practical Innovations, Open Solutions, 8*, 116974–117017. doi:10.1109/ACCESS.2020.3001277

Phifer, L. (2017) What's the diference between licensed and unlicensed wireless? *TechTarget.* https://searchnetworking.techtarget.com/answer/Whats-the-diference-between-licensed-and-unlicensed-wireless

Pinto, T. D., Gonçalves, W. I., & Costa, P. V. (2019). User interface prototype generation from agile requirements specifications written in Concordia. *Proceedings of the 25th Brazilian Symposium on Multimedia and the Web, WebMedia 2019*, (pp. 61-64). ACM. 10.1145/3323503.3360639

Pisano, G. P. (2019). The hard truth about innovative. *Harvard Business Review, 97*(1), 62–71.

Plass, J. L., Homer, B. D., & Kinzer, C. K. (2015). Foundations of game-based learning. *Educational Psychologist, 50*(4), 258–283. doi:10.1080/00461520.2015.1122533

Plattner, H., Meinel, C., & Weinberg, U. (2009). Design-thinking. *Landsberg am Lech.* Mi-Fachverlag.

Ponnana, R. K., & Uppalapati, N. (2022). *Digital Transformation of IKEA's Supply Chain during and after the pandemic.* Diva Portal. https://www.diva-portal.org/smash/record.jsf?pid=diva2:1673117

Pournader, M., Ghaderi, H., Hassanzadegan, A., & Fahimnia, B. (2021). Artificial intelligence applications in supply chain management. *International Journal of Production Economics, 241*(July), 108250. doi:10.1016/j.ijpe.2021.108250

Prahalad, C. K. (1993). The role of core competencies in the corporation. *Research Technology Management, 36*(6), 40–47. doi:10.1080/08956308.1993.11670940

Prasad, R., Rohokale, V., Prasad, R., & Rohokale, V. (2020). Cyber threats and attack overview. *Cyber Security: The Lifeline of Information and Communication Technology*, 15-31.

Prasanthi, B. (2016). Cyber forensic tools: A review. [IJETT]. *International Journal of Engineering Trends and Technology, 41*(5), 266–271. doi:10.14445/22315381/IJETT-V41P249

Pratt, M. K. (2022). Top 12 most commonly used IoT protocols and standards. *IoT Agenda.* https://www.techtarget.com/iotagenda/tip/Top-12-most-commonly-used-IoT-protocols-and-standards

Preuveneers, D., & Joosen, W. (2016). Privacy-enabled remote health monitoring applications for resource constrained wearable devices. In *Proceedings of the 31st Annual ACM Symposium on Applied Computing* (pp. 119-124). ACM. 10.1145/2851613.2851683

Prodi, E., Tassinari, M., Ferrannini, A., & Rubini, L. (2022). Industry 4.0 policy from a sociotechnical perspective: The case of German competence centres. *Technological Forecasting and Social Change*, *175*, 121341. doi:10.1016/j.techfore.2021.121341

Provost, F., & Fawcett, T. (2013). Data Science and its Relationship to Big Data and Data-Driven Decision Making. *Big Data*, *1*(1), 51–59. doi:10.1089/big.2013.1508 PMID:27447038

Purfield, C., & Rosenberg, C. B. (2010). Adjustment under a currency peg: Estonia, Latvia and Lithuania during the global financial crisis 2008-09. *IMF Working Papers*, 1-34.

Qian, M., & Clark, K. R. (2016). Game-based learning and 21st-century skills: A review of recent research. *Computers in Human Behavior*, *63*, 50–58. doi:10.1016/j.chb.2016.05.023

Qiao, L., Zhao, Y., Li, Z., Qiu, X., Wu, J., & Zhang, C. (2021). Defrcn: Decoupled faster r-cnn for few-shot object detection. In *Proceedings of the IEEE/CVF International Conference on Computer Vision* (pp. 8681-8690). IEEE. 10.1109/ICCV48922.2021.00856

Queiruga-Dios, A., Santos Sánchez, M. J., Queiruga Dios, M., Gayoso Martínez, V., & Hernández Encinas, A. (2020). A virus infected your laptop. let's play an escape game. *Mathematics*, *8*(2), 166. doi:10.3390/math8020166

Quimba, F. M. A., Barral, M. A. A., and Carlos, J. C. T. (2021). Analysis of the FinTech Landscape in the Philippines.

Qureshi, Z., & Woo, C. (2022). Economic paradigms are shifting. Digital technologies are driving trans. *Shifting Paradigms: Growth, Finance, Jobs, and Inequality in the Digital Economy*, 1.

Raab, G., Ajami, R. A., & Goddard, G. J. (2016). *Customer relationship management: A global perspective*. CRC Press. doi:10.4324/9781315575636

Rabiey, M., Welch, T., Sanchez-Lucas, R., Stevens, K., Raw, M., Kettles, G. J., Catoni, M., McDonald, M. C., Jackson, R. W., & Luna, E. (2022). Scaling-up to understand tree–pathogen interactions: A steep, tough climb or a walk in the park? *Current Opinion in Plant Biology*, *68*, 102229. doi:10.1016/j.pbi.2022.102229 PMID:35567925

Raghavan, S. (2013). Digital forensic research: Current state of the art. *Csi Transactions on ICT*, *1*(1), 91–114. doi:10.1007/s40012-012-0008-7

Ramchand, S., Shaikh, S., & Alam, I. (2022a, April). Role of Artificial Intelligence in Software Quality Assurance. *Lecture Notes in Networks and Systems*, *295*, 125–136. doi:10.1007/978-3-030-82196-8_10

Randall, N., Šabanović, S., Milojević, S., & Gupta, A. (2022). Top of the class: Mining product characteristics associated with crowdfunding success and failure of home robots. *International Journal of Social Robotics*, *14*(1), 1–15. doi:10.1007/s12369-021-00776-8

Rani, S., Kataria, A., Chauhan, M., Rattan, P., Kumar, R., & Sivaraman, A. K. (2022). Security and privacy challenges in the deployment of cyber-physical systems in smart city applications: State-of-art work. *Materials Today: Proceedings*, *62*, 4671–4676. doi:10.1016/j.matpr.2022.03.123

Rani, S., Pareek, P. K., Kaur, J., Chauhan, M., & Bhambri, P. (2023, February). Quantum Machine Learning in Healthcare: Developments and Challenges. In *2023 IEEE International Conference on Integrated Circuits and Communication Systems (ICICACS)* (pp. 1-7). IEEE. 10.1109/ICICACS57338.2023.10100075

Ranjith Kumar, R., Ganesh, L. S., & Rajendran, C. (2022). Quality 4.0–a review of and framework for quality management in the digital era. *International Journal of Quality & Reliability Management*, *39*(6), 1385–1411. doi:10.1108/IJQRM-05-2021-0150

Rao, S. K., & Prasad, R. (2018). Impact of 5G technologies on smart city implementation. *Wireless Personal Communications, 100*(1), 161–176. doi:10.1007/s11277-018-5618-4

Rappaport, T. S., Daniels, R. C., Heath, R. W., & Murdock, J. N. (2014). Introduction. In *Millimeter wave wireless communication*. Pearson Education.

Rasheed, Y., Azam, F., Anwar, M. W., & Tufail, H. (2019). A model-driven approach for creating storyboards of web-based user interfaces. *ACM International Conference Proceeding Series*, (pp. 169-173). ACM. 10.1145/3348445.3348465

Rath, R. C., Baral, S. K., Singh, T., & Goel, R. (2022). Role of Artificial Intelligence and Machine Learning in Product Design and Manufacturing. *2022 International Mobile and Embedded Technology Conference, MECON 2022*, (pp. 571–575). IEEE. 10.1109/MECON53876.2022.9752455

Ray, P. P., Mukherjee, M., & Shu, L. (2017). Internet of Things for Disaster Management: State-of-the-Art and Prospects. *IEEE Access : Practical Innovations, Open Solutions, 5*, 18818–18835. doi:10.1109/ACCESS.2017.2752174

Razmjoo, A., Østergaard, P. A., Denai, M., Nezhad, M. M., & Mirjalili, S. (2021). Effective policies to overcome barriers in the development of smart cities. *Energy Research & Social Science, 79*, 102175. doi:10.1016/j.erss.2021.102175

Reddy, T. (2017). *How chatbots can help reduce customer service costs by 30% - Watson Blog*. Ibm.Com. https://www.ibm.com/blogs/watson/2017/10/how-chatbots-reduce-customer-service-costs-by-30-percent/

Ren, X., & Wei, C. (2008). Research on the interaction process in use case for automatic generation of user interface prototype. *Proceedings of the International Conference on Computer and Electrical Engineering*. Research Gate.

Revenge Pornography. (2013). Mtsu.edu. https://www.mtsu.edu/first-amendment/article/1532/revenge-pornography

Reyes, P. M., Visich, J. K., & Jaska, P. (2020, March 1). Managing the Dynamics of New Technologies in the Global Supply Chain. *IEEE Engineering Management Review, 48*(1), 156–162. doi:10.1109/EMR.2020.2968889

Reynolds, E. (2017, March 16). Revenge porn: what it is and how can it be stopped? *Wired*. https://www.wired.co.uk/article/revenge-porn-facebook-social-media

Rifkin, J. (2001). *The Age of Access: The New Culture of Hypercapitalism, Where all of Life is a Paid-For Experience*. Amazon. https://www.amazon.com/The-Age-Access-Hypercapitalism-Experience/dp/1585420824

Rijswijk, K., Bulten, W., Klerkx, L. W. A., den Dulk, L. S., Dessein, J., Debruyne, L., & en Nematoden, O. T. E. (2020). *Digital Transformation: Ongoing digitisation and digitalisation processes*.

Rivero, J. M., Grigera, J., Rossi, G., Luna, E. R., Montero, F., & Gaedke, M. (2014). Mockup-driven development: Providing agile support for model-driven web engineering. *Information and Software Technology, 56*(6), 670–687. doi:10.1016/j.infsof.2014.01.011

Rocha Silva, T., Hak, J.-L., Winkler, M., & Nicolas, O. (2017). A Comparative Study of Milestones for Featuring GUI Prototyping Tools. *Journal of Software Engineering and Applications, 10*(6).

Rodgers, W., Murray, J. M., Stefanidis, A., Degbey, W. Y., & Tarba, S. Y. (2023). An artificial intelligence algorithmic approach to ethical decision-making in human resource management processes. *Human Resource Management Review, 33*(1), 100925. doi:10.1016/j.hrmr.2022.100925

Rong, B., Han, S., Kadoch, M., Chen, X., & Jara, A. (2020). Integration of 5G Networks and Internet of Things for Future Smart City. Hindawi. doi:10.1155/2020/2903525

Rosado da Cruz, A. M., & Pascoal-Faria, J. (2010). A metamodel-based approach for automatic user interface generation. *13th International Conference on Model Driven Engineering Languages and Systems*. Springer. 10.1007/978-3-642-16145-2_18

Rossi, R., & Hirama, I. L. (2015). Characterizing big data management. *Issues Inf Sci Inf Technol, 12*, 165–180.

Roubi, S., Erramdani, M., & Mbarki, S. (2016). Modeling and generating graphical user interface for MVC Rich Internet Application using a model driven approach. *International Conference on Information Technology for Organizations Development*. Research Gate.

Rowan, N. J., Murray, N., Qiao, Y., O'Neill, E., Clifford, E., Barceló, D., & Power, D. M. (2022). Digital transformation of peatland eco-innovations ('Paludiculture'): Enabling a paradigm shift towards the real-time sustainable production of 'green-friendly' products and services. *The Science of the Total Environment, 838*(Pt 3), 156328. doi:10.1016/j.scitotenv.2022.156328 PMID:35649452

Roxburgh, C., Gregory, A., Hall, J., Higgins, S., Titus, A., McGill, D., & Ross, C. (2018). Small research and development activity.

Ruane, E., Farrell, S., & Ventresque, A. (2021). User Perception of Text-Based Chatbot Personality. Lecture Notes in Computer Science (Including Subseries Lecture Notes in Artificial Intelligence and Lecture Notes in Bioinformatics), 12604 LNCS(February), 32–47. Springer. doi:10.1007/978-3-030-68288-0_3

Ruggles, R. (1998). The state of the notion: Knowledge management in practice. *California Management Review, 40*(3), 80–89. doi:10.2307/41165944

Russo, L., Høj, J. C., & Borowiecki, M. (2022). Digitalising the economy in Slovenia. https://www.oecd-ilibrary.org/economics/digitalising-the-economy-in-slovenia_9167aa58-en

Rutovitz, J., Visser, D., Sharpe, S., Taylor, H., Jennings, K., Atherton, A., & Mortimer, G. (2021). Developing the future energy workforce. *Opportunity assessment for RACE for, 2030*.

Rutovitz, J., Visser, D., Sharpe, S., Taylor, H., Jennings, K., Atherton, A., & Mortimer, G. (2021). E3 Opportunity assessment: developing the future energy workforce-final report 2021. https://apo.org.au/sites/default/files/resource-files/2021-10/apo-nid314409.pdf

Saber, W., Eisa, R., & Attia, R. (2022). *Efficient Geospatial Data Analysis Framework in Fog Environment*. IEEE., doi:10.1109/ACCESS.2022.3231787

Sabireen, H., & Neelanarayanan, V. (2021). A Review on Fog Computing: Architecture, Fog with IoT, Algorithms and Research Challenges. *ICT Express, 7*(2), 162–176. doi:10.1016/j.icte.2021.05.004

Sadri, A. A., Rahmani, A. M., Saberikamarposhti, M., & Hosseinzadeh, M. (2022). Data reduction in fog computing and internet of things: A systematic literature survey. *Internet of Things : Engineering Cyber Physical Human Systems, 20*, 100629. Advance online publication. doi:10.1016/j.iot.2022.100629

Saha, H. N., Auddy, S., Pal, S., Kumar, S., Pandey, S., Singh, R., Singh, A. K., Banerjee, S., Ghosh, D., & Saha, S. (2017). Disaster management using Internet of Things. *2017 8th Annual Industrial Automation and Electromechanical Engineering Conference (IEMECON)*. IEEE. 10.1109/IEMECON.2017.8079566

Saha, R. K., Saengudomlert, P., & Aswakul, C. (2016). Evolution towards 5G mobile networks—A survey on enabling technologies. *Engineering Journal (New York), 20*(1), 87–112. doi:10.4186/ej.2016.20.1.87

Saharan, S., & Yadav, B. (2022). Digital and cyber forensics: A contemporary evolution in forensic sciences. In Crime Scene Management within Forensic Science: Forensic Techniques for Criminal Investigations (pp. 267-294). Springer. doi:10.1007/978-981-16-6683-4_11

Saidi, A., Nouali, O., & Amira, A. (2022). SHARE-ABE: An efficient and secure data sharing framework based on ciphertext-policy attribute-based encryption and Fog computing. *Cluster Computing*, *25*(1), 167–185. doi:10.1007/s10586-021-03382-5

Said, O., & Tolba, A. (2021). Accurate performance prediction of IoT communication systems for smart cities: An efficient deep learning based solution. *Sustainable Cities and Society*, *69*, 102830. doi:10.1016/j.scs.2021.102830

Sailer, M., & Homner, L. (2020). The gamification of learning: A meta-analysis. *Educational Psychology Review*, *32*(1), 77–112. doi:10.1007/s10648-019-09498-w

Saito, S., & Hagiwara, J. (2012). System prototype generation tool for requirements review. *Frontiers in Artificial Intelligence and Applications*, *240*, 81–87.

Salahdine, F., Han, T., & Zhang, N. (2023). Security in 5G and beyond recent advances and future challenges. *Security and Privacy*, *6*(1), e271. doi:10.1002/spy2.271

Saleem, J., Hammoudeh, M., Raza, U., Adebisi, B., & Ande, R. (2018, June). IoT standardisation: Challenges, perspectives and solution. In *Proceedings of the 2nd international conference on future networks and distributed systems* (pp. 1-9).ACM.

Sánchez-Villarín, A., Santos-Montano, A., & Enríquez, J. G. (2019). Automatic reuse of prototypes in software engineering: A survey of available tools. *Proceedings of the 15th International Conference on Web Information Systems and Technologies*, (pp. 144-150). ACM. 10.5220/0008352900002366

Sánchez-Villarín, A., Santos-Montano, A., Koch, N., & Lizcano-Casas, D. (2020). Prototypes as starting point in MDE: Proof of concept. *Proceedings of the 16th International Conference on Web Information Systems and Technologies*. ACM. 10.5220/0010213403650372

Sankar, C. S., & Sridevi, R. (2019). Artificial Intelligence and Knowledge Management: A Review. *International Journal of Information Dissemination and Technology*, *9*(4), 243–247.

Santosa, K. I., Lim, C., & Erwin, A. (2016). Analysis of educational institution DNS network traffic for insider threats. *2016 International Conference on Computer, Control, Informatics and its Applications (IC3INA)*. Research Gate.

Santos, G. L., Endo, P. T., Sadok, D., & Kelner, J. (2020). When 5G Meets Deep Learning. *Algorithms*, *13*(9), 1–34. doi:10.3390/a13090208

Saravanan, R., & Ravi, V. (2019). Supply chain integration and performance in FMCG industry. *Journal of Advances in Management Research*, *16*(3), 293–314.

Sarnovský, M., Maslej-Krešňáková, V., & Ivancová, K. (2022). Fake news detection related to the covid-19 in slovak language using deep learning methods. *Acta Polytechnica Hungarica*, *19*(2), 43–57. doi:10.12700/APH.19.2.2022.2.3

Sashi, C. M. (2012). Customer engagement, buyer-seller relationships, and social media. *Management Decision*, *50*(2), 253–272. doi:10.1108/00251741211203551

Saurav, A., Kusek, P., & Albertson, M. (2021). World Bank Investor Confidence Survey. https://openknowledge.worldbank.org/bitstream/handle/10986/36581/World-Bank-Investor-Confidence-Survey-Evidence-from-the-Quarterly-Global-Multinational-Enterprises-Pulse-Survey-for-the-Second-Quarter-of-2021.pdf?sequence=1

Schallmo, D., Williams, C. A., & Boardman, L. (2020). Digital transformation of business models—best practice, enablers, and roadmap. *Digital Disruptive Innovation*, 119-138.

Schallmo, D. R., & Williams, C. A. (2018). History of digital transformation. In *Digital Transformation Now!* (pp. 3–8). Springer. doi:10.1007/978-3-319-72844-5_2

Schildkamp, K., van der Kleij, F. M., Heitink, M. C., Kippers, W. B., & Veldkamp, B. P. (2020). Formative assessment: A systematic review of critical teacher prerequisites for classroom practice. *International Journal of Educational Research*, *103*, 101602. doi:10.1016/j.ijer.2020.101602

Schmidhuber, J. (2015). Deep learning in neural networks: An overview. *Neural Networks*, *61*, 85–117. doi:10.1016/j.neunet.2014.09.003 PMID:25462637

Schreieck, M., Wiesche, M., & Krcmar, H. (2022). From product platform ecosystem to innovation platform ecosystem: An institutional perspective on the governance of ecosystem transformations. *Journal of the Association for Information Systems*, *23*(6), 1354–1385. doi:10.17705/1jais.00764

Schumaker, R. P., Ginsburg, M., Chen, H., & Liu, Y. (2007). An evaluation of the chat and knowledge delivery components of a low-level dialog system:The AZ-ALICE experiment. *Decision Support Systems*, *42*(4), 2236–2246. doi:10.1016/j.dss.2006.07.001

Seetha, J., & Raja, S. S. (2018). Brain tumor classification using convolutional neural networks. *Biomedical & Pharmacology Journal*, *11*(3), 1457–1461. doi:10.13005/bpj/1511

Sengan, S., Subramaniyaswamy, V., Indragandhi, V., Velayutham, P., & Ravi, L. (2021). Detection of false data cyber-attacks for the assessment of security in smart grid using deep learning. *Computers & Electrical Engineering*, *93*, 107211. doi:10.1016/j.compeleceng.2021.107211

Šepec, M. (2019). *Revenge Pornography or Nonconsensual Dissemination of Sexually Explicit Material as a Sexual Offence or as a Privacy Violation Offence*. Zenoob. doi:10.5281/zenodo.3707562

Serrano, J. (2021). Decarbonizing energy intensive industries: country study France. *etui.org*. https://www.etui.org/sites/default/files/2022-08/Decarbonizing%20energy%20intensive%20industries%20-%20France%20-%20Serrano.pdf

Shadbolt, N., O'Hara, K., & Schraefel, M. C. (2006). The experimental evaluation of knowledge management system. *Journal of Knowledge Management*, *10*(4), 101–116.

Shafik, W. (2023b). Cyber Security Perspectives in Public Spaces: Drone Case Study. In Handbook of Research on Cybersecurity Risk in Contemporary Business Systems (pp. 79-97). IGI Global.

Shafik, W. (2023d). IoT-Based Energy Harvesting and Future Research Trends in Wireless Sensor Networks. Handbook of Research on Network-Enabled IoT Applications for Smart City Services, 282-306.

Shafik, W. (2023e). Making Cities Smarter: IoT and SDN Applications, Challenges, and Future Trends. In Opportunities and Challenges of Industrial IoT in 5G and 6G Networks (pp. 73-94). IGI Global.

Shafik, W. (2024c). Artificial intelligence and Blockchain technology enabling cybersecurity in telehealth systems. In Artificial Intelligence and Blockchain Technology in Modern Telehealth Systems (pp. 285-326).

Shafik, W., & Kalinaki, K. (2023). Smart City Ecosystem: An Exploration of Requirements, Architecture, Applications, Security, and Emerging Motivations. In Handbook of Research on Network-Enabled IoT Applications for Smart City Services (pp. 75-98). IGI Global.

Shafik, W., Matinkhah, S. M., & Shokoor, F. (2022). Recommendation system comparative analysis: internet of things aided networks. *EAI Endorsed Transactions on Internet of Things, 8*(29).

Shafik, W., Tufail, A., Liyanage, C. D. S., & Apong, R. A. A. H. M. (2024). Medical Robotics and AI-Assisted Diagnostics Challenges for Smart Sustainable Healthcare. In AI-Driven Innovations in Digital Healthcare: Emerging Trends, Challenges, and Applications (pp. 304-323). IGI Global. doi:10.4018/979-8-3693-3218-4.ch016

Shafik, W. (2023a). A Comprehensive Cybersecurity Framework for Present and Future Global Information Technology Organizations. In *Effective Cybersecurity Operations for Enterprise-Wide Systems* (pp. 56–79). IGI Global. doi:10.4018/978-1-6684-9018-1.ch002

Shafik, W. (2023c). *Artificial intelligence and Blockchain technology enabling cybersecurity in telehealth systems. Artificial Intelligence and Blockchain Technology in Modern Telehealth Systems*. IET.

Shafik, W. (2024a). *Wearable Medical Electronics in Artificial Intelligence of Medical Things. Handbook of Security and Privacy of AI-Enabled Healthcare Systems and Internet of Medical Things*. CRC Press.

Shafik, W. (2024b). Introduction to ChatGPT. In *Advanced Applications of Generative AI and Natural Language Processing Models* (pp. 1–25). IGI Global.

Shafik, W. (2024d). Navigating Emerging Challenges in Robotics and Artificial Intelligence in Africa. In *Examining the Rapid Advance of Digital Technology in Africa* (pp. 124–144). IGI Global. doi:10.4018/978-1-6684-9962-7.ch007

Shafik, W. (2024e). Predicting Future Cybercrime Trends in the Metaverse Era. In *Forecasting Cyber Crimes in the Age of the Metaverse* (pp. 78–113). IGI Global.

Shafik, W., & Matinkhah, S. M. (2021). Unmanned aerial vehicles analysis to social networks performance. The *CSI. Journal of Computing Science and Engineering : JCSE, 18*(2), 24–31.

Shafik, W., Matinkhah, S. M., & Shokoor, F. (2023). Cybersecurity in unmanned aerial vehicles: A review. *International Journal on Smart Sensing and Intelligent Systems, 16*(1), 20230012. doi:10.2478/ijssis-2023-0012

Shafi, M., Molisch, A. F., Smith, P. J., Haustein, T., Zhu, P., De Silva, P., Tufvesson, F., Benjebbour, A., & Wunder, G. (2017). 5G: a tutorial overview of standards, trials, challenges, deployment, and practice. *IEEE Journal on Selected Areas in Communications, 35*(6), 1201–1221. doi:10.1109/JSAC.2017.2692307

ShafinR.LiuL.ChandrasekharV.ChenH.ReedJ.ZhangJ. (2019). *Artificial intelligence-enabled cellular networks: a critical path to beyond-5G and 6G*. arXiv 1907.07862. doi:10.1109/MWC.001.1900323

Shah, S. A., Seker, D. Z., Hameed, S., & Draheim, D. (2019). The Rising Role of Big Data Analytics and IoT in Disaster Management: Recent Advances, Taxonomy and Prospects. *IEEE Access : Practical Innovations, Open Solutions, 7*, 54595–54614. doi:10.1109/ACCESS.2019.2913340

Sharma, A., & Verma, R. (2020). Artificial Intelligence and Knowledge Management: An Exploratory Study in Indian IT Firms. In *Proceedings of International Conference on Intelligent Computing and Applications* (pp. 1067-1075). Research Gate.

Sharma, H., Soetan, T., Farinloye, T., Mogaji, E., & Noite, M. D. F. (2022). AI adoption in universities in emerging economies: Prospects, challenges and recommendations. In *Re-imagining Educational Futures in Developing Countries: Lessons from Global Health Crises* (pp. 159–174). Springer International Publishing. doi:10.1007/978-3-030-88234-1_9

Sharma, K., Anand, D., Sabharwal, M., Tiwari, P. K., Cheikhrouhou, O., & Frikha, T. (2021). A Disaster Management Framework Using Internet of Things-Based Interconnected Devices. *Mathematical Problems in Engineering, 2021*, 1–21. doi:10.1155/2021/9916440

Sharma, R., Shishodia, A., Gunasekaran, A., Min, H., & Munim, Z. H. (2022, February 9). The role of artificial intelligence in supply chain management: Mapping the territory. *International Journal of Production Research*, *60*(24), 7527–7550. doi:10.1080/00207543.2022.2029611

Sharma, S. K., Woungang, I., Anpalagan, A., & Chatzinotas, S. (2020). Toward tactile internet in beyond 5G era: Recent advances, current issues, and future directions. *IEEE Access : Practical Innovations, Open Solutions*, *8*, 56948–56991. doi:10.1109/ACCESS.2020.2980369

Sharp, D., Anwar, M., Goodwin, S., Raven, R., Bartram, L., & Kamruzzaman, L. (2022). A participatory approach for empowering community engagement in data governance: The Monash Net Zero Precinct. *Data & Policy*, *4*, e5. doi:10.1017/dap.2021.33

Shashidhara, R., Lajuvanthi, M., & Akhila, S. (2022). A secure and privacy-preserving mutual authentication system for global roaming in mobile networks. *Arabian Journal for Science and Engineering*, *47*(2), 1435–1446. doi:10.1007/s13369-021-05940-w

Shatnawi, A., & Shatnawi, R. (2016). Generating a language-independent graphical user interfaces from UML models. *The International Arab Journal of Information Technology*, *13*(3), 291–296.

Sher, L. (2020). The impact of the COVID-19 pandemic on suicide rates. *QJM*, *113*(10), 707–712. doi:10.1093/qjmed/hcaa202 PMID:32539153

Shi, S., Guo, C., Jiang, L., Wang, Z., Shi, J., Wang, X., & Li, H. (2020). Pv-rcnn: Point-voxel feature set abstraction for 3d object detection. In *Proceedings of the IEEE/CVF Conference on Computer Vision and Pattern Recognition* (pp. 10529-10538). 10.1109/CVPR42600.2020.01054

Shivraj, V. L., Rajan, M. A., Singh, M., & Balamuralidhar, P. (2015, February). One time password authentication scheme based on elliptic curves for Internet of Things (IoT). In *2015 5th National Symposium on Information Technology: Towards New Smart World (NSITNSW)* (pp. 1-6). IEEE.

Shi, Y., Han, Q., Shen, W., & Zhang, H. (2019). Potential applications of 5G communication technologies in collaborative intelligent manufacturing. *IET Collaborative Intelligent Manufacturing*, *1*(4), 109–116. doi:10.1049/iet-cim.2019.0007

Shoeibi, A., Sadeghi, D., Moridian, P., Ghassemi, N., Heras, J., Alizadehsani, R., Khadem, A., Kong, Y., Nahavandi, S., Zhang, Y. D., & Gorriz, J. M. (2021). Automatic diagnosis of schizophrenia in EEG signals using CNN-LSTM models. *Frontiers in Neuroinformatics*, *15*, 58. doi:10.3389/fninf.2021.777977 PMID:34899226

Shokoor, F., Shafik, W., & Matinkhah, S. M. (2022). Overview of 5G & beyond security. *EAI Endorsed Transactions on Internet of Things*, *8*(30).

Sicari, S., Rizzardi, A., Grieco, L. A., & Coen-Porisini, A. (2015). Security, privacy and trust in Internet of Things: The road ahead. *Computer Networks*, *76*, 146–164. doi:10.1016/j.comnet.2014.11.008

Simonyan, K., & Zisserman, A. (2014). Very deep convolutional networks for large-scale image recognition. *arXiv preprint arXiv:1409.1556*.

Singandhupe, A., La, H. M., & Feil-Seifer, D. (2018). Reliable security algorithm for drones using individual characteristics from an EEG signal. *IEEE Access : Practical Innovations, Open Solutions*, *6*, 22976–22986. doi:10.1109/ACCESS.2018.2827362

Singh, A., & Mani, N. (2020). Leveraging Artificial Intelligence for Effective Knowledge Management: A Study of Indian IT Organizations. In *Proceedings of International Conference on Inventive Research in Computing Applications* (pp. 1155-1160). Research Gate.

Singh, S., & Mehrotra, D. (2020). Artificial Intelligence and Knowledge Management: A Study of Indian Banks. In *Proceedings of International Conference on Contemporary Computing and Informatics* (pp. 336-341). Research Gate.

Singh, A., & Hess, T. (2017). How Chief Digital Officers promote the digital transformation of their companies. *MIS Quarterly Executive, 16*(1).

Singh, P., & Singh, N. (2018). Artificial Intelligence and Knowledge Management: A Study of Indian Manufacturing Firms. In *Proceedings of International Conference on Computing, Power and Communication Technologies* (pp. 75-81).

Sinha, A., Kumar, P., Rana, N. P., Islam, R., & Dwivedi, Y. K. (2019). Impact of internet of things (IoT) in disaster management: A task-technology fit perspective. *Annals of Operations Research, 283*(1–2), 759–794. doi:10.1007/s10479-017-2658-1

Smith, M. M., & Davis, R. G. (2021). Can you escape? The pharmacology review virtual escape room. *Simulation & Gaming, 52*(1), 79–87. doi:10.1177/1046878120966363

Solanki, A. S., Patel, C., & Doshi, N. (2019). Smart cities-A case study of Porto and Ahmedabad. *Procedia Computer Science, 160*, 718–722. doi:10.1016/j.procs.2019.11.021

Songhorabadi, M., & Rahimi, M. MoghadamFarid, A. M., & Haghi Kashani, M. (2023). Fog computing approaches in IoT-enabled smart cities. In Journal of Network and Computer Applications, 211. doi:10.1016/j.jnca.2022.103557

Sookhak, M., Yu, F. R., & Zomaya, A. Y. (2017). Auditing big data storage in cloud computing using divide and conquer tables. *IEEE Transactions on Parallel and Distributed Systems, 29*(5), 999–1012. doi:10.1109/TPDS.2017.2784423

Sowmiya, B., & Poovammal, E. (2022). A heuristic K-anonymity based privacy preserving for student management hyperledger fabric blockchain. *Wireless Personal Communications, 127*(2), 1359–1376. doi:10.1007/s11277-021-08582-1

Spohrer, J., Maglio, P. P., Vargo, S. L., & Warg, M. (2022). *Service in the AI Era: Science, Logic, and Architecture Perspectives.* Business Expert Press.

Ståhlbröst, A., Padyab, A., Sällström, A., & Hollosi, D. (2015). Design of smart city systems from a privacy perspective. *IADIS International Journal on WWW/Internet, 13*(1), 1-16.

Stewart, L. (2022). *How Can Company X Effectively Make A Transition From Digitisation To Digital Transformation?* [Doctoral dissertation, University of Liverpool].

Stewart, J., Bleumers, L., Van Looy, J., Mariën, I., All, A., Schurmans, D., & Misuraca, G. (2013). *The potential of digital games for empowerment and social inclusion of groups at risk of social and economic exclusion: evidence and opportunity for policy.* Joint Research Centre, European Commission.

Stracke, C. M., Burgos, D., Santos-Hermosa, G., Bozkurt, A., Sharma, R. C., Swiatek Cassafieres, C., dos Santos, A. I., Mason, J., Ossiannilsson, E., Shon, J. G., Wan, M., Obiageli Agbu, J.-F., Farrow, R., Karakaya, Ö., Nerantzi, C., Ramírez-Montoya, M. S., Conole, G., Cox, G., & Truong, V. (2022). Responding to the initial challenge of the COVID-19 pandemic: Analysis of international responses and impact in school and higher education. *Sustainability (Basel), 14*(3), 1876. doi:10.3390/su14031876

Strmečki, D., Magdalenić, I., & Radosević, D. (2018). A Systematic Literature Review on the Application of Ontologies in Automatic Programming. *International Journal of Software Engineering and Knowledge Engineering, 28*(5), 559–591. doi:10.1142/S0218194018300014

Suleman, M. A., Meyer, N., & Nieuwenhuizen, C. (2022). *Analysis of Top-Ranked South African and International MBA Focus Areas in the 4th Industrial Revolution. In 2022 INTERNATIONAL BUSINESS CONFERENCE.* TSHWANE UNIVERSITY OF TECHNOLOGY.

Sundar, S. S., & Marathe, S. S. (2010). Personalization versus customization: The importance of agency, privacy, and power usage. *Human Communication Research*, *36*(3), 298–322. doi:10.1111/j.1468-2958.2010.01377.x

Sunder, S., Kumar, V., & Zhao, Y. (2016). Measuring the lifetime value of a customer in the consumer packaged goods industry. *JMR, Journal of Marketing Research*, *53*(6), 901–921. doi:10.1509/jmr.14.0641

Surma-Aho, A. O., Björklund, T. A., & Holtta-Otto, K. (2018). Assessing the development of empathy and innovation attitudes in a project-based engineering design course. *Annual Conference and Exposition, Conference Proceedings*. ACM. 10.18260/1-2--29826

Taherdoost, H., & Madanchian, M. (2023). Artificial Intelligence and Knowledge Management: Impacts, Benefits, and Implementation. *Computers*, *12*(4), 72. doi:10.3390/computers12040072

Talking the Talk: The Beginner's Guide to Designing a Chatbot Conversation. (2017). Hubspot. https://blog.hubspot.com/marketing/beginners-guide-to-designing-a-chatbot-conversation

Tan, L., & Wang, N. (2010, August). Future internet: The internet of things. In *2010 3rd international conference on advanced computer theory and engineering (ICACTE)*. IEEE.

Tariq, H., Touati, F., Al-Hitmi, M., Crescini, D., & Mnaouer, A. B. (2019). A Real-Time Early Warning Seismic Event Detection Algorithm Using Smart Geo-Spatial Bi-Axial Inclinometer Nodes for Industry 4.0 Applications. *Applied Sciences (Basel, Switzerland)*, *9*(18), 3650. doi:10.3390/app9183650

Technologies, I. N. (2018, November 21). Blockchain and IoT Revolutionizing Supply Chain Management. How Blockchain and IoT Revolutionizing Supply Chain Management. https://www.indusnet.co.in/blockchain-and-iot-revolutionizing-supply-chainmanagement

Tests, S. (n.d.). *How to Test Validity questionnaire Using SPSS*. SPSS Tests. http://www.spsstests.com/2015/02/how-to-test-validity-questionnaire.htm

Theby, M. (2022). Public Sector Cloud Computing Adoption and Utilization during COVID-19: An Agenda for Research and Practice. [IJMPICT]. *International Journal of Managing Public Sector Information and Communication Technologies*, *13*(1), 1–11. doi:10.5121/ijmpict.2022.13101

Thekkil, T. M., & Prabakaran, N. (2017). *Real-time WSN based early flood detection and control monitoring system*. IEEE. doi:10.1109/ICICICT1.2017.8342828

Thing, V. L. (2014, December). Cyber security for a smart nation. In *2014 IEEE International Conference on Computational Intelligence and Computing Research* (pp. 1-3). IEEE.

Thomas, A. A., & Raja, G. (2019). FINDER: A D2D based critical communications framework for disaster management in 5G. *Peer-to-Peer Networking and Applications*, *12*(4), 912–923. doi:10.1007/s12083-018-0689-2

Thomaz, F., Salge, C., Karahanna, E., & Hulland, J. (2020). Learning from the Dark Web: Leveraging conversational agents in the era of hyper-privacy to enhance marketing. *Journal of the Academy of Marketing Science*, *48*(1), 43–63. doi:10.1007/s11747-019-00704-3

Ting Yan Chan, W., & Hong Leung, C. (2021). Mind the Gap: Discrepancy Between Customer Expectation and Perception on Commercial Chatbots Usage. *Asian Journal of Empirical Research*, *11*(1), 1–10. doi:10.18488/journal.1007.2021.111.1.10

Tiwari, P., Pant, B., Elarabawy, M. M., Abd-Elnaby, M., Mohd, N., Dhiman, G., & Sharma, S. (2022). Cnn based multiclass brain tumor detection using medical imaging. *Computational Intelligence and Neuroscience*, *2022*, 2022. doi:10.1155/2022/1830010 PMID:35774437

Toader, D. C., Boca, G., Toader, R., Măcelaru, M., Toader, C., Ighian, D., & Rădulescu, A. T. (2020). The effect of social presence and chatbot errors on trust. *Sustainability (Basel)*, *12*(1), 1–24. doi:10.3390/su12010256

Todor, R. D. (2016). Blending traditional and digital marketing. *Bulletin of the Transilvania University of Brasov, Series I: Engineering Sciences*, *9*(1), 51–56. http://ezproxy.leedsbeckett.ac.uk/login?url=http://search.ebscohost.com/login.aspx?direct=true&db=a9h&AN=116699220&site=eds-live&scope=site

Torrecilla-Salinas, C. J., Sedeño, J., Escalona, M. J., & Mejías, M. (2015). Estimating, planning and managing Agile Web development projects under a value-based perspective. *Information and Software Technology*, *61*, 124–144. doi:10.1016/j.infsof.2015.01.006

Toujani, R., Chaabani, Y., Dhouioui, Z., & Bouali, H. (2018). The Next Generation of Disaster Management and Relief Planning: Immersive Analytics Based Approach. In Communications in computer and information science (pp. 80–93). Springer Science+Business Media. doi:10.1007/978-3-319-93596-6_6

Trautman, L. J., & Ormerod, P. C. (2016). Corporate directors' and officers' cybersecurity standard of care: The Yahoo data breach. *Am. UL Rev.*, *66*, 1231.

Tsakalidis, G., & Vergidis, K. (2017). A systematic approach toward description and classification of cybercrime incidents. *IEEE Transactions on Systems, Man, and Cybernetics. Systems*, *49*(4), 710–729. doi:10.1109/TSMC.2017.2700495

Tseng, S. H., Chen, S. M., & Yang, C. (2022). Cloud computing-enabled supply chain visibility: A systematic review and future research agenda. *Sustainability*, *14*(2), 372.

Tsui, E. (2005). Knowledge management in the era of artificial intelligence: Can machines really understand knowledge? *Journal of Knowledge Management*, *9*(2), 116–130.

TsvetkovaM.García-GavilanesR.FloridiL.YasseriT. (2016). Even Good Bots Fight. December. http://arxiv.org/abs/1609.04285

Turan, S. G. (2021). Deepfake and digital citizenship: A long-term protection method for children and youth. In *Deep fakes, fake news, and misinformation in online teaching and learning technologies* (pp. 124–142). IGI Global. doi:10.4018/978-1-7998-6474-5.ch006

Turk, Ž., de Soto, B. G., Mantha, B. R., Maciel, A., & Georgescu, A. (2022). A systemic framework for addressing cybersecurity in construction. *Automation in Construction*, *133*, 103988. doi:10.1016/j.autcon.2021.103988

Tuttle, H. (2015). Sony faces lawsuits after data breach. *Risk Management*, *62*(2), 4.

UK. S. (2018). *How Chatbots Can Redefine Your Sales Process*. UK. https://www.salesforce.com/uk/blog/2018/09/how-chatbots-can-redefine-your-sales-process.html

Ulas, D. (2019). Digital transformation process and SMEs. *Procedia Computer Science*, *158*, 662–671. doi:10.1016/j.procs.2019.09.101

Umar, M. A. (2022). Digital Transformation Strategies for Small Business Management. In *Handbook of Research on Digital Transformation Management and Tools* (pp. 435–452). IGI Global. doi:10.4018/978-1-7998-9764-4.ch019

Um, T., Kim, T., & Chung, N. (2020). How does an intelligence chatbot affect customers compared with self-service technology for sustainable services? *Sustainability (Basel)*, *12*(12), 5119. doi:10.3390/su12125119

Understanding revenge porn and how to get justice if affected - People Daily. (2019, September 30). PD. https://www.pd.co.ke/lifestyle/understanding-revenge-porn-and-how-to-get-justice-if-affected-7464/

UNESCAP. (2022). *Asia-Pacific digital transformation report 2022: shaping our digital future.* https://repository.unescap.org/handle/20.500.12870/4725

UNESCAP. (2022). *Building forward together: towards an inclusive and resilient Asia and the Pacific.* UN. https://repository.unescap.org/handle/20.500.12870/4324

Ungureanu, D. M. (2022). Reviving Productivity Growth in Urban Economies. *Annals of Spiru Haret University. Economic Series*, *22*(1), 169–182.

Van Allen, P. (2018). Prototyping Ways of Prototyping AI. *INTERACTIONS*, 46–51. https://github.

Van den Broeck, E., Zarouali, B., & Poels, K. (2019). Chatbot advertising effectiveness: When does the message get through? *Computers in Human Behavior*, *98*, 150–157. doi:10.1016/j.chb.2019.04.009

Vaughan-Whitehead, D., Ghellab, Y., and de Bustillo Llorente, R. (2021). *The new world of work.* doi:10.4337/9781800888050

Veldkamp, A., Daemen, J., Teekens, S., Koelewijn, S., Knippels, M. C. P., & van Joolingen, W. R. (2020). Escape boxes: Bringing escape room experience into the classroom. *British Journal of Educational Technology*, *51*(4), 1220–1239. doi:10.1111/bjet.12935

Veldkamp, A., van de Grint, L., Knippels, M. C. P., & van Joolingen, W. R. (2020). Escape education: A systematic review on escape rooms in education. *Educational Research Review*, *31*, 100364. doi:10.1016/j.edurev.2020.100364

Verma, A., Verma, P., & Verma, N. (2018). Supply chain management practices in FMCG industry: a literature review. *Journal of Advances in Management.*

Verma, V., & Singhal, S. (2019). Artificial Intelligence and Knowledge Management in Indian Public Sector Enterprises. In *Proceedings of International Conference on Machine Learning and Data Engineering* (pp. 619-625). IEEE.

Vial, G. (2019). Understanding digital transformation: A review and a research agenda. *The Journal of Strategic Information Systems*, *28*(2), 118–144. doi:10.1016/j.jsis.2019.01.003

Vide, R. K., Hunjet, A., & Kozina, G. (2022). Enhancing Sustainable Business by SMEs' Digitalization. *Journal of Strategic Innovation & Sustainability*, *17*(1).

Vidergor, H. E. (2021). Effects of digital escape room on gameful experience, collaboration, and motivation of elementary school students. *Computers & Education*, *166*, 104156. doi:10.1016/j.compedu.2021.104156

Vieira, J. C., Sartori, A., Stefenon, S. F., Perez, F. L., De Jesus, G. S., & Leithardt, V. R. Q. (2022). Low-cost CNN for automatic violence recognition on embedded system. *IEEE Access : Practical Innovations, Open Solutions*, *10*, 25190–25202. doi:10.1109/ACCESS.2022.3155123

Vitunskaite, M., He, Y., Brandstetter, T., & Janicke, H. (2019). Smart cities and cyber security: Are we there yet? A comparative study on the role of standards, third party risk management and security ownership. *Computers & Security*, *83*, 313–331. doi:10.1016/j.cose.2019.02.009

Vorderer, P., Klimmt, C., & Ritterfeld, U. (2004). Enjoyment: At the heart of media entertainment. *Communication Theory*, *14*(4), 388–408. doi:10.1111/j.1468-2885.2004.tb00321.x

Vujnovic, M., & Foster, J. E. (2022). Online Instruction and the "Hyflex Teaching 'Shock Doctrine. In *Higher Education and Disaster Capitalism in the Age of COVID-19* (pp. 167–180). Springer International Publishing. doi:10.1007/978-3-031-12370-2_7

Vunnava, R., Bodla, L., Dehury, M. K., & Mohanta, B. K. (2022). Performance Analysis of ML Techniques in Identification of Fake News. *2022 International Conference on Sustainable Computing and Data Communication Systems (ICSCDS)*, Erode, India. 10.1109/ICSCDS53736.2022.9760905

Wang, Z., Vo, H. N. P., Salehi, M., Rusu, L. C., Reeves, C. E., & Phan, A. (2017). *A large-scale spatio-temporal data analytics system for wildfire risk management.* ACM. doi:10.1145/3080546.3080549

Wang, H., Zhang, L., & Yeung, J. H. Y. (2018). The impact of supply chain visibility on supply chain disruption management: A structural equation modeling approach. *International Journal of Production Economics, 195*, 295–301.

Wang, L., & Cheng, J. (2020). Robust disturbance rejection methodology for unstable non-minimum phase systems via disturbance observer. *ISA Transactions, 100*, 1–12. doi:10.1016/j.isatra.2019.11.034 PMID:31818485

Wang, P., & Johnson, C. (2018). Cybersecurity incident handling: A case study of the Equifax data breach. *Issues in Information Systems, 19*(3).

Wang, Q., Ren, K., Yu, S., & Lou, W. (2011). Dependable and secure sensor data storage with dynamic integrity assurance. [TOSN]. *ACM Transactions on Sensor Networks, 8*(1), 1–24. doi:10.1145/1993042.1993051

Wang, X., Peng, Y., Lu, L., Lu, Z., Bagheri, M., & Summers, R. M. (2017). Chestx-ray8: Hospital-scale chest x-ray database and benchmarks on weakly-supervised classification and localization of common thorax diseases. In *Proceedings of the IEEE conference on computer vision and pattern recognition* (pp. 2097-2106). IEEE. 10.1109/CVPR.2017.369

Wang, Y. M., & Elhag, T. M. (2006). Fuzzy TOPSIS for multi-criteria decision making: A comparative study of fuzzy TOPSIS and fuzzy AHP. *European Journal of Operational Research, 179*(1), 1–18. doi:10.1016/0377-2217(89)90055-6

Wang, Y., & Pettit, S. (2022). A Primer on Supply Chain Digital Transformation. *Digital Supply Chain Transformation, 121*, 121–139. doi:10.18573/book8.g

Wang, Y., Wan, J., Guo, J., Cheung, Y. M., & Yuen, P. C. (2017). Inference-based similarity search in randomized montgomery domains for privacy-preserving biometric identification. *IEEE Transactions on Pattern Analysis and Machine Intelligence, 40*(7), 1611–1624. doi:10.1109/TPAMI.2017.2727048 PMID:28715325

Wang, Z., Zhao, L., & Duan, Y. (2021). Enhancing supply chain visibility: An RFID-enabled information system. *Journal of Intelligent Manufacturing, 32*(4), 825–838.

Wan, Z., Hazel, J. W., Clayton, E. W., Vorobeychik, Y., Kantarcioglu, M., & Malin, B. A. (2022). Sociotechnical safeguards for genomic data privacy. *Nature Reviews. Genetics, 23*(7), 429–445. doi:10.1038/s41576-022-00455-y PMID:35246669

Watson, J. (2003). The potential impact of accessing advice on SME failure rates. In The potential impact of accessing advice on SME failure rates (pp. CD-Rom). University of Ballarat.

Wei, H. L., & Wang, E. T. (2010). The strategic value of supply chain visibility: Increasing the ability to reconfigure. *European Journal of Information Systems, 19*(2), 238–249. doi:10.1057/ejis.2010.10

Weinberg, C. (2017). How Messenger and "M" Are Shifting Gears. *The Information.* https://www.theinformation.com/articles/how-messenger-and-m-are-shifting-gears

Wellington, J. J., & Ramesh, P. (2017). Role of Internet of Things in disaster management. *International Conference on Innovations in Information, Embedded and Communication Systems.* IEEE. 10.1109/ICIIECS.2017.8275928

Wiemker, M., Elumir, E., & Clare, A. (2015). Escape room games. *Game based learning, 55*, 55-75.

William, P., Choubey, A., Chhabra, G. S., Bhattacharya, R., Vengatesan, K., & Choubey, S. (2022, March). Assessment of hybrid cryptographic algorithm for secure sharing of textual and pictorial content. In *2022 International conference on electronics and renewable systems (ICEARS)* (pp. 918-922). IEEE. 10.1109/ICEARS53579.2022.9751932

Williams, B. D., Roh, J., Tokar, T., & Swink, M. (2013). Leveraging supply chain visibility for responsiveness: The moderating role of internal integration. *Journal of Operations Management, 31*(7-8), 543–554. doi:10.1016/j.jom.2013.09.003

Wong, L. P., Hung, C. C., Alias, H., & Lee, T. S. H. (2020). Anxiety symptoms and preventive measures during the COVID-19 outbreak in Taiwan. *BMC Psychiatry*, *20*(1), 1–9. doi:10.1186/s12888-020-02786-8 PMID:32677926

Woywode, M. (1998). *Determinanten der Überlebenswahrscheinlichkeit von Unternehmen: Eine empirische Überprüfung organisationstheoretischer und industrieökonomischer Erklärungsansätze*. Nomos.

Wu, K. J., Liao, C. J., Tseng, M. L., Lim, M. K., Hu, J., & Tan, K. (2017). Toward sustainability: Using big data to explore the decisive attributes of supply chain risks and uncertainties. *Journal of Cleaner Production*, *142*, 663–676. doi:10.1016/j.jclepro.2016.04.040

Wunker, S. (2012). Better growth decisions: Early mover, fast follower or late follower? *Strategy and Leadership*, *40*(2), 43–48. doi:10.1108/10878571211209341

Xie, F., Wei, D., & Wang, Z. (2021). Traffic analysis for 5G network slice based on machine learning. *EURASIP Journal on Wireless Communications and Networking*, *2021*(1), 108. doi:10.1186/s13638-021-01991-7

Xie, X., Cheng, G., Wang, J., Yao, X., & Han, J. (2021). Oriented R-CNN for object detection. In *Proceedings of the IEEE/CVF International Conference on Computer Vision* (pp. 3520-3529). IEEE.

Xu, N., Ding, Y., & Guo, J. (2022). Do Smart City policies make cities more innovative: Evidence from China. *Journal of Asian Public Policy*, *15*(1), 1–17. doi:10.1080/17516234.2020.1742411

Xu, P., Lee, J., Barth, J. R., & Richey, R. G. (2021, January 20). Blockchain as supply chain technology: Considering transparency and security. *International Journal of Physical Distribution & Logistics Management*, *51*(3), 305–324. doi:10.1108/IJPDLM-08-2019-0234

Xu, X., Zhang, L., Sotiriadis, S., Asimakopoulou, E., Li, M., & Bessis, N. (2018). CLOTHO: A Large-Scale Internet of Things-Based Crowd Evacuation Planning System for Disaster Management. *IEEE Internet of Things Journal*, *5*(5), 3559–3568. doi:10.1109/JIOT.2018.2818885

Yamin, M. M., Ullah, M., Ullah, H., & Katt, B. (2021). Weaponized AI for cyber attacks. *Journal of Information Security and Applications*, *57*, 102722. doi:10.1016/j.jisa.2020.102722

Yang, Y., Li, X., Liu, Z., & Ke, W. (2019). RM2PT: A tool for automated prototype generation from requirements model. *IEEE/ACM 41st International Conference on Software Engineering: Companion, ICSE-Companion 2019*. ACM. 10.1109/ICSE-Companion.2019.00038

Yang, Z., Jianjun, L., Faqiri, H., Shafik, W., Talal Abdulrahman, A., Yusuf, M., & Sharawy, A. M. (2021). Green internet of things and big data application in smart cities development. *Complexity*, *2021*, 1–15. doi:10.1155/2021/4922697

Yan, Y., Mao, Y., & Li, B. (2018). Second: Sparsely embedded convolutional detection. *Sensors (Basel)*, *18*(10), 3337. doi:10.3390/s18103337 PMID:30301196

Yatsenko, D. (2020). *Project of Introducing a Supportive tool for Establishing and Growing Start-ups in the Environment of Secondary Schools in Zlín Region*.

Yıldız, T. (2019). Human-Computer Interaction Problem in Learning: Could the Key Be Hidden Somewhere Between Social Interaction and Development of Tools? *Integrative Psychological & Behavioral Science*, *53*(3), 541–557. doi:10.1007/s12124-019-09484-5 PMID:30826986

Yu, S., Gu, G., Barnawi, A., Guo, S., & Stojmenovic, I. (2014). Malware propagation in large-scale networks. *IEEE Transactions on Knowledge and Data Engineering*, *27*(1), 170–179. doi:10.1109/TKDE.2014.2320725

Yusif, S., Hafeez-Baig, A., Soar, J., & Teik, D. O. L. (2020). PLS-SEM path analysis to determine the predictive relevance of e-Health readiness assessment model. *Health and Technology*, *10*(6), 1497–1513. doi:10.1007/s12553-020-00484-9

Zack, M. H. (1999). Managing codified knowledge. *Sloan Management Review*, *40*(4), 45–58.

Zeba, G., Dabić, M., Čičak, M., Daim, T., & Yalcin, H. (2021). Technology mining: Artificial intelligence in manufacturing. *Technological Forecasting and Social Change*, *171*(February), 120971. doi:10.1016/j.techfore.2021.120971

Zeferino, N. V., & Vilain, P. (2014). A model-driven approach for generating interfaces from user interaction diagrams. *ACM International Conference Proceeding Series*, (pp. 474-478). ACM. 10.1145/2684200.2684326

Zhang, H., Babar, M., & Tell, P. (2011, June). Identifying relevant studies in software engineering. *Information and Software Technology*, *53*(6), 625–637. doi:10.1016/j.infsof.2010.12.010

Zhang, K., Ni, J., Yang, K., Liang, X., Ren, J., & Shen, X. S. (2017). Security and privacy in smart city applications: Challenges and solutions. *IEEE Communications Magazine*, *55*(1), 122–129. doi:10.1109/MCOM.2017.1600267CM

Zhang, M., Xu, L., & Zhang, J. (2019). Blockchain technology for enhancing supply chain visibility and traceability. *Industrial Management & Data Systems*, *119*(7), 1418–1437.

Zhang, Q., & Fitzek, F. H. P. (2015). Mission critical IoT communication in 5G. In *Future access enablers for ubiquitous and intelligent infrastructures* (Vol. 159, pp. 35–41). Springer International Publishing. doi:10.1007/978-3-319-27072-2_5

Zhang, Q., Xu, F., Li, L., Liu, N. L., & Pan, J. W. (2019). Quantum information research in China. *Quantum Science and Technology*, *4*(4), 040503. doi:10.1088/2058-9565/ab4bea

Zhang, X., & Zhang, Z. (2019). The impact of supply chain visibility on supply chain collaboration: A perspective of Chinese manufacturers. *Sustainability*, *11*(7), 1942.

Zheng, M., Zhi, K., Zeng, J., Tian, C., & You, L. (2022). A hybrid CNN for image denoising. *Journal of Artificial Intelligence and Technology*, *2*(3), 93–99.

Zhou, X., Li, S., Li, Z., & Li, W. (2021). Information diffusion across cyber-physical-social systems in smart city: A survey. *Neurocomputing*, *444*, 203–213. doi:10.1016/j.neucom.2020.08.089

Ziemann, V., & Guérard, B. (2017). *Reaping the benefits of global value chains in Turkey*. OECD. https://www.oecd-ilibrary.org/content/paper/d054af64-en

Ziozias, C., & Anthopoulos, L. (2022, June). Forming Smart Governance under a City Digital Transformation Strategy-findings from Greece and ICC. In *DG. O 2022: The 23rd Annual International Conference on Digital Government Research* (pp. 416-424). 10.1145/3543434.3543491

Ziyadin, S., Suieubayeva, S., & Utegenova, A. (2019, April). Digital transformation in business. In *Digital Transformation of the Economy: Challenges, Trends, New Opportunities* (pp. 408-415). Springer, Cham.

Zouhar, Y., Jellema, J., Lustig, N., & Trabelsi, M. (2021). *Public Expenditure and Inclusive Growth-A Survey*. International Monetary Fund. doi:10.5089/9781513574387.001

Zumstein, D., & Hundertmark, S. (2018). Chatbots : an interactive technology for personalized communication and transaction. *IADIS International Journal on Www/Internet*, *15*(1), 96–109.

About the Contributors

G S Prakasha is an Associate Professor at School of Education, Christ University, Bangalore, India. He has 22 years of teaching and research experience in Education. His areas of interest lie in quantitative research methodology, Teaching-learning, Assessment and Evaluation, Educational Technology, Teacher education, and Higher education. He has published in peer-reviewed journals indexed in reputed databases. He has presented papers in national and international conferences. He is involved in research activities, which have national and international emphasis.

Deepanraj Balakrishnan is currently working as Research Faculty in the Department of Mechanical Engineering, College of Engineering at Prince Mohammad Bin Fahd University, Saudi Arabia. Dr. Deepanraj received his Bachelor's degree in Mechanical Engineering and Master's Degree in Thermal Engineering from Anna University, Chennai and Ph.D degree in Mechanical Engineering from National Institute of Technology, Calicut. He also completed his MBA in Energy Management from Jaipur National University. He has more than 10 years of working experience, which include both teaching and research. Dr. Deepanraj has published more than 100 research articles in peer reviewed international journals and conferences and holds 2 Indian patent. He is serving as guest editor, editorial board member and reviewer for many international peer reviewed journals including well known publishers like Elsevier, Springer and Inderscience. His area of interest includes Renewable Energy Utilization; Energy Conservation and Waste Management with special focus on Bio-Energy.

***

Munir Ahmad Ph.D. in Computer Science, brings over 24 years of invaluable expertise in the realm of spatial data development, management, processing, visualization, and quality assurance. His unwavering commitment to open data, big data, crowdsourced data, volunteered geographic information, and spatial data infrastructure has solidified him as a seasoned professional and a trusted trainer in cutting-edge spatial technologies. With a profound passion for research, Munir has authored more than 30 publications in his field, culminating in the award of his Ph.D. in Computer Science from Preston University Pakistan in 2022. His dedication to propelling the industry forward and sharing his extensive knowledge defines his mission.

Asmat Ali has a PhD in Remote Sensing & GIS. He is Director of Cartography and GIS at Survey of Pakistan. He is also Project Director Feasibility Study for Establishment of National Spatial Data Infrastructure (NSDI) for Pakistan. In, 1998 he earned Professional Master Degree in Geoinformatics from Faculty of Geo-Information Science and Earth Observation (ITC), University of Twente, Enschede

The Netherlands. The title of his IFA was, "DIGITAL PRODUCTION LINE IN THE CONTEXT OF SURVEY OF PAKISTAN". Later on, he got MSc Degree in Geo-information Science and Earth Observation, with Specialization in Geo-Information Management from the same university. The title of his MSc thesis was, "POTENTIAL OF PUBIC PRIVATE PARTNERSHIP FOR NSDI IMPLEMENTATION IN PAKISTAN". In 2022, he got PhD degree in Remote Sensing and GIS from PMAS-Arid Agriculture University Rawalpindi, Pakistan. The title of his dissertation was "SPATIAL DATA INFRASTRUCTURE AS THE MEANS TO ASSEMBLE GEOGRAPHIC INFORMATION NECESSARY FOR EFFECTIVE AGRICULTURAL POLICIES IN PAKISTAN". He has 35 years of experience in geospatial information production and management discipline as practitioner, trainer and educator. He has served on several operational, administrative and instructional appointments. He was in-charge of the team which started GIS mapping and digital cartography at Survey of Pakistan in 1999. His more than 30 research papers including four book chapters and articles on Spatial Data Infrastructure (SDI), GIS, Remote Sensing, E-governance, as well as Land Administration have been published in various internationally renowned journals and conferences. In 2008, SDI Asia-Pacific identified him as FOCAL POINT FOR SDI DEVELOPMENT IN PAKISTAN. GSDI in 2016, acknowledged and awarded him as SDI IMPLEMENTER FROM PAKISTAN. He is on the visiting faculty of Bahria University Islamabad and PMAS- Arid Agriculture University Rawalpindi, Pakistan.

Muhammad Arslan is a dedicated individual currently affiliated with the School of Computer Science at Chenab College of Advance Studies in Faisalabad.

Chandrashekhar Azad has received his MCA from Ranchi University, Ranchi in 2011. In his MCA degree, he has received Gold Medal for Best Master Degree in Professional Courses. He has received Ph.D. from Birla Institute of Technology, Mesra Ranchi the Department of Computer Science & Engineering in 2017. He has qualified GATE (Computer Science & Information Technology) and UGC NET (Computer Science and Applications) examinations. Currently he is working as an Assistant Professor in the Department of Computer Science & Engineering at National Institute of Technology, Jamshedpur. He has published more than 40 research papers in journals and conferences of international repute. He has 5 patents in the domain of computer science and Engineering. He serves as a reviewer for various international journals and conferences. His primary area of research includes Intrusion Detection System, Meta Heuristic Algorithms, Swarm Intelligence, Pattern Recognition, Data Mining, Medical Data Mining and Machine Learning.

Thivashini B Jaya Kumar is a Lecturer at the School of Management & Marketing, Taylors Business School, Taylor's University, Malaysia. She was awarded Bachelor of Business from Victoria University, Australia and Master in Management from Taylors University. Prior to entering academia, she was a business analyst with 3+ years of experience. She holds a PhD in Business with a research interest in service marketing, consumer behavior, international business and entrepreneurship. Currently she teaches service marketing and international business modules.

Debasis Bora has vast experience focused on forensic science, crime scene management, forensic chemistry, research, lecture, laboratory analysis, administration & organization, training programs, student assessment

Sadhna Chauhan Profile linkedin.com/in/dr-sadhna-chauhan-3028051aa76d704f-f5c6-4130-9b7d-a3fc982d6bee

Mohan Kumar Dehury is currently working as Assistant Professor in Amity University Jharkhand. He has more than 10 years of teaching experience. His area of research includes QoS in Wireless networks, AI and ML, and Blockchain. He has published papers in peer-reviewed journals indexed in reputed databases. He has presented papers in national and international conferences.

Rajeev Goyal holds a Doctorate and M.Tech in Computer Science and Engineering. With over 21 years of experience in both academia and industry, he has worked with reputable national and international universities such as VIT and AMITY. Dr. Goyal's expertise is reflected in his 8 publications in renowned academic databases such as Scopus and Web of Science. I am an authorized instructor for CCNA Introduction to Networks and cyber Ops Associate. Additionally, I hold international certifications from Juniper Networks Certified Associate and Microsoft Certified Security Compliance. My teaching expertise has been recognized with the Award for Excellence in Teaching in Higher Education, which was presented to me by Edwin Incorporation in partnership with JYD, International Higher Education Institutes in Thailand. In addition to his academic pursuits, Dr. Goyal is a member of several professional and industrial organizations, including ISTE, IAENG, IET, IRJIE, IRJIET (Reviewer Board Membership), and MTTF. He has also demonstrated his expertise as a speaker at various Faculty Development Programs and has been an active organizer of conferences, workshops, and short-term courses. Currently, Dr. Goyal's area of research is focused on the analysis of online social networks and recommender systems and Federated Learning.

Kassim Kalinaki (MIEEE) is a passionate technologist, researcher, and educator with more than ten years of experience in industry and academia. He received his Diploma in Computer engineering from Kyambogo University, a BSc in computer science and engineering, and an MSc. Computer Science and Engineering from Bangladesh's Islamic University of Technology (IUT). Since 2014, He has been lecturing at the Islamic University in Uganda (IUIU), where he most recently served as the Head of Department Computer Science department (2019-2022). Currently, he's pursuing his Ph.D. in Computer Science at the School of Digital Science at Universiti Brunei Darussalam (UBD) since January 2022 and is slated to complete in August 2025. He's the founder and principal investigator of Borderline Research Laboratory (BRLab) and his areas of research include Ecological Informatics, Data Analytics, Computer Vision, ML/DL, Digital Image Processing, Cybersecurity, IoT/AIoMT, Remote Sensing, and Educational Technologies. He has authored and co-authored several published peer-reviewed articles in renowned journals and publishers, including in Springer, Elsevier, Taylor and Francis, Emerald and IEEE.

Nora Parcus de Koch is a collaborator of the University of Seville, Spain. She formerly worked at the Ludwig-Maximilians-Universität (LMU) München and Fortiss (TUM), and in parallel as a consultant and project manager at F.A.S.T. and NTT DATA GmbH, Germany. Her main research interests include meta-modelling, requirements engineering, model-based software development and web engineering.

Nirmalendu Kumar is currently working as a Director in a National Mapping Organization, Survey of India. He is a core Surveying and Mapping professional, having over 30+ year of experience in geospatial domain like, surveying and mapping, GIS, GPS, CORS, Remote Sensing and Spatial Data

Infrastructure. He has M Tech in Surveying and Mapping from JNT University, Hyderabad and Master degree in geo-information Management from ITC, The Netherlands. He was actively associated in Delhi State Spatial Data Infrastructure (DSSDI) project and has a 5 years tenure in, NSDI, Department of science in Technology. He has published more than 5 research papers and is a member of many professional bodies like, Indian Society of Geomatics, computer Society of India and INCA. His area of interest is SDI, Geospatial Applications and application of AI in geospatial domain.

Sumit Kumar is currently an Associate Professor in the Faculty of Information Technology, Rajan Mamta Degree College, Aurangabad, Bihar, India. He has completed M. Tech. and Ph.D. from School of Computer and Systems Sciences, Jawaharlal Nehru University, New Delhi, India. He received MCA degrees from Ranchi University, Ranchi, Jharkhand, India. His research interest is Internet of Things (IoT). He has published various papers in SCIE, UGC and peer reviewed listed journals and conferences. He is reviewer of following journals: ● International Journal of Research and Analytical Reviews (IJRAR), E-ISSN: 2348-1269, P-ISSN: 2349-5138, An International Open Access Journal, ESTD: 2013 (Approved by ISSN and UGC). ● International Journal of Systems and Software Security and Protection (IJSSSP), IGI Global, ISSN: 2640-4265, EISSN: 2640-4273, DOI: 10.4018/IJSSSP, ESTD: 2018.

Tannisha Kundu is currently working as Assistant Professor in Amity University Jharkhand. She has more than 12 years of teaching experience. Her area of research includes Cybersecurity, AI and ML, and Image processing. She has published papers in peer-reviewed journals indexed in reputed databases. She has also presented papers in national and international conferences.

Mohammad Izzuddin Mohammed Jamil is a PhD Candidate in Management at School of Business and Economics, Universiti Brunei Darussalam, conducting research in the field of Entrepreneurship. He received his Bachelor's Degree in Business Administration (Hons) at Coventry University, United Kingdom, and Master's Degree in Management at Universiti Brunei Darussalam. Prior to academia, his industry experiences started when he first became a salesman and distributor, and has since worked in various professions including becoming a Tutor/Teacher, Website and Application Developer, Business Administrative Officer and has experiences starting-up enterprises. His research areas include Entrepreneurship, Growth, and MSMEs. He teaches at Universiti Brunei Darussalam in the field of Management, Accounting and Economics.

Ipseeta Nanda did her doctorate from CAPGS, Biju Patnaik University of Technology, Rourkela, Odisha, India. Her area of research is System on Chips Design, Internet of Things. Artificial Intelligence, Machine Learning, Automation Design, Data Science etc. She has published many indexed papers in Journals and in international conferences. She holds many patents. Ipseeta Nanda completed her MTech from Kalinga Institute of Industrial Technology (KIIT), Bhubaneswar, Odisha, India in 2010 in Electronics and Telecommunication, with specialization in Communication System. She has 17+ years of experience in teaching in many Engineering Institutes like Silicon Institute of Technology, Sambalpur, Odisha, India, NIIT University, Neemrana, Rajasthan, India. She has worked as a Research Assistant in the Dept. of Microelectronics & Embedded System at Asian Institute of Technology (AIT), Bangkok, Thailand in the year 2016. She has received two Best Paper Award in the field of research work one at Kuala Lumpur, Malaysia and other one at Pune, Maharashtra, India. She is acting as Reviewer, Editor in many International Journals, Plenary speaker, Invited Speaker, Guest of Honor etc. in many International Conferences and Workshop. She is also acting as reviewer in Wiley Publication Books for Internet of Things. On 18th January 2020 she was awarded by IIWA-2020 with Best Women Performer of the Year 2020 by GISR Foundation at Noida, India. She also received Young Professor of the Year 2021 as well as Outstanding Researcher Award 2021. She was also honored by South Central Railway Women Union, Vijayawada on Women's Day 8th March 2020. She is having 13International PatentGranted,1 National Design Patent Granted and4 National Patent Published and She also holds 3 Copyrights. She received outstanding Researcher Award, IARE 2021. Here name is also added in top 100 professors by India Prime. Presently she is presently working as Associate Professor &Dean in Faculty of Information Technology& Engineering, Gopal Narayan Singh University, Jamuhar, Sasaram, Bihar. She also acted as Director Curriculum Design in Innogurus customized learning solution

Hassan Nawaz is an accomplished cloud computing deployment expert who has a bachelor's degree in electrical engineering. He has deployed cloud computing projects in the UAE, Saudi Arabia, and Pakistan. Currently, he has deployed an FSI cloud project for Khazana enterprises, which will support the digital banking industry in Pakistan.

Cagla Ozen has taken her PhD from Computer Science Department of University of York, UK. She has more than 30 publications and one of her publications awarded as Outstanding Paper Award Winner at the Literati Network Awards for Excellence 2011. Her research interests are user experience, user interface, technology adoption and IoT.

Sathish Pachiyappan is currently serving as Assistant Professor at CHRIST (Deemed to be University), Bannerghatta Road Campus, Bengaluru. He has eight years teaching and three years research experience. He has done his doctoral degree from VIT (Deemed to be University), Vellore. He is specialized in Finance and Accounting, doing his research in the same area. He has completed MBA from Anna University and B,Com from SRM University, Chennai. Currently, as a part of his Research work, he had published articles in peer reviewed journals which includes Scopus Indexed Journals; Web of Science Indexed Journals, Australian Business Deans Council (ABDC) listed Journals and EBSCO host Journals. Also, published book chapter in Elsevier, Emerald, Springer and IGI global. Presented research papers in national and international conferences and also attended Faculty development programmes and workshops which are related to SPSS, AMOS and Econometrics. He went as resource person for various FDP, Guest Lecture, Session Chair for Conference and Workshop to various reputed colleges. He is well versed in handling Python, STATCRAFT, E-Views (Econometrics), SPSS for financial data analysis in research area. He is gold medallist and earned first rank in B.Com at SRM University, Chennai and also earned Class topper in MBA and 39th Rank Holder in Anna University. He received Research Award-2017 for publications in VIT University, Vellore. Recently, received award for "Best Researcher-2020" conducted by Pondicherry Research Society in Pondicherry.

Thanuja Rathakrishnan is a Lecturer at Taylor's Business School, Taylor's University, Malaysia. She earned her PhD in Business Economics at Universiti Putra Malaysia (UPM). Prior to this, she obtained a Master of Business Administration from Putra Business School, UPM, Malaysia and was conferred a bachelor's degree in Communication and Management by Upper IOWA University, USA. She has worked on entrepreneurism, family businesses and SMEs and tourism projects thereby expanding her interest in entrepreneurial tourism management. Thanuja also partakes in consultancy projects with government and nongovernment organisations. Her areas of interest are including, but not limited to entrepreneurship, small businesses, family businesses, and tourism. In addition to her academic role, Thanuja is also an Editorial Review Board Member of the Journal of Responsible Tourism Management and a Local Virtual Volunteer for AIESEC.

Baranidharan S specialized in Finance Economics and Econometrics. Having 5 years research experience, 2 years of Industrial experience and 6 years of teaching experience. Published 4 patent, 37 research articles in international and national journal which are indexed in Scopus, WoS, Proquest, ABDC, etc.,

Sameer Saharan is a dedicated researcher in Forensic Science, specializing in fingerprint analysis, cyber forensics, and DNA fingerprinting. He holds a Ph.D. in Forensic Science from Amity University, Haryana, and has authored several research papers and book chapters. With a passion for continuous learning, Dr. Saharan actively contributes to the advancement of forensic science through his expertise and knowledge. He is committed to nurturing the next generation of forensic scientists and making a positive impact in the field.

Nicolás Sánchez-Gómez is a lecturer at the University of Seville and researcher of the ES3 research group of the School of Computer Engineering. I have spent a large part of my professional career in the technology and process consulting sector, both in the private and public sectors. Throughout more than thirty years of professional experience, I have moved from the development, analysis and implementation of systems to the management and supervision of work teams, client management and ICT project management.

Wasswa Shafik is an IEEE member, P.Eng received a bachelor of science in Information Technology Engineering with a minor in Mathematics in 2016 from Ndejje University, Kampala, Uganda, a master of engineering in Information Technology Engineering (MIT) in 2020, from the Computer Engineering Department, Yazd University, Islamic Republic of Iran. He is an associate researcher at the Computer Science department, Network interconnectivity Lab at Yazd University, Islamic Republic of Iran, and at Information Sciences, Prince Sultan University, Saudi Arabia. His areas of interest are Computer Vision, Anomaly Detection, Drones (UAVs), Machine/Deep Learning, AI-enabled IoT/IoMTs, IoT/IIoT/OT Security, Cyber Security and Privacy. Shafik is the chair/co-chair/program chair of some Scopus/EI conferences. Also, academic editor/ associate editor for set of indexed journals (Scopus journals' quartile ranking). He is the founder and lead investigator of Dig Connectivity Research Laboratory (DCR-Lab) since 2019, the Managing Executive director of Asmaah Charity Organisation (ACO).

Deepa Sharma has done Ph.D., MBA in Human Resource Management, currently working as Assistant Professor at MMIM, Maharishi Markandeshwar (Deemed to be University), NAAC Accredited Grade 'A++' University, Mullana, Ambala (Haryana). She has more than 7 years of experience in academics. She has written 45+ research papers for various Scopus and UGC listed referred National & International Journals. And has published two book chapters out of which 1 book chapter is published in Taylor & Francis and has earned 45 citations and an h-index of 4 credentials that may be verified on various research platforms like Google Scholar, SSRN, LinkedIn, and Research gate and 5 papers appear in the Scopus preview. She has actively participated in national and international conferences.

Shailja Singh is an accomplished and dedicated Assistant Professor with a passion for teaching and a strong background in her field. With two years of teaching experience, she has demonstrated a commitment to providing quality education and fostering a positive learning environment for her students. She holds a Master's Degree in Forensic Science from Baba Saheb Bhimrao Ambedkar University, Lucknow, U.P. She is UGC-NET-qualified. She has published five research papers in prestigious journals and various articles in E-magazines and E-newsletters, and she has also presented research papers at conferences. To stay updated with the latest pedagogical practices and advancements in her field, Shailja Singh regularly participates in professional development activities. She has attended workshops, conferences, and seminars, allowing her to enhance her teaching skills and broaden her knowledge base.

Mehul Waghambare is a Product Manager with deep interests in customer touchpoints, experience and UI UX.

İremnaz Yolcu recently graduated with a Bachelor of IT degree from Yeditepe University. Passionate about the ever-advancing technology landscape, İremnaz is dedicated to providing valuable insights to the academic community. With a strong academic foundation and a commitment to lifelong learning, İremnaz is well-positioned to make a meaningful contribution to the field while continually pursuing personal and professional growth.

Index

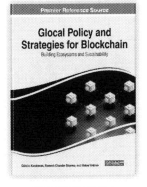
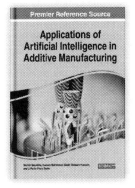
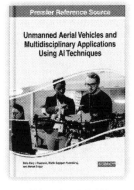

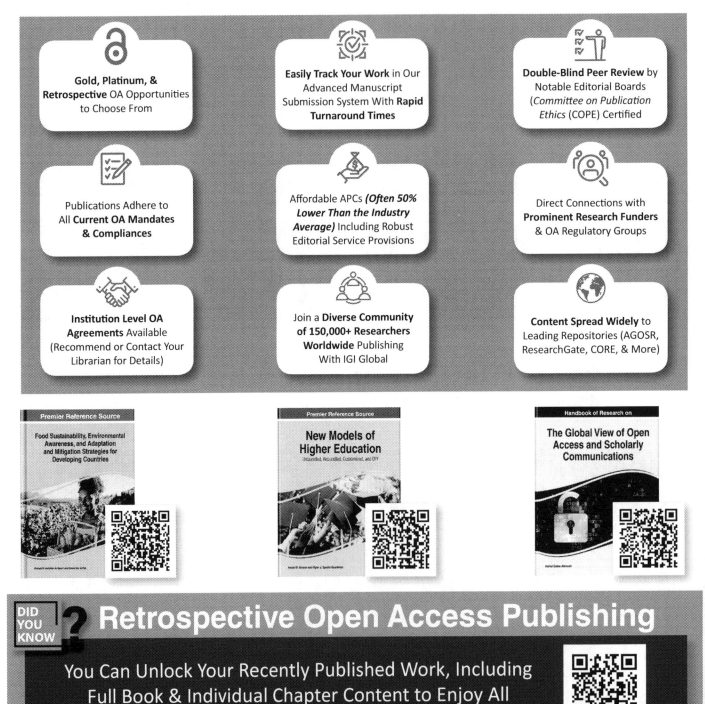

Printed in the United States
by Baker & Taylor Publisher Services